PROCLUS THE SUCCESSOR
ON POETICS AND THE HOMERIC POEMS

Society of Biblical Literature

Writings from the Greco-Roman World

David Konstan and Johan C. Thom, General Editors

Editorial Board

Brian E. Daley
Erich S. Gruen
Wendy Mayer
Margaret M. Mitchell
Teresa Morgan
Ilaria L. E. Ramelli
Michael J. Roberts
Karin Schlapbach
James C. VanderKam

Number 34

Proclus the Successor on Poetics and the Homeric Poems:
Essays 5 and 6 of His *Commentary on the Republic of Plato*

PROCLUS THE SUCCESSOR ON POETICS AND THE HOMERIC POEMS

Essays 5 and 6 of His *Commentary on the Republic of Plato*

Text, translation, notes, and introduction by

Robert Lamberton

Society of Biblical Literature
Atlanta

Proclus the Successor on Poetics and the Homeric Poems:
Essays 5 and 6 of His *Commentary on the Republic of Plato*

Copyright © 2012 by the Society of Biblical Literature

All rights reserved. No part of this work may be reproduced or transmitted in any form or by any means, electronic or mechanical, including photocopying and recording, or by means of any information storage or retrieval system, except as may be expressly permitted by the 1976 Copyright Act or in writing from the publisher. Requests for permission should be addressed in writing to the Rights and Permissions Office, Society of Biblical Literature, 825 Houston Mill Road, Atlanta, GA 30329 USA.

Library of Congress Control Number: 2012952535

Printed on acid-free, recycled paper conforming to
ANSI/NISO Z39.48-1992 (R1997) and ISO 9706:1994
standards for paper permanence.

Contents

Acknowledgments vii
Abbreviations ix

Introduction xi
    1. Proclus: Life and Works   xi
    2. The Commentary on the *Republic*   xiv
    3. Proclus on Poetics and Allegory   xvii
    4. The Defense of Homer   xxvi
    5. The Text   xxxi
    Addendum 1: Table of Contents of Proclus's Commentary
    on the *Republic*   xxxi
    Addendum 2: Wilhelm Kroll's Preface to Volume 1 of His
    Edition of the *Commentary*   xxxiii

Proclus, *In Rempublicam* 5 and 6: Contents xxxvii

Text and Translation 1
    Proclus, On the *Republic*, Essay 5   1
    Proclus, On the *Republic*, Essay 6   57

Bibliography 309
Index locorum 315
General Index 319

Acknowledgments

This book has many debts to the work of scholars of Proclus, some of whom are acknowledged ad loc. in the notes below. Its greatest debts, though, are to John Dillon, who patiently combed out many errors and infelicities of my text, translation, and notes, and to the late A. J. Festugière, whose scholarly translation of the commentary has for decades been my guide through Proclus's thorny Greek. To them goes the credit for much of what I have got right. For the errors that remain, no one but myself is to blame.

Abbreviations

Ancient Works

Alc. 1, 2	Plato, *Alcibiades 1, 2*
Anth. pal.	*Anthologia palatina*
Apol.	Plato, *Apologia*
Coel. hier.	Pseudo-Dionysius, *De coelesti hierarchia*
Def. orac.	Plutarch, *De defectu oraculorum*
Dub. et sol.	Damascius, *Dubitationes et solutiones de primis principiis*
Enn.	Plotinus, *Enneades*
Gorg.	Plato, *Gorgias*
Il.	Homer, *Ilias*
In Alc.	Proclus, *In Platonis Alcibiadem*
In Phd.	Olympiodorus, *In Platonis Phaedonem*
In Somn. Scip.	Macrobius, *In Somnium Scipionis*
In Tim.	Proclus, *In Platonis Timaeum*
Lach.	Plato, *Laches*
Leg.	Plato, *Leges*
Met.	Ovid, *Metamorphoses*
Od.	Homer, *Odyssea*
Or. chald.	*Oracula Chaldaica*
Orph. frag.	*Orphicorum fragmenta*
Phd.	Plato, *Phaedo*
Phdr.	Plato, *Phaedrus*
Plat.	Apuleius, *De Platone*
Prot.	Plato, *Protagoras*
Rep.	Plato, *Respublica*
Rhet.	Aristotle, *Rhetorica*
Sent.	Porphyry, *Sententiae ad intelligibilia ducentes*
Soph.	Plato, *Sophista*

Symp.	Plato, *Symposium*
Theol. Plat.	Proclus, *Theologia Platonica*
Tim.	Plato, *Timaeus*
Var. Hist.	Aelian, *Var. Hist.*
Vit. Isid.	Damascius, *Vita Isidori*
Vit. Plot.	Porphyry, *Vita Plotini*
Vit. Proc.	Marinus, *Vita Procli*
Vitae	Diogenes Laertius, *Vitae philosophorum*

Modern Works

Lampe	*A Patristic Greek Lexicon*, edited by G. W. H. Lampe. Oxford: Oxford University Press, 1961.
LSJ	*A Greek-English Lexicon*, compiled by Henry George Liddell and Robert Scott, revised and augmented throughout by Sir Henry Stuart Jones, 9th edition, with Supplement. Oxford: Oxford University Press, 1968.
PW	*Paulys Real-Encyclopädie der classischen Altertumswissenschaft*. New edition by Georg Wissowa and Wilhelm Kroll. 50 vols. in 84 parts. Stuttgart: Metzler and Druckenmüller, 1894–1980
Sophocles	E. A. Sophocles, *A Glossary of Later and Byzantine Greek*. Memoirs of the American Academy of Arts and Sciences NS 7. Cambridge: Welch, Bigelow, 1860.

Introduction

1. Proclus: Life and Works

Proclus's biographer Marinus made the arrival of the future Successor[1] at Athens into a parable of his promise and importance. After being met at the Piraeus and escorted to the city—with a stop at the "Socrateion"[2]—he meets the "gatekeeper" ready to close the city gate for the night, who says (and Marinus insists that these were his actual words): "Truly, had you not come, I was about to lock the gate" (*Vit. Proc.* 10).[3]

There are a number of rather surprising elements to this story. First, it requires that we imagine Athens in 430 C.E. as a walled, gated city, closed up at night against an at least potentially threatening hinterland. Second, the nineteen-year-old visitor is depicted as radiating an authority that not only impresses those on whose account he has come but even inspires in the gatekeeper an unwitting sententiousness with prophetic overtones. Proclus, as Marinus depicts him, came to an Athens where the study of Platonic philosophy (virtually to be identified with traditional Hellenic polytheism) had reached a low ebb and the "gate" was about to close forever. When he died there in 485, at least one more shrine (the Asklepieion) and the cult statue of Athena in the Parthenon were gone (*Vit. Proc.*

---

1. The leader of the school of Platonic philosophy at Athens held the tile διάδοχος, or Successor. The precise claims inherent in that title were perhaps deliberately vague. The Successor was clearly the one to whom the chair was passed down and was the "successor" of his predecessor (see, e.g., Damascius, *Vit. Isid.* frag. 256 [Zintzen]), but the term suggests as well a (specious) claim to be the successor to Plato himself, the latest in an unbroken line of scholarchs reaching back to the founder.

2. An unlocated and perhaps fictional shrine. On the topography of the Platonists in fifth-century Athens, see Frantz 1988 and Fowden 1990.

3. Ἀληθῶς, εἰ μὴ ἦλθες, ἔκλειον. The biography as a whole, as its most recent editors remind us, belongs to the genre of the funeral eulogy (Saffrey and Segonds 2001, xlii).

29, 30), but the study of Platonic philosophy was, Marinus would have us believe, rejuvenated (*Vit. Proc.* 38).

Before his arrival in Athens, Proclus's career as a student (in Marinus's account) follows a pattern that is familiar in philosophical biography in the Roman Empire. Like Plotinus (Porphyry, *Vit. Plot.* 3) and many others before him, he traveled long in search of the right teacher before he arrived in the Athenian school in 430. What is striking about the trajectory that Marinus describes, however, is the enthusiasm Proclus demonstrated for rhetoric and the depth of his literary training (*Vit. Proc.* 8–9).[4] In the long history of the later Platonists, only Porphyry, two centuries earlier, had a comparable commitment to language, style, and literary pursuits. It is striking that it is largely because of these two thinkers that allegorical reading is so firmly associated with Platonism in late antiquity.

Marinus's eulogy is our principal source for the life of Proclus, but it is supplemented by many passages in the later *Life of Isidore* (or *Philosophical History*) of Damascius.[5] Even if Marinus's account of Proclus's success leads him to exaggerate both the paucity of students in 430 and the numbers of those who came to hear Proclus in the following decades,[6] it seems that the middle of the fifth century was a relatively good time for the polytheist Platonists of Athens. The success of those years may paradoxically have led to their attracting first jealousy and then imperial disfavor two generations later, when the school lost its support and ceased to exist as a formal institution.[7]

The intervening years were, in any case, fraught with difficulties for the Athenian Platonic school. A divisive battle over the succession in the late 480s and the 490s was followed by a period of unknown length in which Hegias as scholarch attracted far too much attention to the school

---

4. The attribution of the *Chrestomathy*, with its unique summaries of much lost early epic, to Proclus seems, from this point of view, highly plausible. See Lamberton 1986, 177 with n. 51.

5. See Athanassiadi 1999.

6. Watts (2006, 98–99 with n. 95) doubts that the numbers were really so small at the beginning of Proclus's stay in Athens, but Synesius's testimony for about the year 400 supports the picture given by Marinus. Certainly the latter mentions only a few individuals in the anecdotes of Proclus's arrival in Athens, then concludes his eulogy with the claim that "many people came to hear [Proclus] from many places" (*Vit. Proc.* 38).

7. See Cameron 1969; Watts 2006, ch. 5.

through his flagrantly illegal religious observations.[8] At some point in the first two decades of the sixth century, Hegias was in turn succeeded by the last scholarch, Damascius, under whose direction the school experienced a last burst of vitality, apparently both lowering its polytheist profile in the increasingly dangerous religious climate and in more properly philosophical matters turning away from the influential positions of Proclus and embracing the tradition of the fourth-century thinker Iamblichus.[9]

The details of these disputes, both religious and philosophical, go far beyond our concerns here, but it is worth noting that the reinstatement of an Iamblichean orthodoxy in the Athenian school may be thought to have marked a distinct falling off of interest in the material treated in the sections of Proclus's *Republic* commentary before us. Some of the reasons for this will be treated below in the next section, but for now suffice it to say that among Iamblichus and his followers there is little evidence of concern with the text of Homer or with poetics generally. Iamblichus is credited with hermeneutic insights of importance for the reading of Plato, as well as with the creation of a standard curriculum for Platonic studies (which, incidentally, does not seem to have included the *Republic*). But a concern with Homer, or other archaic poetry, as privileged texts seems to have had no place in the Iamblichean program, perhaps because less problematic and less ambiguous paths to the truth occupied his attention.[10]

During the half century Proclus spent in Athens, for most of which he was scholarch, he was exceptionally productive, though his remarkable output was cut short in his later years by senility.[11] He started early, in any case, and had completed his massive *Timaeus* commentary by the age of twenty-eight (*Vit. Proc.* 13), which would be in the year 438.[12] We have, in addition, commentaries (some only partially preserved) on the *First Alcibiades*, *Cratylus*, *Parmenides*, and *Republic*, as well as various other works, including the *Elements of Theology* and *Platonic Theology*. Proclus is also a prominent figure in the history of science in late antiquity; his surviving

---

8. Watts 2006, 118–28, esp. 125.
9. Watts 2006, 125–28.
10. Lamberton 1986, 134.
11. His powers were considerably reduced during his last five years (*Vit. Proc.* 26).
12. See Watts 2006, 100 with n. 102, for the idea that this gives us at least a ballpark figure for the date of Syrianus's death and (perhaps) for Proclus's succession.

scientific works include an *Introduction to the Physical Sciences* and a *Commentary on the First Book of Euclid's Elements*.[13]

The commentaries of Proclus all represent, in one form or another, the record of his teaching, which covered Plato, Aristotle (though his commentaries, if in fact ever written, are lost), Plotinus, and the Chaldaean Oracles, as well as mathematics (Euclid) and other scientific subjects. Of particular interest here are the commentaries on the dialogues on Plato, both the five extant ones and the further six that are known to have existed: *Phaedo, Gorgias, Philebus, Phaedrus, Theaetetus,* and *Sophist*. It was the tradition of the later schools of Platonic philosophy for the scholarch to commit to writing his sentence-by-sentence notes on the dialogues studied, and it is this material that forms the core of the commentaries that survive.

We assume that the Athenian school followed in some form or other the curriculum for the study of Plato that was attributed to Iamblichus, in the early fourth century.[14] As reconstructed by Westerink, this curriculum took the beginning student through the *First Alcibiades* (as general introduction), then the *Gorgias, Phaedo, Cratylus, Theaetetus, Sophist, Politicus, Phaedrus, Symposium,* and, finally, the *Philebus*. This will have constituted the elementary cycle, to be followed by the *Timaeus* and the *Parmenides*.[15] In other words, Proclus published commentaries on ten of the twelve dialogues in the Iamblichean canon—all but the *Politicus* and the *Symposium*.

2. The Commentary on the *Republic*

The single dialogue of Plato on which Proclus wrote that has no connection to the Iamblichean canon is the *Republic*. It seems clear that the reason for the exclusion of the *Republic*—and the *Laws*—from the curriculum was a practical one. Their length and complexity made them unmanageable for

---

13. On Proclus's contributions to our knowledge of science on the eve of the Byzantine period, see Siorvanes 1996.

14. The "canon" is presented in its most complete form (though still requiring some restoration) in the "Anonymous Prolegomena" to Plato (Westerink 1990, 39–40 with nn. 215–24). Proclus himself, in his commentary on the *First Alcibiades*, cites with approval Iamblichus's assigning to that dialogue the first place in the list of "the ten dialogues in which he believes the whole of Plato's philosophy to be contained" (Proclus, *In Alc*. 11.11–13 [Westerink]).

15. See Westerink 1990, lxvii–lxxiv.

classroom use, at least for purposes of the basic course. But there was also a question of priorities. From the time of Plotinus, at least, the Platonic schools tended to value metaphysics (and later, theology) at the expense of politics. In the hierarchy of "virtues" associated with the curriculum, the "political virtues" are the starting point, but the emphasis is clearly on the higher levels, the "cathartic" and "contemplative" virtues, which constitute the evident strength of the specifically Platonic curriculum. If the two long dialogues that address the organization of human society were added, the curriculum would be decidedly bottom heavy. For these reasons, or reasons like them, Iamblichus seems to have excluded them.

Does the existence of Proclus's commentary on the *Republic* mean that the Athenian Platonists' curriculum deviated so significantly from the Iamblichean model as to include the *Republic*? The answer to this question is to be found in the commentary itself, which consists of seventeen essays of unequal length (of which the fifth and sixth are included here, representing roughly one quarter of the entire text). The sixteenth book, by far the longest (Kroll 1901, 96–359), consists of a sentence-by-sentence commentary on the Myth of Er in book 10 of the dialogue. Thus 263 pages of the commentary (39.6 percent) are devoted to just eleven pages (or roughly 2.7 percent) of the dialogue, and these are the only pages to receive the sort of treatment that is the norm for the other commentaries. It seems clear from this distribution of labor that the Myth of Er was the portion of the *Republic* that was taught in Athens, and it probably constituted part of the regular curriculum.[16]

The remainder of the *Republic* commentary, when the line-by-line commentary on the Myth of Er is set aside, consists of a series of essays and lectures on various topics relating to the interpretation of the dialogue. In the case of the sixth essay, the one concerning Homer, Proclus tells us explicitly that it was composed (no doubt in a somewhat different form from what we have) as a lecture on the occasion of the celebration of Plato's birthday.[17] Other sections of the commentary doubtless found their place in the pedagogy of the school as well, and quite possibly these lectures were more central to Proclus's teaching than the long essay on

---

16. Westerink (1990, lxix) in fact restored the *Politicus* to the Iamblichean canon on a similar basis: he believed that the myth in that dialogue was the only portion that the Neoplatonists would have required and so presumably the only part that would have been taught.

17. See below p. 59 (K69) with n. 75.

Homer and its briefer predecessor (book 5) on Plato on poetics in general. If the *Republic* was too long to read sentence by sentence, and if large parts of it were far from the concerns of the Athenian Platonists, the dialogue nevertheless treated some issues that were very important to them, and although the bulk of the day-to-day work of the school doubtless consisted of sequential commentary on the (ten or) twelve dialogues that Iamblichus had singled out as containing "the whole of Plato's philosophy,"[18] we should beware of imagining that it was limited to that activity.

The subjects treated in the other topical chapters go some distance toward painting a picture of the *Republic* as taught (and understood) by the Athenian Platonists.[19] The first is among the most interesting, because here Proclus addresses the pedagogical issue of how one is to present to students, not just the *Republic*, but more generally any dialogue of Plato. This lecture is clearly intended for advanced students, those about to become teachers themselves and in need of instruction in the relevant skills. The part of the commentary on the initial attempts to provide a definition of justice is not complete, but it is striking that the only other topic Proclus focuses on before turning to poetics and to Homer is "the theological principles articulated in Book Two."[20]

After the essays presented in this volume (representing the focus of interest of books 2 and 3 of the *Republic*), Proclus goes on to single out basic definitions (e.g., "The Demonstrations in the Fourth Book That the Parts of the Human Soul Are Three and the Virtues in Them Four") and specific arguments (e.g., "The Three Arguments Demonstrating That the Just Man Is Better Off Than the Unjust Man"). This may well, as Anne Sheppard suggested,[21] amount to a "course of introductory lectures" on

---

18. See n. 14, above.

19. See pp. xxi–xxxiii for a table of contents of the entire commentary. Sheppard has a similar table (1980, 203–5), where she emphasizes the coherence of fifteen of the essays as "a course of introductory lectures on the *Republic*" (203) and the independence of Essays 6, 9, 15, and 16 (as well as 17, on Aristotle, which she did not include).

20. In the brief preface to his scholarly translation of the commentary, Festugière suggested that the original may well have been divided into several smaller units, of which Essays 4–6 would have been one. The short fourth essay would then, with its discussion of the theological *typoi* of book 2 of the *Republic*, lead into the discussion of poetics (Essay 5) and finally the defense itself (Essay 6). The logic of this grouping is unimpeachable, but for purposes of the present volume the focus on specifically literary issues has been maintained by omitting Essay 4.

21. Note 19, above.

the *Republic*, and this may be the format in which a series of important topics concerning the *Republic* entered the Athenian curriculum, but clearly other possibilities exist as well.

What is beyond doubt is that several of these essays, including the sixth, stand out as "distinct units,"[22] either exploring the relevant ideas of other thinkers (Theodore of Asine [9] or Aristotle [17]) or expanding on specific points to a degree that sets them apart from the remaining essays. Thus the pairing of 5 and 6 within the commentary may well have been an editorial decision, based simply on the fact that the voluminous exploration of the Socratic criticism of Homer is properly associated with the general principles of poetics and pedagogy explored in more modest format (and in the sequence of the "introductory lectures") in 5. As we shall see in the following section, Essays 5 and 6 are based on two quite distinct views of poetics.

3. Proclus on Poetics and Allegory[23]

If we had only the fifth and not the sixth essay of the *Republic* commentary, Proclus's place in the history of poetics would quickly dissolve into thin air. He would remain one of the early defensive commentators on Plato on poetics, a dry scholar, formulating modest questions and providing reasoned answers, sometimes calling upon relevant outside opinion. The first of the two essays explicitly denies what is most original and most valuable in the second, namely, the claim that poetry's semiotic range extends beyond mimesis and includes modes of representation that make it possible for poetry to designate things and beings that are beyond expression in the mimetic mode.[24]

---

22. Sheppard 1980, 203.

23. In this section I am particularly indebted to Anne D. R. Sheppard, who thirty years ago sorted out the tangled skeins of the fifth and sixth essays of the commentary. The debt is an old one, beginning with the chapter on Proclus in my own *Homer the Theologian* (1986). Building on and correcting the work of Carlo Gallavotti (1929, 1971), she did a great deal to clarify both the relationship of the two essays and the debts of Proclus to Syrianus (Sheppard 1980, esp. 15–38).

24. P. 7 (K44,1–2): μιμητικῆς ἁπάσης οὔσης τῆς τῶν ποιητῶν πραγματείας. Cf. p. 49 (K65,28–29) with n. 61. By contrast, at pp. 259–61 (K178–79), in the tripartite division of poetry, only the third and lowest kind of poetry is conceded to be mimetic.

Essay 5 fits nicely into the sequence of the chapters that form, at least potentially, a Neoplatonic introductory course on the *Republic*. It in fact illustrates the link to the classroom of such comparable collections as Plutarch's *Platonic Questions*.[25] Some of the questions explored would be classed as genuine problems in the interpretation of books 2 and 3 of the *Republic* today (though not, perhaps, the most important ones), some address contradictions that arise from what may be considered stylistic concerns (paradoxes, irreconcilable examples of ignorance on Socrates' part, and other ironies), and, finally, some seem to go beyond this lowly level of *explication de texte* by posing issues that are important to Proclus (and to later Platonist metaphysics) but, to our modern eyes at least, not dictated by the text of Plato. One example from each of these categories will suffice for our purposes.

The first question poses a problem central to the *Republic* and to the entire history of its discussion: Why does Plato prescribe both honor and exile for the poets?[26] Proclus dwells longer on the nature of the "divine" honors involved than a modern commentator would be inclined to do, but overall he patches together an acceptable answer, drawing on passages from the *Timaeus*, *Laws*, and *Republic* (and thus characteristically letting Plato interpret Plato where possible).[27] Proclus breaks down the problem to identify and define two characteristic types of failure of mimesis in the representation of gods and heroes, failures that make the resultant poetry unacceptable for purposes of education. It is one of the paradoxes of Proclus's assessment of Homer that he is consistently willing to concede this point to Plato (or to the Socrates of the *Republic*),[28] yet, Proclus insists, Plato does not reject poetry or Homer outright. With characteristic attention to context (and to the thought experiment of the state characterized by justice in the *Republic*), he argues at the end that Plato is right to exclude poetry from the "first ... state"[29]—it is simply too anarchic—but would recommend poetry as desirable in lesser polities (not characterized by justice), where its vices would shine forth as virtues.

---

25. See Sheppard 1980, 104.
26. Pp. 3 (K42) and 5–17 (K43–49). This is the longest of the ten discussions in essay 5.
27. See Sheppard 1980, 106 with n. 4; Lamberton 1986, 109 with n. 85.
28. See esp. p. 73 (K77) with n. 94, below.
29. P. 15 (K48,25).

The fourth question asks why Socrates professes ignorance of the modes—with some exceptions—and defers to Glaucon in matters of music, and the answer given depends upon an interesting view of Plato's own dramaturgy. It would have been possible simply to point to Socrates' characteristic irony (*eironeia*), but this is not the strategy that Proclus adopts. Rather, he puts the emphasis on Socrates' role in this particular dialogue—the role of the statesman—and answers that there is a certain limited knowledge of music that is appropriate to the statesman, but this falls short of comprehensive understanding. Still, the statesman (in the current argument) is very much concerned with education and so must have knowledge of music to the extent that it contributes to (or, on the contrary, might detract from) effective education. Proclus shows overall a great deal of sensitivity to literary form and diction, a sensitivity that is inseparable from a correct understanding of the content of a text. Again, it is his youthful enthusiasm for and exceptional education in rhetoric that comes out here, in the service of explaining Plato's text.

The last two questions, and particularly the final one, raise issues that do not arise in any obvious way from the *Republic* itself; they would seem to be dictated rather by the metaphysical concerns that constitute the core of later Platonism. The metaphysical model in question certainly arose out of the text of Plato (with a considerable admixture of Aristotle) and by the time of Proclus amounted to an orthodoxy, subject to endless adjustment and rethinking, but fundamentally unimpeachable, that impinged on every aspect of philosophical activity, including hermeneutics. We shall see that in Essay 6 these metaphysical givens inform the elaborate system of classification of kinds of poetry that is Proclus's most characteristic contribution to poetics.

In Essay 5 the closing question ("Who is the poet in the universe, to whom the poet in this world will look?"[30]) is introduced as the logical conclusion to the enterprise of the essay.[31] This, in other words, is the question that will bring closure to the entire enquiry by placing Plato's view of poetics into the largest possible context. It is necessary that all genuine good things in this world preexist among the "whole" (and eternal) entities that

---

30. Pp. 3 (K43,21–25); 53–55 (K68–69).

31. P. 53 (K68,3–4): τούτου δὲ ἡμῖν γνωσθέντος οἶμαι καὶ τὸ τελευταῖον εἶναι δῆλον τῶν προβληθέντων ἡμῖν εἰς ζήτησιν.... This is the most emphatic of the phrases linking one question to the next. Far more characteristic is, e.g., τούτων μὲν οὖν ἅδην· τὸ δὲ ἑπόμενον σκοπῶμεν (p. 29 [K56,20]).

exist beyond change. Here, this model is applied in a rather simple and predictable way. Just as Zeus is the statesman of that realm, Apollo is its poet, organizing his creations according to Zeus's master plan. He presides over celestial mechanics and the various orbits of differing lengths along with the various speeds of the celestial objects borne in those orbits, and so can be described as "the poet of modal and metrical imitations"[32]—which in turn must constitute, in his realm, the so-called music of the spheres.

These three examples from Essay 5 make it clear that, even in his most pedestrian classroom performances, Proclus's readings of Plato bore a characteristic and personal stamp. There is, however, some question whether this "stamp" is that of Proclus himself or a collective accent drawing on the teaching of his predecessors. Plutarch of Athens and Syrianus were both scholarchs, and both taught Proclus, but neither wrote commentaries on the dialogues of Plato that have survived, though Hermias's notes on the *Phaedrus* are heavily dependent on Syrianus.[33] Proclus in his own voluminous commentaries often tells us that a given interpretation or idea belongs to Syrianus, to whom he refers repeatedly as his "guide" or "teacher" (καθηγεμών).[34] In the *Republic* commentary, Proclus invokes Syrianus at least seven times, exclusively in Essay 6,[35] and insists on his own debt to his teacher for much of the interpretive material presented.

Anne Sheppard addressed the question of Syrianus's influence on the *Republic* commentary[36] and concluded that "in his interpretation of particular Homeric passages Proclus is adapting and developing Syrianus rather than striking out in any new directions of his own. He makes no contributions in this area which are comparable with his teacher's devel-

---

32. P. 55 (K69,1): ποιητής ὢν μιμημάτων ἐναρμονίων καὶ ἐνρύθμων. This phrase points up one difficulty of translating such prose. Apollo is a ποιητής in a more general sense ("maker") in his sphere, corresponding to the ποιητής in this world (whom in this context we can call a "poet"). He instills in his creations patterns of pitch (ἁρμονίαι) and rhythm (ῥυθμοί), which are the analogues of the modes and meters, the tools of the poet of this world. In other words, the three central terms in this phrase really require separate translations appropriate to the different spheres where they are applied.

33. Couvreur 1901.

34. On the term, see p. 61 (K71) n. 78, below; at p. 61 (K71,24), he is referred to as the ζηλωτής and ἱεροφάντης of Plato (p. 63 [K71] n. 82).

35. 61, 63, 147, 179, 215 (twice), and 307.

36. Sheppard 1980, 39–103 (= ch. 2, "Proclus's Debt to Syrianus").

opment of metaphysical allegory."[37] Thus the characteristic tone of Essay 6 is to be traced to Syrianus, as well as the specifics of many of the interpretations offered, but Sheppard maintained that the great accomplishment of the essay, the elaboration of a theoretical infrastructure to explain the capacity of poetry to designate its objects by other means than mimesis, is to be attributed to Proclus himself.[38] She attributed to Syrianus a division of poetry into inspired and uninspired, which provided Proclus with a springboard for his own threefold division of poetry, which in turn has proven extraordinarily suggestive and influential.

Rather than duplicate the existing descriptions of Proclus's analysis of poetry,[39] I offer here a tabular presentation of his model.[40]

The Three Levels of Poetry (ποιητική) and the Three Lives (ζωαί) or Conditions (ἕξεις) of the Soul, according to Proclus

SOUL	POETRY
FIRST: Soul on the level of the gods, transcending individual mind (νοῦς) and attaching its "own light to the transcendent light and the most unified element of its own being and life to the One beyond all being and life" (*In Rep.* 257)	NATURE: Absolute fusion of subject and object; inspiration, possession by the Muses; divine madness (μανία) filling the soul with symmetry (*In Rep.* 259, 261–73)
	MEANS: Symbols (σύμβολα), which are nonmimetic [although Proclus is not consistent and sometimes seems to say that images (εἰκόνες) of transcendent patterns (παραδείγματα) occur in this, the highest poetry] (*passim*, esp. *In Rep.* 295)

---

37. Sheppard 1980, 79.
38. Sheppard 1980, 102–3.
39. See Sheppard 1980, 162–202; Lamberton 1986, 188–97; 1992.
40. Based on Lamberton 1992, 121 table 1. In the interest of brevity, the page references refer to the pages of this volume.

	EXAMPLES: The song of Ares and Aphrodite (*Od.* 8.266–366) and the Deception of Zeus (*Il.* 14.153–351) (*In Rep.* 193–99, 177–93, 283–85)
	REPRESENTED IN HOMER BY: Demodocus (*In Rep.* 285–87)
SECOND: Soul turns within itself and focuses on mind (νοῦς) and systematic knowledge (ἐπιστήμη) (*In Rep.* 257)	NATURE: Again, fusion of knower and known—this poetry knows the essential truth and loves to contemplate beautiful actions and accounts of things (λόγοι). It is "packed with advice and the best counsel … offering … participation in thoughtfulness and the other virtues" (*In Rep.* 259–61, 273–77)
	MEANS: Apparently still nonmimetic, based on ἐπιστήμη (*In Rep.* 261)
	EXAMPLES: The description of Heracles in the *nekyia* (*Od.* 11.601–604) and unspecified Homeric passages on the parts of the soul and the arrangement of the elements of the universe (*In Rep.* 285)
	REPRESENTED IN HOMER BY: Phemius (*In Rep.* 287)
THIRD: The lowest life of the soul, based on imagination (φαντασία) and irrational sense perceptions (ἄλογοι αἰσθήσεις) (*In Rep.* 257–59)	NATURE: This poetry is full of opinions (δόξαι) and imaginings (φαντασίαι); it shocks and manipulates the audience and projects a false image of reality; it is a shadow painting (σκιαγραφία), appealing to the emotions. This lowest level of poetry is further divided into: (a) accurately mimetic (εἰκαστικόν); and (b) illusionistic (φανταστικόν) (*In Rep.* 261, 277–83)
	MEANS: Mimetic, using (a) εἰκασία (representation) and (b) an apparent, but not real ἀφομοίωσις (resemblance) (*In Rep.* 261)
	EXAMPLES: (a) Heroes portrayed fighting or performing other activities in character; and (b) descriptions of what *appears* to be; e.g., the sun

rising "out of the sea" (*Od.* 3.1) (*In Rep.* 281–83)

REPRESENTED IN HOMER BY: (a) The bard (ἀοιδὸς ἀνήρ, *Od.* 3.267) left to look after Clytemnestra; and (b) Thamyris (*Il.* 2.595) (*In Rep.* 287–89)

Based on a tripartite metaphysics that has its origins in Plato but is more obviously derivative from Plotinus, this analysis marks out a place for poetry in the map of the human universe. This impulse is already visible in Essay 5, at least in the final question explored (above), but here in Essay 6 the issues at stake are more intricate and engaging. The hierarchy of levels of experience gives birth to a hierarchy of modes of representation, in keeping with the general principle that, in the great translation and fragmentation that constantly generates the world of our immediate experience out of the unchanging, suprasensory realities, all the resulting phenomena are to be understood in terms of ourselves and of our lack of capacity to apprehend an unmediated reality.[41]

The concern with myth, with archaic poetry, and with their interpretation is pervasive in the works of Proclus, and he seems characteristically to have devoted a lost (perhaps early) work "On the Symbols of Myth"[42] to spelling out the principles and procedures that form the basis of such interpretation. The richest articulation of these principles and their application to poetry is undoubtedly to be found in the text translated here, but this is complemented in the surviving corpus by methodological observations in the *Timaeus* commentary and in the *Platonic Theology* that clarify the relationship of these hermeneutic principles to other sorts of interpretive problems.

The *Platonic Theology* probably dates from the latter part of Proclus's career and constitutes an exposition of Neoplatonic theology, largely organized around the interpretation of the *Parmenides*, the dialogue that constituted for the later Neoplatonic curriculum the summation of the theology of Plato.[43] Before turning to the *Parmenides*, however, Proclus needs to establish the range of modes of expression (τρόποι) of Plato's theology,

---

41. See below, 81 n. 100.
42. Περὶ τῶν μυθικῶν συμβόλων, referred to by Proclus in the *Republic* commentary (Kroll 1901, 109,1) and so earlier (though on problems of dating the works of Proclus, see Beutler 1957, 190–91).
43. Saffrey and Westerink 1968, lx–lxxxix; Westerink 1990, 39 with n. 216.

which turn out to be four: (1) the symbolic (characteristic of Orpheus and of myths of the divine generally) and (2) that through images (characteristic of the Pythagoreans, who use number and diagrams as images of the divine); these first two modes use ἔνδειξις (indication, indirect representation)[44] to speak about the gods, whereas the two other modes express the truth regarding the gods in an unmediated, direct manner (ἀπαρακαλύπτως), either (3) through ecstatic inspiration (as in the mysteries) or (4) through systematic knowledge (ἐπιστήμη). Just as the mythic/symbolic mode is most characteristic of Homeric poetry (*In Rep.* 289 [K195], below), it is this last that is most characteristic (ἐξαίρετος) of Plato.[45]

As is often the case with Proclus, this characterization of Homer and Plato amounts to a very elaborate way of saying something quite simple. Plato, the philosopher par excellence, has a characteristic mode of expression for talking about the divine, and it is that of the philosopher, whereas Homer, the mythic poet par excellence, has his own characteristic way of expressing such things, which is that of what Proclus generally calls the "mythoplast." Perhaps the terminology of the *Platonic Theology* is more clearly thought out than that of the *Republic* commentary. It is, in any case, clearer. Of course, both writers can use any of the modes in question, but each has one which he characteristically does use.

Strictly speaking, what is at stake in *Platonic Theology* 1.4 is a series of modes of expression, which correspond broadly with and throw light on the series of poetic modes described in the *Republic* commentary. In the commentary, the goal is explicitly the defense of Homer against Socrates' criticisms and the reconciliation of Homeric and Platonic theology. The modes of expression easily lend themselves to translation into modes of interpretation, as we shall see, and the one hermeneutically problematic mode—the mythic/symbolic—will be found to require its own special technique, associated with what Proclus calls the "secret doctrine" (ἀπόρρητος θεωρία). The correct understanding of myths about the gods will turn out to depend on access to this technique and to the body of knowledge that lies behind it, and broadly speaking there seem to be three ways to understand a mythic poem: (1) literally (that is, remaining at the level of the "screen" [παραπέτασμα] of the fiction and thus missing the

---

44. See below, p. 63 with n. 83.
45. The material summarized here can be found in *Platonic Theology* 1.4.

point, with possibly dangerous consequences), (2) mistakenly (the most frequent examples of which are "physical" readings, which take the gods of myth to be representations of phenomena in the physical universe), and (3) "according to the secret doctrine." This last category—the only correct mode of interpretation—requires either the previous acquisition of a considerable body of knowledge or the sort of hermeneutic assistance that the commentary provides (while reminding its audience that this is privileged information, not to be widely divulged).

There are similarities, of course, with the categories of Christian exegesis,[46] and it is impossible to eliminate the possibility that Clement and Origen lurk somewhere in the distant background of this analysis of poetic language. Certainly, medieval Christian Platonists were the heirs of this complex tradition, which absorbed the ideas of Proclus and the other fifth-century polytheist Platonists of Athens through the corpus of (Pseudo-) Dionysius the Areopagite. It is tempting to believe that some as yet undiscovered chain of influence may have led from polytheist philosophical hermeneutic theory and practice to Origen, who is generally credited with taking the first steps in the direction of the three- and fourfold theories of scriptural exegesis of the high Middle Ages in the West. Whether or not this is the case, Proclus is at least as likely to have been influenced by earlier and contemporary Christian hermeneutic ideas as the reverse, and the influence of Proclan ideas on late medieval Christian thinkers is best understood as stemming from a late antique intellectual world in which Christians and polytheists alike concerned themselves with the interpretation of texts. Their motivations were not the same, but their procedures sometimes resembled one another's, and if indeed hermeneutic ideas were exchanged across the divide, no one seems to have chosen to talk about it.

The influence of Proclus's hermeneutic model did not end with the Middle Ages. It was John Dillon who first noted the most amazing modern manifestation of this tradition: the remarkable resemblance between this system and Charles Sanders Peirce's semiotic triad: icon, index, and symbol.[47] This is unlikely to have been a coincidence, given that the founder

---

46. On the medieval systems of exegesis based on multilayered models, see Lubac 1959–1961.

47. Dillon 1976.

of modern semiotics had considerable knowledge of the Neoplatonists.[48] It is nevertheless striking that this influential innovation is to be found in such an unlikely place, a fifth-century commentary on the *Republic* concerned to defend Homer against Socrates' famous rejection of Homer in that dialogue.

4. The Defense of Homer

If the theoretical innovation that surfaces in Proclus's analysis of poetry is the most enduring accomplishment of this text, it nevertheless remains secondary (or ancillary) to the explicit aim of Essay 6, which is the defense of Homer against the Socrates of the *Republic*.[49]

Socrates' points are familiar enough: held up against the theological principles of book 2 (a god is good, is the cause only of good, is unchanging, and does not lie, 379a–383c), Homer is found wanting again and again. The objections that follow are directed at the portrayal of men (in practice, the heroes, or demigods who are the characters in the poem), and these are based on the assumption that the audience will consider them exemplary and aspire to imitate them. If we want that audience (and we are talking here about the "guardians" of the state) to be brave, we must eliminate all references to death as something to be feared and, along with those, all depictions of these exemplary beings lamenting (book 3: 386c–388c) or overcome by laughter (388e–389b). Numerous examples follow of Homeric descriptions of obnoxious behavior by gods and heroes: Achilles' insubordination, the seduction of Zeus, Achilles' venality, his arrogance (389b–391c). Next comes a series of more difficult criticisms: the best poet should apparently stick to narrative, avoiding scenes where characters speak for themselves (that is, passages of mimesis; 391d–394d). Thus tragedy and comedy are eliminated as mimetic (394d–397e), and the virtuoso poet "able to imitate anything" is imagined visiting the city, meeting with lavish praise, and being expelled as inappropriate in that context. The story is taken up again in book 10, where we learn that mimetic art (the prime example now is painting)[50] is fundamentally defective because the images it creates are "third from the truth" (595a–600e). Homer, because his art

---

48. On Peirce and Neoplatonism and the link through Emerson, see Smyth 1997, ch. 2 *passim*. Other possible links include Victoria Lady Welby (Hardwick 1977).
49. See Kuisma 1996.
50. Annas 1981, 94.

is mimetic, was useless as an educator or an improver of mankind (600c, 606e–607a).[51]

Clearly there are at least two indictments here, and to many readers Plato's twofold attack on Homer and on mimesis has seemed to lack coherence.[52] Proclus does not shy away from apparent contradictions, and it is very much characteristic of this commentary to point to apparent inconsistencies and then to demonstrate that there is an underlying coherence in Plato's thought.[53] In doing so, he taps a long tradition of commentary on Homer, which includes Neoplatonic material such as Porphyry's *Essay on the Cave of the Nymphs in the* Odyssey but extends back as well to Aristotle's collection of *Homeric Problems* and beyond.

Essay 5 is hardly a defense of Homer. His name is never mentioned, though he is once designated by the conventional circumlocution "the Poet."[54] The first question explores the paradox of Plato's simultaneous praise and rejection of poetry and poets, but though it may be obvious that Homer is in question, nevertheless the status of the *Iliad* and *Odyssey* is not put on the table.

Essay 6, by contrast, proclaims from the outset that its goals are the defense of Homer and the demonstration that "a single irrefutable truth is to be seen everywhere in Plato's position on poetics itself and on Homer," so that "each of them would be revealed to us as a thoughtful and knowledgeable contemplator of the divine beings, both of them teaching the same things about the same things, and both interpreters of the same truth about reality."[55] If Plato could reject Homer as a witness to the whole of the truth about reality, Proclus (following in Syrianus's footsteps) could not. He proposes to redeem Homer's credibility even as he restores the coherence of the apparently contradictory things Plato had to say about him. In one sense, the problem will turn out to have been one of rhetoric and of the problematic nature of Homer's language, which often appears to be saying one thing when it is in fact saying something quite different.

---

51. See Annas 1981, esp. 94–101, 336–344, for a synthetic overview of these arguments in the context of the dialogue.
52. Annas 1981 offers perspective on the issues, and Moss 2007 makes a thoughtful argument for reconstructing Plato's goal in the two passages.
53. Note the titles of the first, third, and fifth of the questions treated in Essay 5, as well as 59–61 (K70–71) in Essay 6.
54. P. 33 (K58,14).
55. P. 61 (K71,10–17).

This same ambiguity will form the basis for Proclus's conceding to Plato the unsuitability of the *Iliad* and *Odyssey* for education.[56]

It is worth remembering at this point that (according to Marinus) Proclus "used to say": "If I were in control, of all the ancient books I would keep in circulation only the *Oracles* and the *Timaeus*, and I would hide all the rest from the people of today because some of those who approach them casually and *without interrogating and interpreting them properly* (ἀβασανίστως) are actually harmed."[57] That is to say, Homer and all the other books of the classical tradition (with the exception of the *Timaeus* and the *Chaldaean Oracles*) required hermeneutical assistance. For some of those books, preeminently the *Iliad* and *Odyssey*, hermeneutical assistance was available in every classroom in Greece, in the context of a thoroughly Christianized educational system. In Proclus's judgment, it would clearly have been better to do without the epics entirely than to wander into their outrageous fictions unprepared or to understand them in terms of the benighted and bigoted pedagogic orthodoxy of his own day.

The reading of Homer, then, is for Proclus a curiously subversive process. The literature of Homer interpretation had blossomed in the centuries before his own time, and although Basil of Caesarea,[58] a century before Proclus wrote, had laid out a clear strategy for the use of polytheist texts in Christian education, it is difficult to date the ascendency of a Christian pedagogy of Homer. That it was prevalent in primary and secondary education in Athens by 450 seems, however, unavoidable, and from Proclus's perspective it was these ham-fisted, literalist readers who learned to laugh at the surface of the fiction, and thence to scoff at the gods, who were burning their temples for lime. Hence the privacy of this interpretive discourse.[59] What Proclus is in fact doing is taking what had been for a thousand years the most popular and widely used of elementary textbooks and declaring it to be fit for study only by the equivalent of graduate students, and behind closed doors.

The principal issue, of course, is theology. The strategy of Christian schoolteachers, to judge by the principles set forth by Basil, would be to ignore the theology of Homer and direct their students' attention to the

---

56. P. 73 (K77,4–9).

57. *Vit. Proc.* 38 (the final lines of the biography), emphasis added. On the word ἀβασανίστως, see Saffrey and Segonds 2001, 44 and 181 n. 6.

58. See his essay *Ad adulescentes*.

59. P. 306 (K205,22–23), the conclusion of Essay 6.

edifying passages, those in which an ethical message compatible with Christianity could be read. Much of the behavior of the gods and heroes had been found offensive by the Socrates of the *Republic*, and the passages in question had already generated a substantial literature of commentary, much of it defensive. Proclus taps this literature, but it is important to realize the extent to which the stakes have changed from the time of Plato. For the interlocutors of the *Republic*, the rejection of Homer as a school text was an intellectually stimulating paradox not unlike the education of women, the one as alien to their own society and to any realistic (i.e., pragmatic) program for the reform of Athenian education as the other. In Proclus's Athens, however, Homer remained the "first author" and the core of the (essentially rhetorical) educational process, at the expense of denying that what he said about the gods was to be taken seriously. Proclus's response is not unlike what one might have expected from Julian, that defender of a holistic view of Hellenism.[60] He set out to restore the coherence of Homer and of Homer's account of the world and the gods, but he did so explicitly for a severely restricted group: the few advanced students of Platonism who came to Athens to study in a polytheist environment.

The original context of Essay 6 (or some part of it) was the celebration of Plato's birthday. Little is known about the celebrations of the birthdays of Socrates and Plato in the Platonist philosophical schools of the Roman Empire beyond some comments by Porphyry (relating to Plotinus's school in Rome in the 260s) and the reference here (to Athens, in the mid-fifth century).[61] From this meager evidence, we may conclude that the practice was persistent and long-lived and that it combined a celebration of the lives of the founders with an extension of the intellectual work of the school into a decidedly symposiac setting. The presentations would seem to have been rhetorical performances (perhaps even explicitly taking their cue from Plato's *Symposium*) doubtless expected to be philosophically respectable but at the same time appropriate to the festive environment of the symposium. Nowhere is poetry, and Homer in particular, so at home as in the symposium. The bards of the *Odyssey*—the internalized self-portrait of the Homeric bard at work—sang for the feasts and symposia of the aristocrats of the Homeric age.[62]

---

60. For Julian's insistence on Hellenism as an integral cultural whole, from which no single element could be removed (including religion), see Athanassiadi 1981.
61. See below p. 59 (K69,24–70,7) with n. 75.
62. Proclus is the first of many critics to take Demodocus as a self-portrait of

This is not to trivialize Proclus's symposiac address on poetry and on Homer—far from it. The symposium was a serious institution, in particular that hybrid, the literary symposium, which begins (in the preserved literature) with Plato. But it was also a celebration, with emphasis on the socialization of the participants and the elegance of their performances. Here, again, Homer is where he belongs. To know Homer backward and forward, to be able to cite from memory a vast array of passages, was an indication of high cultural literacy in Proclus's world, as it had been in Plato's. This is a side of the text that it would be a mistake to forget. What Proclus is doing here is to restore a coherent reading of a literary text that had been wrested from the culture that produced it and adapted to the educational needs of a new culture, at considerable cost. That is, certain aspects of the text, including its representation of the traditional gods of Greek polytheism, had been discredited or otherwise attacked. But the important point here is that it is a literary text that is at issue, and even if the matter in dispute is one related to its representation of the gods, the authority of the text is cultural, in the broadest sense, not religious. This is not, in other words, an exercise in exegesis of a scriptural text. It belongs to a society that had no such texts, in the sense that the monotheisms had and have scriptures. A claim might be supported that the poems attributed to Orpheus and the *Chaldaean Oracles* were treated by their adherents in polytheist late antiquity much the way contemporary monotheists treated their scripture, and there is reason to believe that the Athenian Platonists found a place for those texts in their curricula. But the same is not true of Homer, whose poems found themselves at the center of disputes such as these not as competing scriptures but because their immeasurable cultural authority—and most of all the fact that they were the common cultural property of every educated speaker of Greek—made them objects of contention.

The episode in the dispute between Christians and polytheists for the possession of the text of the *Iliad* and *Odyssey* represented by Proclus's essays was proclaimed not by a priest (whether from a pulpit or from a sacrificial altar) but by a philosopher serving as a symposiarch. He spoke in the service of truth rather than belief and in the service of poetry rather than scripture.

Homer. See his typology of the kinds of bards (and of poetry) in Homer, pp. 283–89 (K192–95).

INTRODUCTION

5. The Text

The text of Proclus's commentary that is presented here is by and large the same as that published by Wilhelm Kroll in 1899, with some conjectures and corrections raised from his apparatus to the text and some from his addenda, as well as a very few conjectures of my own. I have introduced a large number of paragraph breaks (in most cases corresponding to the paragraphs of the translation), in the interest both of clarity and of ease in passing from the English to the Greek and vice versa. This has led to some aberrations in the line numbering of the Greek, but I have attempted to retain as much as possible the numbering of the lines in Kroll's text, in order to facilitate reference to that text. Verticals (|) have been added to the Greek text corresponding to the beginning of lines 5, 10, 15, and so on of Kroll's text. Double verticals (||) in both the Greek and English texts represent page breaks in Kroll's text. All other deviations from the text printed by Kroll are underlined in the Greek text and accounted for in the notes. Some typographical errors have also been corrected. For the advisability of many of these improvements in the text I am dependent on the comments of the late A. J. Festugière (1970), to whom not only the text here presented but the translation and notes are deeply and pervasively indebted. The notation "[F.]" is used to indicate notes substantially dependent on those of his exemplary scholarly translation.

Kroll's preface to the first volume of the text he edited is brief (less than three pages), and I have translated what is relevant to the present text below (Addendum 2, pp. xxxiii–xxxv). This gives a description of the unique manuscript, now divided into two parts, of which the portions of the *Commentary* translated here are found in the Florentine codex (Laurentian Library [codex LXXX 9]).

Addendum 1: Table of Contents of Proclus's Commentary on the *Republic*

[Kroll]

Essay 1: What and How Many Are the Principal Topics That a Correct Interpreter Must Articulate Before Reading the *Republic* with a Group?   1:5

[Essay 2: The Arguments of Socrates against Polemarchus' Definition of Justice—MISSING]

Essay 3: The Four Arguments on Justice in the *Republic* Directed against Thrasymachus' Four Notions About It [BEGINNING MISSING]	1:20
Essay 4: The Theological Principles Articulated in Book 2 of the *Republic*	1:27
Essay 5: Plato's Position on the Art of Poetry and its Various Genres and the Best Mode and Meter	1:42
Essay 6: Proclus the Successor on the Things Said by Plato in the *Republic* Regarding Homer and Poetics	
Book 1	1:69
Book 2	1:154
Essay 7: The Demonstrations in the Fourth Book of the *Republic* that the Parts of the Human Soul are Three and the Virtues in Them Four	1:206
Essay 8: The Speeches in the Fifth Book of the *Republic* Showing that the Virtues and Education are Common to Men and Women	1:236
Essay 9: Theodore of Asine's Arguments Maintaining that the Virtue of Men and Women is the Same and an Examination of What Socrates Said [on this Matter]	1:251
Essay 10: The Argument in Book Five of the *Republic* Distinguishing Between the Love of Knowledge [φιλομαθία] of Philosophers and That of the Many	1:258
Essay Eleven: The Argument in the *Republic* Demonstrating What the Good Is	1:269
Essay Twelve: The Cave in the Seventh Book of the *Republic*	1:287
Essay Thirteen: "Melissa" on the Speech of the Muses in the *Republic*	2:1
Essay Fourteen: The Three Arguments Demonstrating That the Just Man Is Better Off Than the Unjust Man*	2:81

* Reading τὸν δίκαιον for τὸ δίκαιον at K. 1:4,22.

Essay Fifteen: The Principal Topics in Book 10 of the *Republic*	2:85
Essay Sixteen: Commentary on the Myth of Er	2:96
Essay Seventeen: An Inquiry into the Objections of Aristotle in Book 2 of the *Politics* to the *Republic* of Plato	2:360

Addendum 2: Wilhelm Kroll's Preface to Volume 1 of His Edition of the *Commentary*

I have little to insert as preface to this first volume of Proclus, containing what is in the Florentine codex; I shall have more to say in preface to the second.

The commentaries on the *Republic* of Plato are extant in a single codex, written in the ninth or tenth century and at some point split in two by some greedy individual, of which one is now in the Laurentian Library (codex LXXX 9) and the other passed from the books of the Salviati to the codices Columnenses and thence to the Vatican collection (Vatic. 2197). The latter lay unexamined for a long time, but the former, though it was available for everyone's use for more than four centuries, was nevertheless fruitfully consulted by virtually no one.[1] The only edition of the first part to appear, published in Basel in 1534 by [Thomas] Grynaeus, came not from the Laurentian manuscript itself but from the Oxford copy (Corpus Christi College 99 chart. saec. XV);[2] a few people have examined the archetype, but no one took down variant readings before Pitram (Analecta sacra et classica V, Rome 1888, part II pp. 197–264), concerning whose meticulousness it is best to say nothing at all.

I therefore collated the Laurentian manuscript as diligently as I could in 1891 and 1893 and reexamined a few passages in 1896 (of one of them,

---

1. I list as an exception Valentinus Rose, who published a list of the titles in *Hermes* 2, 96ff. [Kroll's note; see Rose 1867]

2. Grynaeus in the dedicatory epistle to John More, the son of Thomas, dated March 1, 1534, claims that he received the manuscript from John Claymund [master of Corpus Christi College] in 1531, but Coxe (Catal. II 35) [Henry O. Coxe, Catalogus codicum MSS. qui in collegiis aulisque Oxoniensibus hodie adservantur (2 vols., Oxford, 1852)] says that he bought this same codex from the heirs of William Grocinus in 1521. [Kroll's note]

my friend N. Festa obligingly replied to my request for a reading). The codex is parchment consisting of 164 written pages,[3] 27 x 18 cm., written in the ninth or early tenth century with great care by the same man who wrote the Marcianus 246 of Damascius, the Parisinus 1807 of Plato (A), and the Palatinus 398 of the paradoxographers (I have nothing to report about the Parisinus 1962 of Maximus of Tyre and Albinus, on which cf. Duebner in his preface to Theophrastus, p. viii). Some librarian, from no other source but the archetype, made minuscules of the majuscules without adding accents or breathing marks. He was succeeded by a *revisor* who not only added these but collated the whole book with the archetype and removed nearly all the mistakes. At a later date, perhaps in the eleventh or twelfth century, a *corrector* came along who changed quite a few readings, in part from another manuscript and in part from his own conjectures. A recent hand has been active, chiefly in the first pages, working to restore the lost lines. In the apparatus I have designated the *revisor* as m² and the *corrector* as m³. However, if I had indicated all of his changes, I would have cluttered the apparatus with a great deal of trivia; it is not credible to say how many iotacisms and mistakes of this sort he introduced, especially since in those places where the color of the ink is the same, the one can scarcely be distinguished from the other. And if I had wished, I could with no damage have made my references to this man still less, but I thought it useful to alert the reader that someone of this sort had contributed no small amount to the composition of the manuscript. I warn the reader of one thing: wherever he erased individual letters or a whole word and had nothing to substitute, he filled the empty space with short lines, either plain or with dots above and below (——— and —⋮—), by which certain scholars have been led to quite amazing opinions.

---

3. 165 are numbered, but 177 [77?] occurs twice, 4 is entirely missing, and 1 has been added subsequently. After the first quire, four have fallen out, for the number A' appears on folio 5 and S' on folio 13 (cf. on 19, 25 [where it is observed that the missing pages create a lacuna encompassing the end of the first essay, all of the second, and the beginning of the third]). After quire 24 (folios 156–163) again some pages of the following quire have perished (cf. on 293, 22 [at least one folio is missing]), of which folios 164 and 165 have survived, now joined with two blank pages. Two folios from the 26th quire are preserved in the Vatican codex (folios 151, 152) but in the sixteenth century two more beside these were extant, which have twice been described but have now been removed and carried off somewhere (Diehl mus. Rhen. 54). [Kroll's note; see Diehl 1899]

INTRODUCTION

I have designated the Basel edition with the letter b and added its page numbers in the margin; Grynaeus made several excellent emendations (unless he found the passages already emended in the Oxford copy—the question did not seem to me to be of sufficient importance to travel to Oxford).

In my notes "im." is *in margine*, "ir." *in rasura*, "ss." *supra scripsit*, "exp." *expunxit*, "uv." *ut videtur*. Where I brought in the manuscripts of Plato, I made use of Schanz's notes. It was often necessary to refer to my book on the *Chaldaean Oracles* (Bresl. phil. Abh. vii 1 [Kroll 1894]).

It remains to thank all those who have helped me in the editing of this volume, of whom, after Richard Reizenstein, who was responsible for my editing Proclus, I must first name my friends Ludwig Radermacher and Paulus Wendland, who have earned the greatest credit for this edition by correcting the damaged portions and mistakes of the manuscript and removing my own errors, and, further, Ivo Bruns and Constantine Ritter, who very generously responded to my questions about the *Laws* of Plato at a number of points.

Bratislava   W.K.

Proclus, *In Rempublicam* 5 and 6: Contents

Essay 5: Plato's Position on the Art of Poetry and Its Various Genres and the Best Mode and Meter

1. Introduction: The Ten Questions — 3 [K42]
2. First Question — 5 [K43]
    a. Imitation without resemblance — 7 [K44]
    b. The imitation of human vices — 11 [K46]
    c. Why the art of poetry is exiled with honor — 13 [K47]
3. Second Question (Why are tragedy and comedy not admitted?) — 17 [K49]
4. Third Question (Why are comedy and tragedy produced by the same professional skill in the *Symposium* but not in the *Republic*?) — 21 [K51]
5. Fourth Question (Why does Socrates make conflicting claims about his knowledge of musical modes and meters? — 25 [K54]
6. Fifth Question (What is μουσική-in-itself, and what are the lower forms of μουσική?) — 29 [K56]
    a. The categories of μουσική — 31 [K57]
    b. Solution of the problem — 37 [K60]
7. Sixth Question (Which of the modes does he deem appropriate for education?) — 37 [K60]
8. Seventh Question (What are the failings of the poets known to him, and why does he say the Muses themselves could never fail?) — 45 [K63]
9. Eighth Question (Who, according to Plato, is the best poet?) — 47 [K65]
10. Ninth Question (What, according to him, is the end [τέλος] of correct poetry?) — 51 [K67]

11. Tenth Question (Who is the poet in the universe to whom the poet here looks in order to attain his own goals?)   53 [K68]

Essay 6: Proclus the Successor on the Things Said by Plato in the *Republic* against Homer and Poetry

Book 1

1. Introduction   59 [K69]
2. On the manner in which the divine myths are treated by the theologians, with an explanation of the reasons behind that treatment and answers to the objections raised against them   63 [K71]
   a. Socrates' charges   63 [K71]
   b. Proclus's reply: the correct and incorrect use of myth   67 [K74]
   c. Ugliness and obscenity in Homer's myths   71 [K76]
   d. Socrates distinguished the two types of myth   77 [K79]
   e. The allegorical interpretation of obscene myths   81 [K81]
   f. Proclus's opinion on the function of the monstrous in myth   89 [K85]
3. What are the various ways in which the secret truth in the "Battle of the Gods" of the theologians is brought to light?   91 [K87]
   a. The problem   93 [K87]
   b. First explanation   93 [K87]
   c. Second explanation   97 [K89]
   d. Application to the poets other than Homer   97 [K89]
   e. Application to Homer   99 [K90]
   f. The two explanations and their relevance to Homer   103 [K92]
4. How one might defend the myths about the divine that appear to attribute the causes of bad things to the gods   109 [K96]
   a. The problem   109 [K96]
   b. Interpretation of Homer's two pithoi   113 [K98]
5. How the poem seems to give the gods responsibility for the breaking of the oaths; the true guidance in these matters   117 [K100]

ANALYTICAL TABLE OF CONTENTS

6. What is the [meaning of the] episode of the poem in which Zeus, through Themis, puts the gods into a state of strife? An elaboration of the entire doctrine behind the myth ... 129 [K106]
7. What is [the meaning of] the judgment of the goddesses in the myths of the Poet, and what various sorts of lives does it hint at? ... 133 [K108]
8. What is [the meaning of] the transformations of the gods introduced into the myths, and in how many ways do they attribute these things to them and for what reasons? ... 135 [K109]
   a. The problem ... 135 [K109]
   b. Proclus's reply: Homer supported by theurgy ... 137 [K110]
   c. Transformations representing the multiple powers of the gods ... 141 [K112]
   d. The gods adopt the shapes of the classes of beings into which they descend ... 143 [K113]
9. How we are to defend the episode of the sending of the dream, which appears to attribute falsehood to the gods, and to demonstrate that the gods are free from falsehood ... 145 [K115]
   a. The problem ... 145 [K115]
   b. First reply ... 147 [K115]
   c. Second reply, from Syrianus ... 147 [K115]
   d. Conclusion: Proclus's synthesis ... 149 [K116]
10. A simultaneous defense of the Homeric and Platonic myths in which they speak of a place of correction in Hades and of the various destinies there of the souls that have left their bodies, determined according to the specific qualities of their lives in the body ... 151 [K117]
11. What are the reasons why the poem attributes lamentation both to the heroes and to the gods, and even to the best of the heroes and the greatest of the gods? ... 159 [K122]
    a. The problem ... 159 [K122]
    b. Proclus's response: the heroes ... 161 [K124]
    c. The gods and demons ... 163 [K124]
12. What is the cause of the so-called laughter that in the myths occurs among the gods, and why

did the poem describe the gods as laughing
irrepressibly at Hephaestus? 165 [K126]
13. Response concerning the various ways that the
Homeric poems appear to inspire in their listeners
scorn for moderation 171 [K129]
   a. The problem 171 [K129]
   b. Proclus's response: Achilles 173 [K130]
   c. Proclus's response: Odysseus 175 [K131]
14. What does Zeus's intercourse with Hera hint at:
What is the meaning of Hera's adornment, of the
location of their intercourse, the desire of Zeus, and
the divine sleep? Generally, an explanation of the
entire myth 177 [K132]
   a. The problem: the five questions 177 [K132]
   b. Solution to questions 1 and 2 179 [K133]
   c. Solution to the question of Zeus's sleep (3) 183 [K135]
   d. Solution to the question of the location of their
intercourse 185 [K136]
   e. Solution to the question of Hera's adornment 187 [K137]
   f. Solution to the question of the several occasions
of intercourse 191 [K139]
   g. Conclusion 193 [K140]
15. What does the mythology about Aphrodite and
Ares and the chains with which Hephaestus is said
to have bound them hint at? 193 [K141]
16. What is to be said against Socrates' objections concerning the greed Homer attributes to the heroes? 199 [K143]
17. How must one defend the apparent lack of respect
for the gods in the depiction of the heroes? 203 [K146]
   a. The problem 203 [K146]
   b. Achilles and Apollo 203 [K146]
   c. Achilles and the River Xanthos 207 [K148]
   d. Achilles and the River Spercheios 209 [K149]
18. How one can respond concerning the heroes'
apparent lack of respect for human life in the
poems or generally concerning the extraordinary
narratives that the poets include in their myths? 209 [K150]
   a. The problem 211 [K150]
   b. Reply: Achilles and Hector 211 [K150]

ANALYTICAL TABLE OF CONTENTS   xli

    c. Reply: the sacrifice of the captives   213 [K151]
    d. Other myths   217 [K153]

Book 2

1. Plato is accustomed everywhere to celebrate Homer as the guide to all truth   219 [K154]
2. What are the reasons why, in the *Republic*, Plato judged the poetry of Homer unfit to be heard by the young?   225 [K159]
3. That in all his writings Plato imitates Homer, with regard both to the excellence of his language and to that of his material   231 [K163]
    a. The problem   233 [K163]
    b. Mimesis   233 [K163]
    c. The *Timaeus*   233 [K164]
    d. The *Phaedrus*   237 [K166]
    e. The gods are all-powerful, omniscient, and providential: the *Laws*   239 [K167]
    f. The *nekuias*: the *Republic*, *Phaedo*, *Gorgias*   239 [K168]
    g. Double names: the *Cratylus*   243 [K169]
    h. Organization   245 [K170]
    i. Plato develops and expands ideas briefly stated by Homer: the *First Alcibiades*   247 [K171]
4. How one might answer what is said about Homer in the *Phaedrus*, where [Socrates] seems to judge Stesichorus the greater artist?   249 [K173]
    a. The problem   249 [K173]
    b. Proclus's response   251 [K173]
5. We shall demonstrate the three conditions of the soul and how there are three kinds of poetry divided according to these three conditions within ourselves   257 [K177]
    a. The problem   257 [K177]
    b. The three lives of the soul   257 [K177]
    c. The three kinds of poetry   259 [K178]
6. We shall demonstrate that, according to Plato, there are three kinds of poetry, and their properties are as we have described them   261 [K180]
    a. The problem   261 [K180]

	b.	Inspired poetry: the *Phaedrus*	261 [K180]
	c.	Inspired poetry: the *Ion*	265 [K182]
	d.	Inspired poetry: the *Laws* and *Timaeus*	271 [K185]
	e.	Didactic poetry: the *Laws* on Theognis	273 [K186]
	f.	Didactic poetry: the *Second Alcibiades*	275 [K187]
	g.	Mimetic poetry: the *Sophist*	277 [K188]
	h.	Accurately imitative mimetic poetry: the *Laws*	279 [K190]
	i.	Illusionistic mimetic poetry: the *Republic*	281 [K190]
	j.	Conclusion	283 [K191]

7. The Homeric poems as well exhibit within them these three forms of poetry — 283 [K192]
   a. The types of poetry in Homer — 283 [K192]
   b. The first type is characteristic of Homer — 289 [K195]
8. What is it, precisely, of Homer's poetry that Socrates rejects in the tenth book of the *Republic*, and what are his reasons? He does not reject it entirely, but only the lowest part. — 291 [K196]
9. How can one answer the accusations that Homer is neither educational for humanity nor in any way useful for society? — 297 [K200]
10. What were Plato's reasons for choosing to accuse Homer of being inadequate for the education of humanity? — 301 [K202]

PROCLUS

ON THE *REPUBLIC*, ESSAY 5

Περὶ ποιητικῆς καὶ τῶν ὑπ' αὐτὴν εἰδῶν καὶ τῆς ἀρίστης ἁρμονίας καὶ ῥυθμοῦ τὰ Πλάτωνι δοκοῦντα.

Πρῶτον εἰπεῖν χρὴ καὶ διαπορῆσαι περὶ τῆς αἰτίας, δι' ἣν οὐκ ἀποδέχεται τὴν ποιητικὴν ὁ Πλάτων, ἀλλὰ ἐξοικίζει | τῆς ὀρθῆς πολιτείας, εἰ καὶ μύρον αὐτῆς καταχέας, ὡς τῶν ἐν τοῖς ἁγιωτάτοις ἱεροῖς ἀγαλμάτων θέμις, καὶ ὡς ἱερὰν στέψας αὐτήν, ὥσπερ καὶ ἐκεῖνα στέφειν ἦν νόμος [*Rep.* 3.398a].

Καὶ γὰρ αὐτὸ τοῦτο ζητήσεως ἄξιον, εἰ μέν τι θεῖον ἔχει κατ' αὐτόν, πῶς ἐκβάλλεται τῆς θείας πολιτείας, εἰ δὲ μη|δέν, πῶς τιμᾶται ταῖς τῶν θεῶν τιμαῖς.

Δεύτερον, τί δήποτε μάλιστα τὴν τραγῳδίαν καὶ τὴν κωμικὴν οὐ παραδέχεται, καὶ ταῦτα συντελοῦσαν πρὸς ἀφοσίωσιν τῶν παθῶν, ἃ μήτε παντάπασιν ἀποκλείειν δυνατὸν μήτε ἐμπιμπλάναι πάλιν ἀσφαλές, δεόμενα δή τινος ἐν καιρῷ κινήσεως, | ἣν ἐν ταῖς τούτων ἀκροάσεσιν ἐκπληρουμένην ἀνενοχλήτους ἡμᾶς ἀπ' αὐτῶν ἐν τῷ λοιπῷ χρόνῳ ποιεῖν.

Τρίτον πῶς ἐν Συμποσίῳ [223d] μὲν ἠνάγκαζεν τῆς αὐτῆς ἐπιστήμης εἶναι κωμῳδίαν καὶ τραγῳδίαν ἐργάζεσθαι τοὺς ἀμφὶ Ἀγάθωνα καὶ Ἀριστοφάνη συνομολογεῖν, ἐν Πολιτείᾳ δὲ οὐκ ἐθέλει | τὸν αὐτὸν εἶναι τούτων δημιουργόν, καὶ ταῦτα ἐγγύτατα οὐσῶν, οὐδέ γε ὑποκριτὴν ἀμφοτέρων, οὐχ ὅτι μιμητὴν τὸν αὐτόν [3.395a].

Τέταρτον, τί δήποτε τὰς ἁρμονίας οὔ φησιν [3.398e–399c] εἰδέναι τὰς συμποτικὰς αἵτινές εἰσιν καὶ τὰς θρηνώδεις, οὐδὲ ἃς ὁ προσδιαλεγόμενος ὡς ἀμεί|νους τῶν ἄλλων προτείνει καὶ πρὸς παιδείαν ἀξιοχρεωτέρας,

Essay 5

Plato's Position on the Art of Poetry and Its Various Genres and the Best Mode[1] and Meter[2]

[Introduction: The Ten Questions]

We must first discuss and resolve the problem of the reason for Plato's not admitting poetry but rather exiling it from the rightly constituted state, even though anointing it with myrrh, as it is appropriate to anoint the statues in the holiest rites, and crowning it as holy, just as it was customary as well to crown the statues [cf. *Rep.* 3.398a]. Specifically worthy of inquiry are these points:

[1] If, according to him, poetry has something divine in it, how is it that it is rejected from the divine state? And if it does not, why is it given divine honors?

[2] Second, why does he, most of all, refuse to admit tragedy and comedy, when these contribute to resolving one's debt to the emotions,[3] which it is neither possible to exclude completely nor safe to indulge to satiety, but which require, rather, a timely stimulation,[4] which, fulfilled in the viewing of such spectacles, leaves us subsequently unencumbered by those emotions.

[3] Third, how is it that in the *Symposium* [223d] he has made Agathon and Aristophanes agree that both comedy and tragedy are produced by the same professional skill (ἐπιστήμη), while in the *Republic* [3.395a-b] he is not willing to have the same person write both—although they are very close to one another—nor even be an actor in both, though both the comic and tragic actors are imitators?

[4] Fourth, why on earth does Socrates deny knowing which musical modes are appropriate for the symposium and which are funereal [3.398e-399c], claiming ignorance of the ones his interlocutor proposes as better or more appropriate for education, while he claims he knows something

---

1. ἁρμονία: scale, tuning, mode. On the term in Plato, see West 1992, 174-84. Proclus's use of the term, nearly a thousand years later, is nevertheless not far removed from Plato's, thanks in part to the mathematical foundations of Greek musical theory.

2. ῥυθμός: rhythm, metrical foot.

3. In place of Aristotle's κάθαρσις (*Poetics* 1449b), Proclus uses the term ἀφοσίωσις. The sense is close to "expiation" or "resolution" of a debt.

4. F. saw that ἐν καιρῷ here is explained by ἐμμέτρως (17 [K49,15], "in due proportion," F.)

καίτοι περί γε τῶν ῥυθμῶν εἰδέναι τι προσποιούμενος ἀπὸ τῆς Δάμωνος ὑφηγήσεως ὁ Σωκράτης, καὶ ὀνομάζων οὓς ἐκεῖνος παρεδίδου ῥυθμούς [3.400b].

K43   Πέμπτον τίς ἡ ὄντως κατ' αὐτὸν μουσική, καὶ τίνες αἱ δεύτεραι καὶ τρίται ‖ μουσικαί· δοκεῖ γοῦν ἄλλα ἀλλαχοῦ περὶ τούτων λέγειν, καὶ δὴ καὶ τὴν ποιητικὴν τοτὲ μὲν μουσικήν τινα τίθεσθαι, τοτὲ δὲ διοικίζειν ἀπὸ τῆς μουσικῆς.

5   Ἕκτον, ποῖον ἐγκρίνει τῶν ἁρμονιῶν γένος ὡς παιδείᾳ χρήσιμον, ὃ δεῖ μεταχειρί|ζεσθαι τοὺς παρ' αὐτῷ ποιητάς, καὶ τί τῶν ῥυθμικῶν εἰδῶν ἐκλέγεται· δοκεῖ γὰρ ἀδιόριστα ταῦτα ἀφεῖσθαι, καίτοι δεόμενα διορισμοῦ μάλιστα τοῖς περὶ παιδείας διαλεγομένοις.

10   Ἕβδομον, τίνα ἁμαρτήματα εἶναι τῶν κατ' αὐτὸν φησιν ποιητῶν, καὶ διὰ ποίας αἰτίας μήποτε ἂν τὰς | Μούσας αὐτὰς ἁμαρτεῖν [Leg. 2.669c]. διὰ γὰρ τούτων γνωσθέντων εὑρήσομεν, ὅπως ἄριστος ἦν κριτὴς ποιητικῆς, ἀλλ' οὐχ ὥς τινες ᾠήθησαν τῶν ἔμπροσθεν φαῦλος διὰ τὸν ἐν Τιμαίῳ κατὰ τῶν Σόλωνος ποιημάτων ἔπαινον.

15   Ὄγδοον, τίς ὁ κατὰ Πλάτωνα ποιητὴς ἄριστος, καὶ ἐκ ποίων | τῶν τε πραγματικῶν καὶ τῶν λεκτικῶν χαρακτηριζόμενος πλεονεκτημάτων. δεῖν γὰρ εἶναί τινα πάντως κατωρθωμένον, πρὸς ὃν ἀποβλέποντες κρίνειν οἰόμεθα χρῆναι τὴν ποιητικήν.

Ἔνατον, τί τέλος ἐστὶ κατ' αὐτὸν τῆς ὀρθῆς ποιητικῆς· δεῖ γὰρ
20   τὴν ὀρθότητα παντὸς εἴς τι τέλος ἀναφέρεσθαι, | καὶ δι' ἐκεῖνο ἢ ἁμαρτανόμενον ἢ κατορθούμενον ποιεῖν τὸ ὀρθὸν καὶ διάστροφον ἑκάστου τῶν ἐπιτηδευμάτων.

Δέκατον, τίς ὁ ἐν τῷ παντὶ ποιητής, εἰς ὃν βλέπων καὶ ὁ τῇδε ποιητὴς τεύξεται τοῦ οἰκείου τέλους. οὐ γάρ ἐστιν οὐδὲν τῶν ὡς ἀληθῶς ἀγαθῶν,
25   ὃ μὴ πολλῷ πρότερόν ἐστιν ἐν τοῖς | ὅλοις ἢ τοῖς μέρεσιν.

[1] Ἄνωθεν οὖν ἀρξάμενοι λέγωμεν, δι' ἣν αἰτίαν τὴν ποιητικὴν

of meter, from the tutelage of Damon, and enumerates the meters Damon taught him [400b–c]?

[5] Fifth, what, according to him, is truly music-in-itself,[5] and what are the second and third || sorts of music? He seems to contradict himself about these, specifically positing poetry as a kind of music in one place, while in another he moves it outside of music.

[6] Sixth, which class of the modes does he admit as suitable for education (i.e., which must the poets in his state adopt?), and which of the metrical patterns does he select? He seems to leave these things undefined, while in fact for those discussing education they very much require clear definition.

[7] Seventh, what does he say are the failings of the poets known to him, and why does he claim that the Muses themselves could never fail [*Laws* 669c]? Once these things are understood, we will find that he was the best of judges of poetry and not, as some[6] have previously thought, on account of the praise of Solon's poetry in the *Timaeus*, a poor one.

[8] Eighth, who is the best poet, according to Plato, and by what superior qualities of content and language is he characterized? For we take it that there must be some single poet, perfect in every way, to whom we must look, in order to judge poetry.

[9] Ninth, what, according to him, is the goal (τέλος) of correct poetry, since the correctness of anything must be referred to some goal, which, depending on whether it is achieved or not, will determine the correctness or failure of every undertaking?

[10] Tenth, who is the poet in the universe to whom the poet in this world will look and so will attain his own goal? For there is nothing in the class of truly good things that does not exist in the realm of wholes far previous to its existence in that of partial entities.

[First Question]

[1] Starting from the beginning, then, let us say why, when he is laying

---

5. μουσική is impossible to represent by any single English word, so, at the risk of some confusion, I have simply applied its English derivative wherever possible. In Proclus, the word refers to the entire range of human activity over which the Muses preside, a complex hierarchy with philosophy at the top and what we call music, along with poetry, further down.

6. Callimachus and Douris, according to *In Tim.* 1:90,25–26 (Diehl). [F.]

καὶ ταῦτα εὐδοκιμοῦσαν ὡς παιδευτικὴν ἐν ἐκείνοις τοῖς χρόνοις οὐκ ἀποδέχεται, τῆς παιδείας τοὺς τύπους ‖ αὐτὸς παραδιδούς. ἔοικεν γὰρ μιμητικῆς ἁπάσης οὔσης τῆς τῶν ποιητῶν πραγματείας συνιδεῖν, ὅτι δύο ταῦτα πλημμελοῦσιν ἐν ταῖς μιμήσεσιν, τότε μὲν ἀνομοίως μιμούμενοι τὰ πράγματα, περὶ ὧν ποιοῦνται τοὺς λόγους, τότε δὲ ὁμοίως | μὲν ποικίλων δὲ ὄντες μιμηταὶ ποικίλας παρεχόμενοι τὰς μιμήσεις εἰκότως.

Ὅταν μὲν οὖν τὰ τῶν θεῶν ἢ τὰ τῶν ἡρώων μιμῶνται, λανθάνειν αὐτοὺς ἀνομοίως μιμουμένους, δι᾽ ἐμπαθῶν ὀνομάτων καὶ ἤτοι παρὰ φύσιν ὄντων ἢ παρὰ θεσμὸν ἐπιχειροῦντάς τι λέγειν περὶ αὐτῶν εἴτε ἐν μύθων | πλάσμασιν εἴτε ἄνευ μύθων, ἐξομοιοῦντας μὲν τὰ ἡρωϊκὰ τοῖς ἀνθρωπίνοις ἤθεσιν, καὶ καθέλκοντας εἰς τὰ αὐτὰ τῷ λόγῳ πάθη, φιλοχρηματίαν ἀνελευθερίαν ἀλαζονείαν ἀκολασίαν (εἶναι δὲ ταῦτα τῶν ἡρώων ἀνάξια πάντως, οὓς θεῶν παῖδας ὑπειλήφαμεν), παραπετάσμασιν δὲ χρωμένους | ὀνόμασιν αἰσχροῖς ἐπὶ τῶν θεῶν τῆς περὶ αὐτῶν ἀληθείας, ὧν οὐ ῥᾴδιον τοῖς ἀκούουσιν ἄλλως τε καὶ νέοις οὖσι γενέσθαι κριταῖς.

Ταῦτα δὲ ἀμφότερα δηλοῦν τὴν ἀνόμοιον μίμησιν, τῶν μὲν αὐτόθεν οὐκ ἐφαρμοζόντων, οἷς μιμοῦνται, τῶν δὲ οὐκ αὐτόθεν ἐφαρμοζόντων

down the principles of education, || he rejects poetry, in spite of the fact that it was much respected as educational in those days. He seems to understand that, given that everything the poets write is mimetic,[7] they make the following two mistakes in their representations: sometimes they produce inaccurate imitations of the things they write about, while at other times they produce imitations that are accurate, but as imitators of diverse and complex things, their imitations are, appropriately, diverse and complex.[8]

Thus, whenever they represent the divine or the heroic, they do not realize that their representations are inaccurate when they use language that is emotional and in fact unnatural and illegitimate here, to talk about the gods and heroes—whether in mythic fictions or without myths. By doing this, they make heroic character resemble human character and in their poetry drag the heroes down into the same passions—greed, baseness, pretentiousness, shamelessness (all things utterly unworthy of those whom we take to be the children of the gods)—using disgraceful language as a screen[9] for the truth about the gods, language that it is difficult for the audience, and especially the young, to assess.

[a. Imitation without resemblance]

Both of the following are examples of nonresembling mimesis: on the one hand, when the imitation is immediately maladapted to what it imitates, and on the other, when the imitation is well-adapted, but not immediately so, because of the strangeness that enters as a function of the screen

---

7. The assumption that the entire πραγματεία of poetry is mimetic marks the difference between the underlying models of poetics in this essay and in Essay 6, where the mimetic is found to be just one of three modes, and the least characteristic of Homer.

8. ποικιλία (variety, diversity, complexity) and related vocabulary pose difficulties in translation. In the *Republic*, Plato's Socrates objects to mimetic art, among other reasons, because it destroys the focus and the unity of the individual. Correspondingly, the diversity of representations that mix admirable with reprehensible elements creates dangerous ambiguities that are deemed inappropriate for education. The discussion in *Republic* 3 begins at 394d. See especially 404e. See 11 (K46,5–7).

9. παραπέτασμα (screen, curtain) is a central term in the poetics of Proclus. The fictions of Homer (or any poet) are conceived as screens that serve multiple functions. They mask truths that the poet chooses to represent indirectly and encourage the knowledgeable to seek what lies beyond them. The term was used in this sense several centuries before Proclus. See Lamberton 1986, 80.

διὰ τὴν κατὰ τὸ | πρόσχημα τῆς μυθοποιΐας φαινομένην ἀτοπίαν. δεῖ γὰρ τὸν μιμητὴν καὶ τὰς ἐννοίας οἰκείας παρέχεσθαι τοῖς πράγμασιν, εἰκόνας ἐκείνων εἶναι βουλομένας, καὶ τὰ ὀνόματα πρέποντα ταῖς ἐννοίαις ἐκλέγεσθαι. διὸ περὶ μὲν τῆς τῶν μύθων τῶν θείων ποιήσεως εἴωθεν λέγειν συχνόν, ὅτι <οὐ> καλῶς | ψεύδεται, ψεῦδος ἐκεῖνο καλὸν ὀνομάζων, ὅπερ ἂν ᾖ δι᾽ ὀνομάτων καλῶν ἀποκρύπτον τὴν ἀλήθειαν· περὶ δὲ τῆς τῶν ἡρωϊκῶν πραγμάτων μιμήσεως, οὐχ ὅτι οὐ καλῶς ψεύδεταί φησιν, ἀλλ᾽ ὅλως ὅτι ψεύδεται, τοιούτους εἶναι τοὺς || ἥρωας δεικνῦσα οἵους τοὺς ἀνθρώπους. ὅπου μὲν οὖν δέον τὰ ἀληθῆ λέγειν ψεύδεσθαι διὰ τὴν ἀνοικειότητα τῶν παθῶν, ἅπερ ἐπὶ τοὺς ἥρωας ἀναπέμπουσιν, ὅπου δὲ ψεύδεσθαι δέον μὴ καλῶς ψεύδεσθαι διὰ τὴν ἀνοικειότητα | τῶν ὀνομάτων, ὧν ἐν ταῖς θεομυθίαις παραλαμβάνουσιν, πρὸς τοὺς θεούς.

Αἴτιον δὲ εἶναι τούτων, ὅπερ αὐτὸς ἐν Τιμαίῳ λέγει σαφῶς [19d], ὅτι τὸ μιμητικὸν ἔθνος οἷς ἂν ἐντραφῇ, ταῦτα μιμεῖσθαι δύναται μάλιστα· τὸ δὲ ἐκτὸς τῆς τροφῆς ἑκάστοις γινόμενον χαλεπὸν μὲν ἔργοις μιμεῖσθαι | γίνεται, χαλεπώτερον δὲ λόγοις. οὐκοῦν οὔτε ἔργα πρέποντα τοῖς ἥρωσιν ἀποδιδόναι δύνανται καὶ διὰ τούτων μιμεῖσθαι τὴν ἐκείνων ζωήν, τὰ μὲν ἀνδρικῶς τὰ δὲ σωφρονητικῶς ἐνεργοῦσαν, οὔτε λόγους οὓς ἂν ἐκεῖνοι φθέγξαιντο, ἢ ἐν πολέμοις ἀναστρεφόμενοί τισιν ἢ ἐν εἰρήναις, ἢ πρὸς θεοὺς | ἢ πρὸς ἀνθρώπους, ἀλλ᾽ οὓς οἱ πολλοὶ τῶν ἀνθρώπων, ἢ βλασφημοῦντες εἰς θεοὺς καὶ ἀπαυθαδιζόμενοι, ἢ κολακεύοντες ἀνθρώπους ἢ ὑβρίζοντες.

Διὰ δὲ τὴν αὐτὴν αἰτίαν καὶ περὶ θεοὺς πλημμελοῦσιν, ἀπὸ τῶν συνήθων αὐτοῖς ὀνομάτων λαμβάνοντες καὶ οἷς ἐνετράφησαν, ὅσα πρὸς τὴν | κρύψιν οἴονται συντελεῖν αὐτοῖς, τῶν θεῶν κλοπὰς ἁρπαγὰς πλάνας μοιχείας πολέμους ἐπιβουλάς, πολλοῦ δέοντες ἐκεῖνα τὰ ὀνόματα τοῖς πράγμασιν τιθέναι περὶ ὧν λέγουσιν, ὅσα τῶν εὖ τραφέντων ἐστὶν καὶ ἐν ταῖς ὀρθαῖς ἄνω καὶ κάτω θρυλεῖται πολιτείαις, οἷον θέμιν δίκην νόμον ἀφέλειαν | αἰδὼ πάντα τὰ τοιαῦτα, σύντροφα τοῖς εὖ πολιτευομένοις ὄντα.

of mythification. The imitator (μιμητής) must provide not only concepts (ἔννοιαι) appropriate to the things he represents (since these concepts are intended to be images [εἰκόνες] of those things), but he must also select the language appropriate to the concepts. For this reason, [Plato] always said regarding the poetry of divine myth that it [does not] lie beautifully[10]—calling a "beautiful lie" whatever conceals the truth in beautiful language—but concerning representation of the heroic, he said not that it does not lie beautifully but simply that it lies, in representing the ‖ heroes as the same as humans. And so, where it should tell the truth, [poetry] lies on account of the inappropriateness of the passions that the poets attribute to the heroes, and where it should lie, it does not do so beautifully on account of the inappropriateness to the gods of the language the poets incorporate in the myths about divinity.

The reason for this, as he says clearly in the *Timaeus* [19d] is that the mimetic tribe is best able to imitate that which belongs to the environment of its nurture. Whatever occurs that lies beyond that sphere is difficult for any person to imitate in actions, and yet more difficult to imitate in words. Hence they are able to attribute neither appropriate actions to the heroes—and through those actions to represent their life, which is productive of acts of bravery and moderation—nor appropriate speech that they might actually utter, whether engaged in war or at peace, to gods or to humans—but rather they attribute to the heroes the language of ordinary humans, who are presumptuous and blaspheme the gods and alternately fawn on or insult their fellow mortals.

For the same reason, they strike the wrong note where the gods are concerned, drawing on the language natural to themselves and in which they were nurtured for whatever they think it appropriate to clothe them in[11]—thievery of the gods, rapes, wanderings, adulteries, wars, plotting—failing entirely to apply to the things they are speaking about the language that belongs to the well-bred and that is the common idiom of rightly constituted states: right, justice, law, simplicity, respect, and everything of that sort, things that belong to the nurture of the citizens of well-

---

10. F., citing Kroll's addenda (2:472) and *Rep.* 2.377d9 and e7, added a negative particle here, but as he acknowledged, this does not entirely solve the problems in the passage.

11. Proclus's κρύψις (covering) refers to the necessity of a screen on which to project the divinities of epic, given that the divinities themselves are not visible. Cf. 7 n. 9, above, on παραπέτασμα.

τὰ γοῦν αἰσχρὰ καὶ ἄθεσμα οὐδὲ προφέρεσθαι τούτοις ἀνεκτόν· οὐ γὰρ ἡγοῦνται χρῆναι μολύνειν τὴν γλῶτταν, ὄργανον οὖσαν τῆς θεῶν ὑμνῳδίας καὶ τῆς πρὸς ‖ τοὺς ἀγαθοὺς συνουσίας, διὰ τῆς τούτων φθέγξεως. τὴν μὲν οὖν ἀνόμοιον μίμησιν διπλῆν οὖσαν παρὰ τοῖς ποιηταῖς διὰ ταῦτα ἐπερράπισεν, ὅμοιον ταύτην πράττουσαν, ὡς εἰ ζωγράφος Ἀχιλλέα μιμεῖσθαι προθέμενος Θερσίτην γράψειεν, | ἢ Ἀχιλλέα μὲν οὐ φυλάττοντα δὲ τὴν ἀνδρικὴν ζωήν, ὅπερ ἐν Νόμοις [2.668d] ἐκάλεσεν τὸ εὖ μετὰ τῆς ὀρθότητος.

Τὴν δὲ ἀνομοίαν μίμησιν ἐκάκισεν τὴν παρὰ τοῖς ποιηταῖς καθ' ἕτερον τρόπον διὰ τὴν τῶν παντοίων ἠθῶν καὶ εἰδῶν ζωτικὴν ὁμοίωσιν ὡσαύτως μιμουμένην δειλοὺς | ἀκολάστους ἀνοήτους ὡς ἀνδρείους σώφρονας ἔμφρονας. ταύτην γὰρ τὴν ποικιλίαν παντάπασιν ἀνεπιτήδειον εἶναι πρὸς τὴν παιδείαν, τυποῦν τὰ ἤθη τῶν παιδευομένων ἐν μόνοις τοῖς ἀγαθοῖς ἔργοις τε καὶ λόγοις σπουδάζουσαν.

Φύσει γὰρ τὴν ψυχὴν ἡμῶν χαίρειν τοῖς μιμήμασιν, διὸ | καὶ φιλόμυθοι πάντες ἐσμέν, καὶ παῖδες ὄντες, ἐὰν συνεθιζώμεθα συζῆν μιμήμασι παντοδαποῖς, ἐξομοιούμεθα μὲν αὐτοῖς διὰ τὸ προσπάσχειν, γιγνόμεθα δὲ καὶ ἡμεῖς τοιοῦτοί τινες καὶ ἀποβαίνομεν τὰ ἤθη ποικίλοι διὰ τὸ χαίρειν τοῖς ποικίλοις ὑπὸ τῶν ποικίλων πλαττόμενοι μιμημάτων. αἴτιον | δὲ πάλιν τοῦ τὴν ποιητικὴν τῶν ποικίλων ἠθῶν μᾶλλον εἶναι ποιητικὴν ἢ τῶν ἁπλῶν ταὐτόν, ὃ καὶ ἔμπροσθεν εἴπομεν ἐν Τιμαίῳ γεγραμμένον, τὸ μιμητικὸν ἔθνος ταῦτα μιμεῖσθαι ῥᾷον, οἷς ἂν ἐντραφῇ. τοὺς οὖν ποιητὰς τοιούτοις συντρόφους ὄντας ἀνθρώποις ποικίλοις καὶ παν|τοδαποῖς ἀπᾴδειν τῆς τῶν ἁπλῶν καὶ ἀπλάστων μιμήσεως καὶ τὰ ποιήματα παρέχεσθαι τοιαῦτα, τοιούτους ἄλλους δυνάμενα ποιεῖν τοὺς σπουδάζοντας περὶ αὐτά.

organized societies. It is intolerable for such people to utter shameful and illicit things, since they believe that they should not pollute the tongue, the instrument of hymns to the gods and conversation with || the good, by giving voice to such things. He denounced nonresembling [or inaccurate] mimesis in the poets in the following terms. It does the same thing as if a painter proposed to represent Achilles but actually painted Thersites, or again painted Achilles himself but not cultivating the manly life—[the opposite of] what, in the *Laws* [2.668d] he called "[representing] well" united with "correctness."[12]

He condemned inaccurate mimesis[13] in the poets in another way, on account of their vivid representation of all sorts of characters and models, imitating cowards, shameless people and fools in just the same way as brave, reasonable, and intelligent people. This diversity is completely inappropriate for education, which is concerned to impress upon the characters of those educated exclusively good deeds and good language.

[b. The imitation of human vices]

Our soul naturally enjoys imitations—that is also why we all love stories—and when we are young, if we habitually take in all sorts of imitations, we come to resemble them through empathy, and we ourselves turn out to be people of that sort, our characters complex and diverse because of our enjoying that complexity, ourselves molded by the diversity of the imitations. The reason why poetry is more productive[14] of complex than of simple characters is the same one we referred to above, expounded in the *Timaeus*,[15] that it is easier for the mimetic tribe to imitate what belongs to the environment of their nurture. The poets, who associate with complex people of all sorts, fall short of being able to represent simple, unaffected people and produce poems accordingly, with the capacity to turn those who are enthusiastic about them into more of the same. We will find,

---

12. The *Laws* passage is a discussion of representation, where the ideal specified by Proclus is articulated. Proclus's very compressed reference obscures the fact that the two examples of types of "incorrect mimesis" here are being displayed as violations of Plato's principle.

13. In fact (as F. notes ad loc.), this would appear to fall under *accurate* representation. See, e.g., 13 (K47,16).

14. Kroll's suggestion, μιμητικήν for ποιητικήν, is unnecessary.

15. Above, 9 (K45) (*Tim.* 19d).

τοιγαροῦν εὑρήσομεν καὶ τῶν νῦν ἀνθρώπων τοὺς μάλιστα ζηλωτὰς αὐτῶν μάλιστα τὸ ἦθος ποικίλους· ἔχει γοῦν λόγον παν||ταχοῦ τὸ θαυμάζον ὁμοιοῦσθαι πρὸς τὸ θαυμαζόμενον, καὶ πᾶν τὸ ἡδόμενον συμφύεσθαι πρὸς τὸ ἡδόν. τοῖς τοίνυν παιδευτικοῖς τῶν νέων μάλιστα νόμοις φυλακτέον τὴν τοιαύτην ποιητικήν, ὡς ἡδεῖαν μὲν οὖσαν παισίν, οὐ μέντοι | καὶ πρὸς ἀρετὴν ὠφέλιμον, ἀλλ' ὅσῳπερ ἡδεῖα μᾶλλον, τοσούτῳ βλαβερὰν οὖσαν μᾶλλον· καὶ Μοῦσαν ἐκλεκτέον τὴν αὐστηροτάτην μέν, εὐθὺ δὲ τῆς ἀρετῆς ἄγουσαν. οὐδὲ γὰρ ἰατρικὴν θαυμάζομεν τὴν ἡδοῦσαν, ἀλλὰ τὴν ὑγιάζουσαν· ἔστι δὲ καὶ ἡ παιδεία τῶν ψυχῶν ἰατρική, τὴν ἀνω|μαλίαν ἐξορθοῦσα καὶ τὴν διαστροφὴν τῶν ἐν αὐταῖς παθῶν, ὥστε καὶ ταύτην ἐκλέγεσθαι δεῖ καὶ ποιήματα καὶ ἐπιτηδεύματα πάντα πρὸς τὴν τῶν νέων ἀγωγήν, οὐχ ὅσα τέρπει τὴν νεότητα βλάπτοντα, ἀλλ' ὅσα κοσμεῖ, κἂν ᾖ δυσκολώτερα.

Δύο τοίνυν, ἵνα συλλαβόντες εἴπωμεν, αἴτια | τοῦ μὴ εἶναι παραδεκτέαν τὴν ποιητικὴν εἰς παιδείαν ὀρθήν, <ἐν> οἷς μὲν ἀληθῶς μιμεῖται (ταῦτα δ' ἐστὶν τὰ ἀνθρωπικά), τὸ ποικίλον τῆς μιμήσεως, ἐν οἷς δὲ ψευδῶς μιμεῖται, τὸ ἀπᾷδον τῆς μιμήσεως, καὶ τοῦτο διττόν, ἢ ἐν τοῖς ὀνόμασιν μόνοις ἢ καὶ τοῖς πράγμασιν, ὡς ἐδείκνυμεν. |

Ἐπειδὴ δὲ ὅλως τὴν ποιητικὴν ἱερὰν εἶναι τῶν Μουσῶν ἅπαντες ὑπειλήφαμεν καὶ τὴν ἀρχὴν εἰς ἀνθρώπους παρελθεῖν κατὰ τὴν ἐκείνων ἐπίπνοιαν, εἰκότως δήπου καὶ τῆς ἑαυτοῦ πολιτείας ἐκπέμπων αὐτὴν διὰ τὰς εἰρημένας αἰτίας οὐκ οἴεται δεῖν ἀτιμάσας ἐκπέμπειν, ἀλλ' ὡς ἱερὰν Μουσῶν | ταῖς ὁμοίαις τιμαῖς τῶν ἀγαλμάτων τιμήσας, μύρῳ καὶ στέμματι. μὴ γὰρ δὴ τοῦτο οἰηθῶμεν, ὅτι καὶ τὴν τοιαύτην ποιητικήν, καὶ εἰ τῇ ἀρίστῃ πολιτείᾳ τυγχάνει προσήκουσα μηδέν, πρὸς πᾶσαν ζωὴν ἀνάρμοστον εἶναι θήσεται καὶ βλαβεράν, ἀλλ' εἶναί τινας, οἳ καὶ ἀπὸ τῶν ταύτης ὀνί||ναιντο ἂν λόγων. ὡς γοῦν αὐτός φησιν, καὶ τὴν ψευδῶς τὰ θεῖα μεμιμημένην ἐν μέσοις ἱεροῖς χώραν ἔχειν, ἐν οἷς καὶ τὰ συμβολικῶς λεγόμενα πρέποντα

therefore, among our contemporaries that the greatest admirers of poetry are those who are the most complex in character. There is, in any case, the argument that || everywhere the admirer becomes like what he admires, and the one who experiences pleasure clings to that pleasure's source. Thus the laws that govern the education of the young must keep careful control over such poetry, since it gives pleasure to children but at the same time is useless as far as virtue is concerned—rather, the more pleasurable it is, the more harmful. The Muse to be chosen is the most austere [398a8], but she is also the one who leads directly to virtue. It is not the pleasurable medical treatment that we admire but rather the one that heals. The education of souls is also a form of medicine, setting straight the anomalous and deviant in their passions, and so education as well must select that Muse, and all poetry and all activities generally, with a view to the guidance of children—not what is pleasurable but damaging to the young, but what brings them order, even if it is more difficult.

Therefore, to sum up, there are two reasons why poetry is not acceptable in correct education: in what it imitates truthfully (that is, in human matters), the variety or diversity of the imitation; in what it represents falsely, the inadequacy of the imitation—and this in turn is twofold, as we have shown, lying either in the language alone or in the content as well.

[c. Why the art of poetry is exiled with honor]

Since we all take poetry in general to be sacred to the Muses, and to have come to humanity in the first place through their providence, it was certainly appropriate that, in exiling it from his city for the reasons cited, [Plato] thought it wrong to send it away without honor but rather honored it (as a thing sacred to the Muses) with the same honors as statues receive: incense and a crown. Let us not think that he is going to posit that this sort of poetry—even if it actually has no business at all in the best city—is incompatible with lives of all sorts and universally harmful. Rather, [he will say that] there are some who would || profit even from this sort of discourse. As he himself, in fact, asserts, even poetry that falsely represents the divine has its place in the intermediate mysteries,[16] where that which is expressed in symbols is clearly appropriate to the general service

---

16. Kroll suggested in his apparatus μεγίστοις ("greatest [mysteries]") for the manuscript's μέσοις. Proclus's reference may be to *Rep.* 2.378a.

φαίνεται τῇ συμπάσῃ θεραπείᾳ τῶν θείων καὶ ἡ τούτων ἀκρόασις συντελεῖ πρὸς | τὴν ὅλην ἱερατικήν, αὐτῆς τῆς ζωῆς τῶν ἀκουόντων ἐνιδρυθείσης τοῖς θεοῖς καὶ ἀσφαλῶς ἤδη τῶν τοιούτων ἀκουούσης λόγων, δι' ὧν <u>ἐπάγεται</u> καὶ τὰ τελευταῖα τῶν πνευμάτων, καὶ θέλξαντα τοῖς τοιοῖσδε συμβόλοις ἀκώλυτον προξενεῖ παρ' ἐκείνων εἰς ἡμᾶς προϊέναι τὴν θείαν ἐπίπνοιαν, | οἷον ἀποπλησθέντων οἷς χαίρουσιν ὀνόμασιν καὶ πράγμασιν, οὕτω δὴ καὶ τὴν τῶν ποικίλων μιμητικὴν ἠθῶν εὕροιμεν ἄν πού τισιν ὠφέλιμον, οἷς τὸ μὴ ποικίλον τοῦ ποικίλου βλαβερώτερον· διὸ δὴ πρὸς τὴν τυραννικὴν ἅπασαν πολιτείαν εἶναι χρήσιμον, οὐκ ἐῶσαν ἑνὶ χαίρειν τῷ χειρίστῳ τῆς ζωῆς εἴδει | μόνον, ἀλλ' ἐπεισάγουσαν τὴν ἐκ τῆς τῶν παντοδαπῶν ἠθῶν μιμήσεως ἀγωγήν, [πρὸς] τὴν ὁμοῦ καὶ τὰ ἀμείνω καὶ τὰ χείρω περιπτυσσομένην ἐπιτηδεύματα. καὶ γὰρ ἔοικεν ὡς τῷ βασιλικῷ καὶ θείῳ τῆς πολιτείας εἴδει τοῦτο εἶναι τὸ ποικίλον βλαβερόν, οὕτω τῷ ἐσχάτῳ καὶ τυραννικῷ ὠφέ|λιμον· διττὸν γοῦν τὸ ἁπλοῦν, ἢ τὸ κρεῖττον ἢ τὸ χεῖρον τοῦ ποικίλου, καὶ τὸ μὲν βλάπτοιτο ἂν τῷ ποικίλῳ προσχρώμενον χεῖρον γιγνόμενον, ὡς τοῦ χείρονος ἀναπιμπλάμενον, τὸ δὲ ὠφελοῖτ' ἂν κρεῖττον γινόμενον, ὡς τοῦ κρείττονος ἀπολαῦον.

Εἰ δ' οὖν καὶ ἄλλαις ἐστὶ πολιτείαις τισὶν | ἡ ποιητικὴ χρήσιμος, ὡς μὲν τῇ πρωτίστῃ μὴ προσᾴδουσαν ἀποπεμπτέον, ὡς δὲ Μουσῶν ἄγαλμα οὖσαν τιμητέον. ἐπεὶ καὶ πᾶσαν τέχνην ἱερὰν εἶναι θείου τινός φαμεν, ἀλλ' οὐ διὰ τοῦτο τοὺς παρ' ἡμῖν φύλακας τεχνικοὺς ἐθελήσομεν || ἀποτελεῖν, ἓν ἐπιτήδευμα μόνον ἔχοντας τὴν τῆς πόλεως σωτηρίαν. τὰς μὲν οὖν τέχνας εἰς τὴν κάτω πόλιν ἀπέπεμψεν, τὴν δὲ ποιητικὴν εἰς ἄλλην εἰκότως. αἱ μὲν γὰρ ὀργανικὴν παρέχονται τῷ πολιτικῷ καὶ τοῖς ἄρχουσιν χρείαν, | ὡς ὑποτετάχθαι καὶ μὴ ἀμφισβητεῖν τὴν ἑαυτῶν φυλαττούσας τάξιν πρὸς τοὺς τῆς πόλεως σωτῆρας· τὴν δὲ ποιητικὴν φρονήματος οὖσαν ἀνάπλεων καὶ παιδεύειν ἐπαγγελλομένην οὐκ ἔστι συγκαταλέγειν ταῖς τέχναις, μὴ

of the divinities and the recital of these [symbols] constitutes an element of the hieratic art, since the very lives of the listeners have already been rooted in the gods, and now they listen to such things without danger. Through these utterances, the last of the spirits are also attracted,[17] and [the utterances], working their enchantment with symbols of this sort, provide for the divine concern to flow unhindered from the spirits into us, as if they were saturated with the language and the stories they delight in. Thus, indeed, we might find that the representation of complex characters is a beneficial thing for some, for whom that which is not diverse is more harmful than that which is.

This is why such mimesis is a good thing in all tyrannical states, since it does not permit taking pleasure in the worst form of life alone, but introduces the attraction that comes from the imitation of all sorts of characters, encompassing both better and worse actions, all together. So, just as this variety and diversity seem to be harmful in the regal and divine sort of state, in the last, tyrannical one, they are good. There are two sides to simplicity: it can be either worse or better than diversity. The one sort of simplicity would be harmed by adopting diversity and become worse, as being saturated with the worse, but the other would benefit and improve, as enjoying the better.

So, even if there are some other states in which poetry is good, it is still to be rejected as inappropriate in the first and best, while it is to be honored as a delight of the Muses. We say that every craft (τέχνη) is sacred to some divinity, but we will not on this account want || our own guardians to turn out to be craftsmen, since they have as their unique occupation the preservation of the city. And so [Plato] was right to send the arts down to the lower city and that of poetry to another city. Some of the arts provide instrumental service for the statesman and for the leaders, since they are subordinate and do not compete, respecting their own status with reference to the preservers of the city. But it is not possible to include the art of poetry—full of intellectual content as it is, and specifically adept at educating—among the other crafts, lest without realizing it we erect barricades

---

17. Kroll noted that the passage is corrupt. I follow his suggestion (ἐπάγεται for the manuscript's ἐπανάγεται), as did F. The "last of the spirits"—"last," that is, in the divine hierarchy and hence available and susceptible to such attraction—are identified by F. as those theurgically "attracted" to animate temples, statues, magical stones, and so forth (F. ad loc.).

λάθωμεν ἐπιτειχίσματα κατασκευάζοντες πρὸς τοὺς ἄρχοντας ἐκ τῆς κάτω πό|λεως καὶ τρέφοντες ἐπιτήδευμα πρὸς τὴν τῶν φυλάκων ἐπιτήδευσιν ἐναντιώτατον.

Τὸ μὲν οὖν πρῶτον τῶν προβλημάτων ταύτῃ διαθήσομεν.

[2] Τὸ δὲ δεύτερον (τοῦτο δ' ἦν τὸ τὴν τραγῳδίαν ἐκβάλλεσθαι καὶ κωμῳδίαν ἀτόπως, εἴπερ διὰ τούτων δυνατὸν | ἐμμέτρως ἀποπιμπλάναι τὰ πάθη καὶ ἀποπλήσαντας εὐεργὰ πρὸς τὴν παιδείαν ἔχειν, τὸ πεπονηκὸς αὐτῶν θεραπεύσαντας), τοῦτο δ' οὖν πολλὴν καὶ τῷ Ἀριστοτέλει παρασχὸν αἰτιάσεως ἀφορμὴν καὶ τοῖς ὑπὲρ τῶν ποιήσεων τούτων ἀγωνισταῖς τῶν πρὸς Πλάτωνα λόγων οὑτωσί πως ἡμεῖς | ἑπομένως τοῖς ἔμπροσθεν διαλύσομεν.

Πᾶν τὸ μιμητικὸν τῶν παντοδαπῶν ἠθῶν, διὰ μὲν τὴν μίμησιν ῥᾳδίως εἰσδυόμενον εἰς τὰς τῶν ἀκουόντων διανοίας, διὰ δὲ τὴν ποικιλίαν βλαβερὸν αὐτοῖς γιγνόμενον (ὁποῖ' ἄττα γὰρ ἂν ᾖ τὰ μιμητά, τοιαῦτα ἀνάγκη γίνεσθαι τὸν προσπάσχοντα τοῖς μιμήμασιν), | ἀλλοτριώτατόν ἐστιν πρὸς τὴν εἰς ἀρετὴν τῶν νέων ἀγωγήν. ἁπλοῦν γὰρ ἡ ἀρετὴ καὶ αὐτῷ τῷ θεῷ μάλιστα προσεοικός, ᾧ φαμεν διαφερόντως προσήκειν τὸ ἕν. τὸν οὖν τῷ τοιούτῳ παραπλήσιον γενησόμενον φεύγειν δεῖ τὴν ἐναντίαν τῇ ἁπλότητι ζωήν, ὥστε πάσης αὐτὸν δεήσει καθαρεύειν ποι|κιλίας· εἰ δὲ τοῦτο, καὶ τῶν εἰς ταύτην καθελκόντων πάν||των ὅτι μάλιστα πορρωτάτω νέον ὄντα καὶ διὰ τὴν νεότητα ῥᾳδίως πλαττόμενον ἐπιτηδευμάτων ἀφεστάναι. δῆλον οὖν ὅτι καὶ τὴν τραγῳδίαν καὶ τὴν κωμῳδίαν παντοίων οὔσας μιμητικὰς ἠθῶν καὶ μεθ' ἡδονῆς προσπιπτούσας τοῖς ἀκού|ουσιν διευλαβηθησόμεθα, μὴ τὸ ἐπαγωγὸν αὐτῶν εἰς συμπάθειαν τὸ ἀγώγιμον ἑλκύσαν τὴν τῶν παίδων ζωὴν ἀναπλήσῃ τῶν ἐκ τῆς μιμήσεως κακῶν, καὶ ἀντὶ τῆς πρὸς τὰ πάθη μετρίας ἀφοσιώσεως ἕξιν πονηρὰν ἐντέκωσιν ταῖς

out of the lower city against the rulers and nurture a way of life utterly antithetical to the pursuits of the guardians.

This is how we shall resolve the first of the problems.

[Second Question]

[2] The second problem—that it was irrational to banish tragedy and comedy if in fact it is possible through them to moderately satisfy the emotions and once having satisfied them to create a situation beneficial for education, having treated the irritation they cause—this issue, which provided Aristotle[18] with considerable grounds for complaint and provided those who have taken the side of this sort of poetry with the basis for their writings against Plato, this we shall resolve as follows, working from what has already been said.

Every representation of complex and diverse characters, inasmuch as it easily enters the minds of the audience as mimetic and because of its diversity is harmful to them (since whatever the objects of imitation are, that is what the spectator who empathizes with the imitations will become), is utterly alien to the education of the young to virtue. Virtue is something simple and very similar to the divine itself, to which we say that the One especially belongs.[19] He who is going to approach as closely as possible to such an entity must flee the life that is the opposite of simplicity, and so it will be necessary for him to be pure of all complexity. If this is the case, then the young, who because of their youth are easily molded, must stay as far as possible from all || the activities that attract one to this complexity. And so it is clear that we will be very wary of tragedy and comedy—imitating as they do characters of all sorts and bursting on their audience reinforced by pleasure—lest their seductiveness, drawing the susceptible into sympathy, fill the lives of the children with the evils that stem from imitation and, instead of moderate satisfaction of the emotions, engender in their souls a condition that is wicked and not easily eradicated, destroy-

---

18. This is included in Aristotle, frag. 81 (Rose) (frag. 921 Gigon), along with Iamblichus, *De mysteriis* 1.11 (frag. 893 [Gigon]), which further explores the nature of catharsis.

19. τὸ ἕν (the one, unity, the One) is a metaphysical entity that, from Plotinus onward, took on aspects of divinity in later Platonism. It seems appropriate here to give it the capitalization customary in translating Plotinus.

10   ψυχαῖς καὶ δυσέκνιπτον, τὸ ἓν καὶ τὸ ἁπλοῦν ἀφανίσασαν, | τὰ δ' ἐναντία
τούτων ἐκμαξαμένην ἀπὸ τῆς πρὸς τὰ παντοῖα μιμήματα φιλίας.
   Ἐπεὶ καὶ διαφερόντως αἱ ποιήσεις αὗται πρὸς ἐκεῖνο τῆς ψυχῆς
ἀποτείνονται τὸ μάλιστα τοῖς πάθεσιν ἐκκείμενον, ἣ μὲν τὸ φιλήδονον
ἐρεθίζουσα καὶ εἰς γέλωτας ἀτό|πους ἐξάγουσα, ἣ δὲ τὸ φιλόλυπον
15   παιδοτριβοῦσα | καὶ εἰς θρήνους ἀγεννεῖς καθέλκουσα, ἑκατέρα δὲ
τρέφουσα τὸ παθητικὸν ἡμῶν, καὶ ὅσῳ ἂν μᾶλλον τὸ ἑαυτῆς ἔργον
ἀπεργάζηται, τοσούτῳ μᾶλλον. δεῖ μὲν οὖν τὸν πολιτικὸν διαμηχανᾶσθαί
τινας τῶν παθῶν τούτων ἀπεράσεις καὶ ἡμεῖς φήσομεν, ἀλλ' οὐχ ὥστε
20   τὰς περὶ αὐτὰ προσπαθείας συν|τείνειν, τοὐναντίον μὲν οὖν ὥστε
χαλινοῦν καὶ τὰς κινήσεις αὐτῶν ἐμμελῶς ἀναστέλλειν· ἐκείνας δὲ
ἄρα τὰς ποιήσεις πρὸς τῇ ποικιλίᾳ καὶ τὸ ἄμετρον ἐχούσας ἐν ταῖς τῶν
παθῶν τούτων προκλήσεσιν πολλοῦ δεῖν εἰς ἀφοσίωσιν εἶναι χρησίμους.
25   αἱ γὰρ ἀφοσιώσεις οὐκ ἐν ὑπερβολαῖς εἰσιν, ἀλλ' | ἐν συνεσταλμέναις
ἐνεργείαις σμικρὰν ὁμοιότητα πρὸς ἐκεῖνα ἐχούσαις ὧν εἰσιν ἀφοσιώσεις.
εἰ τοίνυν οὐ δεῖ φιλοθρήνους ἡμῖν ἀποτελεῖσθαι καὶ φιλογέλωτας τοὺς
παιδευομένους, οὐκ ἂν δέοι προσομιλεῖν αὐτοὺς ταῖς ταῦτα ἀμφότερα τὰ
πάθη πολλαπλασιαζούσαις μιμήσεσιν.
K51   Δύο τοίνυν ταῦτα πε||ποίηται τὸν Πλάτωνα μὴ προσέσθαι τραγῳδίαν
καὶ κωμῳδίαν εἰς τὴν ὀρθὴν πολιτείαν ὡς ἀξίας οὔσας σπουδῆς τοῖς
νέοις, ἓν μὲν τὸ ποικίλον ὡς εἴρηται τῶν ἐν ταύταις μιμήσεων, ἕτερον δὲ
5   τὸ τῶν παθῶν ἀμέτρως κινητικόν, ἃ | βούλεται συστέλλειν κατὰ δύναμιν,
τρίτον δὲ ἐπὶ τούτοις τὸ πρὸς πᾶσαν τὴν περὶ τὸ θεῖον καὶ ἡρωϊκὸν γένος
αὐτῶν πλημμέλειαν εὐχερές. οὐδενὸς γοῦν ἀπέχονται τῶν εἰς δυσσέβειαν
τεινόντων ῥημάτων, βλασφημοῦσαι μὲν περὶ τοὺς θεούς, ἀπορρίπτουσαι
10   δὲ εἰς τοὺς ἥρωας ἀναξίους τῶν | ἡρώων λόγους· οἷς εἰ μὲν πιστεύσαιεν
ἡμῖν οἱ νέοι, τὴν Γιγαντικὴν ζωὴν ἐκθρέψουσιν καὶ τὴν ἄθεον φαντασίαν,
ἧς ἐπιταθείσης οἰχήσεται πᾶς ὁ τῆς ἀρετῆς χορός· οὐ γὰρ ἐθέλει συνοικεῖν

ing that which is one and simple and fashioning the opposite out of the affinity to all sorts of imitations.

These poems appeal especially to that part of the soul that is most exposed to the emotions, the one [comedy] inflaming the love of pleasure and leading to irrational laughter, the other [tragedy] developing the love of pain and inducing unseemly lamentation, while both nurture the emotional in us, and more so in proportion to their greater success in fulfilling their own function. We as well will agree that the statesman must contrive some sort of purgation of these emotions, but not so as to intensify our passionate attachment to them but rather to bridle those attachments and make their impulses orderly and harmonious. These poems that are characterized by complexity and variety and are immoderate in their evocation of these emotions are far from useful for their purification. Such purification lies not in excess but in moderate and restricted actions that have a slight similarity to that which they purify.[20] If the children we educate are not going to turn out lovers of lamentation or lovers of laughter, they should not frequent mimetic spectacles that amplify both of these emotions.

Thus these two considerations || made[21] Plato reject tragedy and comedy as things worthy of the enthusiasm of the young in the rightly constituted state: (1) the complexity, as explained, of the imitations they contain, and (2) the immoderate stimulation of the emotions, which he wants to curtail as much as possible. Third in addition to these is the tolerance [of these plays] for false and unseemly representation of gods and heroes. They do not shrink at all from language that tends to impiety, blaspheming against the gods and speaking of the heroes in language unworthy of heroes. If our young people were to believe these things, they will cultivate a life fit for Giants[22] and an atheist vision. When this has grown to a certain point, the whole chorus of virtue will have disappeared, having

---

20. Proclus does not specify the sort of activity in question, but the analogy to modern vaccination is clearly relevant. The individual exposed to the pathogen (emotion), in tiny amounts and rendered harmless by some unspecified agency, gains future immunity.

21. As F. points out, the active πεποίηκε (Wendland's conjecture, cited in Kroll's addenda, 2:472) is more straightforward, but the emendation may be unnecessary.

22. "A life fit for Giants" (Γιγαντικὴ ζωή). The Giants of mythology provide Proclus with a ready metaphor for arrogance, pretentiousness, and lack of intellectual force. Here and below (69 [K74,15]; 99 [K90,8]; 125 [K104,3]; and 271 [K186,2]) I have tried to retain the metaphor, as preferable to "monstrous" or some such transla-

ἀθέῳ ζωῇ καὶ ἀποθρασυνομένῃ πρὸς τοὺς κρείττονας· εἰ δὲ μὴ πιστεύσαιεν, οὐδ' εἴ τι χρηστὸν ἔχουσιν | αἱ ποιήσεις, αὐτὸ πιστὸν ἡγήσονται διὰ τὴν περὶ τὰ μέγιστα πρὸς αὐτὰς ἀπιστίαν. πεφύκαμεν γὰρ ἅπαντες οἷς ἂν ἐπὶ τῶν σπουδῆς ἀξίων διαφερόντως ἀπιστήσωμεν, μηδὲ ἐπὶ τῶν ἀτιμοτέρων ἐνδιδόναι τὴν ἑαυτῶν διάνοιαν· ὥστ' ἢ περιττὰς ἀναγκαίως αὐτὰς ἢ βλαβερὰς τοῖς παιδευομένοις | εἶναι.

Καὶ ταῦτα προϊδόμενος ὁ Πλάτων οὐ δίδωσι χορὸν τοῖς τῶν τοιούτων ποιήσεων δημιουργοῖς, οὐδὲ ἐπιτρέπει νέοις οὖσιν αὐτῶν ἀκροᾶσθαι, τριῶν ὡς εἴρηται φυλακῆς ἕνεκα, δοξῶν πονηρίας, παθῶν ἀμετρίας, τῆς ἐν τῇ πάσῃ ζωῇ ποικιλίας. ὧν τὸ μέν ἐστιν τοῦ ἐν ἡμῖν γνωστικοῦ | κακόν, τὸ δὲ τοῦ ὀρεκτικοῦ, τὸ δὲ τῆς ὅλης ψυχῆς.

[3] Τούτων δὲ διηυκρινημένων ἐκεῖνο προσθῶμεν, ὃ δὴ προὐθέμεθα συγγενὲς ὂν τῷ πρόσθεν, πῶς ἂν αὐτὸς συνᾴδοι πρὸς ἑαυτόν, ἐν Συμποσίῳ μὲν ἀναγκάζων τῆς αὐτῆς εἶναι τέχνης κωμῳδίαν καὶ τραγῳδίαν ποιεῖν, ἐν Πολιτείᾳ δὲ μη||δὲν ταύτας γειτνιώσας ἀλλήλαις <οὐ> τῆς αὐτῆς ἕξεως εἶναι λέγων ἀποτελεῖ, διὰ τὸ τὴν φύσιν ἡμῶν ἄλλην πρὸς ἄλλο πεφυκέναι κατακεκερματισμένην, ὡς μηδὲ ἐπὶ τραγῳδίας μόνης πάντας ὁμοίως ἔχειν

no desire to exist in an environment of atheism and of arrogant rebellion against what is superior. And if, on the other hand, the young were not to believe them, then even if the poems have something sound in them, they will not consider that to be credible, because of their lack of faith in them in larger matters. It is the nature of all of us not to buy into the claims about lesser matters of those we find especially untrustworthy with regard to the important things. The result is that [these plays] are either superfluous or harmful to those being educated.[23]

Anticipating these things, Plato denies a chorus to the writers of such poetry,[24] nor does he allow those who are young to hear them, out of three concerns as enumerated above: falsity of doctrine, excess of emotion, and the complexity that characterizes the whole of life. The first is an evil for the mind, the second for the appetitive element in us, and the third for the entire soul.

[Third Question]

[3] Now that these issues have been examined, let us turn to that other matter that we indicated above is related to the preceding: How can he be consistent, when in the *Symposium* he forces agreement that the writing of comedy and of tragedy belong to the same craft (τέχνη), while in the *Republic* || he gives them no affinity at all with one another and denies that they turn out to be products of the same talent, because of the fact that our natures are fragmented and whittled away in different ways for different things,[25] so that even with regard to tragedy taken by itself, all are not

---

tion for the adjective. The Giants doing battle with Zeus seem more than once, in Proclus, to be a representation of the Christians.

23. It is tempting to see here a tacit refutation of one of the most basic principles of ancient Christian pedagogy of polytheist texts—that the texts retain their ability to teach (for example, ethics), when stripped of their theological authority. This is the influential position, for instance, of Basil in the essay *Ad adulescentes*.

24. In classical Athens, the eponymous archon selected the playwrights who were to compete in the dramatic festivals and granted a chorus (as well as a producer, a χορηγός, to recruit it and finance its training) to those selected. To "deny a chorus," then, would be tantamount to preventing production.

25. Cf. *Rep.* 3.395b, where Socrates uses the distinctive and colorful verb κατακερματίζω (fragment, cut into smaller and smaller parts, fritter away), taken up by Proclus here.

πρὸς πάντα τὰ μέρη τῆς ποιή|σεως ταύτης, ἀλλὰ τοὺς μὲν ἐν ἄλλοις αὐτῆς μέρεσιν τοὺς δὲ ἐν ἄλλοις κατορθοῦν, καὶ κωμῳδίας ὡσαύτως.

Ὅτι μὲν οὖν ἀληθὲς τὸ τὴν ἀνθρωπίνην ψυχὴν διὰ τὴν ἀπόστασιν τῆς ζωῆς καὶ τὴν εἰς τὸ ἔσχατον πτῶσιν ἀπὸ τῆς ὁλικῆς ἐνεργείας εἰς τὴν μερικωτάτην καταντῆσαι, παντός ἐστι συνι|δεῖν. ἐκείνη μὲν γὰρ αὐτὴν ἐποίει κοσμικήν, εἰς τὸ ὅλον βλέπουσαν καὶ τοῖς θεοῖς συνδιοικοῦσαν τὸ πᾶν σμικρὸν ὁρῶσαν τὴν γένεσιν, ὅπου γε καὶ ὁ ἐνταῦθα κορυφαῖος τὴν γῆν εἰωθὼς εἰς τὸ ὅλον βλέπειν· ἡ δὲ εἰς τοῦτο τὸ εἶδος κάθοδος ἀπὸ τοῦ ὅλου καὶ παντὸς εἰς τὸ μερικώτερον ἀγο|μένης γέγονεν, ἀπὸ μὲν τοῦ κοσμικοῦ λόγου καθ' ὃν ἔζη πρότερον <τὸν> τοῦ θνητοῦ ζῴου μόνον προχειριζούσης, ἀπὸ δὲ τούτου μερικώτερον ἄλλον τὸν ἀνθρώπειον προβαλλομένης ἀντὶ <τῆς> τοῦ παντὸς θνητοῦ ζῴου προνοίας ὡς ἑνός, ἀπὸ δὲ τούτου κατὰ τὸν τινὸς ἀνθρώπου βίον ἀπερει|δούσης τὴν ἑαυτῆς ζωήν, οἷον φιλοσόφου, καὶ τὸν κοινὸν τοῦ ἀνθρώπου λόγον ἀφείσης, ἀπὸ δὲ τούτου τὸν ἐν τῷδε τῷ κλίματι καὶ τῇδε τῇ πόλει καὶ τῷδε τῷ γένει βίον ἐνδυσαμένης, καὶ οὕτω δὴ γινομένης μερικῆς ἀντὶ τῆς ὁλικῆς, ἀπὸ δὲ τῆς εἰς τοῦτο πτώσεως λοιπὸν ἐπιτηδειότητας | ἄλλας προσλαβούσης, τὰς μὲν ἐκ τῶν προσεχῶν αἰτίων, οἷον πατέρων καὶ σπερμάτων, τὰς δὲ ἐκ τοῦ περιέχοντος καὶ τῆς ἐν τούτῳ φύσεως ἰδίας, τὰς <δὲ> ἐκ τῶν περιστάσεων τῆς ζωῆς τῆς οἰκείας τοῖς τόποις, ἐν οἷς κατετάχθη πεσοῦσα τὴν τελευταίαν πτῶσιν. ἐκ γὰρ τούτων πάντων ὄντως ἡ φύσις ‖ αὐτῆς κατακεκερματισμένη τὴν πρὸς τὰς διαφερούσας τέχνας καὶ ἐπιστήμας καὶ ἐπιτηδεύσεις ἀπεστένωσεν ἐπιτηδειότητα, καὶ ἄλλη πρὸς ἄλλα πέφυκεν, καὶ οὐδὲ πρὸς ταῦτα ὅλα, διελοῦσα ταῖς ἑαυτῆς δυνάμεσι τὰς περὶ αὐτὰ ζωάς. τοῦτο | μὲν οὖν ὅπερ ἔφην πάντων ἐστὶν ἀληθέστατον καὶ ὡς διὰ τοῦτο τοῖς μὲν κωμῳδίαν τοῖς δὲ τραγῳδίαν ἐργάζεσθαι δυνατὸν καὶ οὐδὲ ὅλην κωμῳδίαν τισὶν ἢ τραγῳδίαν ὡσαύτως πᾶσαν.

Οὐ μὴν ἀλλ' ἐπειδὴ τοῖς ταύτας ἐργαζομένοις τὰς ποιήσεις δυοῖν τούτοιν δεῖ, τῆς τε γνώσεως καὶ τῆς | ζωῆς, τῆς μὲν ὅπως ἂν ἔχωσι τέχνην

equally skilled in the various aspects of that genre, but some succeed in some parts, some in others—and the same for comedy?

Now the truth of the fact that the human soul, on account of its self-alienation from [its true] life and its fall to the outer limits, has descended from total activity to the most fragmented activity, is comprehensible to anyone. That [higher soul] set out to make the [en]cosmic one, which looks into the whole [universe] and shares with the gods in the ordering of the cosmos, scarcely paying attention to the realm of becoming, as the chief of this realm [the sun][26] ignores the earth, accustomed as well to direct his contemplation to the whole. The descent into this form [of existence] came about as she was led from the entire and universal into increasing fragmentation, preferring to the cosmic order (λόγος), by which she had previously lived, that of the mere mortal animal, and next adopting another, yet more partial, one, the human, in place of the providential care (πρόνοια) for the universal mortal animal as a whole, then defining her life after a specific human life—say, that of a philosopher—laying aside the common order (λόγος) of humanity, and from there taking on the life in *this* region, *this* city, *this* family—in all of this becoming partial and no longer whole—and finally acquiring new characteristics because of her fall into this [existence], some from proximate causes—fathers and sperm—some from the environment and specific to its nature, some from the circumstances of the life appropriate to the location in which she was placed, having completed the ultimate fall. From all of this, her ‖ nature, truly fragmented and whittled away, narrowed her capacities for the various arts, sciences, and specialized activities, and she changes with reference to different things, and not to all these things, since she divides up the lives (or aptitudes) that relate to those things, according to her own capacities. This that I have said is the greatest truth,[27] and so in this way some have the capacity to write comedy and others tragedy, and some, not the whole of comedy, nor likewise the whole of tragedy.

Yet, inasmuch as writers of poetry of this sort need these two things: knowledge and aptitude (ζωή)[28]—knowledge, in order to have the skill to

---

26. Kroll made this identification in his addenda (2:472), and F. ad loc. added further supporting evidence.

27. That is, this description of the descent and fragmentation of the soul addresses on the highest level of generality the issues of specialization under discussion.

28. I follow F.'s lead here in translating ζωή "aptitude" (F.: "similitude de vie").

τοῦ πῶς ἑκατέραν μεταχειριστέον καὶ ἐκ τίνων μερῶν διασκευαστέον καὶ πῶς τεταγμένων καὶ ὁποίων προσώπων, ἃ δὴ καὶ λέγειν εἰώθασιν οἱ περὶ αὐτῶν γράφοντες, τῆς δὲ ὅπως ἂν τοιαύτην παράσχωνται τὴν τῶν ἠθῶν μίμησιν, ὁποῖα τά τε πράγματά | ἐστι τὰ ὑποκείμενα καὶ τὰ πρόσωπα, καὶ μὴ ἀνόμοιοι γένωνται μιμηταὶ τῶν προτεθέντων αὐτοῖς, τὴν μὲν γνῶσιν μίαν ἐν ἀμφοτέραις εἶναι τὴν τεχνικὴν δυνατόν, ὃ καὶ ὁ Σωκράτης ὁ ἐν Συμποσίῳ φησίν (οὐ γὰρ μιμεῖσθαι τὸν αὐτόν, ἀλλ' ἐπίστασθαι ποιεῖν κωμῳδίαν καὶ τραγῳδίαν)· | τὴν δὲ διὰ τῶν ἠθῶν ἐπιτηδειότητα πρὸς αὐτὰς τὴν μιμητικὴν ἀναγκαῖον μηκέτι μίαν ὑπάρχειν. <ὃ> καὶ ὁ ἐν Πολιτείᾳ λέγει Σωκράτης· μιμεῖσθαι γὰρ τὸν αὐτὸν κωμικῶς καὶ τραγικῶς οὐκ εἶναι δυνατόν. μάλιστα γὰρ ἠθοποιός ἐστιν ἡ μίμησις, οὐκ ἔστιν δὲ ταὐτὸν ἦθος ἐπιτήδειον πρός | τε τραγῳδίαν φιλόθρηνον οὖσαν καὶ πρὸς κωμῳδίαν φιλόγελων.

Ὥστ' εἰκότως διελὼν ὁ Σωκράτης τὸ τεχνικὸν τοῦ ἠθικοῦ τότε μὲν ἔφατο τὸν αὐτὸν ἐπίστασθαι ποιεῖν ἀμφοτέρας, τότε δὲ οὐ τὸν αὐτὸν μιμεῖσθαι δυνατὸν ἀμφοτέρας· δεῖ γὰρ καὶ τέχνης πρὸς αὐτὰς καὶ ἤθους, ὧν ἡ μὲν κοινὴ || γένοιτ' ἂν ἀμφοῖν, τὸ δὲ ἐξ ἀνάγκης ἐστὶ διάφορον.

Τοσαῦτα καὶ περὶ τούτου.

[4] Τί δὲ δὴ περὶ τοῦ τετάρτου φήσομεν, πῶς ὁ Σωκράτης ἀναίνεται τὰς τῶν ἁρμονιῶν εἰδέναι διαφοράς, καὶ ταῦτα | περί γε τῶν ῥυθμῶν

know how to manage both [comedy and tragedy] and of what parts they are to be composed and how these parts should be arranged and what sort of characters [they require]—what writers on these matters regularly say—and aptitude, in order to provide the sort of representation of character that fits the underlying action and the characters, so that the playwrights do not become inaccurate imitators of what is before them—it is therefore possible that there is a single technical knowledge for both [comedy and tragedy]—as the Socrates of the *Symposium* says [223d]—for he says not that the same person can act both but that the same person "knows how to write" both comedy and tragedy, while of necessity the skill needed for creating the characters in [both of] them is not one and the same. That is what Socrates also says in the *Republic* [395a-b],[29] that for the same person to imitate both in the comic and in the tragic mode is impossible. Imitation (μίμησις) is primarily the creation of characters, and the same aptitude [or predisposition] cannot be suited both for tragedy, which is lament-loving, and for comedy, which is laughter-loving.

Thus Socrates correctly drew a distinction between the technical and the ethical, saying at one point that the same person has the knowledge to write both [comedy and tragedy] and at another that it is impossible for the same person to be a good imitator in both. Both genres require both skill and aptitude, and of these the skill is common to || both, but the other is necessarily different for each.

Enough on this topic.

[Fourth Question]

[4] What, then, shall we say about the fourth question: How does Socrates deny knowledge of the differences between the modes—while saying that he has heard something about the meters from Damon—and

---

According to F., the term is explained below, where ἦθος (character) is used as a virtual synonym (lines 23–26), and one and the same ἦθος is said to be unsuited to both tragedy (which is lament-loving) and comedy (which is laughter-loving).

29. While Proclus's primary inquiry here bears on the question whether one person can be both a comic and a tragic playwright, in the passage in the *Republic* it is clear that μίμησις covers both the activity of the playwright and that of the actor. It is perhaps easier to understand with reference to the actor Proclus's point about the different "aptitudes" required.

ἀκηκοέναι τι παρὰ Δάμωνος λέγων, καὶ εἰς τὸν Γλαύκωνα τὴν γνῶσιν αὐτῶν ἀποπέμπει προστιθείς· σὺ γὰρ μουσικός;

Λέγωμεν τοίνυν καὶ πρὸς ταύτην τὴν ζήτησιν, τῷ πολιτικῷ προσήκειν καὶ περὶ ἁρμονιῶν τι λέγειν καὶ περὶ ῥυθμῶν, ἀλλ' οὐχ ὡς τῷ μουσικῷ. τοῦ μὲν | γὰρ ἔργον ἀφορίσασθαι τὸ εἶδος οἷον εἶναι δεῖ τῶν ἁρμονιῶν τῶν εἰς ὀρθὴν ἀγωγὴν νέων καὶ παιδείαν συντεινουσῶν, τῷ δὲ πάσας ἠκριβωκέναι τὰς ἐν αὐταῖς διαφοράς, ὅσαι τε τὸ φιλόλυπον ἐγείρουσιν τῆς ψυχῆς καὶ ὅσαι χαλῶσι τὸ φιλήδονον καὶ ὅσαι μετροῦσι τὰς ἀμφοτέρων κινήσεις. δεῖ | γὰρ αὐτόν, εἴπερ ἐστὶ τῷ ὄντι μουσικός, ἐπεσκέφθαι τίνες ὠφέλιμοι ταῖς πολιτείαις. διὸ καὶ ὀρθῶς οἱ λέγοντες, ὡς ἄρα δεῖ μήτε τὸν πολιτικὸν ἄμουσον εἶναι μήτε τὸν μουσικὸν ἀπολίτευτον. ὁ μὲν γὰρ ἄμουσος ὢν οὐδ' ὅτι συντελεῖ τις ἁρμονία πρὸς παιδείαν γνώσεται διὰ τὴν ἄγνοιαν τῆς | μουσικῆς· ὁ δὲ ἀπολίτευτος ὢν ὁμοίως ἀσπάσεται πάσας, ὅσαι τε συντείνουσιν εἰς ἀπαιδευσίαν καὶ ὅσαι συντελοῦσι πρὸς παιδείαν· καίτοι τῆς μουσικῆς ἐπαγγελλομένης τὴν ψυχὴν συμπάσχουσαν μὲν τοῖς καλοῖς ἀποφαίνειν, ἀνιλλομένην δὲ ἐπὶ τοῖς αἰσχροῖς.

Τῷ τοίνυν πολιτικῷ τὸ πρέπον | φυλάττων ὁ Σωκράτης ἅτε πολιτείας ὢν δημιουργὸς εἰς ἄλλους ἀποπέμπει τὴν τῶν ἁρμονιῶν διάκρισιν, αὐτὸς τοὺς τύπους μόνον ὑπογράφων τῆς πρὸς παιδείαν συντεινούσης ἁρμονίας. οὕτω δὲ καὶ τῷ στρατηγῷ τὸ μὲν τέλος αὐτὸν προσῆκεν ὁρίζειν τὸν ὡς ἀληθῶς πολιτικόν, τίσιν πολεμητέον, ὅτι τοῖς || ἀδικεῖν ἐγχειροῦσιν, τοὺς δὲ τρόπους τοὺς πολεμικοὺς καὶ τὰς διαφορὰς ἐκείνῳ καταλιπεῖν ὡς εἰδότι, ποῦ καὶ πῶς καὶ διὰ τίνων πολεμητέον. οὕτω καὶ τῷ ἰατρῷ προστάξει μὲν ὁ πολιτικὸς ὑγιάζειν οὓς δέον, μὴ μακρὸν ποιοῦντι | τὸν θάνατον, τοὺς δὲ τρόπους τῆς ὑγιάσεως ἐκείνῳ παραδώσει γιγνώσκειν, εἴτε διαίταις τοῦτο ποιεῖν δυνατὸν εἴτε φαρμακείαις εἴτε χειρουργίαις. οὕτω καὶ τῷ ῥήτορι παρακελεύσεται ῥητορεύειν καὶ πείθειν, ὡς τῶν αὐτῶν ὄντων δικαίων καὶ συμφερόντων, τὰ δὲ εἴδη τῶν λόγων οἷς χρώ|μενος πείθειν δύναται καὶ τὰς ἐν αὐτοῖς διαφορότητας ἐκείνῳ καταλείψει διελέσθαι καὶ ὁρᾶν, εἰ διὰ σεμνῶν λόγων ἢ διὰ ἠθικῶν ἢ διὰ δεινότητα πλείονα ἐχόντων χρὴ πείθειν τοὺς ἀκούοντας· ἑκάστους γὰρ ἐπάξεται διὰ τῶν οἰκείων.

Οὕτω δὴ οὖν καὶ περὶ τῶν ἁρμονιῶν μέχρι τῶν τύπων ὁ | πολιτικὸς ἐστήξεται τῆς ἐκλογῆς αὐτῶν, αὐτὴν δὲ τὴν λεπτουργίαν τῶν ἐν αὐταῖς

why does he defer to Glaucon in knowledge of the modes, adding "you are knowledgeable about music" [398e1]?

Well then, let us say with reference to this inquiry as well that it is appropriate for the expert in statecraft to say something about modes and meters, but not in the same way as the musical expert. It is the statesman's job to define what sort of modes will contribute to the correct upbringing and education of the young, while it is the musician's to be precise about all the differences between them and which ones stimulate the soul's love of pain and which release love of pleasure and which ones moderate both of those impulses. If he is truly a musical expert, he must have considered which modes are useful to the various states. For this reason, they are correct who say that the expert in statecraft must not be unmusical nor the expert in music apolitical. The unmusical statesman, on account of his ignorance of music, will not even understand that a certain mode contributes to education, while the musical expert with no experience of statecraft will embrace all the modes in the same way, the ones that contribute to education and those that tend in the opposite direction, and yet music professes to make the soul sympathetic to the beautiful and repelled by the ugly.

Socrates, then, keeping to what befits the statesman, in his role of creator of a constitution, defers to others on the distinctions among the modes, himself sketching out only the general outline of the mode that contributes to education. In the same way, it is the job of the true statesman to himself define the end for the general (i.e., on whom war is to be waged, that is, on those who undertake ‖ to commit wrongs), but to leave to him, as the expert, the manner of warfare and such distinctions as where, how, and with what resources the war is to be fought. Similarly, the statesman will tell the doctor to cure those who should get treatment (i.e., where he is not simply protracting the process of dying), but he will concede to him knowledge of the manner of treatment, whether this can be achieved by diet, drugs, or surgery. He will also call upon the rhetor to speak and persuade his listeners that what is advantageous is also what is right, but he will leave it to the rhetor to choose the forms of speech by which he will be able to persuade them and to understand the differences among those forms of speech, whether he should persuade his audience with imposing language, with moral harangue, or with more vehement language. He will win over each audience by the means appropriate to it.

And so, in the same way, where the modes are concerned, the statesman will go as far as setting up the principles for their selection, but he

διαφορῶν ἐπιτρέψει τῷ μουσικῷ. διὰ ταῦτ' οὖν ὁ Σωκράτης οὐδ' εἰδέναι φησὶ τὰς ἁρμονίας, οὔτε τίνες θρηνῴδεις οὔτε τίνες συμποτικαί, τοσοῦτον δὲ μόνον ὁρίζειν, ὅτι τὸν παιδεύοντα δεῖ πρὸς ἐκείνην βλέπειν | τὴν ἁρμονίαν, ἥτις ἂν ἀπεργάζηται τὸν παιδευόμενον ἐν πάσαις πράξεσιν καὶ πάσαις περιστάσεσιν καὶ πᾶσιν πάθεσιν τεταγμένον, ἐν μὲν τοῖς βιαίοις καὶ ἀκουσίοις ἀνδριζόμενον καὶ μὴ χαλῶντα τὸν τόνον τῆς ζωῆς, ἐν δὲ ταῖς εὐροωτέραις καὶ ἑκουσίοις σωφρονοῦντα καὶ μὴ ἐκμελῆ γιγνόμενον ὑπὸ | τῆς παρούσης εὐπραξίας. φιλεῖ γὰρ τὰ μὲν ἀβούλητα τῶν συμπιπτόντων ταπεινοῦν, τὰ δὲ βουλητὰ χαυνοῦν τὰς ψυχάς.

Εἰ δὲ [μὴ] τὰς ἁρμονίας ἀναινόμενος εἰδέναι διὰ τὸ τῷ πολιτικῷ προσῆκον λέγει τι περὶ ῥυθμῶν, τούτου δήπου τὴν τοῦ Γλαύκωνος αἰτιατέον ἄγνοιαν· τὰς μὲν γὰρ ἁρμο||νίας εἰδέναι καὶ τὰ εἴδη τὰ ἐν αὐταῖς, τοὺς δὲ ῥυθμοὺς ἀγνοεῖν ἔφατο, καὶ εἰ καὶ τούτων εἰσί τινες ἐπιτήδειοι πρὸς παιδείαν. ἵν' οὖν ἐνδείξηται καὶ τῆς τούτων δυνάμεως πέρι καὶ μὴ ἀτελὴς ὁ λόγος αὐτῷ καταλειφθῇ περὶ τῆς ὅλης | μουσικῆς καὶ τῆς εἰς παιδείαν αὐτῆς συντελείας, βραχέα περὶ τῶν ῥυθμῶν εἰκότως εἶπεν, ἐφιστὰς πῶς ἐστι καὶ ἐν τούτοις παιδευτικὸν καὶ φέρον εἰς ἀρετήν· εἶτ' εὐθὺς τὸν πολιτικὸν φυλάττων, ἀλλ' οὐκ εἰς τὸν μουσικὸν μεταπεσεῖν ἐθέλων, καὶ εἰς Δάμωνα τὴν περὶ τῶν ῥυθμῶν ἀποπέμψας | θεωρίαν ἓν ἐκ πάντων συλλογίζεται, χρῆναι τὸν παιδευτικὸν εὐλογίας στοχάζεσθαι καὶ εὐαρμοστίας καὶ εὐρυθμίας, τάχα κἂν τούτοις εἰς πᾶσαν βλέπων τὴν ψυχήν.

Διὰ μὲν γὰρ τῆς εὐλογίας ὁ ἐν ἡμῖν τελειοῦται λόγος, διὰ δὲ τῆς εὐαρμοστίας καὶ εὐρυθμίας τὸ ἄλογον κοσμεῖται· τῆς μὲν ἀπὸ | τῶν δυνάμεων αὐτῶν ἀρχομένης (ἁρμόζονται γὰρ ἐκεῖναι πρὸ τῶν ἐνεργειῶν), τῆς δὲ ἐν ταῖς ἐνεργείαις μόνως ἐμφαινομένης· τάττονται γὰρ αἱ κινήσεις διὰ τῶν ῥυθμῶν, διότι καὶ τούτων ἐστὶ τάξις ὁ ῥυθμός, καθ' ὅσον χρόνῳ μετροῦνται καὶ τὸ πρότερόν ἐστιν ἐν αὐταῖς καὶ ὕστερον. |

[5] Τούτων μὲν οὖν ἅδην· τὸ δὲ ἑπόμενον σκοπῶμεν, τίνα εἰδέναι χρὴ κατ' αὐτὸν περὶ μουσικῆς καὶ ποιητικῆς, πῶς ἔχουσι πρὸς ἀλλήλας καὶ

will leave to the musical expert the details of the differences among them. This is why Socrates says that he does not even know the modes, or which are funereal and which sympotic, but lays down only the principle that the educator must look to whatever mode makes the student orderly in every action, circumstance, and emotion—in violent and constrained circumstances, courageous and not relaxing his vital intensity, while in more prosperous and unconstrained circumstances, self-controlled and not losing his [inner] harmony to the present sense of well-being. Unwelcome events tend to humble the soul, while getting what one wants relaxes it and fills it with conceit.

If indeed, though he denies knowing the modes out of consideration for what befits the statesman, he says something about meters, Glaucon's ignorance must surely be held responsible for this. He [Glaucon] declared that he knew the modes || and their categories but said he was ignorant of the rhythms [cf. 3.400a] and whether any of these as well are appropriate for education. And so he [Socrates] appropriately spoke briefly about the meters, showing how there is something in them as well that is educational and conducive to virtue, so that he might display the capacities of these as well and so that his account of the whole of music and its contribution to education would not be left incomplete. Then, still respecting the limits of the statesman, and not wanting to fall into being a musician, and referring the theory of meters to Damon, he draws a single conclusion from all of this, that the educator must aim at the eloquent, the harmonious, and the properly rhythmic, perhaps, here as well, looking to the whole of the soul.

Through eloquence, (rational) discourse is perfected within us, while through harmoniousness and good rhythm the irrational is made orderly. Harmoniousness starts with the capacities of the soul, for the capacities are harmonized prior to activity, and rhythm enters only in actions themselves, since movements are ordered by rhythms (rhythm constituting the order of these as well),[30] to the extent that they are measured in time and priority and posteriority are inherent in them.

[Fifth Question]

[5] Enough on these matters. Let us consider the following: According to him, what must we know about music and poetry? What is their rela-

---

30. F. compares *Laws* 2.664e8: τῇ τῆς κινήσεως τάξει ῥυθμὸς ὄνωμα [ἐστίν].

πόσαι τάξεις εἰσὶν μουσικῆς. δόξειεν γὰρ ἂν ὡδὶ μὲν τὴν μουσικὴν συνάπτειν πρὸς τὴν ποιητικήν, ὅταν λέγῃ τὸν ποιητὴν **ἐν τῷ τρίποδι καθῆσθαι | τῆς Μούσης** [Leg. 4.719c] καὶ ὅταν **τὴν ἀπὸ Μουσῶν κατοκωχὴν λαβοῦσαν ἁπαλὴν καὶ ἄβατον ψυχὴν ἀνεγείρειν καὶ ἐκβακχεύειν κατά τε ᾠδὰς καὶ τὴν ἄλλην ποίησιν** [Phdr. 245a], ὡδὶ δὲ διϊστάνειν αὐτὰς ἀλλήλων, ὥσπερ ὅταν τοὺς βίους διορίζων τὸν μὲν μουσικὸν εἰς τὸν πρῶτον φέ‖ρων κατατάττῃ, καθάπερ καὶ πάντα τὸν φιλόκαλον, τὸν δὲ ποιητικὸν εἰς τὸν ἕκτον, καθάπερ καὶ πάντα τὸν μιμητικόν [Phdr. 248d]. ἔοικεν δὴ οὖν πολλὰ τῆς μουσικῆς εἴδη θεασάμενος πᾶν μὲν τὸ ποιητικὸν γένος ὑπὸ τὴν μου|σικὴν ἀναπέμπειν, οὐ πᾶν δὲ τὸ μουσικὸν εἰς τὴν ποιητικὴν κατακλείειν. τίνα οὖν μουσικὴν ἂν φαίη ποιητικήν, ἄξιον ἡμᾶς λέγειν διορισαμένους πρῶτον τὰ εἴδη πάντα τῆς μουσικῆς.

(1) Λέγομεν οὖν καὶ τὴν φιλοσοφίαν αὐτὴν **μεγίστην** εἶναι **μουσικήν**, ὥσπερ καὶ ἐρωτικὴν εἰ βούλει φάναι τὴν | ἐρωτικωτάτην ἁρμοσαμένην οὐ λύραν, ἀλλ' αὐτὴν τὴν ψυχὴν τὴν ἀρίστην ἁρμονίαν, δι' ἣν ἡ ψυχὴ τά τε ἀνθρώπινα πάντα δυνατὸν κοσμεῖν καὶ τὰ θεῖα τελέως ὑμνῳδεῖν, αὐτὸν μιμουμένη τὸν μουσηγέτην, ὃς ὑμνεῖ μὲν τὸν πατέρα ταῖς νοεραῖς ᾠδαῖς, συνέχει δὲ τὸν ὅλον κόσμον τοῖς ἀλύτοις | δεσμοῖς **ὁμοπολῶν πάντα**, καθάπερ ὁ ἐν τῷ Κρατύλῳ λέγει Σωκράτης [405c]. διὸ καὶ τὴν ἔνθεον μουσικὴν παρὰ τῷ φιλοσόφῳ πρώτως ἂν εἶναι φαίη (καὶ γὰρ ὁ φιλόσοφος ἐνθουσιάζων λέληθε τοὺς πολλούς) καὶ τὰ τῆς παιδευτικῆς ἀγαθὰ μουσικῆς μειζόνως καὶ πάντα ἁπλῶς, εἰς ἃ βλέπον|τες ἡγούμεθα τὴν μουσικὴν εἶναι σπουδῆς ἅπασιν ἀξίαν. καὶ ὅ γε τῶν μουσικῶν ἀκρότατος

tionship to one another, and how many categories of music are there? In some passges he would seem to attach music to poetry, when he says that the poet "sits on the tripod of the Muse" [*Laws* 4.719c] and when he says that possession by the Muses, taking hold of a gentle, pure soul, arouses it and instills Bacchic frenzy in odes and other poetry [*Phdr.* 245a]—but elsewhere he seems to distance them from one another, as when in defining the various types of life he takes the musical life (μουσικός) ‖ and puts it in the first rank, along with the other lovers of beauty, but puts the poetic life (ποιητικός) in the sixth rank, along with the whole range of imitators [*Phdr.* 248d–e]. And so he indeed seems to distinguish many sorts of music and to refer the whole of the poetic category to music, but not to include the whole of the musical category within poetry. It is appropriate for us to say which music he would call poetic, after first defining all the categories of music.

[a. The Categories of μουσική]

(1) We give to philosophy itself as well the title of "greatest music" [*Phd.* 61a3–4]—and likewise that of "[greatest] eroticism,"[31] if you are willing to say that the most erotic is that which tunes not the lyre but the soul itself to the best tuning (or mode), through which the soul becomes a thing capable of setting all human matters in order and of perfectly singing the praises of the divine, imitating the leader of the Muses himself, who celebrates his father with odes of intellect, and contains the entire cosmos within insoluble bonds, "moving" the universe "altogether,"[32] as the Socrates of the *Cratylus* [405c] says. He would also say, therefore, that the divinely inspired music dwells first of all with the philosopher (while in fact, most people do not realize that the philosopher is inspired)—and to an even greater degree, the educational benefits of music, and all of these things in simple form,[33] in consideration of which we judge that music is worthy of study for all. And the highest of musicians is this one—the same,

---

31. The adjective ἐρωτικός has a surprising force in later Platonism (see Porphyry, *Vit. Plot.* 11, on Polemon), as in the present passage, where, building on the imagery of the *Phaedrus* (esp. 248d–e) and *Symposium*, philosophy, standing at the pinnacle of μουσική, is likewise at the pinnacle of ἐρωτική.

32. This sentence plays on one of the less-plausible etymologies of Apollo's name in the *Cratylus* (405d): Ἀ-πόλλων < ὁμο-πολῶν (roughly: "together-revolving").

33. ἁπλῶς, i.e., in their simplest, purest form.

οὗτός ἐστιν, ὁ αὐτὸς ὢν ὡς εἴρηται τῷ ὡς ἀληθῶς φιλοσόφῳ, μηδενὶ τῶν κατὰ μουσικὴν ἀγαθῶν ἐλλείπων.

(2) Λέγει δὲ καὶ τὴν ἐκ Μουσῶν κατοκωχὴν μουσικὴν τρόπον ἄλλον ὡς ἐξορμῶσαν καὶ κινοῦσαν εἰς τὴν | ἔνθεον ποιητικὴν τὰς ψυχάς· **ὃς γὰρ ἄν, φησίν, ἄνευ Μουσῶν μανίας ἐπὶ ποιητικῆς θύρας ἀφίκηται, καὶ αὐτὸς ἀτελής ἐστι ποιητὴς καὶ ἡ ποίησις αὐτοῦ ὑπὸ τῆς τῶν μαινομένων ἡ τοῦ σωφρονοῦντος ἠφανίσθη** [Phdr. 245a]· κἀνταῦθα τὸ μουσικὸν || εἰς ταὐτὸν ἥκει καὶ τὸ ποιητικόν, τῆς ἐνθέου μουσικῆς τὸν ἔνθεον ἀποτελούσης ποιητήν· οὐ γὰρ εἰς ἄλλο τί φησιν τὸν ἐκ Μουσῶν κάτοχον ἐνθεάζειν ἢ εἰς τὸ ποιητὴν γενέσθαι, τῶν μὲν ἔμπροσθεν γεγονότων ἔργων ἀγαθῶν ὑμνῳδόν, εἰς | ζῆλον δὲ ἀνεγείροντα παιδείας διὰ τούτων τοὺς ἐπιγινομένους. ὅπου δὴ καὶ τὸ ἔργον μάλιστα τῆς ποιητικῆς ὅσον ἐστὶν εἰς παιδείαν ἀνῆκον ἐξέφηνεν καὶ οἷον, καὶ ὡς οὐ νομοθετικόν ἐστιν, ἀλλ' ὄντως τρίτον ἀπὸ τῆς ἀληθείας, διὰ τῶν εἰς τοὺς ἀγαθοὺς γεγονότας ἐγκωμίων παιδεύον | τοὺς ζηλοῦντας τὰ τῶν ἀγαθῶν ἐπιτηδεύματα. καὶ γὰρ καὶ οὗτός ἐστιν παιδείας τις τρόπος τοῖς ἀρχαίοις μάλιστα συνήθης, διὰ δή τινα πεῖραν τῶν κατ' ἀρετὴν ζησάντων ὁδηγεῖν ἄλλους κατὰ τὴν ἐκείνων μίμησιν εἰς ἀρετήν· οἷον δηλοῖ καὶ ἐκεῖνος ὁ παρὰ τῷ ποιητῇ λέγων οὕτω· |

Καὶ τῶν πρόσθεν ἐπευθόμεθα κλέα ἀνδρῶν [I 524].

καί·

Οὐχ ὁράᾳς οἷον κλέος ἔλλαβε δῖος Ὀρέστης, πάντας ἐπ' ἀνθρώπους [α 298–299]. |

καί·

Οὐ γάρ πω τοίους ἴδον ἀνέρας οὐδὲ ἴδωμαι· κάρτιστοι μὲν ἔσαν [A 262, 267].

as we have said, as the true philosopher—who is deficient in none of the good things associated with music.

(2) And he calls possession by the Muses music in another sense, inspiring and impelling souls into inspired poetry. "For," he says, "whoever arrives without the madness of the Muses at the gates of poetry is himself an incomplete poet, and his poetry—the sane man's—fades into obscurity in the presence of that of madmen" [*Phdr.* 245a]. || Here as well, the musical and the poetic come to the same, inspired music perfecting the inspired poet. He says that possession by the Muses inspires in one and only one thing, namely, becoming a poet, a singer of hymns in praise of the great deeds of the past, and through these arousing in people of later times enthusiasm for education. Here he shows how great and of what sort the function of poetry is, given that it is related to education—and that its role is not that of the lawgiver[34]—rather, it is truly "third from the truth" [*Rep.* 10.597e], teaching, by way of encomia for the good men of old, those who aspire to the pursuit of goodness. This is, in fact, a mode of education that was quite familiar among the ancients: through a certain experience of those who lived according to virtue, to lead others to virtue through imitation of them. The one [Phoenix] who says the following in Homer expresses this:

And we have learned the glorious deeds of men of old.... [*Il.* 9.524]

and [Athena/Mentes]:

Don't you realize what glory godlike Orestes won
among all humanity? [*Od.* 1.298–299]

and [Nestor]:

I never saw, nor will yet see, such men ...
they were the strongest. [*Il.* 1.262, 267]

---

34. The distinction between the work of the poet and that of the lawgiver is further elaborated below (lines 24–27), where it is made explicit that the poet educates through specific examples (or exemplary figures), while the lawgiver does so through "universal, not partial (fragmented) examples." [F.]

ἕκαστα γὰρ τῶν τοιούτων παιδεύει μέν, ἀλλὰ διὰ παραδειγμάτων· νομοθέτου δὲ οὐχ οὗτος ὁ τρόπος, ἀλλὰ τίς ὁ | τῷ ὄντι λέγειν ἀγαθός, καὶ πῶς ἂν ὁ παιδευόμενος γένοιτο τοιοῦτος, καὶ ἡ παιδεία ὑπὸ καθολικῶν οὐχὶ μερικῶν παραδειγμάτων.

(3) Λέγει δὲ ἄρα καὶ τὸ τρίτον μουσικῆς εἶδος, οὐκέτι τοῦτο καθάπερ τὸ προρρηθὲν ἐνθεαστικόν, ἀναγωγὸν δὲ ὅμως ἀπὸ τῶν φαινομένων ἁρμονιῶν εἰς τὸ ἀφανὲς || τῆς θείας ἁρμονίας κάλλος· φιλόκαλος γὰρ καὶ ὁ τοιοῦτος μουσικός, ὥσπερ καὶ ὁ ἐρωτικός, εἰ καὶ ὃ μὲν δι' ὄψεως, ὃ δὲ δι' ἀκοῆς ἀναμιμνήσκεται τοῦ καλοῦ. τοῦτον δ' οὖν καὶ ἐν τῷ πρώτῳ βίῳ συνηρίθμησε τῷ ἐρωτικῷ καὶ τρεῖς | ἐποίησεν τοὺς τὸν ἀναγωγὸν καὶ ἐπιστρεπτικὸν ἑλομένους βίον ἀπὸ τῶν τελευταίων εἰς τὰ πρῶτα πάλιν, ὅθεν δεῦρο κατεληλύθασιν, τὸν φιλόσοφον, τὸν ἐρωτικόν, τὸν μουσικόν, τὸν μὲν περὶ τὶ καλὸν ἐνεργοῦντα τὸ ἐν ἁρμονίαις καὶ ῥυθμοῖς καὶ ἀπὸ τούτου πρὸς τὰς ἀφανεῖς ἁρμονίας ἀνιόντα | καὶ ῥυθμοὺς ἐκείνους οὐκέτι δι' ἀκοῆς ὄντας γνωστούς, ἀλλὰ τῷ τῆς διανοίας λογισμῷ καταφανεῖς, τὸν δὲ περὶ πᾶν τὸ ἐν αἰσθήσει καλόν, ἀναμνηστικὸν ὄντα κάλλους ἁπλῶς, ἀλλ' οὐ τινός, τὸν δὲ ἀπὸ πάντων τῶν αἰσθητῶν εἰδῶν εἰς τὴν θέαν τῶν νοητῶν, ὧν εἰκόνες τὰ αἰσθητὰ | ταῦτα, στελλόμενον καὶ προειληφότα τό τε τοῦ μουσικοῦ καὶ τὸ τοῦ ἐρωτικοῦ τέλος. τὸ γὰρ τὶ καλὸν πάντως δήπου καὶ καλόν ἐστιν καὶ τὸ τὶ εἶδος πάντως καὶ εἶδος· ὁ τοίνυν παντὸς εἴδους θεατὴς οἶδεν ἄμφω, καὶ τὸ ἁπλῶς μὲν καλόν, τὶ δὲ εἶδος, καὶ τὸ τὶ καλόν· ὥστ' εἴη ἂν ὁ τοι|οῦτος μουσικὸς τῷ φιλοσόφῳ σύστοιχος.

(4) Λέγει δὴ οὖν καὶ ἄλλην ἐπὶ ταύταις μουσικήν, τὴν παιδευτικὴν τῶν ἠθῶν διά τε ἁρμονιῶν τῶν εἰς ἀρετὴν καὶ ῥυθμῶν, ἀνευρίσκουσαν τίνες μὲν ἁρμονίαι καὶ ῥυθμοὶ παιδεύειν δύνανται τὰ πάθη τῶν ψυχῶν καὶ πλάττειν ἤθεσι βελτίστοις ἐν | πάσαις πράξεσι καὶ περιστάσεσιν, τίνες δὲ ἐναντίοι τούτοις ἐκμελεῖς αὐτὰς ἀποτελοῦσιν ἐπιτείνουσαι ἢ χαλῶσαι καὶ εἰς ἀναρμοστίαν ἄγουσαι καὶ ἀρρυθμίαν. καὶ ταύτην εἴποις ἂν εἶναι

Each one of these is instructive, but instructive by example. This is not the manner of the lawgiver, but rather [the latter's task is] to say who the truly good man is and how the student might become like him. His education is by universal, rather than partial, models.

(3) He also designates a third class of music. This one is no longer, like the preceding one, inspired, but nevertheless leads upward from perceived harmonies to the || invisible beauty of divine harmony. This sort of musician is a lover of beauty as well, just as the lover (ἐρωτικός) is, though the latter is reminded of beauty through sight, while this musician is reminded through hearing. [Plato] ranked this one in the first type of life along with the lover and made the total of those choosing the life of ascent and return, from the last back to the first from which they have come down here, to be three: the philosopher, the lover, and the musician. The latter acts according to some good that lies in modes and meters and ascends through this to the nonmanifest harmonies and rhythms that are no longer known through hearing but are clear to the reasoning of mind;[35] the lover acts according to the entire beauty of the senses, which recalls that beauty which is simple and not that of any single entity; and the philosopher is sent from all the perceptible shapes to the vision of the noetic forms of which these perceptible ones are images and has reached the goal of both the musician and the lover, ahead of them. A particular beautiful thing is of course beautiful, and a particular form certainly remains a form. The spectator, again, of every form knows both: simple beauty (a particular form) and the particular beautiful thing. This sort of musician would thus be in the same category as the philosopher.

(4) He also clearly designates yet another music in addition to these, the one that educates character through the modes and meters that are conducive to virtue, discovering which modes and meters are capable of educating the emotions of souls and molding them with the best character in all actions and circumstances, and which ones, opposite to these, tightening or slackening the souls, get them out of tune and lead them into discord and arhythmia. You might say that this is the educational

---

35. This sentence points up the difficulty of translating ἁρμονία (tuning, scale, mode) and ῥυθμός (rhythm, meter). Those in use by the poet (and, at least in part, the musician) are the modes and meters of poetry, while their supra-sensory models require different designations.

τὴν παιδευτικὴν μουσικὴν ὑπὸ τῷ πολιτικῷ τεταγμένην τῇ γυμναστικῇ σύστοιχον, εἰς ἣν ὁ ἐν Πολιτείᾳ Σωκράτης ‖ βλέπων τοὺς περὶ ἁρμονιῶν καὶ ῥυθμῶν κεκίνηκεν λόγους, ὥσπερ εἰς τὴν πρὸ ταύτης, ἡνίκα τὰς ἐπιστήμας ζητῶν τὰς ἐχούσας τι πρὸς τὴν ἀλήθειαν ὁλκὸν ἀξιοῖ καὶ τὴν ἁρμονίαν μὴ τὴν αἰσθητὴν ἀσπάζεσθαι ταύτην, ἀλλ' εἰς τοὺς καθο|λικοὺς <u>ἀναγωγὸν</u> λόγους, μεθιστᾶσαν τὸν νοῦν ἡμῶν εἰς τὰ νοητὰ ἀπὸ τῶν αἰσθητῶν.

Τοσούτων τοίνυν ὄντων τῶν παρ' αὐτῷ μουσικῶν ἤδη φανερόν, ὅπως τὴν ποιητικὴν ὑπὸ τὴν μουσικὴν τακτέον, εἴτε τὴν ἔνθεον εἴτε τὴν μὴ τοιαύτην, καὶ τίνος διοριστέον, ὅτι τῆς ἀναγομένης. ταύτην γὰρ εἶχεν | ὁ πρώτιστος βίος, καὶ ταύτην διώριζεν τῆς ποιητικῆς ὡς μιμητικῆς, οὐκ ἐθέλουσαν μιμητικῶς ζῆν, ἀλλὰ ἀπὸ τῶν μιμητῶν ἀναρπάζειν ἑαυτὴν εἰς τὰ παραδείγματα τῶν ἁρμονιῶν τῶν τῇδε καὶ ῥυθμῶν.

[6] Ἀλλ' ἐπειδὴ καὶ ταῦτα διώρισται, μηδὲ ἐκεῖνα παρα|λείπωμεν ἀδιόριστα τούτοις ἑπομένως, τίνας ἁρμονίας ἐγκρίνει δεῖν τὸν ποιητὴν παραλαμβάνειν εἰς τὴν τῶν νέων παιδείαν, καὶ τίνας αὐτὸν ῥυθμοὺς προσαναγκάζει ζηλοῦν, τὴν πασῶν μὲν ἁρμονιῶν πάντων δὲ ῥυθμῶν ἐπιτήδευσιν ἐκτρεπόμενος ὡς ποικιλίας ἀμούσου πρόξενον γιγνομένην | τοῖς ἤθεσιν τῶν παιδευομένων;

Δοκεῖ γοῦν δι' ἃς εἴπομεν αἰτίας ἄλλοις ἐπιτρέπων τὴν τούτων ἐπίκρισιν μετεώρους ἡμᾶς ἀφεῖναι διψῶντας ἀκοῦσαι, τί ποτέ ἐστι τὸ τῷ Σωκράτει περὶ τούτων δοκοῦν, ὅς ἐστιν τῶν μουσικῶν ἀκρότατος· ὥσπερ

music deployed by the statesman and in the same category as gymnastics. This is the music that the Socrates ‖ of the *Republic* has in mind when he speaks about modes and meters, just as he looks to the music previous to this when, seeking those sciences (ἐπιστῆμαι) that have some attraction toward the truth [*Rep.* 7.530c–e], he decides not to embrace that music that is accessible to the senses but rather that which leads upward[36] to the universal ratios (λόγοι), transferring our mind from objects of sense to objects of intellect.

[b. Solution of the problem]

Given that these [four] are the categories of music he acknowledges, it is already clear (1) that poetry is to be ranked lower than music, whether inspired [category 1] or not [categories 2–4],[37] and (2) which sort of music poetry is to be distinguished from, namely, that music which rises upward [to a higher unity, (category 1)]. The first type of life had this [music], and he separated it from poetry (on the basis that poetry is mimetic), since this music is unwilling to exist mimetically but rather wants to snatch itself up from among the imitators and place itself among the models of the modes and meters of this world.

[Sixth Question]

[6] Now that these things have been defined, let us not leave undefined what comes next: Which modes does [Plato] think the poet should adopt for the education of the young, and, in addition, to which meters does he require him to aspire, since he forbids the practice of the full range of modes and meters as conducive to an inelegant [ἄμουσος] diversity in the characters of the students?

He certainly seems, for the reasons already cited,[38] to leave the judgment of these matters to others and so to leave us up in the air, anxious to hear what on earth Socrates thinks about these things—he who is the

---

36. Reading ἀναγωγόν (Wendland), from Kroll's apparatus, for the manuscript's ἀνάγειν.

37. While ambiguous in its reference, this phrase seems to modify music rather than poetry. Indeed, here in Essay 5 an inspired ποιητική seems beyond the realm of possibility.

38. Question 4 above. [F.]

οἶμαι καὶ αὐτὸς ὁμολογεῖ, φιλοσοφίαν μὲν εἶναι | λέγων τὴν μεγίστην μουσικήν, ἑαυτὸν δὲ μηδὲν ἀπολελοιπέναι ταύτης ἐν παντὶ τῷ βίῳ, καὶ ταῦτα διατεινόμενος ὁ εἰρωνικὸς ἐκεῖνος καὶ μηδὲν εἰδέναι λέγων πρὸ τῆς τελευταίας ἡμέρας. Τίνα οὖν αὐτῷ δοκεῖ περί τε ἁρμονίας καὶ ῥυθμοῦ τῶν εἰς παιδείαν φερόντων, ἐν οἷς καὶ τοὺς | ποιητὰς ἀναγκάζει ποιεῖν, <u>ὅσοι προσᾴσονται τοῖς νέοις καὶ || οἷς μόνοις δώσειν χορόν φησιν, ἀλλ' οὐχὶ τοῖς παντοίων ἠθῶν μιμηταῖς;</u>

Τοὺς μὲν οὖν ῥυθμούς, ἐξ ὧν καὶ Δάμωνος ἀκοῦσαι λέγει καὶ ἀποδέχεται τοῦ λόγου, δῆλός ἐστιν τῶν μὲν συνθέτων τὸν ἐνόπλιον ἀποδεχόμενος, ὅς ἐστιν ἔκ τε | ἰάμβου καὶ δακτύλου καὶ τῆς παριαμβίδος· τοῦτον γὰρ ἀνδρικὸν ἦθος ἐμποιεῖν καὶ παρατεταγμένον πρὸς πάσας τὰς ἀναγκαίας καὶ ἀκουσίους πράξεις· τῶν δὲ ἁπλῶν τὸν ἡρῷον δάκτυλον, περὶ οὗ καὶ λόγων φησὶν ἀκοῦσαι Δάμωνος καὶ δάκτυλόν γε καὶ ἡρῷον διακοσμοῦντος, ἐνδεικνύμενος ὡς | ἄρα τὸν τοιοῦτον ῥυθμὸν ἡγεῖται κοσμιότητος εἶναι ποιητικὸν καὶ ὁμαλότητος καὶ τῶν τοιούτων ἀγαθῶν. ἐκ δὲ ἀμφοτέρων ἀποτελεῖσθαι τὴν ψυχὴν ἅμα μὲν εὐκίνητον ἅμα δὲ ἠρεμαίαν· ταῦτα δὲ ἄμφω καλῶς ἀλλήλοις συγκραθέντα παιδείαν τὴν ὡς ἀληθῶς ἐντιθέναι. δεῖν γὰρ καὶ ἐν τῷ | Πολιτικῷ [309b] φησιν μήτε τὸ εὐκίνητον μόνον αἱρεῖσθαι τῶν ἠθῶν, ὀξύρροπον καθ' αὑτὸ καὶ ἄστατον

highest of musicians (as I think he himself admits, when he says that philosophy is the greatest music,[39] and that he never fell short of philosophy, throughout his life—but at the same time, this *eiron*[40] goes on claiming to know nothing, down to his last day).[41] And so, what is his opinion, as far as modes and meters that bear on education are concerned—the ones in which he requires those poets to compose who[42] will sing for the young and || the only ones he says he would give a chorus,[43] to the exclusion of those who represent characters of all sorts?

As for the meters on which he says he has heard Damon [3.400b] and accepts his account, of the synthetic or compound ones he clearly admits the *enoplios* ("military"), which is compounded of an iamb, a dactyl, and a pariambis.[44] This imparts manly character, firm in the face of all actions that are imposed by necessity and external constraint. Among the simple rhythms, he admits the heroic dactyl (on which he says he heard the account of Damon, who "arranged" both dactyl and heroic [3.400b5–6]),[45] showing here that he[46] judges this sort of foot to be productive of orderliness and evenness and good things of that sort, and that from the two of these the soul is made both agile and calm and that these two qualities well mixed together instill true education. He says in the *Statesman* [309b] that in character one should not choose the agile in isolation, since it is unstable and always in motion, nor should one choose the calm [by

---

39. Question 5 (*Phd.* 61a).

40. An εἴρων is someone who understates his knowledge, or claims ignorance of a subject ("[a] dissembler, one who says less than he thinks," LSJ; cf. Theophrastus, *Characters* 1). Socrates is of course the great example of such a character in literature, and he is accused of this sort of deviousness repeatedly in the dialogues, notably by Thrasymachus in *Rep.* 1.337a.

41. *Apol.* 21d. [F.]

42. Reading ὅσοι, with F., from Kroll's addenda (2:472) for the manuscript's ὅσα.

43. See above, 21 n. 24.

44. On the "*en(h)oplion*," see West 1982, 195, s.v.; Dover 1968, 180–81, 271; and Holwerda 1967. According to Photius (see LSJ s.v.), the pariambis was the same as the πυρρίχιος, consisting of two short elements (˘ ˘).

45. Socrates affects a vague understanding of the exact application of the terms, seeming to imply that the two are not one and the same, but the limits of irony here are, as usual, difficult to identify. Proclus, in any case, seems to understand "heroic" and "dactylic" as equivalent terms, designating the same thing.

46. F. takes Damon to be the subject (of ἡγεῖται) here, but grammatically either Damon or Socrates/Plato is a possible candidate, and the latter seems to be a better fit with both the *Republic* passage and the present one.

ὄν, μήτε τὸ ἠρεμαῖον ἀργὸν καὶ ἀδρανὲς ὑπάρχον θατέρου χωριζόμενον. ἄμφω τοίνυν οἱ ῥυθμοὶ τὴν ἀμφοτέρων μετριότητα προξενοῦσιν ἀλλήλοις συμπλεκόμενοι.

Τὰς δὲ αὖ ἁρμονίας | ἤδη μέν τινες τῶν θρηνοποιῶν καὶ συμποτικῶν, ὧν αἳ μὲν τὸ φιλήδονον χαλῶσιν, αἳ δὲ τὸ φιλόλυπον συντείνουσιν, τούτων δ' οὖν ἐκβεβλημένων ἀξιοῦσιν τὰς λοιπάς, ὧν Δάμων ἐδίδασκεν, τήν τε Φρύγιον καὶ τὴν Δώριον αὐτὸν ὡς παιδευτικὰς παραδέχεσθαι· καὶ διαμφισβητοῦσι πρὸς ἀλλή|λους, οἳ μὲν τὴν Φρύγιον εἰρηνικήν, τὴν δὲ Δώριον λέγοντες εἶναι κατ' αὐτὸν πολεμικὴν [εἶναι], οἳ δὲ ἀνάπαλιν, τὴν μὲν Φρύγιον ὡς ἐκστατικὴν εἶναι πολεμικήν, τὴν δὲ Δώριον καταστηματικὴν καὶ εἰρηνικήν. ἡμεῖς δὲ εὑρόντες ἐν Λάχητι [188d] λέγοντα σαφῶς αὐτὸν τὸν ἀγαθὸν || ἄνδρα εἶναι καὶ ὄντως πεπαιδευμένον τὸν ἁρμοσάμενον <οὐ> λύραν οὐδὲ ὄργανα παιδείας, ἀλλ' αὐτὸν τὴν αὐτοῦ ψυχήν, οὐ φρυγιστὶ οὐδὲ αὖ ἰαστὶ ἢ λυδιστί, ἀλλὰ δωριστί, ἥπερ μόνη ἐστὶν ἁρμονία Ἑλληνική, ταύτην μὲν αὐτὸν ἡγούμεθα | μόνην οἴεσθαι τῶν ἁρμονιῶν ἐν παιδείᾳ ἐξαρκεῖν, τὴν δὲ φρυγιστὶ πρὸς ἱερὰ καὶ ἐνθεασμοὺς ἐπιτηδείαν ὑπάρχειν (ὡς καὶ τοῦτο ἐν Μίνωϊ λέγει [318b] σαφῶς, τὰ Ὀλύμπου μέλη μόνα τοὺς εἰς κατοκωχὴν πεφυκότας κινεῖν ἐξιστάντα, πρὸς δὲ παιδείαν μὴ συντελεῖν)· τῶν δὲ ῥυθμῶν | τὸν μὲν ἐνόπλιον οὐκ εἰς τὸ παιδεύειν νέων ψυχάς, ἀλλ' εἰς τὸ ἐξορμᾶν εἰς τὰς πολεμικὰς πράξεις παρέχεσθαι χρείαν ὑπειληφέναι, καὶ τὸ ὄνομα λαβεῖν ἐντεῦθεν τὸν ῥυθμόν· μόνον δὲ τὸν δάκτυλον καὶ ἡρῷον ἁρμόττειν παιδευομένοις καὶ ὅλως τὸν τῇ ἰσότητι κεκοσμημένον. διό μοι δοκεῖ καὶ | οὕτω εἰπεῖν Δάμωνος ἀκοῦσαι τοῦτον διακοσμοῦντος τὸν ῥυθμόν, ὡς εἰς κατακόσμησιν ὡς ἀληθῶς συντελοῦντα τῆς ζωῆς καὶ παιδευτικόν.

Μίαν οὖν ἁρμονίαν τὴν Δώριον καὶ ῥυθμὸν ἕνα τὸν δακτυλικὸν αὐτὸν ἐγκρίνειν ἡμῖν λεκτέον τοῖς παιδεύειν μέλλουσι ποιηταῖς ἐμπρέπειν· καὶ γάρ ἐστι | τούτοις κοινωνία κατὰ τὸν τῆς ἰσότητος λόγον. καὶ γὰρ ὥσπερ <ὁ> δακτυλικὸς ῥυθμὸς ἐν τῷ ἴσῳ συνίσταται τῆς ἄρσεως καὶ θέσεως,

itself], since separated from the other it is idle and weak. But the two meters together favor mutual moderation of these qualities when they are intertwined.

As for the modes, once those that are funereal or sympotic—the latter assuage the love of pleasure and the former intensify the love of pain—have been excluded, some people believe that he accepts as educational the rest of those Damon taught, namely, the Phrygian and the Dorian. They then go on to disagree among themselves, some claiming that according to him the Phrygian is peaceful and the Dorian martial, some the opposite, that the Phrygian, since it is exciting, is martial, while the Dorian is calming and peaceful. But our position—since we find him in the *Laches* [188d][47] saying clearly that the man who is good || and truly educated is the one who has tuned not the lyre or the classroom instruments[48] but his own soul, neither in the Phrygian mode nor the Ionian, nor the Lydian, but in the Dorian, which is the only Greek mode—for this reason, we believe that of the modes he deems this one alone to be adequate for education, while the Phrygian is appropriate for rituals and divine possessions (since he says clearly, as well, in the *Minos* [318b], that the melodies of Olympus alone are able to move those naturally susceptible to possession and to put them in a state of ecstasy, but they are not good for education). [We further believe that], of the rhythms, he maintains that the *enoplios* is of service *not* for educating the souls of the young but rather for providing the stimulus for warlike deeds (and that the rhythm gets its name from this) and that only the dactylic/heroic meter is fitting for those being educated—and generally, the meter structured by equality.[49] This is why, it seems to me, he says that he heard Damon "arranging" this meter, since it brings about the ordering of life and is educational.

Thus we must say that he judges one single mode, the Dorian, and one single meter, the dactylic, to be appropriate for those poets who are going to educate. These also belong together on the principle of equality, since the dactylic rhythm is composed of arsis and thesis in equal parts,[50] in the

---

47. Cf. 87 (K84).

48. F.'s solution here, ὄργανα παιδιᾶς ("des instruments frivoles") for παιδείας (manuscript, Kroll), since it restores a phrase from the *Laches* passage, is very attractive, but assuming that the manuscript reading refers to instruments that the student might be called upon by the teacher to tune, it may well represent what Proclus wrote.

49. See n. 50, below.

50. That is, the initial long syllable of the dactyl (in arsis) is equal in length to

οὕτω καὶ ἡ Δώριος ἁρμονία τὸν ἴσον ἐφ' ἑκάτερα τοῦ τόνου λόγον ἁρμόζει· δύο γὰρ τετράχορδα διοριζόμενα τόνῳ μελῳδεῖται κατ' αὐτήν. ἐμπρέπει δὲ ὁ τῆς | ἰσότητος λόγος ταῖς τῶν ἀλόγων εἰδῶν ἀρεταῖς, τὰς ὑπερβολὰς καὶ τὰς ἐνδείας ἀφελών, αἳ δὴ τῆς τοῦ ἀνίσου μερίδος εἰσίν.

Ταῦτα μὲν οὖν εἰρήσθω δεικνύντα, τίνας ἁρμονίας ἐκλέγεται καὶ τίνας ῥυθμοὺς εἰς ποίησιν παιδευτικήν. ὅτι || δὲ ὥσπερ ἐν τῇ μιμήσει τὴν ποικιλίαν ἀπεσκευάζετο καὶ διὰ τοῦτο τὴν τοιαύτην ποιητικὴν ἐξέπεμπεν, οὕτω καὶ ἐν ταῖς ἁρμονίαις καὶ τοῖς ῥυθμοῖς τὰς παντοδαπὰς αὐτῶν ἕξεις, αἳ δὴ χειροῦνται τὰς τῶν πολλῶν ἀκοάς, ἐκτρέπεται, | δηλοῖ [399c] καὶ τῶν ὀργάνων ἀτιμάζων τὰ καλούμενα παναρμόνια καὶ τοὺς τριγώνους καὶ αὐτὸν τὸν αὐλόν, ἐοικότα τοῖς παναρμονίοις διὰ τὸ πλῆθος τῶν τρυπημάτων, οἷς τὸ ὄνομα γέγονεν ἐκ τοῦ παντοίας ἁρμονίας εἶναι δυνατὸν ἐπιδείκνυσθαι δι' αὐτῶν.

Ὡς οὖν συντόμως εἰπεῖν, | πανταχοῦ δεῖ τὸν παρ' αὐτῷ ποιητὴν εἰς δύο ταῦτα βλέπειν καὶ ἐν ταῖς μιμήσεσιν καὶ ἐν ταῖς ἁρμονίαις καὶ ἐν τοῖς ῥυθμοῖς, τὸ καλὸν καὶ τὸ ἁπλοῦν, ὧν τὸ μέν ἐστι νοερὸν τὸ δὲ θεῖον· καὶ εἰκότως. δεῖν γὰρ ὁμοιωθῆναι τούτοις τὴν ψυχὴν πρὸ αὐτῆς οὖσιν· καὶ γὰρ μετ' αὐτὴν σῶμα καὶ ὕλη, | αὕτη μὲν αἶσχος οὖσα, τὸ δὲ σῶμα σύνθετον.

same way the Dorian mode tunes the same intervals on either side of the tone, since its scale is based on two tetrachords divided by the tone. The principle of equality is appropriate to the virtues of the irrational [parts of the soul],[51] removing the excesses and deficiencies that are characteristic of the portion of the unequal.

And so let these things suffice to indicate which modes and which meters he selects for educational poetry. That || just as in mimesis he eliminated diversity and therefore dismissed poetry of that sort, and in the same way among modes and meters he rejects their manifold forms that captivate the ears of the many—these things he shows also in condemning among instruments the so-called "panharmonic" ones and triangles[52] and the flute (aulos)[53] itself. These are like the panharmonic instruments in the number of holes—the panharmonic instruments getting their name from the fact that all sorts of modes can be played on them.

To sum up: in his account, the poet must everywhere look to these two things in his imitations, his modes, and his meters: the beautiful and the simple,[54] of which the one is intellective[55] and the other divine. And rightly so, since the soul must make herself resemble these things, which are prior to her. And below her are body and matter, the latter a deformity, and the body a composite entity.

---

the second element (in thesis), which can consist either of a long or of two shorts, as explained just below. The principle or ratio of equality (ὁ τῆς ἰσότητος λόγος) is clear enough here, but its application to the Dorian mode less so (but see Winnington-Ingram's comment in F.'s note ad loc.). Cf. the discussion of ἰσότης in Baltzly 2007, 213 n. 432; on the "Damonian scales" and the fifth–fourth century "modes" evoked just below, see West 1992, 174–84. F. rightly saw that Proclus's comments were stimulated by *Rep.* 3.400b6–7, where Damon is described as "arranging the dactyl and the heroic foot, making them equal from above and below in the exchange of long and short."

51. F.'s solution for the puzzling phrase τῶν ἀλόγων εἰδῶν.
52. This τρίγωνος was a multistringed instrument with a triangular body.
53. Traditionally translated "flute," the aulos was in fact a double-reed instrument like the modern oboe and was generally paired, so that the musician produced two tones simultaneously.
54. F. cites *In Alc.* 197.15: "All music is not to be accepted into education, but only that portion of it which is simple [ἁπλοῦν]."
55. For νοερός. I have, in general, used "intellective" in preference to "intellectual," which in English has distracting resonances that obscure the simple sense, "related to intellect (νοῦς)."

[7] Τούτων οὖν ἡμῖν συμπερανθέντων ἴδωμεν, τίνα ποτέ ἐστιν, ἃ τοῖς καθ' ἑαυτὸν ἐπιτιμᾷ ποιηταῖς καὶ δι' ἃ φησιν αὐτοὺς ἀποπίπτειν τῆς ἀληθοῦς μουσικῆς. τὸ γὰρ μὴ ἄν ποτε τὰς Μούσας αὐτὰς ἐξαμαρτεῖν ἅπερ οὗτοι πλημμελοῦ|σιν ἐκβαίνοντας αὐτοὺς δείκνυσι τὴν τῷ ὄντι μουσικὴν καὶ φερομένους εἰς τὴν τὸν πολὺν ὄχλον ἀρέσκουσαν. ἔστι δὴ οὖν τούτων, ὧν φησι τοὺς καθ' ἑαυτὸν ποιητὰς πλημμελεῖν, ἓν μὲν τὸ τοὺς λόγους καὶ τὰς ἁρμονίας καὶ ῥυθμοὺς μὴ ποιεῖν οἰκείους τοῖς εἴδεσι τῆς ζωῆς ἃ μιμοῦνται, περι|άπτοντας γυναιξὶν μὲν ἀνδρικοὺς λόγους, ἀνδράσι δὲ γυναικῶν καὶ οὐδὲ τούτων σπουδαίων· τοῦτο γὰρ οὐκ ἔστιν μιμήσεως ὀρθῆς, ὥσπερ οὐδὲ τὸ δειλοῖς ῥυθμοὺς ἀνδρείων ἢ ἀνάπαλιν διανέμειν.

Ἕτερον δὲ τὸ συγχεῖν τὰς ἁρμονίας καὶ τοὺς ῥυθμοὺς πρὸς τὰ εἴδη τῶν λόγων καὶ τὰ ἀσύγκλωστα || συγκλώθειν, οἷον λόγοις θρηνητικοῖς ἁρμονίαν Δώριον ἐπιφέρειν, καὶ ἀνδρικοῖς Λύδιον γοερὰν οὖσαν. δεῖν γὰρ ἕπεσθαι τῷ μὲν λόγῳ τὴν ἁρμονίαν, τῇ δὲ ἁρμονίᾳ τὸν ῥυθμόν· καὶ εἰ μὲν ἀνδρικὸς ὁ λόγος, καὶ τὰ λοιπὰ εἶναι | τοιαῦτα πάντως, εἰ δὲ θρηνώδης, κἀκεῖνα τῆς ὁμοίας εἶναι δυνάμεως. καὶ ἔοικεν διὰ τούτου [καὶ ταῦτα] κἀκεῖνο διδάσκειν, ὡς ἄρα τῶν ἁρμονιῶν κατὰ τὰ εἴδη διῃρημένων τῆς ζωῆς οἱ ποιηταὶ χρώμενοι πάσαις ἐπὶ πάντων ἀτάκτως δόξαν παρεῖχον, ὡς ἄρα μὴ οὔσης ἐν ταῖς ἁρμονίαις τοι|αύτης διαφορᾶς, ἀλλὰ ἁπασῶν εἰς πᾶν ἦθος ἐναρμόζεσθαι δυναμένων· ὡς θρηνεῖν μὲν ἰαστὶ τυχόν, ἐν δὲ συμποσίοις διαγίγνεσθαι μιξολυδιστί. <ὃ> καὶ εἵλοντο λέγειν τινὲς καὶ ταῦτα συγχωροῦντες εἶναι καὶ λόγων καὶ ῥυθμῶν διαφοράς, καὶ μὴ ἄν τὸν τοῦ ἀνδρικοῦ λόγον ἁρμόσαι τῷ δειλῷ, μηδὲ | τὸν ἀνδρικὸν ῥυθμὸν γενέσθαι ἄν ἐμπρέποντα δειλῷ. γελοῖον γὰρ τῶν ἄκρων ταύτῃ διωρισμένων τὴν ἁρμονίαν μὴ κατὰ ταῦτα διῃρῆσθαι καὶ ἄλλην ἄλλοις ἤθεσιν ἐμπρέπειν. τοῦτο μὲν οὖν ὅπερ ἔφην, τὸ πάντα συγχεῖν, ἔοικεν τοῦτο τοῖς ποιηταῖς ἐπιτιμᾶν.

[Seventh Question]

[7] Now that these things are worked out, let us see what he objects to in the poets known to him and how he says they fall short of true music. The fact that the Muses themselves could never make the mistakes that the poets make [*Laws* 2.669c] demonstrates that the latter abandon true music and are diverted into music that pleases the general crowd. Among the mistakes of which he accuses the poets of his time, one is that of not making their words and modes and meters appropriate to the sorts of lives they imitate, giving manly words to women, and to men, words properly belonging to women and even to frivolous women. This is not characteristic of correct mimesis, nor is giving to cowards the meters of brave men, or the reverse.

Another [of their failings] is to confuse the modes and meters with reference to the types of speeches and to weave together ‖ incompatibles,[56] as when they apply the Dorian mode to lamentations, or the Lydian, which is mournful, to manly things. [He maintains] that the mode must follow the words and the meter the mode. And if the speech is manly, then of course the rest must be similar, and if it is a lamentation, then the other elements must have the same force. He seems here also to tell us that, whereas the modes are divided up according to the sorts of lives, the poets, by using them all indiscriminately for lives of all sorts, conveyed the impression that in fact such differences among the modes did not exist, but rather all could be fitted to every sort of character: that you could lament in the Ionian mode and that there was a place in the symposium for the Mixolydian.[57] This[58] is what some have chosen to say, while admitting that there are differences among speeches and meters and that the speech of a brave man would not be fitting for the coward, nor the brave meter suitable for a coward. It is ridiculous, when the extremes are distinguished in this way, for the mode not to be chosen according to the same principles, and for one mode to be [treated as] fitting for various characters. Thus, as I said, he saw fit to reproach the poets with confusing everything [in this way].

---

56. Lit., "weave together unweaveables"—apparently proverbial. [F.]

57. In 398e, the Mixolydian was classified as θρηνώδης and the Ionian as sympotic.

58. Reading <ὅ> with Kroll's apparatus.

Τὸ δὲ πρότερον, τὸ τοῖς ὑποκειμένοις | ἤθεσι καὶ εἴδεσι τῆς ζωῆς μὴ παρέχεσθαι συνᾴδοντας τοὺς λόγους καὶ τὰς ἁρμονίας καὶ τοὺς ῥυθμούς, εἰ καὶ ἀλλήλοις εἴη ταῦτα μὴ ὡς ἔτυχεν συγκεκλωσμένα, διδάσκοντος ἡμᾶς ἐστιν τὴν πάντων τούτων χρείαν καὶ σύνταξιν εἰς τὰ πράγματα δεῖν ἀναφέρειν. τὰς γὰρ ἐννοίας ἐκείνοις ἕπεσθαι δεῖν, | αἵ προηγουμένην ἐν τοῖς λόγοις ἔχουσι δύναμιν· οἷς ἕπεσθαι προσήκει τὰς ἁρμονίας, ὡς ταύταις τοὺς ῥυθμούς.

Εἰ δὲ ταῦτα ἀληθῶς ἐν Νόμοις [2.669b sqq.] εἰρημένα πεφωράκαμεν, δῆλον δήπουθεν, ὅτι τὸν τοῖς ὅροις τούτοις χρώμενον τῆς ποιητικῆς καὶ διορίζοντα τὰ μέτρα || πάντων τούτων, λόγων ἁρμονιῶν ῥυθμῶν, καὶ μάλιστα ἂν θείμεθα κριτὴν ποιητῶν ἄριστον εἶναι, καὶ οὐχ ὥσπερ ἔδοξέν τισιν κίβδηλον ἐκ τῶν ἐν Τιμαίῳ [21c] περὶ τῶν Σόλωνος ποιημάτων λόγων, οὓς εἰς Κριτίαν ἀνέπεμψεν τὸν | πρεσβύτερον, ὃν ἔδει περὶ ἀνδρὸς προσήκοντος αὐτῷ λέγοντα τὰ αἰσιώτερα λέγειν· πρὸς τῷ καὶ τὸν ἔπαινον ἐστοχάσθαι τῆς Σόλωνος περὶ τὴν ποίησιν τῶν τε ὀνομάτων ἕνεκα καὶ τῶν νοημάτων ἐξουσίας. τὸ γὰρ ἐλευθεριώτατον εἶναι τῶν ποιητῶν τὴν ἐν τούτοις ἄδειαν δηλοῖ, μήτε ὀνομάτων | ὥρας φροντίζουσαν, οἵαν οἱ πολλοὶ περὶ πλείονος ἄγοντες βοστρυχίζουσι τοὺς στίχους, μήτε νοημάτων πέρι τῆς ποικιλίας, οἵας ἀντεχόμενοί τινες τὸ ἦθος ἀμβλύνουσιν τὸ ἀνηγμένον εἰς ἀρετήν. ὥστε ἐμοὶ δοκεῖ καὶ τοῦτο πρέπον ὄνομα τῇ ἰδιότητι τῶν Σόλωνος ποιημάτων εἰς αὐτὸν ἀπορρῖψαι, | κἂν ᾖ Κριτίας ὁ κριτής.

[8] Ἀλλὰ τούτων ἱκανῶν ὄντων εἰς ταύτην τὴν ζήτησιν ἕπεται λέγειν ἡμᾶς, τίς ὁ κατὰ Πλάτωνα ποιητὴς ἄριστος ἂν εἴη, καὶ τίνα μὲν αὐτὸν εἰδοποιεῖ πραγματικά, τίνα δὲ λεκτικὰ καθήκοντα. χρὴ μὲν οὖν τὴν ὡς ἀληθῶς ἐπαινε|τὴν παρ' αὐτῷ ποιητικήν, εἴτε περὶ θεῶν εἴτε περὶ δαιμόνων λέγοι, πρὸς ἐκείνους ὁρᾶν τοὺς τύπους, οὓς αὐτὸς εἶπεν, ὑμνῳδὸν οὖσαν αὐτῶν ὡς ἀγαθοποιῶν μόνως, ὡς ἀμεταβλήτων ταῖς τε οὐσίαις καὶ ταῖς δυνάμεσι καὶ ταῖς ἐνεργείαις, ὡς ἀλήθειαν συμφυᾶ ταῖς ἑνώσεσιν ἀεὶ τὴν

The first [criticism], about not providing words, modes, and meters harmonious with the characters and sorts of lives in question—even if these are not just randomly thrown together with one another—that was the message of someone teaching us that the use and assembly of all these elements must be based on the matter (the actions) and that the concepts, which are of the greatest importance in the speeches, must follow on the actions, and the modes should follow on the words, and the meters on the modes.

And if we have correctly explained these things said in the *Laws* [2.669b–670b], then it is presumably clear that we would take to be the best judge of poetry the one who used these definitions of poetry and found the measure ‖ of all these things—words, modes, meters—and we would not take him to be fraudulent (κίβδηλος), as some have, from the passage in the *Timaeus* [21c] about Solon's poetry, that he puts in the mouth of the elder Kritias, who, since he is speaking about a kinsman, had to say something that erred, if at all, on the side of the auspicious. Moreover, his praise focused on the license of Solon's poetry, in language and ideas. That he was the "noblest and most free" (ἐλευθεριώτατος)[59] of poets is shown in his boldness in these things, not taking care for beauty of language, which most people make so much of, primping up their verses, nor for complexity of ideas, which some cling to at the expense of blunting the quality that elevates to listener to virtue. Thus I think the term "noblest and most free" is appropriately applied to Solon for the salient characteristic of his poetry—even if Kritias is the critic.

[Eighth Question]

[8] This is sufficient for this inquiry, and our next task is to say who, according to Plato, would be the best poet, and what characteristics both of content and of language define him. Now, all poetry that is truly praiseworthy in his judgment, whether it speaks about gods or about *daimones*, must respect those standards (τύποι) he himself has articulated: it must celebrate them as exclusively benevolent, as immutable in their essences, their powers, and their actions, and as having an eternally unchanging

---

59. In this somewhat free account of the *Timaeus* passage, Proclus picks this adjective ("most worthy of a free man," "noblest") among those applied to Solon, in order to make the dubious point that the quality Plato (or rather, Kritias) praised in the poet was precisely a willingness to break, or at least to stretch, the rules of poetry.

αὐ|τὴν ἐχόντων· κἂν πλάττῃ τινὰς περὶ αὐτῶν μύθους, ὥσπερ οὖν δεῖ πλάττειν (πάντως γὰρ τὸ μυθολογικὸν καὶ Πλάτων ἀποδίδωσιν τοῖς ποιηταῖς· **τὸν γὰρ ποιητήν** φησιν [Phd. 61b], **εἴπερ μέλλοι ποιητὴς εἶναι, χρὴ ποιεῖν μύ|θους ἀλλ' οὐ λόγους**), ὁμοίους πλάττειν τοῖς ὑποκειμένοις, ἀλλὰ μὴ διὰ τῶν ἀνομοίων ἐθέλειν αὐτὰ κρύπτειν· λαμβά||νειν δὲ ἀπὸ μὲν τῶν φυσικῶν ὀνομάτων ὅσα κατὰ φύσιν, οἷον γάμους καὶ τόκους καὶ ἐκτροφὰς τῶν γεννηθέντων καὶ συστάσεις κατὰ φύσιν γενομένας, ἀλλ' οὐ τερατώδεις· ἀπὸ δὲ τῶν ἠθικῶν τὰ ἔνθεσμα καὶ ἄξια τῶν ἀεὶ τῷ καλῷ καὶ | τῷ ἀγαθῷ κεκοσμημένων, οἷον νόμον καὶ δίκην καὶ παίδων εἰς πατέρας τιμὰς καὶ πατέρων εἰς παῖδας παραδόσεις τῆς ἀρχῆς. ταῦτα γὰρ ἂν εἴη πρέποντα παραπετάσματα τῶν θείων νοημάτων ἀπὸ τῶν μετ' αὐτοὺς ἑλκόμενα πραγμάτων ἐπ' αὐτούς. εἰ δὲ περὶ ἡρώων ἢ ἀνθρώπων λέγοι, χωρὶς | ἁπάσης κρύψεως τὰ μὲν περὶ ἡρώων προσήκοντα τοῖς ἥρωσι ποιεῖν, ἀπάθειαν αὐτοῖς ἀπονέμοντα τὴν ἡμιθέοις πρέπουσαν, τὰ δὲ περὶ ἀνθρώπων εἰς ἔπαινον τείνοντα τῶν ἀγαθῶν ἀεί, καὶ κοσμοῦσαν λόγοις τὰ ἐκείνων ἔργα καὶ μιμήσει χρωμένην τῶν τοιούτων, τὰ δὲ τῶν κακῶν ἐπιρραπίζουσαν, | ἵν' ᾖ τοῖς νέοις ὠφέλιμα πρὸς ἀκρόασιν, καὶ ἐνδιατρίβουσαν τοῖς περὶ τῶν ἀμεινόνων λόγοις, τὸ δὲ ἁπλοῦν ἀεὶ μεταδιώκουσαν ἦθος ἀντὶ τοῦ ποικίλου κατὰ τὴν μίμησιν.

Τὸ μὲν οὖν πραγματικὸν τῆς ποιητικῆς τοιοῦτον εἶναι δεῖ κατ' αὐτόν· τὸ δὲ λεκτικὸν κατὰ μὲν τὴν λέξιν ἑπομένως | ταῖς διανοίαις μάλιστα μὲν ἀφηγηματικὸν εἶναι τῶν εἰρημένων ἐννοιῶν ἀντεχόμενον, εἰ δέ που δεῖ καὶ μιμήσεως (καὶ γὰρ τοῦτο Πλάτων διώρισεν, ὥσπερ μυθολογικόν, οὕτω καὶ

truth, of the sort that naturally adheres to entities characterized by unity.[60] And if he fabricates stories (μῦθοι) about them, as he must—Plato, in any case, grants mythology to the poets, since he says that the poet "if he is going to be a poet, must write stories (μῦθοι) and not speeches (λόγοι)" [*Phd.* 61b]—then he must fabricate them similar to what they represent and not wish to cover his subjects with things dissimilar to them.[61] He must || take from the terms for natural things whatever is fitting to [their] nature—marriages and childbearing and the raising of offspring, and [generally] formulations that are natural, and not monstrous. From the ethical terms, he must take what is legitimate and worthy of beings eternally adorned by the Beautiful and the Good: laws and justice and honor given by sons to fathers, and transfers of power from fathers to sons. These would be suitable screens for our concepts of the divine, drawing over them things subsequent to them.[62] If, on the other hand, this poetry speaks about heroes or humans, it must, with no dissimulation, compose for the heroes that which befits heroes, giving them the freedom from emotion that is appropriate to demigods—and about humans, it must always compose material tending toward praise of the brave, adorning their deeds with words and imitating people of that sort, while rebuking the actions of the cowardly[63]—in order that the young may benefit from what they hear—and devoting its time to accounts of the better sort, always seeking out in the mimesis that character that is one and focused rather than complex and diverse.

This is what, according to him, the content of poetry should be. The language, literally following the sense, should most of all be narrative and faithful to the concepts explained above. And if at some point there is need of dramatization (μίμησις)[64]—this, too, falls within Plato's definition,

---

60. I.e., the ἑνώσεις (unities) are the divinities themselves, with their affinity to the One (17 [K49,27], above, with n. 19).

61. Here language and thought approach the (later?) formulation, in Essay 6, of a semiotics of poetry. At this point, however, the possibility of a nonresembling alternative to mimesis is still rejected.

62. I.e., because the gods lack perceptible attributes, the depiction of the divine requires attributing to them characteristics that properly belong to lower levels in Proclus's metaphysical hierarchy. On the "screens," see 7 (K44), n. 9, above.

63. The text speaks of the "good" and the "bad" (ἀγαθοί, κακοί), but as F. appreciated, the reference here is to epic poetry, where, within a world of martial values, ἀγαθός is often best translated "brave" and κακός, "cowardly."

64. Proclus here evokes the distinction made in the *Republic* (392d–394d) and

μιμητικὸν εἶναι τὸν ποιητήν), ἐξ ἀνάγκης τὴν μίμησιν μὴ ποικιλίας μετέχειν, ἀλλ' εἶναι τῶν ἀγαθῶν μόνων, κἄν | ποτε μιμήσηταί τινα παθαινόμενον, μήτε ἀνεπίπληκτον ἐᾶν μήτε ἀπολαύειν τῆς μιμήσεως· τούτοις δὲ οἰκείως καὶ μελοποιοῦντα τὴν εἰς ἀρετὴν τείνουσαν ἁρμονίαν τιμᾶν καὶ ταύτῃ προσχρῆσθαι διαφερόντως· εἰ δέ ποτε τῶν ἄλλων τινὰ παραλάβοι τῶν κακῶν τινα μιμουμένη πρὸς ὀλίγον, δή‖λην γίνεσθαι πρὸς τὸ εἶδος ἀνιλλομένην ἐκεῖνο τῆς ἁρμονίας ὡς οὐ σπουδαῖον, ἀλλὰ δυσχεραίνουσαν, ἵν' ᾖ τῇ πολιτικῇ προσήγορος. καὶ δὴ καὶ εἰ ῥυθμοῖς χρῷτο, πρέποντας αὐτοὺς τῇ ἁρμονίᾳ συγκλώθειν, τοὺς μὲν ἐπὶ πλέον | ὡς σπουδάζουσαν, τοὺς δὲ ἐπ' ἐλάχιστον ὡς παίζουσαν· οὕτω γὰρ ἂν εἴη πρὸς ἑαυτὴν σύμφωνος.

Ὥστ' εἴη ἂν ἡ ποιητικὴ κατ' αὐτὸν ἕξις μιμητικὴ διά τε μύθων καὶ λόγων μετὰ ἁρμονιῶν καὶ ῥυθμῶν κατ' ἀρετὴν διατιθέναι δυναμένων τὰς τῶν ἀκουόντων ψυχάς. |

[9] Τὸ μὲν οὖν τῆς ποιητικῆς ἄριστον εἶδός ἐστιν παρ' αὐτῷ τοιοῦτον· ἑξῆς δὲ τούτῳ τί ποτε τὸ τέλος αὐτῆς ἐστι παντὶ συλλογίσασθαι ῥᾴδιον. εἰ γὰρ μιμητής ἐστιν ὁ ποιητής, ὅτι μὲν οὐκ ἔχει τέλος τὴν ἡδονήν, ὥσπερ ὑπέλαβον οἱ πάντα μὲν νομίζοντες πράγματα παραλαμβάνειν εἰς | μίμησιν αὐτόν, πάσαις δὲ ἁρμονίαις χρῆσθαι, πάντων δὲ ῥυθμῶν εἶναι ζηλωτήν, ἵνα ἡδυσμένην ἀποτελῇ τὴν ποίησιν, ὅτι δ' οὖν τοῦτ' οὐκ ἀληθές, ἐν Νόμοις [2.667c] ἔδειξεν οὑτωσὶ συλλογιζόμενος· ὁ ποιητὴς μιμητής· πᾶς μιμητὴς τέλος ἔχει ὅμοιον ποιῆσαι τῷ παραδείγματι, ἄν τε | ᾔδειν μέλλῃ τινὰς ἄν τε μή· δῆλον ἄρα ὅτι καὶ ὁ ποιητὴς οὐ τὸ ᾔδειν ἁπλῶς ποιήσεται τέλος. ὅτι δὲ εἴπερ μέλλοι τοιοῦτος εἶναι μιμητὴς οἷον εἴπομεν, εἰς τέλος βλέψει τὸ ἀγαθόν, καὶ τοῦτο γνώριμον· πάσης γὰρ τῆς κατ' ἀρετὴν ἐπιτηδεύσεως,

that the poet is dramatic/mimetic as well as mythological [*Rep.* 3.392d]—then the dramatization must of necessity be free of complexity and rather constitute imitation exclusively of good people, and if it ever represents a person beset by strong emotion, it must neither leave that person unchastised nor allow pleasure to be taken in the dramatization. In line with these principles, this poetry must in lyric passages respect the mode that tends toward virtue and must especially make use of it. And if ever it adopts one of the other modes, while briefly imitating some inferior person, the poetry must make it || clear—in order to remain in dialogue with politics[65]—that it shrinks from that sort of mode as lacking in seriousness and feels disgust at it. And in particular if it uses meters, it must weave them in in a manner befitting the mode, some in a serious tone (more frequently), and others—very seldom—in a playful one. This is how poetry would be consistent with itself.

And so poetry, according to him, would be a mimetic skill that works through stories, words, modes, and meters capable of disposing the souls of its audience to virtue.

[Ninth Question]

[9] Thus the best type of poetry, for Plato, is of this sort. Next, the question of its goal (τέλος) is an easy one for anyone to think through. If the poet is an imitator, the fact that the goal is not pleasure—as those have maintained who think that the poet takes up any actions he pleases for imitation, uses every mode, and becomes adept at every meter in order to make his poetry more pleasant—[Plato] has shown in the *Laws* [2.667c], reasoning as follows: The poet is an imitator. Every imitator has as his goal making something similar to his model, whether it is going to please people or not. Therefore, it is clear that the poet will not simply make it his goal to give pleasure. It is widely accepted as well that, if he were going to be an imitator of the sort we have been describing, the goal he will look to is the good, for we shall assert that the goal of any virtuous activity—

---

developed in Aristotle's *Poetics* (48a) between narrative and dramatization (μίμησις). Cf Lucas's comments ad loc. (Lucas 1968, 66–71) on Plato's "particular meaning for the word μίμησις" in the *Republic* passage.

65. I.e., poetry will stoop to using trivial musical modes and meters only if required to do so, in order to maintain its subservient, instrumental position with reference to the statesman.

εἴτε ἐν μιμήσεσιν εἴτ' ἄνευ μιμήσεων, οὐκ | ἄλλο τι φήσομεν εἶναι τέλος πλὴν τοῦ ἀγαθοῦ. τοῦτο δὲ δὴ τί ἐστιν, ἄξιον συνιδεῖν, ὅτι πρόδρομον εἶδος τῆς πολιτικῆς ζωῆς, οὐκ εἰς τὸ θεωρητικὸν ἀνάγον τὴν ψυχὴν τέλος, ἀλλ' εἰς τὸ πολιτικόν· διὸ καὶ ἀναγκαῖον ἐλέγομεν εἶναι τῷ ποιητῇ τὰ μέτρα τῶν ἐνεργειῶν ἀφορίζειν τὸν πολιτικόν, | ὡς τῷ στρατηγῷ καὶ ἰατρῷ καὶ ῥήτορι, τὸν δὲ οἷς ἐκεῖνος ‖ διακελεύεται χρώμενον ὅροις τὸν εἰρημένον τρόπον ποιεῖν, εἰς ἐκεῖνο φέροντα τὰ ποιήματα τὸ τέλος.

[10] Τούτου δὲ ἡμῖν γνωσθέντος οἶμαι καὶ τὸ τελευταῖον εἶναι δῆλον τῶν προβληθέντων ἡμῖν εἰς ζήτησιν, τίς ποτε | ἄρα ἐστὶν ὁ ἐν τῷ παντὶ ποιητής, καὶ εἰς τίνα βλέπει καὶ οὗτος πολιτικὸν ὑπὲρ αὐτὸν ὄντα· καθάπερ ἄλλος ὁ ἐν τῷ παντὶ στρατηγὸς καὶ ῥήτωρ ἄλλος καὶ ἰατρός, ὃ μὲν τὸν κοσμικὸν πόλεμον τῷ πατρὶ συνδιακοσμῶν καὶ τὰ ἀμείνω κρατεῖν ἀεὶ τῶν χειρόνων παρασκευάζων, μετὰ τοῦ μηδὲ | τὴν ἐκείνων ἀφανίζειν δύναμιν (δεῖ γὰρ εἶναι κἀκεῖνα πάντως, ἵν' ᾖ τὸ πᾶν ἐκ τῶν ἐναντίων), ὃ δὲ τὴν ἐν τῷ παντὶ φύσιν δυναμῶν, ἵνα συνέχῃ τὰ σώματα πάντα, καὶ ἀγήρων ᾖ καὶ ἄνοσον ἀεὶ τὸ πᾶν κατὰ φύσιν ἔχον, ὃ δὲ τοῖς νοεροῖς λόγοις πείθων ταῦτα ζῆν ἃ βούλεται ὁ πολι|τικὸς ἐν τῷ παντὶ νοῦς. οὕτω γάρ που καὶ ποιητής ἄλλος ἐστὶ κοσμικός, μυθολογικὸς μόνως, μιμήματα ποιῶν τὰ ἐμφανῆ τῶν ἀφανῶν καὶ καλῶν καλά, τῶν κατὰ νοῦν τὰ κατὰ φύσιν, ἁρμονίαις χρώμενος, δι' ὧν ἀρετὴν ἐν τῷ ὅλῳ παρέχεται κρατοῦσαν, ἡττωμένην δὲ

whether it involves imitation or not—is nothing other than the good. And one should pay attention to what this [good][66] is: this is a sort of poetry that is a precursor of the political life,[67] raising the soul not toward the contemplative goal but toward the political one. This is why we said that the statesman has to define the measure of the poet's activity, just as for the general, the doctor, and the rhetor—and that the poet || in turn, following the guidelines he imposes, must write poetry in the manner described, directing the poems toward that goal.

[Tenth Question]

[10] Now that we have recognized these things, I think it is clear what the last of the questions is that we need to look into: Who, then, is the poet in the universe, and to what statesman above him does he look?[68] There is likewise another who is the general in the universe, and another who is the rhetor, and the physician. The general carries on the cosmic war for the father, arranging for the better always to have power over the worse, but arranging as well not to destroy the power of the worse completely (since they, as well, must in any case exist, so that the universe may be constituted of opposites). The physician puts strength into the substance of the universe, so that all the bodies cohere and the universe remains in its natural state, ageless and without ailment. The rhetor uses the words (λόγοι) of intellect to persuade those things to thrive that the statesman-intellect (ὁ πολιτικὸς νοῦς) of the universe wishes to thrive. So, in some such way, there is another poet, a universal one, mythological in a unique manner,[69] fabricating the manifest and beautiful imitations of those things that are both invisible and beautiful, imitations in the natural universe of things that exist in mind, using musical modes (ἁρμονίαι) through which he makes virtue triumphant in the cosmos and evil subordinate. He intro-

---

66. F. (84 n. 1) would have τοῦτο here refer neither to τέλος nor to the ἀγαθόν in question but rather designate "de manière plus vague, ... la tâche propre au poète." He was certainly right that τοῦτο cannot refer to the τέλος, but it seems in fact (if rather imprecisely) to refer to the specific "good" that is the goal of poetry.

67. The expression πρόδρομον εἶδος seems to be unique. Cf. πρόδρομοι ἐλλάμψεις in Plotinus, *Enn.* 6.7.7.

68. This question is rather different from the one announced above (5 [K43]).

69. LSJ cites Damascius for this sense of μόνως.

κακίαν· καὶ ῥυθμίζων | τὰς κινήσεις, ὥστε κατὰ λόγον κινεῖσθαι, καὶ μίαν ἐκ πάντων ζῶσαν ἀποτελῶν ἁρμονίαν καὶ ἕνα ῥυθμόν.

Τοῦτον ἐγὼ τὸν ποιητὴν οὐκ ἄλλον εἶναι φαίην ἂν ἢ τὸν τοῦ μεγάλου πολιτικοῦ μέγαν συνεργὸν καὶ παιδευτικὸν ὡς ἀληθῶς θεόν, εἰς τὸν ἐκείνου βλέποντα νοῦν. ὁ μὲν γὰρ ἐν | τῷ παντὶ πολιτικός ἐστιν ὁ μέγας ὑμνούμενος Ζεύς, παρ' οὗ καὶ αὐτὸς εἶναί φησιν τὴν πολιτικήν [Leg. 1.624a]· ὁ δὲ τούτῳ μὲν συνεργὸς τῆς ἐν τῷ παντὶ πάσης τάξεως ἔν τε ὀξείαις καὶ βαρείαις κινήσεσι καὶ ἐν βραχυπορωτέραις ἢ μακροπορωτέραις περιόδοις οὐκ ἄλλος ἐστὶν ἢ ὁ Ἀπόλλων, || ποιητὴς ὢν μιμημάτων ἐναρμονίων καὶ ἐνρύθμων. ἐκείνων δὲ ὁ μὲν στρατηγὸς ὁ μέγιστος Ἄρης, πολέμων προστάτης θεὸς καὶ ἀνεγείρων πάντα πρὸς τὴν ἐναντίωσιν τὴν κοσμικήν· ὁ δὲ πειθοῦς δημιουργὸς οὐκ ἄλλος ἢ ὁ Ἑρμῆς, | δι' ὃν καὶ δημηγοροῦσιν ἄλλοι θεοὶ κατ' ἄλλους, καὶ πρὸς πάντας ὁ Ζεὺς τὸν ἐν ἑαυτῷ προχειρίσας Ἑρμῆν· ὁ δὲ πάντα κατὰ φύσιν ἔχοντα δεικνὺς Ἀσκληπιός, δι' ὃν οὐ νοσεῖ <τὸ> πᾶν, οὐ γηράσκει, τὰ στοιχεῖα οὐκ ἀνίησι τῶν ἀλύτων δεσμῶν.

Εἰ οὖν με δεῖ τὰ ἀνέξοιστα λαλεῖν, ὁ μὲν | ποιητὴς ὅστις ἐστὶ δῆλον· κινεῖ δὲ τὰς Σειρῆνας ᾄδειν **μίαν φωνὴν ἱείσας ἕνα τόνον**, ὡς ὁ ἐν τῷ δεκάτῳ λέγει τῆς Πολιτείας μῦθος [617b]· κινεῖ δὲ ὡς ὁ Τίμαιος [36c] τοὺς τῶν θείων ψυχῶν κύκλους ἐν λόγῳ περιφερομένους ἐνρύθμως κινεῖσθαι. πάντα δὲ ἀπὸ τῶν | ψυχῶν ἀρξάμενα ποιήματά ἐστιν Ἀπόλλωνος ἐναρμόνια καὶ ἔρρυθμα· καὶ εἰς τοῦτον βλέπων ὁ τῇδε ποιητὴς ὑμνείτω μὲν θεούς, ὑμνείτω δὲ ἀγαθοὺς ἄνδρας ἔν τε μύθοις καὶ ἄνευ μύθων, ἢ περὶ ἄλλα στρεφόμενος γιγνωσκέτω καὶ ποιητικῆς ἁμαρτὼν καὶ Ἀπόλλωνος.

duces meter into the motions, so that they move in measure, and creates out of everything a single living mode and a single meter.

I would say that this poet is none other than the great collaborator of the great statesman, the truly educational god, who looks to the intellect of that statesman. The statesman in the universe is great Zeus, to whom hymns are sung, from[70] whom [Plato] himself says [*Laws* 1.624a] that statesmanship comes. His collaborator, in the whole order of the universe, both in motions fast and slow and in shorter and longer orbits is none other than Apollo, || the poet of modal and metrical imitations. And the general among them is greatest Ares, the god who presides over wars and rouses everything to the cosmic confrontation. The creator of persuasion is none other than Hermes, through whom the gods speak (each using his own Hermes), and Zeus addresses the rest, actualizing the Hermes within him.[71] The one who keeps everything in its natural state is Asklepios, through whom the universe is without illness and neither grows old nor releases its elements from their unbreakable bonds.

And so, if I must express what should not be divulged, it is clear who the poet is. He moves the Sirens to sing "casting a single voice, a single tone" as the myth [of Er] in the tenth book of the *Republic* says [617b]. As Timaeus says [*Tim.* 36c], he sets in motion the cycles of the divine souls, to revolve[72] rhythmically and in an orderly manner—and all things that have souls at their origin are the creations (ποιήματα) of Apollo, harmonious and rhythmic.[73] Looking to him, let the poet of this world celebrate the gods and let him celebrate good men, with or without myths. Alternatively, should he turn to other things, let him recognize that he is failing with respect both to poetry and to Apollo.

---

70. Reading παρ' οὗ for παρ' ᾧ (Kroll and manuscript).

71. There is, then, a λόγος (= Hermes) inherent in each of the deities, through which the νοῦς of each is expressed.

72. Reading (with F.) Kroll's conjecture: περιφερομένους ἐνρυθμῶς κινεῖσθαι for ms. προφερομένους ἐνρύθμους κινήσεις.

73. Or, "modal and metrical".

PROCLUS

ON THE *REPUBLIC*, ESSAY 6

Πρόκλου διαδόχου περὶ τῶν ἐν Πολιτείᾳ πρὸς Ὅμηρον καὶ ποιητικὴν Πλάτωνι ῥηθέντων.

<Βιβλίον Α>

Ἔναγχος ἡμῖν ἐν τοῖς τοῦ Πλάτωνος γενεθλίοις διαλεγομένοις παρέστη διασκέψασθαι, τίνα ἄν τις τρόπον ὑπέρ τε Ὁμήρου πρὸς τὸν ἐν Πολιτείᾳ Σωκράτη τοὺς προσήκοντας ποιήσαιτο λόγους καὶ ἐπιδείξειεν τῇ τε φύσει τῶν πραγμάτων καὶ τοῖς αὐτῷ <τῷ> φιλοσόφῳ μάλιστα πάντων ἀρέσκουσιν συμφωνότατα περί τε τῶν θείων καὶ τῶν ἀνθρωπίνων ἀναδιδάσκοντα, καὶ τὸν Πλάτωνα τῆς πρὸς ἑαυτὸν ἐξέλοι διαφωνίας, καὶ ἀποφήνειεν ὡς ἄρα ἐκ μιᾶς ἐπιστήμης ἅπαντα καὶ νοερᾶς ἐπιβλέψεως καὶ προαιρέσεως θεοπρεποῦς, ὅσα τε ἐγκωμιάζων γέγραφεν τὴν Ὁμήρου ποίησιν καὶ ὅσα ἐπαιτιώμενος ἔφθεγκται. καὶ γὰρ ἄν τις ἀπορήσειεν εἰς ταῦτα ἀποβλέψας, εἰ μὲν ὀρθῶς ὁ Πλάτων αὐτὸν ἐλέγχειν προὔθετο καὶ δεικνύναι τῆς προσηκούσης τοῖς πράγμασιν ἀληθείας ἀπᾴδοντα, πῶς ἔτι δυνατὸν ἐν τοῖς ἐπιστήμοσιν καὶ τόνδε τὸν ποιητὴν καταλέγειν, καὶ ταῦτα τῆς περὶ τῶν θείων γενῶν καὶ τῶν ἀεὶ ὄντων διδασκαλίας· εἰ δὲ τά τε ἄλλα Ὁμήρῳ καὶ ταῦτα τῆς πρεπούσης ἠξίωται παραδόσεως, πῶς ἔτι κατὰ νοῦν τὸν Πλάτωνα καὶ τὴν ἀνέλεγκτον γνῶσιν ἐνεργεῖν συγχωρήσει τις; ἔστιν

Proclus the Successor on the Things Said by Plato in the *Republic* Regarding Homer and Poetics

Book 1[74]

[Introduction]

(1) It recently occurred to me, in my address on Plato's birthday,[75] to examine the problem of how one might compose an appropriate response, on Homer's behalf, to the Socrates of the *Republic*, and show Homer's teachings to be perfectly in harmony with the nature of things, || and most of all, with the positions taken by the philosopher himself, about both divine and human matters, and [so] save Plato from his self-contradictions and show, in sum, that both what he wrote in praise of Homer's poetry and what he says in criticism, all of this comes from a single body of wisdom, a single intellective position, a single marvelous plan. Looking into these things, one might well come up against this problem: If Plato was right to undertake to refute him and to demonstrate that he fell short of the truth that properly belongs to the things he sang about,[76] how, then, is it still possible to list this poet among the wise, and particularly among the wise in their teachings about the classes of the divine beings and the things that exist eternally? And if, on the other hand, both these matters and others have been appropriately treated by Homer, how will one any longer be able to concede that Plato acts intelligently and as guided by irrefutable knowledge? These, as I have said, are matters in need of examination, and

---

74. Book 1 will be concerned primarily with the criticisms leveled by Socrates in books 2 and 3 of the *Republic*.

75. The birthdays of Socrates (6th of Thargelion [Aelian, *Var. Hist.* 2.25]) and of Plato (7th of Thargelion [Diogenes Laertius, *Vitae* 3.2]) were celebrated by the later Platonists (who on this account would be among the last people to believe they could accurately calculate dates in the old Attic calendar—thanks to Tony Grafton for this observation). Porphyry describes the celebration in the school of Plotinus in Rome in the 260s: "[Plotinus refused to reveal his own birthday] although he both performed sacrifices on the traditional birthdays of Socrates and Plato and gave a party for his companions, on which occasion those who were able were required to read a speech to the assembly" (*Vit. Plot.* 2.40–43).

76. πράγματα, here and elsewhere, is regularly used to designate the content, as opposed to the language, of poetry. Cf. Essay 5, Question 8.

μὲν οὖν ὅπερ ἔφην καὶ ταῦτα σκέψεως δεόμενα, μάλιστα δὲ ἁπάντων ἐκεῖνο ἡμῖν δοκεῖ παμπόλλην ἐξέτασιν ἀπαιτεῖν, τὸ καὶ αὐτὸν τὸν Πλάτωνα πρὸς ἑαυτὸν ἐν τοῖς περὶ Ὁμήρου λόγοις διαμάχεσθαι.

Πῶς γὰρ ἂν ἀλλήλοις συμβαίνοιεν ὅ τε ἐν τῷ Φαίδωνι | [95a] λεγόμενος παρ' αὐτῷ θεῖος ποιητὴς καὶ ὁ ἐν Πολιτείᾳ [10.597e] τρίτος ἀπὸ τῆς ἀληθείας δεικνύμενος; οὐ γὰρ λίνον λίνῳ συνάπτειν ἐστὶ τὸ ταῦτα ἀλλήλοις συμπλέκειν, οὐδὲ ἔστιν τις μηχανὴ τὸν αὐτὸν ἑκάτερον τιθέναι. τὸ μὲν γὰρ ἐπέκεινα πάσης τῆς ἀνθρωπικῆς καὶ | μεριστῆς ἐπιβολῆς αὐτὸν ἐνεργήσαντα καὶ τοῖς θεοῖς ἐνιδρύσαντα τὴν ἑαυτοῦ νόησιν ἐπιδείκνυσιν, τὸ δὲ εἰδώλοις συνόντα τῆς ἀληθείας καὶ πόρρω πῃ τῆς περὶ θεῶν ἐπιστήμης πλανώμενον. ἐῶ λέγειν, ὅτι καὶ τὴν ποιητικὴν αὐτὴν τότε μὲν ἐκ Μουσῶν κατοκωχήν τε καὶ μανίαν τιθέμενος καὶ | θεῖον τὸ ποιητικὸν γένος ἀποκαλῶν, τότε δὲ εἰδωλοποιὸν καὶ φανταστικὸν καὶ πολλοστὸν ἀπὸ τῆς ἀληθοῦς γνώ||σεως ἀποφαίνων δόξειεν ἂν κἀν ταῖς περὶ τῶν πραγμάτων κρίσεσιν τῆς πρὸς ἑαυτὸν οὐκ ἀπηλλάχθαι διαφωνίας.

Φέρ' οὖν ὅσα κἀνταῦθα τοῦ καθηγεμόνος ἡμῶν ἠκούσαμεν περὶ τούτων διαταττομένου καὶ τῆς κοινωνίας τῶν δογμάτων, | ἣν ἔχει τὰ Ὁμήρου ποιήματα πρὸς τὴν ὑπὸ τοῦ Πλάτωνος ἐν ὑστέροις χρόνοις καθεωραμένην ἀλήθειαν, συλλαβόντες ἐν τάξει διέλθωμεν καὶ θεωρήσωμεν πρῶτον μέν, εἴ πῃ δυνατὸν τὰς τοῦ Σωκράτους ἀπορίας διαλύειν· δεύτερον δὲ τὸν σκοπὸν τῆς φαινομένης ταύτης πρὸς Ὅμηρον ἀπαντή|σεως· τρίτον δὲ αὖ τὴν τῶν Πλάτωνι δοκούντων περί τε ποιητικῆς αὐτῆς καὶ Ὁμήρου μίαν καὶ ἀνέλεγκτον ἀλήθειαν πανταχοῦ προβεβλημένην. οὕτω γὰρ ἂν ἑκάτερος ἡμῖν ἀποφανθείη τῶν θείων κατὰ νοῦν καὶ ἐπιστήμην θεωρὸς καὶ περὶ τῶν αὐτῶν ἀμφότεροι τὰ αὐτὰ διδάσκοντες καὶ ὡς | ἀφ' ἑνὸς θεοῦ προεληλυθότες καὶ μίαν συμπληροῦντες σειράν, τῆς αὐτῆς περὶ τῶν ὄντων ἀληθείας ὑπάρχοντες ἐξηγηταί.

this matter most of all seems to us to demand a great deal of scrutiny: that Plato himself is at odds with himself in what he says concerning Homer.

How could there be any reconciliation between the man who, in the *Phaedo* [95a] is called by Plato a "divine poet" and the one shown in the *Republic* [10.597e] to be "third in line from the truth"? These cannot be woven together like two linen threads:[77] the same individual could not possibly take both positions. In the first assertion, we have a Homer who has transcended all human and partial notions in his poetry and has rooted his own thought among the gods; in the second, a Homer who knows only images of truth and strays far from wisdom about the divine. This is not to mention that, when Plato at one point calls poetry in general possession by the Muses and madness and calls the race of poets divine [*Phdr.* 245a], and then turns around and says that poetry is a fabricator of images and extravagant and many times removed from true || knowledge, he hardly appears to be free of contradictions, even with regard to judgments about the content of poetry.

Taking all together what I heard from my own guide [Syrianus][78] when he was passing on his teachings on these things as well as on the community of doctrine between the poems of Homer and the truth contemplated in later times by Plato, let us go through it in order and consider first, whether it is in any way possible to resolve the questions raised by Socrates, second, the goal (σκοπός) of this apparent[ly confrontational] response to Homer, and then, third, the fact that a single irrefutable truth is to be seen everywhere in Plato's position on poetics itself and on Homer. In this way, each of them would be revealed to us as a thoughtful and knowledgeable contemplator of the divine beings, both of them teaching the same things about the same things, and both interpreters of the same truth about reality, participating in the procession of the same god and taking their places in the same chain.[79]

---

77. λίνον λίνῳ συνάπτειν was proverbial. [F.]

78. καθηγεμών (guide, leader) is used widely of founders of schools and other teachers and intellectual figures held in high respect. Syrianus became scholarch within a year or two after Proclus's arrival in Athens (430). Proclus succeeded him perhaps six years later. See Watts 2006, 98–100.

79. On the chains of being that proceed from each divinity, see below, 97 (K89).

Περὶ τοῦ τρόπου τῆς τῶν θείων μύθων διασκευῆς παρὰ τοῖς θεολόγοις αἰτίων ἀποδόσεις καὶ λύσεις τῶν | πρὸς αὐτοὺς ἐπιστάσεων.

Τὰ μὲν δὴ προκείμενα τοιαῦτα ἄττα ἐστίν, περὶ ὧν ποιήσομαι τοὺς λόγους. δεῖ δὲ ὅπερ ἔφην ὑμᾶς μὲν καὶ τούτων αἰτιᾶσθαι τόν τε Πλάτωνα αὐτὸν καὶ τὸν ἐκείνου ζηλωτὴν καί, ὡς ἂν ἐγὼ φαίην, ἱεροφάντην· ἐμὲ δὲ τὸν | λέγοντα πειρᾶσθαι πάντα ἀκριβῶς ὑμῖν εἰς δύναμιν τὰ τότε ῥηθέντα διαμνημονεῦσαι καὶ ὅσα καὶ ὕστερον ἡμᾶς περὶ τῶν αὐτῶν διασκοπουμένους ἐπεκδιδάσκειν ἐκεῖνος ἠξίωσεν. ||

Ἐπεὶ δὲ πρὸ τῶν ἄλλων ἁπάντων ὁ Σωκράτης αἰτιᾶται τὸν τῆς μυθοποιΐας τρόπον, καθ᾽ ὃν Ὅμηρός τε καὶ Ἡσίοδος τοὺς περὶ θεῶν παρέδοσαν λόγους, καὶ πρὸ τούτων Ὀρφεὺς καὶ εἰ δή τις ἄλλος ἐνθέῳ στόματι γέγονεν τῶν | ἀεὶ κατὰ τὰ αὐτὰ καὶ ὡσαύτως ἐχόντων ἐξηγητής, ἀνάγκη δήπου καὶ ἡμᾶς, πρὶν τοὺς περὶ τῶν καθ᾽ ἕκαστα δογμάτων ἀνασκεψώμεθα τῆς θεωρίας τύπους, αὐτὴν τὴν τῶν Ὁμηρικῶν μύθων διάθεσιν προσήκουσαν ἐπιδεῖξαι τοῖς πράγμασιν, ὧν δὴ καὶ παρέχονται τὴν ἔνδειξιν.

Πῶς γὰρ δὴ ταῦτα, | φαίη τις ἄν, τὰ πόρρω τοῦ ἀγαθοῦ καὶ τοῦ καλοῦ καὶ τῆς τάξεως ἀποπλανώμενα καὶ αἰσχρὰ καὶ ἔκθεσμα τῶν ὀνομάτων πρέποντα ἂν γένοιτό ποτε τοῖς κατ᾽ αὐτὸ τὸ ἀγαθὸν τὴν ὕπαρξιν λαχοῦσιν καὶ τῷ καλῷ συνυφεστηκόσιν, καὶ ἐν οἷς ἡ τάξις πρώτως ἐστὶν καὶ ἀφ᾽ ὧν πάντα τὰ ὄντα | μεστὰ μὲν καλλονῆς, μεστὰ δὲ τῆς ἀχράντου δυνάμεως ἀνεφάνη; πῶς οὖν τοῖς τοιούτοις ἐφαρμόζει τὰ τῆς τραγικῆς τερατολογίας ἀναπεπλησμένα καὶ τοῖς ἐνύλοις συνυπάρχοντα φαντάσματα, τῆς τε ὅλης

(2) On the manner in which the divine myths are treated by the theologians,[80] with an explanation of the reasons behind that treatment and answers to the objections raised against them.

[a. Socrates' charges]

The material before me, and about which I will compose my presentations,[81] consists of things of this sort. You must, as I said, hold Plato himself responsible for them, as well as his devotee and, as I would say, hierophant.[82] For my part, I the speaker must do my best to give an accurate account of everything he told me then, as well as what he thought to teach me later, when I was looking more deeply into these things. ||

Since Socrates attacks, first of all, the manner in which myths are constructed and in which Homer and Hesiod passed down teachings concerning the gods (and Orpheus before them and everyone else who explained with an inspired tongue those things that are permanent and unchanging), we in turn, then, before we examine the basic principles of the doctrine with regard to specific teachings, must demonstrate that the composition of the Homeric myths fits those things of which they give an indication.[83]

How on earth, one might ask, could these words that depart exceptionally far from goodness, beauty, and order, and are themselves ugly and monstrous, ever be appropriate to things that draw their existence from the Good itself and are of the same substance as the Beautiful, things in which order is primal and from which all those things that exist emerge filled with beauty, filled with undefiled potentiality? What could these fantasies, full of the horror-tales of tragedy and substantially bound to the

---

80. The term in Proclus (as in Aristotle) refers to the poets who wrote myths about the gods: Orpheus, Homer, Hesiod, and the rest.

81. The λόγοι in question are the speeches in reply to Socrates, designated above.

82. In classical Athens, the hierophant was specifically the priest of Demeter and Kore who presided over the Lesser Mysteries, celebrated in the Metroon. The use of the term for Syrianus here is characteristic laudatory hyperbole.

83. Proclus's language here might seem unnecessarily oblique—the πράγματα are in fact the content of the poem—but he is preparing his audience for the notion that a poem can designate its content, can provide an "indication" or "demonstration" of that content, in multiple ways. The noun ἔνδειξις (indication) and the verb ἐνδείκνυμι (indicate, demonstrate) are used by Syrianus, Proclus, and Damascius to designate this sort of symbolic representation (see Saffrey and Westerink 1968, 19 n. 1).

δίκης καὶ τοῦ θείου νόμου στερόμενα· μὴ γὰρ οὐκ ᾖ θεμιτὸν τὰ τοιάδε ταῖς πάντων τῶν ὄν|των ἐξῃρημέναις τῶν θεῶν ὑποστάσεσιν προσφέρειν, μοιχείας λέγω καὶ κλοπὰς καὶ ἀπ' οὐρανοῦ ῥίψεις καὶ πατέρων ἀδικίας καὶ δεσμοὺς καὶ ἐκτομάς, καὶ ὅσα ἄλλα παρά τε Ὁμήρῳ θρυλεῖται καὶ τοῖς ἄλλοις ποιηταῖς.

Ἀλλ' ὥσπερ αὐτοὶ χωριστοὶ τῶν ἄλλων ὄντες οἱ θεοὶ τῷ ἀγαθῷ συνήνωνται καὶ | οὐδὲν εἰς αὐτοὺς παρεισδύεται τῶν χειρόνων, ἀλλ' εἰσὶν ἀμιγεῖς πρὸς πάντα καὶ ἄχραντοι καθ' ἕνα ὅρον καὶ μίαν τάξιν ἑνοειδῆ προϋπάρχοντες, οὕτω καὶ τοὺς περὶ αὐτῶν λόγους προσήκει τὰ ἐξαίρετα τῶν ὀνομάτων καὶ τὰ νοῦ πλήρη καὶ τὰ ἀπεικάζεσθαι δυνάμενα κατὰ τὴν οἰκείαν τά|ξιν πρὸς τὴν ἐκείνων ἄρρητον ὑπεροχὴν ἐπ' αὐτοὺς ἀνα||πέμπειν. καὶ δεῖ καὶ τὰς τῆς ψυχῆς ἐπιβολὰς καθαρεύειν μὲν τῶν ὑλικῶν φαντασμάτων ἐν ταῖς περὶ τοῦ θείου μυστικαῖς νοήσεσιν, ἀποσκευάζεσθαι δὲ ἅπαν τὸ ἀλλότριον καὶ κάτωθεν ἀπὸ τῆς ἀλογίας ὁρμώμενον δόξασμα, μικρὰ δὲ | πάντα πρὸς τὴν ἄχραντον τῶν θεῶν ὑπερβολὴν ἡγεῖσθαι, καὶ μόνῳ τῷ ὀρθῷ λόγῳ πιστεύειν καὶ τοῖς κρείττοσιν τοῦ νοῦ θεάμασιν εἰς τὴν περὶ αὐτῶν ἀλήθειαν. μὴ οὖν λεγέτω τις ἡμῖν τοιαῦτ' ἄττα περὶ τῶν θεῶν, οἷα καὶ περὶ ἀνθρώπων ἁρμόσει λέγειν, μηδὲ τὰ τῆς ἀλογίας τῆς ἐνύλου | παθήματα τοῖς τοῦ νοῦ καὶ τῆς νοερᾶς οὐσίας καὶ ζωῆς ὑπερηπλωμένοις ἐπιχειρείτω προσάγειν· οὐ γὰρ ἐοικότα φανεῖται τὰ σύμβολα ταῦτα ταῖς ὑπάρξεσι τῶν θεῶν.

Δεῖ δὲ ἄρα τοὺς μύθους, εἴπερ μὴ παντάπασιν ἀποπεπτωκότες ἔσονται τῆς ἐν τοῖς οὖσιν ἀληθείας, ἀπεικάζεσθαί πως τοῖς | πράγμασιν, ὧν ἀποκρύπτειν τοῖς φαινομένοις παραπετάσμασιν τὴν θεωρίαν ἐπιχειροῦσιν. ἀλλ' ὥσπερ αὐτὸς ὁ Πλάτων πολλαχῇ διά τινων εἰκόνων τὰ θεῖα μυστικῶς ἀναδιδάσκει, καὶ οὔτε αἶσχος οὐδὲν οὔτε ἀταξίας ἔμφασις οὔτε ἔνυλον καὶ ταραχῶδες φάντασμα παρεμπίπτει τοῖς μύθοις, | ἀλλ' αὐτὰ τὰ περὶ θεῶν νοήματα ἄχραντα ἀποκέκρυπται, προβέβληται δὲ αὐτῶν οἷον ἀγάλματα ἐμφανῆ τοῖς ἔνδον ἀπεικασμένα ὁμοιώματα τῆς ἀπορρήτου θεωρίας, οὕτως

material world, devoid of the whole of justice and divine law, have to do with entities of that sort?[84] No, I rather think that it is not right for such things to be attributed to the essences of the gods that transcend all things that are—adulteries, I mean, and thefts and castings out from heaven and crimes against fathers, tying them up and castrating them, and all the other things Homer and the other poets repeat again and again.

Rather, just as the gods themselves, separate from everything else, are one with[85] the Good, and nothing inferior reaches them, but they are utterly pure and undefiled, preexisting in a single category, a single uniform class, so, in the same way, it is appropriate for discourse about them to refer to them || in exceptional words, words full of intellect and capable of depicting in terms of their own class their ineffable transcendence. Moreover, in mystical contemplation of the gods one must purify the conceptions in the soul of all fantasies bound to matter and get rid of all thoughts that are foreign and surge up from their source below in the irrational and consider everything else trivial beside the undefiled transcendence of the gods, trusting only in right reason and in those visions into the truth about them that transcend intellect. Let no one tell us things about the gods that can appropriately be said about men as well, nor set out to attribute the experiences of the irrationality that is caught up in matter to that which transcends in simplicity the intelligence, the intellective substance, and the life of the intellect: these symbols will never bear any resemblance to the being of the gods.

Thus the myths, unless they are entirely to miss the truth concerning reality, must in some way reflect those things they undertake to hide from contemplation by means of their visible screens. However, just as Plato himself often illuminates divine things mysteriously, through images, and yet nothing ugly, no appearance of disorder nor fantasy deriving from the tumult of matter slips into his myths, yet the essential ideas themselves about the gods remain hidden, undefiled, and what we may call visible representations of them are projected, resembling what lies beyond the screen, and images of the secret doctrine[86]—in this manner, then, the

---

84. Question marks added at line 16 (as implied in F.'s translation) and line 19 (F., n. 3 ad loc.)

85. συνενόω (unite) and in particular its m/p forms (be one with) are very nearly exclusively Christian vocabulary. See LSJ, Lampe, and Sophocles s.v.

86. The term "secret doctrine" (ἀπόρρητος θεωρία) occurs five times in this essay: here, 65 (K73,22), 75 (K78,6), 77 (K79,3-4), 179 (K133,7), and 193 (K140,11)

ἄρα καὶ τοὺς ποιητὰς ἔδει καὶ αὐτὸν Ὅμηρον, εἰ τοῖς θεοῖς προσήκοντας μύθους ἔπλαττον, τὰς μὲν πολυειδεῖς ταύτας | συνθέσεις καὶ διὰ τῶν ἐναντιωτάτων τοῖς πράγμασιν ὀνομάτων συμπληρουμένας ἀποδοκιμάζειν, τὰς δὲ τοῦ καλοῦ καὶ τοῦ ἀγαθοῦ στοχαζομένας προϊσταμένους διὰ τούτων ἅμα μὲν ἀποκλείειν τοὺς πολλοὺς τῆς μηδὲν αὐτοῖς προσηκούσης τῶν θείων γνώσεως, ἅμα δὲ εὐαγῶς περὶ τοὺς θεοὺς | χρῆσθαι τοῖς μυθικοῖς πλάσμασιν.

Ταῦτ' ἐστίν, ἃ καὶ ὁ || Σωκράτης οἶμαι τῇ τε Ὁμήρου μυθοποιΐᾳ καὶ τοῖς ἄλλοις ἐπιπλήττει ποιηταῖς, <καὶ> ἕτερός τις ἴσως ἂν ἐγκαλέσειεν, ταῖς φαινομέναις τῶν ὀνομάτων τερατολογίαις οὐκ ἀρεσκόμενος. καὶ δὴ διαφερόντως οἱ καθ' ἡμᾶς ἄνθρωποι τοῖς | παλαιοῖς μύθοις ἐπιτιμᾶν εἰώθασιν, ὡς πολλῆς μὲν εὐχερείας ἐν ταῖς περὶ θεῶν δόξαις, πολλῆς δὲ ἀτόπου καὶ πλημμελοῦς φαντασίας αἰτίοις γεγονόσιν καὶ οὐδὲν ἀλλ' ἢ πρὸς τὴν παροῦσαν τοὺς πολλοὺς δεινὴν καὶ ἄτακτον σύγχυσιν τῶν ἱερῶν θεσμῶν συνεληλακόσιν.

Ἡμεῖς δὲ πρὸς | μὲν τούτους οὐ πολλοῦ δεησόμεθα λόγου τοὺς τῆς περὶ <τὸ> θεῖον πλημμελείας αἰτιωμένους τὴν τῶν μύθων παραδοχήν·

πρῶτον μὲν ὅτι τοὺς διὰ τὰ φαινόμενα πλάσματα τῆς περὶ τοὺς κρείττους ἡμῶν κατολιγωρήσαντας θεραπείας οὔτε τὸν σκοπὸν τῆς

poets and Homer himself, if they were going to fabricate myths that fit the gods, should have rejected these multiform compositions realized through words diametrically opposed to the things concerned, and on the contrary should have preferred combinations of elements that aim at the Beautiful and the Good, in order simultaneously to bar the many from a knowledge of the divine that has nothing to do with them and still to use mythic compositions legitimately in what concerns the gods.

These, then, I believe, are Socrates' || criticisms of the fables of Homer and the other poets, and someone else might well indict them in the same way out of displeasure with the evident monstrosities of their language. The people of our own day[87] are especially given to denouncing the ancient myths as the cause of extreme license in opinions about the gods and of irrational and mistaken fantasies; they even blame them for having driven the many to their present terrible disorder, where the holiest laws are broken.

[b. Proclus's reply: the correct and incorrect use of myth]

We shall not have to speak at length against those who see in the mythic tradition the cause of error regarding the divine, for the following reasons:

First, because it turns out that those who, on account of the visible fictions,[88] have treated with contempt the cult of the beings greater than

---

(cf. also τὴν ἄβατον τοῖς πολλοῖς θεωρίαν, 69 [K74,23–24]; τὴν ἀφανῆ θεωρίαν, 119 [K101,19]; ἡ συμβολικὴ θεωρία, 181 [K134,2–3]; 295 [K198,18]) and apparently not elsewhere in Proclus. It generally means little more than "hidden sense" or "hidden meaning," i.e., what is meant but expressed only indirectly. This passage, where the "representations" of "intellective apprehensions (νοήματα) hidden in the screen of fiction are said to be "images" (ὁμοιώματα) of the secret doctrine, is the most difficult. Cf. Plato, *Phdr.* 250a–b, where the reactions of embodied souls to the "images" (again, ὁμοιώματα) of things dimly remembered from the other, unmediated, world of forms, are described. On the "screen," see above 7 (K44) n. 9.

87. There is doubtless, as F. (following Kroll) notes ad loc., a reference to the Christians here, but it is complex, as the next section makes clear. The Christians may be the mistaken critics of myth, but it is even more certain that they are the criminals whose behavior is mistakenly understood to be the fault of the myths. See 16 (K75,5–16), below.

88. The fictions are visible in contrast with the truths they conceal. See below. [F.]

μυθοποιΐας οὔτε τὴν δύναμιν | ἐγνωκότας εἰς ταύτην ὑπενηνέχθαι τὴν ἀλόγιστον καὶ Γιγαντικὴν ἀνοσιουργίαν συμβέβηκεν. εἰ γὰρ οἱ μὲν μῦθοι τὴν προβεβλημένην αὐτῶν ἅπασαν σκευὴν ἀντὶ τῆς ἐν ἀπορρήτοις ἱδρυμένης ἀληθείας προεστήσαντο καὶ χρῶνται τοῖς φαινομένοις παραπετάσμασι τῶν ἀφανῶν τοῖς πολλοῖς καὶ | ἀγνώστων διανοημάτων (καὶ τοῦτό ἐστιν, ὃ μάλιστα ἐξαίρετον αὐτοῖς ἀγαθὸν ὑπάρχει, τὸ μηδὲν τῶν ἀληθῶν εἰς τοὺς βεβήλους ἐκφέρειν, ἀλλ' ἴχνη τινὰ μόνον τῆς ὅλης μυσταγωγίας προτείνειν τοῖς ἀπὸ τούτων εἰς τὴν ἄβατον τοῖς πολλοῖς θεωρίαν περιάγεσθαι πεφυκόσιν), οἱ δὲ ἀντὶ μὲν τοῦ | ζητεῖν τὴν ἐν αὐτοῖς ἀλήθειαν τῷ προσχήματι μόνῳ χρῶνται τῶν μυθικῶν πλασμάτων, ἀντὶ δὲ τῆς καθάρσεως τοῦ νοῦ ταῖς φανταστικαῖς ἐφέπονται καὶ μορφωτικαῖς ἐπιβολαῖς, τίς μηχανὴ τοὺς μύθους αἰτιᾶσθαι τῆς τούτων παρανομίας, ἀλλ' οὐκ ἐκείνους τοὺς κακῶς τοῖς μύθοις χρωμένους τῆς | περὶ αὐτοὺς πλημμελείας.

Ἔπειθ' ὅτι καὶ ἐκ τῶν ἄλλων || ἁπάντων, ὅσα δὴ σεμνὰ καὶ τίμια δοκεῖ διαφερόντως εἶναι καὶ αὐτοῖς ἐνιδρυμένα τοῖς θεοῖς καὶ ὑπ' αὐτῶν παραγόμενα, τοὺς πολλοὺς βλαπτομένους ὁρῶμεν, καὶ οὐ διὰ ταῦτα τὴν ἐκείνων αἰτιώμεθα γένεσιν, ἀλλὰ τὴν τούτων | ἀνόητον τῆς ψυχῆς ἕξιν.

Τίς γὰρ οὐκ ἂν συνομολογήσειε τά τε μυστήρια καὶ τὰς τελετὰς ἀνάγειν μὲν ἀπὸ τῆς ἐνύλου καὶ θνητοειδοῦς ζωῆς τὰς ψυχὰς καὶ συνάπτειν τοῖς θεοῖς, ἀφανίζειν δὲ ἅπασαν τὴν ἐκ τῆς ἀλογίας παρεισδυομένην ταραχὴν ταῖς νοεραῖς ἐλλάμψεσιν, ἐξωθεῖν δὲ τὸ ἀόριστον | καὶ τὸ σκοτεινὸν τῶν τελουμένων τῷ φωτὶ τῶν θεῶν; ἀλλ' ὅμως οὐδὲν παραιρεῖται τοὺς πολλοὺς τὸ μὴ οὐχὶ καὶ ἐκ τούτων παντοίας ὑπομένειν διαστροφάς, καὶ τοῖς ἐκ τούτων ἀγαθοῖς καὶ ταῖς δυνάμεσιν κατὰ τὴν οἰκείαν ἕξιν ἐπὶ τὸ χεῖρον χρωμένους ἀφίστασθαι μὲν τῶν θεῶν καὶ τῆς ὄντως | ἱερᾶς θρησκείας, φέρεσθαι δὲ εἰς τὴν ἐμπαθῆ καὶ ἀλόγιστον ζωήν.

Ὅστις οὖν ἡμῶν αἰτιᾶται τοὺς μύθους τῆς δεινῆς ταύτης καὶ πλημμελοῦς τῶν παλαιῶν νομίμων συγχύσεως, καὶ τῶν μυστηρίων αἰτιάσθω τὴν ἔκφανσιν καὶ τῶν τελετῶν τὴν εἰς ἀνθρώπους πάροδον. καὶ τί δεῖ περὶ τούτων λέγειν; | ἀλλὰ καὶ αὐτὴν ἐξέσται τὴν δημιουργίαν αἰτιᾶσθαι τοῦ παντὸς καὶ τὴν τάξιν τῶν ὅλων καὶ πρόνοιαν τῶν τῇδε πάντων, διότι δὴ καὶ τοῖς ἐκ τούτων ἐνδιδομένοις οἱ δεχόμενοι χρῶνται

ourselves were drawn into this unaccountable and Gigantic[89] impiety because they were ignorant of both the goal and the meaning of myth. If myths have set up in front of themselves the whole apparatus they project, rather than the truth that is rooted in secrecy, and use visible screens for the concepts that are obscure and unknowable to the many—and this is precisely their most exceptional virtue, that they expose to the profane nothing of the truth and hold out only traces of the total mystery to those naturally equipped to be led around from these to the kind of contemplation inaccessible to the many—and if these people,[90] rather than search out the truth that lies within the myths, are content with the curtain of mythic fabrications and, instead of purification of the intellect, encounter only fantastic and figurative concepts, how can one blame the myths for their insanity, rather than blame those who misuse the myths for their errors concerning them?

And then [secondly], because we see the many being harmed by everything that || seems exceptionally awe-inspiring and precious and rooted among the gods themselves and brought forth by them, and yet we do not place the blame on the source of these things, but on the ignorant state of these people's souls.

Who would not agree that the mysteries and initiations elevate souls from their embodied and mortal life and attach them to the gods, making all the confusion that enters into them from irrationality disappear through intellective illumination, and expelling all that is undefined and shadowy from those who are initiated into the light of the gods? And nevertheless, nothing prevents the many from undergoing all sorts of perversions, from these things as well, and turning their benefits and potential to the worse, on account of their own state, and abandoning the gods and the truly holy religion and being borne into the most passionate and irrational sort of existence.

Whoever of us blames the myths for this terrible and mistaken destruction of ancient customs, let him also blame the revelation of the mysteries and the introduction of the initiations to humanity. But why talk about these things? At that rate, you will be able to blame the very creation of the universe and universal order and the providential care that extends to everything in this world, because the recipients of the benefits afforded by

---

89. See above, 19 (K51) and n. 22.
90. I.e., those misled by myth (the Christians).

κακῶς. ἀλλ' οὔτε ταῦτα ὅσια φαίην ἂν οὔτε τὴν κατὰ τῶν μύθων διαβολὴν ἀπὸ τῆς τῶν πολλῶν παραφορᾶς | δικαίαν ἄξιον ἡγεῖσθαι. οὐ γὰρ ἐκ τῶν διαστρόφως χρωμένων τὴν τῶν πραγμάτων ἀρετήν τε καὶ κακίαν κριτέον, ἀλλ' ἀπὸ τῆς οἰκείας ἕκαστα φύσεως καὶ τῆς ἐν αὐτοῖς ὀρθότητος δοκιμάζειν προσήκει.

Ταῦτά τοι καὶ ὁ Ἀθηναῖος ξένος [Leg. 1.646a sqq.] οὐδὲ αὐτὴν ἐκβάλλειν || οἴεται χρῆναι τὴν μέθην τῆς εὖ διοικουμένης πόλεως διὰ τὴν τῶν πολλῶν ἄσκοπον καὶ ἀόριστον περὶ αὐτὴν φοράν, ἀλλ' ἀπὸ τῆς ἐναντίας χρήσεως τῆς ὀρθῆς καὶ ἔμφρονος μεγάλην μοῖραν καὶ ταύτην εἰς παιδείαν συμβάλλεσθαί φη|σιν. καίτοι φαίη τις ἂν καὶ τὴν μέθην διαφθείρειν τά τε σώματα καὶ τὰς ψυχὰς τῶν χρωμένων· ἀλλ' οὐχ ὅ γε νομοθέτης διὰ ταῦτα τῆς προσηκούσης αὐτὴν ἀξίας παραιρεῖται καὶ τῆς πρὸς ἀρετὴν συντελείας. οὔτ' οὖν ἡ μέθη φευκτὸν διὰ τοὺς πολλοὺς καὶ ἀπαιδεύτως αὐτὴν καὶ ἀμούσως μετα|διώκοντας, οὔτε αἱ τελεταὶ καὶ αἱ τῶν μυστηρίων δυνάμεις διὰ τὴν τῶν δεχομένων μοχθηρίαν κατηγορίας ἄξιαι τοῖς ἔμφροσιν, οὔτε οἱ μῦθοι διὰ τὴν τῶν εἰκῇ καὶ ἀλόγως αὐτοῖς χρωμένων διαστροφὴν βλαβεροὶ τοῖς ἀκούουσιν ἂν νομίζοιντο δικαίως, ἀλλ' ἐν ἅπασι τούτοις τὴν τῶν μετα|χειριζομένων αἰτιατέον πλημμελῆ καὶ ἀνόητον ἕξιν, δι' ἣν καὶ τοῖς τοῦ ἀγαθοῦ στοχαζομένοις ἐπὶ τὸ χεῖρον χρώμενοι τοῦ προσήκοντος αὐτοῖς τέλους ἀποτυγχάνουσιν.

Εἰ δέ τις τὴν προφαινομένην αἰτιᾶται τῆς μυθοποιίας αἰσχρότητα καὶ τὸ τῶν ὀνομάτων φορτικὸν καὶ διὰ ταῦτα τῆς πρεπού|σης αὐτὸν ἀποστερεῖ τῶν θείων μιμήσεως (ἅπας γὰρ δήπου μιμητὴς διὰ τῶν φύσει προσηκόντων τοῖς παραδείγμασιν ἀπεικονίζεται τὴν ἐκείνων ἰδέαν, ἀλλ' οὐ διὰ τῶν ἐναντιωτάτων καὶ πόρρω τῆς τῶν ἀρχετύπων οὐσίας καὶ δυνάμεως βεβλημένων), πρῶτον μὲν διαιρετέον οἶμαι τὰς τῶν | μύθων προαιρέσεις καὶ χωρὶς ἀφοριστέον τούς τε παιδευτικοὺς λεγομένους καὶ

these things make bad use of them. Neither would I call this pious, nor is it right to consider just the slander of the myths that stems from the madness of the many. The goodness or badness of things is not to be judged on the basis of those who make perverted use of them; rather, it is appropriate to judge each according to its own nature and its inherent rightness.

Consider that the Athenian Stranger [*Laws* 1.646–651] thinks that not even drunkenness should be banned || from of the well-organized city on account of the aimless and ill-defined conduct of the masses under its influence but says that, used in the opposite way, correctly and sanely, even this can make a considerable contribution to education. And yet one could say that drunkenness destroys the bodies and souls of those who practice it, but still the lawgiver will not take away from it the positive value that is properly its own and its contribution to virtue. Thus neither is drunkenness to be rejected on account of the many who pursue it ignorantly and inelegantly, nor do the initiations and the potential of the mysteries deserve to be condemned by those with their wits about them because of the depravity of those who receive them, nor could the myths justly be considered harmful to those who hear them because of the perversity of those who make casual and irrational use of them. Rather, what is to be blamed in all of these instances is the mistaken and wrong-headed and stupid disposition of the agents, through which they miss the goal that is proper to these things by using for the worse even what aims at the good.

[c. Ugliness and obscenity in Homer's myths]

If the apparent obscenity[91] of the myths and the coarseness of the language are the target of criticism, and if it is claimed that on this account Homer does not appropriately imitate the divine—since every imitator, I suppose, copies the forms of his models using things that have a natural affinity with them and not through things that are randomly thrown out that are utterly contrary to the substance and sense of the archetypes and unrelated to them[92]—then first, I think, a distinction is to be made between modes (προαιρέσεις) of myth and a clear division made between

---

91. αἰσχρός and related vocabulary are here and elsewhere used to designate a variety of forms of ugliness and deformity, but Proclus here singles out the obscene stories in Homer.

92. F. notes the difficulty of translating τῶν ... βεβλημένων here. He offers in support and illustration of his understanding of the phrase (which is also mine) an

τοὺς ἐνθεαστικωτέρους καὶ πρὸς τὸ πᾶν ἀποβλέποντας μᾶλλον ἢ τὴν τῶν ἀκουόντων ἕξιν· ἔπειτα διακριτέον τὰς τῶν χρωμένων αὐτοῖς ζωάς, καὶ τὰς μὲν νεαροπρεπεῖς καὶ ἐν ἤθεσιν ἁπαλοῖς τρεφομένας θετέον, ǁ τὰς δὲ ἀνεγείρεσθαι πρὸς νοῦν δυναμένας καὶ πρὸς τὰ ὅλα γένη τῶν θεῶν καὶ τὰς διὰ πάντων προόδους τῶν ὄντων καὶ τὰς σειρὰς καὶ τὰς ἀποτελευτήσεις τὰς ἄχρι τῶν ἐσχάτων ἀνατείνεσθαι σπευδούσας. καὶ τοῦτον δὴ τὸν τρόπον | τάς τε τῶν μύθων ἰδέας διαστήσαντες ἀπ' ἀλλήλων καὶ τὰς τῶν ὑποδεχομένων αὐτοὺς ἐπιτηδειότητας, τὸ μὲν μήτε πρὸς παιδείαν συντελεῖν τοὺς μύθους τούτους, οὓς Ὅμηρός τε καὶ Ἡσίοδος ἐγραψάτην, μήτε τοῖς νέοις προσήκειν αὐτῶν τὴν ἀκρόασιν συγχωρῶμεν τοῖς λέγουσιν· ὅτι δὲ τῇ φύσει | τῶν ὅλων ἕπονται καὶ τῇ τάξει τῶν ὄντων καὶ τοὺς ἀνάγεσθαι δυναμένους εἰς τὴν τῶν θείων πραγμάτων περιωπὴν αὐτοῖς συνάπτουσιν τοῖς ὄντως οὖσιν, τοῦτο προστιθῶμεν.

Κατιδόντες γὰρ οἱ τῆς μυθοποιΐας πατέρες, ὅτι καὶ ἡ φύσις εἰκόνας δημιουργοῦσα τῶν ἀΰλων καὶ νοητῶν εἰδῶν καὶ | τόνδε τὸν κόσμον ποικίλλουσα τοῖς τούτων μιμήμασιν τὰ μὲν ἀμέριστα μεριστῶς ἀπεικονίζεται, τὰ δὲ αἰώνια διὰ τῶν κατὰ χρόνον προϊόντων, τὰ δὲ νοητὰ διὰ τῶν αἰσθητῶν, ἐνύλως τε τὸ ἄϋλον ἀποτυποῦται καὶ διαστατῶς τὸ ἀδιάστατον καὶ διὰ μεταβολῆς τὸ μονίμως ἱδρυμένον, ἑπομένως | τῇ τε φύσει καὶ τῇ προόδῳ τῶν φαινομένως ὄντων καὶ εἰδωλικῶς, εἰκόνας καὶ αὐτοὶ πλάττοντες ἐν λόγοις φερομένας τῶν θείων τοῖς ἐναντιωτάτοις καὶ πλεῖστον ἀφεστηκόσιν τὴν ὑπερέχουσαν τῶν παραδειγμάτων ἀπομιμοῦνται δύναμιν, καὶ τοῖς μὲν παρὰ φύσιν τὸ ὑπὲρ φύσιν αὐτῶν | ἐνδείκνυνται, τοῖς δὲ παραλόγοις τὸ παντὸς λόγου θειότερον, τοῖς δὲ

so-called "educational myths" and the more inspired ones that are more concerned with the universe than with the state or condition of the audience.[93] Next, a distinction is to be made among the lives of those who use the myths. Some of these lives are to be characterized as youthful, and nursed in gentle and childlike manners, || while others have the capacity of being awakened to intellect and to all the ranks of the gods and the processions of beings through the universe and the chains with their ends stretching out to reach the lowest of beings. Having made these distinctions between the basic types of myths along with the capacities of their audiences, let us agree with those who assert that, first of all, these myths of Homer and Hesiod do not contribute to education and, second, they are not fit to be heard by children.[94] But let us add that they are in line with the nature of the universe and the hierarchy of beings and that they put those with the capacity to be led up to the contemplation of the divine in touch with those things that truly exist.

The fathers of myth observed that nature creates images of nonmaterial and noetic forms and embellishes this cosmos with imitations of them, depicting the indivisible in a fragmented manner, the eternal by means of things that proceed through time, the noetic through that which the senses can grasp, and portraying the nonmaterial materially, the nonspatial spatially, and that which is permanently fixed through change. When they saw this, in line with nature and with the procession of those things that have only apparent and image-like existence, they themselves fabricated images of the divine in the medium of language, expressing the transcendent potentiality of the models by those things most opposite to them and furthest removed from them: that which is beyond nature they represent by things contrary to nature; that which is more divine than all reason, by

---

aphorism attributed by Stobaeus (3:684,8–9 [Wachsmuth and Hense]), to Pythagoras: "Rather cast a stone at random than an idle word."

93. This distinction is of crucial importance to Proclus and to other Platonic commentators because the myths of Plato occupy a problematic position for them, clearly "educational" in their concern for their audience and still partaking in the inspired vision that was Plato's.

94. This is perhaps the most unexpected paradox in Proclus's position on Homer. He concedes to the Socrates of the *Republic* what is perhaps the most radical (and itself paradoxical) element in his ironic cultural revolution: the myths of Homer are to be banished from their central role in education. This does, for Proclus, have the convenient consequence of saving them from the classroom hermeneutics of the Christian majority among his fellow citizens.

φανταζομένοις ὡς αἰσχροῖς τὸ παντὸς μεριστοῦ κάλλους ὑπερηπλωμένον· καὶ οὕτω δὴ κατὰ λόγον τὸν εἰκότα τῆς ἐκείνων ἡμᾶς ἀναμιμνήσκουσιν ἐξῃρημένης ὑπεροχῆς.

Πρὸς δὲ αὖ τούτοις καθ' ἑκάστην τάξιν θεῶν ἄνωθεν ἄχρι || τῶν τελευταίων ὑφιζάνουσαν καὶ διὰ πάντων ἐπεξιοῦσαν τῶν ἐν τοῖς οὖσιν γενῶν ἔξεστιν θεᾶσθαι τῶν σειρῶν ἀποτελευτήσεις τοιαύτας ἰδιότητας προστησαμένας, ὁποίας οἱ μῦθοι τοῖς θεοῖς αὐτοῖς ἀπονέμουσιν, καὶ τοιούτων πραγμάτων | ὑποστατικὰς καὶ συνεκτικάς, δι' οἵων ἐκεῖνοι τὴν περὶ τῶν πρωτίστων ἀπόρρητον θεωρίαν κατέκρυψαν. τὰ γὰρ ἔσχατα τῶν δαιμονίων γενῶν καὶ περὶ τὴν ὕλην στρεφόμενα τῆς τε τῶν κατὰ φύσιν δυνάμεων παρατροπῆς καὶ τῆς αἰσχρότητος τῶν ἐνύλων καὶ τῆς εἰς τὴν κακίαν παραφορᾶς καὶ | τῆς ἀτάκτου καὶ πλημμελοῦς προέστηκεν κινήσεως. δεῖ γὰρ εἶναι καὶ ταῦτα ἐν τῷ παντὶ καὶ συμπληροῦν τὴν ποικιλίαν τῆς ὅλης διακοσμήσεως, καὶ τῆς παρυποστάσεως αὐτῶν καὶ τῆς στάσεως καὶ τῆς διαμονῆς ἐν τοῖς ἀϊδίοις γένεσιν περιέχεσθαι τὴν αἰτίαν. ἃ δὴ καὶ οἱ τῶν ἱερῶν θεσμῶν | ἡγεμόνες κατανοήσαντες περιόδοις ὡρισμέναις ἔταξαν γέλωτά τε καὶ θρήνους ἐπιτελεῖσθαι, τοῖς τοιούτοις γένεσιν ἀφοσιούμενοι καὶ τῆς ὅλης περὶ τὸ θεῖον ἁγιστείας τὴν προσήκουσαν μοῖραν ἀποκληρώσαντες.

Ὥσπερ οὖν ἡ τῶν ἱερῶν τέχνη κατανείμασα δεόντως τὴν σύμπασαν θρησκείαν τοῖς θεοῖς καὶ τοῖς | τῶν θεῶν ὀπαδοῖς, ἵνα μηδὲν ἄμοιρον τῆς ἐπιβαλλούσης θεραπείας ἀπολείπηται τῶν ἀϊδίως ἑπομένων τοῖς θεοῖς, τοὺς μὲν ταῖς ἁγιωτάταις τελεταῖς καὶ τοῖς μυστικοῖς συμβόλοις προσάγεται, τῶν δὲ τοῖς φαινομένοις παθήμασιν προκαλεῖται τὰς δόσεις διὰ δή τινος ἀρρήτου συμπαθείας, | οὕτως ἄρα καὶ οἱ τῶν τοιῶνδε μύθων πατέρες εἰς πᾶσαν ὡς εἰπεῖν ἀποβλέψαντες τὴν τῶν θείων πρόοδον καὶ τοὺς μύθους εἰς ὅλην ἀνάγειν σπεύδοντες τὴν ἀφ' ἑκάστου προϊοῦσαν σειρὰν τὸ μὲν προβεβλημένον αὐτῶν καὶ εἰδωλικὸν ἀνάλογον ὑπεστήσαντο τοῖς ἐσχάτοις γένεσιν καὶ τῶν τελευ|ταίων καὶ ἐνύλων προεστηκόσι παθῶν, τὸ δὲ ἀποκεκρυμμένον καὶ ἄγνωστον τοῖς πολλοῖς τῆς ἐν ἀβάτοις ἐξῃρημένης || τῶν θεῶν οὐσίας ἐκφαντικὸν τοῖς φιλοθεάμοσιν τῶν ὄντων παρέδοσαν.

the irrational; that which transcends in simplicity all fragmented beauty, by things that are considered ugly and obscene. They do this, in all probability, to remind us of the transcendent supereminence of that which they treat.

Moreover, it is possible to observe the ends of the chains that descend from the || highest ranks of the gods to the lowest and pass through all the classes that exist, setting [as a screen] before themselves just such identities as the myths attribute to the gods themselves and producing and sustaining just the sort of things they [the myths] use to hide the secret doctrine concerning the primal beings. The lowest of the daemonic[95] ranks, the ones turned toward matter, are set over the perversions of the natural capacities, over ugliness and obscenity in the material world, over distraction into evil, and disorderly and erratic movement. These things, too, must exist in the universe and fill out the diversity of the universal order, and the cause of their epiphenomenal existence,[96] their substance and their continuity must be contained within the ranks of the eternal. In their knowledge of these things, the founders of sacred rites ordained that laughter and lamentation occupy set periods, paying our debt to these classes and allocating to them their due portion of the total worship of the divine.

And so, just as the hieratic art, necessarily distributing cult practices among the gods and their attendants, so that none of those in the eternal following of the gods may be left without an appropriate share of cult, approaches the gods themselves with the holiest initiations and mystical symbols while it invites the gifts of the other class with shows of passion, through some ineffable affinity, in just the same way, the fathers of this sort of myth, taking into consideration, so to speak, the entire procession of divine beings, and desirous of drawing the myths up to the entire chain stemming from each, established that part of them that is projected in front and iconic to correspond to the lowest classes of the divine, those who preside over the lowest, embodied passions, while they passed on that which revealed the transcendent || being of the gods in their sanctuaries, hidden and unknown to the many, to those who are given to contemplation of that which truly exists.

---

95. Broadly speaking, the classes or ranks above the human are the divine and the lower, mediating daemonic, but the daemonic may also be contrasted with the angelic (above) and the heroic (below). Cf. 91 (K86,5–10).

96. παρυπόστασις: F.: *existence épiphénoménale* (as so often, finding the *mot juste*).

καὶ οὕτω δὴ τῶν μύθων ἕκαστος δαιμόνιος μέν ἐστιν κατὰ τὸ φαινόμενον, θεῖος δὲ κατὰ τὴν ἀπόρρητον θεωρίαν. |

Εἰ δὴ ταῦτα ὀρθῶς εἴπομεν, οὔτε τοὺς Ὁμηρικοὺς μύθους διὰ ταῦτα τῆς πρὸς τὰ πράγματα τὰ ὄντως ὄντα οἰκειότητος παραιρεῖσθαι προσήκει, διότι μὴ πρὸς παιδείαν ἡμῖν συντελοῦσιν τῶν νέων (οὐ γὰρ παιδευτικὸν τῶν τοιούτων ἐστὶ μύθων τὸ τέλος, οὐδὲ εἰς τοῦτο βλέποντες αὐ|τοὺς οἱ μυθοπλάσται παρέδοσαν), οὔτε τοὺς παρὰ τῷ Πλάτωνι γεγραμμένους εἰς τὴν αὐτὴν ἰδέαν ἀναπέμπειν τοῖς ἐνθεαστικωτέροις, ἀλλὰ χωρὶς ἑκατέρους ἀφορίζειν· καὶ τοὺς μὲν φιλοσοφωτέρους τίθεσθαι, τοὺς δὲ τοῖς ἱερατικοῖς θεσμοῖς προσήκοντας, καὶ τοὺς μὲν νέοις ἀκούειν πρέποντας, | τοὺς δὲ τοῖς διὰ πάσης ὡς εἰπεῖν τῆς ἄλλης παιδείας ὀρθῶς ἠγμένοις καὶ εἰς τὴν τῶν τοιῶνδε μύθων ἀκρόασιν ὥσπερ ὄργανόν τι μυστικὸν ἱδρῦσαι τὸν τῆς ψυχῆς νοῦν ἐφιεμένοις.

Ἀλλ' ὁ μὲν Σωκράτης καὶ ταῦτα ἱκανῶς ἐνδείκνυται τοῖς συνορᾶν δυναμένοις, καὶ ὅτι τῆς Ὁμήρου | μυθοποιΐας ὡς μήτε παιδευτικῆς μήτε τοῖς τῶν νέων ἀπλάστοις καὶ ἀβάτοις ἤθεσιν συναρμοζομένης ἐπιλαμβάνεται, καὶ ὡς τὸ ἀπόρρητον αὐτῆς καὶ κρύφιον ἀγαθὸν μυστικῆς τινος δεῖται καὶ ἐνθεαστικῆς νοήσεως. οἱ δὲ πολλοὶ τῶν Σωκρατικῶν λόγων οὐκ ἐπηισθημένοι πόρρω ποι τῆς τοῦ | φιλοσόφου διανοίας ἀποπεπτωκότες διαβάλλουσιν ἅπαν τὸ τοιοῦτον τῶν μύθων εἶδος.

Τί δὴ οὖν φησιν ὁ Σωκράτης περὶ αὐτῶν, ἄξιον ἀκούειν, καὶ δι' ἣν αἰτίαν ἀποσκευάζεται τὴν τοιάνδε μυθολογίαν. **ὁ γὰρ νέος οὐχ οἷός τε κρίνειν ὅτι τε ὑπόνοια καὶ ὃ | μή, ἀλλ' ὅσ' ἂν τηλικοῦτος ὢν λάβῃ ἐν ταῖς δόξαις, || δυσέκνιπτά τε καὶ ἀμετάστατα φιλεῖ γίνεσθαι, ὧν δὴ ἴσως ἕνεκα περὶ παντὸς ποιητέον ἃ πρῶτα ἀκούουσιν, ὅτι κάλλιστα μεμυθολογημένα πρὸς ἀρετὴν ἀκούειν.** [2.378d] εἰκότως ἄρα τοὺς Ὁμηρικοὺς | μύθους οὐκ εὖ μεμιμῆσθαι λέγομεν τὸ θεῖον· οὐ γὰρ πρὸς ἀρετὴν καὶ παιδείαν οὐδὲ τὴν ὀρθὴν τῶν νέων ἀγωγὴν συντελοῦσιν τοῖς νομοθέταις, ἀλλὰ ταύτῃ μὲν οὐδὲν ἐοικότες φαίνονται τοῖς οὖσιν, οὐδ' ἂν

Thus, each myth is appropriate to the daemons on its literal level (κατὰ τὸ φαινόμενον), while it is appropriate to the gods according to the secret doctrine.

If we are correct in what we have said, then neither is it right to deny the appropriateness of the Homeric myths to those things that truly exist, on the basis that they do not contribute to the education of the young—since the goal of such myths is not educational, and the mythoplasts did not pass them down to us with this end in view—nor is it right to place the myths of Plato in the same class with the more inspired ones. Rather, we must distinguish between the two, classifying [Plato's] myths as more philosophical and the other sort [Homer's] as more fitting to hieratic custom, the former as appropriate for the young to hear but Homer's appropriate for those who have been correctly guided through, so to speak, the whole of the required education and who wish to firmly establish the intellective part of their soul in the hearing of such myths, using this as a mystical tool.

[d. Socrates distinguished the two types of myth]

For those able to understand, Socrates indicates all of this perfectly clearly, both in that he attacks Homer's mythmaking as noneducational and inappropriate for the unformed and innocent minds of the young and because [, in his account, gaining access to] its secret and hidden good requires some sort of mystical and inspired perception. The many, on the other hand, failing to apprehend Socrates' words and falling far from the philosopher's meaning, denounce this entire class of myths.

One should listen to what Socrates himself says about these myths, along with his reasons for rejecting this sort of mythology:

> The young person is unable to distinguish between what is "second meaning" and what is not, yet whatever opinions he receives at that age ‖ tend to become ineradicable and unchangeable. For these reasons we should certainly make it our highest priority to ensure that those things they hear first will be composed as beautifully as possible to inspire virtue. [*Rep.* 2.378d–e]

Quite reasonably, then, we say that the myths of Homer do not give a good imitation of the divine, for they do not incline to virtue and education and they are not useful to the lawmakers for the correct upbringing of

πρέποιεν τοῖς τῆς πολιτικῆς ἐπιστήμης προϊσταμένοις, τρόπον δὲ ἄλλον συναρμόζονται | τοῖς θεοῖς καὶ ἀνάγουσιν εἰς τὴν ἐκείνων θεωρίαν τοὺς εὖ πεφυκότας· καὶ τὸ ἀγαθὸν αὐτῶν ἐστιν οὐ παιδευτικὸν ἀλλὰ μυστικόν, οὐδὲ νεαροπρεποῦς ἕξεως ἀλλὰ πρεσβυτικῆς στοχαζόμενον. δηλοῖ δέ που καὶ τοῦτο ὁ Σωκράτης λέγων, ὅτι **δι' ἀπορρήτων ἀκούειν ὡς ὀλιγίστους πρέπει τῶν | τοιούτων μύθων, θυσαμένους οὐ χοῖρον ἀλλά τι μέγα καὶ ἄπορον θῦμα.** [2.378a]

Πολλοῦ ἄρα δεῖ κατὰ τὴν πολλῶν δόξαν ἀτιμάζειν τὸν τρόπον τοῦτον τῆς μυθοποιΐας, <ὅτε> ταῖς τε ἁγιωτάταις τῶν τελετῶν καὶ τοῖς τελειοτάτοις τῶν μυστηρίων σύστοιχον αὐτῆς ἀποφαίνεται τὴν ἀκρόασιν | ὑπάρχειν. τὸ γὰρ μετὰ θυσιῶν καὶ τούτων τῶν μεγίστων καὶ τελεωτάτων ἐν ἀπορρήτῳ χρῆναι τοὺς τοιούτους μύθους ἐκφαίνεσθαι μυσταγωγίαν καὶ τελετὴν ἀναγωγὸν τῶν ἀκουόντων εἶναι δηλοῖ τὴν ἐν αὐτοῖς θεωρίαν.

Ὅστις οὖν ἡμῶν τὸ παιδαριῶδες τῆς ψυχῆς καὶ νεαροπρεπὲς ἀπεσκευάσατο | καὶ τὰς τῆς φαντασίας ἀορίστους ὁρμὰς κατεστήσατο καὶ νοῦν ἡγεμόνα προὐστήσατο τῆς ἑαυτοῦ ζωῆς, οὗτος ἐγκαιρότατα ἂν μετέχοι τῶν ἐν τοῖς τοιοῖσδε μύθοις ἀποκεκρυμμένων θεαμάτων, παιδείας δὲ αὖ ἔτι καὶ τῆς τῶν ἠθῶν συμμετρίας προσδεόμενος οὐκ ἂν ἀσφαλῶς ἅπτοιτο τῆς τού|των θεωρίας. οὐ γὰρ δεῖ τι τοῖς τῶν θεῶν μυστικοῖς νοή||μασιν κάτωθεν ἀπὸ τῆς ὕλης προσφέρειν, οὐδὲ κατατεινόμενον ὑπὸ τῶν φανταστικῶν κινήσεων ἐπιπηδᾶν ταῖς τῷ νῷ καταφανέσιν ἐπιβολαῖς, οὐδὲ συγχεῖν ἀλλήλοις τά τε τῆς ἀλογίας παθήματα καὶ τὰ τῆς θεωρητικῆς ἐνεργείας ἐξαίρετα | ἀγαθά, ἀλλὰ τῷ τε Σωκράτει πειθομένους καὶ τῇ τάξει τῆς ἐπὶ τὸ θεῖον ἀναγωγῆς χωρὶς μὲν τῆς ὀρθῆς ἅπτεσθαι τῶν ἠθῶν παιδείας, χωρὶς δὲ τῆς νοερᾶς τῶν ὄντων περιωπῆς ἀντιλαμβάνεσθαι, καὶ ζῆν ἑκατέρᾳ πρεπόντως, ἀρχομένους μὲν ἀπὸ τῆς καταδεεστέρας καὶ πολιτικωτέρας ἀγωγῆς, τελευ|τῶντας δὲ εἰς αὐτὴν τὴν πρὸς τὸ θεῖον μυστικὴν ἕνωσιν.

Ταῦτα μὲν οὖν ἄλλος ἂν εἴη τρόπος λόγων· ὅτι δὲ καὶ τῷ Σωκράτει δέδοκται καὶ τὸ τῶν μύθων εἶδος εἶναι διττόν, ἐκ τῶν εἰρημένων

the young,[97] and in this they appear to bear no resemblance to those things that truly exist and they would be of no use to those concerned with political theory. Nevertheless, in another manner they are in harmony with the gods and raise up to contemplation of the gods those who are naturally suited to it. Their specific virtue is not educational but mystical, and they are aimed not at youth but at maturity. Socrates makes this clear as well, when he says:

> The hearing of such myths should be restricted to a few, in secret, after sacrificing not a pig but some large and rare victim. [*Rep.* 2.378a]

Therefore, this sort of mythmaking is not to be scorned, as many would have us believe, when [Socrates] puts hearing it in the same category with the holiest of initiations and the most perfect of mysteries. The fact that such myths are used in secret and after the greatest and most perfect of sacrifices demonstrates that the doctrine contained in them reveals a holy mystery and constitutes an anagogic initiation for the listener.

Whoever, then, among us has cleared his soul of the puerile and the juvenile and has established order in the uncontrolled impulses of his imagination and made intellect the ordering principle of his life, this is the one who would be at the best point in his life to enjoy the spectacles hidden in such myths, but their contemplation would not be approached without danger by one still lacking in education and symmetry of character. For we must bring nothing from the material world below to the mystical apprehension || of the gods, nor, while still tortured by the impulses of the imagination, must we leap to the concepts perceived [only] by the intellect, nor mix together those things suffered through the influence of the irrational with the transcendent benefits acquired by contemplative activity, but rather, putting our trust in Socrates and in the order of the ascent to the divine, we must separately acquire correct ethical education and grasp the intellective contemplation of true being, and we must live in a manner fitting to each, beginning with the more limited education into the political virtues and finally reaching the mystical union with the divine.

That, however, belongs to another discussion. It has been observed above that it was Socrates' position as well that there are two classes of

---

97. Following F. and supplying a verb (e.g., τείνουσιν) for the first phrase.

ὑπέμνησται, λέγω δὲ ὡς τὸ μέν ἐστι παιδευτικόν, τὸ δὲ τελεστικόν, καὶ τὸ μὲν πρὸς τὴν ἠθικὴν | ἀρετὴν παρασκευάζον, τὸ δὲ τὴν πρὸς τὸ θεῖον συναφὴν παρεχόμενον, καὶ τὸ μὲν τοὺς πολλοὺς ἡμῶν ὠφελεῖν δυνάμενον, τὸ δὲ ἐλαχίστοις συναρμοζόμενον, καὶ τὸ μὲν κοινὸν καὶ γνώριμον τοῖς ἀνθρώποις, τὸ δὲ ἀπόρρητον καὶ ἀσύμμετρον τοῖς μὴ τελέως ἐνιδρῦσθαι τῷ θείῳ σπουδάζουσιν, | καὶ τὸ μὲν ταῖς τῶν νέων ἕξεσιν σύστοιχον, τὸ δὲ μετὰ θυσιῶν καὶ μυστικῆς παραδόσεως μόλις ἐκφαινόμενον.

εἰ τοίνυν ταῦτα καὶ ὁ Σωκράτης ἡμᾶς ἀναδιδάσκει, πῶς οὐχὶ συμφωνεῖν μὲν αὐτὸν πρὸς τὸν Ὅμηρον φήσομεν περὶ ὧν μυθικῶς διεξέρχεται, τοσοῦτον δὲ ἄρα τῆς παρ' αὐτῷ μυθο|ποιΐας ἀποσκευάζεσθαι καὶ διελέγχειν, ὅσον πρὸς τὴν παροῦσαν τῶν λόγων ὑπόθεσιν καὶ τὴν τῆς παιδείας τῶν νέων ὑφήγησιν ἀνάρμοστον αὐτῆς καταφαίνεται;

Ἀλλὰ ταῦτα μὲν μικρὸν ὕστερον· εἰ δὲ δεῖ τῶν μυθικῶν πλασμάτων ἄλλως | μὲν τοὺς νομοθέτας ἐφάπτεσθαι καὶ τὰς ἀτελεστέρας ἕξεις θεραπεύειν ἐπιχειροῦντας, ἄλλως δὲ τοὺς ἐνθεαστικαῖς ἐπι||βολαῖς τὴν ἄρρητον τῶν θεῶν οὐσίαν τοῖς ἕπεσθαι πρὸς τὸ ἄναντες τῆς θεωρίας δυναμένοις ἐνδεικνυμένους, οὔτε τὰς Ἡφαίστου ῥίψεις ἀπορήσομεν ἀνάγειν εἰς τὴν περὶ θεῶν ἀνέλεγκτον ἐπιστήμην οὔτε τοὺς Κρονίους δεσμοὺς οὔτε τὰς | Οὐρανοῦ τομάς, ἃ δὴ ταῖς τῶν νέων ἀκοαῖς ἀσύμμετρά φησιν ὁ Σωκράτης ὑπάρχειν καὶ οὐδαμῶς συναρμόζεσθαι ταῖς ἕξεσιν τῶν παιδείας μόνης δεομένων· ὅλως γὰρ ἐν ἀλλοτρίαις ὑποδοχαῖς ἡ μυστικὴ

myths, the one educational and the other initiatory. The one prepares for moral virtue; the other offers contact with the divine. The one is able to be of some advantage to most of us, but the other is suited to a very small number. The first is shared in common and generally intelligible to humanity, but the other is secret and unsuited to those who are not eager to be perfectly rooted in the divine. The one corresponds to the condition of youth; the other is only revealed through sacrifice and through the mystical tradition.

Now, if Socrates as well teaches us these things, how can we refuse to say that he is in harmony with Homer concerning what Homer describes mythically, and then that all he rejects and finds fault with in Homer's mythmaking is that part of it that is clearly out of harmony with the present discussion[98] and with the direction of the education of the young?

[e. The allegorical interpretation of obscene myths]

We shall return to this a little later. But if lawmakers and those who undertake to look after those further from perfection[99] must approach myth in one way, and in a different way those || who, using inspired concepts, are revealing the hidden existence of the gods to those capable of following on the uphill path of contemplation, we shall not find it impossible to incorporate the casting out of Hephaestus, the binding of Kronos, or the castration of Ouranos into the irrefutable body of wisdom about the gods—all three of them certainly stories that Socrates says are incompatible with a youthful audience and utterly inappropriate to the state of mind of those whose only need is education. The mystical apprehension of the divine would not, after all, come about in entirely alien receptacles,[100]

---

98. I.e., with the discussion of education in the second and third books of the *Republic*.

99. I.e., educators.

100. ὑποδοχαί: in the *Timaeus*, the receptacle is that philosophically dubious matter without quality that receives qualities from the forms. This is an endlessly fascinating relationship for the later Platonists and is described as operative on multiple levels. We ourselves (with our discursive minds) are thought of as the proper receptacles for myths (see 97 [K89,10–24]; 139 [K111,13–19]; 139 [K112,11–12]), where distortions of reality can be understood in terms of our (limited) capacities. Here as well the receptacles in question seem to be the more elementary students, still in need of education and hence not (yet) fit receptacles for the wisdom contained in inspired myth.

τῶν θείων γνῶσις οὐκ ἄν ποτε ἐγγένοιτο. τούτοις δὴ οὖν τοῖς τῶν τοιῶνδε θεαμάτων | ἐπηβόλοις λέγοντες, ὡς ἄρα ἡ μὲν Ἡφαίστου ῥῖψις τὴν ἄνωθεν ἄχρι τῶν τελευταίων ἐν τοῖς αἰσθητοῖς δημιουργημάτων τοῦ θείου πρόοδον ἐνδείκνυται, κινουμένην καὶ τελειουμένην καὶ ποδηγετουμένην ὑπὸ τοῦ πάντων δημιουργοῦ καὶ πατρός, οἱ δὲ Κρόνιοι δεσμοὶ τὴν ἕνωσιν τῆς | ὅλης δημιουργίας πρὸς τὴν νοερὰν τοῦ Κρόνου καὶ πατρικὴν ὑπεροχὴν δηλοῦσιν, αἱ δὲ τοῦ Οὐρανοῦ τομαὶ τὴν διάκρισιν τῆς Τιτανικῆς σειρᾶς ἀπὸ τῆς συνεκτικῆς διακοσμήσεως αἰνίσσονται, τάχα ἂν γνώριμα λέγοιμεν καὶ τὸ τῶν μύθων τραγικὸν καὶ πλασματῶδες εἰς τὴν νοερὰν τῶν θείων | γενῶν ἀναπέμποιμεν θεωρίαν.

Πάντα γὰρ τὰ παρ' ἡμῖν κατὰ τὸ χεῖρον ἐμφανταζόμενα καὶ τῆς καταδεεστέρας ὄντα συστοιχίας ἐπ' ἐκείνων οἱ μῦθοι κατ' αὐτὴν τὴν κρείττονα φύσιν καὶ δύναμιν παραλαμβάνουσιν. οἷον ὁ δεσμὸς παρ' ἡμῖν μὲν κώλυσίς ἐστι καὶ ἐπίσχεσις τῆς ἐνεργείας, ἐκεῖ δὲ | συναφὴ πρὸς τὰ αἴτια καὶ ἕνωσις ἄρρητος. καὶ ἡ ῥῖψις ἐνταῦθα μὲν κίνησίς ἐστι βίαιος ὑπ' ἄλλου, παρὰ δὲ τοῖς θεοῖς τὴν γόνιμον ἐνδείκνυται πρόοδον καὶ τὴν ἄφετον ἐπὶ πάντα παρουσίαν καὶ εὔλυτον, οὐκ ἀφισταμένην τῆς οἰκείας ἀρχῆς, ἀλλ' ἀπ' ἐκείνης διὰ πάντων ἐν τάξει προϊοῦσαν. | καὶ αἱ τομαὶ τοῖς μὲν μεριστοῖς πράγμασιν καὶ ἐνύλοις ‖ ἐλάττωσιν ἐμποιοῦσιν τῆς δυνάμεως, ἐν δὲ ταῖς πρωτουργοῖς αἰτίαις πρόοδον τῶν δευτέρων εἰς ὑφειμένην τάξιν ἀπὸ τῶν σφετέρων αἰτίων αἰνίσσονται, τῶν πρώτων ἀνελαττώτων ἐν ἑαυτοῖς ἱδρυμένων, καὶ μήτε κινουμένων ἀφ' ἑαυτῶν διὰ | τὴν τούτων πρόοδον μήτε ἐλασσουμένων διὰ τὸν τούτων χωρισμὸν μήτε διαιρουμένων διὰ τὴν ἐν τοῖς καταδεεστέροις διάκρισιν.

Ἀλλὰ ταῦτα καὶ ὁ Σωκράτης φησὶν νέοις μὲν ἀνεπιτήδεια ἀκούειν, τοῖς δὲ ἐν ἀπορρήτῳ τὴν περὶ θεῶν ἀλήθειαν συναιρεῖν ἀπὸ τῶν μυθικῶν συμβόλων δυναμένοις | ζητεῖν τε καὶ θεάσασθαι προσήκει· καὶ οὐ διὰ τοῦτο παντελῶς ἐκβλητέα, διότι πρὸς τὰς τῶν νέων ἕξεις ἐστὶν ἀνάρμοστα. πέπονθεν γὰρ τοῦτο καὶ ταῦτα τὰ μυθικὰ πλάσματα, ὅπερ ὁ Πλάτων πού

and so, when we tell those who have experienced such spectacles that the fall of Hephaestus displays the procession of the divine from above to the lowest of the creations in the realm perceived by the senses, begun, brought to completion, and guided along the way by the creator and father of the universe—and that the bonds of Kronos show the union of the whole of creation with the intellective and paternal transcendence of Kronos—and that the castration of Ouranos points to[101] the separation of the Titanic chain from the essential ordering of the universe—in saying all this, we may well be telling a familiar story, referring the theatrical and the fictional [in the myths] to the intellective contemplation of the gods.[102]

Everything that is imagined as pejorative here, and falling into the inferior category, the myths take in its specifically better sense and meaning, when reference is made to the gods. For example, "bondage" among us is hindrance and checking of activity; there, it is contact and ineffable union with the causes. "Casting out" here is violent movement caused by another, but among the gods it indicates generative procession and free and unrestrained attendance on all things, not separated from its own first principle but proceeding from this in an orderly manner through all things. "Castration" in the context of fragmented and material things entails a diminishing of || power, but in the context of the primal causes it points to the procession of secondaries from their own causes to a lower realm, while the primaries remain undiminished in themselves and neither are displaced on account of the procession of these things, nor diminished by their separation from the secondaries, nor divided on account of the division in the lower realms.

All of this Socrates as well says is unfit for the young to hear, but it is the business of those able to grasp in secret, from the mythical symbols, the truth about the gods to seek it out and to contemplate it. It is not to be utterly cast out simply because it is inappropriate to the state of mind of the young. In fact, what happens to these mythic fictions is what Plato

---

101. αἰνίττομαι (hint at, imply, point to) is the verb most frequently chosen to designate the process by which texts designate things other than their most apparent meanings.

102. That is, the "secret doctrine" viewed here as an active process of apprehension through reading.

φησι τὰ θεῖα καὶ παναγέστατα τῶν δογμάτων πεπονθέναι. καὶ γὰρ ταῦτα τοῖς μὲν πολλοῖς | ἐστι καταγέλαστα, τοῖς δὲ εἰς νοῦν ἀνεγειρομένοις ὀλίγοις δή τισιν ἐκφαίνει τὴν ἑαυτῶν πρὸς τὰ πράγματα συμπάθειαν, καὶ τὴν ἐξ αὐτῶν τῶν ἱερατικῶν ἔργων παρέχεται πίστιν τῆς πρὸς τὰ θεῖα συμφυοῦς δυνάμεως· καὶ γὰρ οἱ θεοὶ τῶν τοιῶνδε συμβόλων ἀκούοντες χαίρουσιν καὶ τοῖς κα|λοῦσιν ἑτοίμως πείθονται καὶ τὴν ἑαυτῶν ἰδιότητα προφαίνουσιν διὰ τούτων ὡς οἰκείων αὐτοῖς καὶ μάλιστα γνωρίμων συνθημάτων· καὶ τὰ μυστήρια καὶ αἱ τελεταὶ καὶ τὸ δραστήριον ἐν τούτοις ἔχουσιν καὶ ὁλόκληρα καὶ ἀτρεμῆ καὶ ἁπλᾶ θεάματα διὰ τούτων προξενοῦσιν τοῖς μύσταις καθο|ρᾶν, ὧν ὁ νέος τὴν ἡλικίαν καὶ πολὺ μᾶλλον ὁ τὸ ἦθος τοιοῦτος ἄδεκτός ἐστιν. μὴ τοίνυν λέγωμεν ὡς οὐ παιδευτικοὶ πρὸς ἀρετήν εἰσιν οἱ τοιοίδε μῦθοι τῶν παρ' Ἕλλησιν θεολόγων, ἀλλ' ὡς οὐχὶ τοῖς ἱερατικοῖς θεσμοῖς συμφωνότατοι δεικνύωμεν, μηδὲ ὡς ἀνομοίως μιμοῦνται τὰ θεῖα διὰ | τῶν ἀπεμφαινόντων συμβόλων, ἀλλ' ὡς οὐχὶ συμπάθειαν || ἡμῖν ἄρρητον προπαρασκευάζουσιν εἰς τὴν μετουσίαν τῶν θεῶν.

Οἱ μὲν γὰρ εἰς τὴν τῶν νέων παιδείαν συντείνοντες ἔστωσαν πολὺ μὲν τὸ εἰκὸς ἔχοντες, πολλὴν δὲ τὴν ἐν τοῖς φαινομένοις τύποις τῆς μυθοποιΐας εὐπρέπειαν, πάντῃ | δὲ τῶν ἐναντίων ὀνομάτων καθαρεύοντες καὶ δι' ὁμοιότητος τῶν συμβόλων πρὸς τὰ θεῖα συνάπτοντες, οἱ δὲ ἐνθεαστικωτέρας στοχαζόμενοι ἕξεως καὶ δι' ἀναλογίας μόνης τὰ

somewhere[103] says happens to the most divine and august of doctrines.[104] They are a matter for laughter for the many but to the few who are awakened to intellect they reveal their sympathy with reality and give proof, based on the very operations of the hieratic art, of their powers, which derive from their participation in the nature of the divine. Furthermore, the gods enjoy hearing these symbolic formulas and readily respond to the invokers and reveal their specific properties through these formulas on the basis that they are tokens both appropriate and familiar to them. Both the mysteries and initiations likewise produce their effect through these formulas, and through them they provide entire, calm, and simple visions for the initiates to see, but which the young in age, and much more the young in character, are not equipped to receive. Now, let us not simply say that such myths of the Greek theologians[105] do not educate and incline toward virtue, but let us [if we can] show also that they are not in perfect accord with the hieratic precepts; neither let us say simply that, with their absurd symbols, they give a nonresembling portrait of the divine, but let us demonstrate that they in no way prepare for us a secret || sympathy leading to participation in [the life of] the gods.

Let it be the case that those myths that contribute to the education of children have a good deal of realism in them and a good deal of propriety in the visible patterns of the mythmaking and are everywhere pure of representation through opposite terms,[106] connecting with divinity through the resemblance of their symbols to the divine;[107] nevertheless, those that aim at a more inspired state of mind and compose their whole tale bring-

---

103. But where? F. cites *Theaetetus* 172c–175 (along with several more obviously relevant passages in the *Hermetica*), but in fact the passage in Plato that Proclus has in mind is difficult to identify, and although stories of protecting secret doctrine from the ridicule of the many abound in later Platonism (especially once the "many" can be assumed to be Christian), this is hardly a characteristic theme in Plato. Anne Sheppard (1981) makes a convincing case that Proclus is in fact pointing to the *Second Letter* (314a), a passage she sees as influencing, directly or indirectly, many others.

104. As F. notes ad loc., apparently the doctrines of the hieratic art or precepts (ἱερατικὴ τέχνη, ἱερατικοὶ θεσμοί).

105. Preeminently, Homer and Hesiod.

106. Cf. the formulation below, 295 (K198,13–19), as well as what has just been said above about representation of qualities of the divine in inspired poetry that use expressions diametrically opposite to the true characteristics of the gods.

107. This sentence reinforces Sheppard's position (see 91 n. 117) that iconic representation, based on the relationship called ἀναλογία, is not incompatible with the

ἔσχατα τοῖς πρωτίστοις συναρμόζοντες καὶ τῆς ἐν τῷ παντὶ συμπαθείας τῶν ἀποτελεσμάτων πρὸς τὰ γεννητικὰ αὐτῶν | αἴτια ποιούμενοι τὸν σύμπαντα λόγον εἰκότως δήπου τῶν πολλῶν ἡμῶν ὑπεριδόντες χρῶνται παντοίως τοῖς ὀνόμασιν εἰς τὴν τῶν θείων πραγμάτων ἔνδειξιν.

Ἐπεὶ καὶ τὴν ἁρμονίαν ἄλλην μὲν εἶναι τὴν μιμητικήν φαμεν καὶ διὰ τῶν πρὸς ἀρετὴν ἐγειρόντων μελῶν τὰς τῶν νέων ψυχὰς | θεραπεύουσαν, ἄλλην δὲ τὴν ἔνθεον καὶ κινητικὴν τῶν ἀκουόντων καὶ τῆς θείας μανίας ποιητικήν, ἣν δὴ κρείττονα σωφροσύνης ἐπονομάζομεν· καὶ τὴν μὲν συμπληροῦν τὴν ὅλην παιδείαν ὑπειλήφαμεν, τὴν δὲ ὡς ἀνάρμοστον πρὸς τὴν πολιτικὴν διακόσμησιν ἀποσκευαζόμεθα. ἢ οὐ διὰ τοῦτο | καὶ τὴν Φρύγιον ἁρμονίαν ὁ Σωκράτης ὡς ἐκστατικὴν τῶν ψυχῶν ἐκβάλλειν τῶν πρὸς παιδείαν συντελούντων τῆς μουσικῆς τρόπων ἠξίωσεν [*Lach.* 188d]; ὥσπερ οὖν ἡ ἁρμονία διττή, καὶ ἡ μὲν οἰκεία τοῖς παιδευτικοῖς, ἡ δὲ ἀλλότριος, οὕτως ἄρα καὶ ἡ μυθολογία διῄρηται πρός τε | τὴν τῶν νέων ὀρθὴν ἀγωγὴν καὶ πρὸς τὴν ἱερατικὴν καὶ συμβολικὴν τοῦ θείου πρόκλησιν. καὶ ἡ μὲν δι' εἰκόνων μέθοδος τοῖς γνησίως φιλοσοφοῦσιν προσήκει, ἡ δὲ δι' ἀπορρήτων συνθημάτων τῆς θείας οὐσίας ἔνδειξις τοῖς τῆς μυστικωτέρας ἡγεμόσιν τελεσιουργίας, ἀφ' ἧς δὴ καὶ αὐτὸς | ὁ Πλάτων πολλὰ τῶν οἰκείων δογμάτων ἀξιοῖ πιστότερα καὶ || ἐναργέστερα δεικνύναι. δηλοῖ δὲ ἐν Φαίδωνι [62b, 69c, 108a] **τό τε ἐν ἀπορρήτοις λεγόμενον, ὡς ἔν τινι φρουρᾷ ἐσμεν οἱ ἄνθρωποι**, σιγῇ τῇ πρεπούσῃ σέβων, καὶ τὰς τελετὰς μαρτυρόμενος τῶν διαφόρων λήξεων τῆς ψυχῆς | κεκαθαρμένης τε καὶ ἀκαθάρτου εἰς Ἅιδου ἀπιούσης, καὶ τάς τε σχίσεις αὖ καὶ τὰς τριόδους ἀπὸ τῶν ὁσίων καὶ τῶν πατρίων θεσμῶν τεκμαιρόμενος,

ing the last beings into harmony with the first entirely by analogy and by the sympathy in the universe of resultant things with their generative causes—it is certainly with justification that these myths take little account of most of us and use words in myriad different ways to display the divine.

We say, then, that there exists on the one hand a mode[108] that is mimetic and that cares for the souls of the young with its songs that arouse them to virtue, and another mode that is inspired and stimulates those who listen to it and creates a divine madness, which we declare to be better than sanity.[109] We have said that this first mode has everything in it necessary to education, and we reject the other as incompatible with the orderly arrangement of the state. Yet is this not exactly the reason why Socrates saw fit to banish the Phrygian mode from the musical curriculum, because it was conducive to ecstasy of the soul? [Cf. Plato, *Lach.* 188d.] Now just as there are two musical modes, the one appropriate to education and the other alien to it, in the same way mythology is divided into that which steers the young in the right direction and that which is a hieratic and symbolic evocation of the divine. The [first, the] method that uses images, is appropriate to genuine philosophers, while the demonstration of the true nature of the divine using secret symbols belongs to the guides of the more secret mysteries, on which, of course, Plato himself saw fit to draw to make many of his own doctrines more credible || and clearer. He shows this in the *Phaedo* where he honors with appropriate silence "the esoteric doctrine that we humans are in a prison" [62b],[110] and further where he calls on the initiations to witness to the differing lots of the purified and impure souls going off to Hades [69c], and again in deriving his ideas for the forks and meetings of three roads [in the underworld] from the holy

---

use of symbols and occurs in even the highest of the categories of poetry. Symbols *can* represent through opposites, but they can also represent iconically.

108. The Dorian. Cf. above 41 (K61,28–K62,9). [F.]

109. Better (κρείττονα) in the sense of "stronger," "carrying off the victory." F. took the relative pronoun ἥν above (K84,16) to refer to ἁρμονία, but several factors favor μανία as its antecedent. See in particular the classification of types of μουσική above (33 [K57,25–29]) where Proclus quotes the *Phaedrus* on divine madness and poetry: "his poetry—the sane man's [ἡ τοῦ σωφρονοῦντος]—fades into obscurity in the presence of that of madmen [*Phdr.* 245a]."

110. The first part of the phrase cited is roughly paraphrased, but it is clear that the entire phrase is what is being quoted.

ἃ δὴ τῆς συμβολικῆς ἅπαντα θεωρίας ἐστὶ μεστά, καὶ τῶν παρὰ τοῖς ποιηταῖς θρυλουμένων ἀνόδων τε καὶ καθόδων, τῶν τε Διονυσιακῶν | παθημάτων καὶ τῶν Τιτανικῶν ἁμαρτημάτων λεγομένων, καὶ τῶν ἐν Ἅιδου τριόδων καὶ τῆς πλάνης καὶ τῶν τοιούτων ἁπάντων.

Ὥστ' οὐδ' ἂν αὐτὸς παντελῶς ἀτιμάσειεν τὴν τοιαύτην μυθοποιΐαν, ἀλλ' ὡς πρὸς τὴν παιδευτικὴν τῶν νέων προαίρεσιν ἀλλοτρίαν αὐτὴν ὑπείληφεν· καὶ διὰ ταῦτα | τοὺς τῆς θεολογίας τύπους συμμέτρους τοῖς τῶν παιδευτικῶν ἤθεσιν παραδίδωσιν.

Δοκεῖ δέ μοι καὶ τὸ τῶν ποιητικῶν πλασμάτων τραγικὸν καὶ τὸ τερατῶδες καὶ τὸ παρὰ φύσιν κινεῖν τοὺς ἀκούοντας παντοδαπῶς εἰς τὴν τῆς ἀληθείας ζήτησιν καὶ εἶναι πρὸς τὴν ἀπόρρητον γνῶσιν ὁλκὸν | καὶ μὴ ἐπιτρέπειν ἡμῖν διὰ τὴν φαινομένην ἀπιθανότητα μένειν ἐπὶ τῶν προβεβλημένων ἐννοιῶν, ἀλλ' ἀναγκάζειν εἰς τὸ ἐντὸς τῶν μύθων διαβαίνειν καὶ τὸν κεκρυμμένον ἐν ἀφανεῖ τῶν μυθοπλαστῶν περιεργάζεσθαι νοῦν, καὶ θεωρεῖν ὁποίας μὲν φύσεις, ἡλίκας δὲ δυνάμεις ἐκεῖνοι λαβόντες εἰς | τὴν ἑαυτῶν διάνοιαν τοῖσδε τοῖς συμβόλοις αὐτὰς τοῖς μεθ' ἑαυτοὺς ἐσήμηναν.

and traditional institutions [108a]—all of which[111] indeed is full of symbolic theory and full as well of the things the poets repeat about ascents and descents[112] and of the sufferings[113] of Dionysus, the so-called sins of the Titans, the meetings of three roads in Hades, wanderings, and all such things.

Thus Plato himself would not entirely scorn such mythmaking but judged it alien to the project of educating the young, and it was for this reason that he passed down principles of theology commensurate with the character of education.

[f. Proclus's opinion on the function of the monstrous in myth]

It is my belief that the theatrical, the monstrous, and the unnatural in poetic fictions also move the hearers in all sorts of ways to search after the truth and that they are a device to draw us toward the secret knowledge. Because of their manifest lack of plausibility,[114] they do not permit us to remain at the level of the concepts projected on the surface but rather force us to penetrate[115] into the interior of the myths and concern ourselves with the meaning of the mythoplasts, which is hidden away where it cannot be seen, and to consider what qualities and what great powers they have put into that meaning of theirs[116] and passed on to posterity with these symbols.

---

111. The relative pronoun has a vague antecedent, but "all of this" can be taken to be the Myth of Er (several elements of which are evoked) along with many other passages in Plato that are heavily larded with initiatory language and symbolism.

112. Proclus may have in mind the cave of the nymphs in the *Odyssey* (13.102–112), his ideas on which will have been influenced by Porphyry's reading.

113. Reading (with F.) Abel's conjecture παθημάτων for the manuscript's συνθημάτων, from Kroll's apparatus.

114. Reading my conjecture ἀπιθανότητα for the manuscript's πιθανότητα (cf. 91 [K86,1]).

115. Reading διαβαίνειν for the manuscript's διαβάλλειν with F., from Kroll's addenda (2:472).

116. Reading my conjecture ἑαυτῶν for the manuscript's αὐτῶν. If αὐτῶν is possessive genitive, this position would be quite unusual for a personal pronoun, and as far as I can see, Proclus does not elsewhere break this rule. Just above (lines 22–23) reference has been made to the νοῦς ("meaning") of the mythoplasts (apparently a possessive genitive), and this phrase seems to echo the earlier one.

Ὅτε τοίνυν ἀνεγείρουσιν μὲν οἱ τοιοίδε μῦθοι τοὺς εὐφυεστέρους πρὸς τὴν ἔφεσιν τῆς ἐν αὐτοῖς || ἀποκρύφου θεωρίας καὶ διὰ τὴν φαινομένην τερατολογίαν τῆς ἐν τοῖς ἀδύτοις ἱδρυμένης ἀληθείας ἀνακινοῦσιν τὴν ζήτησιν, τοῖς δὲ βεβήλοις ὧν μὴ θέμις αὐτοῖς <οὐ> συγχωροῦσιν ἐφάπτεσθαι, πῶς οὐ διαφερόντως ἂν προσήκοιεν | τοῖς θεοῖς αὐτοῖς, ὧν εἰσιν ἐξηγηταὶ τῆς ὑποστάσεως; καὶ γὰρ τῶν θεῶν πολλὰ προβέβληται γένη, τὰ μὲν τῆς δαιμονίας τάξεως, τὰ δὲ τῆς ἀγγελικῆς, καταπλήττοντα τοὺς εἰς τὴν μετουσίαν αὐτῶν ἐγειρομένους καὶ γυμναζομένους πρὸς τὴν τοῦ φωτὸς καταδοχὴν καὶ εἰς ὕψος ἐπαίροντα | πρὸς τὴν ἕνωσιν τῶν θεῶν. μάλιστα δ᾽ ἄν τις κατίδοι τὴν τῶν μύθων τούτων πρὸς τὸ τῶν δαιμόνων φῦλον συγγένειαν καὶ διὰ τῆς ἐκείνων ἐνεργείας συμβολικῶς τὰ πολλὰ δηλούσης, οἷον εἴ τινες ἡμῶν ὕπαρ ἐγένοντο δαίμοσιν προστυχεῖς ἢ καὶ ὄναρ τῆς παρ᾽ αὐτῶν ἀπολελαύκασιν ἐπιπνοίας πολλὰ | τῶν γενομένων ἢ καὶ ἐσομένων ἐκφαινούσης.

Ἐν πάσαις γὰρ ταῖς τοιαύταις φαντασίαις κατὰ τοὺς μυθοπλάστας ἄλλα ἐξ ἄλλων ἐνδείκνυται, καὶ οὐ τὰ μὲν εἰκόνες, τὰ δὲ παραδείγματα, ὅσα διὰ τούτων σημαίνουσιν, ἀλλὰ τὰ μὲν σύμβολα, τὰ δὲ ἐξ ἀναλογίας ἔχει τὴν πρὸς ταῦτα συμπάθειαν. | εἰ τοίνυν δαιμόνιος ὁ τρόπος ἐστὶ τῆς τοιαύτης μυθοποιΐας, πῶς οὐ πάντη φήσομεν αὐτὸν ἐξῃρῆσθαι τῆς ἄλλης ἁπάσης τῶν μύθων ποικιλίας, τῆς τε εἰς τὴν φύσιν βλεπούσης καὶ τὰς φυσικὰς δυνάμεις ἀφερμηνευούσης, καὶ τῆς τὰ ἤθη τῶν ψυχῶν παιδεύειν προστησαμένης; ||

**Τίνες οἱ παρὰ τοῖς θεολόγοις θεομαχίας
διάφοροι τρόποι τὴν ἐν αὐτῇ ἀπόρρητον ἀλήθειαν εἰς
φῶς ἄγοντες.**

Thus, since myths of this sort arouse in those of the best natural disposition a longing for the doctrine || hidden within them, and through their superficial monstrosity inspire the pursuit of the truth rooted in their deepest recesses, and at the same time prevent the profane who have no business with that truth from reaching it, how can we say that they do not exceptionally well fit the gods themselves, whose being they interpret? Indeed, many classes of beings are projected in front of the gods, some in the daemonic ranks and some in the angelic, that fascinate those awakened to participation and trained to receive the light and that lift them up to the highest, to union with the gods. The affinity of the myths under discussion to the class of daemons can be seen very clearly as well in the fact that the actions of these daemons are generally also symbolic. For example, when certain of us have met daemons, whether in a waking state or in a dream, those people have had the benefit of the daemons' inspiration, revealing numerous things past or even to come.

In all of these fantasies in the manner of the mythoplasts, one thing is designated by another. This is not always through images representing models; rather, sometimes symbols are used, and sometimes the relationship with the things that are indicated exists by virtue of analogy [that is, through images].[117] If this mode of mythmaking is daemonic,[118] how shall we deny that it is in every way superior to all the other varieties of myth, both that which looks into nature and interprets natural forces and that which proposes to educate the character of the soul? ||

(3) What are the various ways in which the secret truth in the "Battle of the Gods" of the theologians[119] is brought to light?

---

117. I have followed Sheppard here in her important correction of Festugière (who was followed by Coulter). See Sheppard 1980, 197. She is certainly correct that there are in fact three modes of representation discussed (though Proclus, as she also shows, is inconsistent). Her ("rather free") translation of the passage is as follows: "For in all such fictions imagined by the writers of myths one type of entity is shown by another type; it is not a matter of showing models through copies in all these cases; sometimes symbols are used while at other times the sympathy between the two types of entity is expressed by analogy."

118. I.e., intermediate between gods and men.

119. The "theologians," again, are Homer, Hesiod, Orpheus, and the other early poets who told stories about gods. The "Battle of the Gods" (θεῶν μάχη or θεομαχία) is the traditional title of book 20 of the *Iliad*, but various other passages from early epic are brought into the discussion.

Περὶ μὲν οὖν τῆς τῶν μύθων ἰδέας, καθ' ἣν οἵ τε | ἄλλοι ποιηταὶ καὶ Ὅμηρος τὰς περὶ θεῶν μυστικὰς ἐννοίας ἀφανεῖς τοῖς πολλοῖς κατεστήσαντο, τοσαῦτα προειρήσθω. ἕπεται δὲ οἶμαι τοῖς τοῦ Σωκράτους λόγοις τὴν προσήκουσαν ἀποδοῦναι τῶν καθ' ἕκαστα πλασμάτων διάρθρωσιν καὶ θεωρῆσαι, κατὰ ποίας ἄρα τῆς ψυχῆς ἐπιβολὰς ἢ μαχομένους | τοὺς θεοὺς ἢ καὶ ἄλλο τι ποιοῦντας ἢ πάσχοντας Ὅμηρος παραδίδωσι διὰ τῆς ἑαυτοῦ ποιήσεως. καὶ πρῶτον εἰ βούλεσθε τὴν λεγομένην ταύτην θεομαχίαν, ἣν Ὅμηρος μὲν ἐποίησεν, ὁ δὲ Σωκράτης ὡς τοῖς παιδευομένοις ἀκούειν οὐδαμῇ πρέπουσαν ἐπιστάσεων ἠξίωσεν, ἐφ' ἡμῶν | αὐτῶν κατανοήσωμεν.

Ὅτι μὲν γὰρ οὔτε στάσις ἐστὶν ἐν τοῖς θεοῖς οὔτε διαφορὰ καὶ μερισμὸς θνητοειδής, ἀλλ' εἰρήνη καὶ ἀπήμων βίος, δηλοῖ που καὶ αὐτὸς ὁ ποιητὴς περὶ τοῦ Ὀλύμπου λέγων, ὡς ὑπέστρωται μὲν τοῖς θεοῖς, οἳ δὲ εὐφροσύνην ἔχουσι πᾶσαν καὶ θέας ἀμηχάνους τὸ κάλλος· |

τῷ ἔνι τέρπονται μάκαρες θεοὶ ἤματα πάντα [ζ 46].

τίς οὖν διάστασίς ποτε παρεισδύεσθαι δύναται καὶ πόλεμος εἰς τοὺς αἰώνιον λαχόντας τὴν εὐφροσύνην καὶ τὸ ἵλεων ἀεὶ προβεβλημένους καὶ χαίροντας ἐφ' οἷς ἔχουσιν ἀγαθοῖς; | εἰ δὲ δεῖ τῆς τε προνοίας τῶν θεῶν καὶ τῆς τῶν προνοουμένων φύσεως [προβάλλεσθαι] στοχάζεσθαι τοὺς περὶ αὐτῶν λόγους, οὑτωσί πως οἶμαι τὴν μυθικὴν αὐτῶν πρὸς ἀλλήλους ἐναντίωσιν ἀφερμηνεύσομεν. |

Καθ' ἕνα μὲν δὴ τρόπον αἱ τῶν ὄντων ἁπάντων διῃρημέναι πρόοδοι καὶ αἱ κατ' οὐσίαν διακρίσεις ἄνωθεν ἀπὸ || τῆς ἀγνώστου τοῖς πᾶσιν ἄρχονται τῶν πρωτουργῶν αἰτίων διαιρέσεως καὶ κατὰ τὰς ὑπερηπλωμένας τῶν ὅλων ἀρχὰς ὑφιστάμεναι διεστήκασιν ἀπ' ἀλλήλων· αἳ μὲν τῆς τοῦ πέρατος ἑνοποιοῦ μονάδος ἐξηρτημέναι καὶ περὶ ἐκείνην ἀφορί|ζουσαι τὴν ἑαυτῶν ὑπόστασιν, αἳ δὲ τῆς γεννητικῆς τῶν ὅλων ἀπειρίας τὴν

[a. The problem]

Let this preface suffice concerning the form of the myths through which the other poets along with Homer made the secret mystical concepts concerning the gods invisible to the many. The next task, I think, is to offer in response to Socrates' words a suitable articulation of each specific fiction and to examine the problem of what impulses of the soul lie behind Homer's presentation of the gods in his poetry as fighting or doing or experiencing various other things. If you like, let us first examine for ourselves this so-called theomachy that Homer composed and Socrates decided to single out, on the basis that it was in no way suitable to be heard by students.

Now, the Poet himself shows that discord and differences and division of the mortal sort do not exist among the gods, but only peace and a life of ease, when he says about Olympus that it is spread out beneath the gods and that they have every sort of pleasure and spectacles of inconceivable beauty,

> There they take their pleasure, the blessed gods, all their days.
> [*Od.* 6.46]

What division or war could ever intervene among those whose lot is eternal pleasure, who always project happiness and take joy in the good things they possess? If accounts of the gods must always have a view to their providence and the nature of those they watch over, then the following, I think, is the manner in which we must interpret the myth of their strife against one another.

[b. First explanation]

One way [of explaining it] is to say that the distinct processions of all beings and their essential divisions have their source in the division of the primordial causes, which || is beyond the knowledge of us all, and these processions, issuing forth from the first principles of the universe in their transcendent simplicity, are divided from one another. Some processions of beings depend on the unifying monad of Limit, and these define their own existence accordingly; others depend on the Unlimited[120] that gener-

---

120. The terms of the primal division evoked are sometimes "Limit and Unlim-

ἀνέκλειπτον δύναμιν καὶ τὴν πλήθους καὶ προόδων οἰστικὴν αἰτίαν καταδεξάμεναι καὶ περὶ αὐτὴν προστησάμεναι τὴν οἰκείαν ὕπαρξιν.

Ἧιπερ οὖν αἱ πρώτισται τῶν ὄντων ἀρχαὶ διεκρίθησαν ἀλλήλων, ταύτῃ καὶ τὰ θεῖα | πάντα γένη καὶ τὰ ὄντως ὄντα τὴν ἀπ' ἀλλήλων ἔσχεν ἐν τάξει διωρισμένην πρόοδον· καὶ τὰ μὲν αὐτῶν ἐξάρχει τῆς ἑνώσεως τοῖς δευτέροις, τὰ δὲ τῆς διαιρέσεως παρέχεται τὴν δύναμιν· καὶ τὰ μὲν τῆς ἐπιστροφῆς ἐστιν αἴτια τοῖς προελθοῦσιν συνελίσσοντα τὸ πλῆθος αὐτῶν εἰς τὰς οἰκείας | ἀρχάς, τὰ δὲ αὐτῶν ἀφορίζει <τὴν> πρόοδον καὶ τὴν ἐκ τῶν ἀρχῶν ὑφειμένην ἀπογέννησιν. ἔτι δὲ τὰ μὲν τῆς γεννητικῆς ἐστιν περιουσίας χορηγὰ τοῖς καταδεεστέροις, τὰ δὲ τῆς ἀτρέπτου καὶ ἀχράντου καθαρότητος παρεκτικά· καὶ τὰ μὲν τῶν χωριστῶν ἀγαθῶν εἰς ἑαυτὰ τὴν αἰτίαν ἀνα|δησάμενα, τὰ δὲ τῶν συνυφεστηκότων τοῖς μεταλαμβάνουσιν.

Ὅθεν δὴ καὶ ἐν ταῖς τοῦ ὄντος ἁπάσαις διακοσμήσεσιν ἡ τοιαύτη τῶν γενῶν ἐναντίωσις διαποικίλλεται· καὶ ἡ μὲν στάσις ἑδράζουσα σταθερῶς ἐν ἑαυτοῖς τὰ ὄντα ταῖς δραστηρίοις καὶ ζωῆς πλήρεσιν τῆς κινήσεως ἀντίκειται δυνάμεσιν, | ἡ δὲ τῆς ταυτότητος ὁμοφυὴς κοινωνία ταῖς τῆς ἑτερότητος κατ' εἴδη διακρίσεσιν ἀντιδιῄρηται· τὸ δὲ τῆς ὁμοιότητος γένος τῇ ἀνομοιότητι καὶ τὸ τῆς ἰσότητος τῇ ἀνισότητι κατὰ τὴν αὐτὴν ἀναλογίαν τὴν ἐναντίαν ἔλαχεν τάξιν. καὶ τούτων ἁπάντων αἱ διαιρέσεις ἄνωθεν ἀπὸ τῆς ἀρχικῆς | ἀφορίζονται δυάδος, καθ' ἣν ἕκαστα τῶν ὄντων διακρίνεταί || τε τοῖς οἰκείοις ὅροις καὶ ἀντιδιῃρημένα πρόεισιν ἀλλήλοις ἀπὸ τῶν γεννητικῶν αἰτίων, καὶ συμπλεκόμενα μετ' ἀλλήλων ἀπογεννᾷ τὴν ποικιλίαν τῶν δευτέρων.

τί δὴ οὖν ἔτι θαυμαστόν, εἰ καὶ τῶν θεῶν αὐτῶν καὶ τῶν πρωτίστων ἐν τοῖς | οὖσιν τοιαύτην ἐναντίωσιν οἱ μυθοπλάσται κατανοήσαντες διὰ τῶν πολέμων αὐτὴν αἰνίσσοιντο τοῖς ἑαυτῶν τροφίμοις, ἀεὶ μὲν ἡνωμένων

ates the universe and have received from that source limitless power and the capacity to generate quantity and processions, and they project their own existence stemming from that principle.

Just as the first principles of things are divided from one another, in the same way the classes of the divine and of those things that truly exist form orderly processions, divided from one another. These represent respectively, as far as secondaries are concerned, the principle of unity and the power of division. The first group constitutes the cause that makes the projected beings return, rolling their multiplicity together into their first causes; the other defines their procession and their diminished generation downward from their first principles. One class acts as sponsor of their abundance of generative power for the lower stages, while the other produces in them the capacity to maintain their unchanging and uncorrupted purity. The first attach themselves to the cause of the transcendent, unparticipated good things; the others attach themselves to the cause of the good things whose nature is shared by those who participate in them.

Thus, this sort of opposition of classes brings its complexity into every ordering of reality. *Rest*, solidly settling into themselves the things that exist, is opposed to the powers of *Movement*, which are active and full of life, and the communality that shares the nature of *Identity* is correspondingly divided up by the specific distinctions of *Otherness*. The classes of *Sameness* and *Difference* and *Equality* and *Inequality* are opposed to one another by the same analogical principle. All these divisions are defined downwards from the primal || dyad, by which every being has its limits set, and in their fundamental polarity they proceed from the generative causes to be woven together and produce the diversity of the secondaries.[121]

What wonder is it, then, that the mythoplasts, seeing such a fundamental division among the gods themselves and among the most primary of beings, use wars to hint at that division for their disciples, since, although the classes of the divine are eternally united among themselves,

---

ited" (πέρας and ἄπειρον [ἀπειρία]), at other times "monad and dyad" (μονάς and [ἀόριστος] δυάς, see 103 [K93,4–8]). These metaphysical categories are ultimately derived from passages in the *Phaedo* (101c–102a), *Parmenides* (149b–d), and, perhaps most importantly, the *Philebus* (15a–17a; see Burkert 1972, 85–86).

121. At *In Tim.* 1:77,24–78,12 (Diehl), Proclus attributes to Iamblichus and Syrianus a similar interpretation of the war between Athens and Atlantis (Dillon 1973, 110–13; Tarrant 2007, 170–71).

ἀλλήλοις τῶν θείων γενῶν, ὁμοῦ δὲ τὴν ἕνωσιν καὶ τὴν ἀσύγχυτον διάκρισιν ἐν ἑαυτοῖς προστησαμένων. |
 Καὶ ἕτερον δὲ οἶμαι τρόπον ἔξεστιν λέγειν, αὐτοὺς μὲν τοὺς θεοὺς ἀμερίστως ἀλλήλοις συμφύεσθαι καὶ ἑνοειδῶς ἐν ἀλλήλοις ὑφεστηκέναι, τὰς δὲ προόδους αὐτῶν τὰς εἰς τὸ πᾶν καὶ τὰς μεταδόσεις ἐν τοῖς μετέχουσιν διαιρεῖσθαι καὶ μεριστὰς γίνεσθαι κἀνταῦθα τῆς ἐναντιώσεως ἀναπίμ|πλασθαι, τῶν προνοουμένων ἀμιγῶς τὰς ἐκεῖθεν προϊούσας δυνάμεις καὶ ἀσυγχύτως καταδέχεσθαι τὰς πολυειδεῖς ἐλλάμψεις οὐ δυναμένων. ἔτι δὲ τὰς τελευταίας τάξεις τὰς ἐξηρτημένας αὐτῶν τῶν θείων, ἅτε πόρρω μὲν τῶν πρωτίστων αἰτίων ἀπογεννωμένας, προσεχεῖς δὲ τοῖς διοικουμένοις | καὶ προσύλους ὑπαρχούσας, ἐναντιώσεως ἤδη καὶ διακρίσεως παντοίας μετέχειν καὶ μεριστῶς προεστάναι τῶν ἐνύλων, ἀποτεμαχιζούσας καὶ διαιρούσας τὰς ἑνοειδῶς καὶ ἀμερίστως προϋφεστηκυίας ἐν ταῖς ἑαυτῶν πρωτουργοῖς αἰτίαις δυνάμεις. |
 Τοιούτων δὴ οὖν καὶ τοσούτων τρόπων ὄντων τε καὶ λεγομένων, καθ' οὓς αἱ μυστικαὶ τῶν θεολόγων φῆμαι καὶ ἐπὶ τοὺς θεοὺς αὐτοὺς τὸν πόλεμον ἀναπέμπειν εἰώθασιν, τοὺς μὲν ἄλλους ποιητὰς καὶ περὶ τὴν τῶν θείων πραγμά|των ἐξήγησιν ἐνθεάζοντας κατ' ἐκεῖνον φῶμεν τὸν τρόπον ἐν τοῖς θεοῖς ὑποτίθεσθαι πολέμους τε καὶ μάχας, ὃν καὶ || τὰ θεῖα γένη διῄρητο κατὰ τὰς πρωτίστας τῶν ὅλων ἀρχάς.
 τὰ γὰρ ἀναγωγὰ τοῖς γενεσιουργοῖς, καὶ τὰ συνεκτικὰ τοῖς διακριτικοῖς, καὶ τὰ ἑνοποιὰ τοῖς πληθύουσιν τὴν τῶν ὄντων πρόοδον, καὶ τὰ ὁλικὰ τοῖς μεριστῶς δημιουργοῦσι, καὶ | τὰ ἁπλωτικὰ τοῖς τῶν μερικῶν

they simultaneously project both the union and the irresolvable division within them?

[c. Second explanation]

There is, I believe, another way to explain this: the gods themselves are connatural with one another without division and exist uniformly in each other, but their processions into the universe and what they give of themselves to the beings that participate in them is divided and becomes fragmented so that in this world (ἐνταῦθα) they come to be full of contrariety, since the beings providentially overseen by the gods are incapable of receiving unmixed and without confusion the powers proceeding from them and their polymorphic illuminations. Moreover, the last classes suspended from the divine beings themselves,[122] being produced far from the first causes and next to the administered beings, in contact with matter, participate in all kinds of division and contrariety and preside, in a fragmented state, over material realities, parceling out and dividing the forces that previously existed in a unified and indivisible manner in their own primordial causes.

[d. Application to the poets other than Homer]

Now that the nature and the number of the ways in which the mystical utterances of the theologians are accustomed to attribute war to the gods themselves have been stated, let us say that the other poets who have given inspired accounts of divine things have attributed wars and battles to the gods in the first sense, that is, because the classes || of the divine are divided according to the [division in] the first principles of the universe.[123] Disguising the truth, the myths say that the anagogic forces and those that are generative in this world, those that draw together and those that establish distinctions, the unifying and those that produce the multiplicity of the procession of beings, the holistic and those that are creative in the sphere of fragmentation, and finally those that reunite[124] and those that

---

122. I.e., the angelic and daemonic classes (below, 99–101 [K91]). [F.]
123. I.e., the monad and the dyad.
124. F. offers a valuable note in defense of his understanding of the rare and problematic term ἀναπλωτικά ("ceux qui causent l'entier développement"). From Plotinus to Proclus, ἀναπλόω can mean either "deploy" or "simplify," and the first meaning has

προστάταις ἀντικείμενά πως μάχεσθαι καὶ πολεμεῖν ἀλλήλοις οἱ μῦθοι τὴν ἀλήθειαν ἐπικρυπτόμενοι λέγουσιν.

Ὅθεν οἶμαι καὶ τοὺς Τιτᾶνας τῷ Διονύσῳ καὶ Διῒ τοὺς Γίγαντας ἀνταγωνίζεσθαί φασιν· τοῖς μὲν γὰρ ὡς πρὸ τοῦ κόσμου δημιουργοῖς ἥ τε | ἕνωσις προσήκει καὶ ἡ ἀμέριστος ποίησις καὶ ἡ πρὸ τῶν μερῶν ὁλότης, οἳ δὲ εἰς πλῆθος προάγουσιν τὰς δημιουργικὰς δυνάμεις καὶ μεμερισμένως διοικοῦσιν τὰ ἐν τῷ παντὶ καὶ προσεχεῖς εἰσιν πατέρες τῶν ἐνύλων πραγμάτων.

Τὴν δὲ Ὁμηρικὴν θεομυθίαν κατὰ τὸν ἕτερον τρόπον νοήσωμεν | τοὺς ἐν τοῖς θεοῖς πολέμους διαπλάττουσαν. πρῶτον μὲν γὰρ τὴν δημιουργικὴν μονάδα παντὸς ἐξαιρεῖ τοῦ πλήθους τῶν θεῶν καὶ οὔτε προϊοῦσαν ἐπὶ τὴν γενεσιουργὸν ἐναντίωσιν οὔτε ἀνθιστάμενόν τι πρὸς αὐτὴν παραδίδωσιν, ἀλλ' ἐκείνης ἐν ἑαυτῇ σταθερῶς ἱδρυμένης ὁ τῶν θεῶν τῶν ἀπ' | αὐτῆς προεληλυθότων ἀριθμὸς μένων ἅμα καὶ προϊὼν εἰς τὸ πᾶν μερίζεσθαι λέγεται περὶ τὴν πρόνοιαν τῶν ἐγκοσμίων.

Ἔπειτα καὶ τούτων τῶν ἀπὸ τοῦ πατρὸς διῃρημένων θεῶν τοὺς μὲν ἐν τῷ πατρὶ μείναντας καὶ τῆς οἰκείας μονάδος ἀνεκφοιτήτους ὑπάρχοντας, οὓς δὴ καὶ Διὸς ἔνδον ἡ | ποίησίς [Υ 13] φησιν ἱδράσθαι καὶ μετὰ τοῦ πατρὸς τῶν ὅλων προνοεῖν ἐξῃρημένως, οὔτε πολεμεῖν ἀλλήλοις οὔτε ἀνθίστασθαι πρὸς ἀλλήλους ὁ μῦθος οὐδὲ κατὰ τὸ φαινόμενον συγχωρεῖ· τοὺς δὲ ἐκεῖθεν εἰς πολλοστὰς τάξεις ὑφιζάνοντας καὶ μερικωτέρους γενομένους καὶ τοῖς διοι||κουμένοις προσεχεστέρους καὶ ἀγγελικὰς ἢ δαιμονίας στρατιὰς συμπληροῦντας διὰ τὴν πολλὴν πρὸς τὰ καταδεέστερα συμπάθειαν καὶ τὴν τῆς προνοίας μεριστὴν διακλήρωσιν μαχομένους ἀλλήλοις παραδίδωσιν. τούτοις γὰρ οἶμαι καὶ | τὰ τῶν προνοουμένων πάθη συγγενέστερά πώς ἐστιν, πληγαί τε καὶ βολαὶ καὶ ἀντιτυπίαι καὶ ἡ

preside over that which is fragmented are in some sense opposed to one another and fight battles and wars.

This, I believe, is why they depict the Titans fighting against Dionysus and Zeus fighting the against Giants.[125] To Zeus and Dionysus, the creators previous to the cosmos, belong unity and unfragmented creation and the wholeness that precedes the existence of parts. The Titans and the Giants draw the creative powers into multiplicity, govern the beings in the universe in a fragmented manner, and are the immediate fathers of material things.

[e. Application to Homer]

Let us understand that the Homeric myths fabricate wars of the gods in the second mode. First of all, he removes the creative monad from the other gods and does not show [Zeus] entering the conflict of opposites that is productive of this world, nor setting himself up in any way against it. No, the monad rests solidly fixed in itself, while the sum of gods issuing from the monad, simultaneously at rest and proceeding into the universe, is said to split apart over providential care of the beings in the cosmos.

Secondly, of those gods who are separated from the father, the myth does not admit that, even in appearance, those who have remained within their father and have not emanated from their own monad—the poem describes them as fixed "within Zeus" [Διὸς ἔνδον, *Il.* 20.13] and, with their father, taking providential care of the universe while remaining separated from it—that these gods make war with or stand in opposition to each other. He says, however, that those who, from there,[126] have settled to the remotest ranks and become more fragmented and closer to the ‖ administered beings—that these fill out the angelic and daemonic armies and fight with one another because of their immense sympathy for the beings of a lower order and because of the fragmented allocation of providence. I believe that the experiences of the beings over whom providential care is extended—wounds, blows, and counterblows—are somehow more

---

much to recommend it here. I have adopted something closer to the latter, however, taking "reunify" from Harold Tarrant (2007, 320, with loci) as more in line with the preceding list of opposing forces. Tarrant shows that both senses occur in Proclus's *Timaeus* commentary.

125. Cf. above, 19 (K51) with n. 22.
126. I.e., from their source in the monad.

γενεσιουργὸς ἐναντίωσις οὐ πόρρω τῆς τούτων εἰσὶν διακοσμήσεως, τό τε μεριστὸν τῆς εἰς τὰ δεύτερα ποιήσεως καὶ τὸ τῆς προνοίας ἀποτετεμαχισμένον ταῖς τοιαύταις προσήκει δυνάμεσιν, | ἀλλ' οὐ ταῖς ἀρχηγικαῖς καὶ ταῖς ἐξῃρημέναις πάντων τῶν προνοουμένων καὶ [ταῖς] χωρισταῖς αἰτίαις. Ἐπεὶ δὲ καὶ ἀγγελικαὶ τάξεις τῶν κρειττόνων γενῶν τῆς τῶν θεῶν ἡγεμονίας ἐξήρτηνται καὶ τὰς ἰδιότητας τῶν σφετέρων ἡγεμόνων, εἰ καὶ μερικῶς καὶ πεπληθυσμένως, ἀλλ' οὖν καὶ | αὗται διασώζουσιν, τοῖς τε ὀνόμασιν ἀποκαλοῦνται τοῖς ἐκείνων καὶ ὡς τοῖς πρωτίστοις ἀνάλογον ὑποστᾶσαι αἱ αὐταί πως εἶναι τοῖς ὁλικωτέροις ἑαυτῶν καὶ προελθοῦσαι φαντάζονται.

καὶ τοῦτο οὐχ οἱ παρ' Ἕλλησι μῦθοι μόνον δι' ἐπίκρυψιν μεμηχάνηνται, λέγω δὴ τὸ διὰ τῶν αὐτῶν | ὀνομάτων τούς τε ἡγεμόνας καὶ τοὺς ὀπαδοὺς προσαγορεύειν, ἀλλὰ καὶ αἱ τῶν βαρβάρων τελεταὶ παραδεδώκασιν· καὶ γὰρ καλουμένους τοὺς ἐξημμένους τῶν θεῶν ἀγγέλους ταῖς αὐταῖς ἐπωνυμίαις ἐκείνοις χαίρειν διαφερόντως φασὶν καὶ περιβάλλεσθαι τὰ ὀχήματα τῶν ἡγεμόνων τῆς σειρᾶς καὶ | τοῖς θεουργοῖς ἀντ' ἐκείνων προφαίνειν ἑαυτούς.

Εἰ οὖν καὶ Ἀθηνᾶν καὶ Ἥραν καὶ Ἥφαιστον πολεμοῦντας κάτω περὶ τὴν γένεσιν καὶ Λητὼ καὶ Ἄρτεμιν καὶ Ξάνθον τὸν ποταμὸν εἰς ἄλλας τάξεις ἀναπέμποιμεν δευτέρας καὶ προσεχεῖς || τοῖς μεριστοῖς καὶ ἐνύλοις πράγμασιν, θαυμάζειν οὐ χρὴ διὰ τὴν τῶν ὀνομάτων κοινωνίαν. ἑκάστη γὰρ σειρὰ τὴν τῆς μονάδος φέρεται προσηγορίαν, καὶ τὰ μερικὰ πνεύματα τοῖς ὅλοις τὴν αὐτὴν ἐπωνυμίαν δέχεσθαι φιλεῖ. διὸ καὶ | Ἀπόλλωνες καὶ Ποσειδῶνες καὶ Ἥφαιστοι πολλοί τε καὶ παντοδαποί, καὶ οἱ μὲν αὐτῶν χωριστοὶ τοῦ παντός εἰσιν, οἱ δὲ περὶ τὸν οὐρανὸν διεκληρώθησαν, οἱ δὲ τῶν ὅλων προεστήκασιν στοιχείων, οἱ δὲ περὶ ἕκαστον κατενείμαντο τὴν ἐπιστασίαν. καὶ οὐκ ἂν θαυμαστόν, εἰ ὁ μερικώτατος | Ἥφαιστος καὶ τάξιν δαιμονίαν λαχὼν τοῦ ἐνύλου πυρὸς καὶ περὶ τὴν γῆν ὑφισταμένου

akin to these [gods] and that the conflict of opposites that is creative of this world is not foreign to the order that governs their existence. Likewise, the fragmentary quality of creative action upon secondaries and the truncation resulting from providential action belong to powers of this sort, not to the primordial causes, which are transcendent and separate from all the beings over whom providential care is extended. Moreover, since among the superior beings the angelic ranks depend upon the leadership of the gods, and, even in a partial and pluralized way, they still retain the properties of their chiefs and are called by their names, for this reason (as analogous to the first principles) they are imagined as being, even after their procession, somehow identical with what is more universal than themselves.

It is not only the Greek myths that have worked this out cryptically—that is, calling both the leaders and their followers by the same names—but the non-Greek mysteries pass down the same tradition. They say that the angels in the processions of the gods especially rejoice in being called by the same names as theirs[127] and that they put on the vehicles of those at the heads of their processions and make themselves manifest in their place to the theurgists.

So, if we refer Athena and Hera and Hephaestus fighting down below in γένεσις,[128] and Leto and Artemis and the river Xanthos to other classes of beings, secondary ones contiguous || with fragmented and material reality, the shared names should cause no amazement. Each chain bears the name of its monad, and the partial spirits enjoy[129] being called by the same names as their wholes. Thus there are many Apollos and Poseidons and Hephaestuses of all sorts, some of them separated from the universe, some distributed through the heavens, some presiding over the elements in their totality, some assigned authority over specific elements. And it would be no surprise if the most partial Hephaestus, allotted daemonic rank, should have providential care over material and terrestrial fire and should have

---

127. I.e., the names of the gods at the heads of their processions.

128. The term γένεσις in the usage of the later Platonists is very difficult to translate without recourse to the expansive style of a Thomas Taylor, who rendered it as "the realm of coming to be and passing away" (which likewise has precedent in Proclus: 141 [K113,7–8]). Here and below (roughly fifteen times) I have retained the Greek word in this translation, but in a few cases (see pp. 141, 197, 253) I have opted for some variant of Taylor's solution to translate related vocabulary.

129. Cf. Plutarch, *Def. orac.* 421e.

προβεβλημένην ἔχοι τὴν πρόνοιαν ἢ καὶ τέχνης τινὸς ἔφορος εἴη τῆς χαλκευτικῆς (εἰς γὰρ τὸν ἔσχατον μερισμὸν ἡ τῶν θεῶν πρόνοια τὴν ὕφεσιν ἔσχεν, ἄνωθεν ἀπὸ τῶν ὁλικῶν καὶ ἡνωμένων αἰ|τίων τὴν εὔτακτον λαχοῦσα πρόοδον), καὶ οὗτος χαίροι μὲν τῇ σωτηρίᾳ τοῦ σφετέρου κλήρου, πρὸς δὲ τὰ φθοροποιὰ τῆς ἐκείνου συστάσεως αἴτια ἀλλοτρίως ἔχοι. καὶ πόλεμος οὖν ἐν τοῖς τοιούτοις γένεσιν καὶ διαίρεσις παντοδαπῶν δυνάμεων, καὶ οἰκειότης πρὸς ἀλλήλους καὶ ἀλλοτριότης, καὶ ἡ | πρὸς τὰ διοικούμενα μεριστὴ συμπάθεια, καὶ αἱ διὰ λόγων ἐναντιώσεις καὶ διὰ τῶν σκωμμάτων ἄμυναι, καὶ ὅσα τοιαῦτα περὶ τὰς ἀποτελευτήσεις εἰκότως ἐμφαντάζεται τῶν θείων διακοσμήσεων. διὸ καὶ οἱ μῦθοι τὰς τοιαύτας δυνάμεις ὑπὲρ τῶν προνοουμένων στασιαζούσας καὶ διαφερο|μένας ἀλλήλαις ἀναγράφοντες οὐκ ἄν που πόρρω βάλλοιεν τῆς περὶ αὐτῶν ἀληθείας· καὶ γὰρ τὰ πάθη τῶν διοικουμένων ἐπὶ ταύτας ἀναφέρεται προσεχῶς.

Ὡς οὖν συνελόντι φάναι, διττῆς ἐπινοίας θεωρουμένης τῶν παρὰ τοῖς φοιβολήπτοις ποιηταῖς θρυλουμένων πολέ|μων, καὶ τῆς μὲν περὶ τὰς δύο τῶν ὅλων ἀρχάς, ἃς ἡ || τοῦ ἑνὸς ἐξῃρημένη τῶν πάντων αἰτία παρήγαγεν, τὴν διαίρεσιν τῶν θείων γενῶν εὐτάκτως νοούσης καὶ κατὰ τὴν ἐκείνων ἀντίθεσιν καὶ τούτοις τὴν πρὸς ἄλληλα παρεχομένης ἐναντίωσιν (εἴτε γὰρ πέρας καὶ ἄπειρον, εἴτε μονάδα καὶ | ἀόριστον δυάδα χρὴ προσαγορεύειν τὰς πρωτίστας ἐκείνας ὑποστάσεις, πάντως φαίνεταί τις αὐτῶν πρὸς ἀλλήλας ἀντιδιαίρεσις, καθ' ἣν καὶ αἱ τῶν θεῶν διακοσμήσεις ἀπ' ἀλλήλων διεκρίθησαν), <τῆς δὲ> ἐκ τῆς περὶ τὰ ἔσχατα τῶν ὄντων ἐναντιώσεως καὶ τῆς ποικιλίας ἐπ' αὐτοὺς τοὺς | προσεχεῖς αὐτῶν προστάτας ἀναφερούσης τὴν τοιαύτην διάστασιν καὶ οὕτως δὴ προϊόντας εἰς τὴν ἔνυλον φύσιν τοὺς θεοὺς καὶ περὶ ταύτην μεριζομένους πολεμεῖν ἀλλήλοις ὑποτιθεμένης, φανήσεται μέν που καὶ περὶ ἐκείνης τοῖς μὴ παρέργως ἀκούουσιν ἐνδεικνύμενος ὁ ποιητής, ἡνίκα | ἂν λέγῃ [Ξ 203].

**ὅτε τε Κρόνον εὐρύοπα Ζεὺς
γαίης νέρθε κάθισε.**

overseership over a craft, namely, that of the smith, since the providence of the gods receives its orderly procession from the universal, unified causes above and extends down to the last fragmentation. Further, it should be no surprise that this Hephaestus should rejoice in the preservation of his portion [fire] and should be unfavorably disposed toward the causes of the destruction of its substance. Furthermore, war exists in these classes along with divisions of all sorts of powers and harmony and disharmony with one another and fragmented sympathy with the administered beings and verbal disputes and mocking defenses and all the other things of the sort that are realistically imagined concerning the very last of the divine orders. For this reason also, the myths, in describing such powers fighting and opposing one another over the beings for whom they have providential care, would not overshoot the truth about them, since the passions of those under their management are transferred directly back to themselves.

[f. The two explanations and their relevance to Homer]

In summary, there are two [patterns of] meaning that are observed in the wars [of the gods] that the Phoebus-inspired poets narrate again and again, the first of which is concerned with the two principles[130] of the universe, introduced by the cause, || transcendent over everything, of the One, and this conceives in a systematic manner the division of the classes of the divine, attributing the contrariety between them to their antithetical natures. Whether we are to call these first entities "Limit and Unlimited" or "monad and indefinite dyad," there is in any case a sort of natural polarization separating them and according to which the legions of the gods are divided from one another. The other pattern, starting from the contrariety of the [daemonic] beings on the lowest level and their diversity, refers this sort of division back to their immediate superiors, postulating that the gods, by thus entering into material nature and being fragmented by it, "make war" on each other. To careful listeners, the poet will clearly be referring to the first conception when he says,

> ... when farseeing Zeus
> put Kronos beneath the earth... [*Il.* 14.203–204],

---

130. The monad and the dyad.

καὶ περὶ τοῦ Τυφῶνος ἐν ἄλλοις [Β 781]·

**γαῖα δ' ὑπεστενάχιζε Διῒ ὡς τερπικεραύνῳ |
χωομένῳ, ὅτε τ' ἀμφὶ Τυφωέϊ γαῖαν ἱμάσσῃ
εἰν Ἀρίμοις, ὅθι φασὶ Τυφωέος ἔμμεναι εὐνάς.**

πάντως γάρ που τὸν πρὸς τὸν Δία πόλεμον ἐν τούτοις αἰνίσσεται τὸν Τιτανικὸν καὶ τὰς καλουμένας καταταρταρώσεις παρὰ τοῖς Ὀρφικοῖς· διαφερόντως δὲ αὖ κατὰ τὴν | δευτέραν <u>ἐπιβολὴν</u> τοὺς θεοὺς πολεμοῦντας ἀλλήλοις καὶ διαφερομένους περὶ τῶν ἀνθρωπίνων παραδιδοὺς (ἐν οἷς καὶ σφόδρα ἄν τις ἀγασθείη τὴν ἔνθεον τοῦ ποιητοῦ καὶ νοερὰν τῶν πλασμάτων διάθεσιν· ἐπεὶ γὰρ ταῦτα τὰ γένη περὶ αὐτὰ τὸν πόλεμον τοῦτον ὑφίστασθαί φησιν, εἰ καὶ | τὰς ἀποπερατώσεις ἐκληρώσατο τῶν θείων προόδων, ἀλλ' || οὖν καὶ αὐτὰ τῶν θεῶν ἐξήρτηται καὶ ἔστι προσεχῆ μὲν τοῖς διοικουμένοις, συγγενῆ δὲ τοῖς αὐτῶν ἡγεμόσιν) τὴν μὲν πρὸς τὰ καταδεέστερα συμπάθειαν αὐτῶν ἐνδείκνυται τὴν [δὲ] διῃρημένην ζωὴν καὶ τὴν μάχην καὶ τὴν ἀντί|θεσιν ἀπὸ τούτων εἰς αὐτὰ ἀναφέρων (ὥσπερ δὴ καὶ Ὀρφεὺς τοῖς Διονυσιακοῖς εἰδώλοις τὰς συνθέσεις καὶ τὰς διαιρέσεις καὶ τοὺς θρήνους προσῆψεν ἀπὸ τῶν προνοουμένων ἅπαντα ταῦτα ἐκείνοις ἀναθείς), τὴν δὲ πρὸς τὰς σειρὰς ἀφ' ὧν προεληλύθασι συγγένειαν τῶν μεριστῶν τούτων | πνευμάτων παρίστησιν τοῖς τε

and elsewhere, about Typhon,

> The earth beneath groaned as if at the anger of Zeus,
> who delights in thunder, when he heaps the earth high around Typhon
> among the Arimoi, where, they say, is his resting place [*Il.* 2.781–783],

for here at any rate he alludes to the war of the Titans against Zeus and to what the Orphics call "katatartaroseis" [or castings into Tartarus].[131]

[Homer], however, particularly presents the gods fighting with one another and having differences with one another over human matters according to the second of the two conceptions.[132] In these passages one might particularly wonder at the poet's divine and intellective disposition of the fictions. He says that these [daemonic] ranks bring this war upon themselves for the sake of these things [human concerns], and though they have their place in the lowest ranks of the divine processions || these still depend on the gods and are in close proximity with the beings over whom they extend providence, while they are of like nature with their leaders.[133] He demonstrates their sympathy with those below them when he transfers to them, from [the humans], the divided existence and the battles and the oppositions [that properly belong to humanity]. (In the same way, Orpheus associated combinations and separations and lamentations with the images of Dionysus, taking all these things from the beings over whom providential care is extended and attributing them to the images.)[134] Homer furthermore expresses the fact that these fragmented spirits are of

---

131. See *Orph. frag.* 57, 58, 122, 220 (and cf. 215) (Kern).

132. Accepting (with F.) Kroll's conjecture ἐπιβολήν for the manuscript's ὑπερβολήν.

133. That is, the daemonic manifestations of the gods that are depicted in the poems are literally "related" (συγγενῆ) to the leaders of the troops, who are in large part the children of those same gods.

134. The "images" here are, according to F., to be equated with the image of himself that Dionysus sees in the mirror by which the Titans lure him to destruction (= fragmentation, cf. *Orph. frag.* 210 [Kern]; Plotinus, *Enn.* 4.3.12; Olympiodorus, *In Phd.* 111.14–16 [Norvin], etc.; West 1983, 74, 140, and *passim*). The prominence of Dionysus in the Orphic poetry is enough to explain the mention of Orpheus here, but another passage in Proclus (*In Tim.* 1:336,29–337,3 [Diehl], also cited by F.) complicates the reference: "Orpheus fashions replicas (εἴδωλα) of Dionysus which preside

ὀνόμασιν τοῖς αὐτοῖς, δι' ὧν τὰς ἐξῃρημένας δυνάμεις τῶν ἐνύλων ἐξύμνησεν, καὶ τοῖς ἀριθμοῖς καὶ τοῖς σχήμασι προσήκουσι ταῖς ὅλαις αὐτῶν διακοσμήσεσι χρώμενος.

Εἰσὶ μὲν γὰρ οἱ τοῦ πολέμου κοινωνοῦντες ἕνδεκα τὸν ἀριθμόν, μιμούμενοι τὴν ἑπομένην | τῷ Διῒ θεῶν τε καὶ δαιμόνων στρατείαν, κατὰ ἕνδεκα μέρη κεκοσμημένην. τούτων δὲ οἱ μὲν τῆς κρείττονος προεστῶτες συστοιχίας τῇ πεντάδι συνέχονται (καὶ γὰρ τὸ περιττὸν καὶ τὸ σφαιρικὸν καὶ τὸ κατὰ δίκην πάντα ἄγειν τὰ δεύτερα καὶ ἐκ μέσου διατείνειν ἐπὶ πάντα τὸν ἀριθμὸν οἰκεῖόν | ἐστιν τοῖς τὰ νοερώτερα καὶ τὰ τελειότερα καὶ πρὸς τοῦ ἑνὸς ὄντα κρατεῖν ἐθέλουσιν), οἱ δὲ τῆς ὑφειμένης μοίρας κηδεμόνες τῶν ἐνύλων κατὰ τὴν ἑξάδα προεληλύθασιν, τὸ μὲν τελεσιουργὸν τῶν προνοουμένων ἔχοντες διὰ τὸν οἰκεῖον ἀριθμόν, τῷ δὲ ἀρτίῳ καὶ πρὸς τὴν χείρονα φύσιν συστοίχῳ | λειπόμενοι τῶν πρὸ αὐτῶν. οὐ δὴ θαυμαστόν ἐστιν, εἰ καὶ θεούς· τις ἀποκαλοίη ταῦτα τὰ γένη διὰ τὴν πρὸς τοὺς ἡγεμόνας συγγένειαν καὶ πολεμοῦντας παράγοι διὰ τὴν περὶ τὰ τῇδε προσεχῆ κηδεμονίαν.

Ἡ μὲν οὖν τοῦ Ποσειδῶνος καὶ τοῦ Ἀπόλλωνος ἀντίθεσις τὴν τῶν ὑπὸ σελήνην | πάντων ὁλικῶν προΐσταται δοκοῦσαν ἐναντίωσιν (διὸ καὶ || οὐδὲ μάχονται οἵδε οἱ θεοί· σῴζεται γὰρ ὑπὸ τῶν ὁλικῶν τὰ ἐν αὐτοῖς μερικά, καθ' ὅσον ἂν ᾖ χρόνον), ἡ δὲ τῆς Ἥρας καὶ τῆς Ἀρτέμιδος τὴν τῶν ἐνταῦθα ψυχῶν λογικῶν ἢ ἀλόγων, χωριστῶν ἢ ἀχωρίστων, ὑπερφυῶν ἢ φυσικῶν | παρίστησιν ἀντιδιαίρεσιν, τῆς μὲν αἰτίας οὔσης τῶν ἀμεινόνων, τῆς δὲ τὰ χείρω λοχευούσης καὶ εἰς φῶς προαγούσης. ἡ δὲ τῆς Ἀθηνᾶς καὶ τοῦ Ἄρεως τὴν παντὸς τοῦ γενεσιουργοῦ πολέμου διάκρισιν παρίστησιν εἰς τὴν κατὰ νοῦν πρόνοιαν αὐτῶν καὶ τὴν δι' ἀνάγκης ἐπιτελουμένην, |

the same nature as the chains from which they emerge by applying to them the same names he used to sing the praises of the powers that transcend the material and by using the numbers and shapes appropriate to the total orders.

Eleven is the number [of the gods] that take part in the war, imitating the army of gods and daemons that follows Zeus and that is drawn up in eleven divisions [cf. *Phdr.* 246e]. Those who preside over the better column[135] are bound to the *pentad*, for the odd and the spherical, the just management of all secondaries and the capacity to extend from the center to the whole range of number are all appropriate to those who wish to grasp that which is more intellective and more perfect and stems from the One. Those who look after the lower portion[136] of beings bound to matter proceed according to the *hexad*, having the capacity to perfect the beings over whom they extend providential care through the possession of the appropriate number, yet inferior to the previous group because of their association with evenness and the worse nature.

It is no wonder, then, that one should call these classes gods, because of their common origin with those superior to them, and yet depict them at war because of their intimate concern with the things of this world.

The opposition of Poseidon and Apollo projects ‖ the apparent contrariety of all the universals in the sublunary realm (and for this reason these gods do not fight, for the partial realities within the universals are preserved by them for as long as [these universals] exist).[137] The opposition of Hera and Artemis represents the natural dichotomy in this world between souls that are rational and those that are irrational, those detached [from the body] and those undetached, those beyond the natural world and those ensconced in it, since [Hera] is the cause that produces superior beings while [Artemis] acts as midwife to inferior ones and brings them to the light. The opposition of Athena and Ares represents the division that the war that is constitutive of this world creates between that accomplished

---

over the process of becoming" (trans. Runia and Share 2008). The relationship of these "replicas" to the image(s) in the mirror is unclear.

135. I.e., the Greeks.

136. I.e., the Trojans.

137. As F. points out ad loc., Poseidon presides over γένεσις and hence over the cycle of coming to be and passing away and Apollo collaborates with Zeus in maintaining the order of the cosmos. Cf. the description of the role of Apollo above in Question 10 of Essay 5.

τῆς μὲν νοερῶς προεστώσης τῶν ἐναντίων, τοῦ δὲ τὰς φυσικὰς αὐτῶν δυνάμεις ῥωννύντος καὶ κατ' ἀλλήλων ἐγείροντος. ἡ δὲ τοῦ Ἑρμοῦ καὶ τῆς Λητοῦς τὴν κατὰ τὰς γνωστικὰς καὶ τὰς ζωτικὰς κινήσεις τῶν ψυχῶν [τὰς] παντοίαν διαφοράν, τοῦ μὲν τὰς γνώσεις τελειοῦντος, τῆς δὲ | τὰς ζωάς, ᾗ καὶ πολλάκις αὗται διΐστανται ἀπ' ἀλλήλων καὶ ἐναντίως ἔχουσιν πρὸς ἀλλήλας. λοιπὴ δὲ ἡ τοῦ Ἡφαίστου καὶ Ξάνθου τοῦ ποταμοῦ τὰς τῆς σωματικῆς ὅλης συστάσεως ἐναντίας ἀρχὰς διακοσμεῖ δεόντως, τοῦ μὲν τῆς θερμότητος καὶ τῆς ξηρότητος τὰς δυνάμεις συγκροτοῦντος, | τοῦ δὲ τῆς ψυχρότητος καὶ ὑγρότητος· ἐξ ὧν ἡ πᾶσα συμπληροῦται γένεσις. ἐπεὶ δὲ πάσας ἀνάγκη τὰς ἐναντιώσεις εἰς τὴν πρὸς ἀλλήλας ὁμολογίαν τελευτᾶν, πάρεστι καὶ ἡ Ἀφροδίτη, καθάπερ εἴπομεν, φιλίαν ἐμποιοῦσα τοῖς ἀντικειμένοις, συμμαχοῦσα δὲ ὅμως τοῖς χείροσιν, διότι καὶ | ταῦτα μάλιστα κοσμεῖται σύμμετρα καὶ προσήγορα γινόμενα τοῖς ἀμείνοσι τῶν ἐναντίων.

Περὶ μὲν οὖν τῆς παρ' Ὁμήρῳ θεομαχίας τοσαῦτα εἰρήσθω. καὶ γὰρ ἔξεστιν τοῖς περὶ αὐτῆς ἀκριβέστερόν τι πιέσαι βουλομένοις καὶ ταῖς τοῦ καθηγεμόνος ἡμῶν θεωρίαις συγγενέσθαι πολλὰ καὶ θαυμαστὰ | δόγματα ἐκκαλυπτούσαις, ἃς ἐν ταῖς λύσεσιν ἐκεῖνος τῶν Ὁμηρικῶν προβλημάτων ἐπραγματεύσατο.

Πῶς ἄν τις ὑπὲρ τῶν θείων ἀπολογήσαιτο μύθων τῶν δοκούντων τοὺς θεοὺς αἰτιᾶσθαι τῶν κακῶν.

Ἡμεῖς δὲ ἐντεῦθεν ἐπὶ τὰ ἑξῆς τῶν Σωκρατικῶν πρὸς Ὅμηρον ἀπορημάτων μετίωμεν. ἕπεται δὲ οἶμαι διασκέψασθαι, | πῶς τῶν θεῶν κατὰ τὴν ἀγαθότητα διαφερόντως τὴν ὕπαρξιν λαχόντων ἡ ποίησις κακῶν τε καὶ ἀγαθῶν αἰτιᾶται τοὺς θεούς, δέοντος τῶν ἀγαθῶν μόνων ἐπ' αὐτοὺς ἀναπέμπειν τὴν ἀρχηγὸν αἰτίαν. ταῦτα γὰρ ὁ Σωκράτης ἀποδείξας, τὸν θεὸν τῶν ἀγαθῶν ὑποστάτην μόνων, κακοῦ δὲ οὐδενός, | ἐπιστάσεως ἠξίωσεν ἐν τοῖς Ὁμήρου ποιήμασιν· καὶ ἔοικεν τὴν μὲν θεομαχίαν ὡς

through intellective providence and that accomplished through necessity, since she presides intellectively over the opposites and he strengthens their physical powers and urges them on against each other. The opposition of Hermes and Leto represents the whole complex division between the intellectual and the vital in the impulses of the soul (for he brings perfection to wisdom and she to lives), in that[138] these are often separate from one another and stand in opposition. Finally, the opposition of Hephaestus and the river Xanthos necessarily musters the opposing first principles within the whole composition of bodies, with Hephaestus combining the powers of hotness and dryness and Xanthos those of coolness and wetness. These properties complete the whole of γένεσις. Since of necessity all oppositions must end in concord, Aphrodite is also present, as we said, introducing affection between the antagonists, but fighting on the worse side because these are the ones that are drawn into order as they enter into harmony and agreement with the better powers of their enemies.[139]

Enough, then, of Homer's theomachy, for it is possible for those wanting to squeeze something more precise from his account of these things to look likewise into my teacher's theories, which reveal many wondrous doctrines and which he treated at length in his work entitled "Solutions to Homeric Problems." ||

(4) How one might defend the myths about the divine that appear to attribute the causes of bad things to the gods.

[a. The problem]

Let us move on from this to the further Socratic objections to Homer. The next thing to do seems to be to consider how the poetry holds the gods responsible for both good and bad, when it should refer to them the primary cause only of good things, since the gods' existence is preeminently a function of goodness. Socrates, after demonstrating that the god is the creator only of good things and never of bad, thought these things a problem in Homer's poetry. Just as he seemed to censure the theomachy

---

138. Reading, with F., ἦ for the manuscript's εἰ, from Kroll's apparatus.
139. F. refers the reader to the parallel passage *In Tim.* 1:78,26–79,19 (Diehl), in which Proclus gives much the same account of the theomachia he gives here. Both passages are presumably heavily dependent on the lost work of Syrianus to which reference is made just below.

ἀναιρετικὴν τῆς θείας ἑνώσεως εὐθύνειν, ταῦτα δὲ ἃ νῦν πρόκειται ζητεῖν ὡς τῆς ἀγαθότητος τῶν θεῶν ἐλαττωτικὰ διελέγχειν.

**δοιοὶ γάρ τε πίθοι κατακείαται ἐν Διὸς οὔδει, |
κηρῶν ἔμπλειοι ὁ μὲν ἐσθλῶν, αὐτὰρ ὁ δειλῶν** [Ω 527–528].

Πρὸς δὴ τὰς τοιαύτας ἀπαντήσεις λεγέσθω διττὰς εἶναι τὰς συστοιχίας τῶν ἐν τῷ κόσμῳ πραγμάτων, ὃ καὶ πρότερον εἴπομεν, ἄνωθεν ὡρμημένας ἀπ' αὐτῶν τῶν θεῶν. | πάντα γὰρ διῄρηται ταῖς δυοειδέσιν τῶν ὄντων ἀρχαῖς, αἱ τῶν θεῶν διακοσμήσεις, αἱ τῶν ὄντων ὑποστάσεις, τὰ γένη τῶν ψυχῶν, αἱ φυσικαὶ δυνάμεις, αἱ τοῦ οὐρανοῦ περιφοραί, αἱ τῶν ἐνύλων διαφορότητες· τελευτῶσα δὲ ἡ δίδυμος αὕτη τῶν πραγμάτων πρόοδος καὶ τῶν περὶ τοὺς ἀνθρώ|πους συμπιπτόντων καὶ κατὰ δίκην ἀποκληρουμένων διπλῆν προεστήσατο γένεσιν. καὶ γὰρ τούτων τὰ μέν ἐστι τῆς κρείττονος μοίρας, τὰ δὲ τῆς ὑποδεεστέρας· λέγω δὲ οἷον τὰς μὲν τῶν σωμάτων κατὰ φύσιν διαθέσεις, κάλλος καὶ ἰσχὺν || καὶ εὐεξίαν, καὶ τῶν ἐκτὸς τῆς σωματικῆς συστάσεως συγκυρούντων ταῖς ψυχαῖς, τάς τε δυνάμεις καὶ τὰς τιμὰς καὶ τοὺς πλούτους τῆς ἑτέρας εἶναι συστοιχίας, τὰς δὲ αὖ τούτοις ἀντικειμένας ἕξεις τε καὶ περιστάσεις τῆς χείρονος. |

Τούτων δὴ οὖν κατὰ τὸν εἰρημένον τρόπον ἐξ ἀνάγκης διῃρημένων τὰ μὲν ὡς τῆς ἀμείνονος ὄντα μερίδος αὐτόθεν ἀγαθὰ τοῖς παλαιοῖς ἔθος προσαγορεύειν, τὰ δὲ ὡς τῆς ἐναντίας κακὰ προσονομάζουσιν· καὶ οὐχ οὕτω τὸ κακὸν ἐνταῦθα δήπου λέγουσιν, ὡς τὴν ἄδικον καὶ ἀκόλαστον | τῆς ψυχῆς ἕξιν κακὸν ὁμολογοῦμεν ὑπάρχειν· ἀλλ' ὡς τὰ ἐμπόδια τῶν ἐνεργειῶν καὶ τὰ ἐπιπροσθοῦντα ταῖς κατὰ φύσιν ἡμῶν διαθέσεσιν καὶ τὰ διακόπτοντα τῆς ψυχῆς τὴν μετὰ ῥᾳστώνης ἀποτελουμένην τῶν ἀνθρωπίνων πρόνοιαν κακὰ συγχωροῦσιν εἶναι καὶ λέγεσθαι τρόπον ἕτερον τῶν | αὐτῆς τῆς ψυχῆς λεγομένων κακῶν, οὕτως ἄρα καὶ τὴν νόσον καὶ τὴν ἀδυναμίαν καὶ τὴν ἄπορον τῶν ἀναγκαίων ζωὴν ἐν τοῖς κακοῖς εἰώθασι καταλέγειν.

Καὶ τί δεῖ τὴν ποίησιν ἅπασαν μαρτύρεσθαι τῆς τοῦ ὀνόματος ἕνεκα χρήσεως; ἀλλὰ καὶ ὁ τῶν Πυθαγορείων λόγος ὁ τὰς διττὰς | τῶν ὄντων

for destroying the oneness of the divine, he seems as well to want to find fault with the following verses for diminishing the goodness of the gods:

> For two jars lie on Zeus's threshold, the one
> filled with noble fates, but the other with miserable ones.
> [*Il.* 24.527–528][140]

Against such objections let it be said first of all that there are two series of things in the universe, as we said above,[141] coming down from above and having their source in the gods themselves. All things are divided according to the twofold first principles of reality: the orders of the gods, the substances of things that are, the classes of souls, the forces of nature, the orbits of the heavens, the differences in material things. At its extremity, this twin procession of reality has created a dichotomy in those things that happen to men and are justly assigned to them, for of these accidents some belong to the better class and some to the worse. For example, I am speaking of the natural dispositions of the body—beauty, strength, ‖ and well-being—and those things that happen to souls independent of the makeup of the body—powers, honor, riches—these all belong to the first series. The opposite dispositions and circumstances belong to the worse one.

Since these things are, of necessity, divided in the manner just described, the ancients were in the habit of simply calling some things "good," on the basis that they were of the better portion, and others, since they were of the opposite series, "bad." In this they certainly did not use the word as we do when we agree that the criminal and undisciplined condition of the soul is "bad." Rather, as the obstacles to our actions and that which stands in the way of our natural dispositions and the things that prevent the easy accomplishment of the soul's anticipations of human goals are agreed to be "bad" and are so called in a different way from the way things of the soul itself are called "bad"—in this sense, people are accustomed to list sickness and weakness and a life deprived of the necessities among the "bad" things.

But why do we need to call in the whole of poetry to bear witness to the use of this word? The doctrine of the Pythagoreans that divides things

---

140. The citation is from *Rep.* 2.379d and contains substantial variants from the received text of Homer.

141. 93–97 (K87,29– K89,9).

συστοιχίας διαιρούμενος ἐν ἁπάσαις ταῖς διακοσμήσεσιν τὴν μὲν τοῦ ἀγαθοῦ καλεῖν οὐκ ἀπηξίου, τὴν δὲ τοῦ κακοῦ· καίτοι τό γε ἄρτιον ἢ τὸ ἑτερόμηκες ἢ τὴν κίνησιν πῶς ἄν τις ἐν τοῖς τοιούτοις τετάχθαι κακοῖς συγχωρήσειεν, ὅσα τῶν ἀγαθῶν στερήσεις ἀφοριζόμεθα; πῶς δ' ἂν τὸ θῆλυ καὶ τὸ τῆς ἑτερότητος γένος καὶ [τὸ] τὴν ἀνομοιότητα παρὰ φύσιν εἶναι τοῖς οὖσιν φήσαιμεν; ἀλλ' οἶμαι παντὶ δὴ τοῦτο καταφανές, ὅτι τῶν ἀντικειμένων κατὰ πάσας τῶν ὄντων τὰς προόδους τὴν καταδεεστέραν σειρὰν ὡς ἀπολειπομένην τῆς ἑτέρας καὶ οὔτε πρώτως οὖσαν ἀγαθουργὸν οὔτε τὴν αὐτὴν λαχοῦσαν ἀπόστασιν πρὸς τὴν μίαν τῶν καλῶν πάντων καὶ ἀγαθῶν αἰτίαν κακὸν προσηγόρευεν.

Ταύτας τοίνυν τὰς διττὰς συστοιχίας τῶν τε ἀγαθῶν καὶ τῶν κακῶν τῶν ἐν τῷ κόσμῳ γεγονότων τῆς δημιουργικῆς ἐξάπτειν προσήκει μονάδος. καὶ γὰρ αἱ τῶν θεῶν διαιρέσεις καὶ αἱ τῶν μετὰ θεοὺς γενῶν εἰς ἐκείνην ἀνήρτηνται τὴν πρωτίστην ἀρχήν· καὶ τῶν καθ' εἱμαρμένην συμπιπτόντων καὶ κατὰ δίκην ταῖς ψυχαῖς περὶ τὴν γένεσιν ἀποκληρουμένων ἀγαθῶν τε καὶ κακῶν ἐν τῷ διακοσμήσαντι τὸ πᾶν καὶ τὰς ψυχὰς εἰς τὸν θνητὸν τόπον καταπέμποντι τὴν αἰτίαν ὑποθετέον. καὶ γὰρ ἡ τῆς εἱμαρμένης ποίησις τῆς δημιουργικῆς ἐξέχεται προνοίας, καὶ ἡ τῆς δίκης σειρὰ περὶ ἐκείνην ὑφέστηκεν καὶ ἕπεται τοῖς ἐκείνου ὅροις, **τοῦ θείου νόμου τιμωρὸς** οὖσα, φησὶν ὁ Ἀθηναῖος ξένος [Leg. 4.716a], καὶ ἡ τῆς τύχης ἀποπληρωτικὴ τῶν κατὰ δίκην διανεμομένων προμηθία κατὰ τὴν τοῦ πατρὸς ἀφορίζεται βούλησιν. πάντων ἄρα τῶν ἀγαθῶν τε καὶ κακῶν, τῶν τε βελτιόνων ἐν ταῖς δόσεσιν καὶ τῶν χειρόνων, τῶν τε εὐμοιροτέρων ὁμοῦ καὶ τῶν ἐμποδιστικῶν τῆς τῶν ψυχῶν εἰς τὰ ἐκτὸς ἐνεργείας τὴν αἰτίαν ὁ δημιουργὸς καὶ πατὴρ ἐν ἑαυτῷ προεστήσατο καὶ πάντα κατὰ νοῦν ποδηγεῖ, διανέμων ἑκάστοις τὰ προσήκοντα καὶ πρὸς τὴν ἑαυτοῦ πατρονομικὴν ἐπιστασίαν ἀνάγων τὰ πάντα. καὶ γὰρ ταῖς ψυχαῖς τά τε τῆς κρείττονος συστοιχίας καὶ τὰ τῆς καταδεεστέρας διανέμει πρὸς τὸ ἀγαθὸν βλέπων καὶ τῆς τῶν δεχομένων ἕνεκα τελειότητος.

Εἰ δὴ ταῦτα ὀρθῶς εἴπομεν, ἀποδεξόμεθα καὶ τὴν Ὁμηρικὴν διάταξιν ἐν τῷ δημιουργικῷ νῷ τοῦ Διὸς τὰς διττὰς ὑποτιθεμένην καὶ πρωτουργοὺς

into two columns did not refuse to designate one column as that of the "good" and the other of the "bad." Yet how could one agree that "the even," "the rectangle," or "movement" should be placed in that class of "bad" things that we define by deprivation of "good" things? How could we claim that "the female," the category of "otherness," or "dissimilarity" are things that, for real entities, are against nature? No, I think it is perfectly clear to all that, among the columns of opposites throughout all the processions of things, [the doctrine] called the lesser chain "bad" because it was inferior to the other, was not a producer of good in a primary sense, and stood at a greater distance from || the single cause of all good and beautiful things.

Now, these two columns of good and bad things that exist in the world should be set in relation to the creative monad. The divisions of the gods and of the classes below the gods depend on this first cause, and the cause of those things, good and evil, that are the lot of souls in the sphere of γένεσις, and fall to them by fate and justice, is to be assigned to the organizer of the universe and the one who sends souls into the mortal sphere. The action of fate depends on the providence of the creator, and the chain of justice was set up about this and follows his definitions, since, according to the Athenian Stranger, "[Justice] is the avenger of divine law" [*Leg.* 4.716a]. The providence of fortune in accomplishing those things assigned according to justice is defined by the will of the father. Therefore, of all good and bad things, of better and worse gifts, of all that is a better portion and of all those other things that are obstacles to the actions of souls on externals, of all these things the demiurge and father established the cause *in himself* and he directs everything according to his intellect, assigning what is appropriate to each and drawing all things under his paternal government. He assigns to souls the things of the better or worse columns while contemplating the Good and for the sake of the perfection of the recipients.

[b. Interpretation of Homer's two pithoi]

If what we have said is true, we shall also accept the Homeric arrangement, placing the two primally creative causes in[142] the demiurgic mind

---

142. F., in a note ad loc., defends his translation "en presence de" (rather than "dans"), based both on the Homeric verses (24.527–528) and the paraphrases that immediately follow. The issue, however, is the responsibility of the "creative monad"

αἰτίας τῶν τε ἀγα|θῶν, ὧν δίδωσι ταῖς ψυχαῖς, καὶ τῶν κακῶν· ἐπεὶ καὶ ἡ δυὰς πάντων μάλιστα προσήκει τῶν νοερῶν βασιλέων τῷ || δημιουργῷ τοῦ παντός (**δυὰς γὰρ παρὰ τῷδε κάθηται,** φησὶν τὸ λογίον), καὶ τὸ κυβερνᾶν τὰ πάντα καὶ τάττειν ἕκαστον, οὗ ταχθὲν νικῶσαν μὲν ἀρετὴν ἐν τῷ παντί, κακίαν δὲ ἡττωμένην <u>ἀποδείξει</u>. τί γὰρ διαφέρει ταῦτά τε λέγειν | καὶ πεττευτῇ τὸν δημιουργὸν εἰκάζειν, μετατιθέντι τὰς ψυχὰς εἰς τοὺς προσήκοντας αὐταῖς βίους ἑκάστην.

Δύο τοίνυν αὗται πηγαί, τῶν τε βελτιόνων καὶ τῶν χειρόνων μέτρων, οἷς ὁ δημιουργὸς κατὰ δίκην ἄγει τὰς ψυχάς, νοείσθωσαν· ἃς ὁ ποιητὴς μυθολογῶν πίθους προσείρηκεν, εἴθ' ὅτι διὰ | πειθοῦς νοερᾶς πᾶσιν ἐπιβάλλει τὸν οἰκεῖον ὅρον (**ἀρχὴ γάρ,** φησὶν ὁ Τίμαιος [48a], **τῆς ἀνάγκης ὁ νοῦς τῷ πείθειν αὐτὴν πάντα πρὸς τὸ βέλτιστον ἄγειν**), εἴτε καὶ τὸ χωρητικὸν αὐτῶν καὶ περιληπτικὸν τῶν παντοδαπῶν καὶ ποικίλων ἀποτελεσμάτων ἐνδεικνύμενος· τὸ γὰρ διεσπαρμένον | πλῆθος πάντων ὧν διανέμει ταῖς ψυχαῖς ὁ πατὴρ <ἐν> ἐκείναις ἡνωμένως προείληπται.

Ὥστε καὶ κατὰ τοῦτον τὸν λόγον συνᾴδουσιν ἀλλήλοις ὅ τε Πλάτων καὶ ἡ Ὁμηρικὴ ποίησις. ὁ μὲν γὰρ οὐδενὸς κακοῦ φησιν χρῆναι τὸν θεὸν αἰτιᾶσθαι, ἡ δὲ πάντα μὲν ἐκεῖθεν παράγει τὰ ἀγαθά, διττὰ | δὲ ὄντα καὶ ὠφελητικὰ τῶν δεχομένων ἑκάτερα ταῖς διτταῖς συστοιχίαις διελοῦσα καὶ τὴν πρὸς ἄλληλα διαφορὰν αὐτῶν ἐνδεικνυμένη τὰ μὲν ὡς ἀγαθά, τὰ

of Zeus, both that of the good things he gives to souls and that of the bad. The dyad ‖ is also most appropriate, among the intellective kings,[143] to the demiurge of the universe ("for the dyad sits beside him," says the oracle [*Or. chald.* frag. 8, des Places]), as are the governing of all things and placing each thing [in the universal order] where it will make[144] virtue universally victorious and evil the loser. What is the difference between saying this and comparing the demiurge to a petteia player moving each soul to the life that is appropriate to it [*Leg.* 10.903d]?[145]

Now then, imagine two springs, respectively of better and worse measures, by which the demiurge directs souls, according to justice. The poet in his myth called them pithoi, either because through intellective "persuasion"[146] he imposes its proper defining limit on each entity (for Timaeus says, "Mind is the first principle of necessity by virtue of persuading her to draw everything toward the best" [*Tim.* 48a]),[147] or he might be showing their vastness, their capacity to contain the whole enormous variety and complexity of created things, for the father has previously embraced in unity the scattered abundance of all these things he portions out to souls.

Thus, according to this reasoning as well, Plato and Homeric poetry are in harmony. He says that the god must be held responsible for no evil, while the poetry derives all good things from the god, dividing them into the two columns because they are of two sorts, [both] beneficial to their recipients, and showing the difference between them, it established one category as "goods" and separated the other category from them as the

---

(K98,4), which is to say, Zeus, for both columns of "accidentals." In light of this, it seems best to retain the more direct statement.

143. F. refers to *In Tim.* 1:306,1–13 (Diehl; see now Runia and Share 2008, 160–61) for clarification of the doctrine of the three kings/intellects, as articulated by Plotinus's student Amelius (and supported by citations of Plato and Orpheus).

144. Accepting ἀποδείξει in line 4 from Kroll's apparatus, for the manuscript's ἀποδείξειεν.

145. πέττεια was the most widespread of Greek board games (and a favorite metaphor of Plato's, occurring at least ten times in the corpus). In spite of this, the rules and even the goal of the game remain unclear. Proclus's point here, in any case, is that Homer's formulation at *Il.* 24.527–528 is entirely compatible with Plato's (at, e.g., *Leg.* 10.903d).

146. From the similarity of sound between the words *pithos* (storage jar) and *peitho* (persuasion).

147. Again, a paraphrase rather than an exact quotation.

δὲ ὡς ἐναντία τοῖς ἀγαθοῖς ἀπ' ἐκείνων διέστησεν. καὶ ὅτι τὸ λεγόμενον κακὸν οὐ τοιοῦτόν ἐστιν, ὁποῖον ὁ τοῦ Πλάτωνος λόγος τῆς δό|σεως τῶν θεῶν ἀπέφησεν, δηλοῖ που καὶ αὐτὸς ἐπιφέρων ἑξῆς·

**ὡς μὲν καὶ Πηλῆϊ θεοὶ δόσαν ἀγλαὰ δῶρα
ἐκ γενετῆς.
ἀλλ' ἐπὶ καὶ τῷ θῆκε θεὸς κακόν** [Ω 534–535, 538]. ||

τί οὖν τοῦτό ἐστιν τὸ κακόν, αὐτὸς προστίθησιν·

**ὅττι οἱ οὔ τι
παίδων ἐν μεγάροισι γονὴ γένετο κρειόντων,
ἀλλ' ἕνα παῖδα τέκεν παναώριον· οὐδέ νυ τόν γε |
γηράσκοντα κομίζω.** [Ω 538–541]

μή σοι δοκεῖ τῶν ἀληθινῶν κακῶν αἰτιᾶσθαι τὸν θεόν; οὐ τὴν ἐρημίαν τῶν παίδων, οὐ τὴν ἀθεραπευσίαν κακὰ προσείρηκεν. καὶ ὅπως ταῦτα κακὰ προείπομεν, δυσκολίαν περὶ τὸν τῇδε βίον καὶ δυσθυμίαν ἐναπεργαζόμενα ταῖς | ψυχαῖς; ταῦτα γὰρ εἰ καὶ τοῖς γνησίως φιλοσοφοῦσιν κακὰ προσαγορεύειν οὐ θέμις, ἀλλὰ τοῖς τὸν πρακτικὸν βίον ἑλομένοις ἐμπόδια φαίνεται τῆς κατ' ἀρετὴν εἶναι ζωῆς. διὸ καὶ ὁ Ἀθηναῖος ξένος [Leg. 2.661b–d] τὰ τοιαῦτα πάντα τοῖς μὲν ἀγαθοῖς εἶναί που κακὰ διατείνεται, τοῖς δὲ πονη|ροῖς ἀγαθά· καίτοι καὶ τούτων αἰτιᾶται τὸν θεὸν καὶ τῶν ἐκ τοῦ παντὸς ἐνδιδομένων ἁπάντων, ὥστε οὐχ Ὅμηρος μόνος καὶ ὁ παρ' Ὁμήρῳ ταῦτά φασιν Ἀχιλλεύς, ἀλλὰ καὶ ὁ Πλάτων αὐτὸς καὶ ὁ κατ' αὐτὸν νομοθέτης.

**Πῶς τὴν τῶν ὅρκων σύγχυσιν δοκεῖ ἡ ποίησις εἰς |
θεοὺς ἀναπέμπειν, ἡ ἀληθὴς περὶ αὐτῶν ὑφήγησις.**

opposite of "goods." That what the poetry calls "bad" things are not such as the Platonic passage denies belong to the gifts of the gods, Homer himself shows, it seems, in the verses that come just after [the description of the jars]:

> And so, the gods gave dazzling gifts to Peleus, too,
> from birth ...
> but on top of this, the god added a bad one. [*Il.* 24.534–535, 538] ||

What is this "bad" thing [that Achilles says that Peleus received from the gods]? He himself goes on:

> ... that he had no progeny
> of kingly sons grow up in his halls
> but fathered only one son, doomed to die young. And now,
> I am no help to him in his old age. [*Il.* 24.538–541]

Surely it does not seem to you that in this passage he attributes to the gods the cause of true evils, does it? Does he not identify the "bad" things as lack of children, lack of a son to care for him, using "bad" here in the sense we defined above: they produce discontent and discouragement in the soul with regard to this life?[148] Even if it is not right for true philosophers to call such things "bad," to those who have chosen the active life they seem to be obstacles to a life of excellence. Thus the Athenian Stranger maintains that all such things are in a sense bad for the good and good for the wicked [*Leg.* 2.661d].[149] Nevertheless, he blames the god for these things as well as everything else that the universe gives us, so that it is not only Homer and his Achilles who say this but also Plato and his lawmaker.

(5) How the poem seems to give the gods responsibility for the breaking of the oaths; the true guidance in these matters.

---

148. I have followed F.'s lead in adding a question mark after ψυχαῖς in K100,10, but I have also suppressed Kroll's stop and question mark in K100,8.

149. The Athenian Stranger in fact maintains that long life, health, and the like are good things only in the lives of the virtuous and that the best thing for the corrupt man would be to die young. [F.]

Τοσαῦτα καὶ πρὸς ταύτην εἰρήσθω τὴν ζήτησιν· ἐφεξῆς δέ ἐστιν τοῖς εἰρημένοις θεωρῆσαι, πῶς τὴν τῶν ὅρκων σύγχυσιν καὶ τῶν σπονδῶν ἡ ποίησις κατὰ βούλησιν τοῦ μεγάλου Διὸς καὶ τῆς Ἀθηνᾶς ὑπουργούσης τῇ βουλῇ τοῦ | πατρὸς γενέσθαι φησίν· καὶ γὰρ ταύτην ὁ Σωκράτης ᾐτιάσατο τὴν τῶν κακῶν ἀρχὴν ἐπὶ τοὺς πρωτίστους τῶν θεῶν ἀναφέρουσαν. κἀνταῦθα μάλιστα διαπορεῖν ἄξιον, πῶς ὁ τῶν τοιούτων τὸν θεὸν αἰτιώμενος οὐχὶ τῶν μεγίστων αὐτὸν || αἰτιᾶται καὶ ἀληθινῶν κακῶν· οὐ γὰρ ἔτι πενίας καὶ νόσους οὐδὲ τὴν τοιαύτην συστοιχίαν ἐξέσται λέγοντας δοκεῖν τι λέγειν, ἀλλ' αὐτῶν τῶν παρὰ πᾶσιν ὁμολογουμένων ὡς κακῶν τὴν αἰτίαν ἐπὶ τὸν θεὸν ἀνοίσομεν. καὶ ὁ μὲν | Τίμαιος [42d] τὸν δημιουργὸν πρὸ τῆς εἰς γένεσιν καθόδου **διαθεσμοθετῆσαι πάντα** φησὶν **ταῖς ψυχαῖς, ἵνα τῆς ἔπειτα εἴη κακίας ἀναίτιος.** ὁ δὲ λόγος οὗτος καὶ κατελθούσαις αὐταῖς καὶ ἐν τῇ γενέσει στρεφομέναις τῶν μεγίστων κακῶν τὴν ἀρχὴν ἐκεῖθεν ἐνδίδοσθαι συγχωρεῖ. | πῶς οὖν ἄν τις πρὸς ταύτας τὰς ἐπιστάσεις τοὺς προσήκοντας ἀποδοίη λόγους, τῇ τε φύσει τῶν πραγμάτων καὶ τῇ Πλάτωνος ὑφηγήσει τὴν Ὁμήρου διδασκαλίαν συναρμόζοντας.

Ὅτι μὲν οὖν πρὸς τὴν τῶν νέων ἕξιν ἀσύμμετρός ἐστιν | ἡ τῶνδε τῶν μύθων ἀκρόασις, εἴρηταί τε πρότερον καὶ νυνὶ λεγέσθω καὶ παρὰ πάντας τοὺς ῥηθησομένους ὑφ' ἡμῶν λόγους. οὐδὲ γὰρ διακρίνειν τὰς φύσεις τῶν ὄντων τοῖς νέοις δυνατὸν οὐδὲ ἐπανάγειν τὰ φαινόμενα συνθήματα τῆς ἀληθείας πρὸς τὴν ἀφανῆ θεωρίαν οὐδὲ καθορᾶν, ὅπως | ἐν τῷ κόσμῳ πάντα κατὰ βούλησιν ἐπιτελεῖται τοῦ θεοῦ διὰ μέσων τῶν ἄλλων αἰτίων.

Ὅτι δὲ οἰκεῖα ταῦτα τῇ Πλάτωνός ἐστι φιλοσοφίᾳ δεικνύομεν. **Τὸν μὲν δὴ θεὸν ἀρχήν τε καὶ τελευτὴν καὶ μέσα τῶν ὄντων ἁπάντων ἔχειν** καὶ ὁ Ἀθηναῖος ξένος φησίν [Leg. 4.715e], **ἕπεσθαι | δὲ αὐτῷ τὴν δίκην τῶν ἀπολειπομένων οὖσαν τοῦ θείου νόμου τιμωρόν.** οὗτοι δέ εἰσιν, ὡς ὁ ἐκείνου λόγος, **οἱ νεότητι καὶ ἀνοίᾳ φλεγόμενοι τὴν ψυχὴν μεθ' ὕβρεως,** καὶ χρόνον τινὰ δόξαντες κρατεῖν ἔπειτα αὖθις τιμωρίαν ὑπέσχον τῇ δίκῃ πρέπουσαν, ἑαυτούς τε καὶ πόλιν καὶ οἶκον ἄρδην | ἀναστάτους ποιήσαντες. ταῦτα δὴ οὖν ὁ μὲν Ἀθηναῖος ξένος || πολιτικῶς, ὁ δὲ Ὅμηρος

But let us put an end to this discussion. The next matter to examine is how the poem says the violation of the oaths and treaties came about according to the will of Zeus with Athena acting as supporter of the plan of her father. Socrates blamed this [passage] for attributing the first principle of evils[150] to the very first of the gods. At this point, one must wonder how someone who holds the god responsible for such things[151] could avoid ‖ holding him responsible for the greater evils, the true evils, as well. It will no longer be possible to maintain any credibility talking about poverty or sickness or something in that category of "bad" things—here, rather, we will be attributing to god the cause of those evils that by general agreement are true evils. Timaeus says that the demiurge "laid out all the ordinances for souls," before their descent into γένεσις, "so that he should be innocent of the evils that came later" [*Tim.* 42d], while this account concedes that even after they have gone down and entered γένεσις, the cause of the greatest evils for them comes from there [from Zeus]. How might one give adequate answers to these difficulties and bring the Homeric teaching into harmony with the nature of things and with Plato's guidance on this matter?

That hearing this particular myth is incompatible with the condition of youth has already been said, and now let it be said again, along with all that we are about to say. It is not possible for the young to distinguish among the natures of beings nor to refer the visible symbols of truth to the invisible doctrine nor to observe how, in the world, everything is accomplished by the will of the god, acting by means of the other causes.

Let us nevertheless demonstrate that these things [that Homer says] are at home in the philosophy of Plato. The Athenian Stranger says that "the god 'holds the beginning and the middle and the end of all beings' and that justice follows him as the punisher of those who have transgressed the divine law" [*Leg.* 4.715e–716a]. These, as he says, are those who are "burning in their souls with youth and mindlessness, along with arrogant pride," and who, after seeming to triumph for a time, finally undergo the punishment that is appropriate to justice, having completely ruined themselves, their city, and their home. The Athenian Stranger says these things ‖ in the manner of a statesman, but Homer as an inspired guide, says that men

---

150. Or simply, "the beginning of evils."
151. I.e., the "bad" things of ch. 4, above.

ἐνθεαστικῶς ὑφηγούμενος τοὺς πολλὰ πλημμελήσαντας καὶ ἀδικίας τὰς μεγίστας ἠδικηκότας κατὰ τὴν μίαν τοῦ Διὸς βούλησιν δίκην ἀποτιννύναι φησὶν τῶν ἁμαρτημάτων |

σὺν σφῇσιν κεφαλῇσι γυναιξί τε καὶ τεκέεσσιν [Δ 162],

ταύτην δὲ ἄρα τὴν δίκην πρώτως μὲν τὸν Δία πληροῦν καὶ ἐξῃρημένως καὶ ἀφανῶς τοῖς πᾶσιν, δευτέρως δὲ τὴν Ἀθηνᾶν ὑπουργοῦσαν καὶ συναπεργαζομένην τὰ δόξαντα | τῇ πατρονομικῇ προνοίᾳ τοῦ Διός,

(**δεινὴ γὰρ Κρονίδαο νόου κράντειρα τέτυκται**

φησὶν Ὀρφεύς), ἐσχάτως δὲ τοὺς ὑπομένοντας αὐτοῦ τὴν τιμωρίαν· δεῖ γὰρ καὶ τὸ ἐφ' ἡμῖν συμπλέκεσθαι τῇ ποιήσει τῶν ὅλων.

οὗτοι δὴ οὖν ἐν ταῖς σπονδαῖς καὶ τοῖς ὅρκοις | εἰπόντες, ὅτι τῶν παραβαινόντων ταῦτα

ὧδέ σφ' ἐγκέφαλος χαμάδις ῥέοι ὡς ὅδε οἶνος [Γ 300],

καὶ παραβάντες ἑαυτοὺς ὑπάγουσιν τῇ δίκῃ καὶ πρέποντας ἑαυτοὺς ἀποφαίνουσι ταῖς ποιναῖς.

Ἡ τοίνυν σύγχυσις τῶν | ὅρκων καὶ τῶν σπονδῶν ἐπιτελεῖται μὲν ὑπὸ τούτων διαφερόντως τῶν πάσχειν μελλόντων τὰ δοκοῦντα τοῖς θεοῖς κατὰ δίκην τὰ θνητὰ ἄγουσιν ἐπὶ τοῖς ἔμπροσθεν ἁμαρτήμασιν, κινεῖσθαι δὲ λέγεται καὶ εἰς ἐνέργειαν προάγεσθαι παρ' αὐτῶν τῶν θεῶν, οὐχ ὡς ἐκείνων ποιούντων ἀθέους | καὶ ἀδίκους τοὺς τιμωρουμένους, ἀλλ' ὡς ἐπιτηδείους ὄντας αὐτοὺς πρὸς τὰς τοιαύτας πράξεις ἐκκαλουμένων εἰς ἐνέργειαν, ἵνα ποτὲ κατὰ τὴν ἔνδον ἕξιν ἐνεργήσαντες καὶ ἣν ἔχουσιν ὠδῖνα τῶν μοχθηρῶν ἐνεργημάτων προβαλόντες ἄξιοι γένωνται τῆς δίκης. τοῦτο γὰρ δή, φησὶν ὁ Πλάτων [*Leg.* 5.|728c], **δίκη μὲν οὐκ ἔστιν, καλὸν γὰρ τό γε δίκαιον || καὶ ἡ δίκη, τιμωρία δὲ ἀδικίας ἀκόλουθος πάθη**,

who have made many errors and committed the greatest of crimes pay the penalty for those crimes according to the unique will of Zeus,

with their heads, their wives, their children [*Il*. 4.162],

and it is Zeus, then, who in the most primal sense exacts this punishment, acting transcendentally and invisible to all, and then secondarily Athena assists and cooperates in accomplishing what has been decided upon by the patriarchal providence of Zeus,

(for she is the terrible accomplisher of the will of the son of Kronos,

says Orpheus [*Orph. frag.* 177, Kern]), and, lastly, [this punishment is realized] on the level of those awaiting punishment from Zeus, since that which is in our power must also be implicated in activity on the cosmic level.[152]

And so those who, when the libations were poured and the oaths sworn, said about the transgressors of those oaths,

Let their brains run on the ground like this wine [*Il*. 3.300],

and then violated the oaths are bringing themselves to justice and themselves showing that they deserve their punishment.

Now, the breaking of the oaths and treaties is certainly accomplished primarily by those who are going to suffer for their past sins the judgment of the gods who justly manage human affairs, and they are said to be moved and impelled to action by the gods themselves, not because the gods render those who are punished impious and unjust but rather because they activate them to such actions as they are predisposed to, so that, having acted in consequence of their inner disposition and projected their propensity to perform culpable actions, they become worthy of punishment. "For this," says Plato, is not justice, since justice || and that which is just are beautiful; rather, this is punishment, which is the painful conse-

---

152. I.e., Our own actions, the apparent result of our own will, are of necessity bound up with the activity of the "whole" entities, the gods. I have replaced Kroll's periods at lines 5 and 10 with commas.

ἧς ὅ τε τυγχάνων καὶ ὁ μὴ τυγχάνων ἄθλιος.

Πολλὰ δὴ οὖν καὶ τὰ μέγιστα ἀδικήσαντες ἄνθρωποι καὶ ἕξιν ἔχοντες πονηρὰν καὶ ὠδίνουσαν μείζω καὶ χαλεπώτερα κακὰ | τιμωρίαν ὑπέχουσιν πρῶτον, ἣ δοκεῖ μὲν ἐπιτρίβειν τοὺς πάσχοντας ἐπὶ τὰς τῶν ὅρκων ἄγουσα συγχύσεις, ἄγει δὲ αὐτοὺς εἰς τὸ δίκην ὑποσχεῖν τῶν πλημμελημάτων, παραπλήσιόν τι ποιοῦσα ταῖς ἀναστομώσεσιν τῶν ἑλκῶν, αἳ παραχρῆμα μὲν ἐπιτείνουσι τὰ πάθη τῶν σωμάτων, ἐκβάλ|λουσαι δὲ τὸν ὕπουλον καὶ ἐντὸς ἀποκρυπτόμενον χυμὸν αἴτιαι γίνονται τῆς ἐν χρόνοις ὕστερον παραγινομένης ὑγείας. τὴν δὲ δὴ τιμωρίαν ταύτην ἄνωθεν ἀπὸ τοῦ Διὸς ἀρχομένην (ἐκείνῳ γὰρ ἕπεται δίκη τῶν ἀπολειπομένων τοῦ θείου νόμου τιμωρός) διὰ μέσης τῆς Ἀθηνᾶς ἡ ποίησις τελειου|μένην παραδίδωσιν, ἵνα δῶσί ποτε δίκην οἱ Τρῶες ἰδόντες οἷ κακοῦ προήγαγον αὐτοὺς καὶ ὡς ταῖς ὀφειλομέναις ποιναῖς ἐγκατέδησαν τὴν ἑαυτῶν ζωήν. ὃν γὰρ ὅρον ἔθεντο τῆς ἐσχάτης τῶν ἁμαρτόντων κολάσεως, τοῦτον <u>ἀσάλευτον ἐφ'</u> ἑαυτῶν ταῖς τῶν ὅρκων καὶ τῶν σπονδῶν συγχύσεσιν | ἀπέφηναν.

Πρῶτον μὲν <οὖν> οὐχ οἱ θεοὶ τῆς πλημμελοῦς ταύτης καὶ ἀτάκτου πράξεώς εἰσιν αἴτιοι τοῖς Τρωσίν, ἀλλ' ἐκεῖνοι διὰ τὴν ἑαυτῶν πονηρίαν ἀξίους ἑαυτοὺς κατέστησαν τῆς τοιαύτης ἐνεργείας, καὶ τούτων διαφερόντως ὁ Πάνδαρος, φιλότιμός τε ὢν καὶ φιλοχρήματος καὶ τὴν ἄθεον | ζωὴν προβεβλημένος. διὸ καὶ ἡ Ἀθηνᾶ προελθοῦσα κατὰ τὸν νοῦν τοῦ πατρὸς οὐ τὸν ἐπιτυχόντα κινεῖ πρὸς τὴν πρᾶξιν, ἀλλὰ ζητεῖν λέγεται Πάνδαρον, ὡς ἂν μάλιστα πρέποντα πρὸς τὴν τιμωρὸν ἐνέργειαν

Πάνδαρον ἀντίθεον διζημένη εἴ που ἐφεύροι | [Δ 88]. ||

quence of injustice, and wretched is the man who meets with it and likewise he who manages to escape it" [*Leg.* 5.728c].[153]

[In the present instance,] men who have committed many egregious crimes and have a wicked disposition, suffering the birth pangs of yet greater and worse evils, first undergo a punishment that seems to excite the sufferers, leading them to violate the oaths, but actually brings them to undergo punishment for their mistakes. It is a situation very much like the lancing of boils, which in the short term increases the bodily suffering but by driving out the festering pus hidden inside is the cause of the eventual recovery of health. The poem shows this punishment starting from above, from Zeus (since justice follows him as punisher of those who have transgressed the divine law),[154] and accomplished by means of Athena, in order that the Trojans might sometime pay the price, seeing how deeply they had led themselves into evil and how they had burdened their own life with the chains of the penalties they owed. They demonstrated that the terms of extreme punishment they [themselves] set for the offenders, in the event of the breaking of the oaths and treaties, were not to be violated in their own case.[155]

And so, first of all, the gods are not responsible, with reference to the Trojans, for this mistaken and disorderly act, but rather they themselves, who through their own wickedness have made themselves predisposed to such action, and Pandarus, in particular, who was ambitious and greedy and had adopted a godless life. Therefore Athena, going forth according to the will of her father, does not push just anyone to the deed but is said to look for Pandarus, the very most appropriate one to perform the act destined to bring on the punishment:

seeking out Pandarus, enemy of[156] the gods [*Il.* 4.88]. ||

---

153. The passage in the *Laws* goes on to explain: "since the latter does not receive therapy, and the former is himself destroyed, in order that many others may be preserved."

154. See 119 (K100,25–26), above.

155. Following F.'s rejection of Kroll's emendation (σαλευτὸν ὑφ' for the manuscript's ἀσάλευτον ἐφ').

156. Proclus clearly understood the adjective ἀντίθεος ("godlike") to have adversative force. It is surprising that a reader of Proclus's sensitivity to Homer would make this mistake and misconstrue this very frequent epithet, applied to various kings, heroes, and nations, and even to Penelope. Proclus's phrase τὴν ἄθεον ζωὴν

σπάνιον γὰρ καὶ δυσεύρετον ὄντως τὸ τοιοῦτον γένος, τὸ πάντα μὲν δρᾶν ὑπομένον πάντα δὲ πάσχειν, ἀντικείμενον δὲ τῷ θείῳ διὰ δή τινα Γιγαντικὴν καὶ ἀποτετολμημένην ἕξιν τῆς ψυχῆς. ὥσπερ δὴ οὖν οὐχ οἱ ἰατροὶ τῶν τομῶν αἴτιοι καὶ τῶν καύσεων, ἀλλὰ τὰ πάθη τῶν ἰατρευο μένων, οὕτως οὐδὲ οἱ θεοὶ τῶν περὶ τοὺς ὅρκους καὶ τὰς σπονδὰς ἀσεβημάτων, ἀλλ' αἱ ἕξεις τῶν ποιούντων.

Δεύτερον δὲ ἐπὶ τούτῳ κἀκεῖνο κατανοήσωμεν, ὡς οὐδὲ προελθοῦσα ἡ Ἀθηνᾶ καταναγκάζειν λέγεται τὸν Πάνδαρον εἰς τὴν πρᾶξιν, ἀλλὰ πειρᾶσθαι μόνον, εἰ καὶ πρὸς ταύτην ἐπιδίδωσιν ἑαυτὸν τὴν ἐνέργειαν· οὐ γὰρ ἀναιρεῖται τὸ ἐφ' ἡμῖν, οὐδ' ἂν τὰ ἔσχατα πεπλημμεληκότες ὦμεν.

ἦ ῥά νύ μοί τι πίθοιο, Λυκάονος υἱὲ δαΐφρον; [Δ 93]

ὁ δὲ ὑπὸ λαιμαργίας τῶν χρημάτων ἀκούσας καὶ τῆς δυναστείας ἐπιπηδᾷ ταῖς ἀδίκοις ἐνεργείαις, μόνον οὐχὶ τοῦ ποιητοῦ ταῦτα βοῶντος, ἃ καὶ ὁ ἐν Πολιτείᾳ Σωκράτης, ὅτι πολλὰ προτείνεται ταῖς ψυχαῖς ἐκ τοῦ παντός, ἃ καταπλήττειν τοὺς ἀνοήτους καὶ περὶ τὰς αἱρέσεις τῶν βίων ἀποφαίνειν πλημμελεῖς. ὥσπερ οὖν ὁ προφήτης προτείνει τὸν τυραννικὸν βίον καὶ ὁ πρῶτος ἀνελόμενος τοῦτον ἀνόητος εἴρηται, καίτοι τὸ προτεῖναν θεῖόν τι πάντως ἦν, οὕτω δὴ καὶ τῆς Ἀθηνᾶς εἰς αἵρεσιν τὸν Πάνδαρον καταστησάσης τῆς τε δυνατωτέρας καὶ πλουσιωτέρας τάξεως μετὰ ἀθεότη|τος καὶ τῆς ἐναντίας ἐκεῖνος αἱρεῖται τὴν χείρονα. καὶ οὐχ ἡ Ἀθηνᾶ τῆς αἱρέσεως αἰτία, ἀλλ' ἡ μοχθηρία τοῦ αἱρουμένου· οὐδὲ γὰρ ὁ προφήτης τῆς τυραννίδος, ἀλλ' ἡ λαιμαργία τοῦ τὸν βίον τοῦτον προβάλλοντος. διὸ καὶ πειθόμενος ὁ Πάνδαρος τῇ Ἀθηνᾷ δι' ἄνοιαν τοῦτο πάσχειν εἴρηται· οὐ γὰρ ἐκείνῃ πείθεται, ἀλλὰ τῷ φιλοχρημάτῳ καὶ ἀνοήτῳ τῆς ἑαυτοῦ ψυχῆς.

Καίτοι πῶς οὐ θαυμαστόν, εἰ Ἀθηνᾶ μὴ φρονήσεως αἰτία, ἀλλὰ ἀνοίας; ἀλλὰ **καὶ νοῦ ἀπόρροια πανουργία** γίνεται, φησὶν ὁ Πλωτῖνος [2.3.11], καὶ σωφροσύνης ἔλλαμψις ἀκόλαστός ἐστιν καὶ ἀνδρείας δόσις θρασύτης.

This class of men is rare and hard to find, ready to do and suffer anything, and opposed to the divine because of the Gigantic[157] and presumptuous condition of their souls. So, just as doctors are not responsible for incisions and cauterizations, but rather the diseases of their patients, it is not the gods who are responsible for the sacrileges committed over the oaths and treaties but rather the state of the perpetrators.

Second, let us consider in addition that Athena is not said to have gone up to Pandarus and forced him to the act, but only to have tested him to see if he would lend himself to perform it. Our affairs are not entirely taken out of our hands, even if we are the worst of sinners:

Will you do something I tell you, brilliant son of Lycaon? [*Il.* 4.93]

Hearing this, out of greed for possessions and power, he leaps to the criminal actions, and the poet virtually proclaims the same thing Socrates asserted in the *Republic*, that many possibilities are offered souls out of the universe,[158] and these dazzle the mindless and cause them to make mistakes in their choices of lives [*Rep.* 10.618a]. Just as the spokesman of the gods holds out the tyrannical life and the first [soul] to arrive chooses it and is called stupid [*Rep.* 10.619b] (although the one who offered it was, after all, from the ranks of the divine), in the same way, when Athena confronts Pandarus with a choice between the more powerful and richer rank, with impiety, and its opposite, he makes the worse choice. Athena is not responsible for the choice but rather the wickedness of the chooser. Neither is the spokesman [of the gods] responsible for the tyranny but rather the greed of the one who adopts this life. Thus Pandarus is said to have had this happen to him out of stupidity, although he is acceding to Athena, since he is obeying not the goddess but the greed and || stupidity of his soul.

Yet, how is it not amazing, if Athena is a cause not of thoughtfulness but of stupidity? Plotinus observes, nevertheless, that "that which flows forth from intellect becomes wickedness," and that which radiates from

---

προβεβλημένος seems to be an elaborated paraphrase of the epithet as Proclus understood it. Cf. F.'s note ad loc.

157. See 19 (K51) with n. 22, above.

158. The relevance of this phrase to the Myth of Er, where the souls are offered the choice of various "lives" before their return to earth, is clearer than its relevance to the Homeric passage.

ὁποῖ᾽ ἄττα γὰρ ἂν ᾖ τὰ τῆς ζωῆς εἴδη, τοιαύτην ἀνάγκη καὶ τὴν μέθεξιν γίνεσθαι τῶν κρειττόνων· καὶ οἳ μὲν νοερῶς τῶν νοερῶν μετέχουσιν, οἳ δὲ δοξαστικῶς, οἳ δὲ φανταστικῶς, καὶ οἳ μὲν ἀπαθῶς τῶν παθῶν, οἳ δὲ μετριοπαθῶς, οἳ δὲ ἐμπαθῶς· πάντα δὲ ὑπὸ τῶν | θεῶν κινεῖται καὶ κατὰ τὴν ἐπιτηδειότητα τὴν ἑαυτῶν· ὥστε οὐχ ὑπὸ Διὸς καὶ Ἀθηνᾶς ἡ τῶν ὅρκων σύγχυσις, ἀλλὰ ὑπὸ Πανδάρου καὶ τῶν Τρώων. ἐξῆπται δὲ αὕτη τῶν θεῶν ἡ πρᾶξις ὡς πρόδρομος οὖσα τῆς δίκης, καὶ ὡς παρασκευάζουσα τοὺς παρέχοντας πρὸς τὴν τελέαν κόλασιν | τῶν ἁμαρτημάτων (τοιαύτη γὰρ ἡ τιμωρία, καθάπερ ἡμᾶς ὁ Ἀθηναῖος ξένος ἀνεδίδαξεν)· οὐδὲ τῶν ἀληθινῶν κακῶν αἴτιον τὸ θεῖον ταῖς ψυχαῖς, ἀλλ᾽ αἱ μοχθηραὶ τῶν ψυχῶν ἕξεις τῶν πλημμελῶν ἐνεργημάτων εἰσὶν αὐταῖς ἀρχηγοί. πᾶσα δὲ ἐνέργεια, κἂν ᾖ πλημμελὴς εἰς τὸ πᾶν | προϊοῦσα, θεῶν ἐφεστώτων γίνεται καὶ προνοίας ὁλικωτέρας ἢ μερικωτέρας. γίνεται γὰρ ἀδίκως μὲν τῷ δρῶντι δικαίως δὲ τῷ πάσχοντι, φησὶν ὁ Πλωτῖνος [4.3.16], καὶ ὅσον μέν ἐστιν αὐτῆς ἄθεον, ἐκ τῆς μερικῆς αἰτίας ἔχει τὴν γένεσιν τῆς ἀποτελούσης τὴν ἐμπαθῆ πρᾶξιν, ὅσον δὲ ἀγα|θόν, ἐκ τῶν ἐφεστώτων τυγχάνει τοῦ προσήκοντος τέλους.

Ἔδει γὰρ τοὺς τῶν μεγίστων ἀδικημάτων ἄρξαντας ἀνακληθῆναί ποτε πρὸς τὴν δίκην· τοῦτο δὲ οὐκ ἄν ποτε συνέβη, μὴ τῆς μοχθηρίας αὐτῶν ἀναπλωθείσης· πολλαὶ γοῦν τῶν ἕξεων ἀνενέργητοι μένουσαι τῆς προσηκούσης θεραπείας | τυχεῖν ἀδυνάτους ποιοῦσιν τοὺς ἔχοντας. διὸ καὶ βουλεύονται || οἱ θεοὶ περὶ τοῦ παῦσαι τὸν πόλεμον σωζομένων τῶν

reasonableness is lawlessness, and from bravery, arrogance [*Enn.* 2.3.11].[159] Whatever the forms of [human] life, that is the manner in which they must necessarily participate in the higher realities:[160] some participate in the intellective intellectively, others in the mode of opinion, others in the mode of the imagination, and as far as the passions are concerned, some do not experience them at all, others do so moderately, and some embrace them passionately. All things are set in motion by the gods, and[161] [this is done] in accordance with the capacity of the individuals concerned. Thus the dissolution of the oaths was not done by Zeus and Athena but by Pandarus and the Trojans. The action was nevertheless dependent on the gods, in that it was the precursor of justice and prepared the perpetrators for the entire correction (κόλασις) of their sins (for this is what [divine] punishment [τιμωρία] is, as the Athenian Stranger taught us).[162] Neither is the divine a cause of true evils for souls, but rather the wicked dispositions of the souls themselves are the first motivators of their mistaken acts. Every action, even if it is an offense as it devolves in the universe, comes about under the supervision of the gods and of more general or more specific providence. Plotinus says that it is accomplished with injustice for the actor and justice for the sufferer, and whatever part of it is godless has its source in the partial cause that commits the act of passion.[163] Whatever is good attains its appropriate end from the overseeing [gods].

It was necessary for those who had undertaken the greatest crimes to be called someday to justice. This would never have happened if their wickedness had not been opened up. Many conditions of the soul, by remaining inactive, make those who suffer from them unable get the appropriate treatment. Therefore, the gods even discuss || stopping the war and

---

159. Plotinus's point is that astral influences are modified according to the condition of the recipients (as Proclus will state immediately below).

160. F. took τοιαύτην in K105,6 to refer to the earlier description of Pandarus's failed apprehension of the "influence" that reaches him from Athena, but it is more natural (and more consistent with the sequel) to take it with the "whatever" (ὁποῖ' ἄττα) of line 5. I.e., people will participate in the gods according to their own natures.

161. I see little reason for secluding the καί here, as Kroll did.

162. For the Athenian Stranger, see above 115–21 (K99–102). On the two terms, compare Aristotle, *Rhet.* 1369b12–14: διαφέρει δὲ τιμωρία καὶ κόλασις· ἡ μὲν γὰρ κόλασις τοῦ πάσχοντος ἕνεκά ἐστιν, ἡ δὲ τιμωρία τοῦ ποιοῦντος, ἵνα πληρωθῇ.

163. This sentence is a paraphrase of *Enn.* 4.3.16, lines 17–25, where the word ἄθεος ("godless" above) is in fact a Homeric echo (in the distinctively Homeric adverbial form ἀθεεί).

Τρώων, καὶ ἡ τῆς δίκης προστάτις θεὸς κωλύει τὴν τοιαύτην ἐνέργειαν, ἵνα θᾶττον ὑπόσχωσι τῶν ἡμαρτημένων ποινήν· καὶ ἡ ταύτης συνεργὸς κινεῖ πρὸς τὴν σύγχυσιν τοῦ ὅρκου, ἵνα | κατὰ πᾶσαν ἑαυτῶν τὴν μοχθηρίαν ἐνεργήσαντες ὑπὲρ πάσης τὴν κόλασιν δέξωνται. οὔτε γὰρ ἀνιάτους μένειν ἦν ἀγαθὸν οὔτε πρὸ τῶν δευτέρων ἁμαρτημάτων ἰαθῆναι τὴν ὑποικουροῦσαν ἔνδον μοχθηρίαν.

πάσης οὖν τῆς ἀδίκου ζωῆς ἐν αὐτοῖς ἀναστομωθείσης ἕπεται δίκη σωφρονίζουσα | τὴν ὅλην ἀνοσιουργίαν.

Τίς ἐστιν ἡ ἐν τῇ ποιήσει τοῦ Διὸς τῶν θεῶν εἰς ἔριν κατάστασις διὰ Θέμιδος, ἀνάπτυξις τῆς ὅλης τοῦ μύθου θεωρίας.

Πρὸς μὲν οὖν τὴν προειρημένην ἀπορίαν ὧδέ πως ἀπαν|τήσωμεν. ἐπεὶ δὲ καὶ τῆς κρίσεως διαμνημονεύει τῆς παρ' Ὁμήρῳ τῶν θεῶν καὶ τῆς ἔριδος, ἐφ' ἣν ὁ Ζεὺς ἀνακινεῖ τὰ πλήθη τῶν θεῶν διὰ τῆς Θέμιδος πάντα πρὸς ἑαυτὸν ἀνάγων, λεκτέον τι καὶ περὶ τούτων.

Ὅτι μὲν οὖν ὁ Ζεὺς μονάς ἐστι παντὸς τοῦ πλήθους τῶν ἐγκοσμίων θεῶν, | καὶ ὅτι πάντας καὶ παράγειν ἀφ' ἑαυτοῦ δύναται καὶ ἐπιστρέφειν εἰς ἑαυτόν, εἴρηται πολλάκις. διττῆς δὲ οὔσης τῆς εἰς τὸ πλῆθος αὐτοῦ προϊούσης ἐνεργείας, τῆς μὲν ἐπιστρεπτικῆς, τῆς δὲ κινητικῆς εἰς τὴν τῶν καταδεεστέρων προμήθειαν, διττὰς καὶ ἡ ποίησις τοῦ Διὸς πρὸς τοὺς | θεοὺς ἀναγράφει δημηγορίας. καὶ κατὰ μὲν τὴν προτέραν τῆς ἀμίκτου καθαρότητος μεταδιδοὺς ὑπόκειται τῷ πλήθει τῶν θεῶν ὁ εἷς καὶ ὅλος δημιουργός, χωριστάς τε δυνάμεις αὐτοῖς ἐνδίδωσιν ἁπάσης τῆς περικοσμίου διαιρέσεως· διὸ || καὶ παρακελεύεται πᾶσιν ἀφίστασθαι τοῖς

the Trojans' being saved, and the goddess[164] who oversees justice prevents such action, in order that they undergo punishment for their sins more quickly. It is her assistant who moves them to break the oaths, so that they may act out all of their wickedness and receive correction for it all. Neither was it a good thing for them to remain untreated, nor for the wickedness lying hidden inside them to be cured before their further crimes.

Once all the injustice of their lives has come to a head, justice enters and corrects the whole of their impiety.

(6) What is the [meaning of the] episode of the poem in which Zeus, through Themis, puts the gods into a state of strife? An elaboration of the entire doctrine behind the myth.

It is in this way, more or less, that we shall reply to the problem just stated. But since Socrates also mentions the judging [of the goddesses] in Homer and the strife to which Zeus stirs up the multiplicity of the gods, drawing them to him through Themis, something should also be said about these things.

It has often been observed that Zeus is the monad of all the multiplicity of the encosmic gods and that be is able both to draw all of them forth from himself and to cause them to return into himself. Since his activity proceeding into multiplicity is double, on the one hand causing a return to himself and on the other motivating providential care of the lower beings, the poem attributes to Zeus two speeches to the other gods.[165] In the first, the one and universal demiurge is depicted sharing his unmingling purity with the multiplicity of the gods, and he endows them with powers separate from the division[166] that embraces the cosmos and || tells them all to stay away from the war and the contrariety that belong to encosmic things.

---

164. Thus far in this account of the breaking of the oaths, Zeus has been the initiator of the plan acted upon by Athena, and the role of Hera in the *Iliad* passage ignored. But now suddenly there is a goddess behind Athena's action, and that goddess "oversees justice," a role that fits Hera badly. Either Zeus is meant (and some error has found its way into the text—cf. Kroll's apparatus), or perhaps F. is correct that Themis is envisioned as speaking through Hera.

165. Kroll identified the two speeches in question as those at *Il.* 8.5–27 (where Zeus threatens all the other gods with *katatartarosis* if they go into the fighting) and *Il.* 20.20–30 (where Zeus tells the other gods to go and help whichever of the Greeks and Trojans they please).

166. The περικόσμιος διαίρεσις (possibly a unique phrase) refers to an entity (cf.

θεοῖς τοῦ πολέμου καὶ τῆς ἐναντιώσεως τῶν ἐγκοσμίων πραγμάτων. ἐν δὲ τῇ δευτέρᾳ κινεῖ πως αὐτοὺς εἰς τὴν πρόνοιαν τῶν καταδεεστέρων καὶ ἐφίησιν ταῖς διῃρημέναις αὐτῶν εἰς τὸ | πᾶν προόδοις, ἵνα μὴ μόνον καθ' ἕνα συνέχωνται τὸν δημιουργικὸν νοῦν, ὃν οὔτε παρεξελθεῖν δυνατόν, ὥς φησιν ἡ ποίησις, οὔτε ὑπερδραμεῖν, ἀλλὰ καὶ κατὰ τὰς ἑαυτῶν ἰδιότητας ἐνεργῶσιν εἰς τὰ προνοούμενα·

διὸ καί φησιν ὁ Ζεύς· |

ἀμφοτέροισι δ' ἀρήγεθ' ὅπῃ νόος ἐστὶν ἑκάστου [Υ 25].

ἐπειδὴ δὲ καὶ αἱ πρόοδοι τῶν θεῶν οὐκ εἰσὶν ἀπεσπασμέναι τῆς δημιουργικῆς μονάδος, ἐπιστρέφει πρῶτον αὐτοὺς ἡ Θέμις εἰς ἐκείνην. |

Ζεὺς δὲ Θέμιστα κέλευσε θεοὺς ἀγορήνδε καλέσσαι [Υ 4],

ἵνα καὶ προνοοῦντες κατὰ τὴν βούλησιν τοῦ πατρὸς ἐνεργῶσι καὶ τὴν τῆς Θέμιδος κρίσιν.

Ἀλλ' ὁ μὲν ποιητὴς διῃρημένας παραδέδωκεν ἡμῖν τὰς τοῦ ὅλου δημιουργοῦ πρὸς τοὺς | νέους δημηγορίας θεούς· ὁ δὲ Τίμαιος [41a] ἡνωμένως αὐτὸν καὶ ἐπιστρέφοντα ποιεῖ τὸ πλῆθος εἰς ἑαυτὸν καὶ εἰς τὴν πρόνοιαν ἀνεγείροντα τῶν θνητῶν, ἵνα κατὰ δίκην ἄγωσιν τὰ δεύτερα πάντα τῆς ἑαυτῶν γενέσεως. ταῦτα δὲ οὐδὲν διαφέρει τοῦ κινεῖν τε αὐτοὺς ἐπὶ τὸν πόλεμον καὶ | διὰ τῆς Θέμιδος ἀγείρειν εἰς ἑαυτόν. καὶ γὰρ οἱ τῆς γενεσιουργοῦ προϊστάμενοι φύσεως τὸν ἐν τῇ ὕλῃ διακυβερνῶσι πόλεμον, καὶ οἱ κατὰ δίκην ἐνεργοῦντες τῆς ὅλης ἐξήρτηνται Θέμιδος, ἧς ἡ Δίκη

In the second, he is in some sense directing them toward providence on behalf of the lower beings, and he sends forth their separate processions into the universe so that, rather than simply being contained by the single demiurgical intellect (which, according to the poem, it is impossible "to slip past" or to escape)[167] each may act as well according to his own specific qualities upon the beings over whom providential care is extended.

Thus, Zeus says,

> Give help to both sides, wherever the mind of each inclines you [*Il.* 20.25].

On the other hand, since the processions of the gods are not broken off from the creative monad, Themis first draws them back into it:

> Zeus ordered Themis to call the gods to counsel [*Il.* 20.4],

so that their providential action might be according to the will of the father and the judgment of Themis.

Thus the Poet has presented us with the universal demiurge giving two separate speeches to the young gods. Timaeus, on the other hand, shows him in a single speech, drawing their multiplicity to him and sending it forth to providence on behalf of mortals, so that the gods may justly direct all the secondaries of their own creation [*Tim.* 41a–d].[168] This is no different from sending them to war and, through Themis, drawing them back to himself. Those gods who preside over the nature that is creative of this world govern the strife that exists in matter, and those who act according to justice depend on universal Themis ("Right"), whose daughter is Dike ("Justice"), and they mimic the single demiurgical mind, which "has no

---

"division" of an army) rather than an action ("division" in the abstract, and the characteristic meaning of διαίρεσις in Proclus).

167. Proclus clearly has in mind *Od.* 5.103–104 (= 137–138) (Hermes to Calypso): ἀλλὰ μάλ' οὔ πως ἔστι Διὸς νόον αἰγιόχοιο / οὔτε παρεξελθεῖν ἄλλον θεὸν οὔθ' ἁλιῶσαι. This accounts nicely for παρεξελθεῖν ("slip past"), and it is perhaps futile to search further for ὑπερδραμεῖν (ὑποτρέχω, escape), which is not in Homer but occurs several times in tragedy and then fairly commonly in later prose, including Proclus's own.

168. In the *Timaeus*, the gods are told to themselves create a lower class of beings (mortals) and to look after them.

παῖς, καὶ μιμοῦνται τὸν ἕνα δημιουργικὸν νοῦν, ᾧ μὴ θέμις **ἄλλο τι δρᾶν πλὴν τὸ κάλλι|στον**, ὡς αὐτός πού φησιν ὁ Τίμαιος [30a]. ||

Τίς ἡ τῶν θεῶν κρίσις ἡ ἐν τοῖς μύθοις τοῖς τοῦ ποιητοῦ καὶ τίνας αἰνίσσεται βίων διαφοράς.

Ἀλλὰ μὴν καὶ τὴν θρυλουμένην κρίσιν τῶν θεῶν, ἣν παρὰ τῷ Ἀλεξάνδρῳ γενέσθαι φασὶν οἱ μῦθοι κατὰ τὴν | παλαιὰν φήμην, οὐ δεῖ νομίζειν αὐτῶν ὄντως εἶναι τῶν θεῶν ἔριν τε πρὸς ἀλλήλας καὶ ὑπ' ἀνδρὸς βαρβάρου κρίσιν, ἀλλ' ἡγητέον ὅτι καὶ αἱ τῶν βίων αἱρέσεις, ἅς δὴ πολλαχοῦ παραδιδωσιν ὁ Πλάτων, ὑπὸ θεοῖς ἐφόροις γίγνονται τῶν ψυχῶν. καὶ τοῦτο δήπου καὶ αὐτὸς ἐν Φαίδρῳ | [252e–253e, 265b] διδάσκει σαφῶς, τὸν μὲν βασιλικὸν βίον Ἥρας εἶναι λέγων, τὸν δὲ φιλόσοφον Διός, τὸν δὲ ἐρωτικὸν Ἀφροδίτης. ὅταν οὖν αἱ ψυχαὶ πολλῶν αὐταῖς ἐκ τοῦ παντὸς προτεινομένων βίων κατὰ τὴν ἑαυτῶν κρίσιν τούσδε μὲν ἀσπάζωνται, τούσδε δὲ ἀποσκευάζωνται, τηνικαῦτα | οἱ μῦθοι μεταφέροντες ἐπ' αὐτοὺς τοὺς θεοὺς τὰς τῶν βίων ἰδιότητας κρίνεσθαί φασιν ὑπὸ τῶν αἱρουμένων τοὺς βίους τοὺς ἐφόρους τῆς κατ' εἶδος ἐν αὐτοῖς ἐξαλλαγῆς.

Καὶ κατὰ τοῦτον δὴ τὸν λόγον καὶ ὁ Ἀλέξανδρος καταστῆναι λέγεται κριτὴς Ἀθηνᾶς καὶ Ἥρας καὶ Ἀφροδίτης, τριῶν μὲν αὐτῷ | βίων προτεινομένων, ἑλόμενος δὲ τὸν ἐρωτικόν, καὶ τοῦτο οὐ μετὰ φρονήσεως, ἀλλ' ἐπιτρέχων τῷ τῶν φαινομένων κάλλει καὶ τὸ εἴδωλον ἐπιδιώκων τοῦ νοητοῦ κάλλους. ὁ μὲν γὰρ ὄντως ἐρωτικὸς νοῦν καὶ φρόνησιν προστησάμενος καὶ μετὰ τούτων τό τε ἀληθινὸν κάλλος καὶ τὸ φαινόμενον | θεωρῶν οὐχ ἧσσόν ἐστιν Ἀθηναϊκὸς ἢ Ἀφροδισιακός· ὁ δὲ αὐτὸ καθ' αὑτὸ μόνον τὸ ἐρωτικὸν εἶδος ἐπιδιώκων μετὰ πάθους ἀφίσταται μὲν τῶν ἀληθινῶν καλῶν καὶ ἀγαθῶν, ὑπὸ δὲ ἀνοίας καὶ λαιμαργίας ἐπιπηδᾷ τῷ εἰδώλῳ τοῦ καλοῦ καὶ περὶ τοῦτο κεῖται πεσών, οὐδὲ τῆς τῷ ἐρω||τικῷ συμμέτρου τελειότητος τυχών. ὁ γὰρ δὴ τελέως ἐρωτικὸς καὶ Ἀφροδίτῃ μέλων ἐπ' αὐτὸ τὸ θεῖον κάλλος ἀνάγεται τῶν ἐν αἰσθήσει καλῶν ὑπερορῶν· ἐπεὶ δὲ καὶ τοῦ ἐμφανοῦς κάλλους καὶ τοῦ ἐν ὕλῃ τὴν ὑπόστασιν ἔχοντος | εἰσί τινες Ἀφροδισιακοὶ προστάται δαίμονες,

business performing any act other than the most beautiful," as Timaeus himself somewhere says [*Tim.* 30a]. ||

(7) What is [the meaning of] the judgment of the goddesses in the myths of the Poet, and what various sorts of lives does it hint at?

As for the famous judgment of the goddesses that the myths say was performed by Paris, following the ancient account, it is not to be believed that there was truly strife among the goddesses themselves and that they were judged by a [particular] barbarian. Rather, this is to be interpreted as meaning that the choices of lives—to which Plato testifies in many passages—are likewise carried out under the watchful eye of the gods who supervise souls.

Plato himself indeed clearly teaches the same thing in the *Phaedrus*, saying that the regal life belongs to Hera, the philosophical to Zeus, and the erotic to Aphrodite [*Phdr.* 252e–253e, 265b]. Thus souls, when many kinds of lives are offered them out of the universe,[169] accept some and reject others, following their own judgment, while the myths, transferring to the gods themselves the specific qualities of the lives, say that those who preside over the variation in them, form by form, are "judged" by those choosing the lives.

This is the sense in which Paris is said to have been made the judge of Athena, Hera, and Aphrodite: three lives were offered him, and he chose the erotic, not after due thought, but rushing after beauty of the world of appearances and pursuing the phantom of the beauty grasped by the mind. He whose life is truly devoted to Eros sets intelligence and wisdom before him and contemplates the true and the apparent beauty through these and has no less to do with Athena than with Aphrodite. But he who pursues only the erotic form of life, in and for itself and through the passions, departs from true beauty and goodness and out of stupidity and greed leaps upon the phantom of the beautiful and lies there on it, failing to attain that balanced perfection commensurate || with the erotic. The truly erotic individual, who is the concern of Aphrodite, is drawn up to the divine beauty itself, looking beyond the beauties of the senses, but since there are Aphrodisian daemons presiding over the beauty that is visible

---

169. See above, 125 (K104) with n. 158.

διὰ δὴ τοῦτο καὶ ὁ τὸ εἴδωλον περιέπων συνεργοῦ λέγεται τῆς Ἀφροδίτης τυγχάνειν.

**Τίνες εἰσὶν αἱ ἐν ταῖς θεομυθίας μεταβολαὶ
τῶν θεῶν εἰσαγόμεναι καὶ κατὰ πόσους τρόπους |
αὐτὰς διατιθέασιν καὶ διὰ ποίας αἰτίας.**

Ταῦτα καὶ πρὸς ταύτην ἀπαντῶντες τοῦ Σωκράτους τὴν ἐπίστασιν ἐροῦμεν. ἐπειδὴ δὲ οὐ μόνον ἀγαθουργὸν ἡμῖν ἀποδέδεικται τὸ θεῖον, ἀλλὰ καὶ ἀμετάβλητον καὶ ἄμορφον καὶ ἁπλοῦν καὶ ἀεὶ κατὰ τὰ αὐτὰ καὶ ὡσαύτως ἔχον, εἰκό|τως ἐφεξῆς ὁ Σωκράτης τὰ τοιαῦτα τοῦ Ὁμήρου κρίσεως ἀξιοῖ·

**καί τε θεοὶ ξείνοισιν ἐοικότες ἀλλοδαποῖσι
παντοῖοι τελέθοντες ἐπιστρωφῶσι πόληας** [ρ 485–486] |

καὶ αὖ ὅσα περὶ Πρωτέως εἴρηται καὶ Θέτιδος ὡς μεταβαλλόντων τὰς ἑαυτῶν μορφὰς καὶ ποικίλων φανταζομένων. καὶ ὅτι μὲν τῶν τοιῶνδε τοῖς τῆς πολιτικῆς παιδείας γνησίως ἀντιληψομένοις οὐδὲ ἐπαΐειν προσήκει, πάντως που δῆλον· δεῖ γὰρ τῆς ἀκινήτου μελλούσης ἔσεσθαι πολιτείας | αἳ τὸ παράδειγμα ἀμετάβλητον ἑστάναι καὶ τῆς ἐν ἁπλοῖς ἤθεσιν ὑφεστώσης ἁπλοῦν, ἀλλ' οὐ ποικίλον οὐδὲ μεταβολαῖς παντοίαις ἐξαλλαττόμενον. ὅτου γὰρ ἂν ὁ δημιουργός, **εἰς τὸ κατὰ τὰ αὐτὰ ἔχον βλέπων ἀεί, τὴν || ἰδέαν καὶ τὴν δύναμιν ἀπεργάζηται, καλὸν ἐξ ἀνάγκης οὕτως ἀποτελεῖσθαι πᾶν,**

and has its existence in matter, for this reason, of course, even he who pursues the phantom is said to have Aphrodite as his helper.

(8) What is [the meaning of] the transformations of the gods introduced into the myths, and in how many ways do they attribute these things to them and for what reasons?

[a. The problem]

This is what we shall say in answer to this particular objection of Socrates. Now that it has been shown that the divine is not only good in its actions but also unchanging, shapeless, and simple, and that it remains eternally the same and in the same condition, Socrates understandably next sees fit to pass judgment on verses of Homer's such as these:

> The gods take the form of strangers from foreign lands
> and put on various shapes as they visit the cities of men
> [*Od.* 17.485–486],

along with all that is said about Proteus's and Thetis's changing their shapes and manifesting themselves in various ways.[170] I suppose it is entirely clear that those who wish genuinely to lay claim to civic education should not listen to such things, since the model of the city that is to be unchanging must itself be unchangeable, and the model for a state based on simplicity of character[171] must itself be simple and not diverse and undergoing transformations of all sorts.

> [All those objects] whose form || and capacity [the demiurge] created while contemplating that which is eternally unchanging are of necessity created entirely beautiful, but whatever he creates while contemplating that which has come to be, using a created model, is not beautiful,

---

170. Proteus (*Od.* 5.417–419, 454–459) is the preeminent shape-changer of surviving Greek literature, but Thetis clearly performed comparable transformations in the attempt to avoid marriage with Theseus. Ovid (*Met.* 11.229–265) tells the story of her transformations, but lurking here is a lost Greek original.

171. See 7 (K44) with n. 8, above.

ὡς ὁ Τίμαιός φησιν· **ὅτου δὲ ἂν εἰς γεγονός, γενητῷ παραδείγματι προσχρώμενος, οὐ καλόν.** τῶν γὰρ μεταβολὴν | ἐπιδεχομένων καὶ τὰ εἴδωλα πολλῷ μᾶλλόν ἐστιν γενέσεως ἀναπεπλησμένα καὶ ποικιλίας καὶ τῆς ὑλικῆς αἰσχρότητος.

Δεῖ δὲ αὖ καὶ τὴν Ὁμήρου διάνοιαν ἔνθεον οὖσαν τῷ λογισμῷ συνελεῖν· καίτοι με οὐ λέληθεν, ὅτι τὰς προκειμένας ῥήσεις τῶν μνηστήρων τις αὐτῷ πεποίηται λέγων, ἀφ' ὧν | οὐκ ἔστιν τὸν ποιητὴν εὐθύνειν. οὐδὲ γὰρ ἐκ τῶν Καλλικλέους λόγων οὐδὲ τῶν Θρασυμάχου τὴν τοῦ Πλάτωνος δόξαν αἱρεῖν δοκιμάζομεν, οὐδ' εἴ τις ἐλέγχειν ἐπιχειροῖ τὸν Πλάτωνα διὰ τῶν τοῖς σοφισταῖς ἀποτετολμημένων ῥημάτων, κατὰ πόδας αὐτὸν ποιεῖσθαι τοὺς ἐλέγχους φήσομεν, | ἀλλ' ὅταν Παρμενίδης ἢ Σωκράτης ἢ Τίμαιος ἢ ἄλλος τις τῶν οὕτω θείων φθέγγηται, τότε τῶν Πλάτωνος ἀκούειν ἡγούμεθα δογμάτων. καὶ οὖν καὶ τῶν Ὁμηρικῶν ἐπιβολῶν ποιησόμεθα τὴν κρίσιν οὐκ ἐξ ὧν οἱ μνηστῆρες λέγουσιν ἢ τῶν παρ' αὐτῷ τις εἰς πονηρίαν διαβεβλημένων, ἀλλ' ἐξ | ὧν αὐτὸς ὁ ποιητὴς ἢ Νέστωρ ἢ Ὀδυσσεὺς φαίνεται λέγων.

Εἰ δ' οὖν καὶ ταῦτά τις εἰς τὴν Ὁμήρου διάνοιαν ἀναπέμπειν ἐθέλοι, πάντως οὐκ ἀπορήσει λόγων συμφώνων μὲν ταῖς ἱερατικαῖς ἁπάσαις πραγματείαις, συμφώνων δὲ ταῖς τελεταῖς καὶ τοῖς μυστηρίοις καὶ ταῖς τῶν θεῶν ἐπιφανείαις, ἃς ὄναρ τε | καὶ ὕπαρ γινομένας ἄνωθεν ἡ τῶν ἀνθρώπων φήμη παρεδέξατο. ἐν ἅπασι γὰρ τούτοις οἱ θεοὶ πολλὰς μὲν ἑαυτῶν προτείνουσι μορφάς, πολλὰ δὲ σχήματα ἐξαλλάττοντες φαίνονται· καὶ τότε μὲν ἀτύπωτον αὐτῶν προβέβληται φῶς, τότε δὲ εἰς ἀνθρώπου μορφὴν ἐσχηματισμένον, τότε δὲ εἰς || ἀλλοῖον τύπον προεληλυθός. καὶ ταῦτα καὶ ἡ θεοπαράδοτος μυσταγωγία παραδίδωσιν· ταῦτα γάρ φησιν

ἐπιφωνήσας ἢ παιδὶ κατόψῃ
πῦρ ἴκελον σκιρτηδὸν ἐπ' ἠέρος οἶδμα τιταῖνον, |
ἢ καὶ πῦρ ἀτύπωτον ὅθεν φωνὴν προθέουσαν,
ἢ φῶς πλούσιον ἀμφὶ γύην ῥοιζαῖον ἑλιχθέν·
ἀλλὰ καὶ ἵππον ἰδεῖν φωτὸς πλέον ἀστράπτοντα,
ἢ καὶ παῖδα θοοῖς νώτοις ἐποχούμενον ἵππου |

as Timaeus says [*Tim.* 28a-b]. The images from models that themselves accept change are far more infested with γένεσις and diversity and the ugliness of matter.

And yet, one must reflect and realize that the meaning of Homer is also inspired. Further, I realize that, as far as the words before us are concerned, Homer has one of the suitors say them in the poem, and therefore they cannot provide a basis for censuring the poet. We do not think, after all, that we are grasping the opinion of Plato from the speeches of Callicles and Thrasymachus, nor if someone should undertake to blame Plato for the arrogant speeches of the sophists will we say that he is on the right track. Rather, when Parmenides or Socrates or Timaeus or some other who is similarly divine is speaking, then we believe we hear the opinions of Plato. And so, as far as the ideas of Homer are concerned, we shall not judge them on the basis of what the suitors say, or what those say whom he accuses of wickedness, but rather from what the poet himself clearly says, or Nestor or Odysseus.

[b. Proclus's reply: Homer supported by theurgy]

In any case, even if one should want to attribute these things directly to Homer's thought, he would still be by no means at a loss for arguments in harmony with all of the hieratic treatises, with the initiations and mysteries and the apparitions of the gods, which, tradition tells us, come down to us both awake and in dreams. In all of these, the gods extend many forms of themselves, appearing with many changes of shape. At one moment formless light is projected from them, then the next moment this is shaped into human form, and then it has gone on into || some other shape. This is passed down in the mystical doctrine received from the gods. It says the following:[172]

> After making this invocation, you will see a flame
> like a child skipping across the gulf of the air
> or again a shapeless fire, with a voice rushing forth from it,
> or abundant light, whirring and curling around the land.
> Or you might see a horse, more dazzling than the light,
> or a boy borne on the swift back of a horse, a boy

---

172. *Or. chald.* frag. 146, des Places. The editor identifies the speaker as Hekate.

**ἔμπυρον ἢ χρυσῷ πεπυκασμένον ἢ πάλι γυμνόν,
ἢ καὶ τοξεύοντα καὶ ἑστηῶτ' ἐπὶ νώτοις,**

καὶ ὅσα τούτοις ἐφεξῆς τὰ λόγια προστίθησιν, οὔτε ἀλλοίωσιν οὔτε ποικιλίαν οὔτε μεταβολὴν ἐπὶ τὸ θεῖον ἀνα|πέμποντά ποθεν, ἀλλὰ τὰς μεθέξεις αὐτοῦ διαφόρους ἐπιδεικνύοντα. τὸ γὰρ ἁπλοῦν τῶν θεῶν ποικίλον φαντάζεται τοῖς ὁρῶσιν, οὔτε μεταβαλλόντων ἐκείνων οὔτε ἐξαπατᾶν προθεμένων, ἀλλὰ τῆς φύσεως αὐτῆς κατὰ τὰ μέτρα τῶν μετεχόντων τὰς τῶν θεῶν ἰδιότητας ἀφοριζούσης. ἑνὸς γὰρ | ὄντος τοῦ μετεχομένου θεοῦ νοῦς μὲν ἄλλως μεταλαμβάνει, ψυχὴ δὲ ἄλλως νοερά, φαντασία δὲ ἄλλως, αἴσθησις δὲ ἄλλως· ὁ μὲν ἀμερίστως, ἡ δὲ ἀνειλιγμένως, ἡ δὲ μορφωτικῶς, ἡ δὲ παθητικῶς. καὶ ἔστι τὸ μετεχόμενον μονοειδὲς μὲν κατὰ τὴν ὕπαρξιν, πολυειδὲς δὲ κατὰ τὴν μέθεξιν, | καὶ ἀμετάβλητον καθ' αὑτὸ καὶ μονίμως ἱδρυμένον, ἄλλοτε δὲ ἀλλοῖον διὰ τὴν αὐτῶν ἀσθένειαν τοῖς μετέχουσι φανταζόμενον.

Καὶ οὐ ταῦτα μόνον, ἀλλὰ καὶ βάρους τὸ ἀβαρὲς φαίνεται τοῖς πληρουμένοις αὐτοῦ μετέχον· **οὐ φέρει με || τοῦ δοχέως ἡ τάλαινα καρδία**, φησίν τις θεῶν. ὅθεν δὴ καὶ ὁ ποιητὴς ἐν ἄλλοις ἐνθέως καὶ τῶν τοιούτων συνῃσθημένος περὶ τῆς Ἀθηνᾶς πού φησιν·

**μέγα δ' ἔβραχε φήγινος ἄξων |
βριθοσύνῃ· δεινὴν γὰρ ἄγεν θεόν** [Ε 838–839].

καίτοι κἀνταῦθα λέγειν ἔξεστιν· καὶ πῶς βαρύτητος αἴτιον τὸ ἀβαρές; ἀλλ' ὁποῖον ἂν ᾖ τὸ μετέχον, τοιοῦτον ἀνάγκη φαίνεσθαι τὸ μετεχόμενον. εἴτε οὖν ξένοις ἐοικότες φαίνοιντο τῶν θεῶν τινες, εἴτε ἄλλην τινὰ προϊσχόμενοι μορ|φήν, οὐκ ἐν ἐκείνοις ὑποτίθεσθαι χρὴ τὴν φαινομένην μεταβολήν, ἀλλ' ἐν ταῖς διαφόροις ὑποδοχαῖς ποικίλλεσθαι τὴν φαντασίαν.

in flames, or covered with gold, or naked,
or even standing on his horse's back and shooting a bow,

and all that the *Oracles* say in addition to this, never attributing metamorphosis or diversity or change to the divine but rather demonstrating the differing ways of participating in it. That which is simple in the gods is imagined as multiple by those who contemplate them, while they themselves neither change nor intend to deceive—rather, nature itself defines the properties of the gods according to the capacities of the participating beings. The god who is the object of the participation remains single, but the mind (νοῦς) grasps him in one way, the intellective soul (ψυχὴ ... νοερά) in another, the imagination (φαντασία) in another, and sense (αἴσθησις) in yet another, the first indivisibly, the second discursively, the third iconically, and the last experientially. Thus the participated being is single in its true being but multiform as participated in, unchangeable and constantly stable in itself, but envisioned by the participants now in one way, now in another, through their own incapacity.

Moreover, the weightless appears to those who are filled with it to partake of [great] weight: "The wretched heart of the recipient cannot bear me," || says one of the gods.[173] Thus the poet, since he both is generally inspired and is perceptive about things of this sort, says somewhere about Athena,

> ... the oak axle groaned loudly,
> weighted down, for it bore a terrible goddess [*Il.* 5.838–839].

Here one may legitimately ask as well: How can that which is weightless be a cause of weight? [The answer is that,] whatever the qualities of the participating being, that is how the participated being must manifest itself. Hence, whether certain gods should have appeared as foreigners or projecting some other form, one must not take it that the apparent change occurs in them but rather that their image varies according to the various receivers.

---

173. *Or. chald.* frag. dub. 211, des Places.

Ἕνα μὲν οὖν τρόπον τὸν εἰρημένον ἡ ποίησις τῶν ἀμεταβλήτων μεταβολὰς πολυειδεῖς παραδίδωσιν. ἕτερον δὲ | ὅταν καὶ αὐτὸ τὸ θεῖον πολυδύναμον ὑπάρχον καὶ πλῆρες παντοίων εἰδῶν ποικίλα προτείνῃ θεάματα τοῖς εἰς αὐτὸ βλέπουσι. τότε γὰρ αὖ τὴν ἐξαλλαγὴν τῶν δυνάμεων ἐνδεικνυμένη μεταβάλλειν αὐτό φησι τὸ πάσας ἔχον ἐν ἑαυτῷ τὰς δυνάμεις ταύτας εἰς πολλὰς μορφάς, ἄλλοτε ἄλλην | προβαλλόμενον, ἀεὶ μὲν κατὰ πάσας ἐνεργοῦν, ταῖς δὲ μεταβατικαῖς νοήσεσι τῶν ψυχῶν ἀλλοῖον ἀεὶ διὰ τὸ πλῆθος τῶν περιεχομένων φανταζόμενον.

Καὶ κατὰ τοῦτον δὴ τὸν τρόπον ὁ Πρωτεὺς ἐκεῖνος λέγεται μεταβάλλειν τὸ οἰκεῖον εἶδος τοῖς εἰς αὐτὸν βλέπουσιν, ἄλλος καὶ ἄλλος ἀεὶ προ|φαινόμενος. εἰ γὰρ καὶ τῶν πρωτίστων θεῶν ἐστιν καταδεέστερος καὶ ἀθάνατος μέν, οὔπω δὲ θεός, καὶ Ποσειδῶνος μὲν ὑποδμώς, οὔπω δὲ ἡγεμονικὴν ἀξίαν λαχών, ἀλλὰ νοῦς τίς ἐστιν ἀγγελικὸς ἐν τῷ κλήρῳ τοῦ Ποσειδῶνος, ἔχων τε καὶ περιέχων ἐν ἑαυτῷ τὰ εἴδη πάντα τῶν γενητῶν· ὑποτέ||τακται δὲ αὐτῷ πρῶτον μὲν ἡ Εἰδοθέα, ψυχή τις οὖσα δαιμονία συνημμένη πρὸς τὸν οἰκεῖον νοῦν θεῖον ὄντα καὶ τοῖς εἴδεσιν τοῖς ἐκείνου τὰς ἑαυτῆς συνάψασα νοήσεις· ἕπεται δὲ καὶ ἄλλος ἀριθμὸς ψυχῶν, λογικῶν μὴν καὶ ἀϊ|δίων, ἃς ὁ μῦθος προσαγορεύει φώκας. διὸ καὶ ἀριθμῶν αὐτὰς ὁ Πρωτεὺς παραδέδοται, τὸ ἀίδιον αὐτῶν ἐνδεικνυμένης τῆς ποιήσεως· τῶν γὰρ γινομένων δήπου καὶ ἀπολλυμένων ἀόριστόν ἐστιν τὸ πλῆθος.

Νοῦν τοίνυν ὄντα τὸν Πρωτέα καὶ νοῦν πολυδύναμον διακορῆ τῶν εἰδῶν αἱ μερι|καὶ ψυχαὶ θεώμεναι καὶ ἄλλοτε ἄλλοις εἴδεσιν αὐτοῦ προσβάλλουσαι τὴν μετάβασιν τῶν σφετέρων νοήσεων μεταβολὴν τῶν νοουμένων εἶναι φαντάζονται. διὸ καὶ πάντα δοκεῖ γίνεσθαι τοῖς ἀντεχομένοις αὐτοῦ,

ὅσσ' ἐπὶ γαίης |
ἑρπετὰ γίγνονται καὶ ὕδωρ καὶ θεσπιδαὲς πῦρ [δ 417–418].

ὅσα γὰρ ἔχει καὶ περιείληφεν εἴδη, μᾶλλον δὲ ὅσα ἐστὶν ἀεὶ καὶ διαιωνίως, τοσαῦτα παρὰ μέρος γίγνεσθαι δοκεῖ διὰ τὴν τῶν θεωμένων αὐτὸν μεριστὴν ἐπιβολήν. |

[c. Transformations representing the multiple powers of the gods]

This, then, is one manner in which poetry presents polymorphic transformations of those beings that know no change, but there is also a second, in which the divine itself, because of its multiple powers and because it is filled with forms of all sorts, holds out diverse spectacles to those who look at it. Here, in effect, the poem is showing the variations of the powers and says that that which contains all these powers itself changes into many forms, projecting first one and then another, though in fact the being in question is always acting according to all its powers, but because of the multiplicity of those powers it is constantly envisioned as changing by the discursive apprehensions of souls.

It is in this sense that the famous Proteus is said to change his own shape according to those who look at him, constantly appearing as one thing, then another. If he is inferior to the first of the gods, an immortal though something less than a god, and "Poseidon's underling" [*Od.* 4.386] rather than a being with a rank of leadership, still he is an angelic soul allocated to Poseidon, holding and containing in himself the forms of all things that come to be and pass away. Set immediately below him || is Eidothea, a daemonic soul joined to her own intellect, which is divine, and fitting her own thoughts to the forms of that intellect. A number of other souls follow [in his procession], souls that are both rational and eternal and that the myth calls "seals" [*Od.* 4.411]. This is why Proteus is shown counting them, because the poem is indicating that they are eternal, for the number of those things that come to be and pass away is infinite, [and therefore incalculable].

And so, the partial souls that observe Proteus—who is an intellect with multiple powers and glutted with forms—apply the discursiveness of their own intellects now to one of his forms, now to another, and they imagine change in what their mind apprehends. This is why, for those who grasp him, he seems to become everything,

all the
creeping things and water and portentous fire [*Od.* 4.417–418],

and in the partial apprehension of those who contemplate him he seems in turn to become all the forms that he holds and contains, or rather, all those things that he continuously and eternally is.

Τὸ τρίτον τοίνυν λέγωμεν, ὅταν μήτε τοῦ ἑνὸς ποικίλα προφαίνηται σχήματα διὰ τὰς ὑπεστρωμένας ὑποδοχάς, μήτε πολυδύναμον ὂν καὶ ἓν τὸ θεωρούμενον φαντασίαν παρέχηται μεταβολῆς διὰ τὴν ποικιλίαν τῶν δυνάμεων, ἀλλ' ὅταν τὸ αὐτὸ κατὰ διαφόρους τάξεις προέρχηται καὶ μέχρι τῶν | τελευταίων ὑφιζάνῃ, πολλαπλασιάζον ἑαυτὸ κατ' ἀριθμὸν καὶ εἰς ὑφειμένας διακοσμήσεις καταβαῖνον, τότε αὖ πάλιν οἱ μῦθοι μεταβάλλειν φασὶ τὸ προϊὸν εἰς τοῦτο τὸ εἶδος ἄνωθεν, εἰς ὃ πεποίηται τὴν πρόοδον. οὕτω γὰρ καὶ τὴν | Ἀθηνᾶν τῷ Μέντορι καὶ τὸν Ἑρμῆν τῷ λάρῳ τῷ ὄρνιθι καὶ τὸν Ἀπόλλω τῷ ἱέρακί φασιν ἐξομοιοῦσθαι, τὰς δαι||μονιωτέρας αὐτῶν ἐνδεικνύμενοι τάξεις, εἰς ἃς ἀπὸ τῶν ὅλων προεληλύθασιν.

Καὶ διὰ ταῦτα, ὅταν μὲν θείας ἐπιφανείας ἀναγράφωσιν, ἀμορφώτους αὐτὰς καὶ ἀσχηματίστους πειρῶνται φυλάττειν· οἷον καὶ τῆς Ἀθηνᾶς τῆς τῷ | Ἀχιλλεῖ φαινομένης καὶ μόνῳ καταφανοῦς γινομένης, παντὸς τοῦ στρατοπέδου παρόντος. ἐκεῖ γὰρ οὐδὲ κατὰ τὸ μυθικὸν πρόσχημα παραδέδοταί τις τῆς θεοῦ μορφὴ καὶ τύπος, ἀλλ' ὅτι μόνον παρῆν· τίς δὲ ὁ τρόπος τῆς παρουσίας, ἄρρητον ἀφῆκεν ὁ λόγος. ὅταν δὲ ἀγγελικάς, μεταμπισχο|μένους μὲν τοὺς θεοὺς ἀλλοίας μορφὰς εἰσάγουσιν, ἀλλὰ <u>καὶ ταύτας</u> ὁλικάς, οἷον εἰς ἀνθρώπειον εἶδος ἢ κοινὸν ἀνδρὸς ἢ γυναικὸς ἀδιορίστως. οὕτω γὰρ αὖ τῷ Ἀχιλλεῖ πάλιν ὅ τε Ποσειδῶν καὶ ἡ Ἀθηνᾶ συνῆν·

**τῷ δὲ μάλ' ὦκα Ποσειδάων καὶ Ἀθήνη |
στήτην ἐγγὺς ἰόντε, δέμας δ' ἀνδρέσσιν ἔϊκτην** [Φ 284–285].

[d. The gods adopt the shapes of the classes of beings into which they descend.]

Now let us discuss the third [possibility], when various shapes of the single [deity] appear, not because of the receivers subject [to the apparition], nor because what is perceived, being both one and endowed with many powers, creates the illusion of transformation because of the diversity of those powers, but, on the contrary, when the same entity proceeds through the various classes of beings and settles to the very lowest, multiplying itself numerically even as it descends into the lower ranks. Here again the myths say that that which proceeds from above is *changed* into that form into which it has proceeded. It is in this sense that they say that Athena comes to be like Mentor [*Od.* 2.268], Hermes like a "gull-bird" [*Od.* 5.51], and Apollo like a falcon [*Il.* 15.237], indicating the more daemonic || classes of beings into which they have proceeded from the universals.

On account of this problem, when the myths describe epiphanies of the gods themselves they try to keep the apparitions without form and undefined. Take, for example, Athena appearing to Achilles and visible to him alone, though the whole army was present. Here, even in the screen of the mythic account, no form or shape of the goddess is passed down, but simply that she was present. The manner of her presence the text has passed over in silence. When it is an angelic [apparition], on the other hand, the myths introduce the gods taking on alien forms, but even these are universal ones,[174] as, for instance, [they speak of transformations into] a "human form," one that is common to man and woman, indiscriminately. In this way, again, Poseidon and Athena visited Achilles:

> Quickly Athena and Poseidon were beside him
> and stood close by, they had made themselves like men in form[175]
> [*Il.* 21.284–285].

---

174. Reading, with F., Kroll's suggestion, (app. ad loc.): καὶ ταύτας for ταύτας καὶ in K114,11.

175. This seems at first a poor illustration of the claim it is introduced to support, but clearly, for Proclus, ἀνήρ (like ἄνθρωπος) can designate a human being in contrast to a god, though in most occurrences the word designates a man as opposed to a woman.

ὁπόταν δὲ δαιμονίας ἐπιφοιτήσεις ἱστορῶσι, τηνικαῦτα καὶ τὰς μεταβολὰς εἰς ἄτομα καὶ μερικὰ γιγνομένας οὐκ ἀπαξιοῦσιν ἀναγράφειν ἢ καὶ εἰς ἀλλοκότων ζῴων μορφάς· τὰ | γὰρ ἔσχατα τῶν ἀεὶ θεοῖς ἑπομένων γενῶν δηλοῦται διὰ τῶν τοιούτων σχημάτων.

καὶ ὁρᾷς ὅπως κατὰ τὴν τῶν πραγμάτων τάξιν τὰ τοιαῦτα διαπλάττεται. τῷ μὲν γὰρ θείῳ προσήκει τὸ ἁπλοῦν, τῷ δὲ ἀγγελικῷ τὸ καθολικόν, τῷ δὲ δαιμονίῳ τὸ μερικόν· καὶ τῷ μὲν τὸ νοερόν, τῷ δὲ | τὸ λογικόν, τῷ δὲ τὸ τῆς ἀλογίας γένος· ἐν γὰρ τῇ τῶν δαιμόνων διακοσμήσει καὶ ἡ τοιαύτη ζωὴ συνδιαπέπλεκται.

Τοσαῦτα περὶ τῶν τρόπων εἶχον λέγειν, καθ᾽ οὓς οἱ παρ᾽ Ὁμήρῳ μῦθοι τῶν ἀμεταβλήτων μεταβολὰς μηχανῶνται καὶ τοῖς μονοειδέσι πολυειδεῖς ἐπεισάγουσι μορφάς. ||

Περὶ τῆς τοῦ ἐνυπνίου πομπῆς δοκούσης ψεῦδος ἐπὶ θεοὺς ἀναπέμπειν πῶς ἀπολογητέον, ἀψευδὲς τὸ θεῖον δεικνύουσιν.

Ὑπόλοιπον δέ ἐστί μοι περὶ τῆς τοῦ ἐνυπνίου πομπῆς | εἰπεῖν, ἣν ὑπὸ Διὸς ὁ ποιητὴς γεγονέναι τῷ Ἀγαμέμνονί φησιν. καὶ γὰρ ταύτην ὁ Σωκράτης ἐπὶ τέλει τῶν περὶ θεολογίας τύπων ᾐτιάσατο, διότι <τὸ> θεῖον πᾶν καὶ τὸ δαιμόνιον ἀψευδές, ὡς αὐτὸς ταῖς ἀποδεικτικαῖς μεθόδοις συνηνάγκασεν. ὁ δέ γε ποιητὴς ἠπατῆσθαί φησιν τὸν Ἀγα|μέμνονα διὰ τοῦδε τοῦ ἐνυπνίου. καίτοι πῶς οὐκ ἄτοπον, εἰ καὶ **τὸ ὄναρ ἐκ Διός ἐστιν** [A 63] κατὰ τὴν <u>ἑαυτοῦ</u> ψῆφον, τοῦτο μόνον ἐψεῦσθαι σχεδὸν τῶν μνήμης ἠξιωμένων, ὅπερ ἐκ τοῦ Διὸς ἔχει τὴν πρωτίστην γένεσιν;

However, when they relate daemonic visitations, then they do not consider it inappropriate to describe transformations into individuals and partial beings or even into the shapes of strange creatures, for the last of the classes that eternally follow on the gods become manifest in such shapes.

You can see how this fiction is adapted to the classes of reality. The simple belongs to the gods, the universal to the angels, and the partial to the daemons, and likewise the class of the intellective belongs to the gods, that of the rational to the angels, and the irrational to the daemonic, for this sort of [irrational] existence is also interwoven into the rank of daemons.

This is what I have been able to say about the ways in which the myths of Homer manage transformations of the immutable and introduce multiple forms for beings that have only a single form. ||

(9) How we are to defend the episode of the sending of the dream, which appears to attribute falsehood to the gods, and to demonstrate that the gods are free from falsehood.

[a. The problem]

I have still to speak about the sending of the dream that the poet says Zeus sent to Agamemnon. Socrates also found fault with this at the end of the passage on the basic principles regarding theology,[176] for all that is divine and daemonic is free of falsehood, as he showed with apodeictic demonstrations to be necessary. Yet the poet says that Agamemnon was deceived by this dream [cf. *Il.* 2.35–40]. How is it not strange, then, if by his own[177] account "dreams come from Zeus" [*Il.* 1.63], that this dream was virtually unique among all those in human memory in being a liar— this one that had its primal source in Zeus?[178]

---

176. These basic principles are laid down in *Rep.* 2.379–383, and the Homeric passage concerning the deceptive dream is rejected at 383a.

177. Cf. 89 (K85,25). Again, word order suggests that the possessive pronoun in line 11 should be reflexive.

178. Clearly, a question mark is needed after γένεσιν in line 13.

Λεγέσθω μὲν οὖν καὶ οἷς εἰώθασιν οἱ πολλοὶ τῶν ἐξηγητῶν ἀπαντᾶν, ὅτι τὸ | ψεῦδος ἐν τῇ φαντασίᾳ τοῦ Ἀγαμέμνονος ἔσχεν τὴν ὑπόστασιν. τοῦ γὰρ Διὸς ἐν τοῖς πρὸς τὸν ὄνειρον λόγοις καὶ αὖ τοῦ ὀνείρου διὰ τῶν πρὸς τὸν Ἀγαμέμνονα ῥημάτων ἐνδεικνυμένων, ὅτι δέοι πᾶν τὸ στράτευμα κινεῖν καὶ μετὰ πάντων προσβάλλειν τοῖς πολεμίοις (τοῦτο γὰρ αὖ δηλοῦν | ἑκατέρῳ τὸ πασσυδίῃ), τὸν Ἀγαμέμνονα μὴ συνέντα τοῦ προστάγματος τὴν μεγίστην μοῖραν τοῦ στρατεύματος παριδόντα καὶ τῆς Ἀχιλλέως ἐρημωθέντα χειρὸς ὅμως ἐπιχειρεῖν τῷ πολέμῳ, κἀνταῦθα τοῦ τέλους μὴ τυγχάνειν διὰ τὴν ἑαυτοῦ περὶ τὴν κρίσιν τῶν θείων φασμάτων ἀπειρίαν. | ὥστε οὐχ ὁ Ζεύς ἐστιν ὁ τῆς ἀπάτης αἴτιος, ἀλλ' ὁ κακῶς τῶν τοῦ Διὸς προσταγμάτων ἀκούσας.

Λεγέσθω μὲν ὅπερ ἔφην καὶ ταῦτα· προσκείσθω δὲ καὶ ἡ τοῦ καθηγεμόνος ἡμῶν ἐπιβολή, τῆς τε Ὁμηρικῆς διανοίας στοχαζομένη καὶ τῆς τῶν πραγμάτων ἀληθείας. εἰ γὰρ Ζεὺς ὑπό||κειται προνοῶν μὲν τῆς εἰς τὸν ἥρω τὸν Ἀχιλλέα τιμῆς, βουλευόμενος δὲ ὅπως ἂν ἀπολέσῃ πλεῖστον ὅσον τῶν Ἑλλήνων ἀριθμόν, πῶς οὐχὶ καὶ τῆς ἀπάτης αὐτὸν προειληφέναι τὴν αἰτίαν ἀναγκαῖον; οὐ γὰρ ἂν ἀπώλετο τὸ Ἑλληνι|κὸν Ἀχιλλέως συνόντος, οὐδ' ἂν δίκας ἔδοσαν τῆς εἰς αὐτὸν ἀδικίας. βέλτιον οὖν λέγειν, ὅτι καὶ ἡ ἀπάτη θεόθεν ἐπ' ἀγαθῷ τῶν ἀπατωμένων. τὸ γὰρ αὖ ἀγαθὸν κρεῖττόν ἐστιν τῆς ἀληθείας, καὶ ἐν μὲν τοῖς θεοῖς συνέζευκται ἀλλήλοις (οὔτε γὰρ ὁ νοῦς ἄνευ τῆς θεότητος, οὔτε ἡ θεότης ἄνευ | τῆς νοερᾶς οὐσίας), ἐν δὲ τοῖς μετέχουσιν μερίζεται πολλάκις, καὶ τό τε ἀγαθὸν διὰ τοῦ ψεύδους παραγίνεται καὶ τὸ ἀληθὲς ἀποπίπτει τῆς τοῦ ἀγαθοῦ μοίρας.

Ὅθεν δὴ καὶ αὐτὸς ὁ Σωκράτης [Rep. 5.459c] νομοθετῶν τοῖς φύλαξιν συχνῷ τῷ ψεύδει χρῆσθαι προστάττει διὰ τὴν τῶν ἀνοήτων | δόξαν, οὐ δυναμένων ἄλλως τοῦ προσήκοντος αὐτοῖς ἀγαθοῦ τυχεῖν. εἰ οὖν τις

[b. First reply]

Let us then state the argument with which most of the interpreters usually reply,[179] that the lie had its existence in the imagination of Agamemnon. For Zeus in his words to the dream and again the dream in what it says to Agamemnon both indicate that it was necessary to rouse up the whole army and to make use of all of it to attack the enemy—this is shown in both speeches by the use of the word πασσυδίη[180]—but they say that Agamemnon did not understand the order, left the larger part of the army aside, and, unaided by the hand of Achilles, he nevertheless undertook the battle and then failed to accomplish his goal through his own inability to judge divine apparitions. Thus the guilt for the deception falls not on Zeus but on the man who heard Zeus's orders incorrectly.

[c. Second reply, from Syrianus]

Let this stand as stated, but let my teacher's idea be set forth as well, aiming as it does at the meaning of Homer and the truth of the matter. If Zeus is shown || taking providential care, on the one hand, for the honor of the hero Achilles and plotting how to destroy as large a number as possible of the Greeks, how is it possible that he has not also taken on before the fact the responsibility for the deception? The Greek army would not have been destroyed with Achilles present, nor would they have paid the price for the injustice done to him. It is better, then, to say that the deception as well came from the god but for the good of those deceived. The good is greater than truth, and among the gods they are joined to one another—for [there,] there is no intellect without divinity, no divinity without intellective substance—but among the participating beings these are often separated, and the good comes about through falsehood and truth drops from the portion of the good.

Thus, even Socrates himself, as a lawgiver, tells the guardians to use lies extensively on account of the [false] opinions of the stupid, who are unable otherwise to reach the good appropriate to them (*Rep.* 5.459c).

---

179. Cf. (with Kroll and F.) Macrobius, *In Somn. Scip.* 1.7.4–6, with Stahl 1952, 119 n. 3, ad loc.

180. πανσυδίῃ (= πασσυδίῃ) in Homer has been interpreted (as here) as meaning "with full force" or "with the entire army," but it has also been understood to mean "all at once" or "quickly"—a sense that would not support Proclus's argument at this point.

λέγοι καὶ τὸν θεὸν τοὺς μὲν διὰ τῆς ἀληθείας εὐεργετεῖν, τοὺς δὲ διὰ τοῦ ψεύδους, πάντας δὲ ὅμως ἐπανάγειν εἰς τὸ ἀγαθόν, οὐ θαυμαστόν. καὶ γὰρ τῶν γινομένων τὰ μὲν ἄνευ ὕλης ὑφίστησι, τὰ δὲ μεθ' | ὕλης, ᾗ τὸ ψεῦδος ἔνεστι τὸ ἀληθινόν. ὥστε καὶ ἐν τῇ προνοίᾳ τῶν ψυχῶν, εἰ τὰς μὲν ἄλλως κατὰ τὸν εἰρημένον τρόπον εὐεργετοῖ, τὰς δὲ ἄλλως, καὶ τὰς μὲν ἀΰλως διὰ τῆς ἀληθείας, τὰς δὲ ἐνύλως διὰ τοῦ ψεύδους, ἔχοι ἄν που καὶ ταῦτα τὸν πρέποντα τοῖς θεοῖς λόγον.

Εἰ δὲ δεῖ | καὶ τοῦτο λέγειν, τικτέσθω μὲν ἡ ἀπάτη καὶ τὸ ψεῦδος ἐν τῷ μετέχοντι, γιγνέσθω δὲ καὶ τοῦτο κατὰ τὴν τοῦ θεοῦ βούλησιν, ἵνα σωφρονέστερον γένηται διὰ τῆς ἀπάτης τὸ πλημμελῆσαν. ὥσπερ δὴ καὶ γεννᾶται μὲν τὸ ἔνυλον ἐν τοῖς τῇδε τόποις, ὑφίσταται δὲ κατὰ τὴν δημιουργικὴν πρό|νοιαν, ἵνα καὶ γένεσις ᾖ καὶ φθορὰ συμπληροῦσα τὸ πᾶν. ||

Οὔκουν ἀπατᾷ τὸ θεῖον, ἀλλ' ὑφ' ἑαυτοῦ τὸ ἀπατώμενον ἀπατᾶται, καὶ τοῦτο γίνεται κατὰ τὴν ἐκείνου βούλησιν ἐπ' ἀγαθῷ τοῦ πάσχοντος. καὶ γὰρ ἀΰλως τοῦ θεοῦ ποιοῦντος ἐνύλως γίνεται τὸ γιγνόμενον, καὶ ἀμερίστως ἐνεργοῦντος | μεριστῶς ἀποτελεῖται, καὶ νοερῶς σημαίνοντος ἐν τῷ δεχομένῳ τὸ ψεῦδος παρυφίσταται. δηλοῖ δὲ καὶ αὐτὸς ὁ θεῖος ποιητής, ὅτι παρὰ τοῖς θεοῖς <τῆς> ἀληθείας οὔσης ἡ ἀπάτη γεννᾶται διὰ τὴν τῶν δεχομένων ἄνοιαν, ὅταν ποιῇ τὸν Δία τῷ ὀνείρῳ παρακελευόμενον [B 10] **πάντα μάλ' ἀτρε|κέως ἀγορευέμεν**. πῶς οὖν ἐν θεῷ τὸ ψεῦδος καθ' Ὅμηρον; πῶς δὲ ἀπάτης αἴτιος ὁ θεός; εἰ μὴ λέγοι οὕτω τις, ὡς οὐδὲ τῆς ἐνταῦθα παρυφισταμένης ἀπάτης παρὰ τὴν τοῦ θεοῦ βούλησιν γεννωμένης.

Ἀλλὰ ταῦτα διακρίνειν ἡ τῶν νέων ἕξις ἀδύνατός ἐστιν καὶ θεωρεῖν, πῶς τῶν | ὅλων ἀκακώτων μενόντων ἐν τοῖς μεριστῶς αὐτῶν ἀντιλαμβανομένοις ἀναφαίνεται τὸ κακόν, καὶ πῶς τῶν κρειττόνων ἡμῶν οὐκ ἀπατώντων ἡμεῖς ἐξαπατώμεθα πολλάκις, καὶ ὅπως ἐξαπατώμενοι κατὰ πρόνοιαν τοῦτο πάσχομεν. διὸ καὶ ὁ Σωκράτης ἀνηκόους εἶναι τῶν τοιούτων λόγων | θέλει τοὺς νέους, ὡς διηρθρωμένας περὶ αὐτῶν φαντασίας ἔχειν οὐ δυναμένους.

Now, if one should say that the god does good to some through truth and to others through falsehood, though he leads all upwards to the good, this would not be surprising. He constitutes some of the things that come to be without matter, but others with matter, in which genuine falsehood is inherent. And so, even if Zeus should, in the providential care of souls, do good to some in the manner under discussion, to others in another way—to some nonmaterially and through truth and to others materially and through falsehood—these things as well would have a logic appropriate to the gods.

[d. Conclusion, Proclus's synthesis]

If we need to say this as well, let us have it that the deception and the falsehood are begotten in the participant being, but let this happen as well according to the will of the god, so that what has erred may become more reasonable through the deception. In just the same way, that which is embodied is born here, but it comes into being through demiurgical providence, so that coming to be may exist along with destruction, completing and fulfilling the universe. ||

Therefore, the divine does not deceive, but rather he who is deceived deceives himself, and this comes about by divine will for the good of the sufferer. For the god acts nonmaterially, but that which comes to be does so materially; his act is entire, but its effect is fragmented; he gives indications intellectively, and falsehood comes to be secondarily in the receiver. The divine Poet himself indicates that, while truth exists among the gods, deception is produced through the mindlessness of the receivers, when he shows Zeus telling the dream to "tell it all exactly" [*Il.* 2.10]. How, then, is the falsehood in the god, according to Homer? How is the god the cause of the deception? Unless someone should argue that the deception that comes to be secondarily here does not do so against the will of the god.

Nevertheless, the state of mind of the young is unable to distinguish these things and to see how, while the universals remain free of evil, evil makes its appearance in those who grasp them in a partial manner, and how, although the superior beings do not deceive us, we are often deceived, and how when we are deceived we are deceived providentially. Therefore Socrates does not want the young to hear such stories, since they are incapable of forming clearly articulated mental images from them.

Κοινὴ ἀπολογία ὑπέρ τε τῶν Ὁμηρικῶν μύθων καὶ τῶν Πλατωνικῶν, ἐν οἷς περὶ τῶν ἐν Ἅιδου λέγουσι δικαιωτηρίων καὶ τῶν ἐν αὐτοῖς λήξεων τῶν διαφόρων, | ἃς ἔχουσιν αἱ ἐξελθοῦσαι τῶν σωμάτων ψυχαὶ κατὰ τὰ ἰδιώματα τῆς ἐν σώματι ζωῆς.

Ἀλλ' ἐπεὶ καὶ ταῦτα διεπερανάμεθα, πάλιν ἀπ' ἄλλης ἀρχῆς τῶν ἐν τῷ τρίτῳ τῆς Πολιτείας γεγραμμένων ποιησώ||μεθα τὴν ἐξέτασιν. καὶ πρὸ τῶν ἄλλων, ὅσα περὶ τῶν ἐν Ἅιδου διαμυθολογῶν ὁ ποιητὴς ἀνεφθέγξατο, ἢ αὐτὸς λέγων ἢ ἄλλῳ λέγοντι χρώμενος, διασκοπήσωμεν, εἴ πῃ ἄρα ἀληθείας ἔχεταί τινος καὶ ταῖς Πλάτωνος ὑφηγήσεσιν προσ|ήκοντα φαίνεται.

τί δὴ οὖν βούλεται καὶ ὁ τῶν ἐν Ἅιδου πάντων χρημάτων τὴν ἐν τῷ τῇδε βίῳ θητείαν προτιθείς, καὶ τὰ οἰκητήρια τὰ φοβερὰ καὶ ἃ στυγέουσιν οἱ θεοί, καὶ τὸ εἴδωλον καὶ ἡ ψυχὴ τὰ ἔρημα τοῦ νοῦ φερόμενα, καὶ αἱ ταῖς σκιαῖς παραβαλλόμεναι ζωαί, καὶ οἱ θρῆνοι τῶν | ἐνθένδε ἐκεῖσε φερομένων ψυχῶν, καὶ ἡ πρὸς τὰς νυκτερίδας αὐτῶν ἀπεικασία, καὶ ὁ

(10) A simultaneous defense of the Homeric and Platonic myths in which they speak of a place of correction in Hades and of the various destinies there of the souls that have left their bodies, determined according to the specific qualities of their lives in the body.

Now that we have gone through these things, let us go back and, approaching the matter from another starting point, examine ‖ what is written in book 3 of the *Republic*.

First of all, let us look at what the Poet has expressed mythologically about things in Hades, either in his own voice or using those of other characters, and let us consider whether these contain any truth at all and anything that fits with the Platonic accounts.

What, then, is the significance of:[181]

[a] the one who prefers servitude in this life to all the riches Hades has to offer,
[b] the frightful dwelling places "that even the gods hate,"
[c] the ghostly image and soul that go about empty of mind,
[d] the lives compared to shadows,
[e] the wailings of souls being taken there from here,
[f] the representation of them as bats,

---

181. The following are the specific passages cited by Socrates at *Rep.* 3.386c–387b as examples of poetically pleasing but counterproductive poetry, which will have the effect of making its audience fear death more than they fear slavery. Proclus discusses these individually below, and I have keyed the passages to the discussion using lowercase letters in square brackets.

[a] βουλοίμην κ' ἐπάρουρος ἐὼν θητευέμεν ἄλλῳ / ἀνδρὶ παρ' ἀκλήρῳ, ᾧ μὴ βίοτος πολὺς εἴη / ἢ πᾶσιν νεκύεσσι καταφθιμένοισιν ἀνάσσειν (*Od.* 11.489–491 = *Rep.* 3.386c5–7).

[b] οἰκία δὲ θνητοῖσι καὶ ἀθανάτοισι φανείη / σμερδαλέ', εὐρώεντα, τά τε στυγέουσι θεοί περ (*Il.* 20.64–65 = *Rep.* 3.386d1–2).

[c] ὢ πόποι, ἦ ῥά τίς ἐστι καὶ εἰν Ἀΐδαο δόμοισι / ψυχὴ καὶ εἴδωλον, ἀτὰρ φρένες οὐκ ἔνι πάμπαν (*Il.* 23.103–104 = *Rep.* 3.386d4–5).

[d] οἴῳ πεπνῦσθαι· τοὶ δὲ σκιαὶ ἀΐσσουσιν (*Od.* 10.495 = *Rep.* 3.386d7).

[e] ψυχὴ δ' ἐκ ῥεθέων πταμένη Ἄϊδόσδε βεβήκει, / ὃν πότμον γοόωσα, λιποῦσ' ἀνδροτῆτα καὶ ἥβην (*Il.* 16.856–857 = *Rep.* 3.386d9–10).

[f] ὡς δ' ὅτε νυκτερίδες μυχῷ ἄντρου θεσπεσίοιο / τρίζουσαι ποτέονται, ἐπεί κέ τις ἀποπέσῃσιν / ὁρμαθοῦ ἐκ πέτρης, ἀνά τ' ἀλλήλῃσιν ἔχονται, / ὣς αἳ τετριγυῖαι ἅμ' ἤεσαν (*Od.* 24.6–9 = *Rep.* 3.387a5–9).

[g] ψυχὴ δὲ κατὰ χθονός, ἠΰτε καπνός, / ᾤχετο τετριγυῖα (*Il.* 23.100–101 = *Rep.* 3.387a2–3).

καπνὸς καὶ ὁ τρισμός, καὶ ὅσα τοιαῦτα ἐν τοῖς ποιήμασιν γέγραπται, καὶ οἱ ἐν Ἅιδου ποταμοί, καὶ τὰ τραγικώτατα τῶν ὀνομάτων;

Ταῦτα γὰρ δὴ καὶ ὁ Σωκράτης ηὔθυνεν [εἰ] καὶ ἐπὶ πᾶσιν ἕνα κοινὸν | προσέθηκεν λόγον, ὅτι πρὸς μὲν ἄλλο τι εὖ ἔχει, ἡμεῖς δὲ ὑπὲρ τῶν φυλάκων <u>δειδισσόμεθα</u>, μὴ ἐκ τούτων τῶν δειμάτων <τὸν θάνατον> ἡγήσωνται φοβερόν. ἐπεὶ ὅτι γε καὶ αὐτὸς πολλαχοῦ χρῆται τοῖς τοιούτοις ὀνόμασίν τε καὶ αἰνίγμασιν, παντί που καταφανές. ἵνα γὰρ παραλείπω τοὺς ἐν Φαί|δωνι ποταμούς, καὶ τὰς τῶν ψυχῶν πλάνας καὶ τὰς ἀπορίας, καὶ τὰς τριόδους καὶ τὰς κολάσεις καὶ τὰς ἐν τοῖς ῥεύμασιν φοράς, καὶ τοὺς θρήνους τοὺς ἐκεῖ καὶ τὰς ἐκβοήσεις καὶ τὰς τῶν ἠδικημένων ἱκεσίας, ὧν καὶ ὁ Πλάτων μεστὰ εἶναι τὰ ἐν Ἅιδου φησίν, ἀλλὰ τὰ ἐν ταύτῃ τῇ πραγ|ματείᾳ γεγραμμένα πρὸς τῷ τέλει πῶς οὐ τῆς αὐτῆς ἐστι διανοίας τοῖς Ὁμηρικοῖς ποιήμασιν, τὸ στόμιον τὸ μυκώμενον, ὁ Τάρταρος, οἱ διάπυροι δαίμονες οἱ τὸν Ἀρδιαῖον κνάπτοντες, αἱ μεσταὶ κόνεως καὶ αὐχμοῦ ψυχαί; τί γὰρ ἐν τούτοις ἀπολείπεται τῆς μεγίστης τραγῳδίας; ὥστε ὁ || αὐτὸς λόγος καὶ ταῦτα ἐκβάλλειν ἢ μηδὲ τὴν Ὁμηρικὴν αἰτιᾶσθαι διδασκαλίαν.

Λέγωμεν τοίνυν ἐπ' ἀμφοτέρων, εἴτε τῶν Ἐπικουρείων τις ἐγκαλεῖν ἐπιχειροῖ τοῖς τοιούτοις μύθοις εἴτε καὶ ἄλλος τις, ὅτι καὶ τῶν ψυχῶν αἱ ἕξεις εἰσὶ | διάφοροι τῶν ἀπαλλαττομένων τοῦ σώματος καὶ οἱ τόποι τοῦ παντὸς εἰς οὓς ἐνοικίζονται πολυειδεῖς τυγχάνουσιν ὄντες. καὶ τὰς μὲν οὕτω χωριζομένας τῶν ὀργάνων τῶν θνητοειδῶν, ὡς μήτε σχέσιν ἔχειν πρὸς τὰ χείρονα μήτε ἀναπίμπλασθαι τῆς ἐν αὐτοῖς ταραχῆς καὶ τῆς ὑλικῆς | φλυαρίας, καὶ τὰ περιβλήματα τὰ αὐγοειδῆ καθαρὰ φέρειν ἀνάγκη, καὶ μὴ ἐπιθολούμενα ὑπὸ τῶν ἐνύλων ἀτμῶν μηδὲ παχυνόμενα ὑπὸ τῆς γηΐνης φύσεως· τὰς δὲ μὴ τελέως αὑτὰς διὰ φιλοσοφίας καθηραμένας, ἀλλὰ καθελκομένας εἰς τὴν πρὸς τὸ ὀστρέϊνον σῶμα προσπάθειαν καὶ | τὸν μετὰ τούτου διωκούσας βίον, τοιαῦτα καὶ τὰ ὀχήματα τὰ ἐξηρτημένα αὐτῶν δεικνύναι τοῖς ὁρᾶν δυναμένοις, σκιοειδῆ καὶ ἔνυλα καὶ ὀπισθοβαρῆ, καὶ πολὺ τῆς θνητοειδοῦς ἐφελκόμενα [διὰ τοῦτο καὶ] συστάσεως. καὶ διὰ τοῦτο ὅ τε Σωκράτης ἐν τῷ Φαίδωνι [81d] τὰς τοιαύτας φησὶν | περὶ τοὺς

[g] the smoke and the squeaking,
and of all the other comparable things he has written in the poems, including the rivers of Hades, and the most horrific and theatrical of his vocabulary ["Cocytus, Styx, dwellers below, corpses" *Rep.* 3.387b]?

Indeed, Socrates censured these expressions and made a common statement about all of them, that they are alright in another context, but we will fear[182] them for the guardians, lest because of these horrors they decide that death is something fearful. Nevertheless, it is perfectly obvious to everyone that [Plato] himself uses such words and riddles often. Not to mention the rivers of the *Phaedo* [112a–114c] and the wanderings and helplessness of souls [108b–c], the crossroads, the punishments, the being swept away in streams and then the lamentations and screaming there [below], and the prayers they must address to those they have wronged [108a, 113d, 114a–b], of which Plato says Hades is full, how does what is written near the end of the present work [in the Myth of Er] not have the same sense as the Homeric poems, with its howling mouth [*Rep.* 10.615e], Tartarus, the fiery daemons that tear Ardiaeus apart [615e–616a], and the souls full of dust and filth [614d]? What is there in all of this that falls short of the greatest theatricality? Consistent reasoning ‖ must either throw these out or refrain from finding fault with the Homeric teaching.

Let us reply, then, in either case—whether some Epicurean is attacking such myths or someone else—by saying that the conditions of the souls that are leaving the body are various and the places of the universe where they take up residence are actually of many sorts. Those separated from their mortal bodies in such a way that they have no relation to inferior things and are not filled with the troubles inherent in them and with the futility of matter must also wear raiment that is pure and luminous, neither made turbid by material vapors nor thickened by earthly substance; those who have not entirely cleansed themselves through philosophy, however, but rather are drawn down into empathy with their ostraceous bodies and pursue a life bound to these show, to those able to see, vehicles attached to themselves that are of this same quality, shadowy and material and weighted down, dragging along much that belongs to the substance of mortality. On account of this, Socrates in the *Phaedo* says that such souls,

---

182. Reading F.'s conjecture δειδισσόμεθα for the manuscript's δεόμεθα in K118,16 (though Radermacher's αἰδούμεθα will serve as well).

τάφους καλινδουμένας σκιοειδῆ παρέχεσθαι φαντάσματα, καὶ ὁ ποιητὴς σκιαῖς αὐτὰς παραπλησίως ἀΐσσειν ἱστόρησεν.

Ἔτι δὲ καὶ τούτων τῶν ψυχῶν τῶν ἔτι τὸν τῇδε βίον περιπτυσσομένων πολλαὶ διαφορότητές εἰσιν. αἱ μὲν γὰρ πρακτικώτερον ζήσασαι καὶ μηδέπω τῆς τοιαύτης ζωῆς | ἀποστᾶσαι τὸ προσῆκον ὄργανον ταῖς πρακτικαῖς ἐνεργείαις ἀσπάζονται καὶ χωριζόμεναι τούτου δυσχεραίνουσιν, ὥσπερ ἡ Πατρόκλου **λιποῦσα ἀνδρότητά** τε **καὶ ἥβην** [Χ 363], καὶ ἐν Ἅιδου γενόμεναι ποθοῦσιν αὐτοῦ τὴν συνουσίαν, || ὥσπερ ἡ Ἀχιλλέως, διότι καὶ τὴν ἐνταῦθα ζωὴν προτίθησιν τῆς χωριστῆς, ὡς κατ' ἐκείνην μὲν ἐνεργεῖν οὐ δυναμένη, κατὰ δὲ τὸν ἐν πράξει βίον πρωτεύουσα.

Αἱ δὲ διὰ κακοζωΐαν φιλοφρονοῦνται τὸ ὀστρέϊνον σῶμα καὶ τὴν μετ' αὐ|τοῦ ζωήν, οὐδὲν διαφέρειν ἡγούμεναι τῆς ἐν αὐτῷ ζωῆς. ἃς δὴ καὶ νυκτερίσιν ἀπείκασεν ἡ ἔνθεος ποίησις, ὡς εἰς τὸ σκοτεινὸν φερομένας καὶ τὸ ἔσχατον τοῦ παντός, ὃ δὴ θεσπέσιον ἄντρον ἄν τις προσαγορεύσειεν, καὶ ὡς τὸ πτερὸν τὸ ψυχικὸν σαρκῶδες καὶ παχὺ καὶ γήϊνον ἐχούσας. | τί οὖν ἔτι θαυμαστόν, εἰ καὶ Ἀχιλλεὺς πρακτικὴν σχὼν ἀρετὴν ἐφίοιτο τῆς μετὰ σώματος ζωῆς ὑπηρετεῖν αὐτοῦ δυναμένου ταῖς πράξεσιν; ὁ μὲν γὰρ Ἡρακλῆς διὰ τελεστικῆς καθηράμενος καὶ τῶν ἀχράντων καρπῶν μετασχὼν τελέας ἔτυχεν τῆς εἰς θεοὺς ἀποκαταστάσεως· |

αὐτὸς δὲ μετ' ἀθανάτοισι θεοῖσι
τέρπεται ἐν θαλίῃ καὶ ἔχει καλλίσφυρον Ἥβην· [λ 602–603]

καὶ εἴρηται πολλὰ πολλαχοῦ καὶ περὶ τῆς Ἡρακλέους ἐκθεώσεως. ὁ δὲ Ἀχιλλεὺς ἔτι τὸ κατορθοῦν ἐν ταῖς πράξεσιν ἀγαπᾷ καὶ τόνδε τὸν βίον καὶ διώκει καὶ ὄργανον προσῆ|κον αὐτοῦ τῷ βίῳ καὶ ποθεῖ· κατὰ τὰς συνηθείας γοῦν καὶ αὐτὸς ὡς τὰ πολλὰ τὰς ψυχὰς αἱρεῖσθαί φησι τοὺς δευτέρους βίους ὁ Πλάτων [Rep. 10.620a].

Πῶς δὲ οὐ καὶ τοῦτο τῆς Ὁμηρικῆς ἐστιν ἐνθέου παραδόσεως, τὸ διακρίνειν ψυχήν τε καὶ εἴδωλον τὸ ταύτης καὶ τὸν νοῦν τὸν | τῆς ψυχῆς, καὶ τὴν μὲν ψυχὴν χρῆσθαι τῷ εἰδώλῳ λέγειν, τὸν δὲ νοῦν ἀμφοῖν ὑπάρχειν

lurking around tombs, produce shadowy apparitions [81d], and the Poet says that they dart about like shadows [d].

Moreover, there are many differences among these souls that still embrace this life. Some, who have lived a more active life and never abandoned it, cherish the tools appropriate to effective activity and are miserable when separated from them, like Patroclus, "leaving behind bravery and youth" [*Il.* 22.363]. Once they have arrived in Hades, they long for union [with that tool, the body just] || as the soul of Achilles does, and that is why he prefers this life over that separated [from the body], because he is incapable of activity in that other life but was preeminent in this life of action [a].

Others become attached to their ostraceous bodies and to the life in them through bad living, thinking that there is nothing better than that life. These are surely the ones that the inspired poem compares to bats [f], since they are drawn to the shadowy region, the farthest reach of the universe, which one might well call a "wondrous cave,"[183] and since the wings of their souls are fleshy and thick and earthy. What wonder is it, then, that Achilles, who had acquired active virtue, should desire life with a body, which would be able to serve him for accomplishing things? Heracles, purified by initiation and having achieved participation in the pure fruit, experienced a perfect return to the company of the gods:

> he himself is happy among the immortal gods
> in the midst of good cheer, and has slender-footed Hebe as his
>   wife [*Od.* 11.602–603],

and this apotheosis of Heracles has been the subject of much discussion in many places. Achilles, however, is still in love with success in action [a] and with this life, and he longs for and pursues an appropriate tool for this life of his [i.e., a body]. Indeed, Plato himself says that souls usually chose their second lives according to their earlier habits [*Rep.* 10.620a].

How is this as well not part of the inspired Homeric tradition, to distinguish the soul both from its ghostly image[184] and from its intellect and to say that the soul makes use of the image and that the intellect is more

---

183. The phrase occurs at *Od.* 24.6, and this is clearly the passage to which Proclus refers, but the reference to the cave as the universe suggests the cave of Porphyry's essay *On the Cave of the Nymphs*, to which the same phrase is applied at *Od.* 13.363.

184. At this point, the εἴδωλον would appear to be the body; see n. 185 below.

θειότερον; καὶ τὸ μὲν εἴδωλον καὶ τὴν ψυχὴν γνωστά πως εἶναι, καὶ ἔτι κατεχομένην ἐν τοῖς σώμασιν [καὶ] κηδεμόνα φαίνεσθαι τοῦ ὀστρεΐνου ‖ σώματος καὶ τὴν περὶ αὐτοῦ πρόνοιαν καὶ μὴ γιγνομένου ἐπιποθεῖν· τὸν δὲ νοῦν ἄληπτον εἶναι ταῖς φανταστικαῖς ἡμῶν καὶ μορφωτικαῖς κινήσεσιν.

Διὰ γὰρ ταῦτα καὶ ὁ Ἀχιλλεὺς τὸν Πάτροκλον ἰδὼν περὶ τῆς ταφῆς διαλεγόμενον | τοῦ σώματος ψυχὴν μὲν ἐν Ἅιδου καὶ εἴδωλον ἐπίστευσεν εἶναι, νοῦν δὲ οὐκ εἶναι τούτοις μηδὲ φρόνησιν τὴν χρωμένην. τὰ μὲν γὰρ τῆς ἀλογίας ἐνεργήματα πρὸς τὴν τούτων ἐπήγετο θέσιν, τὴν δὲ τῆς νοερᾶς ψυχῆς παραδοχὴν οὐκ εἶχεν ἐκ τῶν ὀνειρωκτικῶν θεαμάτων πιστώσασθαι. |

Πῶς δὲ οὐχὶ καὶ τοῖς πράγμασιν αὐτοῖς ἁπάντων ἐστὶ συμφωνότατον τὸ τὰς πολλὰς τῶν ψυχῶν θρηνούσας ἀφίστασθαι τῶν σωμάτων καὶ δυσαποσπάστως ἐχούσας διὰ τὰς ἐν αὐτῷ ζωὰς καὶ τὰς πολυαράτους ἡδονάς (αὗται γοῦν, φησὶν καὶ ὁ Σωκράτης [Phd. 83d], ὥσπερ ἧλον ἔχουσαι | προσπερονῶσιν αὐτὰς καὶ προσηλοῦσιν τοῖς σώμασιν) καὶ ὀχήμασιν ἐξελθούσας χρῆσθαι σκιοειδέσιν καὶ τεθολωμένοις ἀπὸ τῶν σεληναίων ἀτμῶν καὶ ἐμβριθέσι καὶ γεώδεσιν, καὶ φωνὴν ἄσημον ἀφιέναι καὶ ἦχον ὑλικόν, ὃν ἡ ποίησις τρισμὸν ἀπεκάλεσεν; ὡς γὰρ τῶν ἀναγομένων ψυχῶν τὰ | ὄργανα φωνὴν ἐναρμόνιον ἀφίησιν καὶ ἐμμελῆ,

divine than the other two? And furthermore, that the image and the soul are in some sense knowable and while she is still contained in bodies, [the soul] also appears as caretaker of the ostraceous || body,[185] and, even when the object of this providence no longer exists, she desires to exercise providence on its behalf. The intellect, on the other hand, is impossible to grasp with the shape-imparting impulses of our imaginations.[186]

This is why Achilles [c], seeing Patroclus when he talked with him near the tomb of his body, believed that the soul and the image were in Hades but that they were bereft of intellect and of the thought that depends [on intellect].[187] The actions of the irrational element led [Achilles] to the location of soul and image, but he was not able[188] to confirm from the dream vision the fate of the intellective soul.

Moreover, how are these things not preeminently in harmony as well with things as they are, namely, the fact that most souls leave their bodies lamenting and full of separation anxiety[189] for the lives they led in them and their cherished pleasures—these pleasures, Socrates says, as if they had a spike, penetrate them and nail them to their bodies [*Phd.* 83d]—and when they leave their bodies, that they use vehicles that are shadowy and soiled by lunar exhalations and heavy and earthy, emitting a meaningless sound and a physical noise that the poem called a "squeak" [f and g].[190] Just as the vehicles[191] of souls that are ascending emit a harmonious and musical sound and manifest a rhythmical motion, so souls that are more

---

185. This sentence, in spite of F.'s efforts, still appears to be corrupt. The initial, "inspired" Homeric distinction must be body, soul, and intellect (for the body as εἴδωλον, see the famous anecdote in Porphyry, *Vit. Plot.* 1, along with 247 [K172], below). The simplest solution seems to be κατεχομένην (sc. τὴν ψυχήν) for the manuscript's κατεχομένης in K120,27, with the manuscript's κηδεμόνα in line 28 and in K121,1, γιγνομένου for γιγνομένην. With F., I would bracket the καί in K120,28.

186. I.e., we cannot form a mental image or impression of mind.

187. Or perhaps (F.), of soul.

188. F. took τὰ ... ἐνεργήματα as subject of both verbs, but in spite of the harshness of the change of subject, Achilles' perceptions and mental processes are the topic here.

189. This translation for [the souls] δυσαποσπάστως ἐχούσας admittedly smacks of psychological jargon, but it is faithful to Proclus's point here (which is not simply that the souls are "hard to tear away" from the body but rather that they experience that loss acutely).

190. Adding (with F.) a question mark in line 19, responding to πῶς in line 10.

191. ὄργανα seems to be used here where ὀχήματα might be expected.

καὶ εὔρυθμον ἔχοντα φαίνεται κίνησιν, οὕτω τῶν ὑπὸ γῆς φερομένων καὶ ἀλογωτέρων ὁ ἦχος τρισμῷ παραπλήσιός ἐστιν, τῆς ὀρεκτικῆς μόνης καὶ φανταστικῆς ζωῆς ἴνδαλμα φέρων.

25 Καὶ μὴν καὶ τοὺς τόπους τοὺς ἐν Ἅιδου καὶ τὰ ὑπὸ γῆς δικαι|ωτήρια καὶ τοὺς ποταμούς, οὓς Ὅμηρός τε καὶ Πλάτων ἡμᾶς ἐδιδαξάτην, οὐ κενὰς φαντασίας οἰητέον εἶναι καὶ μυθικὰς τερατείας· ἀλλ᾽ ὥσπερ ταῖς εἰς

K122 οὐρανὸν ἰούσαις || ψυχαῖς πολλοὶ τόποι καὶ παντοδαποὶ τῆς ἐκεῖ λήξεως ἀφωρίσθησαν, οὕτω δεῖ νομίζειν καὶ ταῖς κολάσεως ἔτι καὶ καθάρσεως δεομέναις τοὺς ὑπὸ γῆς τόπους ἀνεῖσθαι, ποικίλας μὲν ἀπορροίας ἔχοντας

5 τῶν ὑπὲρ γῆς στοιχείων, | ἃς δὴ ποταμοὺς καὶ ῥεύματα κεκλήκασιν, δαιμόνων δὲ τάξεις διαφόρους ἐφεστώσας, τὰς μὲν τιμωρούς, τὰς δὲ κολαστικάς, τὰς δὲ καθαρτικάς, τὰς δὲ κριτικάς. εἰ δὲ ἡ ποίησις

σμερδαλέ᾽ εὐρώεντα τά τε στυγέουσι θεοί περ ἐκεῖνα προσ-είρηκεν [Υ 65],

10 οὐδὲ τοῦτο αἰτιᾶσθαι προσήκει. κατα|πλήττει μὲν γὰρ τὰς ψυχὰς διὰ τῆς ποικιλίας καὶ τῆς τῶν ἐφεστώτων φαντασίας, ἀνήπλωται δὲ κατὰ τὰς παντοίας λήξεις τὰς πρεπούσας ταῖς διαφόροις ἕξεσι τῶν ἐκεῖ φερομένων, πορρωτάτω [τὰ] δέ ἐστι τῶν θεῶν ὡς ἔσχατα τοῦ παντός, καὶ πολὺ τῆς ὑλικῆς ἀταξίας ἔχοντα καὶ οὐδὲ τῶν | ἡλιακῶν ἀκτίνων ἀπολαύοντα.

15 Τοσαῦτα καὶ περὶ τούτων εἰρήσθω τῶν στίχων, οὓς ὁ Σωκράτης διαγράφειν ἀξιοῖ, καὶ ὧν τοὺς παρ᾽ αὐτῷ παιδευομένους ἀνηκόους εἶναι παντελῶς δοκιμάζει. διὰ γὰρ τούτων αὔξεσθαι τὸ φιλοσώματον τῆς ψυχῆς

20 καὶ τὸν ἐνθένδε χωρισμὸν παντὸς μᾶλλον ἔτι | φαντάζεσθαι φοβερώτερον.

Τίνες αἰτίαι δι᾽ ἃς ἡ ποίησις ἀναπέμπει θρήνους κἀπὶ τοὺς ἥρωας καὶ ἐπὶ τοὺς θεοὺς καὶ ἐπὶ τὸν ἄριστον αὐτὸν τῶν ἡρώων καὶ ἐπὶ τὸν μέγιστον τῶν θεῶν. |

25 Ἕπεται δέ που τοῖς εἰρημένοις θεωρῆσαι, πῶς οὐχὶ φιλόδακρυν ἕκαστον ἡμῶν ἡ ποίησις ἀπεργάζεται καὶ φιλόθρηνον, ὅταν ποιῇ καὶ τοὺς ἥρωας, καὶ τί λέγω τοὺς ἥρωας; τοὺς θεοὺς αὐτοὺς ἀποδακρύοντας ἐπὶ τοῖς τῶν φιλτάτων θανάτοις.

irrational and are being led below emit a sound very much like a "squeak," having only the traces of the life of the appetites and the fantasies [and not of intellect].

Moreover, the places in Hades and the subterranean places of punishment and rivers, which both Homer and Plato have taught us about, are not to be considered empty fantasies and mythical monstrosities: just as for souls going into heaven many and || various places within that sphere have been defined, so one must believe that for those still in need of punishment and purification the places beneath the earth have been arranged, with various effluents, on the one hand, of elements from the surface of the earth (referred to as "rivers" and "flowings") and various classes of daemons established over them, some of them avengers, some correctors, some purifiers and some judges [b]. If the poem calls these places

terrible, moldy—hated by the gods themselves [*Il.* 20.65],

one should not find fault with this, either. The reason is that these places throw the souls into confusion by their diversity and by the apparitions of the daemons set over them, and they are deployed according to the respective fates fitting the various conditions of the souls carried off there, removed as far as possible from the gods and situated at the last limit of the universe, and thus characterized by a great deal of material disorderliness and not even enjoying the rays of the sun.

Let this suffice concerning these verses that Socrates decided to expunge and that he thought the young educated according to his principles should never hear, on the basis that the soul's love of the body is increased through them and the separation from the body is most assuredly made in imagination to be still more fearful [than it is].

(11) What are the reasons why the poem attributes lamentation both to the heroes and to the gods, and even to the best of the heroes and the greatest of the gods?

[a. The problem]

Next we must examine how, although they portray the heroes (and why do I speak of the heroes?—the gods themselves) weeping over the deaths of those dearest to them, the poems do not make each of us prone to tears and inclined to lamentation.

K123   Καίτοι παρὰ τῷ Πλάτωνι [Phd. 58e] || Σωκράτης μὲν ἄτεγκτος διαμείνας καὶ ἀπροσπαθὴς πρὸς τὰ δάκρυα τῶν οἰκείων ἀνύμνηται, Ἀπολλόδωρος δὲ ἀστακτὶ δακρύων καὶ εἰ δή τις ἄλλος τοιοῦτος ἐπιτιμήσεως ὑπὸ τοῦ καθηγεμόνος ἠξίωται. ἀλλ' ὅ γε θεῖος ποιητὴς τοὺς |
5   ἥρωας ἀσχέτως ὀδυρομένους τὰς τῶν οἰκείων ἀποβολὰς παραδίδωσιν· καίτοι, φαίη τις ἄν, εἰ καὶ Πρίαμον ἔδει τοιαῦτα πάσχειν **κυλινδόμενον κατὰ κόπρον**, καὶ **ἐξονομακλήδην** ὀνομάζοντα ἄνδρα ἕκαστον, βάρβαρον ὄντα καὶ ἀλογώτερον, ἀλλ' οὔτι καὶ Ἀχιλλέα τὸν θεᾶς παῖδα, |
10   τότε μὲν ὕπτιον κατακείμενον, τότε δὲ πρηνῆ, τότε δὲ ἐπὶ πλευρᾶς ἀλύειν, καὶ χευάμενον κόνιν κατὰ τῆς κεφαλῆς ἀποθρηνεῖν παιδικῶς. εἰ δὲ καὶ ἀνθρώποις ἦν προσῆκον φύσιν θνητὴν λαχοῦσι τὸ πάθος, ἀλλ' οὐ τοῖς θεοῖς αὐτοῖς. τί οὖν ἔδει τὴν Θέτιν δακρύειν λέγουσαν· |

15   **ὤμοι ἐγὼ δειλή, ὤμοι δυσαριστοτόκεια;** [Σ 54]

πόρρω γὰρ ἡδονῆς καὶ λύπης ἵδρυται τὸ θεῖον. εἰ δὲ καὶ θεούς τις ἐτόλμα τοιαῦτα πάσχοντας εἰσάγειν, ἀλλ' οὐ τὸν μέγιστον ἐχρῆν τῶν θεῶν τόν τε Ἕκτορα διωκόμενον θρηνεῖν καὶ Σαρπηδόνα τὸν υἱόν, καὶ ὤμοι ἐγὼν ἐπ'
20   ἀμφο|τέρων λέγειν.

ἡ γὰρ τοιαύτη μίμησις οὐδὲν προσήκουσα φαίνεται τοῖς παραδείγμασι, δάκρυα προστιθεῖσα τοῖς ἀδακρύτοις καὶ λύπας τοῖς ἀλυπήτοις ἐκείνοις καὶ ὅλως πάθη τοῖς ἀπαθέσιν. Τοιαῦτα ὁ Σωκράτης ἐγκαλεῖ τῷ ποιητῇ καὶ τῆς
25   τῶν νέων παιδείας ἐκβάλλει, φυλαττόμενος ἐμπόδιον | αὐτῷ γίνεσθαι διὰ τῶν τοιούτων ῥημάτων εἰς τὴν ὀρθὴν πρὸς ἀρετὴν ἀγωγήν. περὶ γὰρ λύπας καὶ ἡδονὰς ἡ παιδεία διαφερόντως ἐστίν, ὧν ἐπιτεινομένων ἀνάγκη τὸν νομοθέτην ἀποτυγχάνειν τοῦ προσήκοντος αὐτῷ τέλους. ||

K124   Λέγωμεν τοίνυν καὶ πρὸς ταύτας τὰς ἐπιτιμήσεις, ὅτι τοὺς μὲν ἥρωας ἐν πράξεσιν ὄντας καὶ τὸν ταύταις προσήκοντα βίον ᾑρημένους ὁ ποιητὴς παραδιδοὺς εἰκότως καὶ παθαινομένους περὶ τὰ καθ'
5   ἕκαστον καὶ ζῶντας ὡσαύτως | εἰσήγαγεν. τοῖς μὲν γὰρ φιλοσόφοις καὶ καθαρτικῶς ἐνεργοῦσιν ἡδοναὶ καὶ λῦπαι καὶ αἱ τούτων μίξεις οὐδαμῇ προσήκουσιν. χωρίζονται γὰρ ἐκ τούτων καὶ πᾶσαν τὴν θνητὴν φλυαρίαν

Now in Plato [e.g., *Phd.* 58e] Socrates ‖ is praised for remaining untouched and unmoved by the tears of those close to him, while Apollodorus, who weeps profusely, is deemed blameworthy by his teacher, as well as anyone else who acts in the same way. The divine Poet, on the other hand, shows the heroes lamenting unrestrainedly at the loss of those close to them. Of course, one might say that, if Priam had to suffer such things, "rolling in dung" and "calling on every man by name" [*Il.* 22.414–415], he was non-Greek and [therefore] less rational, but this will not help to explain Achilles, the son of a goddess, lying on his back, then on his stomach, rolling on his side and pouring dust over his head, howling in grief like a child [*Il.* 24.9–12]. Moreover, even if this emotion is appropriate to men with their mortal nature, it is surely not fitting for the gods themselves. Why, then, did Thetis have to weep and say,

Wretched me, who bore a noble son to an ignoble fate [*Il.* 18.54]?

The divine is beyond pleasure and pain, and even if one could tolerate his bringing in the gods experiencing such emotion, he had no business portraying the greatest of the gods lamenting over Hector when he is pursued [by Achilles] and over his son Sarpedon, and saying "Woe is me" in each case [*Il.* 22.168; 16.433].

This sort of imitation seems utterly inappropriate to its models in attributing tears to the tearless, grief to those beyond grief, and, generally, emotion to those who experience no emotion. Socrates accuses the poet of these things and bars him from educating the young, taking care lest Homer become an obstacle for him in the correct raising of the young to virtue by saying such things. Education is especially concerned with grief and pleasure, and if these become too prevalent, then the lawmaker must fail to accomplish his proper goal. ‖

b. Proclus's response: the heroes]

Now, let us say as well with regard to these criticisms that the poet, describing the heroes in action and as having chosen lives in harmony with such action, appropriately shows them as well to be subject to emotion over day-to-day events and living in this same [passionate] manner. Pleasures and pains and their combinations are utterly inappropriate to philosophers and to those who keep all their actions pure. They separate themselves from these things and reject the triviality of mortal concerns,

ἀποσκευάζονται καὶ γυμνοὶ τῶν περιεστοιχημένων αὐτοὺς εἰδῶν τῆς ζωῆς γενέσθαι σπεύδουσιν, ἑαυ|τοὺς ἀναρπάζοντες ἀπὸ τῶν ἐνύλων καὶ γενεσιουργῶν παθημάτων. τοῖς δὲ ἐν πολέμῳ στρεφομένοις καὶ κατὰ τὸ παθητικὸν ἐνεργοῦσιν ἡδοναί τέ εἰσιν σύστοιχοι καὶ λῦπαι, καὶ συμπάθειαι καὶ ἀντιπάθειαι, καὶ σκηνὴ παντοίων παθῶν. καὶ πῶς ἂν ἡ περὶ τὰς πράξεις συντονία χώραν ἔχοι, | μὴ καὶ τῶν ὀρέξεων ἐπιτεταμένων. καὶ Πρίαμος οὖν καὶ Ἀχιλλεύς, οὔτε φιλόσοφοι ὄντες οὔτε γενέσεως χωρίζειν ἑαυτοὺς ἐθέλοντες οὔτε τὸν τῶν [διὰ] φυλάκων ζῶντες τρόπον, εἰ καὶ θρηνοῦσι τοὺς οἰκείους καὶ οἰκτίζονται, θαυμαστὸν οὐδέν. καὶ γὰρ φίλων ἀποβολαὶ καὶ παίδων ἐρημίαι καὶ | πόλεων ἀφανισμοὶ τοῖς πολεμικοῖς ἀνδράσιν μεγάλην μοῖραν παρέχεσθαι δοκοῦσι τῆς ἀθλιότητος. προσήκει δὲ ἄρα τὸ μεγαλουργὸν αὐτοῖς ὡς φύσιν ἡρωϊκὴν λαχοῦσιν, τὸ δὲ παθητικὸν ὡς περὶ τὰ καθ' ἕκαστα στρεφομένοις·

Ἐπὶ δὲ αὐτῶν θεῶν, ὅταν δακρύειν καὶ ἐκεῖνοι λέγωνται ἢ ὀδύ|ρεσθαι τοὺς φιλτάτους, ἄλλος ὁ τρόπος καὶ τοῖς μυθοπλάσταις πάλαι δεδογμένος, οἳ τὴν περὶ τὰ θνητὰ πρόνοιαν καὶ γιγνόμενα καὶ ἀπολλύμενα τῶν θεῶν διὰ τῶν δακρύων εἰώθασιν ἐνδείκνυσθαι. φύσει γὰρ τὸ προνοούμενον τοῦτο δακρύων ἄξιον ὂν πρόφασιν παρέσχε τοῖς μυθοποιοῖς καὶ | τὴν πρόνοιαν αὐτὴν διὰ τούτων αἰνίττεσθαι· ||

δάκρυα μὲν σέθεν ἐστὶ πολυτλήτων γένος ἀνδρῶν,

φησίν τις τὸν ἥλιον ὑμνῶν [Orph. frag. 354]. καὶ διὰ τοῦτο κἂν τοῖς μυστηρίοις τοὺς ἱεροὺς θρήνους μυστικῶς παρει|λήφαμεν, σύμβολον ὄντας τῆς εἰς ἡμᾶς καθηκούσης ἐκ τῶν κρειττόνων προνοίας.

Καὶ ἡ Θέτις οὖν καὶ ὁ Ζεὺς ὀδύρεσθαι λέγονται τοὺς φιλτάτους αὐτοῖς ἐν ἐσχάτοις ὄντας κινδύνοις, οὐχ ὅτι παθητικῶς διάκεινται τὸν αὐτὸν τοῖς ἀνθρώποις τρόπον, ἀλλ' ὅτι πρόεισιν ἀπ' αὐτῶν διωρισμένη | τις προμήθεια καὶ δόσις εἰς τὰ καθ' ἕκαστα. καὶ ὅταν μὲν τῇ μεριστῇ ταύτῃ προνοίᾳ καὶ ἡ τοῦ παντὸς συντρέχῃ τάξις, ἀνεμπόδιστός ἐστιν ἡ σωστικὴ τοῦ προνοοῦντος ἐνέργεια, ὅταν δὲ ἀνθίστηται καὶ ὡς μέρος ὂν τοῦ

striving to strip themselves of the forms of life that surround them and rescuing themselves from the passions that are linked to matter and the sphere of coming to be and passing away. For those toiling in war, however, and acting in the sphere of experience and emotion, pleasures and pains are perfectly consonant, as are sympathies and antipathies and all the play of varied emotions. How could there be room for intensity in their actions if their appetites, too, were not intense? As far as Priam and Achilles are concerned, since they are not philosophers and neither wish to cut themselves off from γένεσις nor to live in the manner of the guardians, if they lament those near to them and weep, there is nothing surprising in that. Loss of friends and deprivation of children and disappearance of cities seem to warriors to constitute an important part of wretchedness. Great achievement, then, is appropriate to them because of their heroic nature, and emotion, because of their involved concern with particulars.

[c. The gods and daemons]

As far as the gods themselves are concerned, when they as well are said to weep or to lament over those dearest to them, the mode of representation is a different one, and one long dear to the mythoplasts, who are accustomed to depict by means of these tears the providence of the gods for mortal things as they come to be and pass away. Since that over which providence is extended is by nature deserving of tears, this provided the mythmakers with the occasion of [cryptically] designating providence itself, as well, by this means. ||

Your tears are the race of suffering mortals,

someone says in a hymn to the sun [*Orph. frag.* 354, Kern]. Likewise, in the mysteries we have taken over from mystical tradition the holy lamentations as a symbol of the providence that descends to us from the greater ones.

Thus Thetis and Zeus are said to lament for those dearest to them when they are in extreme danger, not because they themselves are subject to emotion in the same way as humans, but because a certain defined providence and largesse proceeds from them into particulars. When the order of the universe coincides with this fragmented providence, the preserving action of the providential being is unimpeded, but when it is in opposition to [that providence] and [the object of providence], as a part

κόσμου καὶ γένεσιν λαχὸν τὴν προσήκουσαν ὑπομένῃ φθοράν, τότε τὴν | ἰδιότητα τῆς προνοίας οἱ μῦθοι παριστάντες, ἧς καὶ τοῦτο κατὰ τὴν αὐτοῦ τάξιν ἀπέλαυεν, θρηνεῖν τοὺς προνοοῦντας λέγουσιν, καὶ τοῦτο <μόνον> οὐχὶ βοῶντές φασιν, ὡς ὁ θρῆνος σύνθημα παρ' αὐτοῖς ἐστιν τῆς ἰδιαζούσης τῶν καθ' ἕκαστα προνοίας.

Τοῖς μὲν οὖν πρωτίστοις θεοῖς τὸν | εἰρημένον τρόπον τοὺς θρήνους ἀποδώσομεν· ἐπεὶ καὶ Κόρης καὶ Δήμητρος καὶ αὐτῆς τῆς μεγίστης θεᾶς ἱερούς τινας ἐν ἀπορρήτοις θρήνους αἱ τελεταὶ παραδεδώκασιν. θαυμαστὸν δὲ οὐδέν, εἰ καὶ τὰ ἔσχατα τῶν ἑπομένων ἀεὶ τοῖς θεοῖς γενῶν καὶ προσεχῶς κηδόμενα τῶν θνητῶν καὶ | ὀρέξεσιν χρώμενα καὶ πάθεσιν καὶ ἐν τούτοις ἔχοντα τὴν ζωὴν χαίροι μὲν ἐπὶ τῇ σωτηρίᾳ τῶν προνοουμένων, ἀνίλλοιτο δὲ καὶ δυσχεραίνοι φθειρομένων καὶ μεταβάλλοι κατὰ τὰ πάθη·

**νύμφαι μὲν κλαίουσιν ὅτε δρυσὶν οὐκ ἔνι φύλλα, |
νύμφαι δ' αὖ χαίρουσιν, ὅτε δρύας ὄμβρος ἀέξει, ||**

φησίν τις ποιητής.

πάντα γάρ ἐστι θείως μὲν ἐν τοῖς θεοῖς, μερικῶς δὲ καὶ δαιμονίως ἐν τοῖς διῃρημένοις ἡμῶν προστάταις. ἀρκεῖ καὶ ταῦτα πρὸς τὴν παροῦσαν πρόθεσιν ὑπὲρ τῶν λεγομένων ἐν θεοῖς θρήνων εἰρῆσθαι. |

**Τίς αἰτία τοῦ ἐν τοῖς θεοῖς λεγομένου γέλωτος
ἐν τοῖς μύθοις, καὶ διὰ τί ἡ ποίησις ἐπὶ τῷ Ἡφαίστῳ
τοὺς θεοὺς ἐποίησε γελῶντας ἀσχέτως.**

Τὸ δὲ αὖ ἐναντιώτατον μὲν τούτοις πάθος τὸ περὶ τοὺς ἀσχέτους γέλωτας, ἐπιστάσεως δὲ ὑπὸ τοῦ Σωκράτους ἠξιω|μένον, εἰ δεόντως ἐπὶ τοὺς θεοὺς αὐτὸ μεταφέρουσιν οἱ μῦθοι, μετὰ ταῦτα σκεπτέον. τί γὰρ δὴ

of the cosmos and something that has come to be, undergoes the concomitant destruction, then the myths, demonstrating the specificity of the providence (which this [its object] enjoyed because of its rank),[192] say that the providential beings lament, and they might as well be proclaiming that the lamentations of the gods are symbols, for them, of that specific providence that concerns particulars, acting on an individual.

We shall attribute lamentation to the highest gods in the manner just stated, since the initiations have passed down secret and holy laments of Kore and Demeter and of the greatest goddess herself.[193] It is no wonder if the last of the classes of beings that perpetually follow the gods and care intimately for mortals and who experience appetites and emotions and have their lives bound up in these should rejoice in the salvation of the objects of their providence and recoil and be pained when these are destroyed, and thus should undergo changes of emotion.

> The nymphs weep when there are no leaves on the oaks;
> the nymphs rejoice when showers make the oaks leaf out. ||

a poet says [Callimachus, *Hymn* 4 (Delos), 84–85].

Everything among the gods exists in a manner fitting for the gods,[194] but among those separate beings that watch over us these same things exist in a partial and daemonic manner.

This treatment of the lamentations said to take place among the gods is sufficient to the present discussion.

(12) What is the cause of the so-called laughter that in the myths occurs among the gods, and why did the poem describe the gods as laughing irrepressibly at Hephaestus?

We should next examine whether or not the myths are correct in attributing to the gods the emotion diametrically opposite to those just discussed, namely, irrepressible laughter, which Socrates thought to be a

---

192. Its "rank" (τάξις) in this case seems to refer to the procession into which the object of providence falls.

193. F. cites Boyancé (1937, 53 n. 3) for the identification of this goddess as Themis (or Themis/Ananke), secured as an Eleusinian deity by an Athenian sacred law of the end of the fifth century (Oliver 1935, 21 line 60).

194. Cf. Porphyry, *Sent.* 10.

καὶ βουλόμενοι γελῶντάς τε καὶ ἀσχέτως γελῶντας αὐτοὺς εἰσάγουσιν, θεωρίας ἄξιον.

ἄσβεστος δ' ἄρ' ἐνῶρτο γέλως μακάρεσσι θεοῖσι, |

15   φησὶν ἡ ποίησις

ὡς ἴδον Ἥφαιστον διὰ δώματα ποιπνύοντα [A 599–600].

Τίς οὖν ὁ τῶν θεῶν γέλως, καὶ τί δήποτε Ἡφαίστου κινουμένου καὶ ἐνεργοῦντος ἐκεῖνοι γελῶσιν;

20   Οὐκοῦν τὸν μὲν | Ἥφαιστον, ὥς που καὶ ἐν ἄλλοις εἴπομεν, δημιουργὸν καὶ ποιητὴν τοῦ φαινομένου παντὸς εἶναί φασιν οἱ θεολόγοι. διὸ καὶ τοὺς οἴκους αὐτὸς λέγεται κατασκευάσασθαι τοῖς θεοῖς

(**ἧχι ἑκάστῳ δῶμα περικλυτὸς ἀμφιγυήεις
Ἥφαιστος ποίησεν** [A 607]) |

25   ὡς τὰς ἐγκοσμίους αὐτοῖς προπαρασκευάζων ὑποδοχάς, καὶ ἄμφω τὼ πόδε χωλεύων παραδέδοται, καθόσον ἐστὶν καὶ τὸ δημιούργημα αὐτοῦ ἀσκελές· τῷ γὰρ τὴν περὶ νοῦν καὶ φρόνησιν κινουμένῳ κίνησιν οὐδὲν

K127   ἔδει ποδῶν, ὥς φησιν || ὁ Τίμαιος [33d]. καὶ χαλκευτικῆς ἔφορος λέγεται καὶ αὐτὸς χαλκεύων ἐνεργεῖ, διότι χάλκεος ὁ οὐρανὸς πολλαχοῦ τῆς ποιήσεως ἀνύμνηται, καὶ ἄλλα ἂν πολλὰ συνέλοις ταύτην πιστούμενα τὴν δόξαν.

5   Ἐπειδὴ δὲ πᾶσα ἡ περὶ τὸ | αἰσθητὸν πρόνοια, καθ' ἣν συνεφάπτονται τῷ Ἡφαίστῳ τῆς δημιουργίας, παιδιὰν τῶν θεῶν εἶναι λέγεται (διό μοι δοκεῖ καὶ ὁ Τίμαιος [42d] τοὺς ἐν τῷ κόσμῳ θεοὺς νέους ἀποκαλεῖν, ὡς ἀεὶ γινομένων καὶ παιδιᾶς ἀξίων προεστῶτας πραγμάτων), ταύτην δὴ τὴν τῆς προνοίας ἰδιότητα τῶν εἰς | τὸν κόσμον ἐνεργούντων θεῶν γέλωτα οἱ

problem. We should look into what they mean by showing the gods not only laughing but laughing irrepressibly.

> Undying laughter sprang up among the blessed gods,

says the Poet,

> when they saw Hephaestus shuffling around the room [*Il.* 1.599-600].

What, then, is the laughter of the gods, and why, in particular, do they laugh at Hephaestus going about and doing his work?

Now the theologians, as we have said elsewhere, say that Hephaestus is the creator and fabricator of the whole phenomenal world.[195] Thus he is also said to have built the houses of the gods

> (There famous Hephaestus, lame in both legs,
> made for each a home [*Il.* 1.607-608])

because he prepared their encosmic receptacles for them. He is said to limp in both legs since his creation is "legless," for that which is moved by the motion generated around intellect and thought "had no need of feet," as Timaeus ‖ said [*Tim.* 33d]. He is said to preside over blacksmithing, and he himself works as a smith, since the heavens are sung of in many places in the poem as being brazen,[196] and you could gather up many other points to support this doctrine.

Furthermore, since all providence concerning the sphere accessible to the senses, in which the gods collaborate in the creation of Hephaestus, is called the "play" of the gods—and for this reason, I believe, Timaeus calls the encosmic gods "young" [*Tim.* 42d], since they are set over things that are continually coming into being and are properly playthings—

---

195. F. (146 n. 3 ad loc.) asserts that θεολόγος is here used not for the poets (as earlier) but for their allegorical interpreters, but the distinction is not so clear as it might seem. These "theologians" might well be either Orpheus and Homer or their (perhaps Orphic) interpreters. Proclus, in any case, goes on in this passage to demonstrate that Homer (certainly a theologian in the usual sense of Proclus, as of Aristotle) made exactly the point specified.

196. Kroll notes *Il.* 5.504; 17.425; and *Od.* 3.2.

μυθοπλάσται προσαγορεύειν εἰώθασι. καὶ δὴ καὶ ὅταν ὁ ποιητὴς τῷ Ἡφαίστῳ κινουμένῳ τοὺς θεοὺς ἐπιγηθοῦντας λέγῃ τὸν ἄσβεστον τοῦτον γέλωτα γελᾶν, οὐδὲν ἄλλο ἢ συνδημιουργοὺς αὐτοὺς καὶ τελεσιουργοὺς τῆς Ἡφαίστου τέχνης ἐνδείκνυται γίνεσθαι | καὶ τῆς εὐθημοσύνης ἄνωθεν τῷ παντὶ χορηγοὺς ὑπάρχειν.

Ὁ μὲν γὰρ ἐξαρτύει πάσας αὐτῶν τὰς ἐγκοσμίους ὑποδοχὰς καὶ προτείνει ταῖς προνοίαις τῶν θεῶν τὰς ὅλας φυσικὰς δυνάμεις, οἳ δὲ μετὰ τῆς αὐτοῖς προσηκούσης ῥᾳστώνης ἐνεργοῦντες καὶ τῆς οἰκείας εὐπαθείας οὐκ ἀφιστά|μενοι καὶ ταύταις ἐπορέγουσι τὰς σφετέρας μεταδόσεις καὶ κινοῦσι τὰ ὅλα ταῖς τελεσιουργοῖς ἑαυτῶν προνοίαις.

Ὡς οὖν συνελόντι φάναι, τὸν γέλωτα τῶν θεῶν τὴν ἄφθονον εἰς τὸ πᾶν ἐνέργειαν καὶ τὴν τῆς εὐθημοσύνης τῶν ἐγκοσμίων αἰτίαν ἀφοριστέον. διότι δὲ <u>ἀκατάληκτός</u> ἐστιν ἡ τοιαύτη | πρόνοια καὶ ἡ τῶν ἀγαθῶν πάντων μετάδοσις παρὰ τοῖς θεοῖς ἀνέκλειπτος, εἰκότως ἄρα καὶ τὸν ποιητὴν ἄσβεστον αὐτῶν <τὸν> γέλωτα προσειρηκέναι συγχωρητέον. καὶ ὁρᾷς πάλιν, ὅπως καὶ ταῦτα τῇ φύσει τῶν πραγμάτων ἑπόμενοι λέγομεν. δακρύειν μὲν γὰρ οὐκ ἀεί φασιν οἱ μῦθοι τοὺς | θεούς, γελᾶν δὲ ἀσχέτως, ἐπειδὴ τὰ μὲν δάκρυα τῆς εἰς τὰ || θνητὰ προνοίας αὐτῶν καὶ ἐπίκηρα πράγματα καὶ ποτὲ μὲν ὄντα, ποτὲ δὲ οὐκ ὄντα συνθήματά ἐστιν, ὁ δὲ γέλως τῆς εἰς τὰ ὅλα καὶ ἀεὶ ὡσαύτως κινούμενα πληρώματα τοῦ παντὸς ἐνεργείας.

Διόπερ οἶμαι καὶ ὅταν μὲν εἰς θεοὺς καὶ | ἀνθρώπους διαιρῶμεν <τὰ> δημιουργήματα, τὸν μὲν γέλωτα τῇ γενέσει τῶν θείων, τὰ δὲ δάκρυα τῇ συστάσει τῶν ἀνθρώπων ἢ ζῴων ἀπονέμομεν·

δάκρυα μὲν σέθεν ἐστὶ πολυτλήτων γένος ἀνδρῶν, |
μειδήσας δὲ θεῶν ἱερὸν γένος ἐβλάστησας·

ὅταν δὲ εἰς τὰ οὐράνια καὶ τὰ ὑπὸ σελήνην, πάλιν κατὰ τὰ αὐτὰ τοῖς μὲν οὐρανίοις τὸν γέλωτα, τοῖς δὲ ὑπὸ σελήνην τὰ δάκρυα συνδιαιρούμεθα.

the mythoplasts are accustomed to designate the specific quality of this providence of the gods that act within the cosmos as "laughter." And in particular, when the Poet says that the gods, delighting in Hephaestus's movements, laughed this "undying laughter," he is simply showing that they are joint creators with him and collaborators in his art and bring it to perfection, and they sponsor the descent of orderliness into the universe.

He is the one who prepares all their encosmic receptacles and provides the entire range of physical powers for the providence of the gods, while they, acting with the ease appropriate to them and not abandoning their accustomed comfort, extend their individual contributions to these powers and move the universe by the their efficacious providence.

In summary, then, the laughter of the gods is to be defined as their generous activity within the universe and the cause of the orderliness of things within the cosmos. It must also be conceded that because such providence is unceasing[197] and the giving of all good things by the gods is inexhaustible, the Poet chose quite rightly to add that their laughter was "undying." You can see again that these explanations are in line with the nature of things: the myths do not make the gods weep incessantly, but they do say that they laugh unrestrainedly, because their tears are symbols of their providence toward || mortal and perishable things, things that exist at one time and at another do not, while their laughter is symbolic of the activity that extends to the universals that fill the universe and are constantly in motion with the same movement.

This, I think, is why, when we divide the creation of the demiurge into gods and men, we allocate laughter to the birth of the divine[198] but tears to the emergence of men and beasts.

> Your tears are the race of suffering mortals
> but smiling you sprouted forth the holy race of gods
> [*Orph. frag.* 354, Kern].[199]

Likewise, when we distinguish between celestial and sublunary things, according to the same principle we attribute laughter to the celestial

---

197. Reading ἀκατάληκτος (F.) in line 24 for ἀκατάληπτος (manuscript and Kroll).

198. Aside from the citation that follows, this may echo *Homeric Hymn* 3 (Apollo), 118, where the earth smiles at the birth of Apollo.

199. Cf. 163 (K125,1–2), above.

ὅταν δὲ καὶ αὐτῶν τῶν ὑπὸ σελήνην τάς τε γενέσεις καὶ τὰς φθορὰς συλλογιζώ|μεθα, τὰς μὲν εἰς τὸν γέλωτα τῶν θεῶν, τὰς δὲ εἰς τοὺς θρήνους ἀναπέμπομεν. καὶ διὰ ταῦτα κἂν τοῖς μυστηρίοις κατὰ χρόνους τεταγμένους ἀμφότερα ταῦτα δρᾶν οἱ τῶν ἱερῶν θεσμῶν ἡγεμόνες παρακελεύονται, <ὡς> καὶ εἴρηται ἐν ἄλλοις.

Καὶ ὁ αὐτὸς τρόπος μήτε τῶν ἐν ἀπορρήτοις δρω|μένων παρὰ τοῖς θεουργοῖς τοὺς ἀνοήτους ἐπαΐειν μήτε τῶν τοιούτων πλασμάτων. ἡ γὰρ ἄνευ ἐπιστήμης τούτων ἀμφοτέρων ἀκρόασις δεινὴν καὶ ἄτοπον ἐργάζεται σύγχυσιν ἐν ταῖς τῶν πολλῶν ζωαῖς τῆς περὶ τὸ θεῖον εὐλαβείας. ||

**Ἀπολογία ὑπὲρ τῶν ἐν τῇ Ὁμήρου ποιήσει
δοκούντων εἰς καταφρόνησιν σωφροσύνης τοὺς
ἀκούοντας κινεῖν παντοδαπῶν τρόπων.**

Τοσαῦτα καὶ περὶ τοῦ γέλωτος εἰρήσθω τῶν θεῶν, ὃν | ἡ ποίησις ἄσβεστον διὰ τὰς ἀναγεγραμμένας αἰτίας προσείρηκεν. ἐφεξῆς δέ ἐστιν τοῖς τοιούτοις προβλήμασιν διασκέψασθαι τοὺς περὶ τῆς σωφροσύνης λόγους, μή πη ἄρα πρὸς ταύτην ἡμᾶς διαλωβᾶται τὰ Ὁμήρου ποιήματα. σωφροσύνης δέ, φησὶν ὁ Σωκράτης [3.389d], μέγιστον | μὲν εἶδος ἡ πρὸς τοὺς ἄρχοντας αἰδώς, δεύτερον δὲ ἡ τῶν ἐπιθυμιῶν τῶν ἐν τῇ ψυχῇ καὶ τῶν ἡδονῶν ἐπικράτεια, καὶ τρίτον ἄλλο τούτοις ἑπόμενον, ὃ δὴ μικρὸν ὕστερον θεωρήσομεν. ἀλλ᾽ οὖν τοῖν δυοῖν τούτοιν ὁ μὲν Ἀχιλλεὺς κατὰ θάτερον ἁμαρτάνων φαίνεται, τοιαῦτα πρὸς τὸν ἄρ|χοντα παρρησιαζόμενος [Α 225]·

οἰνοβαρὲς κυνὸς ὄμματ᾽ ἔχων,

καὶ τὸ ἐφεξῆς τοῦ ἔπους. ὁ δὲ Ὀδυσσεὺς κατὰ τὸ λοιπόν, ὥσπερ ὅταν

beings, tears to the sublunary ones, and when we consider the births and destructions of sublunary things themselves we refer the first to the laughter of the gods, the second to the lamentations. For the same reason, in the mysteries as well, the masters of holy law ordain that we do both of these things at the appropriate times, as already mentioned.[200]

And by the same token, the mindless should not have knowledge of the secret rites of the theurgists, and likewise they should not hear such fictions as these. The witnessing of both of these things without understanding results in a terrible and irrational violation of piety toward the divine in the lives of the many.[201] ||

(13) Response concerning the various ways that the Homeric poems appear to inspire in their listeners scorn for moderation.

[a. The problem]

Let this suffice for the laughter of the gods, which the poem describes as "irrepressible" for the above-mentioned reasons. Next after these problems, we should look at the passages regarding moderation [σωφροσύνη] and ask whether, indeed, the poems of Homer somehow harm us in this regard.

Socrates says that the greatest form of reasonableness is reverence toward rulers, the second, control over the desires of the soul and the pleasures, and that there is a third after these, which we shall examine a little later [*Rep.* 3.389d–390a].[202] Of these two, Achilles clearly violates the first when he openly insults the leader, saying things like this:

drunkard, with a dog's face,

and the rest of the line [*Il.* 1.225], and Odysseus violates the other when,

---

200. Inserting ὡς in line 18 (with F., from Kroll's apparatus). Cf. 75 (K78,14–18), above.

201. Once again, the Christians seem to present the prime example of the disruption of piety in those who see only the surface of religious observation (or of epic poetry), without the knowledge necessary to decipher them.

202. As F. observes, this third category will be sexual self-control, discussed below in chs. 14 and 15, pp. 177–99.

ἀφοριζόμενος τῶν βίων τὸν κάλλιστον λέγῃ τὴν πολιτείαν διαφερόντως
ἐκείνην ἀποδέχεσθαι τῶν ἀνθρώ|πων, ὁπόταν

**εὐφροσύνη μὲν ἔχῃ κατὰ δῆμον ἅπαντα·
δαιτυμόνες δ' ἀνὰ δώματ' ἀκουάζωνται ἀοιδοῦ
ἥμενοι ἑξείης, παρὰ δὲ πλήθωσι τράπεζαι
σίτου καὶ κρειῶν, μέθυ δ' ἐκ κρητῆρος ἀφύσ|σων
οἰνοχόος προχέῃσι καὶ ἐγχείῃ δεπάεσσιν** [ι 6–10].

ἐν γὰρ τούτοις οὐδὲν ἄλλ' ἢ τὴν πολυάρατον ἡδονὴν καὶ τὴν πλήρωσιν
τῶν ἐπιθυμιῶν τέλος προεστήσατο τῆς ζωῆς. ||
Ταῦτα δὴ τοῦ Σωκράτους ἐπιτιμῶντος τοῖς Ὁμήρου λόγοις, πρὸς μὲν
τὴν προτέραν ἐπίστασιν ἀπαντησόμεθα λέγοντες, ὅτι τοῖς μὲν φύλαξιν,
οὓς αὐτὸς ἄρχοντας καθίστησιν τῆς πόλεως, τοσαύτην ὑπεροχὴν λαχοῦσιν
παιδείας | ἕνεκα καὶ ἀρετῆς πρὸς τοὺς ἀρχομένους πρέποι ἄν που τούς
τε ἐπικούρους καὶ σύμπαντας τοὺς ἄλλους πλείστην καὶ μεγίστην τιμὴν
ἀπονέμειν· σωτῆρες γὰρ ὄντως ἐκεῖνοι καὶ εὐεργέται τῆς ὅλης προεστᾶσι
πολιτείας, καὶ οὐδὲν ἀνόσιον οὐδὲ ἄδικον ἄν τις ἀπ' ἐκείνων κατὰ νοῦν
καὶ δίκην | ἀρχόντων εἰς τοὺς ἀρχομένους ἥξειν προσδοκήσειεν. ὁ δὲ δὴ
ποιητὴς οὔτε κατ' ἀρετὴν διαφέροντα τὸν Ἀγαμέμνονα τῶν ὑπηκόων
πάντων εἶναι συγχωρήσας οὔτε ἐν τοῖς εὖ ποιοῦσι τοὺς ἄλλους, ἀλλ'
ἐν τοῖς εὖ πάσχουσι τετάχθαι, καὶ διαφερόντως ὑπὸ τῆς στρατηγικῆς
Ἀχιλλέως ἐπιστήμης, | εἰκότως δήπου καὶ πληττόμενον αὐτὸν ὑπὸ τῶν
κρειττόνων καὶ μείζονα τὴν εἰς τὸ κοινὸν <u>ὠφέλειαν</u> παρεχομένων, ἐν
οἷς πλημμελεῖ καὶ τοῖς ἑαυτοῦ καταχαρίζεται πάθεσιν, εἰσάγει, καὶ μετὰ
παρρησίας τοὺς ἀρίστους αὐτῷ τῶν Ἑλλήνων διαλεγομένους παραδίδωσιν,
οὐδὲν ὑπολογιζομένους τὸ πλῆ|θος τῶν ἑπομένων στρατιωτῶν οὐδὲ τὴν
ναυτικὴν δύναμιν. ἡ γὰρ ἀρετὴ πανταχοῦ τίμιον, ἀλλ' οὐ τὰ ὄργανα τῆς
ἀρετῆς.

for example, defining the best of lives, he says he especially appreciates that society of men where

> good cheer takes hold of the whole assembly
> and the banqueters up and down the hall listen to a bard
> as they sit together beside tables heaped with bread
> and meat, and the cupbearer dips wine from the bowl
> and pours it into the cups [*Od.* 9.6–10].

In these verses [the Poet] has actually set before us as the end of life nothing but precious pleasure[203] and the satisfaction of the appetites. ||

[b. Proclus's response: Achilles]

These are the criticisms leveled by Socrates against what Homer says, and with regard to the first difficulty we shall answer by saying that, as for the "guardians," whom he himself sets as rulers of the city, it would be appropriate for both the underlings and all the others in the city to allocate to them both the most and the highest honors, since they receive their high status on account of their education and their virtue in comparison with the ruled. They preside over the city as genuine preservers and benefactors, and one would never anticipate that any impiety or injustice might come upon the ruled through them, ruling [as they do] with intelligence and justice. On the other hand, the Poet does not concede that Agamemnon stood out over all his underlings in virtue, nor that he was one of those who benefit others, but on the contrary one who receives benefits—and particularly from the martial skill of Achilles—and so it is certainly appropriate that he shows him being berated for his mistakes and his indulgence of his own emotions by those who are his betters and offer more benefits to the community,[204] and shows the best of the Greeks addressing him in outspoken language, taking no account of the number of soldiers under his command nor of his naval power. Virtue itself is everywhere honored, but not the instruments of virtue.[205]

---

203. With τὴν πολυάρατον ἡδονήν here in line 27, compare τὰς πολυαράτους ἡδονάς at 157 (K121,13) (F.).

204. Accepting ὠφέλειαν in line 16 for the manuscript's φιλίαν (cf. F. n. 1, ad loc.).

205. The "instruments [ὄργανα] of virtue" are the troops and ships (of which Agamemnon has more than the other leaders).

Οὐκ ἄρα περὶ τοὺς ἄρχοντας καὶ σωτῆρας τῶν ὅλων ἐξαμαρτάνειν φήσομεν τὸν τὰ τοιαῦτα ὀνείδη προφέροντα τοῖς πλήθεσιν μὲν τῶν
25 ὑπηκόων διαφέρουσιν, ἀρετῇ δὲ | πάμπολυ λειπομένοις. ἐπεὶ καὶ αὐτὸς μικρὸν ὕστερον ὁ τῶν πολλῶν τούτων καὶ δυσαριθμήτων στρατιωτῶν βασιλεὺς ὁμολογεῖ τὴν διαφορὰν τῆς ἀρετῆς καὶ ἀποδύρεται τὴν ἑαυτοῦ δυστυχίαν·

ἀασάμην, οὐδ' αὐτὸς ἀναίνομαι, ||

K131 καὶ

**ἀντί νυ πολλῶν
λαῶν ἐστὶν ἀνήρ, ὅν τε Ζεὺς κῆρι φιλήσῃ,
ὡς νῦν τοῦτον ἔτισε. [H 116–118] |**

5 Πρὸς δὲ αὖ τὴν κατὰ τῶν Ὀδυσσέως λόγων ἐπιτίμησιν λεγέσθω μὲν καί, ὅτι τὰ τοιαῦτα συμβολικώτερον ἀφερμηνεύειν δέδοκται τοῖς τὴν καλουμένην πλάνην ἐπ' ἄλλας ὑπονοίας μεθιστᾶσι καὶ τοὺς Φαίακας καὶ τὴν παρ' αὐτοῖς εὐδαιμονίαν ἀνωτέρω τῆς θνητῆς φύσεως τάττειν
10 ἀξιοῦσιν. καὶ | γὰρ ἡ δαὶς παρ' ἐκείνοις καὶ ἡ θοίνη καὶ ἡ ἐναρμόνιος ᾠδὴ τρόπον ἕτερον ῥηθήσεται καὶ οὐ τὸν τοῖς πολλοῖς συνεγνωσμένον. λεγέσθω δὲ αὖ, ὅτι καὶ τοῖς τὸ φαινόμενον τῆς ποιήσεως μεταθέουσιν ἔξεστιν ἀπαντᾶν πρὸς τοὺς τοιούτους λόγους καὶ δεικνύναι πρῶτον μέν,
15 ὅτι καὶ αὐτὸς ὁ | τῶν Ἑλλήνων σοφώτατος οὐχ ἡδονὴν ἀξιοῖ κρατεῖν ἐν ταῖς ὀρθαῖς πολιτείαις, ἀλλ' εὐφροσύνην· ὅπῃ δὲ ταῦτα διέστηκεν ἀλλήλων, παρ' αὐτοῦ Πλάτωνος μεμαθήκαμεν. ἔπειθ' ὅτι διὰ μουσικῆς ἅπασαν συναρμόζεσθαι τὴν πόλιν καὶ πρὸς ἑαυτὴν ὁμόφρονα γίνεσθαι

We shall not say, then, that as far as the rulers and saviors of the expeditionary force are concerned, a man who delivers such insults to those who are outstanding for the large numbers of their followers but remain entirely inferior in virtue commits a crime. The ruler of all these countless soldiers himself admits a little later the greater virtue [of Achilles] and laments his own mistake:

I was insane; I myself do not deny it [*Il.* 9.116], ||

and

> the man Zeus loves
> in his heart, as he has now honored this one,
> is worth many [*Il.* 9.116–118].

[c. Proclus's response: Odysseus]

Now, with regard to the criticism of the words of Odysseus, let it be said first of all that those who refer what are called the "wanderings" of Odysseus to secondary, allegorical meanings and place the Phaeacians and their "blessedness" beyond the sphere of mortal nature interpret these things more symbolically. Thus "banqueting," among them, "feasting," and "harmonious song" will be said in another sense and not the one generally recognized. It should be emphasized, however, that those who concern themselves with the apparent meaning of the poem are also able to answer such accusations and to point out that, in the first place, the wisest of the Greeks [Odysseus[206]] does not think that "pleasure" should prevail in correctly run states, but rather "good cheer," and we learn this distinction from Plato himself.[207] And then, [second, they can point out] that [Odysseus] approves of the notion that the whole state is brought into harmony through music and becomes unified in its thinking, in obedience to the

---

206. F. (and Kroll) took "the wisest of the Greeks" here to be Homer, but, if so, why does the phrase occur in the essay only here (twice, in lines 15 and 31) in a discussion explicitly of the λόγοι of Odysseus (line 5)? Also note 247 (K172,12): ὁ σοφώτατος Ὀδυσσεύς. Certainly Proclus is concerned to reconcile Homer and Plato here as elsewhere, but for present purposes it is sufficient to reconcile Odysseus and Plato.

207. F. cites, for the distinction between ἡδονή and εὐφροσύνη, *Tim.* 80b5–8.

κατήκοον οὖσαν τῶν πρὸς ἀρε|τὴν ἀγόντων μελῶν δοκιμάζει. τὸ γὰρ ἐπιστῆσαι τῷ πλήθει μὴ τὸν τυχόντα τὴν μουσικήν, ἀλλὰ τὸν θείας μέτοχον κατ' αὐτὴν ἐπιπνοίας, ἄνωθεν ἀπὸ τῶν τῆς μιᾶς ταύτης ἐφόρων ἐπὶ πᾶσαν διατείνει τὴν πολιτείαν παιδείαν τε καὶ ἀρετὴν ἀληθινήν. τρίτον δὲ ὅτι τοῖς τῆς τοιαύτης μετειληφόσιν | ἁρμονίας καὶ τὴν ἀφθονίαν τῶν ἀναγκαίων προστίθησιν, ὧν δεῖται τὸ πλῆθος τὸ πολὺ ἐν ταῖς πόλεσιν. οὐ γὰρ τὸ ἐμπιπλαμένους τῶν τοιούτων ζῆν, ἀλλὰ τὸ μηδενὸς προσδεῖν τῶν τὸν θνητὸν βίον συμπληρούντων [τι] διαφερόντως ἐνεκωμίασεν.

Πρέποντα ἄρα τοῖς ἡμετέροις δόγμασιν καὶ | ταῖς ἀδιαστρόφοις προλήψεσιν περὶ τῆς δημοτικῆς εὐδαιμονίας καὶ ὁ τῶν Ἑλλήνων σοφώτατος φαίνεται λέγων. εἰ || δέ τις τὴν μὲν εὐφροσύνην ἀφέλοι καὶ τὴν διὰ τῆς ἐνθέου μουσικῆς παιδείαν, τραπέζας δὲ καὶ ἀπολαύσεις ἀμέτρους καὶ ἀμούσους καὶ πρὸς ἡδονὴν βλεπούσας αὐτὸν ἀποδέχεσθαι νομίζοι, πόρρω που τὰ τοιαῦτα ὁ Σωκράτης εἰκό|τως εἶναί φησι τῆς ἑαυτοῦ πολιτείας· οὐ γὰρ θέμις ἐν εὐδαιμόνων πόλει τὴν ἀπέραντον κρατεῖν ἡδονὴν καὶ τὸν τοῖς γαστριμάργοις προσήκοντα βίον.

Τί αἰνίττεται ἡ τοῦ Διὸς πρὸς τὴν Ἥραν συνουσία, καὶ τίς ὁ τῆς Ἥρας κόσμος, καὶ τίς ὁ τόπος | ἐν ᾧ ἡ συνουσία, καὶ τίς ὁ ἔρως τοῦ Διός, καὶ τίς ὁ θεῖος ὕπνος, καὶ ἁπλῶς πάσης ἐκείνης τῆς μυθολογίας ἐξήγησις.

Πρὸς μὲν οὖν τὰς τοιαύτας τοῦ Σωκράτους ἐπιστάσεις οὐ χαλεπὸν ἀπαντᾶν. ἐκδέχεται δὲ ἡμᾶς ἀπορία μείζων | ἔτι <καὶ> χαλεπωτέρα καὶ περὶ μεγίστων οὖσα, τῶν τοῦ Διὸς πρὸς τὴν Ἥραν συνουσιῶν. καὶ γὰρ ταύτην ὁ Σωκράτης ἀνεκίνησεν ὡς οὐδαμῇ προσήκουσαν ἀκροᾶσθαι νέοις. καὶ πῶς γὰρ οὐ παντελῶς ἂν δόξειεν ἀθέμιτον εἶναι τοιαῦτα περὶ τοῦ μεγίστου τῶν θεῶν ὑπονοεῖν, ὅτι διὰ τὸν πρὸς | τὴν Ἥραν ἔρωτα τῶν μὲν δεδογμένων ἐπελάθετο πάντων, αὐτοῦ δὲ χαμαὶ συγγενέσθαι τῇ θεῷ, μηδὲ εἰς τὸ δωμάτιον ἐλθεῖν ἀνασχόμενος ἔσπευσεν, καὶ τὰ τῶν ἀνθρωπίνων ἐραστῶν ὑπέμεινεν φράξασθαι. καὶ γὰρ ἐκείνων ἕκαστος πρῶτον μὲν ἁπάντων ὁμοῦ προτίθησι πραγμάτων τὴν πρὸς τὸ | ἐρώμενον

melodies that lead toward virtue. The fact of placing over the many not just anyone, as far as music is concerned, but a divinely inspired musician extends education and true virtue from those concerned exclusively with music down to the entire state. Third, [they can point out] that for those who participate in such harmony,[208] [Odysseus] adds as well abundance of those necessities of life that the many in the cities generally need. What [Odysseus] specifically praises is a life lacking nothing of those things that make mortal existence complete, and not a life glutted with such things.

Thus, the wisest of the Greeks is clearly saying things that are in harmony with our own notions as well as with the incontrovertible received opinions regarding the well-being of the state. If || one should take away the "good cheer" and education through inspired music, and should think that [Odysseus] was considering only pleasure, and was praising feasting and immoderate and inelegant indulgence, then Socrates is perfectly right to say that such things have nothing to do with his state. It is not right for boundless pleasure and a life of gluttony to prevail in a city of men who are truly blessed.

(14) What does Zeus' intercourse with Hera hint at: What is the meaning of Hera's adornment, of the location of their intercourse, the desire of Zeus, and the divine sleep? Generally, an explanation of the entire myth.

[a. The problem: the five questions]

It is not difficult to reply to Socrates' objections of the last sort, but a greater problem awaits us now, a still more difficult one and concerned with things of the greatest importance: the intercourse of Zeus and Hera. Socrates also brought this up as not at all appropriate for the hearing of the young [*Rep.* 3.390b–c]. How indeed could it seem anything but utterly illegitimate to conceive such things about the greatest god as that he utterly forgot all the accepted norms of behavior on account of his desire for Hera, that he was in a hurry to have intercourse with the goddess right there on the ground, not even restraining himself long enough to go into their bedroom, and that he was even willing to say the same things human lovers say? Every human lover, of course, starts out by preferring union with the

---

208. Here social harmony in general is designated by ἁρμονία, but the musical metaphor is pervasive.

συναφήν, ἔπειτα καὶ μείζω πεπονθέναι φησὶν ὧν πέπονθεν ἐν τῷ πρόσθεν χρόνῳ. τοιαῦτα γὰρ καὶ ὁ Ζεὺς πεποίηται λέγων·

οὐ γάρ πώποτέ μ' ὧδε θεᾶς ἔρος οὐδὲ γυναικὸς
30 **θυμὸν ἐνὶ στήθεσσι περιπροχυθεὶς ἐδάμασσεν** | [Ξ 315–316], ||

K133 καὶ ὅτι καὶ αὐτῆς ἐρᾷ μειζόνως ἢ ὅτε τὴν πρώτην

ἐμισγέσθην φιλότητι
εἰς εὐνὴν φοιτῶντε φίλους λήθοντε τοκῆας [Ξ 295–296]. |

5   Ὁ μὲν οὖν ἡμέτερος καθηγεμὼν προηγουμένην καταβαλλόμενος πραγματείαν εἰς τοῦτον ἅπαντα τὸν μῦθον ἐνθεαστικώτατα τὴν ἀπόρρητον αὐτοῦ θεωρίαν ἐξέφηνεν. ἡμεῖς δὲ ὅσον πρὸς τὴν παροῦσαν πρόθεσίν ἐστι τῶν ἐκεῖ γεγραμμένων σύμφωνον παραλαβόντες λέγωμεν
10 ὡς δυνατὸν συντό|μως, τίς μὲν ἡ τῆς Ἥρας πρὸς τὸν Δία συνουσία, τίς δὲ ἡ συναγωγὸς ἀμφοτέρων αἰτία, πῶς δὲ ὁ Ζεὺς καὶ ἐγρηγορέναι λέγεται καὶ καθεύδειν παρὰ μέρος, τίς δὲ ὁ τρόπος τῆς ἀπάτης, καθ' ἣν αὐτὸν ἡ μεγίστη θεὸς ἀπατᾶν μεμυθολόγηται, καὶ ὁ ἔρως οὗτος, ὃν διαφερόντως
15 ἐρᾶν λέγει τῆς | Ἥρας κατὰ ταύτην τὴν συμπλοκήν, τίνα ἔλαχεν δύναμιν· πάντα ταῦτα τῆς πρεπούσης ἀναπτύξεως τυχόντα μόνως ἂν ἡμῖν ἐπιδείξειεν τὸν Ὅμηρον ἁπάσης βλασφημίας ἐν τοῖς προκειμένοις ἔπεσιν καθαρεύοντα.
20   Πάντων τοίνυν τῶν θείων διακόσμων προϊόντων ἔκ τε | τῆς μιᾶς τῶν ὅλων ἀρχῆς, ἣν ἓν καὶ τἀγαθὸν ὁ Πλάτων εἴωθεν ἀποκαλεῖν, καὶ ἐκ τῶν μετὰ ταύτην προσεχῶς ἀναφανέντων δυοειδῶν αἰτίων, ἃ δὴ πέρας καὶ ἄπειρον <ὁ> ἐν τῷ Φιλήβῳ Σωκράτης προσείρηκεν [23c sqq.], ἄλλος δὲ

beloved to absolutely everything else and then says that he has experienced something greater than he has ever experienced before. Zeus, in the poem, says the same sort of thing:

> Never has such desire for any goddess or woman
> poured into my breast and conquered my soul [*Il.* 14.315–316], ||

and moreover that he desires her more than when

> they first made love,
> going to bed when their dear parents were not looking [*Il.* 14.295–296].

My guide [Syrianus] wrote an exemplary treatise on this whole myth, in which he revealed its secret doctrine in a very inspired manner. For my part, let me now take up as much of that material as is relevant to the present discussion and answer the following questions as briefly as possible:[209]

(1) What is the intercourse of Zeus and Hera?
(2) What cause draws them together?
(3) In what sense is Zeus said to be awake at one time and at another, asleep?
(4) What is the sense of the "deception" that the myth says that the greatest goddess perpetrated on him?
(5) Finally, when Zeus claims that he exceptionally desires Hera in this sexual encounter, what is the meaning of this desire?

Only when these points have been developed in an appropriate way can they demonstrate to us that Homer is pure of all blasphemy in the passage under discussion.

[b. Solution to questions 1 and 2]

All the divine orders, then, proceed from the single first principle of the universe, which Plato was accustomed to call "one" and "the Good," and likewise from the twofold causes that appear immediately subsequent to this first principle, and which Socrates in the *Philebus* [16c, 23c] called

---

209. The solutions will follow the stated order only for the first three questions. Thereafter the match is less clear.

ἄλλοις τῶν σοφῶν ὀνόμασιν ἀπεσέμνυνεν, καὶ μεριζομένων | μὲν ἀπ' ἀλλήλων καὶ διακρινομένων κατὰ τὴν πρέπουσαν θεοῖς διάκρισιν ἐκ τῶν δευτέρων ἀρχῶν, ᾗπερ δὴ καὶ εἰώθασιν τὰ μὲν ἄρρενα τοῖς θήλεσιν, τὰ δὲ ἄρτια τοῖς περιττοῖς, τὰ δὲ πατρικὰ τοῖς μητρικοῖς ἀντιδιαιρεῖν οἱ τῆς περὶ θεῶν ἀληθείας ἐξηγηταί, πάλιν δὲ αὖ σπευδόντων εἰς ἕνω|σιν καὶ ὁμοφυῆ κοινωνίαν διὰ τὴν πρωτίστην αἰτίαν πᾶσιν || τοῖς οὖσιν ἐξηγουμένην τῶν ἡνωμένων ἀγαθῶν, ἐντεῦθεν οἶμαί ποθεν οἱ μυθοπλάσται λαβόντες ἀφορμὴν τῆς συμβολικῆς θεωρίας τόν τε γάμον ἐπὶ τοὺς θεοὺς ἀνήγαγον καὶ τὰς συνουσίας καὶ τοὺς ἐκ τούτων τόκους καὶ αὖ τὰς | τῶν ἐγγόνων συμπλοκὰς καὶ συζεύξεις, ἕως ἅπαν τὸ θεῖον πλάτος ταῖς τοιαύταις προόδοις καὶ ταῖς κοινωνίαις διαποικιλλόμενον ἄνωθεν ἄχρι τῶν ἐγκοσμίων τελέως ἐθεάσαντο.

Καθάπερ οὖν ἐν τοῖς πρὸ τῆς δημιουργίας θεοῖς ἀνύμνησαν Κρόνου καὶ Ῥέας καὶ Οὐρανοῦ καὶ Γῆς συνόδους καὶ συνα|πογεννήσεις, κατὰ τὰ αὐτὰ δὴ καὶ ἐν τοῖς δημιουργοῖς τοῦ παντὸς τὴν πρωτίστην σύζευξιν Διὸς καὶ Ἥρας παραδεδώκασιν τοῦ μὲν Διὸς τὴν πατρικὴν ἀξίαν λαχόντος, τῆς δὲ Ἥρας μητρὸς οὔσης τῶν πάντων ὧν ὁ Ζεὺς πατήρ, καὶ τοῦ μὲν ἐν μονάδος τάξει τὰ ὅλα παράγοντος, τῆς δὲ κατὰ | τὴν γόνιμον δυάδα τῷ Διὶ τὰ δεύτερα συνυφιστάσης, καὶ τοῦ μὲν πρὸς τὸ πέρας τὸ νοητόν, τῆς δὲ πρὸς τὴν ἀπειρίαν ἀφομοιουμένων· καθ' ἑκάστην γὰρ τάξιν θεῶν εἶναι προσήκει τὰς ἀνάλογον ἐκείνοις ὑφισταμένας πρωτουργοὺς αἰτίας.

Πρὸς δὴ τὴν ἕνωσιν τῶν μεγίστων τούτων θεῶν | ἀμφότερα δεῖ προϋπάρχειν, τοῦ μὲν μοναδικοῦ καὶ δημιουργικοῦ θεοῦ τὴν ἑνιαίαν ὑπεροχήν, τῆς δὲ γεννητικῆς καὶ δυαδικῆς αἰτίας τὴν πρὸς ἐκεῖνον τελέαν ἐπιστροφήν. ἡ γὰρ ὁμοφυὴς τῶν κρειττόνων κοινωνία τοῦτον ἀποτελεῖται τὸν τρόπον, τῶν μὲν ὑπερτέρων ἐν ἑαυτοῖς ἱδρυμένων καὶ τοῖς | ἑαυτῶν θειοτέροις, τῶν δὲ καταδεεστέρων ἐνδιδόντων ἑαυτὰ ταῖς ἐκείνων δυνάμεσιν.

Καὶ διὰ ταύτας οἶμαι τὰς αἰτίας ἡ μὲν Ἥρα πρὸς τὴν τοῦ Διὸς ἐπειγομένη συνουσίαν τελειοῖ τὴν ἑαυτῆς ὅλην οὐσίαν καὶ προπαρασκευάζει ταῖς

"Limit" and "Unlimited" and other sages have glorified with other names.[210] The divine classes are separated from one another and divided up according to the division appropriate to the gods and, these second ruling principles—by this same [principle of division], the exegetes of the truth about the gods are accustomed to divide male and female, odd and even, maternal and paternal—and then again they are anxious for union and communion in a single nature, because of the first cause that || governs unified good things for all beings.[211] This, I believe, is where the mythoplasts found the material for their symbolic doctrine[212] and attributed both marriage and intercourse to the gods and then represented the subsequent births, and again the intercourse and marriages and unions of the offspring, until they saw the whole divine plane diversified with such processions and unions from above down to [the gods] that are in the cosmos.

Now, just as among the predemiurgic gods they sang of the intercourse and procreation of Kronos and Rhea and of Ouranos and Gaia, by the same token among the demiurges of the universe they relate the tradition of the first union of Zeus and Hera, with Zeus in the role of the father and Hera as the mother of all that which Zeus fathers, [Zeus] in the rank of the monad bringing forth the entire entities and she in the mode of the generative dyad, contributing with Zeus to the production of secondaries—he being assimilated to the Limit perceived by intellect and she to the Unlimited. In each class of gods it is appropriate that there should be established first causes analogous to these.

In order for the union of these greatest gods to occur, then, both of these things must exist in advance: the unified transcendence of the monadic and demiurgic god and the perfect return toward him of the generative dyadic cause. For the union in a single nature of the greater ones comes about in the following way: the higher ones remain fixed in themselves and in what is more divine than themselves, and the lower ones abandon themselves to their powers.

It is on account of these things, I believe, that Hera, driven to union with Zeus, perfects her whole being and equips it ahead of time with all

---

210. See above, 93–95 (K88) with n. 120.
211. Rejecting F.'s supplement τῶν ἡνωμένων <καὶ> ἀγαθῶν as unnecessary.
212. On συμβολικὴ θεωρία, see above 65–67 (K73) with n. 86. For ἀφορμή as "material" ("subject, topic"), see LSJ s.v. 5. Proclus's use of the term in this sense points to the affinities of this text with the rhetorical writers. Here it seems clear that the mythoplasts start from the "secret doctrine" and then invent a fictional vehicle for it.

παντοίαις δυνάμεσιν, ταῖς ἀχράντοις, ταῖς γεννητικαῖς, ταῖς νοεραῖς, | ταῖς ἑνοποιοῖς, ὁ δὲ Ζεὺς ἀνεγείρει τὸν ἐν ἑαυτῷ θεῖον ‖ ἔρωτα, καθ' ὃν καὶ τὰ προσεχῶς αὐτοῦ μετέχοντα πληροῖ τῶν ἀγαθῶν καὶ προτείνει τὴν συναγωγὸν εἰς ἓν τοῦ πλήθους αἰτίαν καὶ τὴν ἐπιστρεπτικὴν τῶν δευτέρων πρὸς ἑαυτὸν ἐνέργειαν. μία δὲ ἕνωσις ἀμφοτέρων καὶ ἀδιάλυτος | συμπλοκὴ τῶν θεῶν τούτων ἀποτελεῖται, χωριστὴ τοῦ παντὸς καὶ τῶν ἐγκοσμίων ὑποδοχῶν ἐξῃρημένη. καὶ γὰρ ὁ Ζεὺς ἐπὶ ταύτην ἀνάγει τὴν κοινωνίαν, τῆς Ἥρας αὐτῷ προτεινούσης τὴν καταδεεστέραν καὶ ἐγκόσμιον, ἀεὶ μὲν καθ' ἑκατέραν τῶν θεῶν ἡνωμένων, τοῦ δὲ μύθου μερίζοντος | καὶ τὰ ἀϊδίως ἀλλήλοις συνυφεστηκότα χωρίζοντος, καὶ τὴν μὲν χωριστὴν τοῦ παντὸς μῖξιν εἰς τὴν τοῦ Διὸς βούλησιν ἀναπέμποντος, τὴν δὲ εἰς τὸν κόσμον προϊοῦσαν αὐτῶν κοινὴν συνεργίαν ἐπὶ τὴν τῆς Ἥρας πρόνοιαν. τὸ δὲ αἴτιον, ὅτι πανταχοῦ τὸ μὲν πατρικὸν τῶν ἐξῃρημένων ἀγα|θῶν καὶ ἑνικωτέρων προκατάρχει, τὸ δὲ μητρικὸν τῶν προσεχῶν τοῖς μετέχουσιν καὶ πληθυομένων κατὰ τὰς παντοίας προόδους.

Εἰκότως ἄρα καὶ ὁ ὕπνος καὶ ἡ ἐγρήγορσις μεμερισμένως ἐν τοῖς συμβόλοις ὑπὸ τῶν μύθων παραλαμβάνονται, τῆς μὲν ἐγρηγόρσεως τὴν εἰς τὸν κόσμον πρόνοιαν | τῶν θεῶν δηλούσης, τοῦ δὲ ὕπνου τὴν χωριστὴν ἁπάντων τῶν καταδεεστέρων ζωήν, καίτοι τῶν θεῶν ὁμοῦ καὶ προνοούντων τοῦ παντὸς καὶ ἐν ἑαυτοῖς ἱδρυμένων. ἀλλ' ὥσπερ ὁ Τίμαιος τότε μὲν ἐνεργοῦντα παραδίδωσι τὸν τῶν ὅλων δημιουργὸν καὶ ὑφιστάντα τὴν γῆν, τὸν οὐρανόν, τὰς | πλανωμένας, τὴν ἀπλανῆ, τοὺς κύκλους τῆς ψυχῆς, τὸν νοῦν τὸν κοσμικόν, τότε δὲ ἐν τῷ ἑαυτοῦ κατὰ τρόπον ἤθει μένοντα [42e] καὶ ἀφ' ὅλων ἐξῃρημένον τῶν εἰς τὸ πᾶν ἐνεργούντων, οὕτω δὴ πολὺ πρότερον οἱ μῦθοι ποτὲ μὲν ἐγρηγορότα τὸν πατέρα τῶν ἐγκοσμίων πάντων, ποτὲ δὲ | καθεύδοντα πρὸς ἔνδειξιν τῆς διττῆς ζωῆς παραλαμβάνουσιν. **νῷ γὰρ κατέχει τὰ νοητά**, φησίν τις θεῶν, **αἴσθησιν** ‖

sorts of powers, transcendent, generative, intellective, and unifying, and on his side Zeus awakens his || divine desire, according to which he fills all that which participates immediately in him with good things, and extends the cause that draws multiplicity together into one and the action that turns secondaries back to him. A single union and indissoluble intercourse of these gods is accomplished, apart from the universe and transcending the encosmic receptacles. Zeus draws her up to this union, while Hera offers him the lower and encosmic one—though in fact the gods are continuously united in each of these sorts of union and the myth makes the distinction, separating those things that in fact coexist eternally and attributing the copulation separate from the universe to the will of Zeus and their shared activity that projects into the cosmos to the providence of Hera. The reason is that everywhere the paternal element is the first ruling principle of the transcendent goods and those that exhibit more unity, and the maternal element, of that which is contiguous with the participants and pluralized[213] according to the various sorts of processions.

[c. Solution to the question of Zeus's sleep (3)][214]

It is therefore quite appropriate for sleep as well and the waking state to be distinguished and incorporated by the myths into their symbolism. The waking state indicates the providence of the gods projected into the cosmos, and the sleep, that life that transcends all lower things—although the gods are in fact simultaneously provident of the universe and transcendent in themselves. Just as Timaeus depicts the demiurge of the universe at one time acting and establishing the earth, the heavens, the planets, the fixed sphere, the orbits of the soul, and the cosmic intellect, and at another time remaining in his accustomed manner within himself, apart from those who are active within the universe [*Tim.* 42e]—in the same way, at a much earlier stage, the myths take the father of all encosmic things to be awake at one time and sleeping at another, in order to demonstrate his double life. One of the gods says:

> The objects of intellection he contains in his mind ||
> and projects sense experience into the worlds,

---

213. Runia and Share 2008 offer this solution for πληθύνειν in Proclus.

214. This explanation is echoed by Pseudo-Dionysius, interpreting a reference to God's "sleep" (probably in Ps 44 (43):23). See Lamberton 1986, 246–47.

δὲ ἐπάγει κόσμοις. οὐκοῦν κατὰ ταύτην μὲν τὴν ἐνέργειαν ἐγρηγορέναι τις ἂν αὐτὸν εἴποι (καὶ γὰρ ἡ παρ' ἡμῖν ἐγρήγορσις ἐνέργεια τῆς αἰσθήσεώς ἐστιν), κατ' ἐκείνην δὲ καθεύδειν ὡς κεχωρισμένην τῶν αἰσθητῶν καὶ κατὰ | νοῦν τέλειον ἀφωρισμένην ζωὴν προστησάμενον· καὶ βουλεύεσθαι μὲν περὶ τῶν ἀνθρωπίνων ἐγρηγορότα (κατ' αὐτὴν γὰρ τὴν ζωὴν προνοεῖ τῶν ἐν τῷ κόσμῳ πραγμάτων), καθεύδοντα δὲ καὶ μετὰ τῆς Ἥρας εἰς τὴν χωριστὴν ἕνωσιν ἀναγόμενον οὐκ ἐπιλελῆσθαι τῆς ἑτέρας, ἀλλ' ἔχοντα κἀκεί|νην ἐνεργὸν μετ' ἐκείνης καὶ ταύτην ἔχειν. οὐ γὰρ ὡς ἡ φύσις τὰ δεύτερα ποιεῖ νοήσεως χωρὶς οὐδ' αὖ διὰ τὴν νόησιν ἐλαττοῖ τὴν εἰς τὰ καταδεέστερα πρόνοιαν, ἀλλ' ὁμοῦ καὶ κατὰ δίκην ἄγει τὰ προνοούμενα καὶ εἰς τὴν νοητὴν ἄνεισι περιωπήν. |

Δηλοῖ δὲ ἄρα τὴν τοιαύτην ὁ μῦθος ἐξῃρημένην ὑπεροχὴν ἐν τῇ Ἴδῃ λέγων αὐτῷ τὴν πρὸς τὴν Ἥραν γενέσθαι συνουσίαν· ἐκεῖ γὰρ καὶ τὴν Ἥραν ἐλθοῦσαν ἑαυτὴν ἐπιδοῦναι τῷ μεγίστῳ Διί. τί οὖν ἄλλο τὴν Ἴδην αἰνίσσεσθαι φήσομεν ἢ τὸν τῶν ἰδεῶν τόπον καὶ τὴν νοη|τὴν φύσιν, εἰς ἣν ἄνεισιν ὁ Ζεὺς καὶ ἀνάγει τὴν Ἥραν δι' ἔρωτος οὐκ ἐπιστρέφων εἰς τὸ μετέχον, ἀλλὰ δι' ὑπερβολὴν ἀγαθότητος καὶ ταύτῃ δευτέραν ἕνωσιν πρός τε ἑαυτὸν καὶ τὸ νοητὸν χαριζόμενος. τοιοῦτοι γὰρ οἱ τῶν κρειττόνων ἔρωτες, ἐπιστρεπτικοὶ τῶν καταδεεστέρων εἰς τὰ πρῶτα | καὶ ἀποπληρωτικοὶ τῶν ἐν αὐτοῖς ἀγαθῶν καὶ τελεσιουργοὶ τῶν ὑφειμένων.

Οὐκ ἄρα τὴν ἀξίαν ἐλαττοῖ τοῦ μεγίστου Διὸς ὁ μῦθος, αὐτοῦ που χαμαὶ συγγινόμενον τῇ Ἥρᾳ παραδιδούς, οὐκ ἀνασχόμενον εἰς τὸ δωμάτιον ἐλθεῖν· ἀντὶ γὰρ τῆς ἐγκοσμίου συμπλοκῆς τὴν ὑπερκόσμιον αὐτὸν ᾑρῆ|σθαί φησιν. ὁ γοῦν Ἡφαιστότευκτος θάλαμος τὴν τοῦ παντὸς ἐνδείκνυται διακόσμησιν καὶ τὸν αἰσθητὸν τόπον· ἐπεὶ || καὶ ὁ Ἥφαιστος δημιουργός ἐστι τοῦδε τοῦ παντός, ὡς εἴρηται καὶ πρότερον.

says one of the gods [*Or. chald.* frag. 8 des Places]. Now, from this last action, one would say that he was awake (since among us being awake is an act of sensation), and from the first that he was sleeping, since there he has preferred a life separated from sense objects and defined according to perfect intellect. In a waking state, he takes counsel about human affairs (for through this sort of life he exercises providence over things in the cosmos), and sleeping and drawn up into transcendent union with Hera he does not forget the other form of union but keeps it active as well and has both the one and the other. He does not, like nature, generate secondaries without thought, the way nature generates secondaries, nor on account of his thought does he diminish his providence over lower things, but he simultaneously guides the objects of his providence according to justice and retires into his noetic vantage point.

[d. Solution to the question of the location of their intercourse]

The myth, then, refers to this transcendent detachment by saying that his intercourse with Hera takes place on Mount Ida, for it is there that Hera goes and gives herself to greatest Zeus. What else shall we say "Ida" [Ἴδη] hints at, if not the place of "ideas" [ἰδεῶν, i.e., forms] and thus the noetic nature? Zeus ascends into this and draws Hera along through desire, not turning toward her in her role as participating being, but through the abundance of his goodness bestowing on her a second union, both with himself and with the noetic. Such are the desires of the greater beings, causing the lower ones to return toward the first and filling them with the good things within themselves, bringing those beneath them to perfection.

The myth therefore does not diminish the dignity of greatest Zeus in depicting him having intercourse with Hera right on the ground, without the patience to go into the bedroom: it is saying that he has chosen the union that transcends the universe over the encosmic one. The bedroom built by Hephaestus indicates the orderly arrangement of the universe and the realm of the senses, since || Hephaestus as well is a demiurge of this universe, as was said earlier.[215]

---

215. Above, 165–71 (K126–28).

Εἰ δὲ βούλει καὶ τὴν τῆς Ἥρας ἐννοῆσαι παρασκευήν, καθ' ἣν συνῆψεν ἑαυτὴν τῷ μεγίστῳ τῶν θεῶν καὶ προεκαλέσατο τὴν πατρικὴν τοῦ Διὸς πρόνοιαν | εἰς τὴν κοινωνίαν τῶν γονίμων ἑαυτῆς δυνάμεων, μειζόνως οἶμαι θεάσῃ τὴν ὑπερβολὴν τῆς ὑμνουμένης ἐν τῷ μύθῳ τούτῳ χωριστῆς ἑνώσεως τῶν θεῶν. ἐξομοιοῖ γὰρ ἑαυτὴν παντοδαπῶς τῇ μητρὶ τῶν θεῶν, ἀφ' ἧς καὶ αὐτὴ προελήλυθεν, καὶ ταῖς μερικωτέραις κοσμεῖται δυνάμεσιν τῶν ὁλι|κῶς ἐν ἐκείνῃ προϋπαρχουσῶν, καὶ μόνον οὐχὶ Ῥέαν αὐτὴν ὑφειμένην ἀποτελέσασα τῷ δημιουργῷ πρόσεισιν τοῦ παντὸς ἐπὶ τὸ σφέτερον ἀνηγμένῳ νοητόν. καὶ γὰρ δεῖ <τὴν> τῷ μιμουμένῳ τὸν πατέρα διὰ τῆς χωριστῆς τῶν ἐγκοσμίων ζωῆς συνάπτεσθαι μέλλουσαν καὶ αὐτὴν πρὸς τὴν μητέρα | τῶν θείων πάντων διακόσμων ἀφομοιῶσαι τὴν ἑαυτῆς τελειότητα, καὶ οὕτω δὴ συμφυῆ τὴν πρὸς αὐτὸν ἐνστήσασθαι κοινωνίαν.

Αἱ μὲν οὖν χαῖται τῆς θεοῦ καὶ οἱ πλόκαμοι διασπειρόμενοί τε πανταχῇ καὶ πάλιν ὑπ' αὐτῆς ἑνιζόμενοι πάντως οὐκ ἄδηλον, ὅτι ταῖς χαίταις εἰσὶν ἀνά|λογον τῆς μητρός.

χαῖται μὲν γὰρ ἐς ὀξὺ πεφρικότι φωτὶ βλέπονται,

φησίν τις θεῶν· καὶ γὰρ τοὺς Ἡραίους πλοκάμους φαεινοὺς ὁ ποιητὴς ἀπεκάλεσεν [Ξ 176]. ἡ δὲ ζώνη τοῖς | προεληλυθόσιν μὲν ἀπ' αὐτῆς, οὐκ ἀποτετμημένοις δὲ θυσάνοις κατακεκοσμημένη πρὸς τὸν ἐκεῖ ζωστῆρα τὸν ὅλον καὶ παντελῆ τὴν ἀφομοίωσιν ἔλαχεν. καὶ ἔστι ζωογόνος τις καὶ αὐτὴ καὶ γεννητικὴ παντὸς τοῦ πλήθους τῶν ψυχῶν, ἃς τῶν ἐξηρτημένων θυσάνων ὁ ἀριθμὸς ἐνδείκνυται συμ|βολικῶς. τὰ δὲ ἕρματα καὶ τὰ ὑποδήματα τάς τε πρωτίστας || καὶ τὰς ἐσχάτας ἀπεικονίζεται τῶν ἐκεῖθεν ἀπορρεουσῶν μερικῶν δυνάμεων, ὧν αἱ μὲν περὶ τὰς ἄκρας ὑφίστανται τῆς θεοῦ δυνάμεις κἀκείνων ἐξέχονται, αἱ δὲ τὰς περιπεζίους αὐτῆς

[e. Solution to the question of Hera's adornment]

If you wish to form a notion as well of Hera's preparation, by which she attached herself to the greatest of the gods and invited the paternal providence of Zeus into union with the generative powers in herself, then I think you will appreciate even more the sublimity of the transcendent union of the gods celebrated in the myth. She in every way makes herself similar to the mother of the gods (from whom she as well is sprung), and she adorns herself with more partial powers than those that previously exist in their entirety in the mother, and she virtually makes of herself a Rhea of a lower rank[216] as she goes to the demiurge of the universe, who has retired into his own noetic realm. As she is going to attach herself to one mimicking their father [Kronos], in his life transcending encosmic things, she must make her own perfection like the mother of all the divine orders and in this way establish her communion with him in a single nature.

It is not at all obscure that the goddess's hair, and the locks scattered every which way and then drawn together, are analogous to those of her mother.

Her hair appears in a sharply bristling light,[217]

says one of the gods [*Or. chald.* frag. 55, des Places], and the poet himself describes the hair of Hera as "radiant" [*Il.* 14.176]. The waistband decorated with a fringe that projects from it and is uncut is modeled on the waistband there, which is entire and perfect.[218] Hera herself is a producer of beings and gives birth to the great multiplicity of souls, which the number of the filaments of her fringe represents symbolically. Her earrings and her sandals are images of the very first ‖ and last of the partial powers that project from her, of which the first are around the upper reaches of the goddess, and are attached there, while the others receive the processions

---

216. F. compares K138,16 below: καὶ οἷον Ῥέα γενομένη μερική.
217. The syntax of this fragment is obscure, and F. suggested a "rather energetic" emendation (156 n. 4 ad loc.).
218. ὁ ἐκεῖ ζωστήρ is clearly a "waistband" in the realm of the hypercosmic gods, perceived by intellect [F.], but its more precise identity is obscure. F., however, offered some elaboration of this idea from Damascius (*Dub. et sol.* 1:241–42 Ruelle), who locates hypercosmic "springs" in the ζωστήρ: "the primal soul and primal virtue [flow from] the partial springs in the waistband."

ὑποδέχονται προόδους. ἡ δὲ ἀμβροσία καὶ | τὸ ἔλαιον τῶν ἀχράντων ἐστὶν τῆς θεοῦ δυνάμεων συνθήματα· καὶ γὰρ αἱ ἀμείλικτοι τάξεις περὶ αὐτὴν ὑφεστήκασιν. ὅπερ οὖν ἐκεῖ τὸ ἀδάμαστόν ἐστιν τῶν θεῶν καὶ τῆς καθαρότητος αἴτιον γένος, τοῦτο ἐνταῦθα διὰ τούτων σημαίνεται τῶν συμβόλων. καὶ γὰρ ἡ ἀμβροσία τὴν πάσης | ἀκαθαρσίας καὶ παντὸς μολυσμοῦ δύναμιν ὑπεραίρουσαν παρίστησιν, καὶ τὸ ἔλαιον ῥώμης ὂν ποιητικὸν καὶ γυμναστικῇ προσῆκον οἰκείως ἔχει τῇ Κουρητικῇ θεότητι. καὶ γὰρ οἱ πρώτιστοι Κούρητες τά τε ἄλλα τῇ τάξει τῆς Ἀθηνᾶς ἀνεῖνται καὶ περιεστέφθαι λέγονται τῷ θαλλῷ τῆς | ἐλάας, ὥς φησιν Ὀρφεύς [frag. 186].

Τοιούτοις δὴ οὖν συμβόλοις ἡ θεὸς αὕτη τελειωθεῖσα καὶ οἷον Ῥέα γενομένη μερικὴ πρόσεισιν τῷ δημιουργῷ τοῦ παντὸς κατὰ ταύτην συναφθησομένη τὴν ζωήν, καθ' ἣν διαφερόντως μιμεῖται τὸν Κρόνον, οὐκ εἰς τὸ πᾶν προϊών, ἀλλὰ χωριστὸς ὢν | ἀπὸ τῶν ἐγκοσμίων, οὐδὲ περὶ τῶν τῇδε βουλευόμενος κατὰ τὴν ἄγρυπνον πρόνοιαν τῶν ὅλων, ἀλλ' ἐξῃρημένος τῶν αἰσθητῶν κατὰ τὸν θεῖον ὕπνον, καὶ ταύτῃ τὸν πατέρα ζηλῶν· καὶ γὰρ ἐκεῖνος καθεύδων πρώτιστος παραδέδοται τῶν θεῶν· |

**ἔνθα Κρόνος μὲν ἔπειτα φαγὼν δολόεσσαν ἐδωδὴν
κεῖτο μέγα ῥέγχων** [Orph. frag. 148].

εἰκότως δὴ οὖν καὶ ἡ τῆς Ἥρας παρασκευὴ πρὸς τὴν ὅλην Ῥέαν ἀποβλέπει, τοῦ Διὸς κατὰ τὸν Κρόνον ἱσταμένου καὶ | διὰ τὴν πρὸς ἐκεῖνον ὁμοιότητα τὴν ἐν τῇ Ἴδῃ συνουσίαν προτιμῶντος τῆς εἰς τὸν κόσμον προϊούσης.

Ἐπεὶ καὶ ὁ || κεστὸς καὶ ἡ τῆς Ἀφροδίτης σύλληψις ἐπὶ πλέον αὐτὴν ἐξομοιοῖ πρὸς τὴν Ῥέαν. ἦν γὰρ καὶ ἐκεῖ τῆς θεοῦ ταύτης προϋφεστῶσα μονάς, ἄνωθεν ἀπὸ τῆς συνεκτικῆς τοῦ Οὐρανοῦ θεότητος διὰ μέσου Κρόνου προελθοῦσα καὶ κατα|λάμψασα πᾶσαν τὴν νοερὰν ζωὴν τῷ φωτὶ

that come from her feet. The ambrosia and the oil are symbols of the pure powers of the goddess and the unrelenting orders of beings submit to her.[219] What *there* constitutes the invincible race of the gods, the cause of purity, is represented *here* through these symbols. The ambrosia reveals the power that rises above all impurity and pollution, and the oil, which produces strength and is associated with gymnastics, has an affinity with the divinity of the Couretes. For the first of the Couretes, aside from the fact that they belong to the portion of Athena, are also said to be crowned with the olive branch, as Orpheus asserts [*Orph. frag.* 186, Kern].

Adorned with these symbols, and perfected and as if changed into a partial Rhea, this goddess goes to the demiurge of the universe to be attached to him in that life in which he most imitates Kronos, not proceeding into the universe but remaining apart from encosmic things, not deliberating on things here below in the mode of awakened providence for the universe but transcending sense-objects in that of divine sleep, and thus imitating his father. [Kronos] was the very first of the gods depicted as sleeping:

Then Kronos, when he had eaten the delusive meal,
lay back, snoring loudly [*Orph. frag.* 148, Kern].

The adornment of Hera thus appropriately looks to the model of the universal Rhea, since Zeus is set up in the manner of Kronos, and it is because of his resemblance to Kronos that he chooses the copulation on Mount Ida over that which proceeds into the cosmos.

Moreover, the || belt [κεστός[220]] and the aid of Aphrodite liken her still more to Rhea. There existed *there* the preexisting monad of this goddess [Aphrodite], proceeding down from the cohesive divinity of Ouranos[221] through the middle of Kronos and illuminating the entire intellective life

---

219. The unrelenting orders (ἀμείλικτοι τάξεις) are obscure. The term is applied to a range of gods in Proclus (e.g., *In Tim.* [Diehl] 1:166,9 (Zeus); 1:167,6 and 1:168,15 (Athena); 1:38,18 (all the gods)—cf. Tarrant 2007). The point seems to be, here, that the ambrosia and oil are "softening" agents, antithetical to the "unrelenting, unsoftened" quality of divinity. I.e., she gets what she wants from Zeus.

220. The *kestos* that Aphrodite gives to Hera (*Il.* 14.214-223) has magical, aphrodisiac powers. Physically similar to the ζωνή, it is to be imagined as worn higher, normally just under the breasts.

221. Taking F.'s identification of the deity in question as Ouranos (based on *In Tim.* 3:99,12-19, Diehl) over Kroll's argument (F., 158 n. 3, ad loc.).

τοῦ κάλλους. ἀλλ' ἡ μὲν Ἀφροδίτη τὸν κεστὸν ἐν τῷ στήθει λέγεται φέρειν, ὡς ἂν προβεβλημένας αὐτοῦ τὰς δυνάμεις ἔχουσα· ἡ δὲ Ἥρα κρύπτει πως αὐτὸν ὑπὸ τοῖς κόλποις, ὡς ἂν ἄλλην μὲν ἰδιότητα λαχοῦσα τῆς ὑπάρξεως,
10 ἔχουσα δὲ καὶ | τὸν κεστόν, καθ' ὅσον καὶ αὐτὴ πεπλήρωται τῆς ὅλης Ἀφροδίτης. οὐ γὰρ ἔξωθέν ποθεν ἐπάγεται τὴν συνάπτουσαν αὐτὴν πρὸς τὸν δημιουργὸν δύναμιν, ἀλλ' ἐν ἑαυτῇ καὶ ταύτην συνείληφεν. δηλοῦσι δὲ <καὶ> αἱ κοιναὶ προλήψεις τὴν τῶν θεαινῶν τούτων κοινωνίαν, ζυγίαν
15 τε καὶ γάμων προ|στάτιν τιμῶσαι τὴν Ἥραν, ὡς ἂν ἀφ' ἑαυτῆς ἀρξαμένην τῶν τοιούτων ἐνεργειῶν. ἑαυτὴν γὰρ συζεύγνυσιν τῷ δημιουργῷ κατὰ τὸν ἐν ἑαυτῇ κεστόν, καὶ διὰ τοῦτο καὶ τοῖς ἄλλοις ἅπασιν αὕτη παρέχεται τὴν ἔνθεσμον πρὸς ἄλληλα κοινωνίαν. |
20 Ἀλλὰ πῶς λέγονται πρῶτον μὲν εἰς εὐνὴν φοιτῆσαι τὴν ἀρχὴν φίλους λήθοντε τοκῆας, ἔπειτα μειζόνως ἀλλήλοις συνάπτεσθαι νῦν δι' ἔρωτος ὑπερβολήν, ὃν ὁ Ζεὺς ἠράσθη τῆς Ἥρας;

ἢ διτταὶ καὶ τῶν ἄλλων ἀγαθῶν εἰσιν αἱ ἰδιότητες καὶ τῆς ἑνώσεως ἡ
25 μὲν συμφυὴς τοῖς ἐνιζο|μένοις, ἡ δὲ ἄνωθεν αὐτοῖς ἀπὸ τῶν τελειοτέρων αἰτίων ἐφήκουσα. καὶ κατὰ μὲν τὴν ἑτέραν λανθάνειν λέγονται τοὺς ἑαυτῶν γεννήτορας, ὡς ἂν ἰδίαν ταύτην λαχοῦσαι τὴν ἕνωσιν, κατὰ δὲ τὴν λοιπὴν ἐπ' αὐτὰ ἀνάγεσθαι τὰ σφέτερα αἴτια· διὸ καὶ μείζονα ταύτην
30 εἶναι καὶ τελεωτέραν | ἐκείνης. ἀμφοτέρων δὲ ὁμοῦ καὶ διαιωνίως οὐσῶν
K140 παρὰ || τοῖς θεοῖς οἱ μῦθοι μερίζουσιν, ὡς τὸν ὕπνον καὶ τὴν ἐγρήγορσιν, ὡς τὴν πρόοδον καὶ τὴν ἐπιστροφήν, ὡς τὴν μετάδοσιν τῶν οἰκείων ἀγαθῶν εἰς τὰ δεύτερα καὶ τὴν μέθεξιν τῶν πρωτουργῶν αἰτίων· καὶ γὰρ ταῦτα
5 συνυπάρ|χοντα ἀλλήλοις οἱ μυθοπλάσται τὴν ἀλήθειαν ἐπικρυπτόμενοι χωρίζουσιν.

with the light of her beauty. Aphrodite is said to wear the *kestos* on her breast as if she had its powers projecting before her, but Hera on the other hand hides it somehow beneath her breasts, as if she had a different aspect of its being,[222] but nevertheless having the *kestos* in her possession, to the extent that she has been filled with the universal Aphrodite. She does not get from some external source the power that joins her to the demiurge, but rather she contains this as well within herself. The common notions as well[223] demonstrate the association of these goddesses, honoring Hera as the "Yoker" [ζυγία[224]] and patroness of marriages, as if she herself were the first cause of such actions. Thus, she "marries herself" to the demiurge through the *kestos* within her and through this she also provides to everyone else legitimate union with one another.

[f. Solution to the question of the several occasions of intercourse]

But in what sense are they said at first to have gone to bed "when their parents were not looking," but now to be joined together even more by the greater desire Zeus has for Hera?

The answer may be that the properties of other good things are double, and likewise those of [sexual] union, the one inherent in those conjoined, the other coming down on them from above from the more perfect causes. In the first, they are said to escape the notice of their own parents, as if this particular union belonged only to them, and in the other one they are said to be drawn up to their own causes. Therefore, the latter is greater and more perfect than the former.

Although both states are simultaneous and eternal among || the gods, the myths divide them, just as with sleep and waking, procession and return, sharing of goods with the secondaries and participation in their own first causes. Disguising the truth, the mythoplasts have separated these things which in fact exist simultaneously.

---

222. Unlike F., I take the ὕπαρξις in question to be that of the *kestos*, in which Hera participates in a different way from Aphrodite herself.
223. Reading (with F.) Radermacher's καί in line 13.
224. An epithet of Hera as patroness of marriage.

Πάντα ἄρα κατὰ τὸν θεολογικὸν τρόπον Ὁμήρῳ τὰ περὶ τῆς συνουσίας λέγεται τοῦ τε μεγίστου Διὸς καὶ τῆς Ἥρας. μαρτυρεῖ δὲ ἄρα τούτοις καὶ ὁ ἐν τῷ Κρατύλῳ Σωκράτης [404b], οὐκ ἀλλαχόθεν αὐτὴν ἐτυμο|λογῶν ἢ ἀπὸ τοῦ ἔρωτος, ὡς τῷ Διί, φησίν, οὖσαν ἐραστήν.

Οὐκ ἄρα κατὰ τὴν ἀπόρρητον θεωρίαν ἐγκαλέσομεν Ὁμήρῳ τοιαῦτα γεγραφότι περὶ τῶν μεγίστων τούτων θεῶν. εἰ δὲ μὴ προσήκοντα νέοις ἐστὶ κατὰ τὸ φαινόμενον ἀκούειν, ἀλλ᾽ ἡμῖν, φαῖεν ἂν οἱ ποιηταὶ τῶν τοιούτων, οὐ πρὸς | νέους ὁ λόγος οὐδὲ παιδευτικῶς τὰ τοιαῦτα γράφομεν, ἀλλὰ μαινομένῳ στόματι· καὶ ταῦτα ἡμᾶς ἡ τῶν Μουσῶν ἐργάζεται μανία, ἧς τὸν στερόμενον τῶν ἐπὶ ποιητικὰς θύρας ἀφικομένων ἀτελῆ καὶ αὐτὸν καὶ τὴν ποίησιν αὐτοῦ προσειρήκασιν.

Ἀλλὰ περὶ μὲν τούτων ἱκανὰ τὰ εἰρημένα· περὶ | δὲ τῶν Ἄρεως καὶ Ἀφροδίτης συνουσιῶν καὶ τῶν Ἡφαίστου δεσμῶν ἐφεξῆς διέλθωμεν. οὐδὲ γὰρ ταῦτα προσίεσθαί φησιν ὁ Σωκράτης [3.390c] οὐδὲ τοὺς τοιούτους μύθους παραδώσειν τοῖς νέοις. τί οὖν καὶ διὰ τούτων ἡ ποίησις αἰνίσσεται, λέγωμεν συντόμως. ||

Τί αἰνίττεται ἡ μυθολογία περὶ Ἀφροδίτης καὶ Ἄρεως καὶ τῶν Ἡφαίστου δεσμῶν, οἷς λέγει συνδεῖν ἀμφοτέρους τὸν Ἥφαιστον.

Ἄμφω μὲν οὖν οἵδε οἱ θεοὶ περὶ πάντα τὸν κόσμον | ἐνεργοῦσιν, ὅ τε Ἥφαιστος λέγω καὶ ὁ Ἄρης, ὁ μὲν διακρίνων τὰς ἐναντιώσεις τοῦ παντὸς καὶ ἀνεγείρων ἀεὶ καὶ σώζων ἀτρέπτως, ἵνα τέλειος ὁ κόσμος ᾖ πᾶσιν τοῖς εἴδεσιν συμπεπληρωμένος, ὁ δὲ τὴν ὅλην αἰσθητὴν διακόσμησιν τεχνικὴν ἀπεργαζόμενος καὶ λόγων φυσικῶν καὶ δυνάμεων | ἀποπληρῶν, καὶ περὶ μὲν τὸν οὐρανὸν εἴκοσι τρίποδας ὑφιστάς, ἵνα τῷ τελεωτάτῳ τῶν

[g. Conclusion]

Thus everything about the copulation of greatest Zeus and Hera is spoken by Homer in the theological mode. The Socrates of the *Cratylus* alludes to this as well when he derives Hera ["Ἥρα] from desire [ἔρως] and from nowhere else,[225] since, as he says, she is the "lover" [ἐραστής] of Zeus [404b–c].

Therefore, viewing them from the perspective of the secret doctrine, we shall not indict Homer for having written these things about the greatest of the gods. If it is not appropriate for the young to hear them and understand them literally, the poets who write such poems might say, "As far as we are concerned, this discourse is not intended for the young, and we do not write such things to serve an educational function, but rather we sing them in an inspired ecstasy. The madness that comes from the Muses does these things to us, and it has been said that whoever arrives at the gates of poetry without this madness will fall short of perfection—both he and his poetry."[226]

Enough has been said about these things. Let us go on to examine in detail the sexual encounters of Ares and Aphrodite and the chains of Hephaestus. Socrates refused to admit these as well or to hand down such myths to children [*Rep.* 3.390c]. Let us indicate briefly what the poem hints at through these things, as well. ||

(15) What does the mythology about Aphrodite and Ares and the chains with which Hephaestus is said to have bound them hint at?

Both of these gods—Hephaestus and Ares—are active in the entire cosmos, the one [Ares] by separating the opposites in the universe and awakening them and maintaining them unchangeably, so that the cosmos may be continuously perfect and filled with all the forms, and the other [Hephaestus] by completing the whole sense realm by the rules of his art, and by filling it with the physical *logoi*[227] and powers, setting up twenty tripods around the heavens [*Il.* 18.373] in order to adorn it with the most

---

225. The popular etymology of Hera's name from "air, mist" (ἀήρ) is also invoked in the passage cited, but Proclus seems to regard it as having been rejected.

226. Cf. Plato, *Phdr.* 245a, and 33 (K57,26–29), above.

227. φυσικοὶ λόγοι are the principles that in this world (governed by φύσις) represent the *logoi* that exist on the level of soul. They are roughly equivalent to the

πολυέδρων αὐτὸν κατακοσμῇ σχημάτων, τὰ δὲ ὑπὸ σελήνην ποικίλα καὶ πολύμορφα διαπλάττων εἴδη·

πόρπας τε γναπτάς θ' ἕλικας κάλυκας τε καὶ | ὅρμους [Σ 401]

κατὰ τὴν ἔντεχνον ποίησιν δημιουργῶν.

Καὶ δὴ καὶ Ἀφροδίτης ἄμφω δέονται κατὰ τὰς ἑαυτῶν ἐνεργείας, ὃ μὲν ἵνα τοῖς ἐναντίοις ἁρμονίαν ἐμποιήσῃ καὶ τάξιν, ὃ δὲ ἵνα τοῖς αἰσθητοῖς δημιουργήμασιν κάλλος ἐναπεργάσηται καὶ ἀγλαΐαν, | ὅση καὶ τόνδε τὸν κόσμον κάλλιστον ἀποτελέσαι τῶν ὁρωμένων ἠδύνατο.

Πανταχοῦ δὲ τῆς Ἀφροδίτης οὔσης ὁ μὲν Ἥφαιστος αὐτῆς ἀεὶ κατὰ τὰς ὑπερτέρας μετέχει τάξεις, ὁ δὲ Ἄρης κατὰ τὰς ὑποδεεστέρας· οἷον εἰ ὁ Ἥφαιστος ὑπερκοσμίως, ὁ Ἄρης ἐγκοσμίως, καὶ εἰ ἐκεῖνος οὐρανίως, ὑπὸ | σελήνην οὗτος. διὸ καὶ ὃ μὲν κατὰ βούλησιν τοῦ Διὸς ἄγεσθαι λέγεται τὴν Ἀφροδίτην, ὃ δὲ μοιχεύειν αὐτὴν μεμυθολόγηται. τῷ μὲν γὰρ δημιουργῷ τῶν αἰσθητῶν κατὰ φύσιν ἐστὶν ἡ πρὸς τὴν καλλοποιὸν αἰτίαν καὶ συνδετικὴν κοινωνία, τῷ δὲ τῆς διαιρέσεως προστάτῃ καὶ τῆς ἐναντιώ||σεως τῶν ἐγκοσμίων ἀλλοτρία πώς ἐστιν ἡ τῆς ἑνώσεως χορηγὸς δύναμις· τοῖς γὰρ συναγωγοῖς τὰ διακριτικὰ γένη τῶν θεῶν ἀντιδιῄρηται.

Ταύτην τοίνυν τὴν τῶν ἀνομοίων αἰτίων σύμπνοιαν οἱ μῦθοι μοιχείαν προσειρήκα|σιν. ἔδει δὲ ἄρα τῷ παντὶ καὶ τῆς τοιαύτης κοινωνίας, ἵνα καὶ τὰ ἐναντία συναρμοσθῇ καὶ ὁ ἐν τῷ κόσμῳ πόλεμος τέλος ἔχῃ τὴν εἰρήνην. ἐπειδὴ δὲ ἄνω μὲν ἐν τοῖς οὐρανίοις τὸ κάλλος προλάμπει καὶ τὰ εἴδη καὶ ἡ ἀγλαΐα καὶ τὰ Ἡφαιστότευκτα δημιουργήματα, κάτω δὲ ἐν τῇ γε|νέσει

perfect of polyhedrons, and fabricating the various and polymorphous sublunary forms,

> pins, spiral buckles, earrings and chains [*Il.* 18.401],

which he fashions by his creative craft.

In particular, both have need of Aphrodite, each in his own activity: the one [Ares] in order to introduce harmony and order into the opposites, and the other [Hephaestus] in order to produce in his creations in the sense realm beauty and brilliance, sufficient to make this world the most beautiful of all visible things.[228]

Now, since Aphrodite is everywhere, Hephaestus always participates in her at the higher levels and Ares at the lower. For example, if the participation of Hephaestus is hypercosmic, then that of Ares is encosmic, and if that of Hephaestus is celestial, the other is sublunary.[229] For this reason, the one [Hephaestus] is said to legitimately marry Aphrodite according to the will of Zeus, while the other [Ares] is said in the myths to commit adultery with her. Union with the cause that binds things together and creates beauty naturally belongs to the demiurge of the sensible world, but to the god who presides over the division and polarity || of encosmic things, the power that encourages union is somehow alien, for the classes of gods that separate are antithetical to those who draw together.

The myths refer to this harmony of disparate causes as "adultery."[230] The universe needed, then, such a joining so that the opposites might be drawn into harmony with one another and the war in the cosmos have its end in peace. And since beauty shines forth from above in the celestial realm and the creations of Hephaestus are up there, along with the forms

---

σπερματικοὶ λόγοι sometimes said to be the shaping principles that express the forms (resident in intellect [νοῦς]) in the material world. Cf. Porphyry, *Sent.* 10.

228. Cf. *Tim.* 29a.

229. One might look for corruption in the somewhat incoherent text here, because the two copulations should both exist on both levels, and in fact the initial description of the relations of Ares, Hephaestus, and Aphrodite (K141,16–21) would appear to put Ares' activity on the higher level (i.e., the level of greater generality), above Hephaestus's activity on the level of the details of the *poikilia* of this world. Proclus (or perhaps Syrianus) seems to be left scrambling to make the former the adulterer and the latter the legitimate spouse.

230. Not in the *Odyssey*, but the term μοιχάγρια ("penalty for adultery," *Od.* 8.332), which does occur here, is perhaps sufficient.

τῶν στοιχείων ἡ ἀντίθεσις καὶ ἡ μάχη καὶ ἐναντίωσις τῶν δυνάμεων καὶ ὅλως τὰ Ἀρεϊκὰ δῶρα, διὰ δὴ τοῦτο καὶ τὴν σύνερξιν τοῦ Ἄρεως καὶ τῆς Ἀφροδίτης ἐφορᾷ μὲν ἄνωθεν ὁ Ἥλιος, μηνύει δὲ τῷ Ἡφαίστῳ, καθ' ὅσον αὐτοῦ συνεργεῖ ταῖς ὅλαις ποιήσεσιν.

15 Ὁ δὲ Ἥφαιστος δεσμοῖς περι|βάλλειν αὐτοὺς λέγεται παντοίοις ἀφανέσι τοῖς ἄλλοις, ὡς ἂν καὶ τὰ γενητὰ κατακοσμῶν τοῖς τεχνικοῖς λόγοις καὶ μίαν σύστασιν ἀπεργαζόμενος ἔκ τε τῶν Ἀρεϊκῶν ἐναντιώσεων καὶ τῶν συναρμοστικῶν τῆς Ἀφροδίτης ἀγαθῶν· δεῖ γὰρ ἀμφοῖν τῇ γενέσει.
20 ἐπεὶ δὲ ἄλλοι μὲν οἱ δεσμοὶ τῶν | οὐρανίων, ἄλλοι δὲ οἱ τῶν ὑπὸ σελήνην (οἳ μὲν γάρ εἰσιν ἄλυτοι, καθάπερ φησὶν ὁ Τίμαιος [43a], οἳ δὲ λυτοί), διὰ δὴ τοῦτο λύει πάλιν ὁ Ἥφαιστος τοὺς δεσμούς, οἷς τὸν Ἄρη συνέδησε καὶ τὴν Ἀφροδίτην, καὶ τοῦτο διαφερόντως ποιεῖ τῷ Ποσειδῶνι πειθόμενος· ὃς
25 δὴ τὴν ἀειγενεσίαν | σῴζεσθαι βουλόμενος καὶ τὸν κύκλον τῆς μεταβολῆς εἰς ἑαυτὸν ἀνακυκλεῖσθαι τά τε γενόμενα φθορᾶς ἀξιοῖ καὶ τὰ φθαρέντα εἰς γένεσιν ἀναπέμπει.

Τί οὖν θαυμαστόν, εἰ καὶ Ὅμηρος ὑπὸ τῶν Ἡφαίστου δεσμῶν τόν
30 τε Ἄρεα καὶ τὴν Ἀφροδίτην συνδεῖσθαί φησιν, ὅπου καὶ ὁ Τίμαιος | τοὺς λόγους τοὺς δημιουργικούς, οἷς οἱ κατ' οὐρανὸν τὰ γενητὰ συνιστᾶσιν,
K143 δεσμοὺς προσείρηκεν [31c]; πῶς δὲ || οὐ κατὰ τὴν <τῶν> πραγμάτων λέγεται φύσιν τὸ λύειν αὐτὸν τὰ δεδεμένα τῶν γενεσιουργῶν δεσμῶν λυτῶν ὑπαρχόντων;

Καὶ ἔοικεν ὅ τε ὅλος δημιουργὸς ἐκ τῶν ἐναντίων στοιχείων τὸν
5 κόσμον συνιστὰς καὶ δι' ἀναλογίας ἐν αὐτῷ | φιλίαν ἀπεργαζόμενος συνάγειν εἰς ταὐτὸν τὰς Ἡφαίστου καὶ Ἄρεως καὶ Ἀφροδίτης ἐνεργείας, καὶ γεννῶν μὲν τὰς ἐναντιώσεις τῶν στοιχείων κατὰ τὸν ἐν ἑαυτῷ γεννῶν Ἄρεα, φιλίαν δὲ μηχανώμενος κατὰ τὴν τῆς Ἀφροδίτης δύναμιν ἐνεργεῖν,
10 συνδέων δὲ τοῖς Ἀρεϊκοῖς τὰ <u>Ἀφροδισιακὰ</u> καὶ τὴν | Ἡφαίστου τέχνην ἐν παραδείγματι προειληφέναι· πάντα γάρ ἐστιν αὐτὸς καὶ μετὰ πάντων ἐνεργεῖ τῶν θεῶν. καὶ δὴ καὶ οἱ νέοι δημιουργοὶ τὸν σφέτερον πατέρα μιμούμενοι ζῷά τε ἀπεργάζονται θνητὰ καὶ φθίνοντα πάλιν δέχονται, τῷ
15 Ἡφαίστῳ συναπογεννῶντες τοὺς ἐνταῦθα δεσμοὺς καὶ | τῆς λύσεως αὐτῶν

and the radiance, while battle and the opposition of powers and generally all the gifts of Ares are down here in γένεσις, with the polarities of the elements—for this reason Helios sees the coming together of Ares and Aphrodite from above and tells Hephaestus, since he collaborates with him in the totality of creation.

Hephaestus is said to cast all sorts of bonds around them, invisible to others, as if he were setting the things of creation in order according to the principles of his craft, creating a single unity from the opposites of Ares and the harmonizing benefits of Aphrodite, since γένεσις has need of both. Since there are, on the one hand, bonds of celestial things and, on the other, those of sublunary things (and the first are indissoluble, the second breakable, as Timaeus says [*Tim.* 43a]), on account of this Hephaestus breaks the chains with which he had bound Ares and Aphrodite, and does so specifically at the urging of Poseidon. He, of course, wishes to preserve perpetual generation and to ensure that the cycle of transformation into itself continues, and he is the one who decides on the destruction of things that have come to be and sends what has been destroyed back up into γένεσις.

What wonder is it, then, that Homer for his part said that Ares and Aphrodite were bound by the chains of Hephaestus, when Timaeus used the word "chains" for the demiurgical *logoi*, through which the celestial beings constitute the things that come to be and pass away [*Tim.*31c]? And how ‖ is it contrary to the nature of things when he says that he freed what was bound, since it is the nature of the bonds that are operative within γένεσις that they are breakable?

The universal demiurge, in bringing the cosmos to be out of opposing elements, and through proportion working attraction into it, seems to be uniting the actions of Hephaestus, Ares, and Aphrodite into one: in producing the opposition of the elements he was creating according to the Ares in him, in contriving attraction he was acting by the power of Aphrodite, and in bonding together the Aphrodisian[231] to the Arean he had taken the craft of Hephaestus as his model. He himself is all things and acts with all the gods. The young demiurges in particular imitate their father in fashioning mortal creatures and receiving them back again when they are destroyed, generating along with Hephaestus the chains of this world,

---

231. The manuscript has Ἀφροδίσια ("sex") for Ἀφροδισιακά (so F, following Kroll's addenda, 1901, 472).

προειληφότες αὐτοὶ τὰς αἰτίας· πανταχοῦ γὰρ ὁ τὸν δεσμὸν <u>παρέχων</u> καὶ τὴν τῆς λύσεως οἶδεν ἀνάγκην.

Τίνα ῥητέον πρὸς τὰς τοῦ Σωκράτους ἐπιστάσεις περὶ φιλοχρηματίας τῆς παρ' Ὁμήρῳ τοῖς | ἥρωσιν ἀποδιδομένης.

Τοσαῦτα καὶ πρὸς ταύτην εἰρήσθω τοῦ Σωκράτους τὴν ἐπίστασιν· μετὰ δὲ ταύτην ἐκεῖνα ἐπισκεπτέον, ὅσα δή φησιν τὸ φιλοχρήματον ἡμῶν αὔξειν τῆς ψυχῆς. τί γὰρ βουλόμενος ὁ Φοῖνιξ τῷ Ἀχιλλεῖ συνεβούλευεν δῶρα μὲν λαβόντι | τῆς μήνιος ἀπαλλάττεσθαι, ἄλλως δὲ μή; τί δὲ Ἀχιλλεὺς ὁ καὶ παρὰ τοῦ Ἀγαμέμνονος δῶρα λαμβάνων ὑπὲρ τῆς ὕβρεως καὶ τὸν τοῦ Ἕκτορος νεκρὸν οὐκ ἄλλως ἀποδιδοὺς ἢ μετὰ χρημάτων λήψεως; ὁ γὰρ τῶν τοιούτων κατήκοος γιγνόμενος δεινὴν καὶ ἀπλήρωτον τὴν ἐπιθυμίαν περὶ τὴν || τῶν χρημάτων κτῆσιν ἀπεργάζεται.

Πρὸς δὴ ταῦτα καὶ ἡμεῖς ἐν βραχεῖ λέγωμεν, ὅτι καὶ ὁ Φοῖνιξ συνεβούλευε χρήματα λαβόντι παύεσθαι τῆς ὀργῆς, καὶ Ἀχιλλεὺς λαβὼν ἀπηλλάττετο, τεκμήριον ἄμφω ποιούμενοι τὴν τῶν χρημάτων | δόσιν τῆς τοῦ διδόντος μεταμελείας, ἀλλ' οὐχ ὡς τὸ φιλοχρήματον ἀποπιμπλάντες τῆς ψυχῆς, οὐδ' ὡς ὅρον τῆς εὐδαιμονίας ἡγούμενοι τὴν τῶν χρημάτων αὔξησιν. οὐδὲ γὰρ τὴν ἀρχὴν αὐτοὶ τὰ χρήματα ᾔτησαν, ἀλλὰ προτεινόμενα ἐδέξαντο. εἰ δὲ καὶ τοῦ Ἕκτορος τὸν νεκρὸν χρημά|των ἀπέδοτο τῷ πατρί, τάχα μὲν καὶ ἔθος τι τοιοῦτον εἶναι φήσομεν, λύτρα δέχεσθαι τῶν πολεμίων σωμάτων. δεῖ δὲ αὖ κἀκεῖνο συννοεῖν, ὅτι στρατηγικὸν καὶ τοῦτο εἴποι τις ἄν, τὸ τῶν ἀνταγωνιστῶν περικόπτειν τὴν εὐπορίαν, αὔξειν δὲ τὰ τῶν οἰκείων ἐν ἀλλοτρίᾳ χώρᾳ πολεμεῖν ἀναγκαζομένων. | ἀλλὰ ταῦτα πάντα καὶ τὰ τοιαῦτα τοῖς μὲν ἥρωσιν ἐκείνοις λόγον τινὰ εἶχεν ὑπ' αὐτῶν πραττόμενα, καὶ περιστατικῶς ἐνεργοῦσιν καὶ κατ' ἄλλα ἔθη τὰς πράξεις μετιοῦσιν· τοῖς δὲ ὑπ' αὐτῷ νομοθέτῃ τρεφομένοις ἀνεπιτήδεια πάντως ἐστὶν ἀκούειν, ὧν αἵ τε φύσεις φιλόσοφοι καὶ ἡ παιδεία πρὸς | ταύτην

themselves anticipating the causes of the breaking of these chains. Everywhere the one who provides[232] the chain recognizes as well the necessity that the chain be broken.

(16) What is to be said against Socrates' objections concerning the greed Homer attributes to the heroes?

So much for this objection on Socrates' part. Next we should examine the passages that he claims increase the greediness of our souls. What did Phoenix mean when he advised Achilles to give up his wrath on receipt of gifts, but not otherwise? And what of Achilles, who also accepts gifts from Agamemnon in recompense for the outrage against him and refuses to release Hector's corpse except in exchange for payment? He who hears such things increases his desire for the || acquisition of possessions so that it becomes terrible and unquenchable.

Let us as well speak briefly about these things and say that Phoenix counseled taking payment and laying aside anger and that Achilles took it and did so, because both took the giving of property as a symbol of the donor's repentance, and not at all to satisfy the greed in their souls, nor because they believed increase of possessions to be a criterion of a successful life. They did not, in the first place, require payment, but accepted it when it was offered. If Achilles gave the corpse of Hector back to his father for payment, we shall respond that there was surely a custom of this sort, to accept ransom for the bodies of enemies. It should be considered, too, that one might say that this was befitting a general, to undercut the prosperity of the enemy and increase that of his own side, when they were compelled to fight in a foreign land. These things and others like them made sense for those heroes when they did them, both acting according to circumstances and conforming to customs different [from ours][233] as they went about their business. At the same time, they are not at all appropriate to be heard by those being raised by the nomothete himself, whose natures are philosophical, whose education is said to be directed toward

---

232. Replacing the manuscript's περιέχων with παρέχων (F.).

233. This traditional form of defensive interpretation ("according to custom" or "according to the time of the events" [Schrader 1880–1890, 1:241]) is widespread in the interpretive literature but relatively uncommon in Proclus. At this point, however, begins a series of such interpretations that, mixed with others, extends to the end of book 1, e.g., 211 (K150,11–13); cf. 217 (K153,18) (πολέμου νόμῳ).

βλέπουσα τὴν ζωὴν παραδέδοται, κτήσεις δὲ καὶ περιουσίαι παντελῶς ἀφῄρηνται.

Εἰ δὲ βούλεσθε, κἀκεῖνα προσθῶμεν τοῖς εἰρημένοις ὑπὲρ Ἀχιλλέως, ὅτι καὶ τῷ Ἀγαμέμνονι φιλοχρηματίαν αὐτὸς ἐγκαλεῖ καὶ ὡς ἐπονείδιστον διαβάλλει τὸ πάθος· |

25   **Ἀτρείδη κύδιστε φιλοκτεανώτατε πάντων** [A 122].

καὶ τὴν ὀλιγωρίαν ἣν ἔχει περὶ τὴν τῶν χρημάτων κτῆσιν αὐτὸς παρίστησι λέγων, ὅτι πάντα κατορθῶν καὶ πόλεις ἀνδραποδιζόμενος καὶ αἰχμαλώτους λαμβάνων σμικρὰ ἐκ πολλῶν κομιζόμενος οὐ διαφέρεται καὶ
30   ὡς τῶν ὅλων ἐπι|τρέπει τῷ Ἀγαμέμνονι τὴν διανομήν, ἐν οὐδενὸς μέρει τήν τε παρουσίαν αὐτῶν καὶ τὴν αὔξησιν τιθέμενος· ||

K145   **ἐγὼ δ' ὀλίγον τε φίλον τε**
         ἔρχομ' ἔχων ἐπὶ νῆας, ἐπὴν κεκάμω πολεμίζων [A 167–168].

5   ἔτι δὲ οὐδὲ προτείνοντος τοῦ Ἀγαμέμνονος τὰ δῶρα προσ|ήκατο [τε] τὴν ἀρχήν, ὅτε μήπω καιρὸν ᾤετο τῆς πρὸς αὐτὸν εἶναι διαλλαγῆς. οὕτως οὐχ ἡ τῶν χρημάτων ὑπόσχεσις ἡμερώτερον αὐτὸν ἐποίει περὶ τὸν ὑβριστήν, ἀλλὰ καὶ ὅτε προσήκειν ὑπέλαβεν καταλῦσαι τὴν μῆνιν, αὐτὸς μὲν
10   ὡς τῷ φίλῳ τιμωρήσων παρεσκευάζετο, τὰ δὲ δῶρα | ὑπ' ἐκείνου μήτε ἐπιστρεφομένου πρὸς αὐτὰ τοῦ Ἀχιλλέως μήτε προστίθεσθαί τι τοῖς αὐτοῦ νομίζοντος ἀγαθοῖς ἀπεπληροῦτο.

Δηλοῖ δὲ αὐτοῦ καὶ τὸ πλῆθος τῶν ἐν τῷ ἀγῶνι προτεθέντων ἄθλων τὴν περὶ ταῦτα ὀλιγωρίαν. καὶ γὰρ ἕκαστον τῶν ἀγωνιστῶν τοῖς προσήκουσιν
15   δώροις ἐφιλο|φρονήσατο, τὸν <δὲ> Νέστορα δι' ἡλικίαν ἀθλεῖν οὐ δυνάμενον τῇ χρυσῇ φιάλῃ τῶν ἄλλων διαφερόντως ἐδωρήσατο.

Πῶς οὖν φιλοχρήματος καθ' Ὅμηρον ὁ χρώμενος εἰς δέον τοῖς χρήμασιν, καὶ παρόντων ὀλιγώρων καὶ ἀπόντα μὴ περιεργαζόμενος καὶ
20   ἐλασσοῦσθαι περὶ αὐτὰ τῶν ἄλλων ἀνεχό|μενος καὶ ὀνειδίζων ἐν μέσοις τοῖς Ἕλλησιν ὡς νόσημα ψυχῆς τὸ πάθος τῷ πλεονάζοντι κατὰ τὴν τῶν χρημάτων ἄμετρον ὄρεξιν; πῶς δὲ ὁ Φοῖνιξ φιλοχρηματίας διδάσκαλος, ἔθος τι παλαιὸν Ἑλληνικὸν ἀποπληροῦν κελεύων; οὕτω γάρ, φησί, |

25   **καὶ τῶν πρόσθεν ἐπευθόμεθα κλέα ἀνδρῶν,**

the philosophical life, and who are entirely without possessions and so without excess property.

If you will, let us add this to what has been said about Achilles, that he himself reproaches Agamemnon with greed and denounces that passion as very shameful:

Greatest son of Atreus and greediest of men [*Il.* 1.122],

and that he himself shows his own lack of concern for the possession of goods when he says that, although he is always the one who is successful in war and enslaves cities and takes prisoners, but has little profit for much effort, still he makes no objection, but allows Agamemnon the distribution of all the goods, putting no stake in property or in its increase: ||

I go to my ships with a small reward but a welcome one, when I am tired with war [*Il.* 1.167–168].

Moreover, when Agamemnon first offered the gifts, he did not accept them, because he did not think it was yet time for reconciliation. Thus the promise of possessions did not make him gentler toward the man who insulted him, and even when he thought suitable to give up his anger [at Agamemnon], he was arming himself to avenge his friend; the promise was fulfilled and the gifts were delivered by Agamemnon without Achilles' paying any attention or thinking about increasing his property.

The great quantity of prizes offered by Achilles in the [funeral] games demonstrates how little he cares for such things. He gratified each of the contestants with appropriate gifts and made a special gift to Nestor, apart from the others, the golden *phiale*, though he was too old to compete.

How, then, in Homer's account, is this man greedy, when he uses wealth as necessary, thinks little of it when it is present, and does not trouble himself over it when it is absent. He is willing to have less than others and, in the midst of the Greeks, denounces greed as a sickness of the soul, addressing a man who goes to excess in his immoderate appetite for possessions? How is Phoenix a teacher of greed, when he tells Achilles to observe an ancient custom of the Greeks? "This is the way [they were]," he says,

"We have learned the glorious deeds of the men of the past—

δωρητοί τ' ἐπέλοντο παραρρητοί τ' ἐπέεσσιν [Ι 524, 526].

ἀλλὰ ταῦτα μὲν τοῖς ἡρωϊκοῖς πρέποντα χρόνοις καὶ τοῖς ἔθεσιν, οἷς ἐκεῖνοι πρὸς ἀλλήλους ἐχρῶντο, τῆς ἀκροτάτης | ἠξίωται παρ' Ὁμήρῳ μιμήσεως. τοῖς δὲ παρ' ἡμῖν τρεφο || μένοις νέοις πολλοῦ δεῖ τὰ τοιαῦτα προσήκειν, οἷς οὐδὲν ἔργον ὑπὸ τοῦ νομοθέτου προστέτακται πλὴν τῆς παιδείας καὶ τῆς εἰς ἀρετὴν ἀγωγῆς· χρημάτων δὲ ἐπιμέλεια καὶ τῶν ἀναγκαίων τοῖς τὸν θνητὸν βίον διαζῶσιν φροντὶς ἄλλοις | παραδέδοται τοῖς εἰς τὴν κάτω πόλιν τελοῦσιν.

Πῶς δεῖ ἀπολογεῖσθαι ὑπὲρ τῆς φαινομένης περὶ τὸ θεῖον ὀλιγωρίας ἐν τῇ ποιήσει τῶν ἡρώων.

Τούτων δὲ αὖ τὸν εἰρημένον τρόπον ἐχόντων ἑπόμενον ἂν εἴη καὶ τὰ ἄλλα ἐφεξῆς ἀνεγεῖραι τῶν ἀπορημάτων, ὅσα | τῷ Ἀχιλλεῖ τὴν περὶ τὸ θεῖον ὀλιγωρίαν ἐγκαλεῖ. πῶς γὰρ <οὐ> τοιοῦτος ὁ πρὸς μὲν τὸν Ἀπόλλω τοιαῦτα ἀποτολμῶν φθέγγεσθαι·

ἔβλαψάς μ' ἑκάεργε, θεῶν ὀλοώτατε πάντων [Χ 15], |

πρὸς δὲ τὸν ποταμὸν Ξάνθον διαμαχόμενος ὄντα θεόν, ἀντὶ δὲ τοῦ Σπερχειοῦ τῷ Πατρόκλῳ νεκρῷ ὄντι προσάγων τὰς τρίχας [Ψ 141–151];

Ὅτι μὲν οὖν εἴπερ τις ἄλλος τῶν ἡρώων καὶ Ἀχιλλεὺς περὶ τὰ θεῖα καθ' Ὅμηρόν ἐστιν ἀσφαλέστατος, δηλοῖ καὶ τὸν Ἀπόλλω θεραπεύειν αὐτὸς συμ | βουλεύων θυσίαν τε πέμπειν τῷ θεῷ παρασκευάζων τοὺς Ἕλληνας καὶ τὸν ἱερέα τοῦ θεοῦ παντοδαπῶς ἐκμειλίττεσθαι, καὶ τοῖς τῆς Ἀθηνᾶς

they accepted gifts and were moved by words" [*Il*. 9.524, 526].

These things, then, were appropriate to the heroic age and to the customs they observed toward one another and so were deemed worthy by Homer of the most exact imitation. They are far from being appropriate for the young people whose education we are ‖ concerned with to hear, those for whom the nomothete sets no task except education and being raised to virtue. Concern for possessions and consideration of the necessities of people living a mortal life have been passed on to others, who belong to the lower city.

(17) How must one defend the apparent lack of respect for the gods in the depiction of the heroes?

[a. The problem]

These things being as stated, we should go on to bring up next the series of problems that bring upon Achilles the charge of lack of respect for the divine. For how could this not be true of a man who dared to address such words as these to Apollo:

You have harmed me, far-shooter, most malicious of the gods [*Il*. 22.15],

and who fought with the river Xanthos although he was a god, and who offered his hair not to the Spercheios [to whom it had been promised] but to the dead Patroclus?[234]

[b. Achilles and Apollo]

That Achilles, according to Homer, gives unfailing attention to things relating to the gods, if any Homeric hero does, [Achilles] himself demonstrates in advising the Greeks to look after Apollo and preparing them to send sacrifices to the god and appease his priest in every possible way.[235] He shows it, moreover, in obeying readily when Athena gives him an

---

234. *Il*. 23.141–151.
235. *Il*. 1.54 and *passim*.

ἐπιφοιτησάσης αὐτῷ προστάγμασιν ἑτοίμως πειθόμενος, καὶ ἐπᾴδων τῷ θυμῷ, καὶ τὸ περὶ τοὺς θεοὺς σέβας καὶ μέχρι τῆς ἀλογίας διατείνων, καὶ πάν|των μάλιστα πεπεισμένος, ὅτι τὸ τοῖς θεοῖς ὑπηρετεῖν καὶ τῆς τῶν κρειττόνων βουλήσεως ἐξάπτειν ἑαυτὸν ἀνυσιμώτατόν ἐστι πρὸς τὴν ἐκείνων εὐηκοΐαν, σπένδων τε τῷ Διὶ ∥ καὶ εὐχόμενος μετὰ τῆς πρεπούσης τοῖς θεοῖς ἐπιστήμης. καὶ γὰρ τὸ προκαθῆραι τὴν φιάλην καὶ τὸ μόνῳ τῷ Διὶ ταύτην ἐξαίρετον ἀνεῖναι καὶ τὸ ἐν μέσῳ ἕρκει στάντα τὸν ἐκ μέσου τοῦ κόσμου πανταχοῦ διήκοντα καλεῖν τῆς περὶ | τὸ θεῖόν ἐστιν εὐλαβείας καὶ τῆς γνώσεως τῶν οἰκείων τοῖς τιμωμένοις συνθημάτων τεκμήριον ἐναργές.

Εἰ δὲ πρὸς τὸν Ἀπόλλω θρασύτερα τοῦ δέοντος ἀπέρριψεν, ἐννοεῖν χρὴ τὰς Ἀπολλωνιακὰς τάξεις ἄνωθεν ἄχρι τῶν τελευταίων διηκούσας, καὶ τὰς μὲν θείας οὔσας, τὰς δὲ ἀγγελικάς, τὰς δὲ δαι|μονίας, καὶ ταύτας πολυειδῶς μεριζομένας· καὶ ὡς οὐ πρὸς τὸν θεὸν ἀποτείνεται διὰ τῶν τοιούτων ῥημάτων, ἀλλὰ πρὸς τὸν δαιμόνιον, καὶ τοῦτον οὐ τὸν πρώτιστον καὶ τοῖς ὁλικὴν ἔχουσιν ἐπικράτειαν συντεταγμένον, ἀλλὰ τὸν τῶν καθ' ἕκαστα προσεχῶς ἐπιστατοῦντα καὶ (τί γὰρ οὐ δεῖ λέ|γειν σαφῶς;) τὸν τοῦ Ἕκτορος αὐτοῦ φρουρόν.

λέγει γέ τοι διαρρήδην ὁ ποιητής·

αὐτῷ γὰρ ἑκάεργος Ἀγήνορι πάντα ἐοικὼς
ἔστη πρόσθ' Ἀχιλῆος [Φ 600–601].

τοῦτον τοίνυν τὸν Ἀπόλλω, καθ' ὅσον αὐτῷ πρὸς τὴν | πρᾶξιν ἐμποδὼν γίνεται φυλάττων ἀπαθῆ τὸν πολέμιον, ὀλοώτατον ἀποκαλεῖ, καὶ οὐ περὶ αὐτὸν πλημμελεῖ τὸν θεόν, ἀλλὰ τὸν ἐν τοῖς μερικωτάτοις τεταγμένον τῆς Ἀπολλωνιακῆς σειρᾶς. καὶ δεῖ μὴ πάντας τοὺς λόγους μηδὲ τὰς ἐνεργείας εἰς ἐκεῖνον ἀναπέμπειν τὸν πρώτιστον, | ἀλλὰ καὶ τὰς δευτέρας αὐτοῦ καὶ τρίτας ἀναλογίζεσθαι προόδους, οἷον τίς μὲν ὁ τῷ Διὶ σύνθακος καὶ τοῖς Ὀλυμπίοις θεοῖς, τίς δὲ ὁ τὴν ἡλιακὴν σφαῖραν ἐπιστρεφόμενος, τίς δὲ ὁ

order,²³⁶ in singing to calm his anger,²³⁷ in extending his reverence for the gods even to the point of irrationality and in believing more than anyone that to serve the gods and attach oneself to the will of the greater ones is the most effective way to ensure that they will listen favorably.²³⁸ He pours libations to Zeus ‖ and makes prayers with a knowledge [of ritual] appropriate to the gods [*Il.* 16.225-232]. Specifically, his cleaning of the *phiale* and offering it specially to Zeus alone and his standing in the center of the courtyard to invoke the god who reaches everywhere from the center of the cosmos,²³⁹ all these things constitute a clear indication of piety toward the divine and of an understanding of the symbols appropriate to the beings honored.

If Achilles said excessively bold things to Apollo, one must consider that the Apollonian classes extend down from above to the very last beings and that some of them are divine, some angelic, and some daemonic, and the latter are divided into many forms; likewise, that Achilles is not attacking the god with words of this sort, but rather the daemon, and this daemon is neither the first nor ranked with those having universal power, but the one who attentively looks after particulars—why not say it clearly?—the one who looks after Hector himself.

Indeed the poet says clearly that

> he who works from afar stood before Achilles
> in the form of Agenor²⁴⁰ [*Il.* 21.600-601].

It is this Apollo, then, inasmuch as he is an obstacle to Achilles' action and guards his enemy free from harm, that he calls "malicious," and he does not speak offensively about the god himself, but rather about the being placed in the most fragmented level of the Apollonian chain. One must not attribute to that first Apollo all Apollo's words and acts, but consider also the secondary and tertiary processions from him: for example, who is the Apollo who sits beside Zeus and the Olympians? Who is the one who

---

236. *Il.* 1.216.
237. *Il.* 9.186-189. F. identifies this as the passage in question, but it is difficult to see why this particular item is in this list at all.
238. *Il.* 1.216-218.
239. *Il.* 16.225-235.
240. The narrative lends a certain support to this claim about Agenor. Before he becomes the disguise of Apollo himself (in the passage cited), he is said to be sent from Troy into the battle by Apollo to prevent the Greeks from taking Troy (*Il.* 21.244).

ἀέριος Ἀπόλλων, τίς δὲ ὁ χθόνιος, τίς δὲ ὁ τῆς Τροίας προστάτης, τίς δὲ ὁ τοῦ Ἕκτορος ἰδίως προνοῶν, | περὶ οὗ καὶ ὁ ποιητὴς λέγει· ||

ᾤχετο δ᾿ εἰς Ἀΐδαο, λίπεν δέ ἑ Φοῖβος Ἀπόλλων [Χ 213].

Εἰς γὰρ ταύτας ἁπάσας βλέποντες τὰς τάξεις δυνησόμεθα καὶ τοὺς τοῦ Ἀχιλλέως λόγους πρός τινα τοιαύτην μερικὴν | δύναμιν ἀναφέρειν, σώζειν μὲν τὸ προνοούμενον ἐθέλουσαν, ἐμποδίζουσαν δὲ τῷ Ἀχιλλεῖ περὶ τὰς κατορθώσεις. καὶ γὰρ τὸ "ἔβλαψας" οἰκείως ἂν ἔχοι πρὸς τὸν τοιοῦτον δαίμονα, τοῦ τέλους τῶν παρόντων πόνων αὐτὸν ἀφαιρούμενον. καὶ τὸ "ὀλοώτατε" δηλοῖ σαφῶς τὸν διαφερόντως αὐτῷ τῶν | ἄλλων θεῶν τε καὶ δαιμόνων ἐναντιούμενον· ὁ γὰρ τὸν μάλιστα λυπήσαντα φυλάττων ἀπαθῆ παντὸς μᾶλλον ἐμποδὼν γίνεται τῷ λυπηθέντι πρὸς τὴν τῆς τιμωρίας ἀπαίτησιν.

Εἰ δὲ μηδὲ οὗτος ὁ τρόπος τῶν λόγων ἀζήμιος τῷ Ἀχιλλεῖ γέγονεν, ἀλλὰ μικρὸν ὕστερον καὶ αὐτὸς ὑπὸ δή | τινος Ἀπολλωνιακῆς δυνάμεως ἀναιρεῖσθαι λέγεται·

**ὅτε κέν σε Πάρις καὶ Φοῖβος Ἀπόλλων
ἐσθλὸν ἐόντ᾿ ὀλέσωσιν** [Χ 359-360],

πῶς οὐχὶ καὶ διὰ τούτων ἡμᾶς ἡ ποίησις περὶ τὸ θεῖον σωφρονεστέρους ποιεῖ καὶ τὸ δαιμόνιον; καίτοι με οὐ λέ|ληθεν, ὅτι τοῖς περὶ τὰς τελετὰς δεινοῖς πολλὰ τοιαῦτα περὶ τοὺς δαίμονας ἀποτετόλμηται· ἀλλ᾿ ἴσως ἐκείνοις μὲν ὑπὸ θειοτέρων δυνάμεων φρουρουμένοις οὐδεμίαν τὰ τοιαῦτα ζημίαν ἐπάγειν ἐστὶν ἱκανά, τοῖς δὲ ἄλλοις ἀνθρώποις ἕπεται δίκη σωφρονίζουσα τὴν ἐν τοῖς λόγοις πλημμέλειαν. |

Καὶ μὴν καὶ περὶ τῆς πρὸς τὸν Ξάνθον αὐτοῦ λεγομένης μάχης οὐ χαλεπὸν ἀπαντᾶν. οὐ γὰρ πρὸς αὐτὸν τὸν θεὸν ἀπειθὴς ἦν, ἀλλ᾿ ἢ πρὸς τὸ φαινόμενον ὕδωρ ἐμποδίζον αὐτῷ τὴν κατὰ τῶν πολεμίων ὁρμὴν ἢ πρός τινα τῶν ἐγχωρίων δυνάμεων μετὰ θεῶν συμμάχων ἠγωνίζετο· | καὶ γὰρ Ἀθηνᾶς καὶ Ποσειδῶνος αὐτῷ παρόντων καὶ || συμπνεόντων ἀνθίστατο.

rotates the sphere of the sun? Who is the aerial Apollo? Who is the chthonian? Who is the protector of Troy? Who is the one who exercises personal providence over Hector, of whom even the poet says, ||

he went to Hades and Phoebus Apollo left him? [*Il.* 22.213]

Considering all of these ranks, we shall be able to say that Achilles' words were addressed to some such partial power, desirous of saving the object of his providence and thus posing an obstacle to the success of Achilles. Indeed the expression "you have harmed [me]" would be appropriate to such a daemon, for he is depriving him of the goal of his present toil. The expression "most malicious" designates clearly the one specifically opposed to Achilles, among all the other gods and daemons. He who protects from harm the one who has done the greatest harm becomes the greatest obstacle to the one who has been harmed, in his quest for vengeance.

Moreover, if not even this sort of language went unpunished in Achilles' case, and we are told just a little later that he as well will be killed by an Apollonian power,

(when Paris and Phoebus Apollo will kill you,
noble as you are) [*Il.* 22.359–360],

how then can one deny that through these things the poem in fact makes us more reasonable concerning the divine and the daemonic? And yet I realize that many such acts of presumption with regard to the daemons are committed by the experts in the mysteries. Perhaps it is because they are guarded by more divine powers that things of this sort do not bring punishment upon them, while for other men retribution imposes restraint on their offensive language.

[c. Achilles and the River Xanthos]

It is not difficult to answer the objection concerning the battle he is said to have fought against the Xanthos. He did not stand up to the god himself, but rather what he attacked was either the physical water, which was an obstacle to his attack on the enemy, or one of the local powers, and he had gods for allies. Athena and Poseidon were || with him and were on his side when he stood up against the river.

Καί μοι δοκεῖ κατὰ πάσας τὰς διαφορὰς ἡ ποίησις τοὺς ἀγῶνας διαπλέκουσα, καὶ τότε μὲν ἀνθρώπων πρὸς ἀλλήλους μάχας ἱστοροῦσα, τότε δὲ τῶν | κρειττόνων γενῶν, ὥσπερ ἐν τῇ καλουμένῃ θεομαχίᾳ, καὶ ταύτην παραδοῦναι τὴν ἀντίστασιν τῶν ἡρώων πρός τινας δαιμονίας φύσεις, ἐνδεικνυμένη τοῖς τῶν τοιούτων ἐπαΐειν δυναμένοις, ὅτι καὶ τὰ πρώτιστα τῶν τελευταίων ἐξισοῦταί πως τοῖς ἐσχάτοις τῶν πρώτων, καὶ διαφερόντως ὅταν ὑπ' αὐτῶν κινῆται καὶ φρουρῆται τῶν θεῶν. καὶ οὐκ | Ἀχιλλεὺς πρὸς τὸν Ξάνθον μόνος, ἀλλὰ καὶ Ἡρακλῆς οὕτω πρὸς τὸν Ἀχελῷον διαγωνίσασθαι λέγεται, πρὸς ὃν καὶ ὁ Ἀχιλλεὺς τὴν ἑαυτοῦ ζωὴν ἐπανάγων οὐδὲ τοὺς τοιούτους ἀγῶνας ἀπεσείετο.

Τὸ δὲ δὴ τρίτον τῶν προκειμένων ζητημάτων διαλύ|σομεν λέγοντες, ὅτι πρώτιστον μὲν ἦν τῷ Ἀχιλλεῖ καὶ προηγούμενον ἀγαθὸν ἐπανελθόντι τῷ Σπερχειῷ τὰς τρίχας ἀποκείρασθαι κατὰ τὴν ὑπόσχεσιν· ἀπογνόντι δὲ ἄρα τῆς ἐπανόδου καὶ τοῦτο πεισθέντι προειπούσης τῆς μητρός·

αὐτίκα γάρ τοι ἔπειτα μεθ' Ἕκτορα πότμος ἑτοῖ|μος [Σ 96],

πῶς οὐχὶ τὸ δεύτερον ἦν ἀναγκαῖον εἰς τιμὴν τοῦ φίλου τὰς κόμας ἀφελεῖν; ἐπεὶ καὶ ὁ παρ' ἡμῖν Σωκράτης δέχεται τοὺς στεφάνους, οὓς ὁ Ἀλκιβιάδης ἔφερεν τῷ θεῷ, καὶ ἀναδεῖται καὶ οὐδὲν οἴεται πλημμελὲς οὔτε αὐτὸς ποιεῖν οὔτε | ποιοῦντα τὸν νεανίσκον περιορᾶν· καὶ ταῦτα ἐν Ἀλκιβιάδῃ δευτέρῳ [151a] παρειλήφαμεν. ἐῶ λέγειν, ὡς οὐδὲ ἱεραί πω τοῦ ποταμοῦ γεγόνεσαν αἱ τρίχες· ὁ γὰρ μετὰ τὴν ἐπάνοδον ἱερὰς αὐτὰς ἀνήσειν ἐπαγγειλάμενος ἀφαιρεθεὶς τῆς ἐπανόδου συναφήρηται καὶ τῆς τῶν τριχῶν ἀφιερώσεως. ||

Πῶς ἀπολογητέον ὑπὲρ τῆς τῶν ἡρώων ἐν τῇ ποιήσει περὶ τὸν βίον φαινομένης ὀλιγωρίας ἢ ὅλως ἀτόπου παρὰ τοῖς ποιηταῖς ἐν τοῖς μύθοις ἱστορίας.

Furthermore, it seems to me that the poem, elaborating the battles with all the variety possible, and telling at one point of men battling each other and at another of the higher powers doing the same (as in the so-called theomachy), passes down as well the tradition of the confrontation of the heroes with certain daemonic powers, demonstrating to those able to understand such things that the very first from the very last classes are somehow the equals of the very last from the first classes, especially when they are motivated and protected by the gods themselves. Not only is Achilles said to have fought against the Xanthos, but likewise Heracles is said to have fought against the Acheloos, and Achilles, modeling his own life on that of Heracles, did not shrink from such struggles as his.[241]

[d. Achilles and the River Spercheios]

We shall resolve the third of the questions before us by saying that it would have been a good thing for Achilles, first of all, to go back to the Spercheios and cut his hair, as he had promised. Having renounced his homecoming, however, and convinced by what his mother had previously said—

Fate is ready for you, immediately after Hector [*Il.* 19.96]—

how was it not necessary, as second best, to cut his hair in honor of his friend? Our Socrates accepts the wreaths that Alcibiades was taking to the god, puts them on his head, and does not think that he has committed any wrong, nor that he is letting the young man commit one. We get this from the *Second Alcibiades* [151a7–c2]. I will not even mention that the hair of Achilles had not become the consecrated property of the river—for he who had promised to consecrate it after his return, when deprived of that return, was likewise deprived of the possibility of dedicating his hair. ||

(18) How one can respond concerning the heroes' apparent lack of respect for human life in the poems, or generally, concerning the extraordinary narratives that the poets include in their myths.

---

241. F., following Kroll, sees here an allusion to *Il.* 18.117–118.

Ἀλλὰ τούτων μὲν ἅδην· ὑπόλοιπον δέ ἐστί μοι περὶ τῶν | εἰς τὸν Ἕκτορα τῷ Ἀχιλλεῖ πεπραγμένων καὶ τῶν περὶ τὸ σῆμα ἕλξεων τοῦ Πατρόκλου, καὶ ὧν εἰς τοὺς ζωγρηθέντας ἔδρασεν ἐμβαλὼν εἰς τὴν πυράν, τὸν εἰκότα λόγον ἀποδοῦναι. ταῦτα γὰρ οὐκ ἀληθῆ περὶ ἀνδρὸς λέγεσθαί φησιν ὁ Σωκράτης [391c], ὃς ἦν θεᾶς παῖς καὶ Πηλέως τοῦ | σωφρονεστάτου, καὶ ἀπὸ Διὸς φύντος καὶ ὑπὸ τῷ σοφωτάτῳ Χείρωνι τεθραμμένου.

Εἴρηται μὲν οὖν καὶ ὑπὸ τῶν παλαιῶν, ὡς Θετταλικόν τι τοιοῦτον ἔθος ἦν (καὶ ὁ Κυρηναῖος μαρτυρεῖ ποιητής·

**πάλαι δ' ἔτι Θεσσαλὸς ἀνὴρ |
ῥυστάζει φθιμένων ἀμφὶ τάφον φονέας)**

[Callimachus frag. 588, Pfeiffer]

καὶ ὡς ταῦτα συμπληροῦντα τὴν περὶ τὸν Πάτροκλον ὁσίαν παρείληπται. εἰ δὲ καὶ ὁ Ἕκτωρ εἷλκε τὸν Πάτροκλον ὄντα νεκρόν, ἵνα

**ἀπ' ὤμοιϊν κεφαλὴν τάμοι ὀξέϊ χαλκῷ, |
τὸν δὲ νέκυν Τρῴῃσιν ἐρυσάμενος κυσὶ δοίη** [Ρ 126–127],

καὶ ταῦτα οὐκ ἠγνόησεν, ἀλλ' εἰπούσης ἔγνω τῆς Ἴριδος·

**μάλιστα δὲ φαίδιμος Ἕκτωρ
ἑλκέμεναι μέμονεν, κεφαλὴν δέ ἑ θυμὸς ἀνώγει |
πῆξαι ἀνὰ σκολόπεσσι ταμόνθ' ἁπαλῆς ἀπὸ δειρῆς.
ἀλλ' ἄνα μηδ' ἔτι κεῖσο· σέβας δέ σε θυμὸν ἱκέσθω, ||
Πάτροκλον Τρῴῃσι κυσὶν μέλπηθρα γενέσθαι** [Σ 175–179],

πῶς οὐ τὴν πρέπουσαν αὐτῷ δίκην ἀποδίδωσιν ἕλκων περὶ τὸν τοῦ Πατρόκλου τάφον καὶ ταύτῃ τὸν φίλον τιμῶν, καὶ | τῆς μὲν ἐννοίας αὐτὸν διὰ τῆς ἕλξεως τὴν τιμωρίαν εἰσπραττόμενος, μὴ ποιήσαντα δὲ ὅσα προύθετο τοῖς οἰκείοις ἀποδιδοὺς καὶ ταφῆς ἀξιωθῆναι συγχωρῶν. ὁ γὰρ

[a. The problem]

Enough of these things. What remains is for me to give an appropriate account of Achilles' treatment of Hector, his dragging [his body] around the tomb of Patroclus, and what he did to the captives, throwing them on the funeral pyre. Socrates claims that these things are not said truthfully of a man who was the son of a goddess and of the very reasonable Peleus and who traced his ancestry to Zeus and was raised by the wise Chiron.[242]

[b. Reply: Achilles and Hector]

It was said by the ancients themselves that the Thessalians had a custom of this sort (and the poet of Cyrene is witness to this:

> Long has a Thessalian hero
> dragged around the tombs of the dead their murderers
> [Callimachus frag. 588, Pfeiffer]),

and that Achilles, in undertaking the ritual for Patroclus, adopted this usage. If Hector as well dragged Patroclus' corpse, in order to

> chop head from shoulders with the sharp bronze
> and haul the corpse off to give to the dogs of Troy [*Il.* 17.126–127],

and Achilles was not ignorant of this (for he had learned it when Iris said,

> brilliant Hector is eager to drag
> the body off, and his heart drives him to stick the head on a stake,
> after he cuts it from the gentle neck.
> Up! Don't lie there. May shame come on your heart, ||
> that Patroclus should become a plaything for the dogs of Troy [*Il.* 18.175–179]),

how, then, does Achilles not assess appropriate punishment by dragging him around Patroclus's tomb and honoring his friend in this way, extracting vengeance for his intentions by dragging him, but then again, because

---

242. *Rep.* 3.391b–c.

τοιαῦτα μέτρα ταῖς πράξεσιν ἐπάγων κατὰ τὴν ὅλην δίκην ἐνεργεῖ καὶ τὴν πρόνοιαν τῶν θεῶν. διὸ καὶ ὁ ποιητὴς ὑπηρε|τοῦντα ταῖς τῶν κρειττόνων βουλήσεσιν αὐτὸν ἡμερώτερα περὶ τὸν Ἕκτορα βουλεύεσθαί φησιν, ὡς καὶ ταῖς ἑαυτοῦ χερσὶν θεραπεῦσαι τὸ λείψανον·

**τὸν δ' ἐπεὶ οὖν δμωαὶ λοῦσαν καὶ ἔχρισαν ἐλαίῳ,
ἀμφὶ δέ μιν φᾶρος καλὸν βάλον ἠδὲ χιτῶνα,** |
αὐτὸς τόν γ' Ἀχιλεὺς λεχέων ἐπέθηκεν ἀείρας [Ω 587–589].

πάντα ἄρα κατὰ τὸ προσῆκον αὐτῷ μέτρον ἀποδέδοται τὰ περὶ τοὺς ἀπελθόντας ἐνεργήματα· τόν τε γὰρ φίλον διαφερόντως ἐτίμησεν οὐ μόνον καταγωνισάμενος τὸν πολέμιον, | ἀλλὰ καὶ τῆς ἐννοίας αὐτὸν τῆς ἀνοσίου δίκην εἰσπραξάμενος· καὶ αὖ πάλιν τῷ πολεμίῳ τῆς ὕβρεως ἀμοιβὴν τήν τε περὶ τὸν Πρίαμον φιλανθρωπίαν καὶ τὴν περὶ αὐτὸν θεραπείαν ἐσχάτην κατεβάλλετο.

Περί γε μὴν τῶν ἐπὶ τῇ πυρᾷ σφαγέντων τοσοῦτον | ῥητέον, ὅτι κατὰ μὲν τὸ φαινόμενον ἥ τε περὶ τὸν Πάτροκλον αὐτῷ τιμὴ καὶ διὰ τούτων τελέως συμπεπλήρωται, καὶ οὐδὲν περὶ ἐκείνους ὠμότερον ἔπραξέν τι, ἢ εἰ πολεμίους ὄντας αὐτοὺς ὥσπερ τῶν ἄλλων τοὺς προστυχόντας ἀπέκτεινεν. τί γὰρ ἂν διαφέροι πρὸς τῇ πυρᾷ τοῦτο πα||θεῖν ἢ πρὸς τῷ ποταμῷ; πῶς δὲ οὐκ ἄμεινον ἔπραξαν ὑπὸ τοῦ πυρὸς ἄρδην αὐτοῖς τῶν σωμάτων ἀφανισθέντων, ἢ ὑπὸ τῶν θηρίων σπαραττόμενοι καὶ ταὐτὰ τῷ Λυκάονι πάσχοντες, πρὸς ὃν φησιν ὁ Ἀχιλλεύς· |

**ἐνταυθοῖ νῦν κεῖσο μετ' ἰχθύσιν, οἵ σ' ὠτειλῆς
αἷμ' ἀπολιχμήσονται ἀκηδέες** [Φ 122–123].

he did not carry out what he proposed, giving him back to his people and allowing him to be buried? He who moderates his actions in such a way acts entirely in accord with justice and the providence of the gods. For this reason, the poet says that, in obedience to the wills of the greater ones, his intentions with regard to Hector are gentler than they might have been, so that he even cares for the corpse with his own hands:

> When the maids had washed him and anointed him with oil
> and wrapped a lovely cloak and chiton around him,
> Achilles himself picked him up and laid him on the bier [*Il.* 24.587–589].

Thus all the things done for the departed were done by Achilles in the measure appropriate to him: he honored his friend greatly by not only fighting his enemy but also inflicting justice upon that enemy for his unholy intention. And again, he compensated the enemy for the outrage both by his kindness to Priam and by giving the last rites to Hector's corpse.

[c. Reply: The sacrifice of the captives]

The following is to be said with regard to those whose throats were cut on the pyre: taken literally,[243] through these things the honors done by Achilles to Patroclus are finally completed, and [Achilles] did nothing more cruel to them than if[244] he had killed them as enemies, just like any of the others he encountered. What difference would it make whether someone suffered this fate on the pyre ‖ or by the river? How, in fact, were they not actually better off, since their bodies were entirely destroyed by fire and not torn apart by beasts, suffering the fate of Lycaon, to whom Achilles says,

> Now lie there with the fish that will
> feel nothing as they lick the blood from your wound [*Il.* 21.122–123]?

---

243. κατὰ μὲν τὸ φαινόμενον ("on the surface" or "taken literally") here is taken up below (215 [K152,7]), where Proclus introduces Syrianus's "more secret" interpretation.

244. Restoring the awkward (but legible) construction corrected by Kroll (and followed by F.).

Εἰ δὲ δεῖ καὶ τῶν ἀπορρητότερον ὑπὸ τοῦ καθηγεμόνος ἡμῶν τεθεωρημένων κἀν τούτοις ποιήσασθαι μνήμην, ῥητέον ὅτι πᾶσα ἡ περὶ τὴν πυρὰν ἐκείνην τοῦ Ἀχιλλέως | πραγματεία μιμεῖται τὸν παρὰ τοῖς θεουργοῖς τῆς ψυχῆς ἀπαθανατισμὸν εἰς τὴν χωριστὴν ζωὴν ἀνάγουσα τὴν τοῦ Πατρόκλου ψυχήν. διὸ καὶ στὰς πρὸ τῆς πυρᾶς ἐπικαλεῖσθαι λέγεται τοὺς ἀνέμους, Βορρᾶν καὶ Ζέφυρον [Ψ 195], ἵνα καὶ τὸ φαινόμενον ὄχημα διὰ τῆς ἐμφανοῦς αὐ|τῶν κινήσεως τύχῃ τῆς πρεπούσης θεραπείας, καὶ τὸ τούτου θειότερον ἀφανῶς καθαρθῇ καὶ εἰς τὴν οἰκείαν ἀποκαταστῇ λῆξιν, ὑπὸ τῶν ἀερίων καὶ τῶν σεληναίων καὶ τῶν ἡλιακῶν αὐγῶν ἀνελκόμενον, ὥς πού φησίν τις τῶν θεῶν, καὶ πάννυχος ἐπισπένδειν παραδέδοται τῇ πυρᾷ. |

**χρυσέου ἐκ κρητῆρος, ἑλὼν δέπας ἀμφικύπελλον,
ψυχὴν κικλήσκων Πατροκλῆος δειλοῖο** [Ψ 219, 221].

μονονουχὶ κηρύττοντος ἡμῖν τοῦ ποιητοῦ, καὶ ὅτι περὶ τὴν τοῦ φίλου ψυχὴν ἡ πραγματεία τοῦ Ἀχιλλέως ἦν, ἀλλ᾽ οὐ | περὶ τὸ φαινόμενον μόνον, καὶ ὅτι πάντα συμβολικῶς αὐτῷ παρείληπται, καὶ ὁ χρυσοῦς κρατὴρ τῆς πηγῆς τῶν ψυχῶν, καὶ ἡ σπονδὴ τῆς ἐκεῖθεν ἀπορροίας κρείττονα ζωὴν ἐποχετευούσης τῇ μερικῇ ψυχῇ, καὶ ἡ πυρὰ τῆς ἀχράντου κα||θαρότητος τῆς εἰς τὸ ἀφανὲς περιάγειν ἀπὸ τῶν σωμάτων δυναμένης·

καὶ ὅλως πολλὰ τῆς ὑπονοίας ταύτης λάβοι τις ἂν τεκμήρια τοῖς τοῦ καθηγεμόνος ἡμῶν ἐντυχών. τοιαύτης δὲ τῆς περὶ τὸν Πάτροκλον οὔσης θεραπείας οὐκ ἂν ἀπὸ | τρόπου τις λέγοι καὶ τοὺς δώδεκα τούτους τοὺς πρὸς τῇ πυρᾷ σφαγέντας ὥσπερ ὀπαδοὺς συντετάχθαι τῇ τοῦ Πατρόκλου ψυχῇ, τὸ ἡγεμονικὸν αὐτῆς τοῦ Ἀχιλλέως εἰδότος καὶ θεραπεύσαντος. διὸ καὶ τὸν ἀριθμὸν τοῦτον ὡς οἰκειότατον τοῖς ἕπεσθαι μέλλουσιν καὶ ταῖς

Furthermore, if we are to mention here the more secret doctrines of my guide [Syrianus], we should say that the whole treatment of Achilles' pyre imitates the procedures of the theurgists for immortalizing the soul and leads the soul of Patroclus up to the life separate from the body. This is why Achilles, standing before the pyre, is said to call on the winds Boreas and Zephyr [*Il.* 23.195], so that the manifest vehicle [of the soul]²⁴⁵ may receive appropriate treatment through their visible movement and the more divine vehicle may be invisibly purified and reestablished in its own domain, drawn up by the aerial, lunar, and solar rays, as one of the gods says somewhere.²⁴⁶ He is also said to pour libations on the pyre all night,

> from a golden krater, dipping with a two-handled cup,
> calling on the soul of wretched Patroclus [*Il.* 23.219, 221].

Here the poet as good as proclaims to us both that Achilles' actions were concerned with the soul of his friend, not with his physical part, his body,²⁴⁷ and that everything he does is done symbolically, the golden krater symbolizing the source of souls, the libation, the pouring forth from above that channels a greater life to the partial soul, and the pyre, || the immaculate purity that is able to lead souls from their bodies into the invisible.

In general, one would find many proofs of this hidden meaning in perusing the works of my guide. Moreover, if this is the sort of care taken over Patroclus, one might say appropriately that the twelve whose throats are cut at the pyre are placed as attendants to the soul of Patroclus, for Achilles recognized, and was paying service to, that soul's quality of leadership.²⁴⁸ Thus he also chose the number [twelve], both because it was the

---

245. See Sheppard 1980, 76–77, on the φαινόμενον ὄχημα and the θειότερον ὄχημα as two separate astral bodies (and not, as one might have expected, and as F. asserts, simply the physical body and a single astral body). See n. 247 below.

246. Cf. *Or. chald.* frag. 61 des Places. Note that the formula ὥς πού φησίν τις τῶν θεῶν generally marks a citation of the *Chaldaean Oracles*, but the present passage has not been so treated by the editors of the oracles.

247. Translation from Sheppard 1980.

248. F. (173 n. 1) took this to mean that Achilles was celebrating Patroclus as a representative of the rational part of the soul, τὸ ἡγεμονικόν ("the leading part," a commonplace in the Stoa, with Platonic precedents), and so gave him appropriate treatment. In context, however, it seems that what is at stake should be a *quality* specific to Patroclus's soul.

παντελέσι προό|δοις ἀνειμένον τῶν θεῶν ἐπελέξατο.

Πολλοῦ ἄρα δεῖ κατά τινα τῆς ψυχῆς ὠμότητα δεινὴν καὶ ἀγριότητα ταῦτα ἐκεῖνος, ἀλλ' οὐ κατά τινας ἱερατικοὺς θεσμοὺς περὶ τὰς τῶν ἐν πολέμῳ τελευτησάντων ψυχὰς ἀφωρισμένους ἅπασαν τὴν πραγματείαν ταύτην πραγματεύσασθαι. μήτ' οὖν ὑπερη|φανίαν αὐτῷ θεῶν τε καὶ ἀνθρώπων ἐγκαλῶμεν μήτε ἀπιστῶμεν, εἰ θεᾶς ὢν παῖς καὶ Πηλέως καὶ Χείρωνος μαθητὴς τοιαῦτ' ἔπραξεν. τὰ μὲν γὰρ ὡς τῆς ὅλης δίκης στοχαζόμενος, τὰ δὲ πολέμου νόμῳ, τὰ δὲ ἱεραῖς μεθόδοις χρώμενος ἔπραξεν. ἐν ἅπασιν δ' ὁ ποιητὴς τὰ μέτρα τῆς | μιμήσεως τελέως διεσώσατο.

Τὰ μὲν δὴ πρὸς Ὅμηρον βλέποντα τῶν Σωκρατικῶν ἐγκλημάτων τοιαύτης <ἂν> ἀπαντήσεως τυγχάνοι. εἰ δὲ Θησέα τις καὶ Πειρίθουν εἰσάγοι τῶν ποιητῶν ἐπὶ τὴν τῆς Ἑλένης ἁρπαγὴν ὡρμηκότας ἢ εἰς Ἅιδου κατεληλυθότας, | τάχα ἂν καὶ ταῦτα μυθικώτερον λεγόμενα τῆς πρεπούσης ἀξιώσαιμεν θεωρίας, λέγοντες τοῦ ἀφανοῦς κάλλους καὶ <οὐ> τοῦ ἐμφανοῦς ἐραστὰς γενομένους τοὺς ἥρωας τούτους μεμυθολογῆσθαι τήν τε Ἑλένην ἡρπακέναι καὶ εἰς Ἅιδου πεπορεῦσθαι, κἀκεῖθεν αὖ τὸν μὲν δι' ὑψηλόνοιαν ὑφ' || Ἡρακλέους ἀνῆχθαι, τὸν δὲ αὐτοῦ που καταμεῖναι πρὸς τὸ ἄναντες ἑαυτὸν ἐπιδοῦναι τῆς θεωρίας ἀδυνατήσαντα.

Εἰ δὲ καὶ ἄλλως πως ἔχει τὰ τοιαῦτα, τῆς Ὁμηρικῆς οὐχ ἅπτεται ποιήσεως, τοῖς τε θεοῖς πανταχοῦ καὶ τοῖς κρείττοσιν ἡμῶν | γένεσιν καὶ ταῖς ἡρωϊκαῖς ζωαῖς τὸ πρέπον ἀποδούσης κατὰ τὴν μίμησιν, καὶ τὰ μὲν ἀπορρητότερον ἐνδειξαμένης, τὰ δὲ καὶ αὐτόθεν σὺν νῷ καὶ ἐπιστήμῃ περὶ τούτων ἡμᾶς διδαξάσης, καὶ οὐδὲν ἀπολειπούσης γένος τῶν ὄντων ἀδιερεύνητον, ἀλλ' ἕκαστα κατὰ τὴν ἑαυτῶν τάξιν ἐνεργοῦντα | πρός τε ἑαυτὰ καὶ τὰ ἄλλα παραδιδούσης.

most appropriate for those who were to attend and because it is consecrated to the perfect processions of the gods.[249]

Therefore, he did not by any means perform these actions out of some terrible cruelty or savagery of the soul, rather than according to certain fixed hieratic rules concerning the souls of those who have died in battle. Let us not accuse him of contempt for gods and men, nor let us be unwilling to believe that he did such things, even though he was the son of a goddess and of Peleus and the student of Chiron. Some of them he did aiming at universal justice, some according to the customs of war, and some using hieratic procedures. The poet has perfectly respected the rules of imitation in all of this.

[d. Other myths]

Socrates' accusations regarding Homer might meet with an answer of this sort. Moreover, if one of the poets should bring in Theseus and Perithous going off to seize Helen or going down to Hades, perhaps we might find these stories with their extremely mythic mode of expression to be worthy of examination as well, saying that it was as lovers of invisible beauty and not the visible that these heroes are said in the myths to carry off Helen and go to Hades and that [Theseus] was brought back by Heracles ‖ because of his highmindedness and the other somehow remained there through his inability to devote himself to the uphill task of contemplation.

If the situation is somewhat different with these last examples, this does not impinge on the Homeric poetry, which everywhere gives their due to the gods, to the ranks of those greater than ourselves, and to the lives of the heroes in its imitation [μίμησις] of them, indicating some things more secretly and teaching us others straightforwardly, with intelligence and authoritative knowledge, and leaving no class of beings unexplored, but depicting each acting in a manner appropriate to its own class, both toward members of that class and toward others.

---

249. *Phdr.* 246e–247a.

<Βιβλίον Β>

Ὅτι πανταχοῦ τὸν Ὅμηρον ὡς ἡγεμόνα πάσης ‖ ἀληθείας ὁ Πλάτων εἴωθεν γεραίρειν [δεύτερον].

Ἃ μὲν τοίνυν ὑπὲρ Ὁμήρου δυνατὸν λέγειν πρὸς τὰς | ἐν Πολιτείᾳ τοῦ Σωκράτους ἐπιστάσεις, τοιαῦτα ἂν εἴη. πάλιν δὲ αὖ ἀπ' ἄλλης ἀρχῆς δεικνύωμεν, ὡς ἄρα καὶ αὐτὸς ὁ Πλάτων πολλαχοῦ, <πανταχοῦ> μὲν οὖν ὡς εἰπεῖν, εἰσποιεῖται τὸν Ὅμηρον καὶ φίλον ἡγεῖται καὶ μάρτυρα καλεῖ τῶν ἑαυτοῦ δογμάτων, τότε μὲν πρὸ τῶν ἀποδείξεων ὥσπερ | εἰς θείαν φήμην ἀναφέρων τὴν τούτου φωνὴν τὴν τῶν ῥηθησομένων ἀλήθειαν, τότε δὲ μετὰ τὰς ἀποδείξεις ἀνέλεγκτον ἀποφαίνων τὴν ἐπιστήμην ἐκ τῆς Ὁμήρου κρίσεως, τότε δὲ καὶ ἐν μέσοις τοῖς περὶ τῶν ὄντων λόγοις ἐπ' αὐ‖τὸν ἀναπέμπων τὴν τῆς θεωρίας ἁπάσης ἀρχήν.

Ἐν Φαίδωνι [94d] μὲν γάρ, ὅπου διαφερόντως ὁ Σωκράτης τὴν ἑαυτοῦ ζωὴν ἀναπλοῖ καὶ πᾶν τὸ τῆς ἐπιστήμης πλάτος ἀνοίγει τοῖς ἑαυτοῦ ζηλωταῖς, πολλοῖς δή τισιν καὶ παντο|δαποῖς λόγοις καταδησάμενος, ὡς ἄρα ἄλλη μέν ἐστιν ἡ ἁρμονία τῶν σωμάτων, ἄλλη δὲ ἡ ψυχῆς φύσις, καὶ διέζευκται ταῦτα κατ' οὐσίαν ἀπ' ἀλλήλων, τελευτῶν ἐπὶ τόνδε τὸν ποιητὴν καταφεύγει καὶ τοῖς ἐκείνου ῥήμασιν ἐναργεστάτοις τεκμηρίοις χρώμενος ἐξῃρημένην ἐπιδείκνυσι τὴν | ψυχὴν τῆς περὶ τὸ σῶμα τῶν κράσεων ἁρμονίας. τὸ γὰρ διαμαχόμενον, φησίν, πρὸς τὴν ἐν τῷ στήθει τεταγμένην ζωὴν κινουμένην καὶ λέγον· **τέτλαθι δὴ κραδίη**, πάντως που κατὰ φύσιν ἐξήλλακται τούτου πρὸς ὃ διαμάχεται, καὶ τὸ κατεξανιστάμενον τοῦ σώματος οὐκ ἂν ἐν τῷ σώματι | τὴν ὑπόστασιν ἔχοι. καὶ οὕτω δὴ προϊὼν ὁ Σωκράτης καὶ συμπεραινόμενος, ὅτι τὴν οὐσίαν τῆς ψυχῆς ἑτέραν χρὴ φάναι τῆς τοῦ σώματος ἁρμονίας, ὥσπερ εἰς ἄφυκτον ἀνάγκην κατακλείων τὸν σύμπαντα λόγον· οὔτε γὰρ ἄν, φησίν, **Ὁμήρῳ θείῳ ποιητῇ ταύτῃ λέγοντες ὁμο|λογοῖμεν οὔτε ἡμῖν αὐτοῖς** [95a]. πολλοῦ ἄρα δεῖ τὴν Ὁμήρου κρίσιν ἀτιμάζειν, τὴν πρὸς αὐτὸν διαφωνίαν ἐν ἴσῳ τοῖς παντελῶς

Book 2[250]

(1) Plato is accustomed everywhere to celebrate Homer as the guide to all truth

What one can say against Socrates' objections to Homer in the *Republic* would, then, be things of this sort. Starting again from another point, let us now show how Plato himself in many passages—one might rather say *everywhere*—adopts Homer and considers him a friend and calls him as a witness to his own opinions, sometimes before his demonstrations, attributing the truth of what is about to be said to Homer's voice as to a divine utterance, and sometimes after the demonstrations, revealing that the knowledge imparted is unimpeachable according to the judgment of Homer, and sometimes in the midst of the discussion of things that truly exist, attributing to him || the origin of his whole doctrine.[251]

In the *Phaedo* [94b-d], where in particular Socrates unfolds his own [intellectual] life and opens the whole breadth of his knowledge to his disciples, after having established securely by many and varied arguments that the harmony that exists in bodies is one thing and the nature of the soul is another, and that these are fundamentally different from one another, he finally takes refuge in this poet and, using his words as clear evidence, demonstrates that the soul is transcendent over the harmony of mixtures relating to the body. For, he says, what opposes itself to the life seated and animated in the chest and says "Bear up, my heart" [*Od.* 20.17], is in any case by nature entirely separate from that with which it struggles, and that which rebels against the body could not have its existence in the body. Going on in this way and finally declaring that it is necessary to say that the substance of the soul is something different from the harmony of the body, he nails down the entire discussion as if with an inescapable conclusion and says, "If we were to speak thus, we would neither be in agreement with Homer the divine poet nor with ourselves" [95a]. He is far from scorning the judgment of Homer, then, and he equates disagreement

---

250. A new beginning. Proclus will establish Plato's admiration for and imitation of Homer (chs. 1–3), then turn to the criticisms in the *Phaedrus* and in book 10 of the *Republic*.

251. It is striking that this would serve well as a description of Proclus's Christian contemporaries' use of scripture (as "prooftexts"), but in fact the description does not match Plato's use of Homer very well at all.

ἀδυνάτοις τιθέμενος. ἀλλὰ μὴν προσήγορον ἑαυτῷ καὶ φίλον ἐνόμιζεν ἐν τοῖς περὶ ψυχῆς λόγοις ὁ τὴν πρὸς ἑαυτὸν ἀναρμοστίαν τῆς πρὸς ἐκεῖνον | οὐδὲν διαφέρειν ἡγούμενος.

Ἐν δὲ τοῖς Νόμοις θειότατόν τε αὐτὸν ποιητὴν ἀποκαλεῖ, καθάπερ ἄλλοις ἄλλο τι τῶν ὀνομάτων, καὶ τούτῳ τὸ θεῖον προσήκειν οἰόμενος· ἔοικεν γοῦν, φησίν, οὗτος ὁ ποιητὴς θειότατος γεγονέναι. || καὶ περὶ τῆς τῶν πολιτειῶν μεταβολῆς διαλεγόμενος, καὶ ὅπως ἐκ τῆς πατρονομικῆς ἐπιστασίας εἰς τοῦτο τὸ σχῆμα προῆλθον τῶν ἀνθρώπων <οἱ> οἰκισμοὶ διδάσκων [3.676a sqq.], πανταχοῦ τὴν Ὁμήρου μαρτυρίαν προστίθησιν, καὶ τέλος | εἰς πᾶσαν ποιητικὴν τὴν ἔνθεον μίαν εὐφημίαν τὴν μεγίστην διέτεινεν·

θεῖον γὰρ οὖν δὴ καὶ τὸ ποιητικὸν ὂν γένος ὑμνῳδοῦν πολλῶν τῶν κατ' ἀλήθειαν γεγονότων σύν τισι Χάρισι καὶ Μούσαις ἐφάπτεται ἑκάστοτε [3.682a].

Ἐν δὲ τῷ Μίνωϊ τὴν περὶ | τοῦδε τοῦ ἥρωος κρίσιν ἣν ἔσχεν Ὅμηρος ἐξηγούμενος ἐπάγει· **καὶ Ὀδυσσείας ἐν Νεκυίᾳ δικάζοντα χρυσοῦν σκῆπτρον ἔχοντα πεποίηκεν** [319d], καὶ ὅτι χρυσοῦν σκῆπτρον οὐδὲν ἄλλο ἢ τὴν παιδείαν λέγει τοῦ Μίνωος ᾗ εὔθυνε τὴν Κρήτην [320d]. καὶ οὐκ ἐν τούτῳ τῷ δια|λόγῳ μόνον Ὁμήρῳ χρῆται μάρτυρι τῆς περὶ τοῦ Μίνωος ἱστορίας, ἀλλὰ καὶ ἐν Νόμοις [1.624a] γράφων·

μῶν οὖν καθ' Ὅμηρον λέγεις ὡς τοῦ Μίνω φοιτῶντος δι' ἐνάτου ἔτους πρὸς τὴν τοῦ πατρὸς ἑκάστοτε συνουσίαν καὶ κατὰ τὰς παρ' ἐκείνου φήμας ταῖς πό|λεσιν ὑμῶν θέντος τοὺς νόμους;

καὶ ὅλως πανταχοῦ τὴν περὶ τῶν ἡρώων ἀλήθειαν παρ' Ὁμήρου δοκιμάζει μανθάνειν.

Ἐν δὲ τῷ Γοργίᾳ μετὰ τοὺς πολλοὺς καὶ μακροὺς ἀγῶνας, οὓς ὑπὲρ σωφροσύνης τε καὶ τῆς ἄλλης ἀρετῆς ἁπάσης πρὸς τὸν Καλλικλέα διηγωνίσατο, μῦθον | διεξιέναι μέλλων, οὐ μῦθον ἀλλὰ λόγον ὄντα, καθάπερ φησὶν αὐτός, καὶ τῶν ἐν Ἅιδου δικαστῶν διαμνημονεύσειν καὶ τῆς ἀφ' ἑνὸς πατρὸς εἰς τρεῖς δημιουργικὰς μονάδας τῶν θεῶν προόδου

with him with the utterly impossible.[252] Indeed, he thought Homer to be in agreement with himself and dear to him, in what he said about the soul, judging that there was no difference between being out of harmony with Homer and being out of harmony with himself.

In the *Laws* he calls him "the most divine poet"[253] as if he thought "divine" appropriate to him just as other epithets are to others. He says that Homer in any case seems to have been the most divine poet. ‖ When he speaks of the transformations of societies and demonstrates how human communities have progressed from patriarchal authority to the present pattern, Plato constantly evokes the testimony of Homer and finally extends his highest praise to all inspired poetry:

> The race of poets is also divine, and when they sing they regularly touch on a great deal that actually occurs, with the help of some of the Graces and the Muses. [*Leg.* 3.682a]

In the *Minos*, explaining Homer's evaluation of this hero, he adds that "in the *nekyia* of the *Odyssey* he depicted him as a judge of the dead with a golden␣scepter" and that "the golden scepter is nothing other than Minos's education, by which he governed Crete" *Min.* 319d, 320d]. This is not the only dialogue in which he uses Homer as a witness to the story of Minos, but he does the same in the *Laws*, where he writes:

> You do not mean to say, do you, with Homer, that Minos used to go to visit his father every nine years and established the laws for your cities based on his father's utterances? [*Leg.* 1.624a–b]

Generally and throughout his works Plato sanctions learning the truth about the heroes from Homer.

In the *Gorgias*, after many long arguments with Callicles over moderation and all the other sorts of virtue, when he is about to tell a myth (which is not a myth at all, he asserts, but a true story [λόγος]) and to speak of the judges in Hades and the procession of the gods from a single father to the three demiurgical monads and of the division of their inheritance in

---

252. Following F. and deleting Kroll's question mark in 155,22.

253. As F. points out, Proclus seems to have mistakenly transferred the expression from the *Ion* (530b, cf. 225 [K158], below) to the passage under discussion in the *Laws* (3.682a), where poets in general are praised.

καὶ τῆς ἐν τῷ παντὶ διακληρώσεως, ἀπὸ τῆς Ὁμηρικῆς ὑφηγήσεως τὰς τῆς θεομυθίας ἀρχὰς καταβάλλε|ται· **ὥσπερ γὰρ Ὅμηρος λέγει, διενείμαντο τὴν ἀρ||χὴν ὅ τε Ζεὺς καὶ ὁ Ποσειδῶν καὶ ὁ Πλούτων** [523a]· καὶ μικρὸν ὕστερον δικαστὴν <ἐν> Ἅιδου καθίζων τὸν Μίνω ταῖς ψυχαῖς τὴν Ὁμήρου περὶ αὐτοῦ διδασκαλίαν ὡς ἔνθεον προστίθησιν [526c]. ἐῶ λέγειν ὅτι καὶ τῶν ἐν Ἅιδου | δικαιωτηρίων παρ' ἐκείνου τὰς ἀφορμὰς εἴληφεν· ἀλλὰ τοῦτο μὲν καὶ εἰσαῦθις μέτιμεν.

ἐν δὲ τῇ Σωκράτους ἀπολογίᾳ [41a] καὶ περὶ τῆς λήξεως ἣν εἶχεν ἐνδείκνυται καὶ τῆς πρὸς αὐτὸν συντάξεως·

ἢ αὖ Ὀρφεῖ συγγενέσθαι καὶ Ἡσιόδῳ καὶ Ὁμήρῳ ἐπὶ πόσῳ ἄν τις δέξαιτο | ὑμῶν;
ἐγὼ μὲν γὰρ πολλάκις ἐθέλω τεθνάναι, εἰ ταῦτά ἐστιν ἀληθῆ.

τίς οὖν μηχανὴ μὴ οὐχὶ σοφὸν ὄντως τὰ θεῖα γεγονέναι τὸν τοιοῦτον νομίζειν, πρὸς ὃν καὶ αὐτὸς ἀφορᾷ καὶ ὃν ζηλωτὸν ἡγεῖται τῆς ἐν Ἅιδου λήξεως ὑπάρχειν; τὸ γὰρ εἰς τὴν ὁμοίαν ἐκείνῳ τάξιν ἀποκατα|στῆναι μακάριον ὄντως ὑπολαμβάνειν ἁπάσης μὲν αὐτὸν ἐπιστήμης, ἁπάσης δὲ ἀρετῆς ἐπήβολον γενέσθαι μαρτυρεῖ.

Ἐν δὲ αὖ τῷ Συμποσίῳ (καὶ γὰρ τῶν ἐνταῦθα γεγραμμένων ἀναμνήσωμεν ἡμᾶς αὐτούς) ἄντικρυς καὶ τὴν ὅλην αὐτοῦ πραγματείαν ἀποθαυμάζει καὶ ζηλωτὴν εἶναί φησιν τοῖς | ἔμφροσι·

καὶ εἰς Ὅμηρον ἀποβλέψας καὶ Ἡσίοδον καὶ τοὺς ἄλλους ἀγαθοὺς ποιητὰς ζηλῶν, ὅσα ἔκγονα καταλείπουσιν, ἃ ἐκείνοις ἀθάνατον κλέος καὶ μνήμην παρέχεται αὐτὰ τοιαῦτα ὄντα [209d].

πολλοῦ ἄρα δεῖ τὰ Ὁμήρου ποιήματα καὶ τῶν ἄλλων ὅσοι | τῆς ἐνθέου κεκοινωνήκασι μανίας (οὗτοι γὰρ ἂν δήπου καὶ ἀγαθοὶ προσαγορεύοιντο ποιηταί) τρίτα παντελῶς ἀπὸ τῆς || ἀληθείας καὶ φαντασίαν παρεχόμενα τῆς γνώσεως τῶν ὄντων ἡγεῖσθαι, ζηλωτὰ καὶ ἀξιομνημόνευτα αὐτὰ τιθέμενος εἶναι καὶ διανοίας οὐ τῆς ἐπιτυχούσης γεννήματα.

Ἐν δὲ τῷ Ἴωνι τά τε ἄλλα ἐξυμνεῖ τόνδε τὸν ποιητὴν καὶ παρα|κελεύεται παντὸς μᾶλλον αὐτῷ συγγενέσθαι καὶ ἀπολαύειν τῆς νοερᾶς αὐτοῦ καὶ ἐπιστημονικῆς ὑφηγήσεως·

the universe [523a], he lays down the fundamentals of his myth about the gods under Homer's guidance. "For," he says, "just as Homer says, Zeus, Poseidon, and Pluto divided up their || domain" [523a], and a little later, when he sets Minos up as a judge for the souls, he adds Homer's teaching about him and takes that teaching as inspired [526c]. I omit the fact that he has taken the essentials of the judgments in Hades from Homer, but we shall come back to that.

In the *Defense of Socrates*, he reveals Homer's fate and talks of being with him:

> What would one of you give to meet Orpheus and Hesiod and Homer?
> If these things are true, I wish to die many times over. [Plato, *Apol.* 41a]

By what means is it possible to think that such a man, to whom even Socrates looks up and whom he judges to be enviable for his lot in Hades, should not have been truly wise concerning the divine? The fact that he considers returning to the same rank as Homer to be true blessedness bears witness that Homer was one who achieved all wisdom and all virtue.

And again in the *Symposium*—let us remind ourselves of what is written there—he openly expresses his wonder at Homer's treatment of his material and says that it is to be emulated by the wise:

> and [anyone], looking to Homer and Hesiod and the other good poets, would be envious of the progeny they leave behind them, which are such as to bring to their parents eternal remembrance and glory. [Plato, *Symp.* 209d].

The poems of Homer, then, and the other poets who have a share of divine madness (and indeed one might as well simply call them the "*good poets*"), Plato is far from considering to be simply "third from the || truth," and purveyors only of phantoms of the knowledge of things that are, since be takes them to be worthy of emulation and citation and to be the offspring of no ordinary intelligence.

In the *Ion* he sings the praises of the poet in various ways and recommends above all else learning from him and enjoying his intellectual and knowledgeable guidance:

ἅμα δὲ καὶ ἀναγκαῖον εἶναι ἔν τε ἄλλοις ποιηταῖς διατρίβειν πολλοῖς καὶ ἀγαθοῖς, καὶ δὴ καὶ μάλιστα ἐν Ὁμήρῳ τῷ ἀρίστῳ καὶ θειοτάτῳ τῶν ποιητῶν, καὶ | τὴν τούτου διάνοιαν ἐκμανθάνειν, μὴ μόνον τὰ ἔπη, ζηλωτόν ἐστιν [530b].

Ἐκ δὴ τούτων τε καὶ τῶν τοιούτων ἁπάντων ἓν ἐκεῖνο συναγάγωμεν, ὅτι καὶ προσήγορον ἑαυτῷ τὸν Ὅμηρον ὁ Πλάτων ὑπείληφεν εἶναι καὶ ἡγεμόνα καὶ διδάσκαλον οὐ | τῶν τραγῳδιοποιῶν μόνον (τούτων μὲν γὰρ ἔστω καθ' ὅσον ἐστὶ μιμητὴς ἡγεμών), ἀλλὰ τῶν ἐν φιλοσοφίᾳ δογμάτων καὶ τούτων τῶν μεγίστων. εἰ γὰρ ἐν μὲν τοῖς περὶ θεῶν λόγοις καὶ περὶ τῆς τριττῆς τῶν δημιουργῶν διανομῆς καὶ περὶ τῶν ἐν Ἅιδου λήξεων καὶ περὶ τῆς ψυχικῆς οὐσίας | ἐπ' αὐτὸν ἀναπέμπει τὴν αἰτίαν τῆς θεωρίας, ἁπάντων δὲ ποιητῶν θειότατον ἀποκαλεῖ καὶ ζηλωτὸν τοῖς ἔμφροσιν καὶ μετὰ τὴν ἐντεῦθεν ἀπαλλαγὴν τὴν πρὸς αὐτὸν συνουσίαν περὶ πολλοῦ τίθεσθαι συνομολογεῖ, πῶς οὐ παντὶ καταφανής ἐστιν τήν τε ὅλην αὐτοῦ ζωὴν ἀποδεχόμενος καὶ τὴν ποίη|σιν ἀσπαζόμενος καὶ ἣν ἔσχεν περὶ τῶν ὄντων κρίσιν οἰκειούμενος;

Μὴ τοίνυν ἐκ τῶν ἐν Πολιτείᾳ γεγραμμένων ἐπαιρώμεθα λέγειν, ὅτι τῆς Ὁμήρου διδασκαλίας ὁ Πλάτων ἐστὶν κατήγορος, μηδὲ ὅτι κατὰ τὰ αὐτὰ τοῖς σοφισταῖς καὶ | τὴν τούτου πραγματείαν εἰδωλοποιὸν ἀποφαίνει, μηδὲ ὅλως διαφέρεσθαι τοὺς ἄνδρας ὑπολαμβάνωμεν. καὶ γὰρ ἐκεῖνος || ἐνθουσιάζων καὶ ὑπὸ τῶν Μουσῶν ἀναβακχευόμενος περὶ τῶν θείων ἡμᾶς ἀναδιδάσκει καὶ τῶν ἀνθρωπίνων πραγμάτων. ταῦτα ὁ Πλάτων ταῖς ἀνελέγκτοις τῆς ἐπιστήμης μεθόδοις κατεδήσατο καὶ διὰ τῶν ἀποδείξεων ἐναργέστερα | τοῖς πολλοῖς ἡμῶν κατέστησεν, οἳ καὶ τῆς τοιαύτης δεόμεθα βοηθείας εἰς τὴν τῶν ὄντων κατανόησιν.

Διὰ τίνας αἰτίας ἐν Πολιτείᾳ τὴν Ὁμήρου ποίησιν ὡς ἀνεπιτήδειον ἀκούειν τοῖς νέοις ἀπεδοκί-| μασεν.

Εἰ δὲ τοῖς ὑπ' αὐτῷ νομοθέτῃ τρεφομένοις καὶ κατὰ τὸ πρώτιστον εἶδος τῆς ζωῆς τελειουμένοις ἄβατόν τε τὴν ψυχὴν ἔχειν ὀφείλουσιν ἁπάσης ποικιλίας καὶ τῆς ἐναντίας διαθέσεως τῷ καλῷ <καὶ> τῷ ἀγαθῷ καὶ πρὸς μόνον τὸν τῆς ἀρετῆς ὅρον ἀποβλέπειν ἀνάρμοστός ἐστιν ἡ τοιαύτη | διδασκαλία, τῆς μὲν ἁπλότητος τῶν θείων πολυειδῆ παραπετάσματα

it is enviable to have to spend time with the many good poets, and particularly with Homer, the best and the most divine of poets, and to learn not only his verses but his meaning. [Plato, *Ion* 530b].

From these passages and all the others like them, let us make this one point, that Plato took Homer to be in harmony with himself and to be a guide and teacher not only for makers of tragedies (still, let him be their leader [as well], inasmuch as he is an imitator), but also a teacher of the doctrines of philosophy and of the greatest among those doctrines. If, in his discourses about the gods and the tripartite division among the demiurges and the lots assigned in Hades and the substance of the soul, Plato traces the source of his theories to Homer, and if he calls Homer the most divine of poets and an object of imitation for the wise, and if he admits that after becoming free of this life he places great value on being with Homer, how can it be anything but perfectly clear to all that he approved of everything about the life of the poet, embraced his poetry, and adopted as his own Homer's judgment concerning the things that exist?

Let us not, then, be induced to say, on account of what is written in the *Republic*, that Plato denounces the teachings of Homer, nor that he makes out his treatment of his material to be productive of illusions (as he does with the sophists), nor, finally, that the two men are utterly at odds.

Homer, for his part, || delivers to us his teachings on divine and human things while raised by the Muses to a state of ecstasy. Plato established these things solidly by the irrefutable methods of systematic thought and by his expositions made them clearer for most of us, who need help of this sort in order to comprehend those things that truly exist.

(2) What are the reasons why, in the *Republic*, Plato judged the poetry of Homer unfit to be heard by the young?

Given that such teaching[254] is unsuitable for those raised by the lawmaker and brought to perfection in the very first life of the soul,[255] needful as they are of keeping their souls inaccessible to all diversity and to the disposition opposite to the good and beautiful, and of contemplating only the single goal of virtue—unsuitable, because it contrives varied and

---

254. I.e. Homer's.
255. The three lives of the soul distinguished below (257–61 [K177,14–178,5]) offer some clarification of what is meant by the "first life" here. Cf. F. ad loc.

μηχανησαμένη, τῆς δὲ ὑπερφυοῦς περὶ αὐτῶν ἀληθείας καὶ τῆς ἐπέκεινα τῶν καλῶν πάντων ὑπάρξεως τὰ φαινόμενα αἰσχρὰ καὶ τὰ παρὰ φύσιν προκαλύμματα ποιησαμένη, πῶς διὰ ταῦτα προσήκει τὴν Ὁμηρικὴν
20 θεωρίαν | διοικίζειν τῆς Πλατωνικῆς φιλοσοφίας, εἰ μὴ καὶ τὴν αὐτοῦ τοῦ Πλάτωνος πραγματείαν διϊστάνειν τῆς Πλάτωνος ἐπιστήμης ἀνεξόμεθα; κατὰ γὰρ τὸν αὐτὸν λόγον καὶ ταύτην οἶμαι τοῖς ἐν ἐκείνῃ τῇ πολιτείᾳ παιδευομένοις οὐδαμῇ προσήκουσαν ἀποφαίνειν δυνατόν. καὶ
25 πῶς γὰρ ἂν πρέποι | τοῖς κατηκόοις μὲν ἐσομένοις τῶν τοῦ νομοθέτου προσταγμάτων, ἀμιγῆ δὲ πρὸς πᾶσαν κακίαν τὴν ζωὴν προστησομένοις, νοῦν δὲ καὶ ἐπιστήμην ἡγεμόνα τῆς ὅλης ἐπιτηδεύσεως ποιησομένοις,
K160 ἀκούειν Θρασυμάχου μὲν τοῦ σοφιστοῦ || βδελυρώτατον ἀποκαλοῦντος τὸν σοφώτατον [Rep. 1.338d], Καλλικλέους δὲ ἠλιθίους τοὺς σώφρονας προσαγορεύοντος [Gorg. 491e], αὐτοῦ δὲ Σωκράτους τὴν ἡδονὴν ἀγαθὸν
5 λέγοντος καὶ προσκατασκευάζοντος, ἄλλου δὲ ἄλλο τι φθεγγο|μένου τῶν ἐν τοῖς διαλόγοις κατὰ τὴν φαινομένην μίμησιν προβεβλημένων;

Ὅλως γὰρ μονοειδεῖς εἶναι χρὴ τοὺς περὶ τῶν ὄντων λόγους καὶ ἁπλᾶς καὶ ἀμιγεῖς πρὸς τὰ ἀντικείμενα τὰς ὑφηγήσεις τῶν ἐκεῖ τρεφομένων νέων
10 καὶ καθαρευούσας ἁπάσης μὲν ἀμφιβολίας, ἁπάσης δὲ ποικιλίας, | ἁπάσης δὲ τῆς ἐναντίας πρὸς τὴν ἀρετὴν διαθέσεως. πότ' οὖν ἡ τοιαύτη τῶν ἠθῶν μίμησις, οἵαν οἱ Πλάτωνος προΐστανται λόγοι, καὶ ἡ πολυειδὴς ἐξαλλαγὴ τῶν δογμάτων τούτων καὶ αἱ παντοδαπαὶ τῶν διαλεκτικῶν ἀγώνων ἐπιχειρήσεις πρὸς τὸ εἶδος ἐκεῖνο τῆς παιδείας συναρμοσθήσονται,
15 μίαν | ἁπλότητα καὶ ὅρον ἕνα ζωῆς ἀεὶ μεταθέον, εἰδώλων δὲ παντοίων καὶ φαντασίας ἁπάσης ἐξῃρημένον; διὰ ταῦτα γοῦν καὶ ὁ Σωκράτης ἐν ἐκείνοις διασκεψάμενος, ὁποῖον εἶδος λέξεως ἂν πρέποι τοῖς παρ' αὐτῷ τρεφομένοις νέοις εἰς τὴν περὶ τῶν ὄντων διδασκαλίαν, μάλιστα μὲν
20 ἀποσκευάζεσθαι | τὴν μιμητικὴν ἰδέαν τῶν λόγων παρακελεύεται καὶ τῆς ποικιλίας τῆς ἐν ταύτῃ καθαρεύειν τοὺς ποιητάς, εἰ δ' ἄρα καὶ δέοι μιμήσει προσχρῆσθαι, τῶν κατ' ἀρετὴν ζώντων καὶ μετ' ἐπιστήμης φθεγγομένων προΐστασθαι δεῖν τὴν μίμησιν, ἀλλ' οὐ τῶν φορτικῶν καὶ ἀγοραίων ἠθῶν
25 οὐδὲ τῶν πολυ|κεφάλων θηρίων οὐδὲ ὅλως τῶν ἐναντίων τοῖς ἀγαθοῖς.

Εἰ τοίνυν καὶ ἡ τοῦ Πλάτωνος αὕτη πραγματεία παντοδαπὰ μὲν εἴδη ζωῆς ἀποτυποῦται, πᾶσι δὲ ἀποδίδωσι τὸ πρέπον ἐν τοῖς λόγοις <καὶ>

polymorphous screens for the unity of divine things and makes apparent obscenities and things contrary to nature veils for the transcendent truth concerning the divine and for the existence that transcends all beautiful things—how on this basis is it appropriate to banish the doctrine of Homer from Platonic philosophy, unless we are also willing to separate Plato's own treatment of his material from his wisdom? By this same reasoning, I think it is possible to show that [Plato's] treatment of his material is in no way appropriate to those being raised in this society. How can it be fitting for those destined to obey the precepts of the lawmaker, who are going to keep their lives free of all evil and make intellect and systematic wisdom the guide of all their activity, to hear Thrasymachus the sophist || calling the wisest of men "absolutely disgusting,"[256] Callicles calling reasonable men "imbeciles,"[257] Socrates himself calling pleasure a "good thing" and then demonstrating it,[258] or others expressing those many ideas that are put forth in the dialogues for dramatic reasons [and not as the actual views of Plato]?

Accounts of the things that exist must, generally speaking, be uniform, and the instructions to the young being raised in Socrates' society must be simple and unmixed with their opposites and pure of all ambiguity, of all diversity, and of the disposition contrary to virtue. Now, when are such imitation of characters as the writings of Plato present, and the polymorphous variations of these ideas and the various kinds of strategies in the dialectical arguments, going to be brought into harmony with that form of education that always pursues a unified simplicity and a single end of life, transcending all images and all fantasy? For these reasons, indeed, Socrates, looking into this problem of what sort of discourse concerning the things that exist would be appropriate to the young people being raised in his society, first of all recommends excluding the mimetic form of discourse and purging the poets of the diversity inherent in it—and, if they should also have to use *mimesis*, they should produce imitations exclusively of those who live virtuously and speak with true knowledge, and not of gross and vulgar characters, many-headed beasts, or, generally speaking, people who are the antithesis of the good.

Now, if Plato's own style also represents various modes of life and assigns appropriate language to each and each speaks, within the limits of

---

256. *Rep.* 1.338d.
257. *Gorg.* 491e.
258. Cf. *Prot.* 351c; *Rep.* 9.581c (Kroll's suggestion).

φθέγγεται ὥσπερ ἐν σκηνῇ κατ' ἐξουσίαν ἕκαστος, καὶ ὁ σοφὸς καὶ ὁ ἀμαθής, καὶ ὁ ‖ σώφρων καὶ ὁ ἀκόλαστος, καὶ ὁ δικαιότατος καὶ ὁ ἀδικώτατος, καὶ ὁ ἐπιστήμων καὶ ὁ σοφιστής, ἀγῶνες δὲ παντοῖοι τῶν ἐν φιλοσοφίᾳ δογμάτων ἀνακινοῦνται, καί που καὶ πιθανώτεροι τῶν τὰ ἀληθῆ κατασκευαζόντων εἰσὶν οἱ τῶν | ἀντικειμένων ὑπερηγοροῦντες, πῶς ἂν χώραν ἔχοι παρὰ τῷ νομοθέτῃ τῆς ἁπλῆς ἐκείνης καὶ νοερᾶς πολιτείας; πῶς δὲ οὐ τὰ αὐτὰ ἂν πάσχοι τοῖς Ὁμήρου ποιήμασιν; καὶ γὰρ ταῦτα διὰ τὴν ποικιλίαν τῶν ἠθῶν οὐ προσιέμεθα καὶ διὰ τὴν φαινομένην εἰδωλοποιΐαν. ὁ αὐτὸς οὖν λόγος καὶ τὸν | Ὅμηρον ἡμᾶς ἐκβάλλειν τῆς πολιτείας καὶ τὸν Πλάτωνα αὐτόν, μᾶλλον δὲ ἑκάτερον μὲν ἡγεμόνα τῆς ζωῆς ἐκείνης καὶ ἀρχηγὸν ἀποφαίνειν, τὸ δὲ μιμητικὸν ἀμφοτέρων διὰ πάσης ὡς εἰπεῖν τῆς ἑκατέρου πραγματείας διῆκον ἀποδοκιμάζειν, ὡς ἀλλότριον τῆς κατ' ἐκείνην τελειότητος.

Πολλὰ | γὰρ τῶν δευτέρων καὶ τρίτων ἀγαθῶν καταδεέστερα τῆς πρωτίστης ὄντα πολιτείας ὁ κατ' αὐτὴν ἱστάμενος νομοθέτης ἀποσκευάζεται· λέγω δὲ οἷον τὴν τῶν κτημάτων διανομήν, ἣν ἐν Νόμοις [5.737c sqq.] παρειλήφαμεν, τὴν κατὰ λόγους ἁρμονικοὺς τῶν ὅλων διαίρεσιν, τὴν τῶν ἀρχόντων | ποικιλίαν, τὴν ἰδίαν τῶν παίδων ἐπιμέλειαν, τὴν διὰ τῆς μέθης παιδείαν [2.672a sqq.]. ἅπαντα γὰρ ταῦτα τοῖς μὲν κατὰ τὴν δευτέραν πολιτείαν βιωσομένοις παντὸς μᾶλλόν ἐστιν προσήκοντα, τοῖς δὲ καὶ εἰς ἐκείνην τὴν πρωτίστην καὶ οὐρανίαν ὄντως τελεῖν μέλλουσιν οὐδαμῇ ἂν πρέποντα | φανείη. ποῦ γὰρ ἡ τῶν κλήρων διαίρεσις τοῖς πάντα κοινὰ κεκτημένοις διαφέρει; ποῦ δὲ ἡ μεριστὴ τῶν παίδων ἐπιστασία τοῖς κοινοῖς τῶν γιγνομένων πατράσιν; ποῦ δὲ ἡ μέθη καὶ τὰ συμπόσια καὶ οἱ παιδικοὶ χοροὶ τοῖς ἀδιάστροφα τὰ ἤθη παντελῶς προβεβλημένοις καὶ οὐδὲν προσδεόμενα τῶν | ἔξωθεν ἐπῳδῶν; Τί οὖν δεῖ θαυμάζειν, εἰ καὶ οἱ Πλάτωνος λόγοι πάντων ἡμῖν τῶν καλῶν **λειμῶνας ἀφθόνους** ‖ προτείνοντες καὶ αἱ τῶν κατόχων ταῖς Μούσαις ποιητῶν πραγματεῖαι τῇ πρωτίστῃ τῶν πολιτειῶν οὐ διαφέρουσιν; τῷ γὰρ ἁπλῷ τὸ ποικίλον, καὶ τῷ μονοειδεῖ τὸ πολυειδές, καὶ τῷ παραδείγματι τῆς ἀρίστης ζωῆς τὸ μιμητικὸν γένος | οὐκ ἄν ποτε προσαρμοσθείη· παράδειγμα δέ, φησὶν ὁ Σωκράτης, πολιτείας ὀρθῆς καὶ τελέας γράφομεν. διὸ καὶ πάντα αὐτῇ

possibility, just as if they were on the stage, both the wise and the ignorant, the || reasonable and the undisciplined, the most just and the most criminal, the wise man and the sophist, and all sorts of struggles are stirred up over philosophical doctrines, and in places those who argue just the opposite are more persuasive than those demonstrating the truth, how could this have any place for the lawmaker of this simple and intellectual state? And how would it not suffer the same fate as the poems of Homer? We are refusing to admit these as well on account of the diversity of their characters and of their projection of images [and not reality]. And so, by the same reasoning, we will throw both Homer and Plato himself out of the state, or rather, make each of them a guide and leader for that sort of life, but reject the *mimesis* that penetrates, we may say, the whole style and approach of each, on the basis that it is alien to the perfection of that life.

The lawmaker concerned with the highest society rejects many of the good things of the second and third orders as beneath that society. I mean, for example, the division of holdings we find in the *Laws* [5.737c], the division of the whole according to principles of harmony,[259] the diversity of magistrates [*Leg.* 6 *passim*], private care of children [*Leg.* 7 *passim*], and education through drunkenness,[260] for all these things are perfectly appropriate to those who are going to live in the society of the second rank, while for those who are going to belong to this first and truly celestial society, they would not seem appropriate at all. What difference would a distribution of portions make for those who [already] own all things in common? And what use is the individual care of children for those who are the common fathers of all those born? And what place have drunkenness and symposia and children's dances for those who have shown that their character is entirely uncorrupted and that they have no need of charms from without? What wonder is it, then, if the dialogues of Plato, offering us "abundant meadows"[261] || of all good things and the works of the poets possessed by the Muses should be out of harmony with the first of societies? The diverse could never be in harmony with the simple, the polymorphous with the uniform, the mimetic genre with the model of the best life. "For," Socrates says, "We are drafting the model of a true and

---

259. F. refers this, no doubt correctly, to the discussion of the distribution of property at *Leg.* 5.737e1–738b1.
260. Cf., e.g., *Leg.* 2.671a–672d.
261. *Soph.* 222a.

πρὸς ἀκρίβειαν τὰ ἀγαθὰ φέροντες ἀποδίδομεν, τὴν ἕνωσιν, τὴν ἁπλότητα, τὴν ἀλήθειαν, τὴν αὐτάρκειαν.

Ὥσπερ οὖν εἴ τις τοῖς νοητοῖς εἴδεσιν, ἃ δὴ παραδείγματα | τῶν ὄντων εἶναι τιθέμεθα, σχῆμα προσάγοι καὶ μέγεθος καὶ χρόαν, καὶ ὅσα ἄλλα προσήκει ταῖς τούτων εἰκόσιν, ἀλλ' οὐ τοῖς πρωτουργοῖς καὶ ὄντως οὖσιν γένεσιν, συγχεῖν αὐτὸν <τὰ> κατ' οὐσίαν διεστῶτα καὶ συγκλώθειν τὰ ἀνάρμοστά φαμεν, οὕτως οἶμαι καὶ τοῖς ἐν τῇ τελεωτάτῃ πολι|τείᾳ φῦσίν τε καὶ τρεφομένοις ἤθεσιν καὶ κατὰ τὸ παράδειγμα τῆς ἀρίστης παιδείας τελειουμένοις μιμήσεις διὰ λόγων καὶ εἴδη παντοίας ζωῆς καὶ σκηνὴν τῶν διαφόρων παθημάτων <τῶν> ἐν τοῖς ἀνθρώποις προτείνειν οὐκ ἄν ποτε συγχωρήσαιμεν. ἄμικτα γὰρ πάντα καὶ ἄχραντα καὶ | τέλεια ἐπιτηδεύματα τῆς πολιτείας ἐκείνης ἐξῆπται *** τῶν ἄλλων ἁπάντων· καὶ ὅσα τῷ νῷ σύστοιχα καὶ τοῖς ἀΰλοις καὶ νοεροῖς λόγοις, ταῦτα πρὸς τὴν παιδείαν μόνα τῶν ἐκεῖ τρεφομένων ἐκλεγόμεθα. πᾶσα δὲ αὖ μίμησις τοῖς φαινομένοις, ἀλλ' οὐ τοῖς ἀληθέσιν, καὶ τοῖς πεπληθυσμένοις, | ἀλλ' οὐ τοῖς ἡνωμένοις τῶν ὄντων, καὶ τοῖς μεριστοῖς τὴν φύσιν, ἀλλ' οὐ τοῖς ἀμερίστως ὑφεστηκόσιν ἐστὶ σύζυγος. ὅπου τοίνυν ἑνοειδὴς μὲν ὁ τῆς ὅλης ζωῆς σκοπός, κοινωνία δὲ ἀδιαίρετος προτιμᾶται διαφερόντως τῆς μεριστῆς περιγραφῆς, ἀλήθεια δὲ ἄμικτος πρὸς τὴν ἐπίπλαστον καὶ || εἰδωλικὴν ἕξιν προέστηκεν, τίς μηχανὴ τὴν πολυειδῆ μίμησιν οἰκείαν ὑπάρχειν τῇ τοιαύτῃ τελειότητι; μήτ' οὖν τὴν Ὁμήρου ποίησιν μόνον τῆς πρωτίστης ἐκβάλλωμεν πολιτείας, ἀλλὰ καὶ τὴν Πλάτωνος πραγματείαν μετ' ἐκείνης, ὡς πολὺ | τῆς μιμήσεως ἀπολαύουσαν, μήτε τὴν μίμησιν ταύτην παντελῶς ἀποδοκιμάζωμεν, διότι τοῖς ἐν ἐκείνῃ τῇ πολιτείᾳ παιδευομένοις ἐστὶν ἀνάρμοστος· οὐ γὰρ τὸ τοῖς πρωτίστοις μηδαμῇ προσῆκον καὶ τῆς δευτέρας ἢ τρίτης τάξεως ἀπεστέρηται τῶν ἀγαθῶν. |

Ὅτι διὰ πάσης τῆς ἑαυτοῦ συγγραφῆς Ὁμήρου ζηλωτής ἐστιν ὁ Πλάτων ταῖς τε λεκτικαῖς ἀρεταῖς καὶ ταῖς πραγματικαῖς.

perfect state. That is also precisely why we bring all good things to it and assign them to it: unity, simplicity, truth, self-sufficiency."[262]

Now just as, if someone should add shape and mass and color to the noetic forms (which, of course, we take to be the models of reality), along with the rest of the qualities that are appropriate to the images or copies of these forms but not to the primordial and truly existing classes, we say that he is mixing together things that are essentially different and weaving together things out of harmony with one another; in this same way, I believe, we would never agree to lay before those, born and raised in this most perfect society, whose character is perfected according to the model of the best education, imitations in words and images of all sorts of ways of life and dramatic representations of the various passions common to humanity. All the activities attached to that society are pure, unmixed, and perfect, [uncorrupted by][263] any others. We select for the education of those raised in that society exclusively those things in the category of intellect and of nonmaterial, intellective logoi. But again, all *mimesis* is bound to appearances rather than truths, to those things that belong to the realm of multiplicity rather than those of the realm of unified things, and to those things that are partial by nature rather than to those that have an entire existence. Now, wherever the goal of the whole of life is uniform, and an indivisible community is especially preferred over a fragmented individuation and unmixed truth prevails over the fabricated and || imitative, how could polymorphous imitation be at home in such perfection? And so, let us throw not just Homer's poems out of the first society but Plato's writings along with them, since they make such use of *mimesis*. At the same time, let us not utterly condemn this *mimesis* on the grounds that it is out of harmony with those being instructed in that society. For that which in no way belongs to the very first category of good things is not also deprived of [participation in] the second and third classes.

(3) That in all his writings Plato imitates Homer, with regard both to the excellence of his language and to that of his material.

---

262. F. points to several passages as the sources for the ideas in this composite speech given to Socrates, including, e.g., *Rep.* 5.472d9–e1.

263. There is a lacuna in the text. Kroll restored (*exempli gratia*) <καὶ καθαρά>.

Ἀλλὰ περὶ μὲν τούτων ἅλις· ὅτι δὲ οὐ μόνον ἡμῖν παρεκελεύσατο ζηλοῦν τὴν Ὁμήρου ποίησιν ὁ Πλάτων, κα|θάπερ ἐν τῷ Ἴωνι [530b] γέγραπται, καὶ πρὸς τὴν ἐκείνου διάνοιαν ἀποβλέπειν, ἀλλὰ καὶ αὐτὸς ὄντως ἐστὶν Ὁμήρου ζηλωτής, μάθοιμεν ἂν τήν τε προβεβλημένην ταύτην τῶν λόγων ἰδέαν καὶ τὴν τῶν δογμάτων ἐπιστήμην, ἣν πανταχοῦ μεταδιώκει, κατανοήσαντες.

Τὸ μὲν γὰρ τῆς | λέξεως εἶδος ὅπως κατ' ἴχνος συνυφαίνεται παρ' αὐτῷ τῆς Ὁμηρικῆς μιμήσεως, καὶ ὡς τὰ ἤθη πάντα τῶν διαλεγομένων ἀνήπλωται καὶ αἱ τῆς ζωῆς ἕξεις μετὰ τῆς ἴσης ἐναργείας ἡμῖν παραδέδονται, μεθ' ὅσης καὶ Ὅμηρος τοὺς περὶ τῶν ἡρώων λόγους διέθηκεν, καὶ ὡς μονονουχὶ παρόν|τας ἑκάτερος καὶ φθεγγομένους τὰ ἑαυτοῦ δόγματα καὶ ζῶντας παρίστησιν τούτους οὓς ἂν μιμῆται, παντὶ καταφανὲς καὶ διὰ τῶν εἰρημένων ὑπέμνησται. καὶ γὰρ τὴν φαντασίαν ἡμῶν κινεῖ παντοίως ἡ τῶνδε τῶν ἀνδρῶν μίμησις || καὶ τὰς δόξας μετατίθησιν καὶ συμμεταμορφοῖ τοῖς ὑποκειμένοις πράγμασιν, ὥστε πολλοὺς μὲν Ἀπολλοδώρῳ συνδακρύειν ἀναβρυχωμένῳ, πολλοὺς δὲ Ἀχιλλεῖ θρηνοῦντι τὸν φίλον, καὶ τοσούτοις ὕστερον χρόνοις τὰ αὐτὰ πάσχειν τοῖς | τότε παροῦσιν. οὐδὲ γὰρ ἡμεῖς ἀπεῖναι δοκοῦμεν τῶν πραγμάτων διὰ τὴν ἐκ τῆς μιμήσεως ἐναργῆ φαντασίαν τῶν μεμιμημένων.

Εἰ δὲ τούτων ἀπαλλαγέντες καὶ τὴν περὶ τὴν λέξιν πολυπραγμοσύνην ἄλλοις ἀφέντες ἐπὶ τὴν τῆς θεωρίας ἀνα|δράμοιμεν τῶν ἀνδρῶν ὁμοιότητα, πάλιν κἀνταῦθα τὴν ἀνέλεγκτον ἐπιστήμην τὴν αὐτὴν παρ' ἀμφοτέροις διαλάμπουσαν γνωσόμεθα καὶ τὸν Πλάτωνα πανταχοῦ μεταθέοντα τὴν πρὸς Ὅμηρον ἀφομοίωσιν.

Εἰ γὰρ βούλεσθε, τῶν ἐν Τιμαίῳ γεγραμμένων ἀναμνησθῶμεν, ἐν οἷς πάντα μὲν | τὰ θεῖα γένη τοῦ κόσμου, πάντα δὲ τὰ θνητὰ παράγων, μίαν δὲ δημιουργικὴν πρόνοιαν ἐπὶ πάντα διατείνων μέχρι τοῦ ποιητοῦ καὶ πατρὸς τῶν ὅλων ἀνάγει τὴν θεωρίαν· τὰ δὲ ἐπέκεινα τῆς ἀρχῆς ταύτης ἀφίησιν ἄρρητα, πλὴν ὅσον τοῦ νοητοῦ παραδείγματος τῆς δημιουργικῆς

[a. The problem]

Enough of these matters. That Plato has not only recommended to us that we admire the poetry of Homer (as he wrote in the *Ion* [530b]) and study his ideas, but moreover that he himself is truly an admirer of Homer, we may learn by paying attention to the outward form of his discourse and to the doctrinal wisdom that he constantly pursues.

[b. *Mimesis*]

It is perfectly clear to all (and has just been observed above) how, first of all, the form of Plato's discourse is woven following the lead of Homeric *mimesis* and how the characters of the speakers are fully developed and the qualities of their lives are given to us with a vividness equal to that Homer put into his accounts of the heroes and that both [Homer and Plato] present those they imitate as virtually living beings, expressing their own ideas. Indeed, the *mimesis* of these men moves our imagination in many ways and || changes our ideas and reshapes them along with the material being treated, so that many are moved to weep along with Apollodorus "howling out loud" [*Phd.* 117d], and many as well with Achilles as he wails over his friend, and at such a great distance in time to experience the same things as those who were then present. We feel we are actually present at the events through the vivid images of the people imitated that are produced by the *mimesis*.

If we leave these matters and let others trouble themselves over style, and move on to the similarity of the theories of the two men, here again we shall find the same unimpeachable wisdom radiating from both and Plato everywhere striving to resemble Homer.

[c. The *Timaeus*]

If you will, let us recall what is written in the *Timaeus*, where Plato brings in all the divine classes of the cosmos and all the mortal ones and extends a single demiurgical providence over all of them, raising our contemplation right up to the maker and father of the universe. He leaves unspoken what lies beyond this first principle, except for what he writes concerning the noetic model, for the sake of [explaining the activity of]

ἕνεκα μονάδος | πεποίηται μνήμην· ὁ γὰρ τοῦ παντὸς ὑποστάτης αὐτὸς δημιουργεῖ τὰ αἰσθητὰ πρὸς τὸ νοητὸν παράδειγμα βλέπων.

Ταύτην τοίνυν ἅπασαν τὴν τῶν ὅλων μέθοδον οὐκ ἀλλαχόθεν ἔμοιγε δοκεῖ συνελεῖν ἢ ἐκ τῆς Ὁμηρικῆς ποιήσεως. καὶ γὰρ Ὅμηρος περὶ τῶν ἐγκοσμίων πραγμάτων ἀναδι|δάσκων καὶ τῆς εἰς τὸ πᾶν καθηκούσης προνοίας τῶν θεῶν μέχρι τοῦ Διὸς ἄνεισιν καὶ τῆς δημιουργικῆς αἰτίας, καὶ εἰς μίαν ταύτην ἀρχὴν ἀκίνητον καὶ ἀεὶ ὡσαύτως ἱδρυμένην ἀναπέμπει τὴν γένεσιν τῶν ἐν τῷ κόσμῳ πάντων, καὶ πατέρα θεῶν τε καὶ ἀνδρῶν διὰ πάσης ὡς εἰπεῖν τῆς πρα|γματείας ἀνυμνεῖ τὸν μέγιστον τοῦτον θεόν· ὥσπερ δὴ καὶ || ὁ Τίμαιος [ὡς] ὕστερον ἀπογεννῶντα μὲν αὐτὸν τοὺς ἐν τῷ παντὶ θεοὺς παραδίδωσιν, ὑφιστάντα δὲ καὶ τὰς μεριστὰς ψυχὰς καὶ εἰς ἀνδρῶν πέμποντα γένεσιν· τοιαύτη γὰρ ἡ πρωτίστη κάθοδος τῶν ψυχῶν, ἣν ἐξ ἀνάγκης ἁπάσαις αὐ|ταῖς προσκεῖσθαι παρὰ τοῦ γεννήσαντος πατρὸς διατείνεται. μέχρι δ' οὖν τῆς μιᾶς δημιουργίας καὶ Ὅμηρος ἀνατρέχει καὶ πάντα ἐξάπτει τῆς τοῦ Διὸς πατρονομικῆς ἐπιστασίας, Κρόνου δὲ καὶ Ῥέας ὡς αἰτίων τοῦ δημιουργοῦ διαμνημονεύει, κατὰ τοὺς δεινοὺς τῶν διαλεκτικῶν ἀπὸ τῆς | προσεχοῦς αἰτίας αὐτῷ τὴν περὶ τοῦ δημιουργοῦ θεωρίαν ὡρμῆσθαι βουλόμενος ὡς ἐκεῖθεν μάλιστα καταφανῆ γενησομένην.

Πάλιν τοίνυν ὁ μὲν θεῖος ποιητὴς διττὰς δημηγορίας τοῦ πατρὸς τῶν ὅλων ἡμῖν ἐξέφηνεν, ὥς που καὶ πρότερον | εἴπομεν [p. 106,21], πρὸς τοὺς ἐγκοσμίους θεούς, καὶ τὴν μὲν αὐτῶν ἐπιστρεπτικὴν καὶ συναγωγὸν τῶν ἀκουόντων εἰς τὸν ἕνα δημιουργικὸν νοῦν, χωριστοὺς ἀπεργαζομένην τῶν προνοουμένων ἁπάντων τοὺς θεοὺς καὶ συνελίσσουσαν τὸ πλῆθος ἐπὶ τὴν ἐξῃρημένην μονάδα καὶ Διὸς ἔνδον, ὥς | φησιν ἡ ποίησις [Υ 13], συλλέγουσαν, τὴν δὲ προνοίας χορηγὸν καὶ δυνάμεων γεννητικῶν καὶ προάγουσαν ἕκαστον εἰς τὴν τῶν δευτέρων ἐπιμέλειαν καὶ κινητικὴν πρὸς τὴν μετάδοσιν τῆς τάξεως, ἵνα δὴ καὶ τὰ ἔσχατα τοῦ παντὸς καὶ ὁ ἐν τῇ φύσει πόλεμος μετάσχῃ τῆς τῶν θεῶν νοερᾶς | ἐπιστασίας.

Ὁ δὲ αὖ Πλάτων, ἢ εἰ βούλεσθε λέγειν ὁ παρὰ τῷ Πλάτωνι Τίμαιος [41a], δημηγοροῦντα μὲν <καὶ> αὐτὸς ἀπὸ τῆς νοερᾶς περιωπῆς τὸν πατέρα τῶν ὅλων παραδίδωσιν εἰς ἅπαντας τοὺς ἀπ' αὐτοῦ προεληλυθότας

the demiurgical monad (for he who is placed over the universe creates sense-objects while contemplating the noetic model).[264]

Now, he seems to me to have taken this entire system of the universe from nowhere else than the Homeric poems. Homer in his teachings about encosmic things and about the providence of the gods that descends into the universe refers this back to Zeus and to the demiurgic cause, and it is to this one first principle, unmoving and eternally, immutably fixed, that he attributes the generation of all things in the cosmos, and everywhere, we may say, in his works he celebrates this greatest god as "the father of gods and men."[265] In just the same way, ‖ Timaeus, later on, also passes down the account that he [the demiurge] not only gave birth to the gods in the universe but also created the partial souls and sent them for the creation of men [*Tim.* 41d–e]. Such is the primal descent of souls, which he maintains is assigned to all by the father who created them. Now Homer also goes back to the single creation and attaches everything to the paternal care of Zeus—he mentions Kronos and Rhea as causes of the demiurge, wishing, like those skilled in dialectic, that the treatment of the demiurge should start from the cause immediately adjacent to the demiurge himself, since that will give it the greatest clarity.[266]

Once again, the divine Poet has shown us two speeches by the father of the universe to the encosmic gods, as we said earlier.[267] One of them draws and gathers those who hear it into the single demiurgical intellect, separating the gods from all the beings under their providence, rolling their multiplicity together into the transcendent monad, and gathering them "within Zeus" [*Il.* 20.13], as the poem says. The other speech supports providence and the powers that operate within γένεσις and sends each [of the gods] forth to care for the secondaries and moves them to offer the secondaries participation in their processions, so that even the last beings of the universe and the war within the natural world may participate in the intellective care of the gods.

Plato himself, on the other hand (or, if you prefer, Plato's Timaeus) passes down an account of the father of the universe addressing all the gods who have issued from him, speaking from his intellective vantage

---

264. *Tim.* 28c–30c.
265. *Il.* 1.544 and *passim*.
266. I.e., Kronos and Rhea are brought in to strengthen the theory by specifying the proximal causes behind the demiurge.
267. Cf. 129 [K106,21–25], above.

K166 θεούς, **τούς τε ἀεὶ περιπολοῦντας καὶ τοὺς φαινομένους** ‖ **καθ' ὅσον ἂν ἐθέλωσιν**, ἀλλ' ἐν τοῖς αὐτοῖς λόγοις καὶ ἐπιστρέφοντα τὸ πλῆθος εἰς ἑαυτὸν καὶ εἰς τὴν πρόνοιαν ἀνεγείροντα τῶν θνητῶν· καὶ τὰ μὲν πρῶτα τῆς δημηγορίας τῆς ἐπιστροφῆς τοῖς ἐγκοσμίοις θεοῖς τῆς εἰς
5 τὸν ἕνα δη|μιουργὸν μεταδίδωσιν, τὰ δὲ τελευταῖα τῆς προνοητικῆς τῶν καταδεεστέρων δυνάμεως. **μιμούμενοι γάρ** φησιν **τὴν ἐμὴν δύναμιν περὶ τὴν ὑμετέραν γένεσιν ζῷα ἀπεργάζεσθε καὶ γεννᾶτε**. πάντη ἄρα φήσομεν αὐτὸν Ὁμήρῳ καὶ τοῖς Ὁμήρου ποιήμασιν ἑπόμενον τὰ τοιαῦτα γράφειν, |
10 ζηλοῦντα τὸν τρόπον τῆς περὶ τῶν ὅλων πραγμάτων ὑφηγήσεως.

 Καὶ μὴν καὶ ὁ ἐν τῷ Φαίδρῳ Σωκράτης ἐνθεαστικῶς ἤδη καὶ ποιητικῶς φθεγγόμενος ἀνάγει μὲν τοὺς ἐν τῷ κόσμῳ θεοὺς εἰς τὴν τῶν νοητῶν
15 περιωπὴν ὑφ' ἡγεμόνι | τῷ μεγίστῳ Διΐ· τούτῳ γάρ, φησίν, **ἕπεται στρατιὰ θεῶν τε καὶ δαιμόνων κατὰ ἕνδεκα μέρη κεκοσμημένη** [246e], δαῖτα δὲ καὶ θοίνην αὐτοῖς προτίθησιν καὶ εὐπαθείας ἀμηχάνους καὶ τὸ νέκταρ καὶ τὴν ἀμβροσίαν, ταῦτα δὴ τὰ παρὰ τοῖς ποιηταῖς θρυλούμενα, καὶ ἐπὶ τὴν |
20 ἑαυτοῦ μετάγει θεωρίαν [247e]. οὐ γάρ ἐστιν μαινομένῳ στόματι λέγοντα τῶν τοιούτων ὀνομάτων ἀπέχεσθαι, ἀλλ' ἡ πρὸς τὸ δαιμόνιον γένος οἰκειότης ἡ προευτρεπίζουσα τὴν τοῦ θείου φωτὸς παρουσίαν ἀνακινεῖ τὴν φαντασίαν εἰς τὴν συμβολικὴν ἀπαγγελίαν.
25 Πόθεν δὴ οὖν ὁ Σωκράτης οἴεσθε | τὴν τοιαύτην τῶν λόγων μέθοδον ἢ ἐκ τῶν Ὁμηρικῶν ποιημάτων ἀνήγειρεν; ἢ οὐχὶ καὶ Ὅμηρος τοιαῦτα ἄττα γράφει περί τε τοῦ μεγίστου Διὸς καὶ τῶν ἑπομένων αὐτῷ θεῶν·

 Ζεὺς γὰρ ἐς Ὠκεανὸν μετ' ἀμύμονας Αἰθιοπῆας |
30 **χθιζὸς ἔβη μετὰ δαῖτα, θεοὶ δ' ἅμα πάντες ἕπονται** [Α 423–424]. ‖

K167 Παντὶ γοῦν τοῦτο καταφανὲς τῷ καὶ μετρίως τῆς τοιᾶσδε θεωρίας ἐπῃσθημένῳ, ὅτι τὸν μέγιστον τῶν θεῶν ἄνωθεν ἐκ τῶν νοητῶν τρέφεσθαι ῥητέον ἐπὶ δαῖτα καὶ θοίνην ἰόντα <καὶ> πρὸς τὰς οἰκείας ἀρχὰς
5 ἐπιστρέφειν καὶ ἀπ' | ἐκείνων πληροῦσθαι τῶν ἐξῃρημένων καὶ ἑνοειδῶν

point, "both those gods that are eternally revolving and those that manifest themselves || as they please" [*Tim.* 41a], but in the same speech both returning the multiplicity back into himself and arousing it to providence over mortal things. The first part of the speech extends to the encosmic gods' participation in the return to the demiurgical One; the latter part extends participation in providential power over the inferior beings. "Imitating the power I exercised in your creation," he says, "make living beings and cause them to be born" [41c–d]. We shall say, therefore, that he is in every way following Homer and the poems of Homer when he writes such things, aspiring to the manner of Homer's description of matters relating to the universe.

[d. The *Phaedrus*]

Moreover, in the *Phaedrus*, Socrates, when he has already begun speaking in an inspired and poetic manner, takes the gods in the cosmos back up to the contemplation of noetic things under the leadership of greatest Zeus. After him, he says, "follows an army of gods and daemons arranged in eleven parts" [*Phdr.* 246e], and Zeus sets a banquet before them, with wondrous delights and nectar and ambrosia—the things the poets are always talking about—and shares with them the contemplation he himself enjoys [*Phdr.* 247]. It is impossible for one speaking in the madness of inspiration to refrain from such language—rather, intimacy with the race of daemons, bringing about the apparition of the divine light, inspires the imagination to move to the symbolic mode of discourse.

Where, then, do you think Socrates got this kind of manner with words, unless it was from the Homeric poems? Or does Homer not also write such things as these about greatest Zeus and the gods who follow behind him:

Zeus went yesterday to feast with
the beautiful Ethiopians, and all the gods went with him [*Il.* 1.423–424]? ||

Indeed, it is perfectly clear to anyone who has even a middling perception of this sort of doctrine that one must say, when the greatest of the gods goes to a banquet, that he is drawing his nourishment from the noetic realm and that he is returning to his own first principles and being satiated with transcendent and uniform goods from that source. And so the

ἀγαθῶν. ἐκεῖ τοίνυν καὶ οἱ Αἰθίοπες οἱ τῷ θείῳ φωτὶ καταλαμπόμενοι καὶ ὁ πρώτιστος Ὠκεανὸς ὁ τῆς νοητῆς πηγῆς ἀπορρέων, καὶ ἡ πλήρωσις ἐκεῖθεν τῷ τε δημιουργικῷ νῷ καὶ πᾶσι τοῖς ἐξηρτημένοις αὐτοῦ θεοῖς. |

10 Ἔτι τοίνυν Ὅμηρος μὲν ἀγαθότητι καὶ ἀνεκλείπτῳ δυνάμει διὰ πάντων φοιτώσῃ τῶν ὄντων καὶ γνώσει περιληπτικῇ τῶν ὅλων ἑνιαίως χαρακτηρίζει τὴν ἰδιότητα τῶν θεῶν· καὶ γὰρ θεοὶ **δωτῆρες ἑάων** φησὶν καί· **θεοὶ δέ τε πάντα δύνανται,** καὶ ἐν ἄλλοις· **θεοὶ δέ τε πάντα ἴσασιν.** |
15 ὁ δὲ Ἀθηναῖος ξένος ἐντεῦθεν ὁρμηθεὶς κατεσκεύασεν ἀδαμαντίνοις ὡς εἰπεῖν λόγοις τὴν ἐπὶ πάντα διήκουσαν πρόνοιαν τῶν θεῶν· καὶ γὰρ βούλεσθαι πάντα πληροῦν ἀγαθῶν τοὺς θεοὺς καὶ δύνασθαι (πάντα γὰρ ποδηγοῦσιν ἀνελάττωτοι κατὰ τὴν δύναμιν ὄντες) καὶ εἰδέναι τὸ
20 προσ|ῆκον αὐτοῖς. προσήκει δὲ ἄρα τοῖς πάντων αἰτίοις τὸ προνοεῖν τῶν σφετέρων γεννημάτων, τοῖς πάντων ἄρχουσιν τὸ κοσμεῖν τὰ ἀρχόμενα ὑπ᾽ αὐτῶν. οὔτ᾽ οὖν δι᾽ ἔνδειαν ἀγαθῶν τὴν πρόνοιαν ἀναιρετέον οὔτε δι᾽ ὕφεσιν δυνάμεως (πολλοῖς γὰρ ἡ μὲν τῆς εὐποιΐας ἔφεσις πάρεστιν, ἡ δὲ
25 | ἀσθένεια παραιρεῖται τὴν εὐεργετικὴν εἰς τοὺς ἄλλους ἐνέργειαν) οὔτε δι᾽ ἄγνοιαν τῶν ἐπιβαλλόντων αὐτοῖς ἔργων· οὔτε γὰρ ἑαυτοὺς οὔτε τὰ μεθ᾽ ἑαυτοὺς ἀγνοοῦσιν. ταῦτα δὴ οὖν ὁ Ἀθηναῖος ξένος τοῖς ἀνελέγκτοις
29 κατεδήσατο λο|γισμοῖς, οὐκ ἀλλαχόθεν ἢ παρ᾽ Ὁμήρου τὰς κοινὰς καὶ διὰ
K168 πάντων τῶν θείων γενῶν διηκούσας ἰδιότητας λαβών, τὴν || ἀγαθοειδῆ βούλησιν, τὴν ἀπερίληπτον δύναμιν, τὴν παντελῆ τῶν ὄντων νόησιν.

Πρὸς δὲ τοῖς εἰρημένοις καὶ τὰς παρ᾽ ἀμφοτέροις νεκυίας ἐνθυμηθῶμεν,
5 καὶ ὅπως Ὁμήρῳ μὲν τά τε ἄλλα | διεσκεύασται ποιητικῶς καὶ κατὰ τὴν

Ethiopians are there, radiant with divine light, and primal Ocean flowing from the noetic spring, and thence also comes satiety for the demiurgical intellect and for all the gods attached to it.

[e. The gods are all-powerful, omniscient, and providential: the *Laws*]

Moreover, Homer characterizes the specific qualities of the gods as goodness, uninterrupted power that moves through all those things that are, and knowledge uniformly embracing the universe. He calls the gods "givers of good things" [*Od.* 8.325] and says "the gods are capable of all things" [*Od.* 10.306], and elsewhere, "the gods know all things" [*Od.* 4.379].[268] The Athenian Stranger, starting from this, established by what we may call adamantine proofs the providence of the gods, penetrating all things,[269] because the gods want to fill everything with good things, and are able to—they guide everything while maintaining their power undiminished—and they know what is appropriate to everything. What is appropriate, on the other hand, for the causes of all things is to be provident over those things that have come to be through them and for the rulers of all things to set in order the things ruled by them. Providence is not to be denied either on the basis of a lack of good things or of capacity (for the impulse to convey benefits comes to many, but weakness deprives them of the capacity to do good to others) or on the basis of ignorance of the acts that would help the administered beings. The gods are ignorant neither of themselves nor of the beings set under them. Indeed, the Athenian Stranger firmly established these things by unimpeachable reasoning, taking from nowhere else but from Homer the specific characteristics that are common to all and penetrate all the classes of the gods: a will || shaped by the Good, unlimited power, and the perfect knowledge of things that are.

[f. The *nekyiai*: the *Republic*, *Phaedo*, and *Gorgias*]

Along with what has been said, let us consider the *nekyiai*[270] of both writers and how, among other things, the tradition of the various fates

---

268. All three phrases are formulaic and are echoed at other places in the poems.
269. *Leg.* 10.900c–907b.
270. Proclus mentions only the first *nekyia* of the *Odyssey*, Odysseus's narrative of his journey to the underworld in book 11, and not the so-called second *nekyia* in book

θείαν μανίαν καὶ ἡ τῶν διαφόρων ἐν Ἅιδου λήξεων παράδοσις (καὶ γὰρ κολαζομένους τινὰς καὶ κρινομένους εἰσήγαγεν, καὶ κρίνοντας ἄλλους καὶ καθαίροντας, καὶ τῶν κολάσεων ποικίλα εἴδη καὶ τῶν καθάρσεων τρόπους ἐξηλλαγμένους), τῷ δὲ αὖ Πλά|τωνι καὶ ταῦτα κατὰ τὸν Ὁμήρου ζῆλον πεπραγμάτευται. καὶ γὰρ ἐν Πολιτείᾳ καὶ ἐν Φαίδωνι καὶ ἐν Γοργίᾳ περὶ τῶν ἐν Ἅιδου ψυχῶν καὶ ὑπὸ τὴν βασιλείαν τοῦ Πλούτωνος τελουσῶν πολλὰ καὶ θαυμαστὰ διελήλυθεν, ἐν Φαίδωνι μὲν τοὺς τόπους διαφερόντως τοὺς ἐκεῖ καὶ τὰ | ὅλα δικαιωτήρια τῶν ψυχῶν ἀφηγούμενος, ἐν Πολιτείᾳ δὲ τὰς παντοίας τῶν κρινομένων τίσεις καὶ τὴν πορείαν αὐτῶν τὴν ὑπὸ γῆν καὶ τὰ δράματα τὰ περὶ αὐτοὺς διεξιών, ἐν δὲ τῷ Γοργίᾳ τῶν δικαστῶν <τὰς> τάξεις καὶ τὰς διαφορότητας προηγουμένως ἡμῖν ἀναφαίνων. καίτοι πανταχοῦ | πάντα ἂν εὕροις αὐτῷ μνήμης ἠξιωμένα, ἀλλ' οὐ μὲν πλείων ὁ περὶ τῶν δικαιωτηρίων λόγος, οὐ δὲ ὁ περὶ τῶν δικαστῶν αὐτῶν, οὐ δὲ ὁ περὶ τῶν κρινομένων ψυχῶν καὶ τῶν ποικίλων περὶ αὐτὰς παθημάτων.

Καὶ ὅτι ταῦτα κατὰ τὸν Ὁμήρου ζῆλον ὁ Πλάτων διέθηκεν, ἐνδείκνυταί που καὶ | αὐτὸς τῷ ποιητῇ τούτῳ μάρτυρι χρώμενος ἐν αὐτοῖς ἐκείνοις τοῖς λόγοις. καὶ γὰρ ὡς ὁ Μίνως χρυσοῦν ἔχων σκῆπτρον δικάζει καὶ ἐπισκοπεῖ τὴν τῶν λοιπῶν δικαστῶν κρίσιν, ἐκ τῆς Ὁμήρου νεκυίας εἰληφέναι συνομολογεῖ [Gorg. | 525d–e], καὶ ὅτι δυνάσται τινές εἰσιν καὶ τύραννοι καὶ βασιλεῖς οἱ τῶν μεγίστων ἁμαρτημάτων τὰς μεγίστας τιμω||ρίας ὑπέχοντες (Τιτυοὶ γὰρ καὶ Σίσυφοι καὶ Τάνταλοι, φησίν, καὶ παρ' Ὁμήρῳ κολάζονται [525d]), καὶ ὅτι μέγιστόν ἐστι τῶν τῆς γῆς χασμάτων καὶ ταῖς ψυχαῖς φρικωδέστατον δικαιωτήριον ὁ Τάρταρος· τούτου γάρ, φησὶν ὁ ἐν τῷ Φαί|δωνι Σωκράτης [112a], καὶ Ὅμηρος διαμνημονεύει λέγων·

τῆλε μάλ' ἦχι βάθιστον ὑπὸ χθονός ἐστι βέρεθρον. [Θ 14]

ἐπεὶ καὶ τῶν ποταμῶν ἐκεῖθεν τὴν ἱστορίαν παρείληφεν· | καὶ γὰρ ὅτι πάντων ἐστὶν Ὠκεανὸς ἐξωτάτω τῶν ῥευμάτων·

allocated in Hades is elaborated by Homer poetically and in the mode of divine madness (for he brought in certain individuals being punished or being judged, and judging others and purifying them, and the diverse forms of punishment and the various modes of purification), and again these things were worked up by Plato in imitation of Homer. In the *Republic*, the *Phaedo*, and the *Gorgias* he reveals many amazing things concerning the souls in Hades subject to the authority of Pluto, describing in the *Phaedo* [110b–115a] in particular the regions below and all of the places of punishment of souls, in the *Republic* [10.614b–621b] elaborating the various punishments of those who have been judged and their travels beneath the earth and the dramatic events that involve them, and in the *Gorgias* [523a–527a] primarily relating to us the classes of judges and their differences. While you would find that he deems all of these things everywhere worthy of mention, still in one place he emphasizes the places of punishment, in another the judges themselves, and in yet another the souls being judged and their diverse sufferings.

That Plato discussed these things in imitation of Homer he himself surely demonstrates when he cites the poet as witness in these very dialogues. He admits that he has taken from the *nekyia* of Homer the account of Minos passing judgment and holding a golden scepter and supervising the judgments of the other judges,[271] along with the idea that there are certain dynasts, tyrants, and kings who endure the greatest punishments for the greatest sins, since the Tityuses, || the Sisyphuses, and the Tantaluses, he says, are punished in Homer as well [*Gorg*. 525d–e], and finally the idea that the greatest of the chasms in the earth and the most horrifying place of punishment for souls is Tartarus.[272] The Socrates of the *Phaedo* says [112a] that Homer is referring to this when he says,

far away, where lies the deepest pit beneath the earth [*Il*. 8.14].

When he undertakes to describe the rivers there [112–113], he likewise borrows the account from Homer. He says that Ocean is the farthest out of all the streams,

---

24. What he calls the *nekyiai* of Plato will be seen to be all of the eschatological myths in the dialogues, but preeminently the Myth of Er in the *Republic*.

271. *Gorg*. 526c–d.
272. *Phd*. 111e, 112a.

Ὠκεανὸς μὲν πρῶτα, τὸν οὔπως ἔστι περῆσαι. [λ 158]

καὶ περὶ τῶν ἄλλων ὡσαύτως·

**Ἔνθα μὲν εἰς Ἀχέροντα Πυριφλεγέθων τε ῥέουσι |
Κωκυτός θ' ὅς δὴ Στυγὸς ὕδατός ἐστιν ἀπορρὼξ** [κ 513-514].

ὅθεν οἶμαι καὶ ὁ Σωκράτης Στύγιον αὐτὸν προσείρηκεν [Phaed. 113c]. ἐν δὲ τῇ Πολιτείᾳ [10,614b] τῆς νεκυίας ἀρχόμενος οὐκ Ἀλκίνου φησὶν ἀπόλογον ἐρεῖν, ἀλλὰ | ἀλκίμου τινὸς ἀνδρὸς Ἠρὸς τοῦ Ἀρμενίου τὸ γένος Παμφύλου, μονονουχὶ λέγων σαφῶς, ὅτι τὴν παρ' Ὁμήρῳ νέκυιαν ἑαυτῷ προθεὶς καὶ ἐκείνην παράδειγμα ποιησάμενος μέλλει καὶ περὶ τούτων διαλέγεσθαι τῶν ἐν ἐκείνῳ τῷ μύθῳ προκειμένων εἰς ἀφήγησιν. |

Ἀλλὰ μὴν καὶ εἰ τῶν ἐν Κρατύλῳ γεγραμμένων ἀναμνησθείημεν, μάθοιμεν ἂν καὶ ἐξ ἐκείνων, ὅτι διὰ πάντων ὡς εἰπεῖν τῶν ἐν φιλοσοφίᾳ σκεμμάτων εἰς τὴν Ὁμήρου ποίησιν ἀποβλέπων ὁ Πλάτων ἐκεῖθεν παραδέχεται τὰς πρώτας ὑποθέσεις τῶν λόγων. πρόκειται μὲν γὰρ αὐτῷ περὶ || ὀνομάτων ἐν ἐκείνῳ τῷ διαλόγῳ τὴν ἀληθεστάτην ἐκφῆναι θεωρίαν· διττῶν δὲ αὖ ὄντων ὀνομάτων καὶ διττοὺς ἐχόντων τῆς αἰτίας ἀπολογισμούς, τοὺς μὲν ἀγνώστους ἡμῖν, τοὺς δὲ γνωρίμους, ἑκατέρων τὸν Ὅμηρον ποιεῖται μάρτυρα | [392a].

Σαφέστατα γὰρ ἐκεῖνον διαστείλασθαι τά τε ἀνθρώπινα καὶ τὰ θεῖα τῶν ὀνομάτων, τὴν Βατίειαν καὶ τὴν Μυρίνην, καὶ Ξάνθον λέγοντα τὸν ποταμὸν καὶ Σκάμανδρον, καὶ τὴν χαλκίδα τὸ ὄρνεον καὶ τὴν κύμινδιν· καὶ τούτων τὰ μὲν νοερώτερα καὶ τῆς φύσεως τῶν ὑποκειμένων | τελέως ἀντεχόμενα πραγμάτων καὶ κατὰ τὸν αἰσθητὸν τύπον εὐπρεπέστερά τε καὶ εὐφωνότερα τῶν θεῶν ἔγγονα τιθέμενον, τὰ δὲ τοῖς εἰρημένοις ἅπασι τούτων λειπόμενα τῶν ἀνθρώπων·

Ocean first, impossible to cross [*Od.* 11.158],

and likewise, concerning the others:

There into Acheron flow Pyriphlegethon
and Cocytus, an outflow of the waters of the Styx [*Od.* 10.513–514].

From this passage, I believe, Socrates also used the adjective "Stygian."[273] In the *Republic*, he says at the beginning of the *nekyia*[274] that he is not going to recount the tale told to Alcinous but rather that of a brave man named Er, son of Armenius of the Pamphylian race, all but saying clearly that, placing the Homeric *nekyia* before him and using that for a model, he is going to talk about the things laid out in that myth in his narrative.

[g. Double names: the *Cratylus*]

If we also called to mind what was written in the *Cratylus*, we would learn there as well that, through the whole range, so to speak, of his speculations in philosophy, Plato contemplates the poetry of Homer and takes over from him the first propositions of his arguments. The task before him in this dialogue is to reveal the truest doctrine on || names. [Saying that] there are names that are double and that the explanations of their causes are double as well, some unknown to us and some known, he cites Homer as witness to both.

Homer, he says, distinguished very clearly between human and divine names, [speaking of a mound called] Batieia [by men] and Myrine [by gods],[275] and giving the river both the [divine] name Xanthos and [the human one] Scamander,[276] and the bird [men call] *chalkis* [the divine name] *kymindis* as well.[277] The more intellective of these, adhering perfectly to the nature of the things designated, and more attractive in their impact on the senses and more euphonious, he takes to be born of the gods, and those inferior to these utterances in all the ways just mentioned he takes to have a human origin.

---

273. *Phd.* 113c, for the region of the Cocytus.
274. *Rep.* 10.614b.
275. *Crat.* 392a7–8; *Il.* 2.811–814.
276. *Crat.* 391e4–392a3; *Il.* 20.74.
277. *Crat.* 392a3–7; *Il.* 14.289–291.

Καὶ τῶν ἀνθρωπείων αὖ τὰ μὲν εἰς ἐμφρονεστέρους ἀνάγοντα νομοθέτας, τῶν δὲ τοὺς ἀφρονε|στέρους ποιοῦντα κυρίους τῆς θέσεως, <ὡς> ἐν τοῖς περὶ τοῦ Ἀστυάνακτος καὶ τοῦ Σκαμανδρίου δεδήλωκε. ταύτας δὴ καὶ τοιαύτας ἀρχὰς ὁ Σωκράτης παρ' Ὁμήρου λαβὼν τῆς περὶ τῶν ὀνομάτων θεωρίας διορίζει, τί μέν ἐστιν αὐτῶν τὸ φύσει, τί δὲ τὸ θέσει, καὶ τίς μὲν ἡ πρὸς τὰ πρά|γματα αὐτῶν ὁμοιότης, τίς δὲ ἡ ἀπολισθάνουσα τῶν δηλουμένων ἀνομοιότης, καὶ ὅπως τὰ μὲν πρώτιστα τῶν ὀνομάτων καὶ ὅσα θεῖα συνυφέστηκεν τοῖς οὖσιν, τὰ δὲ δεύτερα ἀπεικασίαν τινὰ φέρεται τῶν ὄντων, τὰ δὲ πολλοστὰ ἀπὸ τῆς ἀληθείας καὶ τῆς τοιαύτης ὁμοιότητος ἀποπέπτωκεν· καὶ | ὅλως ἅπασαν ἐκείνην τὴν πραγματείαν Ὁμήρῳ καὶ τοῖς ἐνθέοις ποιηταῖς ἑπόμενος διεπραγματεύσατο.

Μὴ τοίνυν μηδὲ ἐκεῖνο παρῶμεν εἰς ἔνδειξιν ἐναργεστέραν τῆς τοῦ Πλάτωνος πρὸς Ὅμηρον φιλίας, ὅτι καὶ || τὴν οἰκονομίαν πολλαχοῦ ζηλοῖ τῶν Ὁμηρικῶν ὑποθέσεων. ὁ μὲν γὰρ τὴν Ὀδυσσέως πλάνην τριπλῆν ἡμῖν ἀφηγήσατο· καὶ γὰρ γινομένην αὐτὴν παραδίδωσι, καὶ ἐν διηγήσεσι τοῦ Ὀδυσσέως πρὸς τὸν Ἀλκίνουν, καὶ αὖ πάλιν ἐν τοῖς πρὸς | τὴν Πηνελόπην λόγοις συνεσπειραμένως ἅπασαν περιλαμβάνοντος. ὁ δὲ τὴν πολιτείαν τριπλασιάσας φαίνεται· καὶ γὰρ ἐν Πειραιεῖ τὴν πρώτην αὐτῆς ἔκφανσιν γενέσθαι φησίν, καὶ ἐν ἄστει διηγουμένου τοῦ Σωκράτους, καὶ ἐκ τρίτων συνοπτικῶς αὐτὴν πρὸ τῆς φυσιολογίας τοῖς ἀμφὶ Τίμαιον | καὶ Κριτίαν ἀπαγγέλλοντος.

Πάνυ γε οὐχ ὁρᾶτε τῆς Ὁμηρικῆς ποιήσεως ὑπερερῶντα τὸν Πλάτωνα καὶ τῶν ἐν αὐτῇ μυστικῶν διανοημάτων, ὃς καὶ τὴν φαινομένην αὐτοῦ ζηλοῖ μεταχείρησιν καί ἐστιν οὐκ ἐνθεάζων μόνον καὶ μύθους συντιθείς, ἀλλὰ καὶ φιλοσοφῶν καὶ ῥητορεύων Ὁμηρικός; | καὶ γὰρ ἡ τῆς μιμήσεως ἐνάργεια καὶ ἡ ποικιλία τῶν ἠθῶν καὶ ἡ τῶν ὀνομάτων ὥρα καὶ ἡ τῆς οἰκονομίας τέχνη καὶ ἡ τῶν σχημάτων ἐξαλλαγὴ τῆς Ὁμηρικῆς ἐστιν ἰδέας μεστή·

Of the human names, again, he attributes some to wiser lawmakers but makes less intelligent ones responsible for the establishment of others, as he shows in the discussion of Astyanax and Scamandrios.[278] Thus, taking these and similar principles of the theory of names from Homer, Socrates defines what part of them exists by nature and what part by convention, in what sense there is resemblance to their objects and in what sense dissimilarity, slipping away from the thing signified, and how the first of names, those that are divine, come to be along with the things, while the secondary ones bear a certain resemblance to those things, and the last fall far from truth and from resemblance of this sort. All in all, he has worked up this entire treatment following Homer and the inspired poets.

[h. Organization]

Let us not leave aside either, in the interest of demonstrating more clearly Plato's affection for Homer, the fact that he || also in many places imitates Homer's arrangement of his material. [Homer] told us the wanderings of Odysseus three times: he recounts them as they are happening, then in Odysseus's narrative to Alcinous, and finally in his account to Penelope, where he takes up the whole story in compressed form. [Plato,] on his side, presents his state three times: he says the first manifestation of it took place in the Piraeus, then [the second] when Socrates sets it out in detail in the city, and for a third time when he reports it comprehensively, before the inquiry into nature, to Timaeus and Critias and that gathering.

Do you not see clearly that Plato loves Homeric poetry deeply, along with the mystical conceptions within it, since he imitates even the superficial qualities of Homer's work and is Homeric not only when he is inspired and making myths but also in his philosophizing and his practice of rhetoric?[279] Indeed, the brilliance of the *mimesis*, the diversity of the characters, the beauty of the words, the craft of the overall organization and the variety of stylistic devices—all are full of the Homeric idea [of literary form].

---

278. *Crat.* 392b1–393b2.
279. Adding a question mark, with F.

Καὶ οὐχ οἱ τραγῳδιοποιοὶ μόνον πολλὰ τῶν παρ' Ὁμήρῳ βραχείας μνήμης ἠξιωμένων σκηνὰς καὶ ὑποθέσεις ἐποιήσαντο | τελείας, ἀλλὰ καὶ αὐτὸς ὁ Πλάτων ἐκ μικρᾶς αὐτῷ δεδομένης ἐκεῖθεν ἀρχῆς πραγματείας ὅλας καὶ διαλόγους πολυστίχους συνεγράψατο.

Φέρε γὰρ ἑνὸς ἐπιμνησθῶμεν, εἰ βούλεσθε, καὶ τοὺς ἐν Ἀλκιβιάδῃ [I 129 sqq.] τοῦ Σωκράτους θεωρήσωμεν λόγους, ἐν οἷς ἄλλο μὲν τὸ χρώ|μενον εἶναί φησιν ἐκεῖνος, ἄλλο δὲ τὸ ὄργανον· καὶ τὸ μὲν ἐν ὑπηρέτου μέρει τετάχθαι, τὸ δὲ ἐξῃρῆσθαι τῆς ἐκείνου φύσεως· καὶ τὸν ἕκαστον ἡμῶν οὔτε ἐν τῇ χείρονι μοίρᾳ τὴν ὑπόστασιν ἔχειν οὔτε ἐξ ἀμφοτέρων συμπεπληρῶσθαι, τοῦ τε ὀργάνου λέγω καὶ τοῦ χρωμένου, ἀλλὰ κατ' αὐτὸ | μόνον τελέως ἀφωρίσθαι τὸ χρώμενον.

Ὅθεν δὴ κατὰ τὴν || ψυχὴν αὐτὸν ὑφεστάναι τὴν τῶν σωματικῶν ὀργάνων ἐξῃρημένην ἐπιδείκνυσιν, καὶ ταύτην οὐ πᾶσαν, ἀλλὰ τὴν νοεράν, ἣν καὶ οὑτωσί πως αὐτὸ τὸ αὐτὸ προσείρηκεν ἐν ἐκείνοις. αὐτὸ μὲν γὰρ καὶ ἡ ψυχὴ πᾶσα πρὸς τὸ ὀστρε|ῶδες ὄργανον, τὸ δὲ ὄντως αὐτὸ τοῦτο ἄρα ἦν ἐκεῖνο τὸ νοερὸν εἶδος τῆς ψυχῆς. ταύτην δὴ οὖν σύμπασαν τῶν δογμάτων τὴν θεωρίαν περὶ τῆς φύσεως ἡμῶν ἐκ τῶν Ὁμηρικῶν ποιημάτων μοι δοκεῖ παραλαβὼν τοῖς ἀποδεικτικοῖς λόγοις ἱκανῶς καταδήσασθαι.

Καὶ γὰρ ἐκεῖνος πρῶτος διέ|κρινεν τὸν ἕκαστον ἡμῶν ἀπὸ τῶν ἐξηρτημένων ὀργάνων καὶ διεστήσατο καλῶς τὰ εἴδωλα τῶν πρωτουργῶν ὑποστάσεων· δηλοῖ δὲ ὁ σοφώτατος Ὀδυσσεὺς ἐν Νεκυίᾳ [λ 601 sqq.] τὸν Ἡρακλέα λέγων ἰδεῖν **γυμνὸν τόξον ἔχοντα** καὶ προστιθεὶς **εἴδωλον,** |

αὐτὸς δὲ μετ' ἀθανάτοισι <θεοῖσιν>
τέρπεται ἐν θαλίῃ καὶ ἔχει καλλίσφυρον Ἥβην,

καὶ οὐδὲν ἄλλο ἐνδεικνύμενος, ἢ ὅτι τὴν μὲν ἀληθινὴν τοῦ Ἡρακλέους οὐσίαν ἐν τῇ ψυχῇ τίθεσθαι προσήκει, τὸ δὲ ἐξημμένον τῆς ψυχῆς εἴδωλον

[i. Plato develops and expands ideas briefly stated by Homer: the *First Alcibiades*]

Not only have the writers of tragedies made scenes and even entire plays out of many things that were thought worthy only of brief mention by Homer, but Plato himself, from small beginnings derived thence, has also composed entire treatises and long dialogues.

Let us call to mind just one, if you will, and let us examine the words of Socrates in the *Alcibiades*,[280] where he makes a distinction between the *user* and the *tool* and places the latter in the category of "servant" while he takes the other out of that category; he goes on to state that each one of us does not have his being in the lower part,[281] nor are we composed of both—the user and the tool, I mean—but [each of us] is perfectly defined as the *user*.

In this, of course, he shows that the existence of each of us is a function || of the soul, which is separate from the body, and not of the entire soul, but the intellective part, which in this dialogue he calls "the thing itself" [αὐτὸ τὸ αὐτό]. For the "thing" [αὐτό] is the entire soul in contrast to the ostraceous tool,[282] and so "that which is truly the thing itself" [τὸ … ὄντως αὐτὸ τοῦτο] is therefore the intellective form of the soul. Indeed, he seems to me to have taken this entire examination of the doctrines concerning our nature from the Homeric poems and to have tied it down securely with apodeictic proofs.

[Homer] was the first to distinguish the individual human being from the tools that depend on it [i.e., the body], and he likewise distinguished "images" from primordial substances. The wise Odysseus reveals this in the *nekyia*, saying he saw Heracles "with a naked bow" [*Od.* 11.607] and adding that this was an "image" because

> he himself, among the immortal [gods]
> is happy in the midst of good cheer, and has Hebe of the pretty
> ankles [*Od.* 11.602–603].

He is demonstrating nothing else here than that it is correct to place the true being of Heracles in his soul, while the "image" attached to the soul

---

280. *Alc.* 1 129b–130c.
281. I.e., the body, the "tool" of the present image.
282. I.e., the body.

ὄργανον ἐκείνου καὶ ἀπει|κασίαν πρὸς ἐκεῖνον φερόμενον, ἀλλ' οὐκ ἐκεῖνον ὑπολαμβάνειν. ἄνωθεν <ἄρα> ἀπὸ τῆς Ὁμηρικῆς ὑφηγήσεως ἤρτηται τὰ περὶ τοῦ ἀνθρώπου τῷ Πλάτωνι δοκοῦντα, μηδὲ τῶν ὀνομάτων ἀποσχομένῳ τῶν Ὁμηρικῶν. τὸ γὰρ αὐτὸ τὸ αὐτὸ πόθεν ἀλλαχόθεν ἂν φήσαιμεν ἢ ἐκ τοῦ **αὐτὸς | δὲ μετ' ἀθανάτοισι θεοῖσιν** ἔχειν τὴν ἀφορμήν, καὶ τὸ τὴν σωματικὴν φύσιν εἴδωλον τῆς ἀληθινῆς οὐσίας ἀποκαλεῖν πῶς οὐχὶ παντὶ δῆλον ἐκεῖθεν μετενηνεγμένον;
ἐπεὶ καὶ τὸ

**ἦλθε δ' ἐπὶ ψυχὴ Θηβαίου Τειρεσίαο
χρύσεον σκῆπτρον ἔχων** [λ 90–91], |

σαφῶς τὸν ἕκαστον ἡμῶν ἐν ψυχῇ διορίζεται τὴν ὕπαρξιν ἔχειν. ‖

**Πῶς ἄν τις ἀπολογήσαιτο πρὸς τὰ ἐν Φαίδρῳ
ῥηθέντα περὶ Ὁμήρου, ἐν οἷς δοκεῖ τὸν Στησίχορον
ὡς μουσικώτερον προκρίνειν.**

Ἀλλὰ τούτων μὲν πολλὰ ἄν εὕροι τις παραδείγματα | πρὸς τὴν ἑκατέρου πραγματείαν ἀποβλέπων. ἐπεὶ δὲ ταῦτα ὑπέμνησται, μικρὰ περὶ τῶν ἐν Φαίδρῳ γεγραμμένων προσθέντες τοὺς περὶ τῆς ποιητικῆς ἀνακινήσωμεν λόγους, οὓς ὁ ἐν Πολιτείᾳ Σωκράτης ἐν τῷ δεκάτῳ διέξεισιν.

Ἴσως γὰρ ἄν τινες καὶ σφόδρα τὸν Πλάτωνα φαῖεν τὴν Ὁμήρου | δόξαν ἀφανίζειν καὶ ἐκ τῶν ἐν τῷ Φαίδρῳ [243a] περὶ τῆς παλινῳδίας εἰρημένων. **ἔστι γάρ**, φησίν,

τοῖς ἁμαρτάνουσιν περὶ μυθολογίαν καθαρμὸς ἀρχαῖος, ὃν Ὅμηρος μὲν οὐκ ᾔσθητο, Στησίχορος δέ. τῶν γὰρ ὀμμάτων στερηθεὶς διὰ τὴν Ἑλένης κακηγορίαν | οὐκ ἠγνόησεν ὥσπερ Ὅμηρος, ἀλλ' ἅτε μουσικὸς ὢν ἔγνω τὴν αἰτίαν, καὶ ποιεῖ εὐθύς· οὐκ ἔστ' ἔτυμος λόγος οὗτος·

should be considered a *tool* of Heracles that bears a resemblance to him but is not he himself. Plato's ideas about man thus, once again, depend on the Homeric precedent, and he has not even rejected Homer's vocabulary. For where else would we say the expression "the thing itself" [αὐτὸ τὸ αὐτό] comes from, except from "he himself among the immortal gods" [αὐτὸς δὲ μετ' ἀθανάτοισι θεοῖσι]? Likewise, to call the substance of the body an "image" of the true being, is it not clear to everyone that this is transferred from the Homeric poems as well?

Furthermore, the verses,

> the soul of Theban Tiresias came upon it,
> holding a golden scepter [*Od*. 11.90–91],

clearly define the position that each of us has our existence in the soul. ||

(4) How one might answer what is said about Homer in the *Phaedrus*, where [Socrates] seems to judge Stesichorus the greater artist?

[a. The problem]

One would find many examples of these things by looking into the works of Homer and Plato. Now that this has been discussed, let us add just a word on the material in the *Phaedrus* and then let us go on to the discussions of poetics that Socrates develops in the tenth book of the *Republic*.

Some might say that Plato utterly destroys the reputation of Homer by what he says in the *Phaedrus* about the palinode.[283] He says,

> There exists an ancient purification for those who are sinners in the matter of mythology, which Homer did not know, but Stesichorus did. Having been deprived of his eyes on account of his slander of Helen, Stesichorus did not remain ignorant of the cause, as Homer did, but inspired by the Muses he perceived it and immediately composed [the poem that begins] "That story is not true" [*Phdr*. 243a],

---

283. Stesichorus, who died in the mid-sixth century, was said by Plato and other later writers to have lost his sight because of some slander of Helen but to have recanted (in his so-called "palinode") and had his sight restored. The *Phaedrus* passage cited above may be the earliest version of the story.

καὶ τὰ τούτοις ἐφεξῆς, ἐν οἷς τά τε ἄλλα δῆλός ἐστιν, ὡς ἂν φαῖεν οἱ τῶν τοιούτων ἀντιλαμβανόμενοι ῥημάτων, τὸν Ὅμηρον λοιδορῶν, καὶ ὅτι Στησιχόρου | καταδεέστερος εἰς τὸ γνῶναί τε τὴν αἰτίαν τῶν δαιμονίων μηνιμάτων καὶ γνόντα διὰ τῆς παλινῳδίας ἱλάσασθαι, ἐπεὶ καὶ τὸ κακηγορῆσαι τὴν Ἑλένην παῖδα τοῦ μεγίστου Διὸς λεγομένην καὶ τὸ δι' ἔνδειαν μουσικῆς ἀγνοῆσαι τὸ πάθος δόξειεν ἂν μεγάλην μοῖραν ἔχειν τῆς περὶ αὐτὸν | βλασφημίας.

Ἀλλ' οὖν καὶ πρὸς ταῦτα λεκτέον, ὅτι Στησίχορος μὲν ὁ Ἱμεραῖος πάντα τὸν περὶ τῆς Ἑλένης μῦθον ὡς λόγον ὄντα καὶ γεγονότων μόνον πραγμάτων ἀφήγησιν παραδεξά||μενος καὶ κατὰ τοῦτον δὴ τὸν τρόπον τὴν περὶ αὐτοῦ ποίησιν διαθεὶς εἰκότως καὶ δίκης τυχεῖν καὶ διὰ τὴν ἐκ τῆς μουσικῆς ὠφέλειαν ἐπιγνῶναι τὴν ἑαυτοῦ πλημμέλειαν λέγεται, Ὅμηρος δὲ κατ' ἄλλην οἶμαι καὶ τελεωτέραν τῆς | ψυχῆς ἕξιν ἀποστὰς μὲν τῶν ἐν αἰσθήσει φερομένων καλῶν καὶ τῆς φαινομένης ἁπάσης ἁρμονίας τὴν ἑαυτοῦ νόησιν ὑπεριδρύσας, εἰς δὲ τὴν ἀφανῆ καὶ ὄντως οὖσαν ἁρμονίαν ἀνατείνας τὸν τῆς ψυχῆς νοῦν καὶ περιαχθεὶς εἰς τὸ ἀληθινὸν κάλλος ὑπὸ τῶν τὰ τοιαῦτα διαμυθολογεῖν | εἰωθότων ἀφαιρεθῆναι τῶν ὀμμάτων εἴρηται καὶ τοιοῦτόν τι παθεῖν, οἷον δὴ καὶ αὐτὸς τὸν Δημόδοκον τὸν παρὰ τοῖς Φαίαξιν ᾠδὸν πεπονθέναι φησίν, ὃν ὁ θεὸς ὁ τῆς μουσικῆς χορηγὸς

ὀφθαλμῶν μὲν ἄμερσε, δίδου δ' ἡδεῖαν ἀοιδήν | [θ 64].

καὶ γὰρ τοῦτον ἄντικρυς τῆς ἐνθεαστικῆς αὐτοῦ ζωῆς παράδειγμα προεστήσατο, καὶ διὰ τοῦτο τῆς μὲν ἐμφανοῦς ἁπάσης αὐτὸν ἁρμονίας καὶ τοῦ κάλλους διὰ τὴν ἐκ τῆς Μούσης κατακωχὴν ἐξῃρῆσθαι λέγει, τοῖς δὲ νοεροῖς περὶ | θεῶν καὶ μυστικοῖς διανοήμασιν τὰς ἑαυτοῦ διαποικίλλειν ἐνεργείας.

Καὶ οὐχ Ὅμηρος μόνον καὶ Δημόδοκος ἐκεῖνος, ἀλλὰ καὶ Ὀρφεὺς μυθολογεῖται τοιαῦτα ἄττα τραγικῶς παθεῖν διὰ τὴν ἐν μουσικῇ τελέαν ζωήν· σπαραχθεὶς γὰρ καὶ μερισθεὶς παντοίως τὸν τῇδε βίον ἀπολιπεῖν, ἐπειδὴ μερι|στῶς οἶμαι καὶ διῃρημένως αὐτοῦ μετέσχον οἱ τότε τῆς μουσικῆς καὶ ὅλην ἅμα καὶ παντελῆ τὴν ἐπιστήμην οὐ δεδύνηνται

and so forth.

It is clear from this, as those who latch onto such remarks might say, that he is insulting Homer because, among other things, he was inferior to Stesichorus in the business of recognizing the cause of the anger of the daemons and then, once he knew it, propitiating them through the palinode. Taken together, the slander of Helen, who is said to be the daughter of greatest Zeus, and his ignorance, stemming from lack of musical ability, regarding what happened to him would seem to constitute the major part of his defamation of Homer.

[b. Proclus's response]

Now one must reply to this that Stesichorus of Himera, accepting the whole myth about Helen as a true account and simply a narrative of events that actually occurred, || and having composed his poem about it in this mode, is rightly said both to have paid the penalty and by virtue of his musical skill to have recognized his error. Homer, on the other hand, I believe acted according to another and more perfect condition of the soul, and, withdrawing from those good things conveyed by the senses and establishing his own thought above and beyond the entire superficial harmony and extending the intellect of his soul into the invisible and truly existing harmony and carried off into the true beauty, he was said, by those accustomed to mythologize such things, to have been deprived of his eyes and to have had happen to himself the same sort of thing he says that Demodocus the bard of the Phaeacians suffered, from whom the god who leads the Muses

took away his eyes, but gave sweet song [*Od.* 8.641].

Homer set this man up as a model of his own inspired existence, and so he says that Demodocus was deprived of the whole visible harmony and beauty through being possessed by the Muses, but that he ornamented his creations with intellective and mystical conceptions concerning the gods.

Not only Homer and this Demodocus but Orpheus as well is said in the myths to have suffered things of this sort, in the tragic mode, on account of the perfection he attained in the art inspired by the Muses. He is said to have left this life by being dismembered and torn to pieces because, I think, his contemporaries participated only partially and in a fragmented manner in his music, and they were unable to receive his wisdom whole

δέξασθαι. τὸ δ' οὖν ἀκρότατον αὐτῆς μέρος καὶ πρώτιστον οἱ τὴν Λέσβον οἰκοῦντες παρεδέξαντο· καί που διὰ τοῦτο καὶ τὴν κεφαλὴν ὁ μῦθος τὴν ἐκείνου σπαραχθέν|τος εἰς Λέσβον ἐξενεχθῆναί φησιν.

Ἀλλ' Ὀρφεὺς μὲν ἄτε || τῶν Διονύσου τελετῶν ἡγεμὼν γενόμενος τὰ ὅμοια παθεῖν ὑπὸ τῶν μύθων εἴρηται τῷ σφετέρῳ θεῷ (καὶ γὰρ ὁ σπαραγμὸς τῶν Διονυσιακῶν ἕν ἐστιν συνθημάτων), Ὅμηρος δὲ ἀφαιρεθῆναι τῶν ὀμμάτων λέγεται, διότι δὴ πᾶν τὸ | φαινόμενον κάλλος ὑπερδραμὼν καὶ τὸν ἐνταῦθα τῶν ψυχῶν ἱστορήσας πόλεμον ἐπὶ τὴν νοερὰν ἑαυτὸν ἀνήγαγεν τοῦ κάλλους θεωρίαν.

τοῦτο γάρ φησιν καὶ ὁ ἐν τῷ Φαίδρῳ Σωκράτης·

τὸ τῇδε κάλλος διὰ τῆς ἐναργεστάτης τῶν αἰσθήσεων κατειλήφαμεν, στίλβον ἐναργέστατα. | ὄψις γὰρ ἡμῖν ὀξυτάτη τῶν διὰ τοῦ σώματος αἰσθήσεων ἔρχεται, ἡ φρόνησις οὐχ ὁρᾶται [250d].

Τὸν τοίνυν ὑπεριδόντα μὲν τοῦ ὁρατοῦ κάλλους, φρονήσει δὲ καὶ νοερᾷ ζωῇ τὴν οἰκείαν ἐνέργειαν ἐπιτρέψαντά φασιν οἱ τραγικώτεροι τῶν μύθων καὶ αὐτῶν ἀφαιρεθῆναι τῶν | ὀμμάτων διὰ τὴν τῆς Ἑλένης κακηγορίαν· ἅπαν γὰρ οἶμαι τὸ περὶ τὴν γένεσιν κάλλος ἐκ τῆς δημιουργίας ὑποστὰν διὰ τῆς Ἑλένης οἱ μῦθοι σημαίνειν ἐθέλουσιν, περὶ ὃ καὶ τῶν ψυχῶν πόλεμος τὸν ἀεὶ χρόνον συγκεκρότηται, μέχρις ἂν αἱ νοερώτεραι τῶν ἀλογωτέρων εἰδῶν τῆς ζωῆς κρατή|σασαι περιαχθῶσιν ἐντεῦθεν εἰς ἐκεῖνον τὸν τόπον, ἀφ' οὗ τὴν ἀρχὴν ὡρμήθησαν.

Τὴν δὲ περίοδον ἄρα ταύτην ὁ μέν τις δεκέτη προσείρηκεν, ὁ δὲ μυριέτη· διαφέρει δὲ οὐδὲν οὕτως ἢ ἐκείνως λέγειν. καὶ γὰρ ἡ χιλιὰς μία περίοδός ἐστιν ἀπὸ γενέσεως αὖθις εἰς γένεσιν ἄγουσα τὰς ψυχάς· | εἴτε τοίνυν ἐννέα χιλιάδας ἐτῶν περὶ γῆν αἱ ψυχαὶ καλινδούμεναι κατὰ τὴν δεκάτην ἀποκαθίστανται, εἴτε ἐννταέτει χρόνῳ τῷ περὶ τὴν γένεσιν προσκαρτερήσασαι πολέμῳ κρατεῖν μὲν τοῦ βαρβαρικοῦ κλύδωνος ἐν τῷ δεκάτῳ, περιάγεσθαι δὲ εἰς || τὰς συννόμους ἑαυτῶν οἰκήσεις λέγονται, πάντως που δῆλον, ὅτι τὸν τῶν τοιούτων ἐν τῷ κόσμῳ πραγμάτων φιλοθεάμονα καὶ ἀπὸ τῶν ἐμφανῶν ἀνηγμένον καὶ τῶν εἰκόνων εἰς τὴν

and entire. In any case, those who live on Lesbos received the first and highest part of that wisdom, and it is for this reason, presumably, that the myth says that when he was torn apart his head was carried off to Lesbos.

Orpheus, because || he was the founder of the rites of Dionysus, is said by the myths to have suffered the same fate as his god (since the *sparagmos* [dismembering] is one of the symbols of the Dionysian rites]), while Homer is said to have ben deprived of his eyes because he transcended all visible beauty and because, telling the story of the battle of souls here below, he drew himself up to the intellective contemplation of beauty.

Socrates says this in the *Phaedrus*:

> We grasp this beauty, radiant with clarity, through the clearest of our senses, vision, for this is the sharpest of the senses of the body—yet we cannot use it to perceive wisdom. [*Phdr.* 250d].

Now, the more theatrical of the myths say that this man who scorned visible beauty and turned over his own activity to wisdom and to the life of the mind had his eyes taken away on account of the slander of Helen. The myths want to indicate, I believe, through Helen the whole of that beauty which has to do with the sphere in which things come to be and pass away and which stems from creation. It is over this beauty that eternal war rages among souls, until the more intellective are victorious over the less rational forms of life and are brought back to the place from which they came in the first place.[284]

The duration of this the one calls ten years[285] and the other ten thousand [*Phdr.* 248e], but it makes no difference which one says. One thousand years is the period that leads souls from one birth to the next. Whether, then, they are said to be tossed about on earth for nine millennia and restored in the tenth, or whether they are said to have persisted in the war over γένεσις for nine years and to have overcome the barbarous flood in the tenth, when they are returned to || their legitimate homes, it is presumably clear, in any case, that the mythoplasts are saying, quite rightly, that he who loved to contemplate such spectacles in the cosmos

---

284. This comprehensive view of the meaning of the Troy tale can be glimpsed elsewhere in Neoplatonist accounts of the *Iliad* and *Odyssey*. See Lamberton 1986, 199–200.

285. Cf. *Il.* 2.134, among other indications that Homer gives ten years as the length of the Trojan War.

ἀφανῆ ταῖς αἰσθήσεσιν ἡμῶν θεωρίαν εἰκότως | τυφλὸν οἱ μυθοπλάσται γεγονέναι λέγουσιν. ἔπρεπεν δὲ ἄρα τοῖς διὰ συμβόλων ἀεὶ τὴν περὶ τῶν ὄντων ἀλήθειαν κατακρύπτουσιν καὶ τὴν περὶ αὐτῶν φήμην συμβολικώτερον παραδοθῆναι τοῖς ὕστερον. Οὐκ ἄρα Ὁμήρου Στησίχορος μουσικώτερος (οὐδὲ γὰρ τὰ αὐτὰ παθήματα περὶ ἑκάτερον | συμβέβηκεν, εἰ μὴ κατὰ τὸ φαινόμενον μόνον τοῦ μύθου πρόσχημα) οὐδὲ Ὁμήρῳ παλινῳδίας ἔδει πρὸς τὸ θεῖον ἐπιστρέψαντι κάλλος, ἀλλὰ Στησιχόρῳ πέρα τοῦ μέτρου τὸν περὶ τῆς Ἑλένης μῦθον φιλοφρονησαμένῳ.

Εἰ δὲ ὁ Σωκράτης ἐν ἐκείνοις τῷ φαινομένῳ χρώμενος ἡμαρτηκέναι | φησὶν τὸν Ὅμηρον καὶ ἁμαρτόντα τὰ αὐτὰ τῷ Στησιχόρῳ παθεῖν, οὐ θαυμαστόν, ἐπεὶ καὶ ἑαυτὸν ὡσαύτως ἁμαρτεῖν περὶ τὸν πρότερον λόγον φησὶν οὐχ ἁμαρτὼν σαφῶς·

— **νῦν δ' ᾔσθημαι τὸ ἁμάρτημα.**
— **λέγεις δὲ δὴ τί;**
— **δεινόν, ὦ Φαῖδρε, δεινὸν λόγον αὐτός τε ἐκόμισας ἐμέ | τε ἠνάγκασας εἰπεῖν.**
— **πῶς δή;**
— **εὐήθη καὶ ὑπό τι ἀσεβῆ, οὗ τί ἂν εἴη δεινότερον** [242d].

ὥσπερ οὖν αὐτὸς ὡς λοιδορήσας τὸν ὑβριστὴν ἔρωτα καὶ ὃν οἱ θεοὶ **πνιγμὸν ἔρωτος ἀληθοῦς** προσειρήκασιν ἡμαρτηκέναι λέγει, καθ' ὅσον ἀντὶ τῆς τοῦ θείου καὶ ἀναγωγοῦ τῶν | ψυχῶν ἔρωτος θεωρίας περὶ τὸ ἔσχατον αὐτοῦ καὶ ἔνυλον εἴδωλον ἐστράφη, τὸν αὐτὸν τρόπον καὶ Ὅμηρον περὶ τὴν Ἑλένην ἁμαρτεῖν ἂν λέγοι, καθ' ὅσον τὸν τῆς ψυχῆς νοῦν εἰς τὴν θέαν τοῦ ἐμφανοῦς κάλλους κατήγαγεν· ἁμάρτημα γάρ ἐστιν ψυχῆς ἡ τῶν ἐσχάτων κατανόησις ὡς πρὸς τὴν || ἄχραντον καὶ τελείαν τῶν ὄντως ὄντων περιωπήν. τοσαῦτα

καὶ περὶ τῶν ἐν Φαίδρῳ γεγραμμένων εἰς Ὅμηρον εἴχομεν λέγειν.

and who was borne up from the visible and from images to that contemplation that is beyond our senses "became blind." It was fitting that the traditions regarding those who habitually concealed with symbols the truth regarding reality should also be passed down to those who came later in a more symbolic manner. Stesichorus was not a more inspired poet than Homer (nor did the two experience the same things, except according to the visible screen of the myth), nor did Homer, directed as he was toward the divine beauty, have any need of a palinode, though Stesichorus, who embraced the myth of Helen in an immoderate way, did.

If Socrates, looking only at the literal meaning of these stories, says that Homer made a mistake, and in consequence suffered the same fate as Stesichorus, this is no wonder, for he himself admits that he made a similar mistake in the speech immediately preceding, though it was not clear that he had done so:

— Now I see my mistake.
— What mistake do you mean?
— That was a terrible speech, Phaedrus, that you brought along, and you forced me to deliver an equally terrible one.
— How so?
— It was a silly thing, and rather blasphemous—what could be more terrible? [*Phdr.* 242d].

Just in the same way that he says that he has made a mistake by railing at domineering love (which the gods call "stifling of true love"[286]), in that he turned his attention to the furthest removed, material image of love, rather than contemplate that love that is divine and elevates souls, he might say that Homer made the same mistake about Helen, in that he drew the intellect of his soul down to the contemplation of physical beauty. It is a mistake for the soul to take cognizance of the lowest things, as against the || pure and perfect transcendent contemplation of those things that truly exist.

This is what we are able to say about the things written in the *Phaedrus* about Homer.

---

286. *Or. chald.* frag. 45, des Places.

Τίνες εἰσὶν αἱ τρεῖς ἕξεις τῶν ψυχῶν, καὶ πῶς |
τὴν ποιητικὴν τριττὴν ἀποδείξομεν κατὰ ταύτας συν-
διαιρουμένην τὰς τρεῖς ἕξεις ἐν ἡμῖν.

Εἶεν· ἀλλ' ἐπὶ τοὺς περὶ τῆς ποιητικῆς λόγους ἐντεῦθεν τραπώμεθα καὶ θεωρήσωμεν, τίνα μὲν γένη τῆς κατὰ Πλάτωνα ποιητικῆς ἐστιν, εἰς ποίαν δὲ ἀποβλέπων ἐν τῷ δε|κάτῳ τῆς Πολιτείας τοὺς κατ' αὐτῆς ἐλέγχους διεξελήλυθεν, ὅπως δὲ ἄρα κἂν τούτοις Ὅμηρος ἐξῃρημένος ἀποδείκνυται τῶν τοῖς πολλοῖς ποιηταῖς προσηκόντων ἐλέγχων.

Ἵν' οὖν καὶ ταῦτα γένηται σαφῆ, τὴν ἀρχὴν τῆς περὶ τούτων διδασκαλίας ἐντεῦθεν λάβωμεν. τριττὰς ἐν | ψυχῇ εἶναί φαμεν ὡς τὸ ὅλον εἰπεῖν ζωάς·

τὴν μὲν ἀρίστην καὶ τελεωτάτην, καθ' ἣν συνάπτεται τοῖς θεοῖς καὶ ζῇ τὴν ἐκείνοις συγγενεστάτην καὶ δι' ὁμοιότητος ἄκρας ἡνωμένην ζωήν, οὐχ ἑαυτῆς <u>οὖσα</u>, ἀλλ' ἐκείνων, ὑπερδραμοῦσα μὲν τὸν ἑαυτῆς νοῦν, ἀνεγείρασα δὲ τὸ ἄρρητον | σύνθημα τῆς τῶν θεῶν ἑνιαίας ὑποστάσεως καὶ συνάψασα τῷ ὁμοίῳ τὸ ὅμοιον, τῷ ἐκεῖ φωτὶ τὸ ἑαυτῆς φῶς, τῷ ὑπὲρ οὐσίαν πᾶσαν καὶ ζωὴν ἑνὶ τὸ ἑνοειδέστατον [τὴν] τῆς οἰκείας οὐσίας τε καὶ ζωῆς.

Τὴν δὲ ταύτης μὲν δευτέραν πρεσβείᾳ τε καὶ δυνάμει, μέσην δὲ ἐν μέσῃ τῇ ψυχῇ τε|ταγμένην, καθ' ἣν ἐπιστρέφει μὲν εἰς ἑαυτὴν ἀπὸ τῆς ἐνθέου καταβᾶσα ζωῆς, νοῦν δὲ καὶ ἐπιστήμην προστησαμένη τῆς ἐνεργείας ἀρχὴν ἀνελίττει μὲν τὰ πλήθη τῶν λόγων, θεᾶται δὲ τὰς παντοίας τῶν εἰδῶν ἐξαλλαγάς, εἰς ταὐτὸν δὲ συνάγει τό τε νοοῦν καὶ τὸ νοούμενον, ἀπεικονίζεται δὲ || τὴν νοερὰν οὐσίαν ἐν ἑνὶ τὴν τῶν νοητῶν φύσιν περιλαβοῦσα.

Τρίτην δὲ ἄλλην ἐπὶ ταύταις τὴν συμφερομένην ταῖς καταδεεστέραις

ESSAY 6, BOOK 2   257

(5) We shall demonstrate the three conditions of the soul and how there are three kinds of poetry divided according to these three conditions within ourselves.

[a. The problem]

Now, then, let us turn from this to the discourses on poetics and let us consider, first, what kinds of poetry there are, according to Plato, and then which sort he was referring to when, in the tenth book of the *Republic*, he elaborated the accusations against it, and, finally, how even here Homer is shown to be exempted from the criticisms that apply to most poets.

[b. The three lives of the soul]

So that these things may be clear, let us take up our instruction about them from this point of departure: generally speaking there are, we say, three kinds of life of the soul:

(1) The best and the perfect life, in which the soul is contiguous with the gods and lives the life that is most closely related to them and made one by its extreme resemblance to them. The soul belongs not to the itself but to them,[287] surpassing its own intellect and awakening in itself the secret symbol of the unified substance of the gods, and attaching like to like, the soul's own light to the transcendent light and the most unified element of its own being and life to the One beyond all being and life.

(2) The life that comes after this one in rank and power, situated as a mean in the middle of the soul, in which the soul returns within itself, coming down from the divine life and setting intellect and wisdom as the first principle of its activity, elaborates the multiplicity of logoi and contemplates the varied transformations of the forms, draws together the knower and the known into the same entity, and reproduces the image of the || intellective substance, drawing together into one the nature of the noetic objects.

(3) Another, third life after these, drawn along with these lower powers [in our immediate environment] and acting with them. It makes use of

---

287. Reading οὖσα in 177,18, with b (the Basel edition of 1534: see addendum 2 to the introduction, xxxiii, and F.'s comments ad loc.).

δυνάμεσιν καὶ μετ' ἐκείνων ἐνεργοῦσαν, φαντασίαις τε καὶ αἰσθήσεσιν ἀλόγοις προσχρωμένην καὶ | πάντη τῶν χειρόνων ἀναπιμπλαμένην.

Τούτων δὴ οὖν τῶν τριττῶν τῆς ζωῆς εἰδῶν ἐν ταῖς ψυχαῖς θεωρουμένων κατὰ τὴν ὁμοίαν τάξιν καὶ τὴν τῆς ποιητικῆς νοήσωμεν διάκρισιν ἄνωθεν συμπροϊούσης ταῖς πολυειδέσι τῆς ψυχῆς ζωαῖς καὶ εἰς πρῶτά τε καὶ μέσα καὶ | ἔσχατα γένη τῆς ἐνεργείας ποικιλλομένης.

Καὶ γὰρ ταύτης ἡ μέν ἐστιν ἀκροτάτη καὶ πλήρης τῶν θείων ἀγαθῶν, καὶ αὐτοῖς ἐνιδρύουσα τὴν ψυχὴν τοῖς αἰτίοις τῶν ὄντων, κατά τινά τε ἕνωσιν ἄρρητον εἰς ταὐτὸν ἄγουσα τῷ πληροῦντι τὸ πληρούμενον, καὶ τὸ μὲν ἀΰλως καὶ ἀναφῶς ὑποστρων|νύουσα πρὸς τὴν ἔλλαμψιν, τὸ δὲ προκαλουμένη πρὸς τὴν μετάδοσιν τοῦ φωτός,

μιγνυμένων δ' ὀχετῶν πυρὸς ἀφθίτου ἔργα τελοῦσα

κατὰ τὸ λόγιον, ἕνα δὲ σύνδεσμον θεῖον ἀπεργαζομένη τοῦ | μετεχομένου καὶ μετέχοντος καὶ σύγκρασιν ἑνοποιόν, ὅλον μὲν τὸ καταδεέστερον ἑδράζουσα ἐν τῷ κρείττονι, τὸ δὲ θειότερον μόνον ἐνεργεῖν ὑπεσταλμένου τοῦ καταδεεστέρου καὶ ἀποκρύπτοντος ἐν τῷ κρείττονι τὴν σφετέραν ἰδιότητα παρασκευάζουσα. αὕτη δὴ οὖν μανία μέν ἐστιν σωφροσύνης | κρείττων ὡς συνελόντι φάναι, κατ' αὐτὸ δὲ τὸ θεῖον μέτρον ἀφορίζεται· καὶ ὥσπερ ἄλλη πρὸς ἄλλην ὕπαρξιν τῶν θεῶν <ἀνάγει>, οὕτω δὴ καὶ αὕτη τῆς συμμετρίας ἀποπληροῖ τὴν ἐνθεάζουσαν ψυχήν· διὸ δὴ καὶ τὰς ἐσχάτας αὐτῆς ἐν|εργείας μέτροις τε καὶ ῥυθμοῖς κατεκόσμησεν. ὥσπερ οὖν κατὰ μὲν τὴν ἀλήθειαν τὴν μαντικήν, κατὰ δὲ τὸ κάλλος ‖ τὴν ἐρωτικὴν μανίαν ὑφίστασθαι λέγομεν, οὕτως ἄρα καὶ κατὰ τὴν συμμετρίαν τὴν θείαν τὴν ποιητικὴν ἀφωρίσθαι φαμέν.

Ἡ δὲ ταύτης μὲν τῆς ἐνθεαστικῆς καὶ πρωτίστης ὑποδεεστέρα, μέση δὲ ἐν τῇ ψυχῇ θεωρουμένη κατ' αὐτὴν | δήπου τὴν ἐπιστήμονα καὶ νοερὰν ἕξιν ἔλαχεν τὴν ὑπόστασιν, γιγνώσκουσα μὲν τὴν οὐσίαν τῶν ὄντων καὶ τῶν καλῶν καὶ ἀγαθῶν ἔργων τε καὶ λόγων ὑπάρχουσα φιλοθεάμων, εἰς δὲ τὴν ἔμμετρον προάγουσα καὶ ἔνρυθμον ἕκαστα τῶν πραγμάτων

imaginings and irrational sense-perceptions and is entirely infested with lower things.

[c. The three kinds of poetry]

Since these may be considered to be the three forms of life for souls, let us understand that, according to the same pattern, there is likewise a division of the kinds of poetry, radiating downward with the multiform lives of the soul and diversified into first, intermediate, and last kinds of action:

(1) The first kind is highest and full of divine goods. It establishes the soul in the very causes of those things that exist, drawing the vessel and that which fills it into a single entity in an ineffable union, spreading the former out, nonmaterially and impalpably, to receive the illumination, and summoning the latter to give a share of its light,

> accomplishing the works of the mingled vehicles of deathless fire
> [*Or. chald.* frag. 66, des Places],

according to the oracle. It creates a single divine bond and unifying mixture of that which is participated in and that which participates, rooting all that is inferior in that which is better, arranging that what is more divine, alone, is active, while the lower has contracted and hidden its own individual identity in that which is greater. And so, to sum up, this is indeed a madness that is greater than reasonableness[288] and is defined by the measure of the divine itself. And since the different kinds of poetry lead the soul up to different qualities of the divine, this one fills the inspired soul with symmetry. Therefore, it has ornamented even its very lowest activities with meter and rhythm. Just as we say that the art of prophecy exists as a function of truth and erotic madness is constituted as function of beauty, || thus also we say that poetry is defined by divine symmetry.

(2) Below this inspired and primal poetry is another kind, which may be conceived as having a middle place in the soul and certainly has its existence as a function of the soul's wise and intellective condition. Knowing the essence of the things that exist and loving the spectacle of good and beautiful deeds and discourses, it draws each matter it treats into metrical

---

288. See *Phdr.* 245a and 33 [K57,26], 61 [K70,29], 87 [K84,16] with n. 109, and 193 [K140], above.

ἑρμηνείαν. οἷα δὴ πολλὰ τῶν ἀγαθῶν ποιη|τῶν εὕροις ἂν γεννήματα, ζηλωτὰ τοῖς εὖ φρονοῦσιν, νουθεσίας καὶ συμβουλῶν ἀρίστων πλήρη καὶ νοερᾶς εὐμετρίας ἀνάμεστα φρονήσεώς τε καὶ τῆς ἄλλης ἀρετῆς προτείνοντα τὴν μετουσίαν τοῖς εὖ πεφυκόσιν, ἀνάμνησίν τε παρεχό μενα τῶν τῆς ψυχῆς περιόδων καὶ τῶν ἀϊδίων ἐν αὐταῖς | λόγων καὶ τῶν ποικίλων δυνάμεων.

Τρίτη δὲ ἐπὶ ταύταις ἐστὶν ἡ δόξαις καὶ φαντασίαις συμμιγνυμένη καὶ διὰ μιμήσεως συμπληρουμένη καὶ οὐδὲν ἀλλ᾽ ἢ μιμητικὴ καὶ οὖσα καὶ λεγομένη καὶ τότε μὲν εἰκασίᾳ προσχρωμένη μόνον, τότε δὲ καὶ φαινομένην προϊσταμένη τὴν ἀφομοίωσιν, ἀλλ᾽ | οὐκ οὖσαν, εἰς ὄγκον μὲν ἐπαίρουσα τὰ σμικρὰ τῶν παθημάτων, ἐκπλήττουσα δὲ τοὺς ἀκούοντας τοῖς τοιοῖσδε ὀνόμασι καὶ ῥήμασιν, καὶ ταῖς ἐξαλλαγαῖς τῶν ἁρμονιῶν καὶ ταῖς τῶν ῥυθμῶν ποικιλίαις συμμεταβάλλουσα τὰς τῶν ψυχῶν διαθέσεις, καὶ τὰς τῶν πραγμάτων φύσεις οὐχ οἷαίπερ εἰσίν, | ἀλλ᾽ οἷαι φαντασθεῖεν ἂν τοῖς πολλοῖς ἐπιδεικνύουσα· σκιαγραφία τις οὖσα τῶν ὄντων, ἀλλ᾽ οὐ γνῶσις ἀκριβής, τέλος τε προϊσταμένη τὴν τῶν ἀκουόντων ψυχαγωγίαν, καὶ πρὸς ἐκεῖνο διαφερόντως βλέπουσα τὸ παθητικὸν καὶ χαίρειν καὶ λυπεῖσθαι πεφυκὸς τῆς ψυχῆς.

Ἔστιν δὲ ὅπερ ἔφαμεν καὶ | ταύτης τὸ μὲν εἰκαστικόν, ὃ καὶ πρὸς τὴν ὀρθότητα τοῦ μιμήματος ἀνατείνεται, τὸ δὲ τοιοῦτον οἷον εἴπομεν, φανταστικὸν καὶ φαινομένην μόνον τὴν μίμησιν παρεχόμενον. ||

Ὅτι κατὰ Πλάτωνα τὰς τρεῖς ἰδέας τῆς ποιητικῆς ἀποδείξομεν τοιαύτας οὔσας καὶ τοσαύτας.

Τὰ μὲν τοίνυν γένη τῆς ποιητικῆς τοσαῦτά ἐστιν, ὡς συντόμως διελέσθαι. δεῖ δὲ καὶ τὸν Πλάτωνα τούτων ἐπι|δεῖξαι τὴν μνήμην ποιησάμενον καὶ καθ᾽ ἕκαστον ἐπελθεῖν τὰ ἐκείνῳ περὶ αὐτῶν ἀρέσκοντα. καὶ πρῶτον περὶ τῆς ἐνθέου ποιητικῆς, ὅσα θαυμαστὰ διανοήματα λάβοι τις ἂν μὴ παρέργως ἀναλεγόμενος τὰ γεγραμμένα, διαπερανώμεθα· τούτων γὰρ οἶμαι προδιορισθέντων ῥᾴδιον καὶ περὶ τῶν | ἐχομένων ἔσται τοὺς προσήκοντας ἀποδοῦναι λόγους.

Ταύτην τοίνυν τὴν ἔνθεον ποιητικὴν ἐν Φαίδρῳ [245a] κατοκωχὴν

and rhythmic expression. You would find that many of the productions of the good poets are in this category, admired by the right-minded, packed with advice and the best counsel and full of intellective moderation, and offering to those with a natural aptitude participation in thoughtfulness and the other virtues and providing recollection of the cycles of the soul and of the timeless logoi and the various powers in these cycles.

(3) The third along with these is the kind of poetry that has opinions and imaginings mixed into it and is made up of *mimesis* so that it is and is called nothing other than "mimetic." Sometimes it simply proceeds by representation, while at other times it projects a resemblance that is apparent but not real. Stirring up the trivial passions to enormous volume and impressing the listener with such words and expressions and changing the various dispositions of the soul as it goes, through changes of mode and variation of meter, it shows the natures of things to be not as they are but as they might be imagined by the many to be. It is a shadow painting of things that are, and not a clear perception, and sets itself the goal of entertaining its listener and looks especially to the passionate element in the soul, which is naturally disposed to rejoice and to grieve.

There are, as we have said, within this last category the accurately imitative type [of mimetic poetry], which aspires as well to correctness of imitation, and the type we have described, the illusionistic, which provides only the appearance of an imitation. ||

(6) We shall demonstrate that, according to Plato, there are three kinds of poetry and that their properties are as we have described them.

[a. The problem]

Dividing them up concisely, then, these three are the classes of poetry. Now it is necessary to demonstrate that Plato has also written about these things and to examine one by one the positions he adopted on each of them. First, with regard to inspired poetry, let us examine in detail all the wondrous concepts one might find in Plato, if one read through his writings with care. Once these are clearly defined it will, I think, be easier to give an appropriate account of what follows.

[b. Inspired poetry: the *Phaedrus*]

In the *Phaedrus*, then, he calls this inspired poetry "possession by the

μὲν ἀπὸ Μουσῶν καὶ μανίαν προσείρηκεν, εἰς ἁπαλὴν δὲ καὶ ἄβατον ἄνωθεν δίδοσθαι ψυχήν, ἔργον δὲ αὐτῆς εἶναί φησιν ἀνεγείρειν τε καὶ ἐκβακχεύειν κατά τε | τὰς ᾠδὰς καὶ τὴν ἄλλην ποίησιν, τέλος δὲ τὸ μυρία τῶν παλαιῶν ἔργα κοσμοῦσαν τοὺς ἐπιγιγνομένους παιδεύειν.

Ἐν οἷς δὴ παντὶ καταφανές, ὅτι πρῶτον μὲν τὴν ἀρχηγικὴν καὶ πρωτουργικὴν αἰτίαν τῆς ποιητικῆς τὴν τῶν Μουσῶν εἶναί φησιν δόσιν. ὡς γὰρ τὰ ἄλλα πάντα τά τε ἀφανῆ | καὶ τὰ ἐμφανῆ δημιουργήματα τοῦ πατρὸς τῆς ἁρμονίας πληροῦσιν καὶ τῆς ἐνρύθμου κινήσεως, οὕτως δὴ καὶ ταῖς κατόχοις <ἐξ> αὐτῶν ψυχαῖς τὸ τῆς θείας συμμετρίας ἴχνος ἐλλάμπουσαι τὴν ποιητικὴν ἀποτελοῦσιν τὴν ἔνθεον. ἐπεὶ δὲ ὅλη μὲν ἡ ἐνέργεια τοῦ ἐλλάμποντός ἐστιν ἐν ταῖς | θείαις παρουσίαις, τὸ δ' ἐλλαμπόμενον ἑαυτὸ ταῖς ἐκεῖθεν κινήσεσιν ἐπιδίδωσιν καὶ τῶν σφετέρων ἠθῶν ἐξιστάμενον ὑπέστρωται ταῖς τοῦ θείου καὶ μονοειδοῦς ἐνεργείαις, διὰ ταῦτα οἶμαι κατοκωχήν τε καὶ μανίαν ὁμοῦ τὴν τοιαύτην προσείρηκεν ἔλλαμψιν· ὡς μὲν κρατοῦσαν τῶν ὑφ' ἑαυτῆς | κινουμένων ὅλων κατοκωχὴν αὐτὴν ὀνομάσας, ὡς δὲ ἐξιστᾶ||σαν τῶν οἰκείων ἐνεργημάτων εἰς τὴν ἑαυτῆς ἰδιότητα τὰ ἐλλαμπόμενα μανίαν προσειπών.

Δεύτερον δὲ ὅτι καὶ αὐτὴν τὴν κάτοχον ἐσομένην ταῖς Μούσαις ψυχὴν ὁποίαν εἶναι δεῖ προσδιώρισεν, ἁπαλήν γε φησὶν λαβοῦσα καὶ ἄβα|τον ψυχήν. ἡ μὲν γὰρ σκληρὰ καὶ ἀντίτυπος καὶ δυσπαθὴς πρὸς τὴν θείαν ἔλλαμψιν ἐναντίως ἔχει πρὸς τὴν τῆς κατοκωχῆς ἐνέργειαν· ἑαυτῆς γάρ ἐστιν μᾶλλον ἢ τοῦ ἐλλάμποντος καὶ οὐκ εὐτύπωτος πρὸς τὴν ἐκεῖθεν δόσιν. ἡ δὲ ὑπ' ἄλλων παντοδαπῶν κατεχομένη δοξασμάτων καὶ | ποικίλων καὶ ἀλλοτρίων τοῦ θείου πεπληρωμένη διαλογισμῶν ἐπισκιάζει τὴν θείαν ἐπίπνοιαν, συμμιγνῦσα ταῖς ἐκ ταύτης κινήσεσιν τὰς ἰδίας ἑαυτῆς ζωάς τε καὶ ἐνεργείας. δεῖ δὴ οὖν ἀμφότερα ἅμα τὴν ψυχὴν προειληφέναι ταύτην, ἥτις ἂν μέλλῃ ταῖς Μούσαις ἔσεσθαι κάτοχος, ἁπαλήν τε αὐτὴν | ὑπάρχειν καὶ ἄβατον, ἵνα πρὸς μὲν τὰ θεῖα παντελῶς εὐπαθὴς ᾖ καὶ συμπαθής, πρὸς δὲ τὰ ἄλλα πάντα ἀπαθὴς καὶ ἄδεκτος αὐτῶν καὶ ἀμιγὴς πρὸς αὐτά.

Τρίτον τοίνυν τὸ κοινὸν ἔργον τῆς τε τοιαύτης ἐπιτηδειότητος καὶ τῆς τῶν Μουσῶν κατοκωχῆς καὶ μανίας προστίθησιν. τὸ γὰρ | ἀνεγείρειν τε καὶ ἐκβακχεύειν τοῦτο δή ἐστιν τὸ ἐκ τῆς ἀμφοτέρων <ἐνεργείας> εἰς ταὐτὸν συμπληρούμενον ἔργον, λέγω δὴ τοῦ τε ἐλλαμπομένου καὶ ἐλλάμποντος· τοῦ μὲν ἄνωθεν κινοῦντος, τοῦ δὲ ὑπεστρωμένου τῇ ἐκείνου δόσει. ἔστι

Muses" and "madness" [245a], saying that it is granted from above to a gentle and pure soul and that its task is to awaken and enrapture the soul with odes and other poetry, and its goal is to set in order the myriad acts of the ancients, in order to educate posterity.

In this text it is perfectly clear to all, in the first place, that the original and primordial cause of poetry is the gift of the Muses. Just as [the Muses] fill all the other creations of the father, both visible and invisible, with harmony and rhythmic motion, even so, by illuminating the souls of which they take possession with a trace of divine symmetry, they bring to perfection divine poetry. Since the entire action of the illuminator consists in divine presence, and the one illuminated gives himself over to the impulses that come from the illuminator and steps out of his own character and subjects himself to the actions of the divine and uniform, this, I believe, is why [Plato] calls such illumination both "possession" and "madness." He calls it "possession" because it takes power over the entirety of what is moved by it and "madness" because it causes || those illuminated to abandon their own activities and enter into its identity.

Second, it is clear that Plato has even defined the qualities that the soul destined to be possessed by the Muses must have, when he says "taking a pure and gentle soul." The hard and resistant soul, insensitive to the divine illumination, is opposed to the action of possession, for she belongs more to herself than to the illuminator and is not readily receptive of its gifts. Moreover, the soul that is possessed by all sorts of other conceptions and filled with considerations that are diverse and the opposite of the divine obscures the divine inspiration, mingling her own states and actions in the impulses coming therefrom. Therefore it is necessary for this soul that is to be possessed by the Muses already to have acquired both these qualities in advance: she must already be gentle and pure so that, on the one hand, she may be entirely docile and sympathetic toward the divine and unmoved, unreceptive, and impermeable toward other things.

Third, Plato adds the shared task belonging to such a capacity [of the soul] and to possession and madness from the Muses. Awakening and enrapturing indeed constitute this accomplishment to which both contribute with their actions[289]—the illuminated and the illuminating, I mean—the one moving downward and the other spread out below it to

---

289. Reading <ἐνεργείας>, following Kroll's apparatus.

δὲ ἡ μὲν ἔγερσις ἀνάτασις <u>ἄυπνος</u> τῆς ψυχῆς καὶ ἀδιάστροφος ἐνέργεια | καὶ ἀπὸ τῆς ἐν τῇ γενέσει πτώσεως ἐπιστροφὴ πρὸς τὸ θεῖον, ἡ δὲ βακχεία κίνησις ἔνθεος καὶ χορεία περὶ τὸ θεῖον ἄτρυτος, τελεσιουργὸς τῶν κατεχομένων. δεῖ δὲ αὖ πάλιν καὶ τούτων ἀμφοτέρων, ἵνα ἄπτωτοι μὲν ὦσιν οἱ | κάτοχοι πρὸς τὸ χεῖρον, εὐκίνητοι δὲ πρὸς τὸ κρεῖττον.

Τέταρτον δὴ οὖν τὸ μυρία τῶν παλαιῶν ἔργα κοσμεῖν καὶ || διὰ τούτων τοὺς ἐπιγινομένους παιδεύειν πρόδηλον, ὅτι τά τε ἀνθρώπινα διὰ τῶν θείων αὐτὴν τελειότερα <u>ἀποδεικνύναι</u> καὶ λαμπρότερά φησιν, καὶ παιδείαν ἀπ' αὐτῆς ἀληθινὴν παραγίνεσθαι τοῖς κατηκόοις αὐτῆς γινομένοις. πολλοῦ ἄρα | δεῖ τὴν ποιητικὴν ταύτην τὴν ἔνθεον τῆς παιδευτικῆς δυνάμεως ἀποστερεῖν· ἀλλ' οἶμαι τὸ τῆς παιδείας οὐ ταὐτὸν εἶναι πρός τε τὰς τῶν νέων ἕξεις καὶ τὰς τῶν ἤδη τελεωθέντων ἐκ τῆς πολιτικῆς καὶ δεομένων τῆς μυστικωτέρας ἤδη περὶ τῶν θείων ἀκροάσεως. ἔστιν ἄρα ἡ τοιαύτη ποίη|σις παντὸς μᾶλλον παιδευτικὴ τῶν ἀκουόντων, ὅταν ἔνθεος ᾖ καὶ ὅταν τὸ θεῖον αὐτῆς τοῦτο κατάδηλον γίνηται τοῖς ἀκούουσιν· ἡ γὰρ ἐπιπολῆς αὐτῆς ἐπαφὴ τῆς ἔνδον ἀποκρυπτομένης μυστικῆς ἀληθείας οὐκ ἀντιλαμβάνεται.

Ταύτην δὴ τὴν ἐκ τῶν Μουσῶν ὑφισταμένην ἐν ταῖς ἁπαλαῖς | καὶ ἀβάτοις ψυχαῖς ποιητικὴν ἁπάσης ἄλλης τέχνης ἀνθρωπίνης εἰκότως προτίθησιν· τὸν γὰρ ἄνευ τῆς τοιαύτης μανίας ποιητὴν ἀτελῆ καὶ αὐτὸν καὶ τὴν ποίησιν αὐτοῦ [καὶ] ὑπὸ τῆς τῶν μαινομένων ἀφανίζεσθαι τὴν τοῦ σωφρονοῦντος διϊσχυρίζεται· τῆς γὰρ θείας δόσεως τῷ παντὶ τὴν ἀν|θρωπίνην ἐπιβολὴν ἀπολείπεσθαι.

Τοιάδε μὲν οὖν ὁ ἐν τῷ Φαίδρῳ Σωκράτης ὑπὲρ τῆς ἐνθέου ποιητικῆς ἡμᾶς ἀνεδίδαξεν, τῇ τε θείᾳ μαντικῇ καὶ τῇ τελεστικῇ συντάττων αὐτὴν διαφερόντως καὶ τὴν πρώτην ἔκφανσιν αὐτῆς εἰς θεοὺς ἀναπέμπων.

receive its gift. The "awakening" is a wakeful[290] straining by the soul and inexorable movement, a return from the fall into γένεσις back toward the divine; the "rapture" is inspired movement, and a tireless dance around the divine, bringing the possessed to perfection. And again there is need of both of these so that the possessed will not be subject to fall back into the inferior and will easily moved toward the better.

And so, fourth, as far as setting in order the myriad deeds of the ancients is concerned, and || through these instructing posterity, it is clear in advance that he is saying that this kind of poetry renders[291] human things more perfect and more radiant through the divine and that true education comes from this poetry for those who hear it. This inspired kind of poetry should by no means be deprived of its capacity to educate. I believe the whole matter of education to be different with reference to the state of mind of the young and to that of those already educated in civic life[292] and now needing to hear a more mystical teaching about the divine. Indeed, this sort of poetry is preeminently educational for its audience when it is inspired and when this divine element in it is clearly perceptible to them. Superficial contact with it, however, does not grasp the mystical truth hidden within.

This poetry, then, created by the Muses in gentle and pure souls, [Plato] appropriately places before every other human art. He maintains that the poet who does not have this sort of madness is imperfect himself and that his poetry, which is that of a reasonable man, fades into obscurity in the presence of that of the madman, because human conceptions are in every way inferior to the gift of the gods.

[c. Inspired poetry: the *Ion*]

These are the things, then, that the Socrates of the *Phaedrus* taught us about inspired poetry, in particular establishing its connections with divine prophecy and initiation and attributing its first revelation to the gods. He also says things in harmony with these about such poetry to

---

290. Accepting Kroll's suggestion, ἄυπνος for ὑπό [K181,24].
291. Accepting, with F., ἀποδεικνύναι for the manuscript's δεικνύναι above [K182,2]. Cf. Kroll ad loc.
292. The Neoplatonic educational canon, traceable to Iamblichus, called for education first of all in the "political virtues" and subsequently in higher levels of knowledge.

σύμφωνα δὲ | τούτοις καὶ ἐν τῷ Ἴωνι πρὸς τὸν ῥαψῳδὸν διαλέγεται περὶ αὐτῆς, οὗ δὴ καὶ ἐμφανέστατα τὴν Ὁμήρου ποιητικὴν ἔνθεον ἀποφαίνει καὶ ἄλλοις ἐνθουσιασμῶν αἰτίαν τοῖς περὶ αὐτὴν διατρίβουσιν.

Εἰπόντος γὰρ οἶμαι τοῦ ῥαψῳδοῦ [531a] περὶ μὲν τῶν Ὁμήρου ποιημάτων εὐπορεῖν τι λέγειν, περὶ | δὲ τῶν τοῖς ἄλλοις ποιηταῖς γεγραμμένων οὐδαμῶς, ὁ Σω∥κράτης τὴν αἰτίαν ἀποδιδοὺς τοῦ τοιούτου παθήματος· **ἔστι γὰρ τοῦτο, φησίν, τέχνη μὲν οὐκ ὂν παρὰ σοὶ περὶ Ὁμήρου εὖ λέγειν, θεία δὲ δύναμις ἥ σε κινεῖ** [533d]. καὶ ὡς τοῦτο ἀληθές, παντί που καταφανές. | οἱ μὲν γὰρ τέχνῃ τι ποιοῦντες ἐπὶ πάντων ὡς εἰπεῖν τῶν ὁμοίων τὸ αὐτὸ δύνανται ἀπεργάζεσθαι, οἱ δὲ θείᾳ τινὶ δυνάμει περί τι συμμέτρως ἔχοντες οὐκέτι καὶ πρὸς τὰ ἄλλα τὴν αὐτὴν ἐξ ἀνάγκης ἔχουσι δύναμιν.

Πόθεν οὖν ἡ τοιαύτη τῷ ῥαψῳδῷ δύναμις ἐφήκει, πρὸς μὲν Ὅμηρον | αὐτὸν διαφερόντως συνάπτουσα, πρὸς δὲ τοὺς ἄλλους οὐκέτι ποιητάς, ἐφεξῆς ὁ Σωκράτης ἀναδιδάσκει, τῇ λίθῳ χρώμενος ἐναργεστάτῳ παραδείγματι τῆς τελευταίας ἐκ τῶν Μουσῶν κατοκωχῆς, ἣν Ἡρακλείαν οἱ πολλοὶ καλοῦσιν. τί οὖν αὕτη ἡ λίθος ἀπεργάζεται;

οὐ μόνον δή φησιν αὐ|τοὺς ἄγει πρὸς ἑαυτὴν τοὺς σιδηροῦς δακτυλίους, ἀλλὰ καὶ δύναμιν αὐτοῖς ὁλκὸν τῶν ὁμοίων ἐντίθησιν, ὥστε ἄλλους ἄγειν δακτυλίους· καὶ πολλάκις φησὶν ὁρμαθὸς δακτυλίων ἢ σιδηρίων ἐξ ἀλλήλων ἤρτηται· πᾶσι δὲ ἄρα τούτοις ἀπ' ἐκείνης τῆς | λίθου ἡ δύναμις ἐξήρτηται.

τίνα μὲν οὖν τρόπον τὰ τοσαῦτα πάθη περὶ τοὺς δακτυλίους συμβαίνει καὶ τίς ἡ τῆς λίθου δύναμις, οὐ πρόκειται λέγειν ἐν τούτοις· τὰ δὲ τούτοις παραπλήσια καὶ ἐπὶ τῆς ἐνθέου ποιητικῆς τοῦ Σωκράτους προστιθέντος ἀκούσωμεν.

οὕτω δὲ καὶ ἡ Μοῦσα | ἐνθέους μὲν ποιεῖ αὐτούς, διὰ δὲ τῶν ἐνθέων τούτων ἄλλων ἐνθουσιαζόντων ὁρμαθὸς ἐξαρτᾶται.

Ἐν οἷς πρῶτον μὲν τὴν θείαν αἰτίαν ἑνικῶς προηνέγκατο, Μοῦσαν αὐτὴν προσειπών, ἀλλ' οὐχ ὥσπερ ἐν τῷ Φαίδρῳ τὴν ἐκ Μουσῶν κατοκωχήν τε καὶ μανίαν εἰς ἅπαν αὐτῶν | τὸ πλῆθος ἐπέτρεψεν, ἵνα πάντα τὸν τῶν ἐνθεαστικῶς κινου∥μένων ἀριθμὸν οἷον εἰς μονάδα μίαν ἀνάγῃ τὴν πρωτουργὸν τῆς ποιητικῆς ἀρχήν. ἔστι γὰρ ἡ ποιητικὴ μονοειδῶς μὲν ἐν τῷ πρώτῳ κινοῦντι καὶ κρυφίως, δευτέρως δὲ καὶ ἀνειλιγμένως ἐν τοῖς ποιηταῖς ὑπὸ τῆς μονάδος ἐκείνης κινου|μένοις, ἐσχάτως δὲ καὶ

the rhapsode in the *Ion*, where indeed he very clearly treats the poetry of Homer as inspired and a cause of inspiration for those who devote time to it.

When the rhapsode has said, I believe, that he is quite able to speak about the poems of Homer but not at all about the composition of the other poets, Socrates, in || giving an explanation of this experience, says, "This faculty of yours of speaking well about Homer is not, as it turns out, a skill, but rather a divine power that moves you" [533d]. That this is true is, I suppose, entirely clear to all. Those who bring something about by skill are able to do it, we may say, to all similar things, but if it is by some divine power that they are capable of doing something, then it no longer follows that they have the same ability with regard to other things.

Socrates next explains whence such a power, relating specifically to Homer himself and not to other poets, has come upon the rhapsode, using as a vivid image of the most perfect possession by the Muses the stone that most call "the stone of Heracleia." What does this stone do?

> Not only (he says) does it attract iron rings to itself, but it also induces in them the power of attraction over similar things, so that they attract other rings, and often a string of rings or other iron objects is hung together, so that for all these things the force depends on that stone. [533d–e]

Now, the manner in which this business about the rings comes about and the nature of the power of the stone are not things to be discussed here, but let us listen to Socrates adding closely related things with regard to inspired poetry:

> And in this way also the Muse makes them inspired, and from these inspired ones hangs a chain of other beings in a state of inspiration. [533e]

First of all, in this passage he introduced the divine cause as single, calling it "Muse," and did not, as in the *Phaedrus*, attribute "possession and madness stemming from the Muses" to all of them [collectively]. [He did this] in order to draw the whole || number of those moved to inspiration back up to, so to speak, a single monad, the primordial first principle of poetry. Poetry resides, uniformly and cryptically, in the first mover, then secondarily and explicitly in the poets moved by this monad, and in the

ὑπουργικῶς ἐν τοῖς ῥαψῳδοῖς, διὰ μέσων τῶν ποιητῶν ἐπὶ τὴν μίαν αἰτίαν ἀναγομένοις.

Ἔπειτα τὴν θείαν ἐπίπνοιαν ἄνωθεν ἄχρι τῶν τελευταίων μεθέξεων διατείνων δῆλός ἐστιν ὁμοῦ μὲν τὴν περιουσίαν τῆς πρωτίστης ἀρχῆς τῆς κινούσης ἀνυμνῶν, ὁμοῦ δὲ τὴν τῶν πρώ|των μετεχόντων μέθεξιν δεικνὺς ἐνεργεστάτην. τὸ γὰρ διὰ τῶν σφετέρων ποιημάτων ἀνεγείρειν καὶ ἄλλους εἰς ἐνθεασμὸν τρανεστάτην ἐν αὐτοῖς τὴν τοῦ θείου παρουσίαν ἐπιδείκνυσιν. τούτοις δὴ οὖν ἑπομένως καὶ τὰ ἐφεξῆς προστίθησιν περὶ τῆς τῶν ποιητῶν κατοκωχῆς.

πάντες γὰρ οἵ | τε τῶν ἐπῶν ποιηταὶ οἱ ἀγαθοὶ οὐκ ἐκ τέχνης, ἀλλ' ἔνθεοι ὄντες καὶ κατεχόμενοι πάντα ταῦτα τὰ καλὰ λέγουσιν ποιήματα, καὶ οἱ μελοποιοὶ οἱ ἀγαθοὶ ὡσαύτως καὶ πάλιν ἑξῆς· κοῦφον γὰρ χρῆμα ποιητής ἐστι καὶ πτηνὸν καὶ ἱερόν, καὶ οὐ πρότερον οἷός | τε ποιεῖν, πρὶν ἂν ἔνθεός τε γένηται καὶ ἔκφρων [534b].

καὶ τέλος, ὅτι διὰ ταῦτα

ἅτε οὐ τέχνῃ ποιοῦντες καὶ πολλὰ λέγοντες καὶ καλὰ περὶ τῶν πραγμάτων, ὥσπερ σὺ περὶ Ὁμήρου, ἀλλὰ θείᾳ μοίρᾳ, τοῦτο μόνον ἕκαστος οἷός τέ ἐστι ποιεῖν καλῶς, ἐφ' | ὃ ἡ Μοῦσα αὐτὸν ὥρμησεν.

Ἐν δὴ τούτοις ἅπασιν τὴν ἔνθεον ποιητικὴν μέσην ἀτέχνως ἱδρῦσθαί φησιν τῆς τε θείας αἰτίας—ἣν Μοῦσαν προσείρηκεν, καὶ ταύτῃ τὸν Ὅμηρον ζηλῶν, καὶ ποτὲ μὲν εἰς τὸ πλῆθος, ποτὲ δὲ εἰς τὴν ἕνωσιν ἀποβλέπων τῆς τῶν Μουσῶν σειρᾶς (**ἔσπετε | νῦν μοι, Μοῦσαι,** καὶ **ἄνδρα μοι ἔννεπε Μοῦσα** φησὶν ἐκεῖνος)—ταύτης δ' οὖν τῆς πρωτίστης ἀρχῆς τῶν || ἐνθεαστικῶν κινήσεων καὶ τῶν τελευταίων ἀπηχημάτων τῆς ἐπιπνοίας τῶν ἐν τοῖς ῥαψῳδοῖς κατὰ συμπάθειαν ὁρωμένων ἐν μέσῳ τὴν τῶν ποιητῶν μανίαν ἔταξεν, κινουμένην τε καὶ κινοῦσαν καὶ πληρουμένην ἄνωθεν καὶ εἰς ἄλλα δια|πορθμεύουσαν τὴν ἐκεῖθεν ἔλλαμψιν, ἕνα τε σύνδεσμον παρεχομένην τοῖς ἐσχάτως μετέχουσι πρὸς τὴν μετεχομένην μονάδα.

lowest degree and in an auxiliary manner in the rhapsodes, who are drawn up to the single cause by means of the poets.

Then, when he extends divine inspiration down from above to the lowest participants, it is clear that he is simultaneously celebrating the superabundance of the first moving principle and showing very clearly the nature of the participation of the first participants. Their capacity, through their own poetry, to arouse others as well to inspiration demonstrates the manifest presence of the divine in them. He then adds the following on the possession of the poets:

> All the good epic poets deliver all these good poems of theirs not out of skill but when inspired and possessed, and just the same is true for the good lyric poets … etc. [533e–534a]. A poet is a delicate thing, winged and holy and incapable of writing his poetry until he becomes inspired and beside himself [534b].

Finally, for these reasons,

> since it is not by skill that they create and say so much that is beautiful about things, as you do about Homer, but rather by divine fate, each is capable of doing well only that one thing to which the Muse has aroused him [534b–c].

Thus, in absolutely all these passages, he says that inspired poetry is seated right in the middle, between the divine cause—which he calls "Muse" in imitation of Homer as well, looking now to the group, now to the united chain of the Muses ("Tell me now,[293] Muses" [*Il.* var. loc.] and elsewhere "Muse, sing me the man," [*Od.* 1.1] says Homer)—between this first cause, then, of || inspired impulses, and the last echoes of inspiration seen operating by sympathy in the rhapsodes, here in the middle Socrates has placed the madness of the poets. This madness receives its impulse from outside and imparts it to others, brought to fulfillment from above and transferring the illumination it receives from above to other things, providing a single bond between the most remote participants and the participated monad.

---

293. Correcting ἔσπετε at K184,29 to ἔσπετε.

Τούτοις δὴ οὖν καὶ ὅσα ὁ Ἀθηναῖος ξένος ἐν τῷ τρίτῳ τῶν Νόμων λέγει περὶ τῆς ποιητικῆς καὶ ὅσα ὁ | Τίμαιος περὶ τῶν ποιητῶν που συναρμόσωμεν. ὃ μὲν γὰρ **θεῖον**, φησίν,

καὶ τὸ ποιητικὸν ἐνθεαστικὸν ὂν γένος ὑμνῳδοῦν σύν τισι Χάρισιν καὶ Μούσαις πολλῶν τῶν κατ' ἀλήθειαν γεγονότων ἐφάπτεται ἑκάστοτε [*Leg.* 3.682a].

<ὃ> δὲ ἕπεσθαι παρακελεύεται τοῖς φοιβο|λήπτοις ποιηταῖς τῶν θεῶν οὖσι παισὶν καὶ εἰδόσιν τὰ τῶν σφετέρων προγόνων, καίπερ ἄνευ τε εἰκότων καὶ ἀποδείξεων λέγουσιν [*Tim.* 40d].

Ἐξ ὧν καὶ παντὶ ῥᾴδιον ἐννοῆσαι, τίνα μὲν οἴεται εἶναι τὴν ἔνθεον ποιητικήν, ὁποίους δὲ τοὺς κατ' αὐτὴν ἱσταμένους ποιητάς, καὶ ὡς οὗτοι μάλιστα | τῶν θείων εἰσὶ καὶ μυστικῶν νοημάτων ἄγγελοι τὰ τῶν πατέρων διαφερόντως εἰδότες. ὅταν ἄρα τῶν μυθικῶν πλασμάτων ἐπιλαμβάνηται καὶ εὐθύνῃ τὰ τραγικώτερα τῶν ἀναγεγραμμένων, δεσμοὺς καὶ τομὰς καὶ ἔρωτας καὶ μίξεις καὶ δάκρυα καὶ γέλωτας, αὐτὸν ἂν μάλιστα τῶν τοιούτων | ἔχοιμεν λόγων ὡς εὖ ἐχόντων κατὰ τὴν ἐν τοῖς συμβόλοις τούτοις ἀποκρυπτομένην ὥσπερ προκαλύμμασι θεωρίαν μάρτυρα. ὁ γὰρ διαφερόντως αὐτοῖς πιστεύειν ἐν ταῖς περὶ θεῶν πραγματείαις ἀξιῶν, κἂν ἄνευ ἀποδείξεως λέγωσιν, διὰ τὴν ἐκ τῶν θεῶν ἐπίπνοιαν, οὗτος δή που θαυμάσεται | τὴν ἐν τοῖς μύθοις δι' ὧν ἐκεῖνοι τὰ θεῖα παραδιδόασιν || ἀλήθειαν· καὶ ὁ θεῖον τὸ ποιητικὸν γένος ἀποκαλῶν οὐκ ἂν τὴν ἄθεον ἐπ' αὐτὸ καὶ γιγαντικὴν ἀναπέμποι περὶ τῶν θείων πραγμάτων ὑπόνοιαν· καὶ ὁ σύν τισι Χάρισιν καὶ Μούσαις τοὺς ποιητὰς λέγειν ἃ λέγουσιν ἀποφαινόμενος | τὴν ἐκμελῆ καὶ ἀνάρμοστον καὶ ἄχαριν φαντασίαν πόρρω τῆς θεωρίας αὐτῶν διῳκίσθαι πάντως προείληφεν.

Ὅταν οὖν τὴν ποιητικὴν καὶ τὴν διὰ τῶν μύθων ἔνδειξιν μὴ προσάγειν ταῖς τῶν νέων ἀκοαῖς νομοθετῇ, πολλοῦ δεῖ τὴν ποιητικὴν αὐτὴν ἀτιμάζειν, ἀλλὰ τὴν τῶν νέων ἕξιν ὡς | ἀγύμναστον πρὸς τὴν τούτων ἀκρόασιν

[d. Inspired poetry: the *Laws* and *Timaeus*]

Let us then establish some sort of harmony between these passages and both what the Athenian Stranger says in the third book of the *Laws* about poetics and what Timaeus says about poets. The stranger says,

> The race of poets is also divinely inspired, and when they sing they regularly touch on a great deal that actually occurs, with the help of some of the Graces and the Muses [*Leg.* 3.682a],[294]

and Timaeus recommends following the poets who are in the grip of Apollo since they are children of the gods and know the things that relate to their own forebears, even though they speak without either plausible propositions or conclusive demonstrations.[295]

From these passages it is easy for all to perceive what [Plato] thinks inspired poetry to be and how he conceives the poets who create in this mode: they are primarily the messengers of divine and mystical conceptions because of their exceptional knowledge of those things that relate to their fathers. Therefore, when Plato attacks the mythic fabrications and censures the more theatrical things described—the chainings and castrations and loves and copulation and tears and laughter—we can certainly take him as a witness that such accounts are good things in terms of the doctrine that is hidden behind these symbols, as if behind a screen. The man who thinks it right, on account of their divine inspiration, to give the poets special credence in things concerning the gods, even if they speak without conclusive demonstrations, will, I suppose, surely admire the truth that lies in the myths the poets use to hand down their ideas about the divine, || and the man who called the race of poets divine would not attribute to it atheistic and Gigantic[296] insinuations about divine matters. Moreover, he who makes the poets say what they say with the help of the Graces and the Muses surely assumes that unmusical, inharmonious, graceless fantasy is far from their doctrines.

Thus, when he lays down the law that poetry and demonstration through myths must not be brought to the hearing of the young, he is far from condemning poetry itself, but rather he is deflecting the state of

---

294. Cf. above, 221 [K156], where the text is cited slightly differently.
295. Cf. *Tim.* 40d.
296. See 19–21 (K51) with n. 22, above.

ἀπάγει τῆς τοιᾶσδε μυθοποιΐας. ὡς γάρ που καὶ ἐν Ἀλκιβιάδῃ δευτέρῳ φησίν [147b], τοιοῦτόν ἐστιν τὸ τῆς ποιητικῆς γένος·

φύσει γάρ ἐστιν σύμπασα αἰνιγματώδης καὶ οὐ τοῦ προστυχόντος ἀνδρὸς γνωρίσαι.

15 τοιαῦτα δὲ καὶ ἐν Πο|λιτείᾳ σαφῶς ἔλεγεν [2.378d], ὡς ὁ

νέος οὐκ ἔστι δυνατὸς κρίνειν ὅ τι τ' ἔστιν ὑπόνοια καὶ ὃ μή.

πάντῃ ἄρα φήσομεν αὐτὸν τὴν ἔνθεον ἀποδέχεσθαι ποιητικήν, ἣν θείαν ἐπονομάζει καὶ τοὺς ἔχοντας αὐτὴν σιγῇ σέβειν ἀξιοῖ [Rep. II
20 378a]. τοσαῦτα μὲν οὖν περὶ ταύτης εἰρήσθω τῆς | πρώτης καὶ θεόθεν ὑφισταμένης ἐν ταῖς ἁπαλαῖς καὶ ἀβάτοις ψυχαῖς.

Μετὰ δὲ ταύτην τὴν ἐπιστήμονα τῶν ὄντων καὶ κατὰ νοῦν καὶ φρόνησιν ἐνεργοῦσαν θεωρήσωμεν, ἣ πολλὰ μὲν περὶ τῆς ἀσωμάτου
25 φύσεως νοήματα τοῖς ἀνθρώποις ἐξέ|φηνεν, πολλὰ δὲ περὶ τῆς σωματικῆς ὑποστάσεως εἰκότα προήγαγεν εἰς φῶς δόγματα, διηρευνήσατο δὲ καὶ τὴν καλλίστην καὶ τοῖς ἤθεσιν πρέπουσαν συμμετρίαν καὶ τὴν ἐναντίαν πρὸς ταύτην διάθεσιν, πάντα δὲ ταῦτα μέτροις τε καὶ ῥυθμοῖς κατεκόσμησεν
30 οἰκείοις. τοιαύτην γάρ που καὶ | τὴν Θεόγνιδος ποιητικὴν εἶναί φησιν ὁ
K187 Ἀθηναῖος ξένος || [Leg. 1.630a], ἣν ἐγκωμιάζει τῆς Τυρταίου μειζόνως, διότι τῆς ὅλης ἀρετῆς ἐστιν ὁ Θέογνις διδάσκαλος καὶ τῆς εἰς ἅπασαν διατεινούσης τὴν πολιτικὴν ζωήν. ὁ μὲν γὰρ τὴν πιστότητα τὴν ἐκ τῶν
5 ἀρετῶν ἁπασῶν συμπληρουμένην | ἀποδέχεται καὶ τὴν ἀληθεστέραν κακίαν ἐκβάλλει τῶν πόλεων τὴν στάσιν καὶ εἰς μίαν ὁμόνοιαν περιάγει τὰς τῶν πειθομένων ζωάς, ὁ δὲ αὐτὴν καθ' ἑαυτὴν τὴν ἀνδρείαν ἕξιν

mind of the young from this mythopoeia, since it is untrained for hearing such things. As he says in the *Second Alcibiades*, poetry as a class is something of this sort:

> By nature, all of it is riddling and enigmatic, and he who happens upon it casually will not grasp it [147b].

Moreover, he said the same thing clearly in the *Republic*:

> The young man is not able to judge what has a second meaning and what does not [2.378d].

We shall say, then, that he altogether accepts the inspired class of poetry, which he calls "divine," and moreover says that those who possess it should be given silent reverence.[297]

This will be sufficient on this first category of poetry, stemming from the gods and coming upon gentle and pure souls.

[e. Didactic poetry: the *Laws* on Theognis]

Next let us examine that kind of poetry that has systematic knowledge concerning the things that are and acts with intellect and thought and has revealed to men many ideas about the nonmaterial realm and brought to light many plausible teachings about the substance of the material world. It has also looked into the most beautiful [internal] symmetry that is fitting for character, as well as the state that is its opposite, and ornamented all these things with meter and rhythm appropriate to them.

The Athenian Stranger says that the poetry of Theognis is of this sort,[298] and || he praises it above that of Tyrtaeus because Theognis is a teacher of that total virtue that extends into the whole of civic life. [Theognis] in fact expresses approval of "fidelity," which is the fulfillment of all the virtues, and he banishes from the cities the truest evil, discord, and draws into uniform agreement the lives of those who take his advice. [Tyrtaeus,] on the other hand, praises the condition of valor in and for itself and encourages

---

297. Cf. *Rep.* 2.378a.
298. *Leg.* 1.630a.

ἐγκωμιάζει καὶ εἰς ταύτην προτρέπει τῶν ἄλλων ἀμελήσας ἀρετῶν.
κάλλιον δὲ ἀκούειν αὐτῶν τῶν τοῦ Πλά|τωνος ῥημάτων [*Leg*. 1.630a–b]·

> **ποιητὴν δὲ καὶ ἡμεῖς μάρτυρα ἔχομεν Θέογνιν, πολίτην τῶν ἐν Σικελίᾳ Μεγαρέων, ὅς φησιν·**
> > **πιστὸς ἀνὴρ χρυσοῦ τε καὶ ἀργύρου ἀντερύσασθαι |
> > ἄξιος ἐν χαλεπῇ, Κύρνε, διχοστασίῃ.**
> **τοῦτον δὴ φαμεν ἐν πολέμῳ χαλεπωτέρῳ ἀμείνονα ἐκείνου πάμπολυ γενέσθαι, σχεδὸν ὅσον ἀμείνω δικαιοσύνη καὶ σωφροσύνη καὶ φρόνησις εἰς ταὐτὸν ἐλθοῦσαι μετὰ ἀνδρείας αὐτῆς μόνον ἀνδρείας. | πιστὸς γὰρ καὶ ὑγιὴς ἐν στάσεσιν οὐκ ἄν ποτε γένοιτο ἄνευ ξυμπάσης ἀρετῆς.**

ἐνταῦθα τοίνυν ἀποδέχεται τὸν Θέογνιν ὡς πολιτικῆς ἐπιστήμης μετέχοντα καὶ τῆς ὅλης ἀρετῆς, ἣν δὴ πιστότητα κέκληκεν, ἡγεμόνα καὶ σύμβουλον·

ἐν δὲ Ἀλκιβιάδῃ δευτέρῳ [142e] τὸν ὀρθό|τατον τῆς εὐχῆς τρόπον ἀφοριζόμενος καὶ ἀσφαλέστατον εἰς τὴν ποιητικὴν αὐτὸν ἀναπέμπει τὴν ἔμφρονα.

> **κινδυνεύει γοῦν, ὦ Ἀλκιβιάδη, φησίν, φρόνιμός τις || εἶναι ἐκεῖνος ὁ ποιητής, ὃς δοκεῖ φίλοις ἀνοήτοις τισὶ χρησάμενος, ὁρῶν αὐτοὺς καὶ πράττοντας καὶ εὐχομένους ἅπερ οὐ βέλτιον ἦν, ἐκείνοις δὲ ἐδόκει κοινῇ ὑπὲρ ἁπάντων εὐχὴν ποιήσασθαι. λέγει δέ | πως ὡδί·**
> > **Ζεῦ βασιλεῦ, τὰ μὲν ἐσθλὰ καὶ εὐχομένοις καὶ ἀνεύκτοις ἄμμι δίδου, τὰ δὲ λυγρὰ καὶ εὐχομένων ἀπέρυκε.**

Τὴν γὰρ διάκρισιν τῶν ἀγαθῶν καὶ τῶν κακῶν καὶ τὴν | πρέπουσαν ταῖς μέσαις ἕξεσιν τῶν ἀνθρώπων πρὸς τὸ θεῖον ὁμιλίαν μόνος ὁ ἐπιστήμων ἀφορίζειν κύριος· καὶ διὰ τοῦτο καὶ τὸν τῶν στίχων τούτων ποιητὴν φρόνιμον ὁ Σωκράτης ἀπεκάλεσεν, ὡς οὔτε δι' ἐνθουσιασμὸν οὔτε δι' ὀρθὴν δόξαν, ἀλλὰ δι' ἐπιστήμην κρίνοντα μὲν τὰς τῶν αἰτουμένων

his listener toward that, neglecting the other virtues. But it is better to hear Plato's words themselves:

> We also have a poet to call to witness, namely, Theognis, a citizen of Megara in Sicily, who says,
>> Kyrnus, a man who remains faithful in bitter discord is worth his weight in gold and silver. [Theognis 77–78, West]
>
> Indeed, we say that this man, in bitter war, is much better than the other, virtually as much better as justice, moderation, and prudence coming together into union with bravery are better than bravery alone. No one would ever be faithful and sound in the midst of strife without total virtue [*Leg.* 1.630a–b].

Here, then, he accepts Theognis as having a share in civic wisdom and as a guide and counselor in total virtue, which he has called "fidelity."

[f. Didactic poetry: the *Second Alcibiades*]

In the *Second Alcibiades*, defining the most correct and efficacious manner of prayer, he sends [Alcibiades] to the poetry of wisdom:

> For indeed, there is a possibility, Alcibiades, (he says) that that ‖ poet is a thoughtful man, who seems to have had some stupid friends, and when he saw them doing and praying for things that were not the best but seemed so to them, he made for them a single, common prayer to cover everything. He says something of this sort:
>> King Zeus, that which is good, whether we pray for it or not, grant to us, and keep away the bad, even if we ask for it [Plato, *Alc.* 2 142e–143a].[299]

Only someone who has systematic knowledge is able to define the difference between goods and evils and the appropriate manner of addressing the divine for people of the intermediate dispositions. This is why Socrates called the poet of these lines "thoughtful," since it is neither through inspiration nor through correct opinion but rather by systematic

---

299. Cf. *Anth. pal.* 10.108.

φύ|σεις, στοχαζόμενον δὲ καὶ τῆς τῶν αἰτούντων ἕξεως, σώζοντα δὲ τὸ πρέπον ταῖς ἀγαθουργοῖς τῶν θεῶν δυνάμεσιν. καὶ γὰρ τὸ πάντας ἐπιστρέψαι διὰ τῆς εὐχῆς εἰς τὴν μίαν τοῦ Διὸς βασιλικὴν πρόνοιαν, καὶ τὸ τῶν ἀγαθῶν τὴν ὑπόστασιν ἐξάψαι τῆς τοῦ θεοῦ δυνάμεως, καὶ τὸ τῶν ἀλη|θινῶν κακῶν τὴν γένεσιν ἀφανίσαι διὰ τῆς τοῦ κρείττονος εὐμενείας, καὶ ὅλως τὸ ταῦτα τοῖς μὲν εὐχομένοις ἄγνωστα φάναι, τῷ δὲ θεῷ κατὰ τοὺς προσήκοντας ὅρους διακεκριμένα, φρονήσεώς ἐστι καὶ ἐπιστήμης οὐ τῆς τυχούσης ἔργον.

Εἰκότως δὴ οὖν τὴν τοιαύτην ποιητικὴν ἔμφρονα καὶ | ἐπιστήμονά φαμεν ὑπάρχειν· ἡ γὰρ ταῖς μέσαις ἕξεσιν τὰς ὀρθὰς ἀφορίζειν δυναμένη δόξας αὕτη δή που κατὰ τὴν τελέαν ἐπιστήμην ὑφέστηκεν.

Τὸ τρίτον δὴ οὖν περὶ τῆς μιμητικῆς λέγωμεν, ἣν ποτὲ μὲν εἰκάζειν τὰ πράγματα, ποτὲ δὲ φαινομένως ἀποτυ|ποῦσθαι προείπομεν. ταύτης γὰρ δὴ τὸ μὲν ὅσον εἰκαστι||κόν ἐστιν ὁ Ἀθηναῖος ξένος ἐναργῶς ἡμῖν παραδίδωσιν, τὸ δὲ ὅσον φανταστικόν, ὁ ἐν τῇ Πολιτείᾳ Σωκράτης παρίστησιν. ὅπως δὲ ταῦτα διενήνοχεν ἀλλήλων, τό τε εἰκαστικὸν λέγω τῆς μιμητικῆς εἶδος καὶ τὸ φανταστικόν, | ὁ Ἐλεάτης ξένος ἡμᾶς ἱκανῶς ἀναδιδάσκει. **δύο γάρ**, φησί [Soph. 235d],

— **φαίνομαι καθορᾶν εἴδη τῆς μιμητικῆς, μίαν μὲν τὴν εἰκαστικὴν ὁρῶν ἐν αὐτῇ τέχνην. ἔστιν δὲ αὕτη μάλιστα, ὁπόταν κατὰ τὰς τοῦ παραδείγματος συμμετρίας τις ἐν μήκει καὶ πλάτει καὶ | βάθει καὶ πρὸς τούτοις ἔτι χρώματα ἀποδιδοὺς τὰ προσήκοντα ἑκάστοις τὴν τοῦ μιμήματος γένεσιν ἀπεργάζηται.**
— **τί δέ; οὐ πάντες οἱ μιμούμενοί τι τοῦτ' ἐπιχειροῦσι δρᾶν;**
— **οὔκουν ὅσοι γε τῶν μεγάλων πού τι πλάττουσιν ἔργων ἢ γράφουσιν. εἰ | γὰρ ἀποδιδοῖεν τὴν τῶν καλῶν ἀληθινὴν συμμετρίαν οἶσθ' ὅτι σμικρότερα μὲν τοῦ δέοντος τὰ ἄνω, μείζω δὲ τὰ κάτω φαίνοιτ' ἂν διὰ τὸ τὰ μὲν πόρρωθεν, τὰ δὲ ἐγγύθεν ὑφ' ἡμῶν ὁρᾶσθαι.**

knowledge that he distinguishes the natures of the things prayed for and tries to make out the disposition of those offering the prayer, still keeping in mind what is appropriate to the beneficial powers of the gods. All of these actions bespeak thoughtfulness and uncommon systematic knowledge: returning all people through prayer to the unique and regal providence of Zeus, connecting the existence of goods to the power of the god, obliterating the origins of true evils through the goodwill of the greater one, and, generally, saying that these things are unknown to those offering the prayer while they are distinguished by the god according to their appropriate boundaries.

Thus it is appropriate that we say that such poetry is intelligent and systematic in its knowledge. This sort of poetry, which is able to define correct opinions for people of the intermediate dispositions, must surely in some sense have come to be through the perfection of systematic knowledge.

[g. Mimetic poetry: the *Sophist*]

Third, let us talk about mimetic poetry, which we have already said sometimes makes [accurate] images of things and sometimes gives an illusory impression of them. The Athenian Stranger gives us a clear reference to the category within this type of poetry that creates || [accurately] imitative copies, and Socrates in the *Republic* presents the illusionistic kind. How these things differ from one another—the [accurately] imitative and the illusionistic types of the mimetic category, that is—is adequately described by the Eleatic Stranger:

— For it seems to me (he says) that I can distinguish two types of *mimesis*.... One I view as a craft that produces accurate copies. This one occurs mainly when someone brings about the creation of the imitation according to the proportions of the model in mass and width and depth and on top of these adds the appropriate colors.
— What? Don't all the mimetic artists try to do that?
— Not at any rate those who sculpt or paint something of huge dimensions, for if they should reproduce the true proportions of the beautiful things, the higher part, you see, would appear smaller than it should and the lower part larger, on account of their being seen, respectively, from farther away and from closer.

— πάνυ μὲν οὖν.
— ἆρ' οὖν οὐ χαίρειν τὸ ἀληθὲς ἐάσαντες | οἱ δημιουργοὶ νῦν οὐ τὰς οὔσας συμμετρίας, ἀλλὰ δοξούσας εἶναι καλὰς τοῖς εἰδώλοις ἐναπεργάζονται;

ταῦτα δὴ διελόμενος ὁ Ἐλεάτης ξένος εἰκότως οἶμαι καὶ ἐπὶ τέλει τοῦ διαλόγου [264c] τὸν σοφιστὴν ἐνδῆσαι τῇ ὁριστικῇ μεθόδῳ βουλόμενος τῆς εἰδωλουργικῆς τὸ | μὲν εἰκαστικὸν ἔθετο, τὸ δὲ φανταστικόν· τὸ μὲν οἷόν ἐστι τὸ παράδειγμα, τοιοῦτον ἀπεργαζόμενον τὸ μίμημα, τὸ δὲ φαίνεσθαι τοιοῦτον τὸ γενόμενον οἷον τὸ μιμηθὲν παρασκευάζον. καὶ τῆς μιμητικῆς τοίνυν τῆς ποιητικῆς τὸ μὲν εἰκαστικόν ἐστιν, αὐτὰ τὰ πράγματα περὶ ὧν ποιεῖται τοὺς | λόγους ἀποτυπούμενον, τὸ δὲ μείζω καὶ ἐλάττω τὰ αὐτὰ || φαίνεσθαι καὶ τὴν ὁμοίωσιν ἐν φαντασίᾳ κειμένην ἔχειν, ἀλλ' οὐκ ἀληθείᾳ παρεχόμενον.

Τὸ μὲν δὴ μιμητικὸν ἅμα καὶ εἰκαστικὸν ὁ Ἀθηναῖος ξένος μνήμης ἠξίωσεν. τὴν γὰρ μουσικὴν οὐ τὴν ἡδονὴν τέλος ποιουμένην, ἀλλὰ τὴν | πρὸς τὸ παράδειγμα ἀφομοίωσιν, καὶ τὴν ὀρθότητα τοῦ μιμήματος ἐπιδεῖξαι προθέμενος οὑτωσί πως φησίν [Leg. 2.667c]·

τί δέ; τῇ τῶν ὁμοίων ἐργασίᾳ, ὅσαι τέχναι εἰκαστικαί, ἆρ' οὐκ, ἂν τοῦτο ἐξεργάζωνται, τὸ μὲν ἡδονὴν ἐν αὐτοῖς γίνεσθαι, παρεπόμενον ἐὰν γί|νηται, χάριν αὐτὸ δικαιότατον ἂν ἡμῖν προσαγορεύειν; ... τὴν δὲ ὀρθότητά που τῶν τοιούτων ἡ ἰσότης ἄν, ὡς ἐπὶ τὸ πᾶν εἰπεῖν, ἐξεργάζοιτο....

— Definitely.
— Isn't it true, then, that present-day artists abandon the truth and work into their images not the true proportions but rather those that *seem* beautiful? [*Soph.* 235d–236a].

Having made this distinction, the Eleatic Stranger is right, it seems to me, at the end of the dialogue, when he wants to tie down the sophist by the method of definition, to establish two categories of image-making: the accurately imitative and the illusionistic.[300] The first type fashions the imitation exactly after the model, but the other aims at making that which is produced *appear* like what it imitates. Likewise, then, there are two modes of poetic *mimesis*, the accurately imitative, reproducing the things themselves that the words are about, and the other, taking those same things and making them appear larger || or smaller than they are and creating a resemblance that lies in the imagination but does not exist in reality.[301]

[h. Accurately imitative mimetic poetry: the *Laws*]

The Athenian Stranger mentions that mimetic mode which is also accurate in its imitations. Undertaking to describe that μουσική that makes its goal not pleasure but rather resemblance to the model and correctness in the reproduction, he says something of this sort:

> What, then? As far as the creation of likenesses is concerned, is it not true in all the image-making arts that, if they manage to produce pleasure with their imitations—if it is just a by-product—that we would be perfectly correct to call this a "grace"? Still, I suppose that the correctness of such imitations is due, in general terms, to their own likeness [in dimensions, etc., to their model, and not to any pleasure they might provide] [*Leg.* 2.667c–d];

---

300. *Soph.* 264c.

301. This description depends on the notion that the φαντασία—roughly, the capacity of forming mental images or the locus of such images (at the lowest point in the soul, in touch with sense impressions)—may contain images that are real or false and that the φανταστικὸς mimetic artist (the "imaginative" or "illusionistic" artist) tricks the viewer by distorting the proportions of the object imitated to create a realistic mental image.

οὐκοῦν καὶ μουσικήν γε πᾶσάν φαμεν εἰκαστικήν τε εἶναι καὶ μιμητικήν; ἥκιστα ἄρα ὅταν τις μου|σικὴν ἡδονῇ φῇ κρίνεσθαι, τοῦτον ἀποδεκτέον τὸν λόγον.

καὶ ἐφεξῆς [668b]·

— καὶ μὴν τοῦτό γε πᾶς ἂν ὁμολογοῖ περὶ μουσικῆς, ὅτι πάντα τὰ περὶ αὐτὴν ἐστι ποιήματα μίμησίς τε καὶ ἀπεικασία. καὶ τοῦτό γε μῶν οὐκ ἂν ξύμπαντες ὁμολογοῖεν ποιη|ταί τε καὶ ἀκροαταί;
— καὶ μάλα.

τὴν ἄρα ποιητικὴν ταύτην, ὅση τῇ μουσικῇ συντέτακται τῇ παιδευτικῇ τῶν ἠθῶν καὶ τάς τε ἁρμονίας δύναται κρίνειν καὶ τοὺς ῥυθμούς, εἰκαστικὴν ἄν τις ἐν δίκῃ προσείποι καὶ οὕτω μιμητικήν· διὸ καὶ οὐ τὴν ἡδονὴν τέλος ἔχει, ἀλλὰ τὴν ὀρθό|τητα τῶν εἰκασθέντων.

Τὸ μὲν οὖν εἰκαστικὸν αὐτῆς τοιοῦτον· τὸ δὲ φανταστικὸν ἐκ τῶν ἐν Πολιτείᾳ γεγραμμένων κατανοήσωμεν. ἀποδείξας γὰρ ὁ Σωκράτης, ὅτι τρίτος ἀπὸ || τῆς ἀληθείας καὶ μιμητικός ἐστιν ὁ τοιοῦτος ποιητής, οἷον ἐπισκοπεῖν προύθετο, καὶ τοῦτο ἑξῆς προστίθησιν, ὅτι μιμεῖται φανταστικῶς τῷ τῆς ζωγραφίας παραδείγματι προσχρώμενος.

— τὸν μὲν δὴ μιμητὴν ὡμολογήκαμεν. εἰπὲ | δέ μοι περὶ τοῦ ζωγράφου τόδε, πότερα ἐκεῖνο αὐτὸ τὸ ἐν τῇ φύσει ἕκαστον δοκεῖ σοι ἐπιχειρεῖν μιμεῖσθαι ἢ τὰ τῶν δημιουργῶν ἔργα;
— τὰ τῶν δημιουργῶν, ἔφη.
— ἆρα οἷα ἔστιν ἢ οἷα φαίνεται; τοῦτο γὰρ ἔτι διόρισον.
— πῶς λέγεις; ἔφη.
— ὧδε. | κλίνη ἐάν τε ἐκ πλαγίου αὐτὴν θεᾷ ἐάν τε καταντικρὺς ἄν τε ὅπῃ οὖν, μή τι διαφέρει αὐτὴ αὑτῆς, <ἢ> διαφέρει μὲν οὐδέν, φαίνεται δὲ ἀλλοία; καὶ τὰ ἄλλα ὡσαύτως;

[and]

> Do we not say that all μουσική is both "productive of images" and "mimetic"? ... Consequently, when someone says that μουσική is judged by the standard of pleasure, this account is absolutely not to be accepted [*Leg.* 2.668a];

and so forth. And later,

> — Indeed, everyone would agree, concerning μουσική, that all the creations that relate to it are both *mimesis* and copying. Would not everyone, composers and audiences, agree on this?
> — Yes, indeed. [*Leg.* 2.668b–c].

One might, then, correctly use the terms "[accurately] imitative" and (in that sense) "mimetic" for this kind of poetry, to the extent that it is associated with music that educates character and is able to distinguish among modes and meters. Therefore it does not have pleasure as its goal but rather the accuracy of the representations.

[i. Illusionistic mimetic poetry: the *Republic*]

So much for [accurately] imitative mimetic poetry. Let us develop an idea of the kind of poetry that produces an illusionistic image from what is written in the *Republic*.

Socrates, having demonstrated that a poet of the sort he proposed to examine is at the third || remove from the truth and mimetic, then adds that he imitates in an illusionistic manner, using the example of painting:

> — Then we have agreed on the imitator. Tell me, concerning the painter, whether he seems to you to imitate the unique object as it exists in nature or the creations of the craftsmen.
> — The creations of the craftsmen.
> — As they are or as they seem? Make this further distinction.
> — What do you mean? he said.
> — This: if you look at a bed from the side, or right in front or any other way, it does not really change, does it—rather, it does not change and yet appears different? And likewise for other things?

> — οὕτως, ἔφη, φαίνεται, διαφέρει δὲ οὐδέν.
> 15 — τοῦτο δὴ αὐτὸ σκόπει· πρὸς πότερον γρα|φικὴ πεποίηται περὶ ἕκαστον, πότερα πρὸς τὸ ὂν ὡς ἔχει μιμήσασθαι, ἢ πρὸς τὸ φαινόμενον ὡς φαίνεται, φαντάσματος ἢ ἀληθείας οὖσα μίμησις;
> — φαντάσματος ἔφη [I 597e–598b].

διὰ δὴ τούτων ἐναργέστατα παρίστησιν ὁ Σωκράτης, ὅτι τὸ φανταστικὸν
20 τοῦ | μιμητικοῦ γένους τῆς ποιητικῆς ἀποτεμόμενος ἡδονῆς τε στοχάζεσθαι μόνης καὶ τῆς τῶν ἀκουόντων αὐτὸ ψυχαγωγίας φησίν. καὶ γὰρ ταύτης τῆς μιμήσεως τὸ φανταστικὸν ἀπολείπεται τοῦ εἰκαστικοῦ, καθ' ὅσον ἐκεῖνο
25 μὲν πρὸς τὴν ὀρθότητα βλέπει τοῦ μιμήματος, τοῦτο δὲ ἄρα πρὸς | τὴν ἐκ τῆς φαντασίας τοῖς πολλοῖς γινομένην ἡδονήν.

Τὰ μὲν οὖν γένη τῆς ποιητικῆς τοιᾶσδε καὶ παρὰ τῷ Πλάτωνι διακρίσεως ἠξίωται, τὸ μὲν ὡς κρεῖττον ἐπιστήμης, τὸ δὲ <ὡς> ἐπιστημονικόν, τὸ δὲ ὡς ὀρθοδοξαστικόν, τὸ δὲ ὡς καὶ τῆς ὀρθῆς δόξης ἀπολειπόμενον.
30 λέγει γοῦν περὶ τοῦ | ἐσχάτου σαφῶς [602a], ὡς **οὔτε ἄρα εἴσεται οὔτε ||**
K192 **ὀρθοδοξάσει ὁ τοιόσδε μιμητής, οἷον τὸν ποιητὴν τοῦτον ἐλέγομεν, περὶ ὧν ἂν μιμῆται πρὸς κάλλος ἢ πονηρίαν.**

Ὅτι καὶ ἡ Ὁμήρου ποίησις | ἐπιδείκνυσι τὰς τρεῖς ἰδέας ἐν ἑαυτῇ τῆς ποιητικῆς.

5

Τούτων δὲ αὖ διωρισμένων ἐπὶ τὴν Ὁμήρου ποίησιν ἀναδράμωμεν καὶ θεωρήσωμεν πᾶσαν ἐν αὐτῇ ποιητικῆς ἕξιν διαλάμπουσαν, διαφερόντως δὲ τὰς τοῦ ὀρθοῦ καὶ τοῦ καλοῦ στοχαζομένας.
10 Ὅταν μὲν γὰρ ἐνθουσιάζων ἐνεργῇ καὶ | ταῖς Μούσαις κάτοχος ὢν καὶ τὰ μυστικὰ περὶ αὐτῶν τῶν θεῶν ἀφηγῆται νοήματα, τηνικαῦτα κατὰ τὴν πρωτίστην ἐνεργεῖ καὶ ἔνθεον ποιητικήν· ὅταν δὲ αὖ τὴν τῆς ψυχῆς ζωὴν

— Yes. It seems different but is no different.
— Now, consider this: toward which end, with regard to each object, is painting directed, toward representing the real as it is or toward representing the appearance as it appears to be? And so, is it imitation of a fantasy or of the truth?
— Of a fantasy, he said. [*Rep.* 10.597e–598b]

Socrates indeed shows very clearly here that he distinguishes the illusionistic element of the mimetic class of poetry and says that it aims only at pleasure and at entertaining its listeners. In this sort of mimesis, the illusionistic is inferior to the accurately imitative inasmuch as the latter looks to the correctness of the imitation, the former to the pleasure that comes to the many from the illusion.

[j. Conclusion]

Thus in Plato as well, the classes of this kind of poetry are similarly distinguished: the one higher than systematic knowledge, another characterized by systematic knowledge, another by correct opinion, and the last, inferior even to correct opinion. Indeed, he says clearly, concerning the lowest poet, that "such an imitator (as we have said this poet is) will have neither knowledge nor || correct opinion concerning what he imitates, with reference to its goodness or its badness" [*Rep.* 10.602a].

(7) The Homeric poems as well exhibit within them these three[302] forms of poetry.

[a. The types of poetry in Homer]

Now that these have been defined, let us go back to the poetry of Homer and let us observe resplendent within it every one of the types of poetry, but especially those that aim at the correct and the good.

Whenever he acts under inspiration and possessed by the Muses and relates mystical conceptions about the gods themselves, at that point Homer is active according to the first and divinely inspired type of poetry.

---

302. The third type, mimetic poetry, is of course further divided into "accurately imitative" and "illusionistic," but Proclus clings to the threefold division as primary, doubtless out of a preference for the triad.

καὶ τὰς ἐν τῇ φύσει διαφορὰς καὶ τὰ πολιτικὰ καθήκοντα διεξίῃ, τότε δὴ μάλιστα κατὰ τὴν ἐπιστήμην διατί|θησιν τοὺς λόγους· ὅταν δὲ ἄρα τοὺς προσήκοντας ἀποδιδῷ τῆς μιμήσεως τύπους τοῖς τε πράγμασι καὶ τοῖς προσώποις, τηνικαῦτα κατὰ τὴν εἰκαστικὴν προΐσταται τὴν μίμησιν· ὅταν δὲ οἶμαι πρὸς τὸ φαινόμενον τοῖς πολλοῖς, ἀλλ' οὐ πρὸς τὴν ἀλήθειαν τοῦ ὄντος ἀποτείνηται καὶ οὕτω δὴ | τὰς τῶν ἀκουόντων ἐπάγηται ψυχάς, τότε που κατὰ τὸ φανταστικόν ἐστιν ποιητής.

Λέγω δὲ οἷον, ἵν' ἀπὸ τῆς ἐσχάτης ἀρξώμεθα τοῦ ποιητοῦ μιμήσεως, τὸν ἥλιον ἔστιν ὅπου λέγει τὰς ἀνατολὰς ἀπό τινος ποιεῖσθαι λίμνης καὶ τὰς δύσεις ὡσαύτως οὐχ ὡς ἔστιν ἑκάτερον τούτων οὐδ' ὡς | γίνεται λέγων οὐδὲ ταύτῃ μιμούμενος διὰ λόγων, ἀλλ' ὡς φαίνεται ταῖς αἰσθήσεσιν ἡμῶν διὰ τὴν ἀπόστασιν· τοῦτο τοίνυν καὶ πᾶν τὸ τοιόνδε φανταστικὸν τῆς ποιήσεως φαθί με λέγειν.

Πάλιν ὅταν τοὺς ἥρωας μιμῆται πολεμοῦντας ἢ || βουλευομένους ἢ λέγοντας κατὰ τὰ εἴδη τῆς ζωῆς, τοὺς μὲν ὡς ἔμφρονας, τοὺς δὲ ὡς ἀνδρείους, τοὺς δὲ ὡς φιλοτίμους, τῆς εἰκαστικῆς ἂν εἴποιμι τὸ τοιοῦτον ἔργον ὑπάρχειν. καὶ μὴν καὶ ὅταν ἢ τὰς διαφόρους ὑποστάσεις τῶν | μορίων τῆς ψυχῆς εἰδὼς ἀναφαίνηται [καὶ] διδάσκων, ἢ τὴν ἐξαλλαγὴν τοῦ εἰδώλου πρὸς τὴν χρωμένην ψυχὴν ἢ τὴν τάξιν τῶν ἐν τῷ παντὶ στοιχείων, γῆς ὕδατος ἀέρος αἰθέρος οὐρανοῦ, ἢ ἄλλο τι τοιοῦτον, τὴν ἐπιστήμονα τῆς ποιητικῆς δύναμιν ταύτην ἂν ἐγὼ θαρρῶν ἀποφηναίμην. |

Ἐφ' ἅπασι δὲ τούτοις ὅταν περί τε τῆς δημιουργικῆς ἡμᾶς ἀναδιδάσκῃ <μονάδος> καὶ τῆς εἰς τρία διανομῆς τῶν ὅλων, ἢ ὅταν περὶ τῶν Ἡφαίστου δεσμῶν, ἢ ὅταν περὶ τῆς πατρικῆς τοῦ Διὸς ἑνώσεως πρὸς τὴν γόνιμον θεότητα τῆς Ἥρας δι' ἀλύτου συμπλοκῆς, τότε δὴ φαίην ἂν αὐτὸν ἐνθουσιά|ζειν σαφῶς καὶ διὰ τὴν ἐκ τῶν Μουσῶν κατοκωχὴν τὰ τοιαῦτα διατιθέναι μυθολογήματα.

Δηλοῖ δέ που καὶ αὐτὸς ἐπὶ τοῦ Δημοδόκου τὴν ἐκ θεῶν ὡρμημένην ἐνέργειαν, λέγων πρὸ τῆς ᾠδῆς ὅτι **ὁρμηθεὶς θεοῦ ἤρχετο** καὶ ὅτι ἔνθεος

Whenever he tells of the life of the soul, on the other hand, and the distinctions within the natural world[303] and civic obligations, there he is certainly arranging his discourse under the guidance of systematic knowledge. Whenever he gives the appropriate sorts of imitation to events and characters, he is composing in the [accurately] imitative type of *mimesis*, and when he alludes to that which seems to the many to be the case, and not to the truth of reality and thus entices the souls of his listeners, then, I believe, he is a poet of the illusionistic type.

For example, starting from the lowest form of the Poet's *mimesis*, there is a passage where he says the sun rises from the sea,[304] and says the same sort of thing about its setting, but in neither case does he describe these things as they are or as they occur, nor does he use words to imitate in this way, but rather he describes them as they appear to our senses, because of the distance. You can take it, then, that this is what I mean, and everything of this sort, when I speak of the illusionistic type of poetry.

Next, when he imitates the heroes fighting or || taking counsel or speaking according to their various characters, some as wise men, some as brave, some ambitious, I would say that work of this sort belongs to the [accurately] mimetic type. Moreover, in his teaching[305] when he reveals from knowledge the various substances of the parts of the soul or the distinction between the "image" and the soul that uses it, or the arrangement of the elements in the universe (earth, water, mist, *aither*, and heaven), or anything else of this sort, I would presume to put this in the category of poetry based on systematic knowledge.

On top of all of these, whenever he offers us teachings on the creative monad[306] or on the tripartite division of the universe or about the bonds of Hephaestus or the paternal union of Zeus with the generative divinity of Hera in an indissoluble embrace, then I would say that he is clearly in a state of inspiration and that he composed these myths through being possessed by the Muses.

He himself, in fact, makes it clear, with reference to Demodocus, that the activity stems from the gods. He says at the beginning of the song that

---

303. Cf. the third paragraph below, K193,7–9. [F.]
304. Cf. *Od.* 3.1. [F.]
305. Bracketing καί at K193,5.
306. Supplying <μονάδος> at K193,11, with Kroll (apparatus), followed by F.

ἦν καὶ ὅτι ἡ Μοῦσα αὐτὸν ἐφίλησεν ἢ ὁ μουση|γέτης θεός·

> ἤ σέ γε Μοῦσ' ἐδίδαξε Διὸς παῖς ἢ σέ γ' Ἀπόλλων·
> λίην γὰρ κατὰ κόσμον Ἀχαιῶν οἶτον ἀείδεις,
> ὅσσ' ἔρξαν τ' ἔπαθόν τε καὶ ὅσσ' ἐμόγησαν Ἀχαιοί | [θ 488-490].

Καίτοι γε ὅτι τὸν Δημόδοκον ὡς ἑαυτὸν τρόπον τινὰ προΐσταται καὶ τῶν περὶ ἑαυτὸν παθημάτων παράδειγμα ποιεῖται, τῶν διατεθρυλημένων ἐστὶν ἱκανῶς, καὶ τὸ ||

K194

> ὀφθαλμῶν μὲν ἄμερσε, δίδου δ' ἡδεῖαν ἀοιδὴν [θ 64]

ἄντικρυς τὸν κατ' αὐτὸν μῦθον εἰς ἐκεῖνον ἀναπέμπειν ἔοικεν. τοῦτον δ' οὖν ἐνθεάζοντα λέγειν ἃ λέγει σαφῶς | διϊσχυρίζεται.

Ἀλλ' εὖ γε ὅτι Δημοδόκου καὶ τῆς ἐνθεαστικῆς ᾠδῆς ἐπεμνήσθημεν· δοκεῖ γάρ μοι κατὰ τὰ πρόσθεν εἰρημένα τῆς ποιήσεως γένη διελεῖν τοὺς παρ' αὐτῷ μνήμης ἠξιωμένους μουσικούς. ὁ μὲν γὰρ Δημόδοκος ἔνθους ἦν, ὥσπερ | εἴρηται, καὶ τὰ θεῖα καὶ τὰ ἀνθρώπινα ἀφηγούμενος, καὶ θεόθεν ἐξάψασθαι λέλεκται τὴν ἑαυτοῦ μουσικήν· ὁ δὲ Φήμιος ὁ ἐν Ἰθάκῃ κατὰ τὴν γνῶσιν μάλιστα τῶν τε θείων καὶ τῶν ἀνθρωπίνων ἐχαρακτηρίζετο·

> Φήμιε, πολλὰ γὰρ ἄλλα βροτῶν θελκτήρια οἶ|δας,
> ἔργ' ἀνδρῶν τε θεῶν τε, τά τε κλείουσιν ἀοιδοί [α 337-338]

λέγει που πρὸς αὐτὸν ἡ Πηνελόπη· τρίτος δὲ ἄλλος ὁ τῆς Κλυταιμνήστρας ᾠδός, μιμητικός τις ὡς ἔοικεν καὶ ὀρθῇ | δόξῃ χρώμενος καὶ τὰ τῆς σωφροσύνης μέλη προτείνων τῇ γυναικί·

> πὰρ γὰρ ἔην καὶ ἀοιδὸς ἀνήρ, ᾧ πόλλ' ἐπέτελλεν
> Ἀτρεΐδης Τροίηνδε κιών [γ 267-268]. |

"he began under [the inspiration of] the god" [*Od.* 8.499][307] and that he was divinely inspired and that the Muse or the god who leads the Muses loved him:

> Either the Muse, daughter of Zeus, taught you, or Apollo,
> you sing the fate of the Greeks so perfectly—
> all they accomplished and experienced and toiled at [*Od.* 8.488–490].

In fact, that he is presenting Demodocus in some sense as himself and creating him as a model of the experiences that were his own is something that has been said often enough, and the verse ||

> [The Muse] took away his eyes but gave sweet song [*Od.* 8.64]

seems to refer the myth about Homer directly to Demodocus. In any case, Homer clearly insists that he says what he says in a state of inspiration.

It is fortunate that we have brought up Demodocus and his inspired song, since it seems to me best to divide the singers whom Homer chose to mention according to the previously mentioned classes of poetry. Demodocus was inspired, as has been said, in his treatment both of the human and of the divine, and he is said to have attached his own art to the gods. Phemius, in Ithaca, was characterized especially by his knowledge of divine and human things.

> Phemius, you know many other means to bewitch men,
> and works of men and gods that bards sing of [*Od.* 1.337–338],

says Penelope to him, at one point. There is another, a third, Clytemnestra's bard, who seems to be accurately mimetic and to have correct opinion and provide songs of moderation for the woman:

> Beside her was a singer, whom Agamemnon
> gave many orders as he left for Troy [*Od.* 3.267–268],

---

307. Proclus's understanding of these three words (reflected in the translation above) is largely discredited. See Hainsworth ad loc. (Heubeck, West, and Hainsworth 1988, 379).

25 καὶ μέχρι τῆς τούτου συνουσίας οὐδὲν ἀνόσιον ἔργον τῇ Κλυταιμνήστρᾳ πέπρακτο, ταῖς παιδευτικαῖς ᾠδαῖς σωφρονίζοντος αὐτῆς τὴν ἄλογον ζωήν. τέταρτος δὲ εἰ βούλει μουσικὸς ἀνάλογον τῇ φανταστικῇ τῆς ποιήσεως ἰδέᾳ τεταγμένος Θάμυρις ἐκεῖνος, ὃν αἱ Μοῦσαι λέγονται
30 παῦσαι τῆς | ᾠδῆς· ||

K195 **αἱ δὲ χολωσάμεναι πηρὸν θέσαν** [B 599]·

πολυτροπωτέραν γὰρ καὶ αἰσθητικωτέραν καὶ τοὺς πολλοὺς ἀρέσκουσαν οὗτος μουσικὴν μετεχειρίζετο. διὸ καὶ φιλονικῆσαι λέγεται ταῖς Μούσαις,
5 ὡς ἂν τῆς ἁπλουστέρας | μουσικῆς, καὶ ταῖς Μούσαις οἰκειοτάτης τὴν ποικιλωτέραν ἐπίπροσθεν ποιησάμενος, καὶ ἀποπεσεῖν τῆς τῶν θεαινῶν εὐμενείας. ὁ γὰρ τῶν Μουσῶν χόλος οὐκ εἰς ἐκείνας ἀναπέμπει τι πάθος, ἀλλὰ τὴν τούτου δείκνυσιν ἀνεπιτηδειότητα τῆς ἐκείνων μεθέξεως. οὗτος
10 οὖν ἐστιν ὁ πολλοστὸς | ἀπὸ τῆς ἀληθείας ᾠδὸς καὶ τὰ πάθη τῶν ψυχῶν προκαλούμενος καὶ φανταστικὸς καὶ οὔτε δόξαν ὀρθὴν οὔτε ἐπιστήμην ἔχων περὶ τῶν μιμημάτων.

Πάντα ἄρα τὰ γένη τῆς ποιήσεως παρ' Ὁμήρῳ τεθεάμεθα, διαφερόντως
15 δὲ τὸ ἐνθουσιαστικόν, καθ' ὃ δὴ καὶ | μάλιστα χαρακτηρίζεσθαί φαμεν αὐτόν (καὶ οὐχ ἡμεῖς μόνον, ἀλλὰ καὶ αὐτὸς ὁ Πλάτων θεῖον ποιητὴν καὶ θειότατον τῶν ποιητῶν καὶ παντὸς μᾶλλον ἄξιον ζηλοῦν πολλαχοῦ προσαγορεύων αὐτόν, ὡς ἐν τοῖς ἔμπροσθεν ἐδείκνυμεν)· ἀμυδρότατον
20 δὲ τὸ μιμητικὸν ἅμα καὶ φανταστικόν, ἵνα καὶ | τοῖς πολλοῖς ᾖ πιθανός, καὶ ὅτι μὴ πᾶσα ἀνάγκη πᾶν τὸ τοιοῦτον τῆς ποιήσεως ἐξῃρῆσθαι.

Ἀλλ' Ὅμηρος μὲν τοῦτον τὸν τρόπον· οἱ δὲ τῆς τραγῳδίας ποιηταὶ φανταστικοὶ μόνον ὄντες καὶ τῆς τῶν πολλῶν στοχαζόμενοι ψυχαγωγίας
25 εἰκότως κατὰ τοῦτο πλεονάζουσιν τῆς ποιήσεως τὸ εἶδος. ὥσπερ | οὖν εἴ τις εἰς πόλιν εὐνομουμένην εἰσελθὼν καὶ θεασάμενος ἐκεῖ, καθάπερ φησὶν ὁ Ἀθηναῖος ξένος [Leg. 2.673e], καὶ τὴν μέθην ἕνεκά τινος χρησίμου παραλαμβανομένην μὴ τὴν φρόνησιν τὴν ἐν τῇ πόλει μηδὲ τὴν ὅλην τάξιν

and as long as he is with her, Clytemnestra does not commit a single unholy act, since he keeps her irrational disposition reasonable with his instructive songs. And, if you like, there is a fourth bard corresponding to the illusionistic type of mimetic poetry: that Thamyris whom the Muses are said to have stopped from singing: ||

In their rage, they left him maimed [*Il.* 2.599],

for this poet undertook a form of art that was too devious and too much addressed to the senses and pleasing to the many. For this same reason, he is also said to have competed with the Muses—as having placed the more varied kind of poetry before that kind which is simpler and more appropriate to them—and so to have fallen from the favor of the goddesses. For the "rage" of the Muses does not attribute to them any sort of emotion but rather demonstrates Thamyris's unsuitability to participate in them. This singer is the furthest from the truth, arousing the emotions of the soul, and an illusionist, having neither right opinion nor wisdom concerning the things that he imitates.

[b. The first type is characteristic of Homer]

We have seen, therefore, all the kinds of poetry present in Homer, but particularly the inspired, which we indeed say is most characteristic of him (and not only we, but Plato himself, who at many points calls him a "divine poet" and the "most divine of poets" and the most worthy to be emulated, as we have demonstrated above). Least conspicuous is the mimetic and illusionistic mode, which he uses to be persuasive to the masses of men—and moreover because there is no necessity to remove this sort of thing entirely from poetry.

This is how it stands as far as Homer is concerned, but the poets of tragedy, being exclusively illusionists and aiming at entertaining the many, naturally go overboard on this type of poetry. Just as, then, if someone coming into a well-governed city and observing (as the Athenian Stranger says[308]) that drunkenness is accepted there for some useful purpose should emulate *not* the thoughtfulness of the city, nor the total order, but only the

---

308. As F. points out, Proclus seems to have conflated two passages in the *Laws* here, 1.640d, and 2.673e–674c, the latter of which is singled out by Kroll as the passage referred to.

30 ζηλώσειεν, ἀλλ' αὐτὴν καθ' αὑτὴν μόνην τὴν μέθην, | οὐκ ἐκείνην ἂν αἰτίαν
K196 ἔχοι τῆς ἑαυτοῦ παρανοίας ἀλλὰ || τὴν οἰκείαν ἀσθένειαν τῆς κρίσεως,
οὕτως οἶμαι καὶ οἱ τραγῳδιοποιοὶ τὸ ἔσχατον τῆς Ὁμηρικῆς ποιήσεως
ζηλώσαντες οὐκ εἰς ἐκεῖνον τὴν ἀρχὴν τῆς σφετέρας πλημμελείας, ἀλλ'
εἰς τὴν ἑαυτῶν ἀναπέμπουσιν ἀδυναμίαν.

5   Λεγέσθω | τοίνυν ἡγεμὼν τῆς τραγῳδίας Ὅμηρος, καθόσον αὐτὸν
ἐζήλωσαν οἱ τῆς τραγῳδίας ποιηταὶ τά τε ἄλλα, καὶ ὅτι μέρη τῆς ἐκείνου
κατενείμαντο ποιήσεως, τὰ μὲν εἰκαστικῶς εἰρημένα φανταστικῶς
μιμησάμενοι, τὰ δὲ ἐπιστημόνως συντεθέντα ταῖς τῶν πολλῶν ἀκοαῖς
10 προσαρμόσαντες. ἀλλ' οὐ | τραγῳδίας μόνον ἐστὶν διδάσκαλος (ταύτης
μὲν γὰρ κατὰ τὸ ἔσχατον τῆς ἑαυτοῦ ποιήσεως), ἀλλὰ καὶ τῆς Πλάτωνος
ἁπάσης πραγματείας τῆς μιμητικῆς καὶ τῆς φιλοσόφου θεωρίας ὅλης.

Τί ἐστιν, ὅπερ ὁ Σωκράτης ἐν τῷ δεκάτῳ τῆς |
15 **πολιτείας ἐκβάλλει τῆς Ὁμήρου ποιητικῆς, καὶ διὰ**
τίνας αἰτίας, καὶ ὅτι οὐχ ὅλην αὐτήν, ἀλλ' ὅτι τὸ
ἔσχατον αὐτῆς ἀποδοκιμάζει μόνον.

Περὶ μὲν δὴ ποιητικῆς αὐτῆς καὶ τῆς Ὁμήρου τελεωτάτης ποιήσεως
20 ἱκανὰ τὰ εἰρημένα. τούτοις δὲ τοὺς τοῦ | Σωκράτους ἀντιπαρατείνωμεν
λόγους καὶ θεασώμεθα, τίνα μὲν ἐλέγχει ποιητικὴν ἰδέαν, ὅπως δὲ αὐτὸν
Ὅμηρον ἐξαιρήσωμεν τῶν πολλῶν ἐκείνων καὶ παντοδαπῶν ἐλέγχων·
καὶ πρῶτον ὅτι μὴ πᾶσαν εὐθύνει τὴν ποιητικὴν ἐκ τῶν γεγραμμένων
25 ἐπιδείξωμεν. ἐν ἀρχῇ μὲν οὖν εὐθὺς τοῦ δε|κάτου βιβλίου·

καὶ μήν, ἦν δὲ ἐγώ, φησίν, πολλὰ μὲν καὶ ἄλλα περὶ αὐτῆς ἐννοῶ
(τῆς εἰρημένης πολιτείας λέγων), **ὡς παντὸς ἄρα μᾶλλον ὀρθῶς**
ᾠκίζομεν τὴν πόλιν, οὐχ ἥκιστα δὲ ἐνθυμηθεὶς περὶ ποιήσεως, ||
K197 **τὸ μηδαμῇ παραδέχεσθαι αὐτῆς ὅση μιμητική. παντὸς γὰρ**
μᾶλλον οὐ παραδεκτέον νῦν καὶ ἐναργέστερον, ὡς ἐμοὶ δοκεῖ,
φαίνεται [595a].

καὶ πάλιν ἑξῆς·

5   **ὡς μὲν πρὸς ὑμᾶς εἰρῆσθαι** (οὐ γάρ μου κατε|ρεῖτε πρὸς τοὺς
τραγῳδίας ποιητὰς καὶ τοὺς ἄλλους πάντας τοὺς μιμητικούς),
λώβῃ ἔοικεν εἶναι πάντα τὰ τοιαῦτα τῆς τῶν ἀκουόντων
διανοίας [595b].

drunkenness, in and for itself, he would not be able to say that the city was the cause for his own madness but rather || would have to blame his own weakness of judgment—in just this way, it seems to me, the tragic poets, by emulating the lowest form of Homeric poetry, are locating the source of their mistake not in Homer but rather to their own weakness [of judgment].

Let it be said, then, that Homer was the founder of tragedy inasmuch as the poets of tragedy emulated him generally and that they divided up and parceled out his poetry, imitating in an illusionistic manner that which he described in the [accurately] imitative mode and adapting that which was composed through systematic knowledge to the ears of the many. However, he is not only the originator of tragedy (and indeed he is this by the lowest level of his poetry), but likewise of the whole mimetic style of Plato and of the whole of his philosophical perspective.

(8) What is it, precisely, of Homer's poetry that Socrates rejects, in the tenth book of the *Republic*, and what are his reasons? He does not reject it entirely, but only the lowest part.

On poetics itself and on the exquisitely perfect poetry of Homer, that which has already been said will be sufficient. Now, let us hold Socrates' words up against what has been said here and let us see what form of poetry he finds wanting and how we may exempt Homer from those many and varied refutations. First, let us demonstrate from his writings that he does not find fault with all of poetry. Right at the beginning of the tenth book he says,

> Indeed, I said, I have many other thoughts concerning it (meaning the state under discussion)—how we were constructing the city as correctly as possible—and particularly when I think about poetry, || and the decision absolutely not to accept any of it that is mimetic. It now seems even clearer to me that, above all else, it is not to be admitted [*Rep.* 10.595a],

and then, next,

> Speaking only to you—for you will not denounce me to the tragic poets and all the other mimetic artists—all such things seem an outrage against the understanding of the audience [*Rep.* 10.595b].

Τὸ μὲν οὖν προκείμενον αὐτῷ τοῦτό ἐστιν, τὴν μιμητικὴν μόνον ποίησιν καὶ ταύτης ὡς δειχθήσεται διαφερόντως τὴν | φανταστικὴν ἐκβάλλειν. ἡμεῖς δέ, εἰ μὲν πᾶσαν ποιητικὴν τοιαύτην ἐνόμιζεν εἶναι, τάχ' ἂν ὑπελαμβάνομεν αὐτὸν ὁμοίως ἅπασαν ἐλέγχειν· εἰ δὲ τὴν ἔνθεον ποίησιν καὶ τὴν μετ' ἐπιστήμης τοὺς λόγους ποιουμένην ἑτέραν ἀπολείπει τῆς ἀτελοῦς καὶ μιμήσει χρωμένης, πρὸς μὲν ταύτην | τείνειν οἰησόμεθα τοὺς ἐλέγχους, ἐκείνην δὲ ἐξαιρήσομεν τῶν προκειμένων λόγων. δηλοῖ δέ που καὶ αὐτὸς εἰπὼν ἐν ἀρχῇ καὶ διορισάμενος [595a], ὡς οὐ χρὴ τῆς ποιητικῆς ἀποδέχεσθαι ταύτην ὅση μιμητική. τό τε γὰρ πᾶσαν οἰόμενον εἶναι μιμητικὴν τοῦτο προστιθέναι περιττόν, καὶ | τὸ κατὰ πάσης τοὺς αὐτοὺς ἐφαρμόττειν λόγους ὑπολαμβάνοντα πρὸς τὴν μιμητικὴν ἀποτείνεσθαι μόνην ἄλογον. λείπεται ἄρα τοσοῦτον φάναι τῆς ποιητικῆς εὐθύνεσθαι μόνον, ὅσον περὶ τὴν μίμησιν τὴν πᾶσαν ἔχει σπουδήν.

Ἐπεὶ κἀν τοῖς ἐφεξῆς οὑτωσί πως προάγει τὸν ἔλεγχον· ὁ | ποιητὴς μιμητής· πᾶς μιμητὴς τρίτος ἀπὸ τῆς ἀληθείας· ὁ ἄρα ποιητὴς τρίτος ἀπὸ τῆς ἀληθείας.

διὸ καὶ ἐξ ἀρχῆς ὡρίσατο, τί ποτέ ἐστι μίμησις, λέγων·

τὸν τοῦ τρίτου ἄρα γεννήματος ἀπὸ τῆς φύσεως μιμητὴν καλεῖς [597e],

καὶ συνάγων ἀμφοτέρας τὰς προτάσεις οὑτωσί | πως φησίν·

τοῦτ' ἄρα ἔσται καὶ ὁ τραγῳδιοποιός, ‖ εἴπερ μιμητής ἐστιν, τρίτος ἀπὸ βασιλέως καὶ τῆς ἀληθείας πεφυκὼς καὶ οἱ ἄλλοι πάντες μιμηταί.

εἶτ' ἐπὶ τούτοις δείκνυσιν, ὡς οὐδὲ πάσης μιμήσεως ἐπιλαμβάνεται, ἀλλὰ τῆς φανταστικῆς, καὶ συνάγει· **πόρρω | ἄρα τοῦ ἀληθοῦς ἡ μιμητική ἐστιν** [598b], καὶ ὅτι ὁ κατὰ ταύτην μιμητὴς **οὐδὲ ὀρθοδοξάσει περὶ ὧν ἂν μιμῆται πρὸς κάλλος ἢ πονηρίαν** συλλογίζεται [602a].

Τί οὖν ταῦτα πρὸς τὴν καθ' Ὅμηρον ποιητικήν; πρὸς μὲν γὰρ τὴν τραγικὴν ποίησιν καὶ κωμικήν | ἱκανά· τούτων γὰρ τὸ ὅλον μίμησίς ἐστιν

What he is looking at, then, is this: the banishment of mimetic poetry alone, and within this category, as will be shown, especially the illusionistic. If he thought that the whole of poetry was of this sort, then we would probably think that Plato was condemning poetry in general, but if he accepts the distinction between inspired poetry and poetry composed according to systematic knowledge, on the one hand, and the imperfect type that makes use of *mimesis*, on the other, we shall take it that his refutations apply to the latter, and we shall exempt the former from the accusations before us. But he himself makes this clear, I think, at the beginning, when he specifies "not to accept any of it that is mimetic." It would be superfluous for one who thinks that all poetry is mimetic to add this point, and it would be absurd to apply the same arguments to the whole of poetry when he set out to refer only to the mimetic type. Consequently, what is left to say is that only that kind of poetry is attacked that is entirely concerned with *mimesis*.

In what follows, then, he proceeds with the accusation more or less in this way: The poet is an imitator. Every imitator is third in line from the truth. Therefore, the poet is third in line from the truth.

This is why, from the beginning, he has defined what *mimesis* is, saying,

> He who belongs to the third creation removed from nature you call an imitator [*Rep.* 10.597e],

and bringing together the two premises he says something of this sort:

> This, then, is what the tragic poet will be, || if indeed he is an imitator: third, by nature, from the king and from truth. The same is true of all other imitators [*Rep.* 10.597e].

Then, moreover, he demonstrates that this poet does not undertake every kind of imitation, but specifically the illusionistic, and he draws the conclusion that "mimetic art is indeed outside the realm of truth" [*Rep.* 10.598b] and says in summary that the imitator who works in this mode "will not even have correct opinion concerning the goodness or badness of what he imitates" [*Rep.* 10.602a].

What, then, is the relationship of these accusations to the poetry of Homer? As far as tragic and comic poetry are concerned, they are valid, since these are nothing but *mimesis*, contrived entirely to entertain the

πρὸς τὴν τῶν ἀκουόντων ἐξειργασμένη ψυχαγωγίαν· πρὸς δὲ τὴν Ὁμήρου ποιητικὴν τὴν ἀπὸ θεῶν ὡρμημένην καὶ τῶν ὄντων ἐκφαίνουσαν τὴν φύσιν οὐδὲν ἂν προσήκοι.

Καὶ πῶς γὰρ ἂν ἡ διὰ συμβόλων τὰ θεῖα ἀφερμηνεύουσα μιμητικὴ προσαγο|ρεύοιτο; τὰ γὰρ σύμβολα τούτων, ὧν ἐστι σύμβολα, μιμήματα οὐκ ἔστιν· τὰ μὲν γὰρ ἐναντία τῶν ἐναντίων οὐκ ἄν ποτε μιμήματα γένοιτο, τοῦ καλοῦ τὸ αἰσχρόν, καὶ τοῦ κατὰ φύσιν τὸ παρὰ φύσιν. ἡ δὲ συμβολικὴ θεωρία καὶ διὰ τῶν ἐναντιωτάτων τὴν τῶν πραγμάτων ἐνδείκνυται φύσιν. | εἴ τις ἄρα ποιητὴς ἔνθους ἐστιν καὶ διὰ συνθημάτων δηλοῖ τὴν περὶ τῶν ὄντων ἀλήθειαν, ἢ εἴ τις ἐπιστήμῃ χρώμενος αὐτὴν ἡμῖν ἐκφαίνει τὴν τάξιν τῶν πραγμάτων, οὗτος οὔτε μιμητής ἐστιν οὔτε ἐλέγχεσθαι δύναται διὰ τῶν προκειμένων ἀποδείξεων. |

Σκοπεῖτε δέ, εἰ βούλεσθε, καὶ τῶν λόγων ἕκαστον ἐφ' ἑαυτοῦ θεωροῦντες· ὁ ποιητὴς μιμητής· ὁ μιμητὴς τρίτος ἀπὸ τῆς ἀληθείας. <ὁ ποιητὴς ἄρα τρίτος ἀπὸ τῆς ἀληθείας>. ἀλλ' οὐχ ὁ πρώτιστος ποιητὴς φαῖμεν ἂν τοιοῦτος, οὐδὲ ὁ τῶν ποιητῶν ὡς φῂς θειότατος, ἀλλ' ἡ μὲν κάτο||χος ταῖς Μούσαις, αὐτοῖς σύνεστι τοῖς οὖσιν καὶ θεᾶται τὴν περὶ τῶν ὄντων ἀλήθειαν, ἡ δὲ μιμητής, τρίτος ἐστὶν ἀπὸ τῆς ἀληθείας. δεῖ δὲ ἕκαστον ἐκ τοῦ κρατίστου χαρακτηρίζειν, ὧν [μὲν] ἐνεργεῖ, καὶ οὐκ ἐκ τοῦ τελευταίου· ἐπεὶ | καὶ Πλάτωνα μιμητὴν ἂν οὕτως τις ἀποφήνειε καὶ τρίτον ἀπὸ τῆς ἀληθείας. ἔστι γὰρ ἐν τοῖς διαλόγοις [ἡ] μίμησις τῶν διαλεγομένων συμπινόντων, ἔστι δὲ καὶ πολεμούντων καὶ εἰρηνευόντων μίμησις, ὡς ἐν Τιμαίῳ καὶ ἐν Κριτίᾳ τεθεάμεθα· ἀλλὰ τοῦτο μὲν πάρεργον, τὸ δὲ ἐξαίρετον ἀγα|θὸν τοῦ Πλάτωνος ἡ φιλόσοφός ἐστι θεωρία. καὶ Ὁμήρου τοίνυν ὁ μὲν ἐνθεασμὸς τὸ πρώτιστόν ἐστιν ἀγαθὸν ἐν τῇ ποιήσει, τὸ δὲ μιμητικὸν ἔσχατον· τοῖς δὲ τραγῳδιοποιοῖς τοῦτο προηγουμένως ἐσπούδασται καὶ τὸ ὅλον αὐτοῖς ἡ μίμησις δύναται.

audience. But against the poetry of Homer, which springs from the gods and reveals the nature of things that exist, they would have no force at all.

How, moreover, could the term "mimetic" be applied to that poetry which interprets the divine by means of symbols? For symbols are not imitations of those things they symbolize. Things could never be imitations of their opposites (good imitating bad, natural imitating unnatural), but the symbolic mode[309] indicates the nature of things even by means of their complete opposites.[310] Therefore, if a poet is inspired and reveals to us through symbols[311] the truth about the things that are, or if he uses systematic knowledge to reveal to us the order of things, this poet is not an imitator and cannot be found wanting by the arguments we are discussing.

But look here, if you will, and examine in itself each part of the arguments: The poet is an imitator. Every imitator is third in line from the truth. Therefore the poet is third in line from the truth.

No!—we would not say that the very first poet was of this sort, nor that poet whom you[312] call "most divine." Rather, to the extent that he is possessed || by the Muses, he frequents those things themselves that truly exist and contemplates the truth concerning them. At the same time, to the extent that he is an imitator, he is third in line from the truth. One must characterize each individual by the best thing that he does, not by the least. Otherwise, on this basis one might make Plato an imitator and third in line from the truth, since in the dialogues one finds imitations of the speakers drinking together and imitations of men at war and men at peace, as we see in the *Timaeus* and the *Critias*. But this is incidental, and the special virtue of Plato is his philosophical doctrine. On the other hand, divine inspiration is the very highest virtue of the poetry of Homer, and the mimetic element is the lowest. This element, on the contrary, is the primary concern of the tragic poets, and, generally speaking, *mimesis* is everything to them.

---

309. ἡ συμβολικὴ θεωρία.

310. Proclus elsewhere (*In Tim.* 1:30 [Diehl], *Theol. Plat.* 1.4) and his follower "Dionysius" (*Coel. hier.* 2.2) repeat this point, and through the latter it enters medieval literary theory. See Lamberton 1986, 190 with n. 99, 245. (I am grateful to John Dillon for the references.)

311. συνθήματα, here a virtual synonym for σύμβολα.

312. Proclus literally draws Plato into the debate in this *prosopopoeia*.

15 Ἀλλ' εἰ καὶ μιμεῖσθαι, φησίν | [599a], Ὅμηρος ἱκανὸς καὶ πρὸς τῷ παραδείγματι τὸν νοῦν ἔχειν καὶ ποιεῖν ταῦτα ἃ μιμεῖται, πῶς οὐκ ἄτοπον αὐτὸν ἐπὶ τῇ δημιουργίᾳ τῶν εἰδώλων ἑαυτὸν τάξαι καὶ τοῦτο προστήσασθαι τοῦ βίου τέλος; ἀλλ' οὐδὲ ἡμεῖς συγχωρήσομεν τέλος εἶναι
20 τοῦ βίου τῷ θείῳ ποιητῇ τὴν μίμη|σιν, ἀλλὰ πάρεργον, καὶ δεύτερον, ἀλλ' οὐ πρῶτον, καὶ μιμεῖσθαι μὲν αὐτὸν πολλὰ ὧν οὐ δύναται ποιεῖν διὰ τὸ ψιλὴν αὐτὸν πεῖραν λαβεῖν τῶν μιμημάτων, μιμεῖσθαι δὲ αὖ καὶ ὅσα οἷός τε ποιεῖν ἦν. καὶ γὰρ ναυπηγοῦντα τὸν Ὀδυσσέα καὶ ἡνιοχοῦντα ἄλλον
25 μιμεῖται, <εἰ> καὶ οὐ πάν|τως ἡνιοχεῖν ἠδύνατο καὶ ναυπηγεῖν· γνωστικῶς γὰρ εἶχεν ταῦτα καὶ οὐ χειρουργικῶς· ἀλλὰ καὶ συμβουλεύοντα καὶ περὶ τῶν δικαίων εἰσηγούμενον· ταῦτα δὲ οὐ μιμεῖσθαι μόνον, ἀλλὰ καὶ ποιεῖν ἱκανὸς ἦν. ||

K200 **Τίνα ἄν τις ἀπολογήσαιτο πρὸς τοὺς ἐλέγχοντας λόγους ὡς οὐκ ὄντα τὸν Ὅμηρον ἀνθρώπων παιδευτικὸν οὐδὲ ὅλως πολιτικόν.**

5 Ἐνταῦθα δὴ λοιπὸν ἐπιρρεῖ παντοίων ἐρωτήσεων πλῆ|θος, τίνας ἐπαίδευσεν Ὅμηρος, εἴπερ μὴ μιμητὴς μόνον, ἀλλὰ καὶ δημιουργὸς παιδείας ἀληθοῦς, τίσι τῶν πόλεων ἔθετο νόμους, τίς πόλεμος δι' ἐκεῖνον ἐπράχθη καλῶς, τίνες ἰδίᾳ τῆς Ὁμήρου παιδείας ἀπολελαύκασιν.
   Πρὸς δὴ ταῦτα πάντα καὶ τὰ τοιαῦτα φήσομεν, ὅτι καὶ τὸ μῆκος τοῦ |
10 χρόνου τὴν ἐν ταῖς διαδοχαῖς τῶν ἀνθρώπων μνήμην ἀφῄρηται, καὶ τὸ μὴ εἶναι κατ' ἐκείνους τοὺς καιροὺς ἄνδρας ἱστορεῖν τὰ τοιαῦτα δεινοὺς τῆς διὰ τούτων ἡμᾶς διδασκαλίας ἀπεστέρησεν, ὧν Ὅμηρος ἰδίᾳ τε καὶ
15 κοινῇ ταῖς πόλεσιν εἰς παιδείαν καὶ εὐνομίαν συνετέλεσεν. ἐπεὶ | ὅτι γε τῶν πόλεών τινες ἐν τοῖς ὕστερον χρόνοις διαμφισβητήσασαι πρὸς ἀλλήλας Ὁμήρῳ δικαστῇ καὶ τοῖς Ὁμήρου γράμμασιν ἐχρήσαντο τῶν δικαίων, ἐκ τῆς ἱστορίας παρειλήφαμεν. τί οὖν θαυμαστόν, εἰ καὶ ζῶντα νομοθέτην τινὲς προεστήσαντο καὶ ἰδίᾳ διδάσκαλον ἐποιήσαντο καὶ ταῖς
20 ἐκεί|νου συμβουλαῖς ὥσπερ ἐπῳδαῖς ἐχρήσαντο; ταῦτα δὴ ἠγνόηται τοῖς ὕστερον. καὶ γὰρ ὅτι Πυθαγόρας πολλοὺς ἐπαίδευσεν καὶ ὅτι Λυκοῦργος

If, moreover, Plato says Homer is capable of imitation[313] and of directing his mind to the model and creating what he imitates, how is it not absurd for him to place himself in the category of creators of images and to set this up as the goal of his life? For ourselves, we shall not agree that the goal of the life of the divine poet is *mimesis*, which is, on the contrary, something incidental and secondary for him, and not of primary importance, and we shall agree that, on the one hand, he imitates many things that he was not able to do, on account of his having minimal experience of the thing imitated, but we shall insist also that he imitates some things that he was able to do. For example, he portrays Odysseus building a ship and another character driving a chariot, while he was in no way able to drive a chariot or to build a ship. He grasped these things theoretically but had no practical knowledge of them. Taking counsel and making some point about justice, however—these are things that he was able not only to imitate but to do himself. ‖

(9) How one can answer the accusations that Homer is neither educational for mankind nor in any way useful for society.

At this point, a flood of questions of all sorts arises: Whom did Homer teach, if he was not simply an imitator but truly an educator? For what cities did he establish laws? What war was well conducted through him? Who benefited privately from his instruction?[314]

To all of these and similar charges, we shall say both that the huge amount of time that has passed has obliterated the memory of these things from the successive generations of men and that the absence in those times of men skilled in giving accounts of such things has deprived us of information concerning what Homer, in private and in public, accomplished for the cities in education and good government. Still, we learn from history that in later times certain cities at war with one another used Homer and the writings of Homer as a judge of what was right. What wonder would it be, then, if during his lifetime some had actually set him up as their lawmaker and made him a teacher, in private, and used his advice as incantations? Of course, these things remain unknown to later generations. We have learned that Pythagoras taught many men and that

---

313. Cf. *Rep.* 10.599a, d.
314. Cf. *Rep.* 10.599d–600b.

Λακεδαιμονίοις ἐνομοθέτησεν ἢ Σόλων Ἀθηναίοις, ἐκ τῶν πολυστίχων ἡμεῖς ἔγνωμεν συγγραμμάτων, ὅσοι τῶν χρόνων ἐκείνων ἀπελείφθημεν.

Ἀλλ' ὅ | γε μιμητής, φησίν, οὔτε δόξαν ὀρθὴν ἔχει περὶ ἐκείνων ἃ μιμεῖται, ὥσπερ ὁ δημιουργός (οὐ γὰρ σύνεστιν τῷ χρησομένῳ), οὔτε ἐπιστήμην· οὐ γάρ ἐστιν ὁ χρησόμενος. τρεῖς γὰρ αὗται τέχναι νοείσθωσαν περὶ τὸν χαλινόν, εἰ τύχοι, ἡ χρησομένη, ἡ ποιήσουσα, ἡ μιμησομένη· δῆλον οὖν ὡς ἣ || μὲν ἐπιστήμην ἔχει τῆς τοῦ χαλινοῦ χρείας, ἣ δὲ δόξαν ὀρθήν, ὑπ' ἐκείνης διδασκομένη ποῖον εἶναι δεῖ τὸν χαλινόν, ἣ δὲ οὐδέτερα τούτων· γράφει γὰρ ὁ ζωγράφος χαλινὸν οὔτε ἱππέως οὔτε χαλινοποιοῦ παρόντος. ταῦτα καὶ | ἡμεῖς ἀληθῆ φήσομεν ἐπὶ τῶν μιμητῶν μόνον· εἰ δέ τις τοῦτο μὲν προστήσαιτο ὡς πάρεργον, ἄλλην δὲ ἐπιστήμην ἔχοι καὶ γνῶσιν τῶν πραγμάτων, πῶς οὐκ ἀνάγκη τοῦτον καὶ ὧν μιμεῖται τὸ κάλλος εἰδέναι καὶ τὴν πονηρίαν; δηλοῖ δέ που τοῦτο καὶ αὐτὸς ὁ θεῖος ποιητής, πανταχοῦ | τοῖς πραττομένοις τὴν ἑαυτοῦ κρίσιν ἐπιφέρων, ὅτι καλὰ καὶ ὅτι αἰσχρά, **τῷ δὲ φρένας ἄφρονι πεῖθεν**, καὶ **νήπιος** λέγων, καὶ **φρεσὶ γὰρ κέχρητο ἀγαθῇσιν** καὶ ὅσα τοιαῦτα, ταῖς πράξεσιν τὸ κάλλος καὶ τὴν μοχθηρίαν ἀφορίζων.

Ἀλλ' ὁ μιμητής, φησίν, καὶ εἰδωλοποιὸς οὗτος ποιη|τὴς πρὸς τὸ παθητικὸν τῆς ψυχῆς ἀποτείνεται καὶ τούτου προκαλεῖται τὰς κινήσεις· καὶ ἡμεῖς συμφήσομεν, εἰ τὴν τραγῳδίαν λέγοι καὶ τὴν κωμῳδίαν καὶ τὴν ἐν ταύταις μίμησιν. εἰ δὲ τὴν Ὁμήρου ποίησιν, τὸ μέγιστον αὐτῆς ἔργον εἰς τὴν τοῦ νοῦ καὶ τῆς διανοίας ἡμῶν τελείωσιν ἀποκεῖσθαι δια|τεινόμεθα, καὶ οὐχ ἡμεῖς μόνον, ἀλλὰ καὶ αὐτὸς ὁ Πλάτων, ὅταν λέγῃ [Ion 533e] τῷ ποιητῇ τῷ κατόχῳ ταῖς Μούσαις καὶ τοὺς ἀκούοντας συνενθουσιᾶν καὶ συνεπαίρεσθαι πρὸς τὴν θείαν μανίαν. εἰ μὲν οὖν τὸ παθητικόν ἐστι τὸ ἐνθουσιάζον, πρὸς τοῦτο καὶ Ὅμηρος προσεχέτω τὴν ἐνέργειαν· εἰ δὲ | νοῦς ἢ τοῦ νοῦ θειότερον, πολλοῦ ἂν δέοιμεν ταὐτὸν ἐκ τῆς Ὁμήρου

Lycurgus made laws for the Lacedaemonians and Solon for the Athenians, from the extensive written accounts that have come down to us from those times.

But [Plato] says, the imitator has neither correct opinion concerning what he imitates, like the craftsman (since he is not in the presence of the future user), nor systematic knowledge (since he is not himself the future user).[315] Imagine, for example, that there are three skills relating to the bit: that which will make use of it, that which will create it, and that which will imitate it. Now, it is clear that the || first is based on systematic knowledge of the use of the bit, the second on correct opinion (since it has learned from the first how the bit should be), and the last on neither of these. A painter paints a bit without the assistance either of a horseman or of a bit-maker. We shall agree that these observations are valid with regard to those who are exclusively imitators. But if someone should set [*mimesis*] up as something only incidental to his work, while [on another level] he had systematic knowledge and understanding of things, then how could he fail to understand the goodness or badness of the things he imitates? The divine Poet of course gives clear indications of this himself when everywhere he applies his own judgment to the things done and calls some good and some bad: "She persuaded him in his stupidity," he says, [*Il.* 4.104], and "fool" [var. loc.], and "he had a good heart" [*Od.* 14.421; 16.398], and all the rest, specifying the beauty or the depravity of the actions.

But, [Plato] says, this mimetic and image-making poet addresses himself to the emotional part of the soul and stimulates it.[316] We shall agree, if he means tragedy and comedy and the *mimesis* in them. But if he means the poetry of Homer, we maintain that the major work of this poetry is reserved for the perfection of our minds and understanding, and we are not alone in maintaining this—Plato does so himself when he says that, along with the poet who is inspired by the Muses, the audience as well is enraptured and is raised with him to divine madness.[317] Now, if the emotional is the same part that is inspired, then let it be said that Homer directs his activity to that part. But if it is intellect, or something more divine than intellect,[318] that is inspired, then there would be a great difference between

---

315. Cf. *Rep.* 10.602a. Proclus paraphrases *Rep.* 10.601–602 in this passage.
316. Paraphrase of *Rep.* 10.603e–605c.
317. Paraphrase of *Ion* 533e.
318. Kroll's conjecture, ἢ τὸ νοῦ θειότερον for the manuscript's ἢ τοῦ νοῦ θειότερον, followed by F., seems unnecessary. Either way, the reference is presumably

ποιήσεως πάσχειν, ὅπερ ἐκ τῆς τραγικῆς μιμήσεως. ὅταν οὖν ὁ Σωκράτης λέγῃ σαφῶς·

ὁ δὴ μιμητικὸς ποιητὴς οὐ πρὸς τὸ λογιστικὸν τῆς ψυχῆς πέφυκεν, εἰ μέλλει εὐδοκιμήσειν ἐν τοῖς πολλοῖς, ἀλλὰ πρὸς | τὸ ἀγανακτητικὸν καὶ ποικίλον ἦθος [605a],

ἀπαν||τησόμεθα λέγοντες· ἀλλ' ὁ ἐνθουσιαστικὸς πρὸς τὸ θεῖον τῆς ψυχῆς ποιεῖται τοὺς λόγους, ὅταν δὲ καὶ κολάζῃ τὰ πάθη διὰ τῶν ἐπιπλήξεων, πῶς ἄν φήσειέν τις αὐτὸν προκαλεῖσθαι καὶ τρέφειν τὸ παθητικόν;

Τοσαῦτα μὲν πρὸς τὰς | Σωκρατικὰς ἐφόδους ὑπὲρ Ὁμήρου δικαιολογούμεθα καὶ τῆς ἐνθέου ποιήσεως.

Διὰ ποίας αἰτίας ὁ Πλάτων ἐλέγχειν εἵλετο τὸν Ὅμηρον ὡς μὴ ὄντα παιδευτικὸν ἀνθρώπων ἱκανόν.

Πάλιν δὲ ἐπὶ θάτερα μεταβάντες αὐτὸ τοῦτο ζητήσωμεν, | διὰ ποίαν οὖν αἰτίαν ὁ Πλάτων τοιαῦτα περὶ Ὁμήρου καὶ ποιητικῆς εἵλετο λέγειν· οὔτε γὰρ ἐλάνθανεν αὐτὸν τὰ παρ' ἡμῶν ῥηθέντα καὶ ὅσα αὐτὸς ἐν ἄλλοις ἀνέγραψεν, οὔτε διὰ πάθος πεποίηται τὴν σύστασιν τῶν εἰρημένων λόγων· οὐ γὰρ θέμις αὐτῷ. τί οὖν τὸ αἴτιον, προσθῶμεν τοῖς | ἔμπροσθεν.

Δοκεῖ δή μοι τὴν τῶν καθ' ἑαυτὸν ἀνθρώπων περὶ φιλοσοφίαν καὶ τοὺς τῆς ἐπιστήμης λόγους ὀλιγωρίαν πολλὴν καὶ ἀμήχανον οὖσαν ὁρῶν, τῶν μὲν ἀχρηστίαν πάντων τῶν περὶ αὐτὴν ἐσχολακότων καταψηφιζομένων, τῶν δὲ καὶ φευκτὸν εἶναι τὸν ἐν φιλοσοφίᾳ βίον ἡγουμένων, | ποιητικὴν δὲ πέρα τοῦ μέτρου θαυμαζόντων καὶ τὴν μίμησιν αὐτῆς ζηλούντων καὶ μόνην πρὸς τὴν παιδείαν ἐξαρκεῖν οἰομένων, τοὺς ἀγῶνας ἐνστήσασθαι τούτους, ἐν οἷς ἐπιδείκνυσιν τὸ μὲν ποιητικὸν καὶ μιμητικὸν γένος πόρρω πῃ τῆς ἀληθείας πλανώμενον, τὴν δὲ ἀληθῆ σωτηρίαν τῶν ψυ|χῶν

what we experience from the poetry of Homer and what we experience from tragic *mimesis*. And so, when Socrates says clearly,

> The mimetic poet has no natural link to the rational part of the soul, if he is going to be appreciated by the many, but rather to the irritable and diverse temperament,[319]

we shall || answer by saying: On the contrary, the inspired [Poet] addresses his discourse to the divine part of the soul, and since he corrects the passions with his rebukes, how could one say that he evokes and nurtures the emotional?

This much, then, we shall say against the attacks of Socrates and in defense of Homer and of inspired poetry.

(10) What were Plato's reasons for choosing to accuse Homer of being inadequate for the education of mankind?

Now let us go back to the other side[320] and look into this problem: Why did Plato choose to say such things about Homer and about poetry? He was not ignorant of what we have been discussing, nor of what he himself wrote elsewhere, nor is it out of emotion that he created this conflict within his writings, because that is not characteristic of him. Let us then add to what has already been said the question: What, then, was the cause?

It seems to me that he saw that the scorn of the men of his time for philosophy and words of wisdom was enormous and irreversible, with some condemning the uselessness of all those who devoted themselves to it and others considering the philosophical life something to be avoided, and he saw as well that they had excessive admiration for poetry and were very enthusiastic about its *mimesis* and considered it to be adequate by itself for education. Therefore, he instituted these debates, in which he shows that the poetic and imitative genre wanders, in some sense, far from the truth, and that philosophy offers the true salvation of the soul. In line with

---

to the most unified part of the soul, the One of the soul, so to speak. (Thanks for this observation to John Dillon.)

319. Though emphatically presented by Proclus as a quotation, this is likewise a paraphrase of *Rep.* 10.605a.

320. In this final chapter the defense of Homer is complete, and in his closing words Proclus sets out to put in context the Socratic critique itself. [F.]

φιλοσοφίαν παρεχομένην. κατὰ γὰρ τὴν ἀγαθοειδῆ ταύτην βούλησιν καὶ τοὺς σοφιστὰς ἐλέγχει καὶ τοὺς δημαγωγούς, ὡς οὐδὲν πρὸς ἀρετὴν συντελεῖν δυναμένους. ||

Οὕτως οὖν οἶμαι καὶ τοὺς ποιητὰς εὐθύνει, διαφερόντως μὲν τοὺς τῆς τραγῳδίας δημιουργούς, καὶ ὅσοι μιμηταὶ ψυχαγωγίαν τινὰ μεμηχανημένοι τῶν ἀκουόντων, ἀλλ' οὐκ ὠφέλειαν πρὸς ἀρετήν, καὶ γοητεύοντες τοὺς πολλούς, ἀλλ' | οὐ παιδεύοντες· Ὅμηρον δὲ ὡς ἀρχηγὸν τῆς τοιαύτης Μούσης καὶ τοῖς τραγῳδιοποιοῖς τὰ σπέρματα τῆς μιμήσεως παρασχόμενον ἀξιοῖ τῶν ὁμοίων ἐλέγχων, ἀπάγων τοὺς πολλοὺς τῆς περὶ τὴν ποίησιν πτοίας, οἳ τῆς ἀληθινῆς παιδείας ἀμελήσαντες περὶ τοὺς ποιητὰς ὡς πάντων ἐπιγνώ|μονας διέτριβον. ὅτι δὲ ἀπὸ ταύτης ὁ Πλάτων τῆς προαιρέσεως πάντας καταβέβληται τοὺς περὶ ποιητῶν λόγους, ἐκ τῶν γεγραμμένων δῆλον·

οὐκοῦν, ἦν δ' ἐγώ, μετὰ ταῦτα σκεπτέον τήν τε τραγῳδίαν καὶ τὸν ἡγεμόνα αὐτῆς Ὅμηρον, ἐπειδή τινων ἀκούομεν, ὅτι οὗτοι | πάσας μὲν τέχνας ἐπίστανται, πάντα δὲ τὰ ἀνθρώπεια τὰ πρὸς ἀρετὴν καὶ κακίαν, καὶ τά γε θεῖα. ἀνάγκη γὰρ τὸν ἀγαθὸν ποιητήν, εἰ μέλλοι περὶ ὧν ἂν ποιῇ καλῶς ποιήσειν, εἰδότα ἄρα ποιεῖν, ἢ μὴ οἷόν τε εἶναι εὖ ποιεῖν. δεῖ δὴ ἐπισκέψασθαι, | πότερον μιμηταῖς τούτοις οὗτοι ἐντυχόντες ἐξηπάτηνται καὶ τὰ ἔργα αὐτῶν ὁρῶντες οὐκ αἰσθάνονται τριττὰ ἀπέχοντα τοῦ ὄντος καὶ ῥᾴδια ποιεῖν μὴ εἰδότι τὴν ἀλήθειαν. φαντάσματα γάρ, ἀλλ' οὐκ ὄντα ποιοῦσιν· ἤ τι καὶ λέγουσιν καὶ τῷ ὄντι οἱ | ἀγαθοὶ ποιηταὶ ἴσασιν περὶ ὧν δοκοῦσι τοῖς πολλοῖς εὖ λέγειν [598d–599a].

αὐτὸς γὰρ ἐν τοῖσδε τοῖς ῥήμασιν λέγει τὴν αἰτίαν σαφῶς, δι' ἣν τὸν κατὰ τῆς ποιητικῆς ταύτης ἐνεστήσατο λόγον, διότι δὴ τοὺς πολλοὺς ἑαλωκότας ὑπὸ τῆς μιμήσεως ἑώρα καὶ πάντων ἐπιστή||μονας οἰομένους εἶναι τοὺς πάντα χρήματα μιμουμένους καὶ εἰδωλοποιούς. παιδευτικῶς ἄρα τῶν πολλῶν καὶ διορθωτικῶς τῆς ἀτόπου φαντασίας καὶ προτρεπτικῶς εἰς τὴν φιλόσοφον ζωὴν τούς τε τραγῳδιοποιοὺς κοινοὺς παιδευτὰς | ὑπὸ τῶν τότε καλουμένους ὡς οὐδὲν ὑγιὲς ἐπεσκεμμένους διήλεγξεν, καὶ τῆς πρὸς Ὅμηρον ὑφῆκεν αἰδοῦς καὶ συντάξας αὐτὸν τοῖς τραγικοῖς ὡς μιμητὴν ἐν τοῖς λόγοις ηὔθυνεν.

this desire, which is basically a good one, he also lays blame both on the sophists and on the demagogues for being unable to accomplish anything contributing to virtue. ||

It is thus, I believe, that he censures the poets as well, and especially the creators of tragedies and those who are imitators and contrive to entertain the audience but not to contribute to their virtue and who enchant the many but do not instruct them. He judges Homer worthy of the same refutation, as the leader of this Muse and the one who provided the tragic poets with the seeds of their *mimesis*. [In so doing, Plato is] trying to lead the many away from their excitement with poetry, those who neglected true education and used to spend their time with the poets, as if the poets were knowledgeable about everything. That Plato set down all his writings about the poets with this purpose in mind is clear from what he writes:

> Now, I said, after this we must examine tragedy and its master Homer, since we hear from some that these not only know all skills but also all human things related to virtue or vice, and all divine things. It is necessary for a good poet [they argue], if he is going to treat his subjects well, to compose from a basis of knowledge, or he will be unable to compose well. Thus, we must consider whether those who meet up with such imitators have not been deceived and, looking at their works, have not realized that they were third in line from reality and could easily be composed by someone utterly ignorant of the truth—for poets fabricate illusions and not real things—or whether, in fact, they are saying something and the good poets are knowledgeable concerning that on which they seem to the many to speak well [*Rep.* 10.598d–599a].

In this passage Plato clearly states the cause that led him to institute this discourse against poetry: it is because he saw the many captivated by imitation and thinking that those who imitated everything and made images of everything were wise || about everything. And so, therefore, in a manner simultaneously educational for the many and corrective of their irrational fantasies and protreptic to the philosophical life, he argued that the tragic poets, whom the people of that time called their common educators, had not a single sound idea, and he even put aside his reverence for Homer, lumping him with the tragic poets and censuring him, in the course of the discussion, as an imitator.

Οὐ δὴ θαυμαστόν ἐστιν ἔτι, πῶς ὁ αὐτὸς καὶ θεῖος ποιητής ἐστι καὶ τρίτος ἀπὸ τῆς ἀληθείας. ὡς μὲν γὰρ | κάτοχος ταῖς Μούσαις θεῖός ἐστιν, ὡς δὲ μιμήσεως ἐφαψάμενος τρίτος ἀπὸ τῆς ἀληθείας. ὡδέ πως καὶ πρὸς τὰ μέγιστα τῶν δογμάτων αὐτῷ χρῆται μάρτυρι καὶ τῆς πολιτείας αὐτὸν ἐκβάλλει. ὡς μὲν γὰρ ἐπιστήμων τὴν αὐτὴν ἔχει τῷ Πλάτωνι περὶ τῶν ὄντων γνῶσιν, ὡς δὲ τοῖς τρα|γῳδιοποιοῖς ἔχων τι κοινὸν τῆς εὐνομουμένης ἐκβάλλεται πόλεως· **εἰ γὰρ τὴν ἡδυσμένην,**

φησὶν ὁ Σωκράτης,

παραδέξει Μοῦσαν ἐν μέλεσιν ἢ ἔπεσιν, ἡδονή σοι καὶ λύπη ἐν τῇ πόλει βασιλεύσετον [607a].

ὅτι δὲ καὶ Ὅμηρον, καθόσον ἐστὶν ἐν τῇ ποιήσει τῆς τραγῳδίας | τις ἀρχή, συμπεριλαμβάνει τοῖς ἐλέγχοις καὶ ὁ προηγούμενος λόγος εἰς τὴν τοιαύτην τείνει μίμησιν, διὰ πάντων ὡς εἰπεῖν [τῶν ἐκ] τῶν τοῦ Σωκράτους ῥημάτων ἐστὶν καταφανές.

ἔοικεν γάρ, φησίν, **Ὅμηρος τῶν καλῶν πάντων τούτων τῶν τραγικῶν διδάσκαλος καὶ ἡγεμὼν | γενέσθαι. ἀλλ' οὐ γὰρ πρό γε τῆς ἀληθείας τιμητέος ἀνήρ** [595c].

καὶ ἑξῆς·

τοῦτο ἄρα ἐστὶ καὶ ὁ τραγῳδιοποιός, εἴπερ μιμητής ἐστι, τρίτος ἀπὸ τοῦ βασιλέως καὶ τῆς ἀληθείας πεφυκώς [597e].

οὐ μὲν γὰρ τὴν αἰτίαν εἶπεν, δι' ἣν καὶ πρὸς Ὅμηρον ἂν αἱ||ρεῖται παρρησιάζεσθαι διὰ λόγων· οὐ δὲ ὡς προηγουμένως περὶ τραγῳδίας ἀγωνιζόμενος αὐτὸν διαφερόντως τὸν τραγῳδιοποιὸν μνήμης ἠξίωσεν ὡς τρίτον ἀπὸ τῆς ἀληθείας. καὶ ἔοικεν οὐδὲν ἄλλο κατασκευάζειν ἐν τούτοις ὁ Πλάτων | ἢ τοῦτο, ὃ καὶ Σωκράτης αὐτῷ πρῶτον ἐντυχὼν περὶ τραγῳδίαν σπουδάζοντι καὶ ἀποδείξας, ὡς οὐδὲν ἀγαθὸν ὑπάρχει τοῖς ἀνθρώποις, ἀπέτρεψεν τῆς τοιαύτης μιμήσεως, καὶ τρόπον τινὰ τοὺς

Thus it is no longer surprising that the poet who is "divine" is also "third from the truth." To the extent that he is possessed by the Muses, he is divine, and to the extent that he is an imitator, he is third from the truth. This is how Plato is able to call him as a witness to the greatest of doctrines and also to expel him from his state. In that he has systematic knowledge, he shares Plato's knowledge of the things that exist, but in that he has something in common with the tragic poets, he is expelled from the well-governed city.

Socrates says,

> If you are going to admit the honeyed Muse, either lyric or epic, pleasure and pain will rule in your city [*Rep.* 10.607a].

It is perfectly clear virtually everywhere in the speeches of Socrates that he includes Homer in the criticisms to the extent that in his poetry there is a precedent for tragedy, and the passage just cited refers to that sort of imitation.[321]

> For, he says, Homer seems to have been the teacher of all these fine tragic poets and their guide. But a man is not to be honored above truth [*Rep.* 10.595b–c],

and later,

> This, then, is what the tragic poet is, if indeed he is an imitator: third, by nature, from the king and from truth [*Rep.* 10.597e].[322]

In the first citation, he told the reason why he chose ‖ to speak out openly against Homer as well, while in the second, since he was primarily contending with tragedy, he specifically said that the tragic poet was "third from the truth." Plato seems to be concerned here with precisely that very thing that Socrates pointed out to him when they first met[323] and Plato was enthusiastic about tragedy: that it is no good for people. [And so Socrates] turned him away from imitation of that sort and in the direction, one way

---

321. *Rep.* 10.598d–599a, cited on 303 (K203), above.
322. Cf. above, 293 (K197,30–198,2), with ἔσται for ἐστί.
323. The same anecdote occurs in Apuleius, *Plat.* 1.2 (89–90 Moreschini) and in the Anonymous Prolegomena, 3 (Westerink).

Σωκρατικοὺς ἐκείνους ἀναγράφειν λόγους, ἐν οἷς ἀπέφαινεν οὔτε παιδευτικὴν οὖσαν οὔτε ὠφέλιμον τὴν | τραγῳδίαν, ἀλλὰ τρίτην ἀπὸ τῆς ἀληθείας, καὶ οὔτε ἐπιστήμης οὔτε ὀρθῆς δόξης μετέχουσαν περὶ ὧν μιμεῖται πραγμάτων οὐδὲ τῆς διανοίας ἡμῶν, ἀλλὰ τῆς ἀλογίας στοχαζομένην. ταῦτα δέ, εἰ καὶ ἔστι πως παρ' Ὁμήρῳ συνηρημένως καὶ ἀρχοειδῶς, ἀλλὰ μὴ διὰ ταῦτα τὴν Ὁμήρου ποίησιν | αἰτιώμεθα.

Οὐδὲ γὰρ Πλάτωνα διὰ τὴν ἐν τῇ λογογραφίᾳ καλλιέπειαν αἰτιατέον καὶ τὴν περὶ τὴν λέξιν ἐπιμέλειαν, εἰ καὶ ἄλλοι περὶ ταύτην διαφερόντως ἐσπούδασαν, τὰς τελευταίας ἐνεργείας μιμούμενοι τοῦ Πλάτωνος, οὐδὲ αὐτὸν τὸν δημιουργὸν τῶν θνητῶν ἕνεκα πραγμάτων καὶ τῆς περὶ τὴν | γένεσιν κακίας, ἐπειδήπερ αἱ μερισταὶ ψυχαὶ καλινδοῦνται περὶ αὐτήν.

Ταῦτα, ὦ φίλοι ἑταῖροι, μνήμῃ κεχαρίσθω τῆς τοῦ καθηγεμόνος ἡμῶν συνουσίας, ἐμοὶ μὲν ὄντα ῥητὰ πρὸς ὑμᾶς, ὑμῖν δὲ ἄρρητα πρὸς τοὺς πολλούς.

or another, of writing those Socratic dialogues in which he revealed that tragedy is neither educational nor useful, but third in line from the truth, with a share neither of systematic knowledge nor of correct opinion concerning the matters it imitates, and is aimed not at our understanding but rather at our irrational part. Even if these things are present in Homer in a very general way and in the form of a precedent, yet let us not hold the poetry of Homer responsible on this account.

Neither is Plato to be blamed for his beautiful use of language in the dialogues and the care he takes of expression, even if others have concentrated their efforts particularly on this, in imitation of the lowest of the activities of Plato[324]—nor is the demiurge to be blamed for mortal things and for the evil that is associated with γένεσις because the partial souls come to wallow about in it.

Dear friends, may these things be made a tribute to the memory of my conversations with my guide,[325] things fit for me to tell you, but which you must keep secret from the many.[326]

---

324. One is reminded that Plato was read as a stylistic model in the rhetorical schools of the Roman Empire. Cf. Libanius, *Ep.* 569 (Foerster).

325. Syrianus.

326. This closing flourish may be largely conventional (F.), but it is yet another instance of *hoi polloi* here referring to the Christians, who were surely in control of the teaching (and so the meaning) of Homer in Proclus's time and just as surely would treat the "secret doctrine" with ridicule and contempt should they be told of it.

Bibliography

Editions

Kroll, Wilhelm, ed. 1899. *Procli Diadochi in Platonis Rem publicam commentarii.* Vol. 1. Bibliotheca scriptorum Graecorum et Romanorum Teubneriana. Leipzig: Teubner.

Translations, Entire

Festugière, A. J., trans. 1970. Proclus, *Commentaire sur la Republique.* Bibliotheque des textes philosophiques. Paris: Vrin.

Translations, Partial

Taylor, Thomas, trans. 1804. In Floyer Sydenham and Thomas Taylor, trans. *The Works of Plato.* 5 vols. London: T. Taylor. In this work, said to be the first complete translation of Plato into English, Taylor included nearly the whole of the first book of Essay 6 (pp. 63–217 [K72–154] in this volume) as an "Introduction to the Second and Third Books of the Republic" under the title *An Apology for the Fables of Homer.* His translation is reprinted in Raine and Harper 1969, 447–520.

Bychkov Oleg V., and Anne Sheppard, trans. and eds. 2010. *Greek and Roman Esthetics.* Cambridge Texts in the History of Philosophy. Cambridge: Cambridge University Press. This collection includes the fifth section of the second book of Essay 6 (pp. 257–61 [K177,7–179,32] in this volume).

Secondary Works

Annas, Julia. 1981. *An Introduction to Plato's Republic.* Oxford: Oxford University Press.

Athanassiadi, Polymnia. 1981. *Julian and Hellenism: An Intellectual Biography*. Oxford: Oxford University Press.

———, ed. and trans. 1999. *Damascius, the Philosophical History*. Athens: Apamea Cultural Association.

Baltzly, Dirk, trans. 2007. Proclus, *Commentary on Plato's* Timaeus, Volume 3: Book 3, Part 1: *Proclus on the World's Body*. Cambridge: Cambridge University Press.

———, trans. 2009. Proclus, *Commentary on Plato's* Timaeus, Volume 4: Book 3, Part 2: *Proclus on the World Soul*. Cambridge: Cambridge University Press.

Beutler, Rudolf. 1957. Proklos 4. PW 23.1:186–247.

Boyancé, Pierre. 1937. *Le Culte des Muses chez les philosophes grecs: Études d'histoire et de psychologie religieuses*. Paris: Boccard.

Burkert, Walter. 1972. *Lore and Science in Ancient Pythagoreanism*. Translated by Edwin L. Minar Jr. Cambridge: Harvard University Press.

Cameron, Alan. 1969. The Last Days of the Academy at Athens. *Proceedings of the Cambridge Philological Society* 195:7–29.

Couvreur, Paul, ed. 1901. *Hermeias von Alexandrien in Platonis Phaedrum Scholia*. Paris: Bouillon. Repr., Hildesheim: Olms, 1971.

des Places, Edouard. 1971. *Oracles chaldaiques: Avec un choix de commentaires anciens*. Paris: Belles Lettres.

Diehl, Ernst. 1899. Subsidia Procliana. *Rheinisches Museum* 54:171–200.

———. 1903–1906. *Procli Diadochi in Platonis Timaeum commentaria*. 3 vols. Leipzig: Teubner.

Dillon, John. 1973. *Iamblichi Chalcidensis in Platonis dialogos commentariorum fragmenta*. Philosophia antiqua 23. Leiden: Brill.

———. 1976. Image, Symbol, and Analogy: Three Basic Concepts of Neoplatonism. Pages 247–62 in *The Significance of Neoplatonism*. Edited by R. Baine Harris. Norfolk Va.: International Society for Neoplatonic Studies, Old Dominion University; Albany: State University of New York Press.

Dover, K. J., ed. 1968. Aristophanes, *Clouds*. Oxford: Oxford University Press.

Festugière, A. J. 1944–1954. *La révélation d'Hermès Trismégiste*. Études bibliques. 4 vols. Paris: Gabalda.

Fowden, Garth. 1990. The Athenian Agora and the Progress of Christianity. *Journal of Roman Archaeology* 3:494–500.

Frantz, Alison. 1988. *The Athenian Agora XXIV: Late Antiquity; A.D. 267–700*. Princeton: American School of Classical Studies.

Gallavotti, Carlo. 1929. Eterogeneità e cronologia dei commenti di Proclo alla Republica. *Rivista di Filologia e d'Istruzione Classica* 57:208-19.

———. 1971. Intorno ai commenti di Proclo alla Republica. *Bollettino del Comitato per la Preparazione dell'Edizione nazionale dei Classici greci e latini* NS 19:41-54.

Gigon, Olof. 1987. *Librorum deperditorum fragmenta*. Vol. 3. of *Aristotelis Opera*. Berlin: de Gruyter.

Hardwick, Charles S., ed. 1977. *Semiotic and Significs: The Correspondence between Charles S. Peirce and Victoria Lady Welby*. Bloomington: Indiana University Press.

Heubeck, Alfred, Stephanie R. West, and John Bryan Hainsworth. 1988. *A Commentary on Homer's Odyssey*. Vol. 1. Oxford: Oxford University Press.

Holwerda, Douwe. 1967. De artis metricae vocabulis quae sunt ΔΑΚΤΥΛΟΣ et ΕΝΟΠΛΙΟΣ. Pages 51-58 in ΚΩΜΩΙΔΟΤΡΑΓΗΜΑΤΑ: *Studia Aristophanea viri Aristophanei W. J. W. Koster in Honorem*. Amsterdam: Hakkert.

Kern, Otto. 1922. *Orphicorum fragmenta*. Berlin: Weidmann.

Kroll, Wilhelm. 1894. *De Oraculis Chaldaicis*. Breslauer philologische Abhandlungen 7.1. Breslau: Koebner.

———, ed. 1899-1901. *Procli Diadochi in Platonis Rem publicam commentarii*. 2 vols. Bibliotheca scriptorum Graecorum et Romanorum Teubneriana. Leipzig: Teubner.

Kuisma, Oiva. 1996. *Proclus' Defence of Homer*. Commentationes humanarum litterarum 109. Helsinki: Societas Scientarum Fennica.

Lamberton, Robert. 1986. *Homer the Theologian: Neoplatonist Allegorical Reading and the Growth of the Epic Tradition*. Transformation of the Classical Heritage 9. Berkeley: University of California Press.

———. 1992. The Neoplatonists and the Spiritualization of Homer. Pages 115-33 in *Homer's Ancient Readers: The Hermeneutics of Greek Epic's Earliest Exegetes*. Edited by Robert Lamberton and John J. Keaney. Princeton: Princeton University Press.

Lubac, Henri de. 1959-1961. *Exégèse médiévale: Les quatre sens de l'écriture*. 2 vols. Paris: Aubier.

Lucas, Donald William, ed. 1968. Aristotle, *Poetics*. Oxford: Oxford University Press.

Manolea, Christina-Panagiota. 2004. *The Homeric Tradition in Syrianus*. Thessalonike: Ant. Stamoulis.

Moreschini, Claudio, ed. 1991. *Apulei Platonici Madaurensis operae quae supersunt.* Vol. 3. Leipzig: Teubner.

Moss, Jessica. 2007. What Is Imitative Poetry and Why Is It Bad? Pages 415–44 in *The Cambridge Companion to Plato's Republic.* Edited by Giovanni R. F. Ferrari. Cambridge: Cambridge University Press.

Oliver, James H. 1935. Greek Inscriptions. *Hesperia* 4:1–107.

Pépin, Jean, and Henri-Dominique Saffrey, eds. 1987. *Proclus lecteur et interprète des anciens: Actes du colloque international du CNRS, Paris, 2–4 Octobre 1985.* Paris: Editions du Centre national de la recherche scientifique.

Pfeiffer, Rudolf. 1949–1953. *Callimachus.* 2 vols. Oxford: Oxford University Press.

Raine, Kathleen, and George Mills Harper. 1969. *Thomas Taylor the Platonist: Selected Writings.* Princeton: Princeton University Press.

Rose, Valentin 1867. Der Index zu Proclus Abhandlungen über die Republik des Plato. *Hermes* 2:96–101.

———. 1886. *Aristotelis qui ferebantur librorum fragmenta.* Bibliotheca Teubneriana. Leipzig: Teubner.

Ruelle, Charles Émile. 1889. *Dubitationes et solutiones de primis principiis, in Platonis Parmenidem.* 2 vols. Paris: Klincksieck.

Runia, David T., and Michael Share, trans. 2008. Proclus, *Commentary on Plato's* Timaeus, Volume 2: Book 2: *Proclus on the Causes of the Cosmos and Its Creation.* Cambridge: Cambridge University Press.

Saffrey, Henri-Dominique. 1975. Allusions antichrétiennes chez Proclus le diadoque platonicien. *Revue des Sciences Philosophiques et Théologiques* 59:553–63.

Saffrey, Henri-Dominique, and Alain-Philippe Segonds, eds. 2001. Marinus, *Proclus ou Sur le bonheur.* Collection des universités de France. Paris: Belles Lettres.

Saffrey, Henri-Dominique, and Leendert G. Westerink, ed. and trans. 1968. Proclus, *Théologie Platonicienne.* Vol. 1. Collection des universités de France. Paris: Belles Lettres.

Schrader, Hermann, ed. 1880–1890. *Porphyrii quaestionum Homericarum ad Iliadem pertinentium reliquias.* 2 vols. Lepizig: Teubner.

Sheppard, Anne D. R. 1980. *Studies on the 5th and 6th Essays of Proclus' Commentary on the Republic.* Hypomnemata 61. Göttingen: Vandenhoeck & Ruprecht.

———. 1981. Two Notes on Proclus. *Classical Quarterly* NS 31:470–71.

Siorvanes, Lucas. 1996. *Proclus: Neo-Platonic Philosophy and Science.* New Haven: Yale University Press.
Smyth, Richard A. 1997. *Reading Peirce Reading.* Lanham Md.: Rowman & Littlefield.
Stahl, William Harris. 1952. Macrobius, *Commentary on the Dream of Scipio.* Records of Civilization, Sources and Studies 48. New York: Columbia University Press.
Tarrant, Harold, trans. 2007. Proclus, *Commentary on Plato's Timaeus, Volume 1: Book 1: Proclus on the Socratic State and Atlantis.* Cambridge: Cambridge University Press
Wachsmuth, Curt. 1897. *Ioannis Laurentii Lydi Liber de ostentis et calendaria graeca omnia.* Leipzig: Teubner.
Wachsmuth, Curt, and Otto Hense, eds. 1884–1923. *Ioannis Stobaei anthologium.* 5 vols. in 4. Berlin: Weidmann.
Watts, Edward J. 2006. *City and School in Late Antique Athens and Alexandria.* Berkeley: University of California Press.
West, M. L. 1982. *Greek Metre.* Oxford: Oxford University Press.
———. 1983. *The Orphic Poems.* Oxford: Oxford University Press.
———. 1992. *Ancient Greek Music.* Oxford: Oxford University Press.
Westerink, Leendert G., ed. 1990. *Prolégomènes à la philosophie de Platon.* Translation by Jean Trouillard, with the collaboration of Alain Philippe Segonds. Paris: Belles Lettres.

Index Locorum[1]

Aristotle
    frag. 893 Gigon (81 Rose): 49,17; 17 n. 18; **frag. 921** Gigon (81 Rose): 49,17; 17 n. 18

Callimachus
    Hymn 4 (Delos), 84–85: 125,29–30; **frag. 588** Pfeiffer: 150,14–15

Chaldaean Oracles (des Places)
    frag. 8: 99,1; 135,31–136,1; **frag. 45**: 176,23; **frag. 55**: 137,22; cf. **frag. 61**: 152,17–18; **frag. 66**: 178,17; **frag. 146**: 111,3–11; **frag. dub. 211**: 111,28–112,1

Homer
    Iliad 1: cf. **54, 127 and** *passim*: 146,19; **122**: 144,25; **167–168**: 145,1–2; cf. **216–217**: 146,21–22 with 205 n. 236; **225**: 129,16; **262, 267**: 58,21; cf. **281**: 130,19–20; **423–424**: 166,28–29; **599–600**: 126,14–16; **607–608**: 126,23–24
    2: cf. **1–40**: 115,4–6; **10**: 117,9–10; **599**: 195,1; **781–783**: 93,19–21
    3: **300**: 102,16
    4: cf. **14–19**: 105,30; **88**: 103,30; **93**: 104,13; **104**: 201,11; **162**: 102,5
    5: **838–9**: 112,4–5
    8: cf. **5–27**: 106,24 with 129 n. 165; **14**: 169,7
    9: **116–118**: 130,29; **524**: 58,15; **524, 526**: 145,25–26
    14: **176**: 137,24; **203–204**: 93,16–17; cf. 165,8; **295–296**: 133,2–3; **315–316**: 132,28–29

---

1. This index is based on that in Kroll (2:416–24), with additions and omissions. Page and line numbers refer to Kroll's Greek text (reproduced in the margin of this volume); note numbers are cited according to the pages of the English translation in this volume.

15: cf. **187**: 165,8-9
16: cf. **225-232**: 147,1; **433**: 123,19-20; **856-857**: 118,9-10 with 151 n. 181
17: **126-127**: 150,19-20; cf. **425**: 127,2-3
18: cf. **22-27**: 164,3-4; **54**: 123,15; **96**: 149,19; cf. **117-118**: 149,10 with 209 n. 241; **175-179**: 150,23-151,1; **401**: 141,14
20: **4**: 107,15; **13**: 90,24; 165,19; cf. **20-30**: 106,24 with 129 n. 165; **25**: 107,10; **64-65**: 118,7 with 151 n. 181; 122,7; **67-74**: 91,25
21: 122-123; 152,5-6; **284-285**: 114,14-15; **600-601**: 147,17-18
22:**15**: 146,13; **168**: 123,19-20; **213**: 148,1; **359-360**: 148,16-17; **363**: 119,27; **414-415**: 123,7-8
23: **100-102**: 118,11; 121,22 with 151 n. 181; **103-104**: 118,8; 122,3-7 with 151 n. 181; **141-151**: 146,17 with 203 n. 234; **195**: 152,13; **219, 221**: 152,20-21
24: **9-12**: 123,9-12; **527-528**: 96,14-15; **534-538**: 99,27-29; **587-589**: 151,13-15
Odyssey 1: **1**: 184,30; **298-299**: 58,17-18; **337-338**: 194,15-16
3: **1**: 192,22-23 with 285 n. 304; cf. **146**: 201,11; **267-268**: 194,22-23
4: **379**: 167,14; **386**: 112,27; **411**: 113,5; **417-418**: 113,14-15
6: **46**: 87,20
8: **64**: 174,15; 194,1; cf. **302**: 142,12; **326**: 126,13; **488-490**: 193,21-24; **499**: 193,18
9: **6-10**: 129,21-26
10: **306**: 167,14; **495**: 118,9; 119,20-21 with 151 n. 181; **513-514**: 169,13-14
11: [*nekyia*]: 168,3-169,24; **90-91**: 172,28-29; **158**: 169,11; **207-208**: 119,21-22; **488-491**: 118,5-6 with 151 n. 181; 120,1-2; **601-608**: 172,13-14; **602-603**: 120,15-16
14: **421**: 201,12
17: **485-486**: 109,17-18
24: **6-9**: 118,10-11; 120,6; 121,19-23 with 151 n. 181

ORPHEUS (often ὁ θεολόγος or οἱ θεολόγοι) (Kern)
frag. 52: 125,21; **frags. 57, 58, 122, 220, cf. 215**: 93,24 with 105 n. 131; **frag. 148**: 138,25; **frag. 177**: 102,11; **frag. 186**: 138,13; **frag. 210**: 94,5; **frag. 221** (= frag. 221 Abel): 85,10 with 89 n. 113; **frag. 354**: 125,1; 128,8

PLATO

Alcibiades 1: **129c**: 171,23; **130d**: 172,1–6
Alcibiades 2: **142e**: 187,24; **147b**: 186,11; **151a**: 149,26
Apology: **41a**: 157,6–11
Cratylus: **391a–393b** (double names): 169,25–170,26; **404b**: 140,8–12; **405c**: 57,14–16
Critias: general: 199,6–9
Gorgias: **491e**: 160,2–3; **523a–527a**: 156,22–157,1; 168,17–19; **525d–526c**: 157,2–4; 168,26–169,2
Ion: **530b**: 158,3–11; 163,15; **531a**: 182,28–30; **533d–e**: 163,1–26; 201,21–23; **534b–c**: 184,14–25
Laches: **188d**: 61,28–62,6; 84,19–22
Laws: 1: **624a**: 68,21–26; 156,16–20; **629e–630b**: 186,30–187,24; **646–651**: 75,28–76,5
    2: **661b–d**: 100,12–15; **667c–668c**: 67,11–27; 190,2–25; **668d**: 46,5–7; **669c**: 43,10; 64,27; **672a**: 161,18; **673e**: 195,25–26
    3: **676a**: 156,3–4; **682a**: 155,25–156,9; 185,10–14
    4: **715e–716a**: 101,22–26; **716a**: 98,12–14; **719c**: 56,24–25
    5: **728c**: 102,29–103,2; **737e**: 161,17–18
    6: **751a**: 161,19–20
    7: **788a**: 161,20
    10: **900c–907b**: 167,15–17
    uncertain *loci*: 105,15–16
Minos: **318b**: 62,6–9; **319d**: 156,9–12; **320d**: 156,12–14
Phaedo: **58e–59b**: 122,28–123,4; **61a**: 60,24; **61b**: 65,26–29; **62b**: 85,1–3; **69c**: 85,3–5; **81d**: 119,18–21; **83d**: 121,13–15; **94b–d**: 155,1–15; **95a**: 70,19–20; 155,15–20; **108a**: 85,5–7; **108a–114c**: 118,18–24; **110b–115a**: 168,13–15; **112a**: 169,2–5; **113c**: 169,16–17; **117d**: 164,2–3
Phaedrus: **242d**: 176,14–21; **243a**: 173,8–25; **244a**: 57,16–18; **245a**: 56,25–28; 57,25–29; 70,28–30; 140,16–19; 180,10–12; **246e–247a**: 153,5–8; 166,12–18; **248d**: 56,28–57,3; **248e**: 175,21–22; **249d**: 57,17–18; **250c**: 83,23–26; **250d**: 175,7–11; **252e–253e**: 108,9–12; **265a**: 108,9–12
Philebus: **16c, 23c**: 133,22–23
Politicus: **309b**: 61,14–18
Republic: 1: **338d**: 159,28–160,1
    2: **371e**: 162,5 with 231 n. 262; **376e**: 59,28–29; **377d**: 44,23–25 with 9 n. 10; **378a**: 48,1–2 with 13 n. 16; 80,13–16; 186,16–18;

378d: 79,27–81,4; 186,14–16; **381b**: 109,15; **383a**: 115,6–7 with 145 n. 176

3: **386c–387b**: 117,26–118,13; **389d–390a**: 129,8–13; **390c**: 140,21–23; **390d–e**: 143,22–23; **391b–c**: 150,8–9; **392d**: 66,22–23; **395a**: 42,19–22; **395a–b**: 51,29–52,3 with 21 n. 25; **398a**: 42,6–7; **398e–399c**: 42,22–24; 54,3–7; **399a**: 61,24–27; **399c**: 62,5–9; **399e ff.** (meter): 42,3; 60,17–20; **400b**: 42,26–28; 62,14–17; **406b**: 55,3

5: **459c**: 116,12–16; **472d9–e1**: 162,5–8 with 231 n. 262

7: **530e**: 60,2–6

9: **581c** (?): 160,3–4

10: **595a–b ff.** (rejection of mimetic poetry): cf. 66,22; 177,7–11; 196,24–197,8; **595b–c**: 204,23–26; **597e–598b**: 70,20–21; 191,4–18; 197,26–198,5; 204,26–28; **598b**: 198,4–5; **598d–599a**: 203,10–26; **599a, d**: 199,14–15; **602a**: 191,29–192,2; 198,5–8; **603e–605c**: 201,14–16 with 299 n. 315; **605a**: 201,27–30; **607a**: 204,16–19; **614b**: 169,18–24; **614b–621b** (Myth of Er): 118,23–29; 168,15–17; **617b**: 69,9–12; **618a**: 104,17–20; **620a**: 120,20–22

Sophist: 235d–236a: 189,5–22; **264c**: 189,22–25

Symposium: 209d: 157,17–23; **223d**: 42,16–19; 51,28–52,3; 53,17–19

Timaeus: gen. 199,6–9; **19d**: 45,6–8; 46,19–23 with 11 n. 15; **21c**: 43,12–13; **28a**: 109,27–110,4; **28c–30c**: 164,13–21; **30a**: 107,30; **30c**: 164,20–21; **31c**: 142,29–31; **33d**: 126,27–127,1; **36c**: 69,12–14; **40d**: 185,14–17; **41a–d**: 107,20–23; 165,25–166,11; **41d**: 164,30–165,3; **42d**: 127,6–9; **42e**: 135,22–28; **43a**: 142,20–21; **48a**: 99,10–12; **80b**: 131,17 with 175 n. 207

PLOTINUS

Enneads **2.3.11**: 105,2–5
    4.3.16: 105,21–25

General Index

Acheloos, 209
Achilles, xxvi, xl, 11, 117, 143, 147, 155, 157, 161, 163, 171, 173–75, 199–215, 233
Agamemnon, 145–49, 173–75, 199–203, 287
Alcibiades, 209, 275
allegory, xii, xvii, xxi, 81, 167 n. 195, 175
Amelius, 115 n. 143
Aphrodite, xxii, xl, 109, 133–35, 189–93, 193–99
Apollo, xx with n. 32, xl, 31 n. 32, 55, 101, 107 with n. 137, 143, 169 n. 198, 203–7, 271, 287
Apollodorus, 161, 233
Ares, xxii, xl, 55, 107, 193–99
Aristotle, xiv, xvi, xvii, xix, xxvii, xxxiii, 3 n. 3, 17, 51 n. 64, 63 n. 80, 127 n. 162, 167 n. 195
Homeric Problems, xxvii
Athena, xi, 33, 101, 107, 119–29, 133, 139, 143, 189, 203, 207
Athenian Platonic school, xi n. 1, xii–xvi, xxviii, xxix, 61 n. 78
curriculum, xiii–xvii, xxiii

Basil of Caesarea, xxviii, 21 n. 23

Callicles, 137, 221, 227
Callimachus, 5 n. 6, 165, 210, 211

Calypso, 131 n. 167
catharsis, 17 n. 18
Chaldaean Oracles, xiv, xxviii, xxx, xxxv, 115, 137 with n. 172, 139 with n. 173, 185, 187, 215 n. 246, 255 n. 286, 259
Chiron, 211, 217
Christians, xxv, xxviii, xxix, xxx, 19–21 n. 22, 21 n. 23, 65 n. 85, 67 n. 87, 69 n. 90, 73 n. 94, 85 n. 103, 171 n. 201, 219 n. 251, 307 n. 326
Clytemnestra, xxiii, 287, 289
Critias, 245

Damascius, xi n. 1, xii–xiii, xxxiv, 53 n. 69, 63 n. 83, 187 n. 218
Damon, 5, 25, 29, 39–43
Demodocus, xxii, xxix n. 62, 251, 285, 287
[Ps.-]Dionysius the Areopagite, xxv, 183 n. 214, 295 n. 310
Dionysus, 89, 99, 105 with n. 134, 253

Euclid, xiv

foot/feet, metrical, 3 n. 2, 39, 41–43 n. 50
dactyl, 39 with n. 45, 41–43
enoplios, 39, 41

foot/feet, metrical (cont.)
  iamb, 39
  pariambis, 39 with n. 44

Giants, 19 with n. 22, 69, 99, 125, 271

Hades, xxxix, 87, 89, 151–59, 207, 217, 221–25, 241
Hector, xl, 161, 199, 205–13
Hegias, xii–xiii
Helen, 217, 249–55
Hephaestus, xxxix–xl, 81–83, 101–3, 109, 165–69, 185, 193–99, 285
Hera, xl, 101, 107, 129 n. 164, 133, 177–93, 285
Heracles, xxii, 155, 209, 217, 247–49
Hermes, 55 with n. 71, 109, 131 n. 167, 143
Hesiod, 63 with n. 80, 73, 85 n. 105, 91 n. 119, 223
Homer, xiii–xxiv, xxvi–xxx, xxxviii–xliii, 7 nn. 7 and 9, 33, and 59–307 *passim*
  Iliad, xxvii, xxviii, xxx, 91 n. 119, 129 n. 164, 253 n. 284 and *passim*
  Odyssey, xxvii, xxviii, xix, xxx, 89 n. 112, 195 n.230, 221, 239 n. 270, 253 n. 284 and *passim*
  Nekyia in the *Odyssey*, xxii, 221, 239–43, 247
  Theomachy (Battle of Gods in the *Iliad*), xxxviii, 91 n. 119, 93, 109, 209

Iamblichus, xiii–xvi, 17 n. 18, 95 n. 121, 265 n. 292

Julian the Apostate, xxix with n. 60

Leto, 101, 109

Macrobius, 147 n. 179
Marinus, xi–xii, xxviii
Mentor, 143
meter. *See* metrics; foot/feet, metrical
metrics, xx n. 32, xxxii, 5, 25–29, 35–47, 51, 55, 259, 261, 273, 281
mimesis/mimetic, xvii–xviii, xxi–xxii, xxvi–xxvii, xli–xlii, 7–11, 15–19, 37, 43, 45, 49–51, 87, 227–33, 245, 261, 277–303
Minos, 221–23, 241
mode(s), musical, xxxii, xxxvii, 3 n. 1, 25–31, 35 n. 35, 41–45, 51, 55, 87, 261
  Dorian, 41–45, 87 n. 108
  Ionian, 41, 45 with n. 57
  Lydian, 41, 45
  Mixolydian, 45 with n. 57
  Phrygian, 41, 87
μουσική, xxxvii, 5 with n. 5, 31–37, 87 n. 109, 279–81
Muses, xxi, xxxii, xxxvii, 5 with n. 5, 13, 15, 31, 33, 45, 61, 193, 221, 225, 229, 249, 251, 263–71, 283–89, 295, 299, 303, 305

Nestor, 33, 137, 201

Odysseus, xl, 137, 171, 175–77, 239 n. 270, 245–47, 297

GENERAL INDEX 321

Olympiodorus, 105 n. 134
Orestes, 33
Orpheus, xxiv, xxx, 63 with n. 80, 91 n. 119, 105 with n. 134, 115 n. 143, 121, 167 n. 195, 189, 223, 251, 253
Ovid, 135 n. 170

Paris (Alexander), 133, 207
Parmenides, 137
Patroclus, 155, 157, 203, 211–15
Peirce, Charles Sanders, xxv, xxvi n. 48
Peleus, 117, 211, 217
Perithous, 217
Phemius, xxii, 287
Phoinix, 33, 199–201
Plato, *passim*
　Alcibiades, 1 xiii, xiv, xli, 247
　Alcibiades, 2, xlii, 209, 273, 275–77
　Cratylus, xiii, xiv, xli, 31 with n. 32, 193, 243
　Critias, 295
　Gorgias, xiv, xli, 221, 239–41
　Ion, xli, 221 n. 253, 223, 225, 233, 265–69, 299
　Laches, 41 with n. 48
　Laws, xiv, xviii, xxxv, xli–xlii, 5, 11 with n. 12, 29 n. 30, 31, 45, 47, 51, 55, 71, 123 n. 153, 221 with n. 253, 229, 239, 271–75, 279–81, 289 n. 308
　Letters: Second Letter, 85 n. 103
　Minos 41, 221
　Parmenides, xiii, xiv, xxiii, 93–95 n. 120, 137

Phaedo, xiv, xli, 61, 87, 93–95 n. 120, 153, 219, 239–41
Phaedrus, xiv, xx, xli, 31 n. 31, 87 n. 109, 133, 219 n. 250, 237–39, 249–55, 261–65, 267
Philebus, xiv, 93–95 n. 120, 179
Politicus, xiv, xv n. 16
Republic, xiii–xx, xxiii–xxiv, xxvi. xxix, xxxi–xxxiii, 3, 7 n. 8, 21, 25 with n. 29, 37, 39 n. 46, 49–51 n. 64, 55, 59–61, 73 n. 94, 81 n. 98, 125, 151, 219 with n. 250, 225, 239–43, 249, 257, 273, 277, 281–83, 291; Myth of Er: xv, xxxiii, 55, 89, 125 n. 158, 239–41 n. 270
Sophist, xiv, xlii, 277–79
Symposium, xiv, xxix, xxxvii, 3, 21, 25, 31 n. 31, 223
Theaetetus, xiv, 85 n. 103
Timaeus, xiii, xiv, xviii, xxiii, xxviii, xli–xlii, 5, 9, 11, 47 with n. 59, 55, 81 n. 100, 97–99 n. 124, 115, 119, 131 with n. 168, 133, 137, 167, 183, 197, 233–37, 245, 271–73, 295
Plotinus, xii, xiv, xv, xxiii, xxix, 17 n. 19, 53 n. 67, 59 n. 75, 97 n. 124, 105 n. 134, 115 n. 143, 125, 127 with n. 159
Plutarch of Athens, xx
Plutarch of Chaironeia, xviii
　Platonic Questions, xviii
　Disappearance of Oracles, 101 n. 129

poetics, xiii–xxvii, xxxii, 7 n. 7, 9, 59, 61, 249, 257–91
polytheism, xi–xiii, xv, xxv, xxviii–xxx
Porphyry, xii, xxvii, xxix, 31 n. 31, 59 n. 75, 89 n. 112, 155 n. 183, 157 n. 185, 165 n. 194, 193–95 n. 227
   Essay on the Cave of the Nymphs in the Odyssey, xxvii, 89 n. 112, 155 n.183
Priam, 161, 163, 213
Proclus, *passim*
   commentaries, xiii–xiv
   Commentary on the Republic, xiv–xvii and *passim*
   Elements of Theology, xiii
   Introduction to the Physical Sciences, xiv
   Platonic Theology, xiii, xxiii–xxiv
   "On the Symbols of Myth," xxiii with n. 42
   tripartite division of poetry, xxi–xxvi, xxvii n. 24, 259–297
Proteus 135 with n. 170, 141

Socrates, xviii–xix, xxiv, xxvi, xxix, xxxi–xxxii, xxxvii–xlii, 2–307 *passim*
Stesichorus, xli, 249–255
symbol, xxi, xxiii–xxv, 13–15, 63 n. 83, 65, 75, 83–91, 119, 163, 165, 169, 175, 181, 183, 187, 189, 199, 205, 215, 237, 253, 255, 257, 271, 295
symposium, xxix–xxx, 3, 45

Syrianus, xiii n. 12, xvii n. 23, xx–xxi, xxvii, xxix, xxxix, 61 with n. 78, 63 nn. 82–83, 95 n. 121, 109 n. 139, 147–49, 179, 195 n. 229, 213 n. 243, 215, 307
"Solutions to Homeric Problems," 109 with n. 139

Thamyris, xxiii, 289
Theodore of Asine, xvii, xxxii
Theseus, 135 n. 170, 217
Thetis, 135 with n. 170, 161, 163
Thrasymachus, xxxii, 39 n. 40, 137, 227
Timaeus, 115, 119, 133, 137, 167, 183, 197, 235, 245, 271
tragedy, 21, 25, 63, 131 n.167, 289, 291, 303, 305, 307
tragedy and comedy, xxvi, xxxvii, 3, 17, 19, 23, 25, 299

Xanthos, xl, 101, 109, 203, 207–9, 243

Zeus, xx, xxii, xxvi, xxxviii, xl, 21 n.22, 55, 99, 103–9, 111, 115, 119, 121, 127–33, 145–49, 163, 175–95, 205, 211, 223, 235, 237, 251, 275, 277, 285, 287

www.ingramcontent.com/pod-product-compliance
Lightning Source LLC
Chambersburg PA
CBHW021116300426
44113CB00006B/169